PORTRAITS of GOD

A BIBLICAL THEOLOGY of HOLINESS

ALLAN COPPEDGE

InterVarsity Press
Downers Grove, Illinois

InterVarsity Press

P.O. Box 1400, Downers Grove, IL 60515-1426

World Wide Web: www.ivpress.com

E-mail: mail@ivpress.com

InterVarsity Press® is the book-publishing division of InterVarsity Christian Fellowship/USA®, a student movement active on campus at hundreds of universities, colleges and schools of nursing in the United States of America, and a member movement of the International Fellowship of Evangelical Students. For information about local and regional activities, write Public Relations Dept., InterVarsity Christian Fellowship/ USA, 6400 Schroeder Rd., P.O. Box 7895, Madison, WI 53707-7895.

Scripture quotations, unless otherwise noted, are from the Revised Standard Version of the Bible, *copyright 1946, 1952, 1971 by the Division of Christian Education of the National Council of the Churches of Christ in the U.S.A., and are used by permission.*

Cover photograph:

ISBN 0-8308-1560-0

Printed in the United States of America ∞

Library of Congress Cataloging-in-Publication Data

Coppedge, Allan.
    Portraits of God : a biblical theology of holiness / Allan Coppedge.
        p.m.
    Includes bibliographical references and index.
    ISBN 0-8308-1560-0 (alk. paper)
    1. God—Biblical teaching. 2. God—Holiness. 3. Trinity. I. Title.
    BS544.C656 2001
    231—dc21

                                                                                            00-054446

27 26 25 24 23 22 21 20 19 18 17 16 15 14 13 12 11 10 9 8 7 6 5 4 3 2 1

24 23 22 21 20 19 18 17 16 15 14 13 12 11 10 09 08 07 06 05 04 03 02 01

To my father-in-law
Dennis F. Kinlaw

Teacher, Mentor, Friend
who has modeled for me so effectively the role of God as Father
and through that role challenged and encouraged me
in my intellectual and spiritual pursuit
of knowing the triune God in all his roles.

CONTENTS

Abbreviations

BAGD	W. Bauer, W. F. Arndt, F. W. Gingrich and F. W. Danker, *Greek-English Lexicon of the New Testament*
BDB	F. Brown, S. R. Driver and C. A. Briggs, *Hebrew and English Lexicon of the Old Testament*
BDT	*Beacon Dictionary of Theology*, ed. R. S. Taylor
BETS	*Bulletin of Evangelical Theological Society*
BibW	*Biblical World*
BTLNT	*Biblical Theological Lexicon of the New Testament*, Cremer
BSAC	*Bibliotheca sacra*
CD	*Church Dogmatics*, Karl Barth
CBQ	*Catholic Biblical Quarterly*
EBS	*Encyclopedia of Biblical Study*, ed. Johannes B. Bauer
EBT	*Encyclopedia of Biblical Theology*, ed. Johannes Bauer
EDT	*Evangelical Dictionary of Theology*, ed. W. A. Elwell.
EvQ	*Evangelical Quarterly*
ExpT	*Expository Times*
HDB	*A Dictionary of the Bible*, ed. J. Hastings.
ICC	International Critical Commentary
IDB	*Interpreter's Dictionary of the Bible*
Int	*Interpretation*
ISBE	*International Standard Bible Encylcopedia*
ISBE (rev.)	*International Standard Bible Encyclopedia* (rev. ed.)
JBL	*Journal of Biblical Literature*
JR	*Journal of Religion*
NIDNTT	*New International Dictionary of New Testament Theology*, ed. Colin Brown
NBD	*New Bible Dictionary*, ed. J. D. Douglas
NDT	*New Dictionary of Theology*, ed. S. Ferguson, D. F. Wright and J. I. Packer
NSRE	*The New Schaff-Herzog Religious Encyclopedia*
PTR	*Princeton Theological Review*
RelS	*Religious Studies*
SJT	*Scottish Journal of Theology*
SV	*Sacramentum Verbi*
TD	*Theology Digest*
TDNT	*Theological Dictionary of the New Testament*, ed. G. Kittel and G. Freidrich

TDOT	*Theological Dictionary of the Old Testament*, ed. G. Botterweck and H. Ringgren
THAT	*Theologisches Handwörterbuch Aum Altem Testament*, ed. E. Jenni
TWB	*Theological Wordbook of the Bible*, ed. A. Richardson
TWNT	*Theological Wordbook of the New Testament*
TWOT	*Theological Wordbook of the Old Testament*, ed. R. L. Harris and G. L. Archer Jr.
VT	*Vetus Testamentum*
VTSup	Supplements to Vetus Testamentum
Works	Works of John Wesley
WTJ	*Wesleyan Theological Journal*
ZAW	*Zeitschrift für die alttestamentliche Wissenschaft*
ZPEB	*Zondervan Pictorial Encyclopedia of the Bible*, ed. M. C. Tenney

Introduction

God wants to be known! He goes to great lengths for us to know him, because from his perspective this is the most important thing in life. Therefore, he spares no pains to help us understand what he is like and how we may enter into a relationship with him. So the two crucial questions we must not miss are "What is he like?" and "How do we know him?"

Portraits/Roles of God

The first thing we know about God is his personal nature. The Christian God is a personal being, not a force, not an energy field, not even the "ground of being." To relate to him is not to relate to a power but to a person. An important implication of this is that knowledge of other persons is different from any other knowledge we have. We know others through our relationships with them, and one key thing we know about persons is that they are always known by their interlocking relationships. It is this personal, relational, triune God, who desires for people to enter into relationship with him and with other persons, who is the focus of our concern.

This personal God has made himself known by both his words and his acts. As a master teacher God knows the best way to communicate with us is to use the different parts of our learning faculties. He knows that we need some explanation of what he is like, and accordingly, he speaks to our reason through words. He also knows that we learn through our imaginations, so he makes himself known through his actions, which are described to us as pictorial events. In other words, he gives us logical explanations of what he is like (word), while he adds a pictorial vision as a complement to it (act).

This dual pattern of communication is obvious as soon as we open the Bible and observe the balance of the genre of literature that we have in Scripture.

There are logical and analytical sections (word), like the prophets and wisdom literature of the Old Testament and the epistles of the New Testament. But these are balanced by the historical, biographical sections (act) that include the Pentateuch and the historical books in the Old Testament, and the Gospels and Acts in the New. Neither is complete without the other, and the two serve in a complementary way to make God's revelation available to us.

In the same way he balances his means of communication in the description of who he is. Sometimes he makes himself known to our minds in logical categories as he describes his attributes: he is love, he is the Almighty, he is everlasting, he is faithful, etc. At the same time he makes himself known by his acts in the world, and it is his way of acting that gives us the roles that he uses in relating to us. Drawing from images both from his own nature and from our world, he makes himself known as Father, Redeemer, Creator, Friend and so forth. As an effective teacher, he often brings together word and act so we do not miss the lesson, and at times he provides a rational description of himself to go with these visual portraits of himself (e.g., loving Father, powerful Redeemer, faithful Friend).

The first major purpose of this book then is to identify these portraits of God and examine the implications of each one. We will be asking ourselves, How do these "roles of God" illuminate our understanding of him and affect our relationship to him? Understanding God is not just an academic exercise; its design is to lead to an appropriate relationship with him. This means the next issue is, How can we learn more about God so that we might know him better? Accordingly, we will identify the major and minor ways in which God reveals himself through these portraits or roles and then show how these can open the door for a better understanding of God and so lay the groundwork for a deeper, personal knowing of him.

How Roles Connect Biblical Studies to Systematic Theology

A second purpose is to show how these roles link biblical materials with Christian theology. This is related to two contemporary movements in Christian scholarship. The first is an attempt to connect work in the Old Testament with work in the New Testament and both with systematic theology. Francis Watson has correctly identified major splits in academic circles between Old Testament studies and New Testament studies, and between both of these and

Christian theology. Appropriately, he is calling for a reuniting of these three disciplines that are currently operating as separate entites,[1] and he is being joined by others who have also begun to see creative ways to unite the three areas of concern.[2] A basic conviction for many is that if Christian theology is to be credible, it must demonstrate first its scriptural foundation. Theology does not begin with philosophy, tradition or experience. It begins with revelation. But how does this revelation from the Old Testament lead to the New, and how do both flow into Christian theology? Part of our purpose will be to show how the roles of God assist in this transition from one Testament to the other and then from Scripture to Christian doctrine.

This procedure is possible because each of the roles of God appears in both Testaments and thus becomes a key bridge between the Old and New Covenants. For example, the roles serve as a tie between the Old Testament view of God and the New Testament view of God in Jesus Christ because both persons are identified in all of the major roles. This makes it possible for one view of God to lead to an understanding of the other (Old Testament preparing the way for the New Testament). But then the second view of God in Jesus gives a greater and clearer picture of the first perspective (New Testament illuminating the Old Testament). The result is a theological bridge between the two Testaments based on these roles.[3]

Not only do the roles of God tie the two Testaments together, but also they lead to a theological bridge with Christian doctrine. For example this approach aids us in constructing an understanding of the Trinity. Since all three persons of the Godhead are identified in each role, there is significant data available

---

[1]Francis Watson, *Text and Truth* (Grand Rapids, Mich.: Eerdmans, 1997), pp. 1-9.

[2]Joel Green and Max Turner, *Between the Horizons: Spanning New Testament Studies and Systematic Theology* (Grand Rapids, Mich.: Eerdmans, 2000); Christopher Seitz, *Word Without End* (Grand Rapids, Mich.: Eerdmans, 1998); Gerald O'Collins and Daniel Kendall, *The Bible for Theology: Ten Principles for the Theological Use of Scripture* (Mahwah, N.J.: Paulist, 1997); Trevor Hart, *Faith Thinking: The Dynamics of Christian Theology* (Downers Grove, Ill.: InterVarsity Press, 1995); Charles J. Scalise, *From Scripture to Theology: A Canonical Journey into Hermeneutics* (Downers Grove, Ill.: InterVarsity Press, 1996); N. T. Wright, *The New Testament and the People of God* (Minneapolis, Fortress, 1992), pp. 121-44.

[3]A variation of the same approach comes from Richard Bauckham who refers to the roles as the "Identity of God." He distinguishes this from the more philosophical interest in divine essence or nature that defines God in terms of his attributes. Bauckham feels the "Identity of God" better describes the biblical portraits of God like Creator and Ruler. He uses the concept to open the door for understanding Christology within the uniqueness of Jewish monotheism, i.e., for connecting Jesus (New Testament) with the God of Israel (Old Testament). See Richard Bauckham, *God Crucified* (Grand Rapids, Mich.: Eerdmans, 1998), pp. 6-13.

related to Father, Son and Holy Spirit to serve as a basis for building a Christian doctrine of the Trinity. This allows for materials that have been mined from the Old and New Testament to be coordinated as the first step in establishing this central Christian truth.

This book then is a part of the tie between biblical and systematic theology. It comes at the junction between a diachronic reading of Scripture, with its progressive unfolding of God's revelation through his word, and a synchronic understanding of truth that gathers a holistic understanding of revelation by themes. Both are important ways of reading Scripture and understanding truth, and it is hoped that a proper understanding of the roles of God will assist in the transition from one to the other.

In order to assist with this movement from Old Testament materials to New Testament concepts to Christian doctrine, I have tried to use evidence from a variety of sources throughout Scripture. So in identifying different words and terms that are used in relationship to each of the roles of God in the Old Testament, I have tried to draw representative examples from the Pentateuch, the historical books, the wisdom and poetical literature and the prophets. In the New Testament I have also tried to balance the Synoptic Gospels with John and both of these with the Pauline materials, the Catholic Epistles and Revelation. Much of the material for the roles of God is spread over a variety of books and therefore is written in different genres of literature. Sometimes a particular author or book will accent one role and therefore one language category, but I will attempt to take representative examples of how these appear in multiple places (in most instances) throughout Scripture.

Any view of God that shows how the Father works, how the Son works and how the Holy Spirit works forces us back to a fresh consideration of the doctrine of the Trinity. Fortunately, along with new attempts to reconnect biblical studies with theological studies, there is a second contemporary movement in Christian theology that relates to this concern with trinitarian materials. It is the revived interest in the Trinity as a foundational doctrine for the Christian faith. Here significant work is being done across denominational lines, a reality that is possible because every major Christian church has a commitment to trinitarian faith. Its possible fruitfulness for ecumenical dialogue is significant because the focus is not on ecclesiology, as has been the case for so many years, but rather on theology. For some generations theological questions have been shunned in ecumenical dialogue because they seemed more divisive, and the result has been a focus on organizational and structural issues. With a return to trinitarian thinking as a part of the classical theology of the Christian church, a new approach may be unfolding.[4]

The focus on the doctrine of the Trinity inevitably means returning to the fourth century and the classical formulation established by the Nicene/Constantinopolitan Creed. This has meant a revisiting of the writings of the leaders of the church as they wrestled with how to express trinitarian beliefs. In this process it has become obvious that the thinking of the early church was firmly grounded in the biblical materials about God the Father, God the Son, and God the Holy Spirit. The Scriptures were their starting point for shaping the Christian doctrine of the Trinity, and therefore a fresh look at these biblical materials should be foundational for all contemporary attempts to examine the Trinity.[5]

It is at this point that the roles of God assume a place of particular importance. Since the three persons of the Trinity are described in all the major roles of God, this means that not only do the roles tie Old and New Testament material together, they also provide an introduction to the ways we must envision God in any doctrine of the Trinity. The data about God the Father, the Son and the Spirit from each role supply a very impressive amount of material that must underlie any doctrine of the Trinity. A focus on this approach will have the effect of shifting the theological discussion from a few trinitarian formulas or triadic forms in Scripture to a much larger base of trinitarian thought which uses the

---

[4]See Thomas F. Torrance, *Theology in Reconciliation* (Grand Rapids, Mich.: Eerdmans, 1975), pp. 15-81, 215-66; *The Incarnation: Ecumenical Studies in the Nicene-Constantinopolitan Creed* (Edinburgh: Handsel, 1981); *Theological Dialogue Between Orthodox and Reformed Churches* (Edinburgh: Scottish Academic Press, 1985), pp. 79-156.

[5]For contemporary discussions regarding the Trinity see Thomas F. Torrance, *The Christian Doctrine of God* (Edinburgh: T & T Clark, 1995); *The Trinitarian Faith* (Edinburgh: T & T Clark, 1995); Colin Gunton, *The Promise of Trinitarian Theology* (Edinburgh: T & T Clark, 1991); *The One, the Three, and the Many* (Cambridge: Cambridge University Press, 1993); Walter Kasper, *The God of Jesus Christ* (New York: Crossroad, 1999); William J. Hill, *The Three-Personed God: The Trinity as a Mystery of Salvation* (Washington, D.C.: Catholic University of America Press, 1982); Christopher Schwöbel and Colin Gunton, *Persons, Divine and Human* (Edinburgh: T & T Clark, 1991); John Zizioulas, *Being as Communion* (Crestwood, N.Y.: St. Valadimir's Seminary Press, 1997); Ronald J. Feenstra and Cornelius Plantinga Jr., *Trinity, Incarnation, and Atonement* (Notre Dame, Ind.: University of Notre Dame Press, 1989); Christopher Schwöbel, *Trinitatian Theology Today* (Edinburgh: T & T Clark, 1995); Aladair I. C. Heron, ed., *The Forgotten Trinity* (London: BBC/CCBI, 1991); Thomas A. Smail, *The Forgotten Father* (London: Hodder-Stoughton, 1980); Jürgen Moltmann, *The Trinity and The Kingdom of God*, trans. Margaret Kohl (New York: Harper & Row, 1981) ; Alvin F. Kimel Jr., ed., *Speaking the Christian God* (Grand Rapids, Mich.: Eerdmans, 1992); James R. White, *The Forgotten Trinity* (Minneapolis: Bethany House, 1998).

whole picture of God in three persons revealing himself and his work through these various roles. For example, if it is the prerogative of deity to give life and if the role of God as Creator demonstrates that the Father gives life, the Son gives life, and the Spirit gives life, then this combination of materials has very significant implications for the full divine nature of all three persons. Accordingly, a synthesis of the whole picture of each of the persons of God in all of his roles will be one of the significant tasks underlying any fresh, holistic understanding of the Trinity.

My hope is that this study will assist in supplying primary scriptural data that is foundational for the formulation of trinitarian theology. An added benefit will mean that the use of the roles of God will be an approach that helps keep any doctrine of the Trinity firmly rooted in Scripture while historical and philosophical issues are considered in formulating this doctrine.

Understanding the Centrality of God's Holiness

A third purpose of this book is to propose a fresh examination of the holiness of God and its multiple dimensions. Never has the Christian church needed to place a greater emphasis on holiness of character than in our own day. But human holiness can not be properly understood without reference to divine holiness. Many branches of the church have long felt this to be a central concept for understanding God, and it certainly seems to bracket the biblical materials about how God describes himself (Lev 11:44-45; 1 Pet 1:15-16). Just how significant is this attribute of God? How central does he intend it to be for our understanding of men and women and what he wants to do for them? This study will attempt to explore the breadth of the concept of holiness by looking at its multiple aspects. We will do this by showing how different aspects of holiness are related to the major roles of God.

This discussion of the holiness of God in relationship to his roles will set the stage for showing how this central aspect of God's being affects the rest of our theological categories. The result will be an indication of how large and overarching the idea of holiness is for understanding God, ourselves, and our relationship to each other.

Providing a Fresh Approach to Dialogue

In addition to these three major purposes for our study, there are two other practical concerns. One is how the use of these roles may assist us in dialogue across Christian traditions on theological issues. The roles of God give us a vehicle for agreement on certain ideas when we realize that many truths in Scripture are described in multiple ways. Some may be coming to a biblical truth using language from one of the roles of God, while other branches of the church are approaching the same truth using other terms. Sometimes the issue is not which one is right or wrong, but where to begin or what to emphasize. It may be that the different terms describing the same truth provides complementary and therefore illuminating understandings of the concept discussed. The use of the roles of God and related language can help us think holistically, and often this means acknowledging that other segments of the Christian church are legitimately approaching a biblical truth.

A recent example of how an understanding of the roles would be helpful in contemporary dialogue is in relationship to a proposed evangelical creed published in *Christianity Today*. The framers of this creed desire a fresh evangelical statement of basic Christian principles in our day, but apparently the largest number of framers are from a Reformed orientation. Accordingly, when they formulate the work of God's saving grace, they describe it in terms of justification.[6] The Reformed leanings toward legal and magisterial language (God as Judge and King) shape the focus of the whole creed with an emphasis on justification and imputed righteousness as its primary framework. While this approach would be fine for the purpose of writing a new Reformed creed, the stated desire of the framers was to offer a broadly based evangelical creed, which would allow those from a variety of traditions to join in a common witness to a basic statement of Christian truth.

A more helpful approach would be to pick a broader theological term for the saving grace of God, like "salvation," and then indicate how this concept may be described in multiple ways (using the language categories from the various roles of God) such as justification, receiving new life, reconciliation, new birth, entering the kingdom, receiving Christ, etc. The use of the vocabularies from the various roles would not have prejudiced such a statement as coming from any one branch of the church and would have made it much more likely that others from different traditions could readily agree to its declaration of faith. As the

---

[6]"The Gospel of Jesus Christ: An Evangelical Celebration," *Christianity Today* 43, no. 7 (1999): 51-56.

creed stands now, many will not be able to affirm it in spite of a strong desire for a common creedal statement as a witness to our generation. It is simply too slanted in one theological direction, and this could have been prevented by a more holistic view of salvation, using the language from the roles of God to describe its multiple dimensions.

Indicating Practical Implications of Theology

Another practical issue arises out of the strong conviction that theology should be done within the church and in the service of the church. Theological discussion divorced from its family moorings among God's people has lost its reason to be. Accordingly, some suggestions need to be made about how the roles of God affect the spiritual lives of men and women and how they are related to doing ministry in the church. For example, by identifying how the roles of God supply various approaches to salvation, it means there are a variety of options concerning how we present the gospel. As a result, our evangelism and apologetics can be enriched by a study of the various roles that give us multiple ways to share the Christian faith. This is only a hint at the many, practical implications of the roles of God for ministry. Most of our suggestions in this area will come in the last chapter.

Finally, as an addendum to the practical implications of the roles, let me add a personal word about how understanding God in his roles has impacted my own life. I began to work with three of the roles twenty-five years ago as a means of unraveling the scriptural data on the doctrines related to predestination. I found the use of these roles in sorting out how God works enormously helpful in settling my own theology on these related issues. In the process of using a few of the roles to understand this particular point in Christian theology, I was led to an exploration over several years of other roles that I had seen in Scripture. In the midst of this study I began trying to relate to God personally in several roles that were less familiar or previously little used in my own spiritual life. The increase of my personal understanding of God in this way has inspired in me a concentrated effort to relate directly to him in all the roles. It has had an incredibly broadening and deepening effect on my whole relationship with him.

I am still finding it a wonderfully enriching experience in my personal worship and devotion to come before him with a focus on one of his roles one day and another the following, etc. Focusing on passages of Scripture that accent a particular role helps concentrate attention on God in this way, with the result that I have found him making himself known in a far richer and personal way than ever before as Father, Creator, Shepherd, etc.

The implications did not stop with this. I soon began to find how valuable the roles were in a variety of practical ministries, including family devotions, preaching and teaching. I discovered people responding to the presentations about God in this way at all levels: children in the family, laity in local congregations and graduate students in seminary. Part of the appeal is learning to relate to God in ways that capture the imagination through the pictorial nature of the roles. People get excited about knowing God when he is a Priest, Father, Shepherd or Redeemer. Apparently this is a lot more attractive than when he is described in the abstract as Grace, Love, Goodness or Power. The visual images produced by the roles invite us into a working relationship with God that a focus on God's attributes themselves does not.

An additional appeal of the roles I discovered is that it organizes familiar biblical terms and ideas in a way that is simple and easy to remember. For those who have read their Bible and have sat under some biblical preaching, it provides a way to conceptually put together many biblical terms and ideas in a manner that does not seem too complicated or too abstract. The language categories that accompany each role are a tremendous help to many in this regard, and I found, particularly for nonacademics, that people are open to a great deal more theology when it comes wrapped in this package.

As a result of my own experience, I am sending forth this book with the hope it will assist others in similar ways: knowing about God and the theology that comes from this knowledge; knowing God personally at another level of spiritual development; and having a tool available to present him to others in a positive and attractive way.

ONE

BIBLICAL ROLES OF GOD

An Overview

The concept of God is the most determinative factor for all Christian theology and spiritual life. A right understanding of the nature of God sets a proper pattern for systematic theology as well as for personal knowledge of God. Wolfhart Pannenberg can boldly state, "Everything else remains insecure in theology, before one has made up one's mind on the doctrine of God."[1] In other words our view of God is the single most influential part of our theology. But knowing about God is only the beginning. It is this correct knowledge of God that leads to a proper relationship with him. This is why some argue that the gravest question before the church and each individual is what they conceive God to be like. For individuals as well as for the church, the most revealing thing about them is their idea of God. Many would agree with A. W. Tozer: "There is scarcely an error in doctrine or a failure in applying Christian ethics that cannot be traced finally to imperfect and ignoble thoughts about God."[2] The most crucial question then for any individual or church is, "What is God like?" The answer to this question will determine both their doctrine and experience.

The Place of Revelation
Historic Christian orthodoxy has always believed that a proper understanding

---

[1]Philip Clayton and Carl E. Braaten, *The Theology of Wolfhart Pannenberg* (Minneapolis: Augsburg, 1988), p. 16.

[2]A. W. Tozer, *The Knowledge of the Holy* (New York: Harper & Row, 1961), pp. 7-8.

of the nature of God must come by revelation. By its very nature Christianity is based not primarily on what we think about God but on what God has made known about himself. Biblical faith is rooted not in our discovery of God but in his disclosure of himself. However, if he is what he declares himself to be, that is, the supranatural, transcendent and personal God who stands outside of the universe of space and time, then human powers of reason and perception, which are limited to this world, cannot comprehend this God without assistance. So if God is who he says he is, and he is like what he says he is like, we can really only understand him through his special revelation to us.[3] The church has always believed this special revelation has come to us in Scripture. This means the Bible becomes the sourcebook for any attempt to comprehend the nature and character of the God whom we desire to know.

If we accept that God reveals himself in Scripture, the next question is, How are we to view the wholeness of this revelation? Given our premise, the obvious answer is that correct theology must be drawn from all the biblical data. A partial use of biblical materials will yield only an incomplete picture of God. Yet different parts of the Christian church at various times in her history have emphasized only select aspects of the nature of God while neglecting some others. Part of the reason for this has been certain historical circumstances that made it easier to see certain portions of the revelation about God more clearly than others. For example, during the Reformation when the battle raged over the question of authority (who decides the way of salvation: the church or God through his word?), it was natural for leaders like Martin Luther to focus on God's role as Sovereign King. It was God the King who exercised the right to offer salvation on his own terms. The result of emphasizing God as the kingly authority in that historical period is that even today many tend to see God through royal language, One who relates to people as a king to his subjects.

While varying historical circumstances make it understandable that people have viewed God in a particular way, yet we must be clear that a truly biblical and therefore fully Christian theology must encompass the whole of biblical

---

[3]"A human knowledge of God can be a true knowledge that corresponds to the divine reality only if it originates in the Deity itself. God can be known only if He gives Himself to be known. The loftiness of the divine reality makes it inaccessible to us unless it makes itself known. Hence the knowledge of God is possible only by revelation" (Wolfhart Pannenberg, *Systematic Theology*, trans. Geoffrey W. Bromiley [Grand Rapids, Mich.: Eerdmans, 1988], 1:1; cf. Emil Brunner, *The Christian Doctrine of God* [London: Lutterworth, 1949], p. 118).

revelation. Such a holistic theology must not be content with the parts of Scripture accented by a particular tradition, nor must it focus only on those portraits of God that are most naturally attractive. Rather, it must provide as complete a picture as is possible from the whole of Scripture. Such a task grows out of a conviction that the whole Bible is the Word of God and his revelation to people. Furthermore, it presupposes that God's revelation in Scripture is fully reliable, and therefore it is able to serve as a basis for right thinking about him.

Understanding the Transcendent, Supranatural God

Because God is a supranatural being and human perceptive powers are limited to the natural world, how are people to understand the supranatural world beyond? How can God be known if he is outside the world of space and time? Human descriptive language is necessarily confined to the world of creation. Recognizing our dilemma (particularly the finiteness of our perception), God has condescended to use language from the created world to describe his own transcendent being. Working with terms from creation and personal relations, God tells us what he is like in language familiar to us.[4]

In using the language of this world to talk about a transcendent God, the best way to describe God in relation to reality is by the use of *analogical language* (i.e., using terms that are alike in some ways, but not in all ways).[5] So, for example, from the natural world we understand what "power" is, and that assists us (by comparison) to understand the work of God as all-powerful (Almighty) or omnipotent. So by *analogy* the use of "power" in relation to God is similar to our use of "power" in this world. Analogy is particularly helpful in comparing the way God works in relationships. Philip Rolnick declares that because analogy is inherently expressive of relationships, "Our view of the world, ourselves and our God is wrapped in the way we use analogy."[6]

There are many kinds of analogies. For our purposes the one that has particular

---

[4]For discussion of how terms about God are related to both special revelation (Scripture) and general revelation (creation, reason and experience) see the section on general and special revelation in chapter eleven.

[5]On analogy see Thomas Aquinas, *Summa Theologica*, ed. Thomas Gilby (Garden City, N.Y.: Image, 1969), 1.Q.13; *Summa Contra Gentiles* (Notre Dame, Ind.: University of Notre Dame Press, n.d.), 1:32-34; Eric L. Mascall, *Exsitence and Analogy* (Hamden, Conn.: Archon, 1967); P. Sherry, "Analogy Reviewed," *Philosophy* 51 (1976): 337-45; P. Sherry, "Analogy Today," *Philosophy* 51 (1976): 431-46.

[6]Philip A. Rolnick, *Analogical Possibilities: How Words Refer to God* (Atlanta: Scholars Press, 1993). Rolnick also provides an introductory history on the use of analogy to the time of Aquinas.

relevance for this study is *metaphor*. A metaphor is a more specialized form of analogical language in which one thing (a subject) is compared to another (a symbol). When God is described using metaphors, there is an analogy between God (subject) and something in the created world (symbol) that is based on some similarity of being, action or relationship.[7] An example of God described with a metaphor is when he is called a "rock" (Ps 18:2; 18:31). While the comparison is limited, this metaphor helps us understand that God is unchanging and provides a firm foundation for whatever he wants to do in our lives or in the world. Because of the multiple use of these metaphors in the Bible, it may well be that metaphorical analogy is used more frequently than any other mode of description of God.[8]

A narrower kind of analogical language, then, is the use of metaphor.[9] There is also an even narrower use of metaphor to describe God. The metaphors that imply the greatest degree of correspondence between God (subject) and the symbols from this world are those in which the symbol is taken from personal relations. These personal metaphors describe God's being, God's actions and God's relationships as being similar in many respects to a human's being, a human's actions and a human's relationships. This kind of "human" metaphor for God may be called a *portrait* or *role*. These portraits (a metaphor borrowed from painting) or roles (a metaphor borrowed from the theater) indicate some things about God from the way people are, the way people act and the way people relate to others. Each of these indicates that this is the way God *is*, the way God *acts* and the way God *relates to others*. It is the use of these portrait or role metaphors that allows the Bible to talk about God so graphically when it is describing him as King, Father, Judge and so forth. These portraits or roles of God then are basically a specialized form of metaphor that are in turn one dimension of analogical language.[10]

The choice of either the term *portrait* or the term *role* has both advantages and limitations. The idea of a *portrait* is initially more vivid and catches the

---

[7]See Peter W. Macky, *The Centrality of Metaphors to Biblical Thought* (Lewiston, N.Y.: Edwin Mellen, 1990), pp. 26, 49. Mackey lists ten different types of metaphor used in Scripture.

[8]Battista Mondin, *Principle of Analogy in Protestant and Catholic Theology* (The Hague: Martinus Nyjhoff, 1963), p. 94. For significant discussion of metaphors and God see Walter Kasper, *The God of Jesus Christ* (New York: Crossroad, 1999), pp. 93-99.

[9]On limits on using analogy and metaphor, see Humphrey Palmer, *Analogy: A Study of Qualification and Argument in Theology* (London: Macmillan, 1973), pp. 85-96.

[10]Cf. Richard Baukham's use of "the identity of God" as an alternative label in *God Crucified* (Grand Rapids, Mich.: Eerdmans, 1998), pp. 7-8.

imagination. Its limitation is that a picture is more static in nature and has more difficulty showing interaction between the subject and other persons. The strength of the concept of *role* is that it is more full orbed in showing how a person acts and relates to others in a variety of situations. There is a dynamic nature to the use of roles that is very attractive. The limitation of the use of role is that actors can play different roles that may have contrary character traits and sometimes people view a role as arbitrary and perhaps disconnected from the person actually playing the role. This disadvantage may be overcome if the concept of role is not limited to the language of the theater but is expanded to include the way persons have a variety of responsibilities (like roles) within of their lives. So a father may also be understood as carrying out a variety of roles. He leads, he teaches, he may be a friend, an intermediary and so on. If we understand that a father is playing certain more limited roles within the context of his overarching fatherly role, we have a better understanding of the way the term *role* may be used without the limitations of it as a theater metaphor only.

In making the choice between the term *portrait* or the term *role*, we observe that traditionally different portraits are painted of people as they are known in certain roles, for example, the king, my father, a shepherd. An artist paints a portrait to remind his viewers of the fuller role in life that the subject plays. In other words, portraits lead to understanding people in their life roles. This seems to suggest that perhaps the better choice of these terms is the concept of *role*. It certainly seems to fit the description of the living God in Scripture, whom we see acting and relating to people in a variety of ways. It is this active doing, speaking and relating that seems best captured with the word *role*. Accordingly, we are going to use *roles* as the primary term to describe these personal pictures of God, while *portraits, metaphors* and *analogies* will be used as secondary terms.[11]

G. B. Caird in his significant study *The Language and Imagery of the Bible* calls attention to the fact that God uses human categories to begin to help people understand himself. He points out that these metaphors/roles derived from human relationships are of special significance because they lend themselves to a two-way traffic in ideas.

---

[11]Three kinds of metaphors are used for God: inanimate objects (God is a rock), animals (the Lion of the tribe of Judah) and persons (King, Father, Shepherd). On a scale of increasing comparison, the inanimate objects are clearly where the comparison is least like God, and the personal metaphors are the ones that are most like him.

When the Bible calls God Judge, King, Father or Husband it is, in the first instance using the human known to throw light on the divine unknown, and particularly on God's attitude to his worshipers. But no sooner has the metaphor traveled from earth to heaven than it begins the return journey to earth, bearing with it an ideal standard by which the conduct of human judges, kings, fathers and husbands is to be assessed.[12]

God uses multiple metaphors/roles because no single category is fully adequate to explain himself. In addition, people's perception of the ideal in each role is also often distorted, so that from a human point of view there is no ideal judge, king or father. Yet enough is known about each of these human categories to give us a better understanding of some aspect of the nature of God.[13] God is like them in some ways but (in accord with the way analogy works) not in every way.

Once we begin to reflect on the nature and character of God as revealed in his roles, a much more perfect model is given to us of what an earthly judge, king or father ought to be. While we begin to understand God with the use of these extended metaphors, our more comprehensive understanding of him is not conditioned on our knowledge of any of these human portraits, which might be faulty. In fact, a proper understanding of the human roles must be corrected in the light of a larger understanding of what God is like.[14]

The Major Roles

It is now time to turn our attention to the primary roles of God that are

---

[12]G. B. Caird, *The Language and Imagery of the Bible* (Philadelphia: Westminster Press, 1980), pp. 19.

[13] There is a growing list of literature on metaphor in general. Some of the more significant works include: I. A. Richards, *The Philosophy of Rhetoric* (New York: Oxford University Press, 1936); Edwin Robert Bevan, *Symbolism and Belief* (London: Collins, 1938); Max Black, *Models and Metaphors* (Ithaca: Cornell University Press, 1962); Ian Barbour, *Myths, Models and Paradigms* (New York: Harper & Row, 1974); Paul Ricoeur, *The Rule of Metaphor* (Toronto: University of Toronto Press, 1977); George Lakoff and Mar Johnson, *Metaphors We Live By* (Chicago: University of Chicago Press, 1980); Earl R. MacCormac, *A Cognitive Theory of Metaphor* (Cambridge, Mass.: MIT Press, 1985). Several works specifically relate metaphor to religious language. In addition to the sources cited in the text see C. S. Lewis, *Miracles: A Preliminary Study* (New York: Macmillan, 1947); "Bluspels and Flalanfferes," in *Rehabilitations and Other Essays* (New York: Oxford University Press, 1939), pp. 135-58; Earl R. MacCormac, *Metaphor and Myth in Science and Religion* (Durham, N.C.: Duke University Press, 1976); Janet M. Soskice, *Metaphor and Religious Language* (Oxford: Clarendon, 1985).

[14]For discussion of the biblical figures of speech, including metaphor, see Benjamin Keach, *Preaching from the Types and Metaphors of the Bible* (Grand Rapids, Mich.: Kregel, 1972); E. W. Bullinger, *Figures of Speech Used in the Bible: Explained and Illustrated* (Grand Rapids, Mich.: Baker, 1968); C. F. Pfeiffer, "Figures of Speech in Human Language," *BETS* Vol. 2, no. 4 (fall 1959), pp. 17-21.

emphasized in Scripture. Eight major roles that describe God seem to dominate the biblical data. This is not to say there are not other roles/portraits that are used to describe God and our relationship with him, but in terms of quantity of material and theological significance, eight of them seem to stand out. The eight roles are *Creator, King, Personal Revealer, Priest, Judge, Father, Redeemer* and *Shepherd*. Each of these roles has a language category that describes not only God but people and the divine-human relationship. The language category connected with each term forms an extended metaphor system that helps illuminate the relationship depicted in each role. For example, when speaking of God as *Creator* we use the language of creation with a focus on giving life. In describing God as *King* we use the language of the royal court that describes his majesty. Here the focus is on authority. It is the *King* who rules. The full picture of the roles and their language categories may be seen in table 1.1.

Table 1.1. Roles of God with Language and Focus Emphases

Role	Creator	King	Personal Revealer	Priest	Judge	Father	Redeemer	Shepherd
Language	Creation	Majesty	Personal Communication	Sanctuary	Legal	Family	Slavery/ Freedom	Pastoral Scene
Focus	Life	Authority	Fellowship/ Communication/ Truth	Grace/ Purity	Law	Love	Deliverance/ Service	Care

From the chart one can see that the chief focus of God as Personal Revealer is that of fellowship and personal communication of truth in interpersonal relationships. This role is the least specific of the eight we are using but the most pervasive in Scripture. Part of the reason is that God is "revealing" himself as a person through each of the other seven roles. But this category refers primarily to that person-to-person communication in verbal form when God is not speaking in some other role. Often he does not communicate as a King or Father, but he just speaks to people in a personal, linguistic way. The subcategories under this role (table 1.2) give it a bit more definition. They are the roles of God as Teacher, Prophet and Friend. Each focuses on a personal God communicating with and entering into relationships with other persons.

When God functions as *Priest*, the language is borrowed from the temple or the sanctuary, and the focus is on grace and purity. When he is described as *Judge*, the language is from the courtroom and is legal in nature. Here law is the focus. When God appears as *Father*, it is language from the family which describes him. This is the portrait of intimacy and of the home, and naturally has its focus on love. The language of slavery and freedom describes God as *Redeemer*, and it focuses first on deliverance and then on service. Finally, it is the extended metaphor from the pastoral scene that assists us in understanding God as a *Shepherd* with its focus on his care.

The Subroles

These eight major roles of God do not exhaust the personal biblical metaphors that describe him. But these eight are among the most extensively used in Scripture, and certain other metaphors are really subcategories of these eight. For example, God's role as *Physician* or *Healer* is a picture of one who restores health and life, and thus may be reasonably understood as a subcategory of God's role as the Creator and giver of life.

Likewise, the concept of God as the *Lord of Hosts*, or *God of the Armies*, is really a subcategory of God's ruling function as King of the universe. The picture of the husband-and-wife relationship is a significant analogy that describes the relationship of God to his people. Yet, the *Husband* role is really another part of the family analogy that describes God's relation to his people in the language of the home. Table 1.2 includes the key subroles along with their language categories and the major focus of each.

Why So Many Roles?

Each of the roles/portraits conveys significant information as to what God is like, but no single one is complete by itself. This is the reason Scripture uses many different metaphors to describe God and our relationship to him.[15] Because no one portrait of God is fully adequate to describe him, multiple images are necessary for a holistic picture of God. It may well be that one of the

---

[15]See Vern S. Poythress, *Symphonic Theology* (Grand Rapids, Mich.: Zondervan, 1991), pp. 16-17.

major problems in the history of the Christian church has been the tendency of different segments of the church to emphasize different analogies or roles. By emphasizing one or two roles at the expense of the others, an unbalanced picture of God has resulted. In an extreme form this approach leads to heresy. In milder forms it leads to various groups within the Christian church focusing on only part of the truth.

Table 1.2. Roles with Their Subroles

Role	Creator	King	Personal Revealer	Priest	Judge	Father	Redeemer	Shepherd
Language	Creation	Majesty	Personal Communication	Sanctuary	Legal	Family	Slavery/Freedom	Pastoral Scene
Focus	Life	Authority	Fellowship/Communication	Grace/Purity	Law	Love	Deliverance/Service	Care
Subrole	Physician	Lord of Hosts	Teacher		Lawmaker	Husband		
Language	Medicine	Military	Learning		Legislation	Home		
Focus	Healing	Warfare	Truth		Giving law	Love		
Subrole	Farmer		Prophet			Bridegroom		
Language	Agriculture		Proclamation			Marriage		
Focus	Growing		Revelation			Intimacy		
Subrole	Builder		Friend					
Language	Construction		Friendship					
Focus	Building		Faithfulness					
Subrole	Potter							
Language	Pottery							
Focus	Shaping							

It is our desire that in articulating the major categories in which the Bible analogically describes God, a fuller picture of what he is like will lead to a more balanced Christian theology. Further, since incomplete, as well as distorted, views of God ultimately lead to a stunted or imbalanced Christian experience, it is hoped that a more complete understanding of God will lead each member of the Christian church to a deeper personal knowledge of God in his own life. Caird is right when he expresses his conviction that this type of theological knowledge of God should ultimately lead to our being conformed into God's image.

Man begins with the familiar situations of home and community and derives from them metaphors to illuminate the activity of God; but the application of these terms to God establishes ideas and absolute standards which can be used as instruments for the remaking of man in God's likeness. Man is created to become like God, and the ultimate justification of anthropomorphic imagery lies in the contribution it makes to the attainment of that goal.[16]

One of the purposes of this book is to provide a fuller understanding of who God is from his roles so that we will be drawn into a deeper relationship with him that results in being more perfectly conformed to God's likeness.

The Roles and Themes from Christian Theology

An examination of each role and its accompanying language category reveals that a significant amount of Christian theology is described under each one. This is because the metaphors at the heart of each role have an extended language system. Caird spells out how this works.

Some metaphors readily lend themselves to a high development because they belong to a metaphor system, i.e., a group of metaphors linked together by their common origin in a single area of human observation, experience or activity which has generated its own particular sublanguage or jargon. Farming, commerce, law, welfare, family, weather, love, health, nature, sport—each of these has a recognizable language of its own and any metaphor drawn from any one of these areas invites embellishment by the addition of others.[17]

Because of these metaphor systems, each of the roles we are going to examine provides biblical terms or theological language that explicates a number of themes in Christian theology.[18] The biblical materials reveal that in each role category there is language that describes the *triune God* (Father, Son and Holy Spirit), but there is also language that describes *men and women, sin, salvation, atonement, growth in Christian experience, the church, full sanctification* and *glorification.*

It works like this: In the role of God as Creator, not only is God the *Father* described as Creator but so is the *Son* and the *Holy Spirit. Men and women* are

---

[16]Caird, *Language and Imagery of the Bible*, pp. 177-78.

[17]Ibid., p. 155.

[18]For a different use of metaphor to build Christian theology from a contemporary feminist perspective see Sallie McFague, *Metaphorical Theology* (Philadelphia: Fortress, 1982). For a critique of McFague's restricted use of "Metaphorical Theory" see Colin Gunton, "Proteus and Procrustes: A Study in the Dialectic of Language in Disagreement with Sallie McFague," in *Speaking the Christian God*, ed. Alvin Kimel Jr. (Grand Rapids, Mich.: Eerdmans, 1992), pp. 65-80.

described as creatures who are persons created in the image of God. *Sin* is described in terms of marring the image of God in people, and *salvation* is that which begins to remake the image of God in them. The *atonement* has to do with Christ as the new head (recapitulation) of the human race. *Growth* in Christian experience is a progressive rebuilding of the image of God. The *church* is seen as the body of Christ, while *full sanctification* is a more complete remaking of the moral image of God in individuals. *Glorification* is described in terms of a final restoration of persons as well as the creation of a new heaven and new earth. The complete set of terms relating to creation language may be outlined as in table 1.3.

Table 1.3. Example of Theological Themes Described in One Role

Father	Son	Spirit	Persons	Sin	Salvation	Atonement	Growth	Church	Full Sancti-fication	Glorifi-cation
Creator	Creator	Agent of creation	Made in image of God	Marred image/ idolatry	Remaking image Regenera-tion	Recapitu-lation	Growth in image of God	Body of Christ	Full remaking of image	New heaven/ earth

In addition to the major themes in Christian theology under each role we are including an introduction to the *attributes* of God that relate to each one. These include the *absolute attributes* (e.g., spirituality and infinity), the *relative attributes* (e.g., omnipotence and wisdom) and the *moral attributes* (e.g., righteousness and love). Some attributes are related to more than one role in the biblical material, but most have at least a close association with one major role (e.g., loving Father). We will use these close connections as a means of introducing all the major attributes of God. There has always been some uneasiness in Christian theology that the attributes of God were more abstract categories that did not convey the more personal dimensions of the way God describes himself in Scripture. By identifying certain attributes with certain roles of God we are hoping to bridge the gap between the more narrative descriptions of God that are pictorial in nature (the roles of God) and the more systematic delineations of his nature normally connected with a discussion of his attributes. The two should provide complementary forms of describing God so that we might relate to him more adequately.

When all the roles are put together with all the themes of Christian theology under each role, a very full conception emerges of God and how we relate to him. *Who God is* obviously dominates the whole of Christian theology and is the connecting link between its various themes.[19] We are going to examine this

Table 1.4. Roles of God with Theological Themes

Role	Creator	King	Personal Revealer	Priest	Judge	Father	Redeemer	Shepherd
Language	Creation	Majesty	Personal communication	Sanctuary	Legal	Family	Slavery/Freedom	Pastoral scene
Focus	Life	Authority	Fellowship/Communication/Truth	Grace/Purity	Law	Love	Deliverance/Service	Care
Son	Creator	King	Emmanuel/Word/Teacher	High priest/Mediator	Judge/Advocate/Witness	Son/Bridegroom	Savior	Good Shepherd
Spirit	Agent of creation	Executive of Godhead	Spirit of truth	Intercessor	Advocate	Agent of new birth	Spirit of power	Good Spirit
Man/Woman	Creature in God's image	Subject/Citizen	Person	Worshiper	Made for law/Order	Child	Freedman/Servant	Sheep
Sin	Marred image/Idolatry	Rebelliousness/Rebellion	Alienation/Rejection	Defilement/Uncleanness	Lawlessness/Transgression	Self-love/Disobedience	Bondage/Yielding	Lostness/Straying
Salvation	Regeneration/Life	Pardon/Entering kingdom	Reconciliation/Accepting Christ	Forgiveness/Cleansing	Justification	New birth/Life	Redemption/Ransom/Delivery	Being found
Atonement	Recapitulation	Governmental/Anselmic satisfaction	Reconciliation	Propitiation	Penal satisfaction	Moral influence	Ransom	Example
Growth	Growth in image	Kingly rule	Developing relationship	Continuous cleansing	Obeying law	Maturity	Serving God	Following
Church	Body/Building	Assembly/Kingdom	Communion of saints	Kingdom of priests	Community under law	Family/Household	Community of Redeemed	Flock
Sanctification	Full remake of image	Full submission/Lordship	Fullness of God/Infilling of Spirit	Cleansing from sin/Purification	Full obedience/Blamelessness	Perfect love/Perfection	Full redemption	Total following/Rest of faith
Glorification	New heaven/New earth	King of kings	Eternal fellowship	Eternal worship	Final judgment	Final inheritance	Final redemption	Eternal rest

as a whole, using the data under each role in some detail in the following chapters, but an abbreviated outline of the total picture appears in table 1.4.

This data leads us to the conviction that there are many theological truths that are described biblically and theologically in multiple ways. The pattern is clearly set

[19]William B. Pope, *A Compendium of Christian Theology* (London: Wesleyan-Methodist Book Room, 1880), 1:233. "God is all in all throughout the whole compass of theology: everywhere both its subject and its object and the unity of these."

for this in Scripture. Part of the reason for this is to give us the full picture, not only of God himself, but also of other crucial truths we need to understand. The use of the roles of God gives us language categories which in turn introduce us to a means of understanding Christian theology in a very holistic way. After seeing the multiple roles we cannot be content, for example, with describing sin or salvation in only one or two ways. In order to have a full biblical theology each subject needs to be described in all of these language categories as well as by using any additional terms that may be used in Scripture for that particular theological truth. We will return in chapter eleven to more discussion of this use of the roles to develop Christian doctrine after we have examined each role.[20]

How Roles Are Used in Scripture

Throughout the biblical text these extended metaphors or roles are often mixed together in the same passages. Rarely do you get only one portrait used in any single passage, although certain authors tend to use one or two of the roles more frequently than the others. Our purpose will be to separate these roles for the sake of analysis, which we hope will lead to a clearer picture of God and our relationship to him. God's nature, of course, is not separable or neatly divisible, and so the biblical passages that mix these roles come as a healthy corrective to our analytic treatment of them. God is one God, and so he is, in some measure, like all of these portraits. Each role has certain elements that cause it to modify the others. A holistic view of God must include all of the roles of God and also must consider their mutual impact on one another.

No analogy or role from this world will be perfectly adequate to explain a transcendent God. That is one of the reasons why so many different analogies are used to describe him. The various roles condition one another and help us see God more perfectly.[21] We will try to press these roles of God as far as Scripture

---

[20]For a discussion of how roles are a unique combination of metaphorical and conceptual language that provide grids for interpreting a relationship between God and people see McFague, *Metaphorical Theology*, pp. 117-29. McFague also helpfully notes, "Many models, both dormant and subsidiary, as well as many kinds of models (some more metaphorical and others more conceptual) will constitute a Christian theology" (p. 129). The difference between this study and McFague's is that she sees a greater validity in the use of "many kinds of models" that may come from Scripture *or* any other kind of relationship in creation. Our study is based on a more traditional view of revelation as the authoritative standard for theology which carries with it the conviction that the multiple kinds of roles (models) need to all be biblically based.

[21]On how metaphor and analogy qualify one another see J. F. Bethune-Baker, *Introduction to the Early History of Christian Doctrine* (London: Metheun, 1942), p. 160.

does, and there may be certain circumstances when the theological implications of certain roles may be pressed even further. But in this second part of the task we need to proceed very cautiously, lest we fall into misunderstanding by pressing an analogy too far. After all, an analogy is by definition like something in some respects, but not in all respects.

In our study of the various roles we will notice that there is some overlap from one role to another. This means that some things described as done by God in one role are also done by him in another role. God brings life into being both as Creator and as Father. Both the roles of King and Judge have some responsibility for law and order in society. Thus while we try to categorize the language in each of these roles, it must be remembered that some activities of God and some relationships of people to God may fit in more than one category. The lines between these categories must not be drawn too rigidly, but must be seen as flexible and porous because many times the categories "bleed" into one another. An effort will be made in each chapter to indicate which part of each analogy may also be applicable to other roles in our discussion.

A Whole View of God Is Essential

In the following chapters each of the eight major roles will be discussed in sequence. When this task has been completed, then it will be possible to synthesize the data under each theme in Christian theology (Christ, the Holy Spirit, men and women, sin, salvation, atonement, growth, the church, sanctification and glorification) for application in knowing God and for ministry. There can be no holistic theology of any of these truths without biblical materials from all eight roles and their language categories. This means the church must "package" a holistic portrait from each of these categories for preaching, teaching and other ministry purposes. It simply is not sufficient to speak of "Isaiah's view of God" or "Paul's view of sin." For those in the church who are convinced that the whole Bible is the word of God, a holistic understanding of this data must be at the heart of their theology. This does not mean to imply that there was never a progressive revelation of materials, nor that there ought not to be significant consideration given to how much revelation had been given at any particular period in biblical history. Yet, for teaching, preaching and discipling purposes today, the entire biblical picture must be taken into account if the church is going to call men and women to properly understand God and adequately respond to him. It is this full, whole, biblical understanding that is one of the first parts of the work of systematic theology.[22]

In relation to the data, our task is not to gather everything the Bible has to say about sin, for example, but we hope to be provisionally comprehensive about how the Bible pictures sin under each of the major roles we are describing. The next step in the process would be to put together a holistic doctrine of sin from these eight major roles (plus any other data that might not be included in these or their subcategories) for a complete and realistic picture of sin. It is hoped that our analysis of these biblical language categories will facilitate the process of pulling together what the Scripture has to say about sin and each of the other subject headings described. This is part of the way we hope to facilitate the movement from biblical materials to systematic theology.

Further, it has been observed that many people find it much easier to obtain a grasp of the categories of Christian theology if there is a way for them to see how they fit together. Helping people understand Christian truth in categories of creation language, legal language, family language, etc., makes it much easier for them to conceptualize truth in their own minds and apply it in their own lives. Since it is the application of biblical truth to life that is a matter of special concern for the church, we hope the following analysis will make a significant contribution to that end.

Analogical Language *Religious Language*

Since this whole book is wrapped up with the language of analogy, a further word is in order about how analogy functions. In the history of the Christian church it was Thomas Aquinas who made the most effective case for analogi-

---

[22]This approach to the biblical data fits between the final stages of biblical theology and beginning stages of systematic theology. It is the task of biblical theology to collect the fruits of exegesis, first within books and then within authors. But most biblical theology stops with the collection of certain significant data under authors or time periods. An exception to this is Donald Guthrie's *New Testament Theology* (Downers Grove, Ill.: InterVarsity Press, 1981), in which he attempts to summarize the biblical data under the categories of systematic theology. As valuable as Guthrie's work is, it is limited only to the New Testament data. The next step must be to include the Old Testament materials in order to gain a holistic view of subjects like God, men and women, sin, salvation, the atonement, growth, the church, sanctification and glorification. The task of this book is located between the final responsibilities of biblical theology and the initial task of systematics.

cal language as the best means of speaking about God.[23] He argued that since God is infinite, it follows that none of our finite concepts can be applied to him univocally (with one voice), i.e., expressing entirely the same meaning as they do in ordinary usage. Further, he insisted that since God created the world, then he cannot be totally distinct in every way from it, for that would make the descriptive terms of him equivocal (in a different voice), i.e., expressing totally different meanings. The creature must bear some similarity to the Creator. It is this similarity, said Aquinas, that makes it possible for the creature to speak analogically of the Creator, using the language of creation in order to describe him.[24]

For example, we may say God is a King, meaning there is an analogy (comparison) between the way God works and the way a king works, i.e., sometimes he acts like a king but not all the time. Since God is a purely spiritual King, there will always be dissimilarities between him and any earthly king. If we said God is a King using univocal language, we would be saying that he is exactly like a king in all respects. If we used theological language equivocally, we would say that the concept of an earthly king will tell us nothing about God's work as a King. God as a King and "King George" would be as unrelated in meaning as the word "ball" when used of Cinderella or a sporting event. So in terms of the options of language when speaking about God (univocal, equivocal or analogical), clearly analogous language seems to be best.

This analogical language may be divided into two types: metaphysical and metaphorical. While the former apply literally to God, the latter do not. A metaphysical analogy has to do with the essence of God's being, whereas a metaphorical analogy describes the way God works in relationship to others. Up to this point we have been referring primarily to metaphorical analogy in our discussion of the way God works. Six of the eight roles of God we have described are metaphorical analogies: Creator, King, Priest, Judge, Redeemer and

---

[23]For a discussion of the significant role of Aquinas in the use of analogical language about God see the excellent study by Mondin, *Principle of Analogy*. Also see Mascall, *Existence and Analogy*; and Ralph M. McInerny, *The Logic of Analogy: An Interpretation of St. Thomas* (The Hague: Nijhoff, 1961).

[24]"A word has the same sense (univocal) if it has all the same synonyms, contraries, determinates and so on; similar sense (analogical) if it has many of the same synonyms and so on; unrelated sense (equivocal) if it has none of the same synonyms and so on" (Richard Swinburne, *Revelation: From Metaphor to Analogy* [Oxford: Clarendon, 1992], pp. 39-40).

Shepherd. However, a word needs to be said about metaphysical analogy and the two roles associated with it.

Metaphysics has to do with the essence or being of something. When we talk about a metaphysical nature of God, we are talking about that which belongs to the essence of his nature. In our discussions we will be talking about the essence of God's nature in relation to his holiness. We will also be talking about the expression of his holiness in attributes like purity, righteousness, love and goodness. When we use any of these expressions in relationship to God (e.g., God is good), we will be talking about a metaphysical analogy that is literally true of God's being.

Metaphysical analogy is also related to two of the roles that we are discussing: God as Personal Revealer and God as Father. While both of these analogies include metaphorical elements (that is, God is like a person who verbally communicates [Personal Revealer] and like a Father), he is not perfectly like either. He does not have a physical body like all other persons in the created world, nor does he have a consort with which to beget children. So like the other metaphorical analogies, God is like a Personal Revealer and like a Father in some ways but unlike them in other ways. The added dimension in these two roles is that there is something within the inner being of the triune God that each of these roles describes, something of his essence. As Personal Revealer the three members of the Trinity are relating to each other as three persons within one Godhead, and particularly, they are communicating with each other. This person-to-person relation and communication within God himself has to do with the very essence or being of God. The same is true with regard to the relationship between the Father and the Son in the Trinity. Classic Christian theology has understood the distinction between the first and second persons of the Trinity as basically that which relates to Fatherhood and Sonhood, One begets and One is eternally begotten. This means that the role of God as Father in Scripture sometimes relates to his Fatherhood within the triune Godhead and sometimes to his role as Father over persons within creation. Since a designation of God as Personal Revealer and as Father have to do with the very essence of God's being, these two roles are designated as metaphysical analogies.

Because these two roles are metaphysical analogies and have to do more with the basic essence of God's nature, there is a sense in which God is more like these two roles than any of the others. Or to put it another way, these roles describe who he is, as well as the way he works, more accurately and more fully than any of the others. They might be referred to as foundational roles for the Christian faith.

In the light of what we have said in this chapter about definitions, it may be valuable to summarize the way we are going to use significant terms:[25]

1. *Analogy.* A relationship between two realities in which there are significant similarities but also recognizable differences.

2. *Symbol.* A reality that stands for and gives insight into some other reality because of the analogy between the two.

3. *Metaphor.* A figurative way of speaking in which the subject (God) is spoken of in terms of a symbol (e.g., lion), which is related to it by analogy.

4. *Role.* A specialized use of metaphor when referring to God (subject) in terms of human beings (symbol): Creator, King, Priest, Judge, Redeemer, Shepherd; with metaphysical dimensions when referring to God in terms of Personal Revealer and Father. Roles may also be labeled as portraits, models or the identity of God.

Having defined our terms, one more issue remains before we can look in detail at each of the roles of God. Is there a characteristic of God's nature that ties together the various roles we are going to study? It is to this issue that we now turn our attention.

---

[25]I am indebted to Peter W. Macky for his preciseness in defining some terms in his valuable study *The Central-ity of Metaphors to Biblical Thought* (pp. 49-56). Mackey does not speak, however, of roles, but models, which he defines as "an established symbol, one that has become conventionally used to illuminate a particular subject" (p. 56). Our use of role is closer to Sallie McFague's description of models as "systematic and relatively perma-nent metaphors" (*Metaphorical Theology*, pp. 39, 103, 117, 125, 129, 193).

Two

The Unity of the Roles

In the light of the introduction to the roles it is clear that these portraits of God give us multiple ways of understanding him. By themselves they tend to accent diversity because God is using so many different pictures of himself. But he is not diverse, he is one God. There is a unity in his nature behind all these various descriptions of himself. We are dealing with the same God whether he describes himself as King, Judge, Father or in other roles.

The question for us then becomes whether or not there is one revealed characteristic of God that accents this unity. Is there one concept that ties together the many roles and corresponding attributes of God's character? Is there one part of his nature that describes more fully his being and thus serves as an overarching category for understanding all the attributes of God and all the roles that God plays in relationship to people?

Not comprehensive enough

The Options

Certain groups within the Christian church have tended to view the sovereignty of God as the most significant characteristic of his being. It is not difficult to understand why many have focused on this characteristic of God's nature. On opening the book of Genesis we are immediately struck with the sovereignty of God that is expressed in creation, in his providential government of the universe and in his preservation of Abraham's descendants in Egypt. Furthermore, the picture of the sovereignty of God runs straight through Scripture in terms of the accomplishment of his overall purposes in history. This attribute appears all the way to the closing pictures of God's final sovereign rule over earth and heaven.

The concept of God's sovereignty is able to encompass many activities of the roles of God in Scripture that reveal him as Creator, King, Judge and Redeemer, and therefore, it is justifiably conceived as one of the most pervasive concepts for understanding the whole nature of God.

Yet other parts of God's revelation about himself are not so easily incorporated under the concept of sovereignty. Certain roles (e.g., that of Teacher, Prophet, Friend, Priest, Shepherd and Father) that God has in relationship to people are not so readily subsumed under the category of sovereignty. While the data related to each of these roles of God is not unconnected with sovereignty, neither is it immediately apparent how sovereignty serves as an all-encompassing concept for these pictures of God. This leads us to ask whether or not there is in Scripture another concept related to God's nature that is even more all-encompassing than his sovereignty.

Emil Brunner raises this question when he discusses the relationship of God's sovereignty with his holiness. Brunner notes, "From the standpoint of revelation the first thing which has to be said about God is his Sovereignty. But this first point is intimately connected with a second one—so closely indeed that we might even ask whether it ought not to have come first: God is the Holy One."[1]

There is in fact significant biblical data that supports the view that the holiness of God ought to come first in understanding God. This biblical material indicates that holiness serves the function of describing the essence of God's being and is the unifying element for all the rest of his attributes and roles. Because of the pervasive nature of this data on holiness and its implications for the unity behind the roles of God, we are going to review its key elements. This should properly set the stage then for a look at each of the eight major roles of God.

The Biblical Centrality of Holiness

the thing that identifies unity of God

Holiness in the beginning. The question may be raised that if holiness is the most pervasive concept of the nature of God in Scripture, why does it not receive more attention earlier in Scripture? In short, why must one wait for the books of Exodus and Leviticus for any focus on God's holiness, when one might expect that the most significant thing said about God's character would be said first,

---

[1]Emil Brunner, *The Christian Doctrine of God* (London: Lutterworth, 1952), p. 157.

i.e., in Genesis. However, it may be that, in God's providence, the first thing that needed to be said about himself in the ancient Near Eastern world had to do with his supranatural nature. The first question to be settled in the ancient world may well have been the supranatural, monotheistic character of God over against the immanent polytheist gods of that world. The picture of God in Genesis certainly makes the case for one transcendent God who created the universe but is not a part of it. The first theological battle that had to be fought (supranatural monotheism vs. naturalistic polytheism) may only begin to introduce the nature of God. A fuller understanding of him follows in other biblical books, built on this important presupposition about his being.

Related to this question of when the concept of holiness appears in Scripture (and in particular in the light of an earlier focus on God's role as Creator), it will be helpful to distinguish between an *Order of Knowing* and an *Order of Being*. The *Order of Knowing* refers to the unfolding knowledge that God gives through his revelation. Different parts of what we can and need to know about God will be unfolded in his wisdom as people are ready to receive them. This is why the concept of progressive revelation is significant for God's unfolding self-revelation throughout Scripture. But as it relates to knowledge of God himself, it is only when the totality of this knowledge has been revealed in all Scripture that we then have a full picture of what God is like.

When all of the revelation God gives about himself is made known at the end of special revelation (the Scriptures), we are then in a position to understand the wholeness of God's nature, a wholeness that would have been true about God even before he began to make it known. This means that there is an *Order of Being* (i.e., what God is in himself) that is prior to God's making known anything about himself. This allows for the fact that God exists in himself (Order of Being) and existed before any progressive revelation of himself (Order of Knowing). So it is perfectly conceivable that concepts of God (like his holiness) may well be more central to our understanding of his being, while in the unfolding knowledge of himself, this truth is not made known at first.

Yet when God begins to reveal his holiness in the context of the Exodus-Sinai events, he may be giving an even larger concept about himself, one that encompasses his sovereignty and also his immanence and his moral character. It is possible that the holiness of God includes all those things normally subsumed under the category of his sovereignty, and also many other roles and attributes that are not as easily understood as manifestations of sovereignty. If a survey of the biblical materials indicates that God's holiness is the overarching tie within his nature, this would certainly not deny the sovereignty of God. However, it may show that sovereignty alone does not adequately unify all of the attributes or roles of God. Rather, it may indicate that holiness is a more complete concept for encompassing the full description of what God is like. It was just this conclusion that holiness is the most pervasive concept of Hebrew faith that led Hänel to describe the faith of the Old Testament as the "religion of holiness."[2]

The holiness of God: Mount Sinai. The centrality of holiness for understanding the nature of God begins at Mount Sinai when God tells Israel that he is looking for a holy people (Ex 19:6). He then explains why he wants them to be holy, viz., because they are to be like himself. He declares, "I am the LORD your God; consecrate yourselves therefore, and be holy, for I am holy" (Lev 11:44). In describing the character of the people who are to be his "own possession," He makes clear what his own basic character is like, i.e., it is holy, and he continues to reiterate this same understanding of himself throughout the book of Leviticus (19:2; 20:7, 26; 21:8).

Earlier at Mount Sinai God had revealed himself to Moses as "I AM WHO I AM" (Ex 3:14). This revelation of his "name" is also a revelation of his nature. At first reading this appears to focus on his creative sovereignty, i.e., he is the one responsible for all being. This declaration is followed repeatedly in Exodus and Leviticus by the declaration of God, "I am Yahweh," or as in most of our English translations, "I am the LORD." This may well be a repeated emphasis on himself as the only God, as well as the One who is the source of all existence.

However, a fuller picture of God begins to emerge as he starts to qualify this declaration. When an adjective begins to be placed in relationship to the "I AM," it is in God's statement, "I am holy" (Lev 11:44, 45). Since his name is so intimately bound up with his nature, the connection of holiness with the name is very significant. It seems to indicate that holiness is the most important thing Israel needed to know about this One who was revealing himself to them. Furthermore, in Leviticus 11:44, 45 the phrases "I am the LORD" and "I am holy" seem to be used interchangeably. The parallelism is so striking that it is difficult

[2]J. Hänel, *Die Religion der Heiligkeit*, cited in Walther Eichrodt, *Theology of the Old Testament*, 6th ed. (London: SCM Press, 1964), 1:270.

not to see the two as synonymous throughout the book (19:2-4, 10, 12, 14, 16, 18, 25, 28, 30-31, 34, 36, 37; 20:7, 8, 24, 26; 21:8, 15, 23; 22:2-3, 8-9, 16, 30-33). The recurrence of these two expressions all through the Sinai story strongly indicates that the chief idea being revealed about God is his holiness.

This seems to be underlined elsewhere in the Old Testament through the references to the "name" of God. In Leviticus 20:3 the first modifier connected with the "name" of God appears. God pronounces judgment on those who profane his "holy name." The sequence of revelation seems to be "I am the LORD," then "I am holy," followed by references to "my holy name." This is certainly the most characteristic adjective connected with the "name" of God throughout the Old Testament. There are five references to a "glorious" name and four references to a "great name" of God, but all the others (23) refer to God's "holy name."

Edmond Jacob points out that "the name" is synonymous with Yahweh. So the name "always expresses the essential nature of a being, manifests the totality of the divine presence." Since "name," in fact, does refer to the essence of God's being, then holiness seems to be most characteristic of his nature. In Jacob's words, "the relation between holiness and the name reveals the identity of holiness with deity."[3] Given the fact that "glory" is one of the manifestations of holiness (Is 6:3), it may be that even the references to his "glorious name" are really only an alternate rendering of "holy name."

In addition to the revelation of his name, God gave Israel at Mount Sinai a pictorial representation of the holiness of his character. It came in the form of the tabernacle that was to be pitched in the center of the camp of Israel. Within the tabernacle precincts, the place that most clearly represented the personal presence of God among his people was the Holy of Holies (Ex 26:33-34). Thus Israel had a visual reminder every day of not only the presence but the holiness of God.

The holiness of God: Throughout Israel's history. The revelation of God's holiness to Israel is not limited to the Exodus/Sinai events, but the fact that it receives such emphasis at this point means that it was foundational for all Israel's understanding of God. The nature of biblical revelation is that it is progressive

---

[3]Edmond Jacob, *Theology of the Old Testament*, trans. Arthur W. Heathcote and P. J. Allcock (New York: Harper & Row, 1950) pp. 82, 85, 88.

in character and built on the foundation of what has been made known earlier. Further revelation elaborates our understanding of the character of God, but does not abrogate that which has gone before. It builds on the foundation of what has been revealed. Thus it was not necessary for the holiness of God's character to receive the same emphasis at all points in Israel's history. The Exodus/Sinai events were so crucial for all Israel's life and thought that from that time onward the picture of a holy God that had been revealed was understood as a "given." A fuller understanding of what that holiness was like would come with additional revelation, but it would continue to be rooted in the name and nature of God.

There are significant points in Israel's history when further glimpses into the essential character of God are given. One of these comes with the vision of the prophet Isaiah when he sees the creatures around the throne of God crying, "Holy, holy, holy is the LORD of hosts; the whole earth is full of his glory" (Is 6:3). It is interesting to note that while Isaiah sees God as the sovereign King, his description of his essential being is not in terms of sovereignty, or even righteousness, mercy or love. Rather, it is the holiness of God that stands at the very heart of his nature.

The impact of this understanding of God is why the prophet uses as his characteristic designation for God the term "the Holy One of Israel." The title fits well Israel's reverence for the name of God. God had warned Israel about profaning his name by taking it in vain (Ex 20:7). The taking of the name of the Lord in vain had to do with claiming the holiness of his character while not reflecting that character as a holy people. Ezekiel declares God's judgment on Israel because they took his "holy name" in vain and profaned it among the nations. When they did this, God said it became his concern to "vindicate the holiness of my great name" (Ezek 36:20-23). Further, the holiness of God is so identified with the very nature of his divinity that, as Skinner points out, when God swears by himself, he swears by his own nature, i.e., by his holiness (Ps 89:35).[4]

The holiness of God: New Testament. By the time we get to the New Testament the holiness of God is assumed to have been established. As E. F. Harrison

---

[4]*HDB*, vol. 2, p. 396. Helmer Ringgren remarks that throughout the development of Israelite religion "the notion of holiness seems to have been surprisingly constant" (*The Prophetical Conception of Holiness* [Uppsala: A. B. Lundequistska Bokhandeln, 1948], p. 30).

remarks, "The lesser emphasis in the New Testament is readily accounted for on the assumption that the massive presentation under the Old Covenant is accepted as an underlying presupposition."[5] Nevertheless, the holiness of God is mentioned at strategic points. In the Lukan birth narrative, Mary exclaims, "He who is mighty has done great things for me, and holy is his name" (Lk 1:49). At the beginning of his ministry Jesus instructs his disciples to pray to their heavenly Father, "hallowed be thy name" (Mt 6:9), and at the very end of his time with the disciples he prays in his own high priestly prayer to "Holy Father" (Jn 17:11). Thus it would seem that the holiness of God receives special mention at the Incarnation as well as the beginning and end of Jesus' ministry. These emphases take on particular meaning in the light of Jesus' purpose to make known the character of God (e.g., Jn 1:18). Apparently, the New Testament writers meant for believers to see the connection between the holiness of God and the character of God revealed in Jesus.

Peter caught the implications of all of this very well and so instructed the early Christians to be holy in all their conduct, "since it is written, 'You shall be holy, for I am holy'" (1 Pet 1:15, 16). The holiness of God is highlighted again when the book of Revelation repeats the vision of Isaiah, where the creatures cry day and night, "Holy, holy, holy, is the Lord God Almighty, who was and is and is to come!" (Rev 4:8). It is as though Revelation is saying that the character of God *has been* holy, *is* holy, and *will be* holy. Indeed, the essence of God's Being is timeless; he is the same in the past, the present and the future. The same God who reveals himself in the Old Testament as holy, is still holy at the end of the New Testament.

The holy Trinity. It is important to note, however, that the New Testament picture is augmented by the references to the second and third persons of the Trinity as holy. Jesus is introduced as "holy" in the angel's announcement to Mary, "The child to be born will be called holy, the Son of God" (Lk 1:35). This is not surprising in the light of the biblical witness to the divine nature of Christ. If he is divine and divinity at its essence is holy, then he will be holy. At the outset of his ministry Jesus is recognized as "the Holy One of God" (Mk 1:24), and after a period of time the disciples come to recognize the holiness of his character. Peter, speaking for the Twelve, exclaims, "We have believed, and have come to

---

[5] *ISBE rev.*, vol. 2, p. 725.

know, that you are the Holy One of God" (Jn 6:69). Likewise, the early church recognizes this in their description of Jesus as God's holy servant (Acts 3:13-14; 4:26, 30).[6]

In reference to the Spirit of God the adjective *holy* is only attached to that title three times in the Old Testament (Ps 51:11; Is 63:10, 11). However, it is found in the New Testament no less than ninety-one times, and is by far the most common expression for God's Spirit. It is not an accident that in the New Testament and the vocabulary of the Christian church the Spirit of God is almost always referred to as the *Holy Spirit*. Its familiarity has obscured the fact that it represents the essential nature of the triune God: Father, Son and Spirit.

As Emil Brunner astutely observed, "Although in the New Testament the idea of the holiness of God as a divine attribute is emphasized somewhat less than in the Old Testament, yet it is everywhere presupposed, and it appears at decisive points where the whole revealing and saving work of Christ is gathered up as the revelation of the Name." He concludes that "the whole of the Old Testament is the revelation of the holy God."[7] Otto Procksch agrees: "The holiness of God the Father is everywhere presumed in the New Testament, though seldom stated. It is filled out in Jesus Christ as the *hagios tou theou* (ἅγιος τοῦ θεοῦ), and in the *pneuma hagion* (πνεῦμα ἅγιον)."[8]

The significance of God's holiness. In the light of this biblical data it is not surprising that many scholars from a wide variety of traditions believe that holiness is the most central concept for understanding the nature and being of God. Gerhardus Vos describes divine holiness as something which

> is not really an attribute to be coordinated with the other attributes distinguished in the divine nature. It is something coextensive with and applicable to everything that can be predicated of God; He is holy in everything that characterizes Him and reveals Him, holy in His goodness and grace, no less than in His righteousness and wrath.[9]

Walther Eichrodt agrees: "Of all the qualities attributed to the divine nature there is one which in virtue both of the frequency and the emphasis with which

---

[6]"The Holy One" is used of Jesus in Mk 1:24; Lk 4:34; Jn 6:69; Acts 2:27; 3:14; 13:35; 1 Jn 2:20; Rev 3:7; see also Lk 1:35, Heb 7:26.

[7]Brunner, *Christian Doctrine of God*, p. 157.

[8]*TDNT*, 1:101. See also *IDB*, 2:623; *ZPEB*, 3:180.

[9]Geerhardus Vos, *Biblical Theology* (Grand Rapids, Mich.: Eerdmans, 1948), p. 266.

it is used, occupies a position of unique importance—namely, that of holiness." Because of that he declares, "'Holy' is the epitaph deemed fittest to describe the Thou whose nature and operations are summed up in the divine Name; and for this reason it comes to mean that which is distinctively characteristic of God, that which constitutes his nature."[10]

The concept of holiness is seen at the heart of the picture of God in both testaments. Theodorus Vriezen claims holiness to be "the central idea of the Old Testament faith in God,"[11] and E. F. Harrison states, "It is no exaggeration to state that this element overshadows all others in the character of the deity so far as the Old Testament revelation is concerned."[12] Otto Procksch holds to the same views regarding holiness in the New Testament. "In the New Testament the holiness of God is thought of as his essential attribute in which the Christian must share and for which the heavenly Father prepares him by his instruction." Therefore, "the nature of Christianity is thus centrally determined by the concept of the holy."[13] The same biblical data leads Rudolf Kittle to assert that the idea of holiness is not just one side of God's essential being, but "rather it is the comprehensive designation for the total content of the divine being in his relationship to the external world."[14]

Gustaf Aulén in his *Faith of the Christian Church*, expresses his conviction that "holiness is the foundation on which the whole conception of God rests." It is not as though these scholars would ignore the other attributes of God, but simply that all other characteristics need to be qualified by his holiness. Aulén states, "It gives specific tone to each of the various elements in the idea of God and makes them part of a fuller conception of God. Every statement about God, whether in reference to his love, power, righteousness . . . ceases to be an affirmation about God when it is not projected against the background of his holiness."[15] So while God is righteousness, love and mercy, and expresses wrath and jealousy, these are always understood in Scripture as holy righteousness, holy love, holy mercy, holy wrath and holy jealousy. Holiness is that which qualifies and conditions all

---

[10]Walther Eichrodt, *Theology of the Old Testament*, trans. J. A. Baker, 6th ed. (London: SCM Press, 1961), 1:270, 274.

[11]Theodorus C. Vriezen, *An Outline of Old Testament Theology*, trans. S. Neuijen (Bristol: John Wright, 1911), p. 151.

[12]*ISBE* (rev.) 2:725.

[13]*TDNT*, 1:114, 110. See also pp. 93, 100.

[14]*NSRE*, 5:317.

[15]Gustaf Aulén, *The Faith of the Christian Church* (Philadelphia: Muhlenberg, 1960), p. 103.

the other attributes of God. For this reason P. T. Forsyth can say, "Everything in Christian theology begins and ends with the holiness of God."[16] The holiness of God must be viewed as being at the heart of any truly biblical theology[17]

⚹ Holiness: Original and Derived

A corollary to the fact that the essence of the character of God is his holiness is the biblical picture that only God is originally holy. He is the only one who is inherently holy in himself, and as the only naturally holy One, it is he who transfers things into the category of the holy.[18] There are other things in Scripture referred to as holy, but theirs is a derived holiness. This derived holiness arises out of a right relationship to God the holy One. Certain *places* are described in Scripture as holy, for example, Jerusalem (Is 52:1) and Zion (Is 27:13), the camp of Israel (Deut 23:14), and heaven (Is 57:15). In addition, certain *things* are described as holy, for example, the tabernacle/temple, which houses both the Holy Place and the Holy of Holies (Ex 26:33); the garments of the priests (Lev 16:4); and the vessels of the tabernacle (Num 3:31). Certain *times* and *seasons* are also designated as holy, for example, the sabbath (Gen. 2:3; Ex 20:8; Is 58:13), the annual festivals (Lev 23), and the year of jubilee (Lev 25:12).

Furthermore, *people* are declared to be holy in Scripture. Sometimes their holiness has reference to ceremonial holiness (Lev 22:1-9), and at other times it references moral holiness (Ex 19:6; Lev 21:6-7; 1 Pet 1:15-16). While all the above (places, things, times and people) may be described as holy, theirs is a derived holiness, not a natural holiness. According to Helmer Ringgren, "No thing, or person is holy in itself, but becomes holy when it is placed in relation to God."[19] Thus it may be proper to describe the holiness of things other than God as an imparted holiness or a given holiness that comes from the Holy One.

This means the holiness of all other things becomes a secondary holiness, not a primary holiness.[20] One of the consequences of this fact is that while God is

---

[16]P. T. Forsyth, *The Cruciality of the Cross* (London: Hodder & Stoughton, 1909), pp. 23-24.

[17]See also Jacob, *Theology of the Old Testament*, pp. 8, 6; Hermann Schultz, *Old Testament Theology* (Edinburgh: T & T Clark, 1892), 2:167; A. B. Davidson, *The Theology of the Old Testament* (Edinburgh: T & T Clark, 1904), p. 151.

[18]Eichrodt, *Theology of the Old Testament*, 1:272.

[19]Ringgren, *The Prophetical Conception of Holiness*, p. 9.

[20]See also Gustave F. Oehler, *Theology of the Old Testament*, ed. George E. Day (Grand Rapids, Mich.: Zondervan, 1883), p. 106; *HDB*, 2:395.

holy always and forever, persons and things may lose their holiness. Thus, Jerusalem was not the holy city when it was controlled by the Jebusites, and when the glory of God departed from it (Ezek 10:11), it ceased to be the holy city. So we may safely say that derived holiness is not automatically a permanent possession.

Ceremonial and moral holiness. While many are convinced that holiness is the essence of God's being, there is less unanimity with regard to the meaning of this holiness. The first major division over the meaning of holiness in Scripture has to do with its ceremonial and ethical dimensions, particularly in the Old Testament. The debate over this question has been heavily influenced by Rudolph Otto's contention that the "holy" originally had no ethical connotations. Otto, following the history of religion's school, wanted to reduce the original biblical materials to their most primitive form. This would then allow him to identify holiness as a primal element with similar phenomena in other religions of the ancient Near Eastern world. Thus, he desired for the original concept of the holy to stand for that which did not include either a moral factor or a rational factor. This holiness, without any moral or rational content, he designates as the "numinous."[21] Otto's influence has been so widespread that many see holiness in the early stages of Israel's faith as nonethical or nonmoral, with the ethical element only coming through the eighth-century prophets and later.[22]

The problem with Otto's view is that it does not adequately represent the biblical data as we have it. The holiness of God in Scripture is never depicted apart from its moral and rational dimensions. A holy God is always moral, and he communicates in rational language. It does not mean there may not be other dimensions involved in his relationships with people, but the moral and the rational are always connected with God who is the Holy One at every stage of biblical history.

This fact has not gone unnoticed by a number of scholars. Heinisch writes, "The holiness of God as an attribute which is ethical in nature and opposed to sin was proclaimed long before the time of the prophets."[23] The moral character of God is revealed early in places like the Ten Commandments which, as Vriezen

---

[21]Rudolf Otto, *The Idea of the Holy* (London: Oxford University Press, 1928), pp. 1-7.

[22]Cf. Brunner, *Christian Doctrine of God*, pp. 158, 165. Eichrodt agrees that the ethical element comes through the influence of the prophets; however, he sees a personal element in the concept of holiness much earlier. Because he feels holiness is used primarily of God, the personal dimension he feels is at the heart of what holiness originally meant in Israel (*Theology of the Old Testament*, 1:271-78).

[23]Paul Heinisch, *Theology of the Old Testament*, trans. William G. Heidt (St. Paul: North Central, 1955), p. 69.

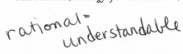
rational = understandable

points out, ranks first in the narrative of the revelation at Mount Sinai. These moral demands, he declares, "did not spring up after the appearance of the major prophets but at a much earlier date."[24] J. C. Lambert states that "the injunction, 'Be ye holy; for I am holy' (Lev 11:44; 19:2), plainly implies an ethical conception. Men cannot resemble God in his incommunicable attributes. They can reflect his likeness only along the lines of those moral qualities of righteousness and love in which true holiness consists." He sees the concept of God's declaration of his own holiness intimately bound up with the call to the holiness of individuals. "While the idea of ceremonial holiness runs through the Old Testament, the ethical significance which Christianity attributes to the term is never wholly absent, and gradually rises in the course of the revelation into more emphatic prominence."[25]

Kittel believes that from the beginning of the establishment of the covenant in Exodus 19 holiness in terms of "separation" is only secondary and that the heart of the event is God's concern for the character of his people whom he desires to be holy. "Whatever belongs to God must have the essential character which accompanies such relationship," Kittel argues. Therefore, he feels the concept of separation and its accompanying ceremonial regulations concerning holiness are clearly secondary.[26] Even a critical scholar such as J. Muilenburg believes that the Ten Commandments are included in the earliest dated sections of the Pentateuch, and therefore the ethical element in holiness must have come very early.[27]

Otto and others have failed to see the moral and ethical dimensions of holiness coming early in Scripture, and part of their failure is due to their desire to find a "primitive holiness" easily identifiable with "the holy" in other religions of the ancient near eastern world. Ceremonial holiness, without ethical or rational overtones, certainly is easier to identify in this way. Unfortunately, this position has failed to understand the unique relationship between ceremonial and moral holiness in Israel. The ceremonial does not just represent that which is "separated" from the common or profane and dedicated to deity, as it might in other religions. Rather, ceremonial holiness is designed to promote moral holiness. It is an object lesson that places theological truth in concrete experience.

---

[24]Theodorus C. Vriezen, *An Outline of Old Testament Theology*, trans. S. Nueijen (Bristol: John Wright, 1911), pp. 159-60.
[25]ISBE, 3:1403-4.
[26]NSRE, p. 316.
[27]IDB, 2:620.

God is holy, and therefore certain things are clean, acceptable and holy, while certain other things are unclean, unacceptable and unholy. When this case is made, for example, in the dietary restrictions, it reinforces the lesson for every Israelite that some things are acceptable to God and some things unacceptable, i.e., some things are holy and some things unholy. This strengthens one's understanding then of moral and ethical questions; they too are either in the category of acceptable or unacceptable to God. Ceremonial holiness in Israel is designed as a teaching tool to communicate certain basic principles and theology that relate to the moral realm. Heinisch observes, "Ordinances regarding foods, ritual purifications and sacrifices were not meant as ends in themselves but as means to a moral life, to promote that inner sanctity demanded by God."[28] This is seen clearly in such passages as Leviticus 19 and 21 where an intimate interweaving of both moral and ceremonial holiness occurs. This close relationship between the two was not the accidental result of a later editor, but was part of the original design of the passages as they were given.

The Meaning of Holiness

In some discussions of the meaning of holiness the categories of moral and non-moral holiness may be helpful. Yet this must not be the only approach taken in the discussion of the full range of meaning for this central biblical concept. A survey of the data (as the following chapters will show) indicates that the meaning of holiness has six major components. They include the concepts of separation, brilliance, righteousness, love, power and goodness. Their relationship to holiness may be pictured as in figure 2.1.

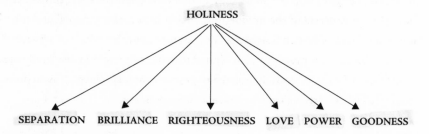

HOLINESS

SEPARATION   BRILLIANCE   RIGHTEOUSNESS   LOVE   POWER   GOODNESS

Figure 2.1. Components of holiness.

---

[28]Heinisch, *Theology of the Old Testament*, p. 69.

For those who like to focus their attention on the nonmoral elements in holiness, the meanings of holiness as "separation" and "power" usually receive attention. But the practice of making holiness mean only separation or power (as Otto does) leads to a truncated view of the biblical concept of holiness. For the holistic view of holiness that Christian theology must have for the application of this truth to life, the entire range of meanings must be given full consideration, including those that refer to its rational and moral content.[29]

Holiness and the roles of God. The six major dimensions of the meaning of holiness (separation, brilliance, righteousness, love, power and goodness) each require an explanation and a documentation from the biblical materials. This will be done in the following chapters. The important factor to note at this point is how the various meanings of holiness are very closely correlated with certain roles of God and the language connected with each of these roles throughout Scripture. The matching of six parts of the meaning of holiness with eight of the major roles is possible because two of the meanings of Christian holiness are related to more than one role.

Thus when holiness is understood as separation, it seems to apply to God in terms of his transcendent supranaturalism and is closely tied with his role as Creator. But other passages that refer to God's holiness as separation are more intimately bound up in his sovereignty over the creation, and so are related to God's role as King or Ruler of the universe. So holiness as separation encompasses two roles: God as Creator and God as King.

In Scripture the uses of holiness that imply brilliance also seem to be divisible into two categories. The brilliance of God's holiness is often closely related to his immanent personal presence in the communication of truth, and this dimension is tied to his role as Personal Revealer. But holiness as brilliance is also associated with matters of purity and grace, and these passages seem to be correlated with God's role as Priest. Thus holiness as brilliance may be expressed in concepts of truth, purity and grace, which relate to two major roles: God as Personal Revealer and God as Priest.

The passages that describe God's holiness in terms of righteousness are most

---

[29]On how the meaning of brilliance reflects the rational dimension of holiness see chapter 5, and for a discussion on how righteousness, love and goodness reflect the moral side of holiness see chapters 7, 8 and 10 respectively.

often associated with his role as Judge, while those that depict holiness as love are usually connected with his role as Father. Holiness as goodness is intertwined with the picture of God as Shepherd. The idea of holiness as power is repeatedly associated with the image of God as Redeemer, although in some degree it is related to the roles of Creator and King. The full picture that correlates God's holiness with God's roles is set out in figure 2.2.

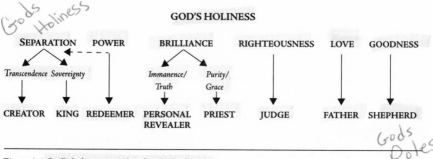

Figure 2.2 God's holiness correlated with God's roles

The close relationship among these six meanings of holiness and the eight roles in which the Scripture describes God means that a significant part of the biblical data about God, people and the relationship between the two are tied together by the idea of holiness. No other category that describes God is so pervasive in holding together these major metaphors about God and his relationship to individuals.

G. B. Caird is convinced that almost all of the language used by the Bible to refer to God is metaphor. The one possible exception that he mentions is the word "holy."[30] The concept of the holy is the exception is because this is the word that most effectively ties together so many of the metaphorical descriptions of God. In the following chapters we will see how the biblical data connects the concept of holiness with each of the roles (metaphors) of God.

This understanding of the tie between God's holiness and each of these roles strengthens the conviction that the concept of holiness is one, and perhaps the greatest, overarching tie in all biblical truth. This makes even more convincing the argument of some that the holiness of God is the central dimension of his own nature.

---

[30]Caird, *The Language and Imagery of the Bible*, p. 18.

THREE

HOLY GOD AS
TRANSCENDENT CREATOR

[handwritten margin note: Transcendent & separate from the world]

The Unity Factor

The first of the roles of God to be studied is that of Creator. In the previous chapter we saw that this role is tied with God's other roles by means of his holiness. To explore more fully the relation of holiness to creation, we will look at the concept of "separation" as the first of the key meanings of holiness and then allow that to serve as a basis for exploring God's role as Transcendent Creator.

Other attributes of God will be discussed later in the chapter; however, we are beginning our study of God as Creator within the context of his holiness for two reasons. The first is because of the pervasive nature of God's holiness. The second is because the attribute of holiness both unifies the Creator role with other roles and also ties together so many parts of the language of creation. Accordingly, we will look at the meaning of holiness as separation, then at how holiness as separation is tied to creation, and finally, we will be ready to examine God's role as Creator.

Holiness as Separation

Hebrew word for holiness: qodesh. Any understanding of biblical holiness must be centered around the Old Testament word *qodesh* (קֹדֶשׁ) and its derivatives. The exact meaning of the root *qds* has been a matter of extended debate.

There are two basic possibilities for its etymological meaning. One is related to the Babylonian *quddushu*, which is the syllabary equivalent to *ellu*, meaning bright or clear.[1] This explanation leads to an understanding of holiness as originally symbolizing brightness or brilliance, which would relate it closely to purity. Delitzsch even indicates the root may mean freedom from defect. This possibility easily leads to an understanding of holiness with ethical overtones. However, since many modern scholars do not consider the ethical element of holiness significant until late in Israel's history, they tend not to prefer this explanation. As Norman Snaith observes, the etymological choice for many scholars depends "upon *a priori* considerations as to the development of religion in general." Snaith contends that the scholarly swing away from the earlier meaning of "bright, or clear," or the similar idea of "freedom from defect," is

> due largely to the modern view that the development of religion must be traced from below and not from above. That is, the conclusion of the modern scholars is ultimately dependent on the view that religion is a movement from man to God rather than a revelation of God to man. This is the leading motif in the modern study of the history of religion, being a product of the application to the study of religion of the New Scientific Method with its rigid evolutionary hypothesis.[2]

The second etymological alternative is that *qodesh* comes from the root *qd*, which means to divide or separate. This alternative would make the basic meaning of holiness that which is "cut off, withdrawn or set apart," and the central focus would be on "separation." This seems to be the most widely accepted explanation.[3]

Because *qodesh* rarely occurs in a secular sense, it may be that any concrete conclusion regarding its etymology will be difficult to arrive at with any certainty. This is not an absolute stumbling block, however, because, as James Barr points out, the etymology of a word provides the past of a word but it is not

---

[1]Norman H. Snaith, *The Distinctive Ideas of the Old Testament* (New York: Schocken, 1964), p. 24; Ludwig Koehler, *Lexicon in Veteris Testamenti Libros*, ed. Walter Baumgartner (Leiden: E. J. Brill, 1959), p. 825. T. C. Vriezen recognizes that the etymology is unclear, but he thinks brilliance is the most plausible meaning (*An Outline of Old Testament Theology*, trans. S. Neuijen [Bristol: John Wright, 1911], p. 149). This view is supported by W. Gesenius, A. Dillmann, H. Zimmern, T. K. Cheyne and others.

[2]Snaith, *The Distinctive Ideas of the Old Testament*, pp. 24-25.

[3]Ibid. Snaith declares that the monograph by Von Baudissin, *Der Begriff der Herligkeit im Alten Testament* to be the most comprehensive and searching analysis of the subject. *IDB*, 2:617; *ISBE*, 3:1403; *BDB*, p. 871; Marcus Jastro, *A Dictionary of the Tarqumim, The Talmud Babli and Yerushalmi, and the Midrashic Literature* (New York: Pardes, 1950), p. 1319; *HDB*, 2:395. A. B. Davidson, *The Theology of the Old Testament* (Edinburgh: T & T Clark, 1904), p. 150. The case for this option has been carefully laid out by W. W. Graf von Baudissin and supported by Snaith. Others have agreed including J. Muilenburg, J. C. Lambert, the authors of *BDB* and J. Skinner.

an infallible guide to its present meaning. "Etymology is not, and does not profess to be, a guide to the semantic value of words in their current usage, and such value has to be determined from the current usage and not from the derivation."[4] The limited relevant evidence on which to base the comparison may mean that we should best describe *qodesh* as a state that belongs to the sphere of the sacred.

Since the exact etymological explanation of any word is not the conclusive factor in deciding its meaning in any particular context, its actual usage in various contexts becomes that which finally determines its significance. The occurrence of this word in many contexts of Scripture suggests that the factor of "separateness" is basic to some texts, but there may also be crucial elements such as brilliance and purity in other texts.[5] So although separateness may not be provable as the last word on the etymology of *qodesh*, it is certainly one of the meanings that emerges in our examination of its use in the Old Testament. Accordingly, in this chapter and the next we will focus on the concept of holiness as separation, and return in chapters five and six to examine the concept of holiness as brilliance.

Holiness as separation relates to two roles. Since the concept of *qodesh* is used exclusively in relationship to God or that which is in a certain relationship to God, we will begin by focusing on the concept of the holiness of God.[6] The data that speaks about the holiness of God in terms of separation can be seen in two categories. Both are identified by Isaiah's reference to "the LORD, your Holy One, the Creator of Israel, your King" (Is 43:15). The first of these categories relates the concept of holiness to God's transcendence ("Your Holy One, the Creator") and is particularly connected to God's role as Creator, both of his people and his creation. The second category relates to God's sovereignty ("Your Holy One . . . your King"). This connotation is especially related to God's role as King or Ruler and will be the focus of consideration in the next chapter. It is the first of these, i.e., the role of God as the transcendent Creator, that will be the center of our attention in this chapter. The connection of holiness as separation to the two roles (Creator and King) may be pictured as in figure 3.1.

---

[4]James Barr, *The Semantics of Biblical Language* (London, Oxford University Press, 1961), p. 107.
[5]A. S. Wood, "Holiness," *ZPEB*, 3:174.
[6]On the *hagios* word group as the predominant translation of *qodesh*, see *NIDNTT*, 2:224ff.

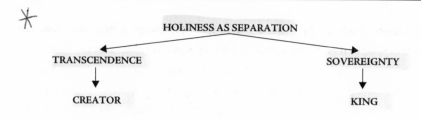

Figure 3.1 Holiness as separation connected to Creator and King

Holiness as transcendence separate from natural world. When the concept of holiness as separation is applied to God, it has reference to God's transcendence of the world of space and time. He is not a part of the natural world, but he is the supranatural One, or as Vriezen says, he is the "Wholly Other One."[7] Hosea states it succinctly "I am God and not man, the Holy One in your midst" (11:9). God is distinct from the created world and from humanity. It is true he relates to it and interacts with it, and this dimension of his holiness will be discussed under the rubric of his immanence. Yet, God is clearly seen as separate and distinct from the created order. Emil Brunner describes holiness as "the Nature of God, that which distinguishes him from everything else, the Transcendence of God in his very nature, as the 'Wholly Other.' Hence, holiness is not a quality which God possesses in common with other beings; on the contrary, it is that which distinguishes Him clearly and absolutely from everything else."[8]

The connection between God's holiness and his transcendence is illustrated in the Lord's prayer. The opening address "Our Father who art in heaven," begins the prayer with an emphasis on God's transcendence, and is immediately followed by the petition "hallowed be thy name" (Mt 6:9). The One whose name and nature is holy, is also the One who transcends the world of space and time.[9]

Uniqueness of Supranatural God

It is holiness as transcendence that distinguishes God from everything else.

---

[7]Vriezen, *Outline of Old Testament Theology*, p. 149. Also George A. F. Knight, *A Christian Theology of the Old Testament* (Richmond, Va.: John Knox Press, 1959), p. 90.

[8]Brunner, *Doctrine of God*, p. 158. See *TDNT*, 1:91; *NSRE*, 5:317.

[9]For the link between holiness and transcendence see CD 1/1, p. 360; Davidson, *Theology of the Old Testament*, p. 145; Snaith, *Distinctive Ideas of the Old Testament*, pp. 79-82; Carl F. H. Henry, *God, Revelation and Authority*, vol. 6, *God Who Stands and Stays*, pt. 2 (Waco, Tex.: Word, 1983), pp. 35-51.

This is not something he possesses in common with other things; rather it is that which separates him from everything else. Because he is in a unique sense "wholly other," he cannot be understood as being identified with any single part of creation. He is, in short, a supranatural being. As Yehezkel Kaufmann has made clear, the basic distinction between the God of Israel and all the gods of the ancient Near Eastern world is that Yahweh is a single, sovereign, supranatural being that is not a part of the created order.[10] All of the other gods of the ancient world were nature gods, i.e., they were identified with some aspect of the natural world. Each of the gods corresponded to one physical dimension of the universe. Thus, the sun god was not just symbolized by the sun, but corresponded exactly with the sun, so that in the ancient mind the sun god *was* the sun and the sun *was* the sun god. Each major aspect of the natural world was likewise identified with one of the gods of the pantheon. This meant that in the stories of creation like the Babylonian *Enuma Elish*, the narrative opens with the gods as natural forces. *Apsu* and *Tiamot* are the salt water and sweet water that mingle their waters together and give birth to other gods. From those gods come the natural world and finally the creation of people. In each of the extrabiblical creation accounts there is a continuity between the gods, the natural elements of the world, the created universe and humanity. They all come from the same primeval "stuff."[11]

In contrast, the biblical picture is one of God who is not identified with any single part of the created order but rather is a supranatural God. He is a Creator who stands outside of (i.e., separate from) the world of space and time, and there is no continuity between himself and creation. There is rather a discontinuity. Creation is not an extension or an emanation of himself but is something created wholly and distinctly apart from him.[12] This is one of the reasons behind the commandment forbidding the worship of images in biblical religion (Ex 20:4-5; Deut 5:8-9). Since God is not any one part of creation, he cannot be fully

---

[10]Yehezkel Kaufmann, *The Religion of Israel* (Chicago: University of Chicago Press, 1960), p. 60.

[11]See Kaufmann's excellent discussion of non-Israelite religion. Ibid., pp. 21-59. Also George E. Wright, *The Old Testament Against Its Environment* (London: SCM Press, 1950), pp.16-19.

[12]See Kaufmann's exceptional picture of the uniqueness of Israel's God in *Religion of Israel*, pp. 60-121. See also Daniel O'Connor, "The Human and the Divine," in *Creation: The Impact of an Idea* (New York: Charles Scribner's Sons, 1969), pp. 107-19; Walther Eichrodt, *Theology of the Old Testament*, trans. J. A. Baker, 6th ed. (London: SCM Press, 1961), 2:98-9, 113-17; Jacob, *Theology of the Old Testament*, pp. 138-42.

represented by any created element. As the transcendent One, he cannot be represented adequately by any aspect of nature.[13]

The Role of God as Transcendent Creator
The Father - Role

Creator. The transcendence of a holy God immediately emphasizes the role of God as Creator of the universe. Isaiah is particularly helpful in identifying a holy God with his role as Creator: "Thus says the LORD, the Holy One of Israel, and his Maker: . . . I made the earth, and created man upon it; it was my hands that stretched out the heavens" (45:11-12). Again he declares, "For your Maker is your husband, the LORD of hosts is his name; and the Holy One of Israel is your Redeemer, the God of the whole earth he is called" (54:5). Further he reminds Israel, "In that day men will regard their Maker, and their eyes will look to the Holy One of Israel" (17:7).[14] In the New Testament when we come to the final biblical pictures of God, we find a recurrence of Isaiah's vision of the one who is described as "holy, holy, holy," and we learn that this is also the one who is described as worthy to receive glory and honor and power "for thou didst create all things, and by thy will they existed and were created" (Rev 4:8, 11). It is clear that God the Holy One is also God the Creator of the universe.[15]

The language figure then that most closely identifies God's transcendence is the language of creation. Beginning with the first chapter of Genesis, God is described as the Creator of the universe. "In the beginning God created the heavens and the earth."[16] This creation was out of nothing (*creatio ex nihilo*)[17] and was accomplished by the word of God.[18] Hebrews asserts that "by faith we understand that the world was created by the word of God, so that what is seen was made out of things which do not appear" (Heb 11:3).

---

[13]Wright, *Old Testament Against Its Environment*, pp. 20-25.

[14]See also Is 40:25-28, 43:1-3, 15; 45:7-12; 57:15-16.

[15]Gustave Friedrich Oehler, *Theology of the Old Testament*, ed. George E. Day (Grand Rapids, Mich.: Zondervan, 1883), p. 106, and Helmer Ringgren, *The Prophetical Conception of Holiness* (Upsalla: A. B. Lundequistska Bokhandeln, 1948), pp. 26-27.

[16]Other references to God as Creator of universe: Gen 2—4; Ps 89:11-12; 90:2; 148:5; Is 40:22, 26, 28; 42:5; 45, 18; 48:13; 51:13; 65:17-18; Jer 33:2; Zech 12:1; Mk 13:19; Eph 3:9; Rev 4:11; 10:6.

[17]On *creatio ex nihilo* see Gerhard von Rad, *Old Testament Theology*, trans. D. M. G. Stalker (New York: Harper & Row, 1962), 1:142; Eichrodt, *Theology of the Old Testament*, 2:101-6; Emil Brunner, *The Christian Doctrine of Creation and Redemption* (London: Lutterworth, 1952), pp. 9-12; Henry, *God, Revelation and Authority*, 6:120-32.

[18]Gen 1:1, 3; Ps 33:6, 9; 148:5; Jn 1:1-3; 2 Pet 3:5.

Elohim is the key name used for God in association with his role as Creator (Gen 1), and it is connected with a *focus* of the language of creation on *life*. The focus of Genesis 1 is on the creation of all life in the universe,[19] and especially the creation of human beings (1:27).[20] The creation of people, however, not only describes the creation of physical life, but also the spiritual life that sets them apart from all other forms of life on earth. When God formed Adam from the dust of the earth, he "breathed into his nostrils the breath of life; and man became a living being" (2:7). It was the breath or spirit of God breathed into humankind that made them unique of all the creatures of the universe.

But it is also a foreshadowing of God's ability to create or recreate spiritual life in individuals. Isaiah proclaims, "Thus says God, the LORD, who created the heavens and stretched them out, who spread forth the earth and what comes from it, who gives breath to the people upon it and spirit to those who walk in it" (Is 42:5). The prophet adds that it is the Creator of life who also gives his Spirit for the creation of spiritual life. "Thus says the LORD who made you, who formed you from the womb and will help you: . . . I will pour my Spirit upon your descendants, and my blessing on your offspring." (44:2-3; cf. Ezek 37:5-6, 10, 14). This is why the New Testament can talk about God as "the source of your life in Christ Jesus" (1 Cor 1:30).[21]

In addition to the biblical materials that speak of God as Creator, there are pictures of him doing creator-like things but using different language categories to describe his activity. Three of these "subroles" are God as Cultivator, God as Builder, and God as Potter. We will elaborate on these in the following sections. A fourth subrole, God as Physician, is more extensive than the other three and is treated as a separate section at the end of the chapter.

✳ *Cultivator.* The God who made creation is also sometimes described as the one who cultivates the land he has made. So in the parable of the vineyard, God is described as a *geōrgos* (γεωργός), a cultivator of the soil (Mt 21:33-43). This role has various translations. Sometimes God is depicted as a vinedresser and sometimes a husbandman. But the basic image is the work of a farmer.

---

[19]Ps 33:6, 9; Is 42:5, 12.

[20]For creation of people: Gen 5:1, 2, 6, 7; Deut 4:32; Job 15:7; Ps 51:5; 89:47; 139:13-16; Is 43:1, 7; 45:12; Zech 12:1; Mal 2:10, 15; 1 Cor 11:9; Col. 3:10.

[21]For God's creation of Israel as his own see Is 27:11; 29:16; 43:1, 7, 21; 44:2, 21, 24; 49:5; Ezek 21:30; Deut 32:18.

The *language category* used to describe this role is from the world of *agriculture.* Its *focus* is on *growth* from the physical creation, whether that growth is described in terms of vines, fields, trees or other plants. The Creator who gives life also causes it to grow.

The first picture of God in this role comes as a part of the creation story, and it is an additional reason for understanding this metaphor to be a subrole of God's work as Creator. God breathed life into Adam, and then he "planted a garden in Eden." Accordingly, "out of the ground the LORD God made to grow every tree that is pleasant to the sight and good for food" (Gen 2:8-9).

The Old Testament has some other graphic pictures of God in this role. One of them is Isaiah's parable of the vineyard where God is depicted as the vinedresser who planted a vineyard expecting a yield of choice grapes, only to receive a harvest of wild grapes. The application to Judah and Jerusalem as a means of conveying promise and judgment provides a very vivid picture of what God not only expected but what he will do in the light of their disobedience (Is 5:1-7). Jesus uses the same picture in his description of the vineyard and the wicked tenants where God expects fruit from his vineyard but those whom he has entrusted with its care plot to keep it from him. As in Isaiah, the point of the parable is judgment (Mt 21:33-43; Mk 12:1-12; Lk 20:9-19).

Jesus shifts the figure in John 15 when he describes God as the vinedresser, himself as the true vine and his disciples as branches that are expected to bear fruit. His purpose here is to talk about the crucial importance of abiding in him, so that the nourishment from the vine may flow through the branches to produce the fruit the vinedresser desires (Jn 15:1-8).

The people in relationship to God as Cultivator may be described as branches connected to vines (Jn 15); as the vineyard itself (Jer 12:10) or as God's field (1 Cor 3:9). The use of the Hebrew verb *nata* (נָטַע), "to plant," sometimes depicts God as the one great planter. In addition to the garden of Eden, he also plants aloes (Num 24:6) and the cedars of Lebanon (Ps 104:16). In this role God brought a vine, Israel, out of Egypt and then planted it with his own hand (Ps 80:8, 15). In spite of his efforts, God's vineyard turned into a wild vine (Jer 2:21). His judgment on Israel for their disobedience meant they must be uprooted from their land. "What I have planted I am plucking up—that is, the whole land" (Jer 45:4).

God's plan for his people was spelled out in the Davidic covenant. "I will appoint a place for my people Israel, and will plant them, that they may dwell in their own place" (2 Sam 7:10). So God promises that again in the future, "I will plant them upon their land, and they shall never again be plucked up out of the land which I have given them" (Amos 9:15).

Jesus picks up this analogy when he declares, "Every plant which my heavenly Father has not planted will be rooted up" (Mt 15:13). Further, Jesus' analogies of sowing and reaping, while without direct reference to God, may reflect his understanding of God in this role by implication (Mt 13:1-23; Mk 4:1-9, 13-20; Lk 8:4-8, 11-15).

Coupled with the planting analogy depicting God as Cultivator are the references in Scripture to God's work in the harvest. Jesus refers to his Father as "the Lord of the harvest" (Mt 9:37-38; Lk 10:2). In the parable of the wheat and the tares God is likened to the householder who sends his reapers out into the harvest (Mt 13:24-30). And Jesus describes a group of people who are very open to receive a word from God as fields that "are already white for harvest" (Jn 4:35, 38). Lastly, the final judgment is described in terms of "the harvest of the earth" (Rev 14—15).

While God plants and ultimately desires a harvest, he is also the one who gives the growth. Paul describes the work of apostles in relationship to God's work of spiritual cultivation. "I planted, Apollos watered, but God gave the growth. So neither he who plants nor he who waters is anything, but only God who gives the growth" (1 Cor 3:6-7).[22]

Builder. The role of God as Builder relates to his role as Creator in that both have to do with the making of something new. While creation is something brought into existence from nothing, building is done out of existing materials God has already made. But both have to do with making, shaping, and constructing according to God's plan. Whereas the role of Creator relates to creation, uses creation language and focuses on the giving of life, the builder role uses the *language* of *architecture* and *construction* and the *focus* is on *buildings*.

Early in biblical materials God in his creative act "built" (*bana,* בָּנָה) the rib which he had taken from Adam and made into Eve. Elsewhere God is pictured

---

[22]For נָטַע see *TWOT,* 2:575. Seock-Tae Sohn connects this role with God's election of Israel (*The Divine Election of Israel* [Grand Rapids, Mich.: Eerdmans, 1991], pp. 80-84).

as building the ordered universe, the one "who builds his upper chambers in the heavens, and founds his vault upon the earth" (Amos 9:6; cf. Ps 104:2-3). God's capacity to build (i.e., create) was seen by Abraham as he looked forward to the city "whose builder and maker is God" (Heb 11:10). In addition to creation, God also exercises his sovereignty in building up a kingdom through kings he has chosen. He promised Jeroboam an enduring house if he would walk in obedience before the Lord (1 Kings 11:38). He chose Solomon to be the one to build his own house, representing his personal presence among his people (8:16-21). God is also concerned about building individual families and a "house" in the sense of a line of descent. "Unless the LORD builds the house, those who build it labor in vain" (Ps 127:1). In these cases the Builder role also overlaps with family categories.

God declares that he will both pluck up and tear down any kingdom or nation that has consistently walked in disobedience to him, but conversely what he longs to do is to "build and plant it" (Jer 18:7-10; 42:10). His future rebuilding comes as a promise to those in exile, "Again I will build you, and you shall be built, O virgin Israel" (Jer 31:4).

God's work as a builder has reference to the coming of the Messiah (Ps 118:22-23). "The stone which the builders rejected has become the head of the corner. This is the Lord's doing." This Psalm is quoted five different times in the New Testament as a reference to Jesus (Mt 21:42; Mk 12:10; Lk 20:17; Acts 4:11; 1 Pet 2:7). Clearly God as the master Builder of his kingdom has selected Jesus for a key cornerstone role.

Christians are described as "God's building" by Paul (1 Cor 3:9). Sometimes he equates God's work of building with the believers being the temple of God. "Do you not know that you are God's temple and that God's Spirit dwells in you? If any one destroys God's temple, God will destroy him. For God's temple is holy, and that temple you are" (1 Cor 3:16, 17). In an additional reference to believers as "a holy temple in the Lord" Paul declares, "in whom you also are built into it for a dwelling place of God in the Spirit" (Eph 2:22).[23]

In one place both the Father and the Son are described in a building role. "Jesus has been counted worthy of as much more glory than Moses as the builder of a house has more honor than the house. (For every house is built by some one,

---

[23]Sohn, *Divine Election of Israel*, pp. 256-59.

but the builder of all things is God)" (Heb 3:3, 4). This focus has to do particularly with the building of the house of God as the church of God. Jesus indicated his own building responsibility when he declared of Peter's confession of him as the Messiah, "on this rock I will build my church" (Mt 16:18).

✗ *Potter.* An additional subcategory of the role of God as Creator relates to his ability to fashion and to make things, and pictures God as a Potter. The chief description of this comes in a vision to Jeremiah. The Lord sends the prophet to the potter's house to observe how he works, and then God compares himself to the potter, as one who can do with the clay as he pleases (Jer 18:1-11). The strength of the figure of speech is its graphicness in creating pottery, often beautifully. The limitation of the figure is that it has God as a personal potter working with an inanimate substance from physical creation. The key purpose is to communicate that God has the power to do what seems good to him to do (18:4).

The word for potter comes from *yasar* (יָצַר), meaning to fashion or form. It overlaps on certain occasions with *bara* (בָּרָא), to create.[24] Isaiah in particular connects the role of the potter with God's role as creator or maker (Is 45:12). He also talks about the futility of the clay arguing with the potter, the passage that Paul uses to describe God's providential direction of his people (Is 29:16; Rom. 9:19-21). The role of potter is also connected with God's role as Father. Apparently, the comparison has to do with the work of a Father fashioning or shaping his children in their growth (Is 45:10-11; 64:8).

The Son - Role

✗ *Creator.* Not only is God the Father identified with the role of Creator, but so is Jesus. The New Testament writers clearly see this identification as one of the evidences of the divinity of Jesus. Jesus is described by John as the "Holy One of God" (Jn 6:69), and it is this One who is clearly connected with the Father at creation in John 1. "The Word was God. He was in the beginning with God; all things were made through him, and without him was not anything made that was made" (1:1-3).[25] Similarly, Paul identifies Jesus in his role as Creator. "For in him all things were created, in heaven and on earth, visible and invisible,

---

[24]For יָצַר see *TWOT,* 1:396.

[25]On Christ as the creative Word see Ethelbert Stauffer, *New Testament Theology* (London: SCM Press, 1955), pp. 55-58, and Wolfhart Pannenberg, *Jesus, God and Man,* trans. Lewis L. Wilkins and Duane A. Priebe (Philadelphia: Westminster Press, 1968), pp. 390-98.

whether thrones or dominions or principalities or authorities—all things were created through him and for him" (Col 1:16-17). In writing to the Corinthians Paul connects the Father and the Son in their dual role at creation. "For us there is one God, the Father, from whom are all things and for whom we exist, and one Lord, Jesus Christ, through whom are all things and through whom we exist" (1 Cor 8:6). Further, Hebrews clearly identifies Jesus as "a Son, whom he appointed the heir of all things, through whom also he created the world" (Heb 1:2).

ⲭ *Giver of life.* John's description of Jesus' role as Creator is certainly intended as an introduction to Jesus' role in the creation of spiritual life. Thus after John spells out Jesus' role in creation (Jn 1:1-3) he declares that

> in him was life, and the life was the light of men. . . . He was in the world, and the world was made through him, yet the world knew him not. He came to his own home, and his own people received him not. But to all who received him, who believed in his name, he gave power to become children of God. (Jn 1:4, 10-12)

Throughout the entire book John makes it clear that his purpose in writing is to show that Jesus as the Son of God can give life to those who believe in his name (Jn 20:30-31). In the debate over Jesus' identification with the Father in John 5, Jesus states that "the Son gives life to whom he will." The reason is because "as the Father has life in himself, só he has granted the Son also to have life in himself," and therefore, Jesus can declare, "He who hears my word and believes him who sent me, has eternal life" (Jn 5:21, 26, 24). In like manner Paul connects the creation of the physical with the spiritual when he writes, "If there is a physical body, there is also a spiritual body. Thus it is written, 'The first man Adam became a living being'; the last Adam became a life-giving spirit" (1 Cor 15:44-45). So the Son, like the Father, is a creator who gives life.

The Holy Spirit – Role

In addition to the Father and the Son, the Spirit of God is also identified with the work of creation very early in the biblical data. Genesis 1:2 says, "the Spirit of God was moving over the face of the waters." The Spirit of God is particularly involved in the creation of people and the giving of life,[26] so that one man can properly confess, "The Spirit of God has made me, and the breath of the

---

[26]On the role of the Spirit in creation and in giving, see Davidson, *Theology of the Old Testament*, pp. 120-22.

Almighty gives me life" (Job 33:4).[27] It is the Spirit of the living God who in the New Testament gives life (2 Cor 3:3, 6). Paul makes further reference to the life-giving power of the Spirit in re-creating the spiritual lives of individuals. "If the Spirit of him who raised Jesus from the dead dwells in you, he who raised Christ Jesus from the dead will give life to your mortal bodies also through his Spirit which dwells in you" (Rom 8:11, cf. Gal 5:25).

So when the entire biblical picture is put together it is clear that God the Father, God the Son, and God the Spirit are all understood as being a part of the godhead who is the Creator of everything. [28] The picture of God as the Creator of the universe in general then sets the stage for an understanding of God's relationship to people as a part of the created order. The chief concern of Scripture is not creation but redemption. Creation, according to von Rad, comes as a preface to understanding the saving work of God. Before humans and their needs can be discussed thoroughly, along with the solution to their dilemma, certain basic questions about the universe and the original design of a relationship between God and people must be explicated.[29] Then, with a proper theological understanding of creation and the Creator, the stage is set throughout the rest of Scripture to understand this God who is so intimately involved in the ongoing existence and life of his creation.[30]

Man and Woman

Made in the image of the Creator. The climax of the story of creation in Genesis 1 deals with the making of man and woman.[31] Having created the universe and all other forms of life, God surveys his work and declares that it is good (Gen 1:25).

---

[27]See also Gen 2:7. For a discussion of the Spirit in creation, see Oehler, *Theology of the Old Testament*, pp. 118-19.

[28]For further discussion of God's role as Creator see Vriezen, *Outline of Old Testament Theology*, pp. 183-94; Walter Kaiser, *Toward an Old Testament Theology* (Grand Rapids, Mich.: Zondervan, 1978), pp. 72-76; Ronald E. Clements, *Old Testament Theology* (Atlanta: John Knox Press, 1978), p. 53; Donald Guthrie, *New Testament Theology* (Downers Grove, Ill.: InterVarsity Press, 1981), pp. 78-79.

[29]Rad, *Old Testament Theology*, pp. 136-53. Barth also sees the doctrine of creation subordinated to redemption (CD 3/1, pp. 3-94).

[30]For the theology of creation see Brunner, *Christian Doctrine of Creation and Redemption*, pp. 3-39; Koehler, *Old Testament Theology*, pp. 85-88; Eugene Carpenter, *A Contemporary Wesleyan Theology*, ed. Charles W. Carter (Grand Rapids, Mich.: Zondervan, 1983), 1:156-68, 171-74.

[31]For a discussion of man in the Old Testament see Vriezen, *Outline of Old Testament Theology*, pp. 199-207. For a discussion of man in the New Testament see Guthrie, *Theology of the New Testament*, pp. 150-87. For theological discussion see Brunner, *Christian Doctrine of Creation and Redemption*, pp. 46-78. For the contemporary debate over the origin and nature of man see Henry, *God, Revelation and Authority*, 6:197-228.

Then he says, "'Let us make man in our image, after our likeness'; ... So God created man in his own image, in the image of God he created him; male and female he created them" (1:26-27). Apparently the writer of the story thought it was particularly significant that God created individuals in his own image. He emphasizes this fact by repeating the phrase.[32] The uniqueness of this part of creation is further highlighted by the fact that this is the only part of creation that is described as being made like God.[33]

Further, it is clear that all of humanity is made in the image of God, for it very specifically states that both male and female are made in his likeness (1:27). The reference to man and woman being created in the likeness of God gives them a special role in relation to the rest of creation. This is symbolized by God's declaration that they be given dominion over the earth. God, as the one who is separate from his creation and yet rules over it, has now made men and women in his image to do the same. Thus, in a unique sense, human beings are separate from all the rest of creation and are given dominion over it under God's ultimate authority. They are not separate from creation in the same transcendent sense that God is, but they are separate from creation in the sense that they are the only part of the created order that bears the image and likeness of the Creator.

The image of God, or the *imago Dei*, is not only found in the first chapter of Genesis before sin enters into the world, but it is also described in Genesis 5:1. "When God created man, he made him in the likeness of God." This second reference appears to be a deliberate attempt to indicate that at least some significant part of the image of God still remains even after the fall into sin (Gen 3). The next reference comes in Genesis 9:6 after the flood and apparently is an indicator that even after that cataclysmic event people continue to retain the image of the Creator. The New Testament likewise picks up this theme when it describes individuals "who are made in the

---

[32]We are treating "image" and "likeness" from a basically Protestant position which understands the two words as a Hebrew parallelism and therefore to be treated like synonyms. Others in the history of the church have wanted to divide the two Hebrew words as a means of understanding the different parts of the image of God. For discussion of this debate in the church see David Cairns, *The Image of God in Man* (London: SCM Press, 1953); Emil Brunner, *Man in Revolt* (Philadelphia: Westminster Press, 1947), pp. 92-96. See also Eichrodt, *Theology of the Old Testament*, 2:60ff.; James Orr, *God's Image in Man* (London: Hodder & Stoughton, 1907), p. 54.

[33]For the biblical data on image see *TDNT*, 2:381-97.

likeness of God" (Jas 3:9).[34]

The content of the image of God may be subdivided in various ways. The best approach seems to focus on two parts that are identified as the moral image and natural image. If the organizing characteristic of God's attributes is holiness, then it should not surprise us that the heart of the image of God is also related to his holiness. The moral image of God is more directly reflective of the holy character of God, but even the natural image of God is related to God's holiness is significant ways.[35]

The *moral image* of God in men and women are those parts of the character of God that require choices on the part of persons so that they might reflect this holy character. There are six key elements that constitute the category of moral holiness. Among them are the concept of (1) righteousness and its corresponding standard of (2) moral purity. The (3) truth of God is reflected in both his speech and his faithfulness in personal relationships. The (4) grace of God involves both his favor and his self-giving, and stands in close relationship to both the (5) love and the (6) goodness of God, which round out the picture of his moral image. The whole picture is presented in figure 3.2.

Figure 3.2. Elements of moral image of God

The other broad category that identifies ways in which men and women reflect the nature of God may be described as the *natural image*.[36] It contains four significant components. The first of these is the social nature of people. They are social beings, made for personal relationships in parallel to the triune God who

---

[34]For a discussion of the biblical materials on the image of God see Vriezen, *Outline of Old Testament Theology,* pp. 143-47, 208-9; Rad, *Old Testament Theology,* 1:144-47; Eichrodt, *Theology of the Old Testament,* 2:122-31; Heinisch, *Theology of the Old Testament,* pp. 169-71; Jacob, *Theology of the Old Testament,* pp. 166-72; J. Barton Payne, *The Theology of the Older Testament* (Grand Rapids, Mich.: Zondervan, 1962), pp. 226-28; Knight, *Christian Theology of the Old Testament,* pp. 22-39.

[35]Wesley divides the image of God into three parts: the Moral Image, the Political Image and the Natural Image (*Works VI,* p. 66). Others speak of the material and formal aspects of the image, which corresponds to our use of moral and natural dimensions. See Brunner, *Christian Doctrine of Creation and Redemption,* pp. 55-61.

[36]I develop more this explanation of the moral and natural images in *Holy Living: Godliness in the Old Testament* (Willmore, Ky.: Barnabas Foundation, 1999), chap. 1.

himself is a social being. A second dimension includes the capacities of personhood and has to do with the make-up of individual persons that includes their reason, imagination, emotions and will.

The third component relates to the expressions of these capacities of personhood in several areas:

☐ freedom of the will to make choices

☐ the ability to take responsibility over the created order (sometimes referred to as the political image that gives men and women dominion over creation)

☐ creativity (reflected in people's ability to work and to raise children) and aesthetics (expressed in beauty and music)

☐ conscience: the ability to distinguish things that are right from things that are wrong

The last dimension of the natural image is its spirituality and immortality. Persons, like God, are spiritual beings (although unlike God they also have a physical body), and they are made for immortality (though unlike God they have a beginning). The cluster of components under that natural image of God is expressed in figure 3.3.

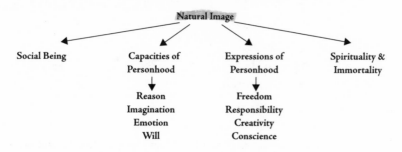

Figure 3.3. Elements of natural image

Reflecting the likeness of God. The image of God in people is closely related to the second commandment. In Exodus 20:4 God forbids any graven images of himself among his people. A holy people were not to have any wooden, stone or metal representations of the Creator, because the Creator was not like any of the natural elements in creation. This was in stark contrast to the gods of the ancient Near Eastern world who were all nature gods and were identified with some natural element in the universe. Since God is not like the heavens, the earth, the storm, the river or the sky, he is not represented by any of these things. He is the Creator who transcends all that he has made. Yet he has not left himself without some representation of his likeness in the created order and that representation is found in men and women. It is humanity that reflects the image of the Creator in the universe, so that the New Testament can declare that man "is the image and glory of God" (1 Cor 11:7).[37]

Under the New Covenant Jesus in his divinity comes as the full revelation of the image of God that people need to see and understand. John tells us that "the Word became flesh and dwelt among us, full of grace and truth; we have beheld his glory, glory as of the only Son from the Father. . . . No one has ever seen God; the only Son, who is in the bosom of the Father, he has made him known" (Jn 1:14, 18). Paul echoes that sentiment when he writes that Jesus "is the image of the invisible God. . . . For in him all the fulness of God was pleased to dwell" (Col 1:15, 19; cf. 2 Cor 4:4-6). Stauffer describes Jesus as "the image of God in a full and final sense."[38] Hebrews, after explaining that it was through Jesus that the Father created the world, observes, "He reflects the glory of God and bears the very stamp of his nature" (Heb 1:3). The word used is χαρακτήρ, from which we get our English word *character*, and it may suggest that Jesus particularly reflects the moral character of the Father.

Jesus, however, is not only the full reflection of the image of God, but he is also the image of what God desired people to be when he created them. Here we see one purpose for the humanity of Jesus. Hebrews describes Jesus as one who "partook of the same nature" and was "made like his brethren in every respect" (Heb. 2:14, 17), so that he might identify with humanity. Paul says Jesus did not count equality with God a thing to be grasped but "emptied himself, taking the form of a servant, being born in the likeness of men" (Phil 2:7).[39] So Jesus, in a unique sense, reflects in his divinity the divine image of the Creator, and in his

---

[37]For a theological discussion of the image, see CD 3/3, pp. 183-206. See also Cairns, *Image of God in Man*; Philip E. Hughes, *The True Image* (Grand Rapids, Mich.: Eerdmans, 1989), pp. 51-70; Richard Watson, *Theological Institutes* (London: John Mason, 1832), 2:169-74; Pope, *A Compendium of Christian Theology* (London: Wesleyan-Methodist Book Room, 1880), 1:423-28; Harald G. Lindstrom, *Wesley and Sanctification* (Stockholm: Nya Bokförlags Aletiebolaget, 1946), pp. 25-26.

[38]Stauffer, *New Testament Theology*, p. 111.

[39]For the relationship of Jesus and humanity see CD 3/1, pp. 55-71, 132-222; Wolfhart Pannenburg, *Systematic Theology*, trans. Geoffrey W. Bromiley (Grand Rapids, Mich.: Eerdmans, 1991), 2:297-323; George E. Ladd, *A Theology of the New Testament* (Grand Rapids, Mich.: Eerdmans, 1974), pp. 251, 253; Guthrie, *New Testament Theology*, pp. 202, 228.

humanity he reflects the image of the persons God desires to see serving him in the created order. He is the Son of God, and he is also the Son of man, the perfect image of both.

Sin

Image lost/marred. When sin enters into the created order in Genesis 3, there are three dimensions of its existence. The first of these has to do with the state of sin caused by the Fall. This is referred to as the sin principle, the sin nature, the carnal nature, or the state of sinfulness in people.[40] Its chief focus has to do with its impact on the image of God in people. The content of the moral image of God in individuals has been completely lost, although the capacity for it has not. People still remain moral beings, but they no longer appear holy as God is holy and do not manifest that holiness of character in moral dimensions such as righteousness or love. Unrighteousness is clearly evidenced in their conduct according to God's law from Genesis 3 onward. The failure to love as God loves is first demonstrated in Adam's accusation against Eve regarding the cause of their disobedience. The absence of holy character is described when "the LORD saw that the wickedness of man was great in the earth, and that every imagination of the thoughts of his heart was only evil continually" (Gen 6:5). He is no longer pure or good, truthful or self-giving (gracious). This sinfulness not only affected Adam, but also all people born after him. So while Adam himself was originally created in the likeness of God, Genesis 5:3 says that Adam begot a son in his own likeness! This is among the earliest indications that a sinful nature is being passed from one generation to another.[41]

This failure to continue to walk according to God's standard for righteous living and to love as God loves continues to be evidenced over and over again throughout the first eleven chapters of Genesis. It is this fall into a state of sinfulness that God later describes when he says, "You were blameless in your ways from the day you were created, till iniquity was found in you" (Ezek 28:15). This first effect of sin on the creature has to do with the subjective impact of sin

---

[40]For a biblical discussion of the state of sin, see Davidson, *Theology of the Old Testament*, pp. 224-25; Schultz, *Old Testament Theology*, 2:242-69; "Harmatia," *TDNT*, 1:267-316; Donald Metz, *Studies in Biblical Holiness* (Kansas City, Mo.: Beacon Hill, 1971), pp. 83-85; Pope, *Compendium of Christian Theology*, 2:1-19.

[41]On the transmission of sinfulness, see Louis Berkhof, *Systematic Theology* (Edinburgh: Banner of Truth, 1958), pp. 237-43; John Miley, *Systematic Theology* (New York: Methodist Book Concern, 1892), 1:463, 467; H. Orton Wiley, *Christian Theology* (Kansas City, Mo.: Beacon Hill, 1941), 2:109-19.

in his own being. Sin is not original to humanness, and therefore sinfulness and humanness must never be equated. But after the Fall into sin and the subsequent passing of that sinfulness to future generations (Ps 51:5; Rom 5:12-21), all mankind has ceased to reflect the moral character of God.[42]

Yet in spite of the Fall, men and women retain their character as humans. Although the moral image of God was lost, the natural image seems to be only marred.[43] This comes as an inference from the biblical data that continues to describe individuals after the Fall as still having some use of the capacities categorized under the natural image, in spite of the drastic impact of sin.[44] So they still have some dominion over creation, although not a perfect rule over the rest of the creatures in the universe. They still remain social beings, although all of their social relationships and interactions have been seriously affected. They continue to be spiritual beings with immortality, although affected by the entrance of death into the world. People retain their personality in the sense that they continue to reason and to have imagination; they still have human emotions and continue to make willful choices. All of these traits of personhood are adversely affected by sin, but still remain as a part of the human make up. People no longer are able to reason perfectly, their imaginations are distorted, their emotions are often damaged, and their ability to make willful choices is somewhat impaired. Nevertheless, they do continue to function with all these capacities.

Last, their expressions of personhood in creativity, responsibility and creativity have been affected by sin. They still have some sense of the beautiful, as well as the capacity to create, and they are still designed for work. But their sense of beauty is not perfect. The ability to create has been severely limited in some cases, and the desire for work and the delight in it have been seriously undermined. Responsibility often has become domination or exploitation, and their freedom has been limited by a fallen, self-centered will.

The Scripture implies that there is a kind of grace that God gives to everyone

---

[42]For a discussion of the history of the doctrine of sin, see Brunner, *Christian Doctrine of Creation and Redemption*, pp. 113-17. For the origin and nature of sin, see Pope, *Compendium of Christian Theology*, vol. 2, pp. 20-42.
[43]See Lindstrom, *Wesley and Sanctification*, p. 26.
[44]On the retention of some part of the image of God in persons after the impact of sin, see Vriezen, *Outline of Old Testament Theology*, pp. 208-9; Rad, *Old Testament Theology*, 1:147; Heinisch, *Theology of the Old Testament*, p. 170; Guthrie, *Theology of the New Testament*, p. 210; Brunner, *Christian Doctrine of Creation and Redemption*, p. 57.

that makes the retention of this natural image of God possible.[45] God seems to give to all a universal grace that has an effect even before redemption. It is described as prevenient grace or the grace that comes before salvation.[46] It is this grace that allows people to retain a significant portion of the natural image of God in themselves, and in particular, restores enough freedom of the will to further respond to God's offer of salvation.[47]

Idolatry. The second major dimension of sin and its effect on the creature has to do with sin as an act. Sin's entrance into the world not only causes a state of sinfulness, but that state then leads to certain actions that are described as sins.[48] In the language of creation an act of sin is described as the worship of the creature or the creation. This is what the Bible means when it describes an act of idolatry. Paul speaks of those who "exchanged the truth about God for a lie and worshiped and served the creature rather than the Creator" (Rom 1:25). This is one of the reasons for the second commandment (Exod 20:4-5; Deut. 5:8-9). People were not to make any graven image or likeness of anything in the heavens or in the earth or in the water because no part of inanimate creation was representative of a transcendent Creator. God was bigger than either the heavens, the earth, the water or anything contained in them, and his only adequate representation on the earth was persons made in his own image. So when people begin to worship or seek their fulfillment in any part of the creation other than the Creator, it is described as idolatry and is strictly forbidden.

Infirmities. The third dimension of sin and its impact on people is known as general depravity. This has to do with the general effect of the Fall on individuals, particularly their natural image, and it refers to those "infirmities" of human nature which are not related to an act of the will. These infirmities may be defined as all those inward and outward imperfections from God's absolute standard that are not of a moral nature.[49] They are things that may be wrong in people according to God's perfect design for them or wrong according to the

---

[45]Lindstrom, *Wesley and Sanctification*, p. 44-50.

[46]For theological discussion of prevenient grace, see Pope, *Compendium of Christian Theology*, pp. 358-62; Miley, *Systematic Theology*, 2:244-46; John Wesley, *Wesley's Standard Sermons*, ed. Edward H. Sugden (London: Epworth, 1921), 2:445; Thomas C. Oden, *The Transforming Power of Grace* (Nashville: Abingdon, 1993).

[47]For passages implying prevenient grace, see Acts 13:48; 18:27; Jn 1:9; Rom 1:19-21; 2:15-16.

[48]On the dual nature of sin see Herman Schultz, *Old Testament Theology*, trans. J. A. Patterson (Edinburgh: T & T Clark, 1892), 2:292-306; W. T. Purkiser, *God, Man and Salvation* (Kansas City, Mo.: Beacon Hill, 1977), pp. 83-86.

[49]Wesley, *Standard Sermons*, 2:155.

absolute standard of God's moral law, but which do not spring from a willful choice by an individual.

General depravity may be divided into four different categories. The first includes physical infirmities, such as the natural decline of the body in old age, the hardening of arteries, the dimming of eyesight, the malfunction of certain organs with age, physical birth defects and so on.

The second are mental infirmities that have to do with the imperfectness of our reason and logic. Even with the impact of sin people retain their capacity to think and to speak, but it is not always with perfect reason. Lack of information or faulty data can lead to wrong understandings and then to mistakes. This happens irrespective of the will at times, and thus, while one may choose to do the will of God in many situations, a faulty reasoning process or misinformation will lead to certain mistakes and sometimes, as a consequence, to a breaking of the absolute law of God.

There are also emotional infirmities that come from living in a fallen world. These include things like stage fright, shyness, and heightened or depressed emotions due to certain physical states, for example, periodic cycles in life. Many of these emotional infirmities arise out of a fallen environment.

Finally, there are social infirmities that have to do with the way we interact with other people. This too may be largely related to the fallenness of the environment in which an individual is raised. Many do not know how to relate to people well. They may be reserved or more introverted in personality, finding it difficult to make conversation or to know the appropriate use of humor. This category includes failure in adequate communication between people with the resultant breakdown in relationships.

None of these infirmities involve a willful disobedience on the part of the individual, and therefore, in a strict sense, may not be properly called acts of sin.[50] Many use an ethical definition of the act of sin which describes sin as a willful transgression of a known law of God by a morally responsible agent. Since infirmities are not deliberate transgressions, they do not qualify. Other theological traditions sometimes use a legal definition of an act of sin as any transgression of the law of God, voluntary or involuntary, whether the law was known or unknown. In that case, these infirmities would be classified as acts of sin.[51]

---

[50]Ibid., 1:45, 171.

[51]Merne Harris and Richard Taylor, "The Dual Nature of Sin," in *The Word and the Doctrine*, ed. Kenneth Geiger (Kansas City, Mo.: Beacon Hill, 1965), p. 45.

However, regardless of one's theological tradition, any and every transgression of the law of God, voluntary or involuntary, needs atonement. The Scriptures indicate that one of the general affects of Christ's atonement is the covering of these infirmities (Rom 5:11-21).[52] Because they do not involve an act of the will on the part of the individual and because Christ has paid the penalty for any guilt involved in them, people are not directly responsible for them. They will continue to exist as a part of fallen humanity until glorification. Individuals do not have the power to remove them, and therefore, in the strict (ethical) sense, they do not constitute acts of sin.

While a person may not by a choice of the will remove infirmities from his life, there are certain parts of general depravity that one may choose by grace to modify. This is particularly true with intellectual, emotional and social infirmities. While these will not be erased entirely from any life, they may be modified by grace. For example, a person may learn to think more logically and thus make fewer mistakes in reasoning and judgment. Or one may learn to modify certain emotional ups and downs in his life, and everyone has grace available to work at social relationships. A shy, reserved individual may learn to be more outgoing in relating to people. Thus, while grace will not eliminate all these infirmities short of heaven, it will make possible some moderation of their effects on life in this world. This is a part of maturity as one grows in grace.

Salvation

Remaking image of God. A proper relationship between the Creator and people begins with saving grace in the initial remaking of the image of God in individuals. God made people to be like himself, and the whole process of redemption has to do with re-creating them to be like himself. Indeed, the purpose of God in redeeming people is that they may "be conformed to the image of his Son" (Rom 8:29). Thus Paul can say, "Just as we have borne the image of the man of dust, we shall also bear the image of the man of heaven" (1 Cor 15:49). This relates primarily to restoration of the lost moral image. In salvation[53] God begins to make people like himself, holy as he is holy. This is sometimes described as initial sanctification

---

[52]John Wesley, *A Plain Account of Christian Perfection* (London: Epworth, 1952), p. 45; Leo G. Cox, "The Imperfections of the Perfect," in *Further Insights into Holiness* (Kansas City, Mo.: Beacon Hill, 1963), pp. 191-95.

[53]The term *salvation* here is used in the narrow sense of initial salvation, that act of God's saving grace that establishes a relationship to God and begins to transform the nature of the individual.

ini tial sanctification. Now the individual begins to reflect the moral nature of a holy God through attitudes and conduct toward others that reflect God's holiness in purity, righteousness, truth, self-giving (grace), goodness and love.

Recapitulation theory of atonement. The remaking of men and women in the image of God is based on the biblical passages that talk about Christ coming into the world to unite people to himself so that they might be remade according to the purpose of God. Paul talks about God making known his will "which he set forth in Christ as a plan for the fulness of time, to unite all things in him, things in heaven and things on earth" (Eph 1:9-10).

The reference to Christ as head of the race has given rise to that theory of the atonement called recapitulation, meaning a "new head" or "re-heading." This specifically is connected with the role of Christ superseding the old headship of Adam and undoing the work of his fall into sin. So as Adam's disobedience brought sin and resulting death into the world, in reversal of that process by a new head, Christ's work of obedience brings life for all. "As one man's trespass led to condemnation for all men, so one man's act of righteousness leads to acquittal and life for all men" (Rom 5:18). It is just this parallel between Adam and Christ that Paul elaborates in Romans 5:12-21.

It is this data that led Irenaeus to formulate the recapitulation theory of the atonement according to which Christ gathered up (re-headed) all things in himself. This means that Christ's incarnation involved identifying with each of the stages of human life and in so doing reversing the course initiated by Adam.[54] The parallels between Christ and Adam are interesting. Adam was made from virgin soil, tempted by the devil and through disobedience brought death and sin into the world. Christ, reversing the process, was born of a virgin, resisted temptation and by obedience defeated sin by death on the cross and brought life to humanity. Christ, passing through infancy, childhood, youth and adulthood, sanctified every stage of human life for all those who are born again to God through him. In other words he became fully human in order to make men and women fully like the image of God. This was part of his role as Creator, says Hebrews, "in bringing many sons to glory" (Heb 2:10). According to Irenaeus, as a result of Christ's life, death and resurrection, all that was lost in Adam is

---

[54]Irenaeus, "Against Heresies," in *Ante-Nicene Fathers* (New York: Charles Scribners, 1925), 2:455-58. For a good discussion of this view see Gustaf Aulén, *Christus Victor* (London: SPCK, 1965), pp. 16-35.

regained in Christ. The ultimate purpose, of course, was that having made people in his own image, God now desires to remake them according to his original purpose.[55]

Regeneration. This re-creation of people in the image of God is described in several other ways.[56] The first of these is that of regeneration, i.e., the act of generating life again. This is that subjective experience whereby the Spirit of God remakes the spiritual life of the individual.[57] So we are saved "not because of deeds done by us in righteousness, but in virtue of his own mercy, by the washing of regeneration and renewal in the Holy Spirit" (Tit 3:5). Regeneration means that we become new creatures in Christ. "If any one is in Christ, he is a new creation; the old has passed away, behold, the new has come" (2 Cor 5:17; see Gal. 6:15; Ps 33:15). Or, to alter the figure slightly, Paul says, "We are his workmanship, created in Christ Jesus for good works" (Eph 2:10). The connection between holiness and regeneration is seen in the nature of the regenerate state. As Miley describes it, "It is a state of subjective holiness."[58] God actually makes people holy internally.

Life. This initial recreating of the image of God is also described in terms of giving or restoring life. Thus, the Lord can declare, "See now that I, even I, am he, and there is no god beside me; I kill and I make alive" (Deut 32:39). Hannah exclaims in her song of praise, "There is none holy like the LORD, there is none besides thee. . . . The LORD kills and brings to life" (1 Sam 2:2, 6). Likewise, Hosea declares, "After two days he will revive us; on the third day he will raise us up, that we may live before him" (6:2; cf. Ps 71:20).

This focus on giving of new life is even clearer in the New Testament. John opens his Gospel with a deliberate parallel to Genesis 1:1, "In the beginning was the Word, and . . . in him was life, and the life was the light of men" (Jn 1:1, 4). He clearly means for us to understand that Jesus is the Word, who originally participated in the creation of the universe with God (v. 2), and is now the one who comes to re-create life. He who was responsible for physical life is also

---

[55]Thomas C. Oden, *The Word of Life* (San Francisco: Harper & Row, 1989), pp. 128-129; *EDT*, pp. 916-17; Berkhof, *Systematic Theology*, p. 385.

[56]For a general discussion of the restoration of the moral image of God in man, see Orr, *God's Image in Man*, pp. 249-83.

[57]For a theological discussion of regeneration see Watson, *Theological Institutes*, 2:476-78; Pope, *Compendium of Christian Theology*, 3:5-13.

[58]Miley, *Systematic Theology*, 2:327-38.

responsible for giving spiritual life. Thus, John's ultimate purpose in writing the whole Gospel is that persons might "believe that Jesus is the Christ, the Son of God, and that believing you may have life in his name" (Jn 20:31). Accordingly, throughout the whole Gospel record one finds the theme, "He who believes in the Son has eternal life; he who does not obey the Son shall not see life" (Jn 3:36). This is particularly illustrated in John 5 when Jesus claims equality with the Father and describes as one of the evidences of his divinity that the Father has given him the power of life: "For as the Father raises the dead and gives them life, so also the Son gives life to whom he will. . . . Truly, truly, I say to you, he who hears my word and believes him who sent me, has eternal life; he does not come into judgment, but has passed from death to life. . . . For as the Father has life in himself, so he has granted the Son also to have life in himself" (Jn 5:21, 24, 26).

This new life is bound up with one's relationship to Jesus. The one who responds by believing in Christ has available to him this gift of newly created life. Thus, it is "the testimony, that God gave us eternal life, and this life is in his Son. He who has the Son has life; he who has not the Son of God has not life" (1 Jn 5:11-12).[59]

In a similar fashion Paul can state, "the first man Adam a living being" while "the last Adam became a life-giving spirit" (1 Cor 15:45). He writes to the Romans that if Christ is in them their spirits are alive because of righteousness. "If the Spirit of him who raised Jesus from the dead dwells in you, he who raised Christ Jesus from the dead will give life to your mortal bodies also through his Spirit which dwells in you" (Rom 8:11). He exhorts them, "You also must consider yourselves dead to sin and alive to God in Christ Jesus" (Rom 6:11). In like manner he declares to the Ephesians, "You he made alive, when you were dead through . . . trespasses and sins" (Eph 2:1).[60] The means of obtaining this life is the same for Paul as it was for John as he makes clear in his declaration of the theme of Romans the "righteous live by faith" (Rom 1:17).

Jesus also describes this coming into the experience of a regenerate spiritual life in terms of moving from death to life. In the parable of the prodigal son he closes with that fitting declaration, "This your brother was dead, and is alive"

---

[59]For a discussion of new life in Christ, see Ladd, *Theology of the New Testament*, pp. 479-80; see Jn 2:1-11 for creation of wine as a sign leading to life; also 3:15-16; 4:14; 6:40, 47, 51, 53-58, 67-69; 12:25-26; 14:6; 17:2.

[60]See Paul's references to regenerated life, Rom 8:6, 13; 14:9; 2 Cor 13:4; Phil 1:21; 2:16; 2 Tim 1:1.

(Lk 15:32).[61] Further, Peter understood this well when he proclaimed that Christ's "divine power has granted to us all things that pertain to life and godliness" (2 Pet 1:3).

While the whole understanding of the giving of life is intimately bound up with God's role as the Creator who gives both physical and spiritual life to his creatures, it is not the only role that relates to life. Of special significance is the role of a Father who begets or gives life to his children (e.g., Jn 1:12-13), and according to Jesus, even the Shepherd has some role in the giving of life (Jn 10:10, 27-28). It would seem, however, that in the Shepherd figure the role is more as a midwife of the sheep than as a life-giving source.

Separation. A final reference within this category to the experience of saving grace has to do with an initial separation of people from the world when they come into an experience of regeneration or the receiving of new life. Because they belong to God, who himself is separate, they become, at least in an initial way, a separated people. Thus, when the Lord calls a holy people to himself in the Old Testament (Ex 19:5-6), one of the implications has to do with their separateness. It is separateness *from* the nonbelieving world around them, and it is separateness *unto* God. So it has both a negative connotation of that which distinguishes a person from an unbelieving world, and it also carries a positive connotation of commitment to the one who is separated from all the universe as its Creator. Thus, the Lord commands his people, "Come out from them, and be separate from them" (2 Cor 6:17).

Growth in Christian Experience

The experience of saving grace is the initial change in the creature that begins to make him holy as God is holy. This regeneration begins to re-create the moral image of God in people, and this process continues in a further growth in likeness to God. This is what is known as progressive sanctification. It is an ongoing growth in holiness. It involves a progressive conformity to the likeness of the moral image of God in Christ. Thus, Paul can talk about "the new nature, which is being renewed in knowledge after the image of its creator" (Col 3:10).

Increasing conformity to image of God. Notice the relationship between "being renewed in knowledge" and increasing in conformity to the image of God. It is a

---

[61]Cf. Jesus' response to questions about eternal life, Mt 19:16-30; Lk 10:25-37. See also Mt 25:46.

more accurate knowledge of God through the revelation of himself in Scripture that allows an individual to conform his life more perfectly to that likeness. The more one lives in the light of Scripture, the more one sees impurity and unholiness which must be removed from his life. On the positive side, as one sees more clearly the implications of loving as God loves, he may be led by God and enabled by grace to more fully conform his attitudes to that of a loving heavenly Father. Further, the standard of goodness becomes more clear in his mind, and his character begins to change through an increasing manifestation of righteousness and love. Finally, being renewed in knowledge affects his understanding of the truth as it is revealed in God's Word, making it possible for him to more fully conform his life to the truth that God has made known, thus reflecting that truth as a part of the moral image of God in him.

So holiness dominates this progressive growth in the Christian experience as a holy Creator works to further shape the moral image of God in people that it may be like his own nature. A person's character is progressively developed into the holiness of God's character and is expressed in terms of righteousness, love, purity, self-giving, goodness and truth. Paul makes it clear that the Holy Spirit is the agent who continues to change a believer into the likeness of a holy God. "We all, with unveiled face, beholding the glory of the Lord, are being changed into his likeness from one degree of glory to another; for this comes from the Lord who is the Spirit" (2 Cor 3:18).[62]

The Church

The context for growth in grace and a continued relationship with the Lord is found in relationship with other believers. People are made in the image of a tri-une God and are therefore social beings. People need other people. One place where this need is obvious is in one's spiritual life. People need others to help them come to know God, and then they need others in order to continue to live in a right relationship with him. Because of our social nature, God has designed an organization of people that joins persons with other persons so that they might know him better and continue to follow after him.

Body of Christ. In the creation category the group of believers known as the church may best be described as the body of Christ. The Creator has made all

---

[62] See also 2 Cor 4:16, which refers to the continual renewal of our inner nature every day.

things, including the physical body. But this is only symbolic of his capacity to create a spiritual body as well. The created human body becomes a concrete illustration of the way he desires for believers to relate to one another, i.e., interdependent and joined together in a permanent way (Eph 4:16). It is a masterful analogy that shows how unity and diversity exist together.

The body analogy is most extensively developed in three separate New Testament passages, all in the context of discussing spiritual gifts. The Creator endows every human being with certain natural gifts, such as personality, physical traits, intelligence, and abilities to do certain tasks well. But the focus of these three passages of Scripture (Rom 5; 1 Cor 12, Eph 4) is chiefly to illustrate how spiritual gifts are supranaturally given by God to allow believers to contribute to and build up other believers in the church. The illustration that best describes how these gifts work in concert with one another is the analogy of the spiritual body to the physical body. As Paul puts it, "For just as the body is one and has many members, and all the members of the body, though many, are one body, so it is with Christ. For by one Spirit we were all baptized into one body" (1 Cor 12:12-13).

The analogy of the body as a symbol of the church of Christ serves as the context for three significant discussions of spiritual gifts. In Ephesians 4 it relates to gifts in terms of *positions* within the church. "His gifts were that some should be apostles, some prophets, some evangelists, some pastors and teachers, for the equipment of the saints, for the work of ministry, for building up the body of Christ" (Eph 4:11-12). In Romans Paul talks about our *functional* or *basic gifts* and lists seven: prophecy, service, teaching, exhortation, giving, aiding, and mercy (Rom 12:3-8).

The most extensive discussion of spiritual gifts and their relationship to the body of Christ occurs in 1 Corinthians 12 and 14. Here Paul lists the *manifestation gifts* that seem to come occasionally to any member of the body of Christ as they are needed. The Creator gives through the Spirit the gifts of a word of wisdom, a word of knowledge, faith, gifts of healing, miracles, prophecy, the ability to distinguish between spirits, tongues/languages, and interpretation of tongues/languages.[63]

---

[63]On this approach to spiritual gifts see Allan Coppedge and William Ury, *A Workbook on Spiritual Gifts* (Wilmore, Ky.: Barnabas Foundation: 1999).

So the Creator who made physical bodies also has created the church. It is likened to the body of Christ as the extension of his continued work on the earth. Each member of the church is uniquely gifted to carry out his part of the ministry to other believers and to the world.

It is this context that describes Christ as the head of the body and therefore the head of the church. So Paul remarks that "Christ is the head of the church, his body, and is himself its Savior" (Eph 5:23). Since he is the head of the body (Eph 1:22-23; 4:15), he is also responsible for directing the other members of the body. Here the role of God as Creator bleeds over into the category of God as Sovereign King or Ruler. Headship clearly implies directing or ruling for Paul, and Christ's role is to direct his body, that is, the church.

Building. A second way in which the church is described relates to one of the subroles of God as Creator. God as Builder constructs according to his plan. So sometimes the people of God are described as "God's building" (1 Cor 3:9). Paul likens his work of building the church to that of a master builder. He begins by laying a foundation in Christ and then building on that foundation. He warns others to be careful how they build on this foundation. The building Paul is doing seems to be evidenced in his work of bringing lives into a right relationship with God (1 Cor 3:10-15). In like manner Peter describes believers as those who are "like living stones" which are "built into a spiritual house" for God. The cornerstone or the keystone for this spiritual building is the person of Christ (1 Pet 2:5-7).

Full Sanctification

The nomenclature for the category of full sanctification is found in the closing of Paul's first letter to the Thessalonians, where he prays for them, "May the God of peace himself sanctify you wholly," that is, fully or entirely (5:23). The verbal form of Paul's prayer is turned into the nominal form for this descriptive term of "entire sanctification" or "full sanctification." God's work in the believer's total being—including his spirit, soul and body—is necessary to make the believer entirely holy. Paul is praying that God, in his creative role, will more fully make holy every part of the creature he has made and already regenerated. The definiteness of Paul's prayer would seem to imply an expectation that God would act in as clear-cut a manner to sanctify a believer fully as he would to regenerate a person in conversion.[64]

---

[64]Miley describes the incompleteness of regeneration, *Systematic Theology,* 2:357-71.

Put off old nature, put on new nature. Full sanctification is described in this creator role from various perspectives. The first of these Paul mentions in his letter to the Ephesians when he exhorts them to "put off your old nature which belongs to your former manner of life and is corrupt through deceitful lusts, and be renewed in the spirit of your minds, and put on the new nature, created after the likeness of God in true righteousness and holiness" (Eph 4:22-24). He is clearly talking here to the Ephesian *believers*. He has already prayed that they might "be strengthened with might through his Spirit in the inner man" and that they might "know the love of Christ which surpasses knowledge." Then he prays that they "be filled with all the fulness of God" (Eph 3:16-19). To these new believers, he now writes about putting off their old natures and putting on their new natures, although in theory this has already been done in their experience of initial salvation. Yet, he encourages them to do this with the definiteness of putting off or putting on a coat.[65]

Further, this new nature which he desires to see in these believers is that which is "created after the likeness of God" (Eph 4:2) and seems to imply a further creation in the likeness of God's moral character. He connects this likeness with righteousness and holiness in the same verse. God's holiness is the larger theological category in Paul's mind and that explains why there follows in the immediate context a number of particular examples of righteous conduct. Since righteousness is an expression of holiness, then it is the righteousness that needs further elaboration (Eph 4:25-26, 28-29, 31-32). In addition to righteousness, the passage also shows how purity is a part of the new nature created after the likeness of God. Thus Paul wants them to "put off your old nature which belongs to your former manner of life and is corrupt through deceitful lusts" (4:22). Both purity and righteousness are reiterated again when he warns, "But immorality and all impurity or covetousness must not even be named among you, as is fitting among saints" (i.e., the holy ones, 5:3).

In the context of this section of his letter Paul also includes love as a part of the likeness of God. In 5:1 he exhorts them to "be imitators of God, as beloved

---

[65]The word ἀποθέσθαι is aorist middle infinitive of ἀποτίθημι, "to put off, to remove," as one puts off clothes. "The aorist tense denotes a once and for all, definite, concluding action: the stripping off is to be done at once, and for good." (Barth, cited in Fritz Eienecker, *A Linguistic Key to the Greek New Testament* [Grand Rapids, Mich.: Zondervan, 1982], p. 533). ἐνδύσασθαι is aorist middle infinitive of ἐνδύομαι, "to put on," in the sense of putting on a garment.

children." The children are to be like the image of their Father, and they are also to imitate his character. This is followed by the exhortation, "Walk in love, as Christ loved us and gave himself up for us" (5:2). His case is that the likeness of God is revealed in Christ's sacrificial love and self-giving grace. Accordingly, sacrificial love is to be a part of the lives of those who put on the new nature, created after the likeness of God. Further, the goodness of God's moral character may be suggested when those who are now being made like his image are exhorted to "be kind to one another, tenderhearted, forgiving one another, as God in Christ forgave you" (4:32). While the word goodness is not used, manifestations of goodness of character seem definitely to be implied here.

Finally, the concept of truth as a part of moral holiness is implied as that which Paul desires in these who are being created after the likeness of God. He speaks about "the truth . . . in Jesus" (4:21), about "putting away falsehood," and speaking "the truth with his neighbor" (4:25). If the holy God is a God of truth, then those whose moral nature reflects his character must also be people of the truth. Paul here appears to be calling the Ephesian believers to a deeper level of commitment to truth as a part of reflecting God's character. Such a commitment is part of putting on this new nature.

This same dealing with an old nature is the deeper kind of heart cry that comes from the mouth of David after the confession of his sin in Psalm 51. He asks God to deal with his transgressions and iniquities that relate to his specific sins (Ps 51:1, 3-4, 9), but he also prays fervently for something deeper in the very nature of his being. "Create in me a clean heart, O God, and renew a right spirit within me" (Ps 51:10). It is this creation of a clean heart that implies a desire after a heart more fully like the heart and spirit of God. In this context the clean heart is closely bound up with the concept of purity and power. David's desire for cleanness of heart includes a desire for ability or power for righteous conduct and purity from sin.

Abundant life. The whole concept of a deeper work of the Creator in the life of the individual Christian also seems to be implied in some of the references to life "in Christ" in the New Testament. Certain passages appear to be more than just the initial life of regeneration that is spoken of so frequently. For example, Jesus talks about coming to provide life, but it is life with a dimension of abundance (Jn 10:10). Paul seems to speak of this fuller dimension of life that results from a fuller death to self when he says, "I have been crucified with Christ; it is no longer

I who live, but Christ who lives in me; and the life I now live in the flesh I live by faith in the Son of God, who loved me and gave himself for me" (Gal 2:20).[66] These references seem to relate more to a "state" of deeper life than to the manner of getting into it. Nevertheless, they set a standard that was clearly attainable for New Testament believers.

Fuller separation. Lastly, full sanctification is referred to sometimes as a more complete separation from the world than that which occurs at conversion. Thus, to the Corinthian Christians Paul raises the question about being mismated with unbelievers and having partnership with iniquity. "What fellowship has light with darkness? What accord has Christ with Belial? Or what has a believer in common with an unbeliever? What agreement has the temple of God with idols? For we are the temple of the living God; as God said '. . . Therefore come out from them, and be separate from them, says the Lord.'" Therefore, Paul concludes, "since we have these promises, beloved, let us cleanse ourselves from every defilement of body and spirit, and make holiness perfect in the fear of God" (2 Cor 6:14—7:1). It would appear that Paul is calling for a deeper kind of separation from nonbelievers as a part of cleansing oneself from every defilement and perfecting holiness of character before the Lord.

This is also the thrust of Peter's comments when he speaks about the divine power that has "granted to us all things that pertain to life and godliness, through the knowledge of him who called us to his own glory and excellence, by which he has granted to us his precious and very great promises, that through these you may escape from the corruption that is in the world because of passion, and become partakers of the divine nature" (2 Pet 1:3-4). It is clear that becoming full partakers of the divine nature involves in some significant way a further separation from the corruption that is in the world, and this is related to the power available to Christians to pursue godliness of character.

So full sanctification under the category of God as the holy Creator is expressed in three principle ways. The first is putting on a new nature that is more perfectly conformed to the image and likeness of God's character. The second involves a fuller participation in abundant life in Christ where the individual ceases to live in himself but finds his total existence wrapped up in

---

[66]Paul may be referring to this kind of life of self-sacrifice when he writes, "For to me to live is Christ, and to die is gain" (Phil 1:21).

Christ so that Christ may be described as living through him. This is only possible for those who, third, are willing to be completely separated from the world in an even greater way than when they came to an experience of conversion. It is a deeper separation from sin and unholiness, and a fuller separation unto God.

Further Growth

Ongoing transformation. After one comes to an experience of full sanctification there is still further growth in God's grace. In this category growth after full sanctification is described as a continual transformation of the mind with result-ant change in character. In full sanctification there is a complete conformity of the will to the full moral image of God. One chooses to be made wholly like a holy God. But the working out of the implications of a fully surrendered will to God takes place in the understanding, in attitudes, and in personal behavior in the years that follow such an experience. This further growth after full sanctification is what Paul is calling for in Romans 12:2. After challenging the justified to a total presentation of their lives as a living sacrifice to God, holy and acceptable to him, Paul enjoins them, "Do not be conformed to this world, but be transformed by the renewal of your mind, that you may prove what is the will of God, what is good and acceptable and perfect" (Rom 12:2). For those whose lives have been totally yielded or separated to God in full sanctification, there is still the question of not being conformed to the image of the world. There must be an ongoing transformation that flows out of full yielding of the life and will to God that is a part of being a living sacrifice. Paul's exhortation is a present imper-ative that can be translated "keep on being transformed by the renewal of your mind."[67] There is a continual process of working out the conformity to God's image beginning with the mind, so that one may know and then do the perfect will of God in every area of life.

Glorification

New heaven/new earth. The final dimension of God's transforming grace in the remaking of persons in his own image comes at the time of glorification. Glorifica-tion is a broad term describing what happens either when a believer dies and is

---

[67] The verb is μεταμορφοσθε from which comes "metamorphosis." Cf. 2 Cor 4:16.

taken into the presence of God or when believers are resurrected at Christ's second return to earth. As John puts it, "we know that when he appears we shall be like him" (1 Jn 3:2). Glorification is often described in Scripture as a part of God's final re-creation of the universe.[68] This will be a time of restoration of the natural world,[69] and the creation of a new heaven and earth.[70] This involves a final transformation when even infirmities of body, mind, emotions and social relationships will be taken away. It is the last dealing with the effects of the fall on the human race. In this experience even that which is a part of general depravity will be restored. This is the import of Paul's declaration when he says, "We know that the whole creation has been groaning in travail together until now; and not only the creation, but we ourselves, who have the first fruits of the Spirit, groan inwardly as we wait for adoption as sons, the redemption of our bodies" (Rom 8:22-23). This is possible because God "who raised the Lord Jesus will raise us also with Jesus and bring us with you into his presence" (2 Cor 4:14).

Resurrection life. It is this ultimate resurrection life that Paul speaks about when "that what is mortal may be swallowed up by life" (2 Cor 5:4). He describes it more fully in discussing the whole question of the resurrection with the Corinthians. Speaking of the body with all its infirmities, Paul writes:

> What is sown is perishable, what is raised is imperishable. It is sown in dishonor, it is raised in glory. It is sown in weakness, it is raised in power. It is sown a physical body, it is raised a spiritual body. If there is a physical body, there is also a spiritual body. Thus it is written, "the first "Adam became a living being." . . . As was the man of dust, so are those who are of the dust; and as is the man of heaven, so are those who are of heaven. Just as we have borne the image of the man of dust, we shall also bear the image of the man of heaven. (1 Cor 15:42-45, 48-49)

The whole concept of resurrection life is implicit even in the Gospel record. Thus, John's emphasis on life is sometimes focused on a future life in heaven. Glorification will consist of that final, future, eternal life when God has fully remade his image in people and given them life like himself for all eternity.

Final separation. Finally, glorification will involve an element of separation. Jesus teaches that at the close of the age the angels will separate the evil from the

---

[68] Jacob, *Theology of the Old Testament*, pp. 141-42.

[69] See Acts 3:20-21; Rom 8:19-23; and 2 Pet 3:13.

[70] Knight, *Christian Theology of the Old Testament*, pp. 334-48.

righteous (Mt 13:49), and thus he depicts the final judgment as a separation of the sheep from the goats (25:32), wheat from tares (13:30).

So in glorification the holy Creator, who is in the process of making his creatures like himself, will do three things. One, he will remove the final effects of sin or unholiness from people made in his own image. Two, by bringing them into his immediate presence he is able to give them the fullness of resurrection life to enjoy for all of eternity. Three, this means a final separation of those who belong to him from those who do not, as well as a separation from this present world in order to live in his presence forever. Glorification then becomes the confirmation of God's efforts to re-create people so that they might share his character for eternity.

Attributes of God

The attributes of God[71] are normally divided for purposes of clarification into the absolute attributes, the relative attributes and the moral attributes.[72] The *absolute attributes* have to do with the qualities related to God's mode of existence, that is, those that belong to him apart from his created work. The *relative attributes* are qualities arising out of the relationship existing between the Creator and the created, and which of necessity require the creature for their manifestation. The *moral attributes* are qualities relating to God's direction over free and intelligent creatures who are created with the capacity for moral decisions. While the classification of God's attributes is somewhat arbitrary, such classification is nevertheless helpful in terms of understanding the different facets of God's being.

In relating the attributes of God to the various roles God plays in his relationship to people, certain roles seem to have a special relationship to certain attributes. While there is a good deal of overlap between the attributes and various roles, some of the attributes appear to be more closely associated with some roles than others. This close (though not exclusive) association provides the opportunity to introduce these attributes and thus begin to bridge the gap between a more narrative-oriented presentation of God (biblical theology) in his

---

[71] Of the possible terms for this heading, *appellationes, virtues, attributa, proprietates* or *perfectiones*, I have chosen the traditional *attributa* or "attributes." Others have chosen "perfections." CD 2/1, p. 322ff.

[72] Pope, *Compendium of Old Testament Theology*, 1:289-91. For alternative classifications see Berkhof, *Systematic Theology*, pp. 52-56; 88 n. 72; Thomas Oden, *The Living God*, (San Francisco: Harper & Row, 1987) p. 50.

roles with the more thematic presentation of his attributes (systematic theology).

Spirituality. Almost all the absolute attributes and two of the relative attributes are very closely related to God's role as transcendent Creator, and therefore are appropriately discussed in this chapter. The first of the absolute attributes is God's spirituality. The truth that God is a spiritual being has two components: his unity and simplicity. The unity of God focuses on the oneness of his essence and on monotheism as a description of his being. Thus, the Lord declares:

> I am the LORD, and there is no other, besides me there is no God; . . . I form light and create darkness, I make weal and create woe, I am the LORD, who do all these things. . . . Thus says the LORD, the Holy One of Israel, and his Maker: . . . I made the earth, and created man upon it; it was my hands that stretched out the heavens, and I commanded all their host. . . . For thus says the LORD, who created the heavens (he is God!), who formed the earth and made it (he established it; he did not create it a chaos, he formed it to be inhabited!): I am the LORD and there is no other (Is 45:5, 7, 11-12, 18).

Thus, God's people are enjoined, "Know therefore this day, and lay it to your heart, that the LORD is God in heaven above and on the earth beneath; there is no other" (Deut 4:39). This fact produces the great *shema* as a declaration of faith by God's people: "Hear, O Israel: the LORD our God is one LORD" (6:4).[73] This is echoed by the New Testament doxology "to the King of ages, immortal, invisible, the only God" (1 Tim 1:17). Thus the New Testament as well as the Old Testament teaches "there is one God" (2:5).

But the spirituality of God includes not only the unity of God but his simplicity, i.e., that he is invisible and incorporeal. When the Scriptures teach that God is pure spirit, it means that he does not have a literal body or functions. As Jesus describes him, "God is spirit, and those who worship him must worship in spirit and truth" (Jn 4:24). Paul reinforces this with his declaration about the only God as immortal and invisible (1 Tim 1:17). This is further implied by the whole picture of God as not being identified with any single part of the natural creation or its constituent parts. Rather, he is pictured as the transcendent Creator who is discontinuous with the physical universe of space and time.

---

[73] Other references to monotheism: Ex 3:14; 20:3; Deut 4:35; 5:7; Is 43:10-11; 44:6, 8; 45:21-22; 46:9.

This does not mean that God may not enter into his universe and take on certain forms. In particular, he may adopt a human form in a theophany or come in an incarnation for his own purposes. Further, it does not mean that God may not be described in one or more of his roles in an anthropomorphic manner that would seem to connect him with some physical form. But these physical descriptions of God (e.g., God's arm) are not to be understood literally, but figuratively.

Infinity. Not only is the spirituality of God connected with his role as Creator, but his infinity is also connected to the Creator role. The infinity of God has reference to his being without bounds or limits in the divine nature. It encompasses the eternity of God, i.e., infinity in relationship to time, so that God is without beginning or end and stands outside of time. He is the great timeless I AM.[74] Thus, it is the Creator of the ends of the earth who is described as the everlasting God (Is 40:28). He is the one who is the Lord, the first and the last (Is 41:4; 44:6).[75] The psalmist also connects God's role as Creator with his eternity when he exclaims, "Before the mountains were brought forth, or ever thou hadst formed the earth and the world, from everlasting to everlasting thou art God" (Ps 90:2).

In the New Testament John sends grace and peace from "him who is and who was and who is to come" (Rev 1:4). This is the same one who declares of himself, "'I am the Alpha and the Omega,' says the Lord God, who is and who was and who is to come, the Almighty" (Rev 1:8).

The infinity of God not only encompasses his eternity but also his immensity. Whereas the eternity of God had to do with infinity in relationship to time, immensity has to do with the relationship of infinity to space. God is not limited or circumscribed by space any more than he is by time; he transcends both of these. As the Hebrews put it, "Behold, heaven and the highest heaven cannot contain thee" (1 Kings 8:27). While God transcends the universe of space, he also is described as filling the universe without being localized in any particular part (cf. Deut 4:39; Is 40:22; 66:1; Jer 23:24).

Self-sufficiency. The third absolute attribute of God particularly associated with his role as Creator is his self-sufficiency. This is described as his asiety or his

---

[74] Ex 3:14-15; cf. Jesus, "Before Abraham was, I am" (Jn 8:58).
[75] Other references to his eternity: Deut 33:27; Ps 102:25-27; 1 Tim 1:17.

self-subsistence, meaning that he is the one who is in possession of life in himself. He is not dependent on any other outside of himself for his own existence. So Jesus can state, "As the Father has life in himself, so he has granted the Son also to have life in himself" (Jn 5:26). This is surely part of what God had in mind with the revelation of his name to Israel as the "I AM WHO I AM" (Ex 3:14). Thus he may declare, "Before me no god was formed, nor shall there be any after me" (Is 43:10), and "I am He, I am the first, and I am the last" (Is 48:12; see also 44:6; Gen 1:1). It is the self- sufficiency of God along with his spirituality and infinity that make up the heart of his transcendence. These dimensions are the basis of what is referred to as the supranatural being of God.

Immutability. A fourth of the absolute attributes related to God's role as Creator is his immutability. This refers to the fact that there is no change in the essence of any attribute of God's nature. As the psalmist declares, "Thou art the same, and thy years have no end" (Ps 102:27; Heb 1:12). This is the Lord's declaration about himself as well when he says, "For I the LORD do not change" (Mal 3:6; also Jas 1:17; Heb 6:17-18). Jesus, who is the full reflection of the Father, is described as "the same yesterday and today and for ever" (Heb 13:8). The biblical picture of the unchangeableness of God is the guarantee for God's people that the One in whom they have confidence and trust today will not be different tomorrow. Their faith is built on the trustworthiness and sameness of his character. While some of the descriptions of God's work in terms of the various roles with which he is described may seem to imply certain changes in relationship to him (e.g., God repented of an action), this is not to be understood in terms of a change in his essence of attributes, purposes or character.

Freedom. One of the relative attributes of God that seems most closely related to his creatorship is the freedom of God. When the Scripture opens with the story of creation in Genesis 1 and 2, there is no hint of any necessity of God to create the universe. He is free to create or not to create, and he is free to create according to his own will. There is no force or "metadivine" above or beyond God that determines his choices or forces him into action as is the case in all the other creation stories of the ancient Near Eastern world. Thus he declares, "I am God, and also henceforth I am He; there is none who can deliver from my hand; I work and who can hinder it?" (Is 43:13). Or as the Hebrews understood it, "Our God is in the heavens; he does whatever he pleases" (Ps 115:3).

God, of course, does not have the freedom to do that which is contrary to his nature. His willful choices are determined by the nature of his character, and in particular his moral character. Thus, God is not free to be something that he himself is not. A good God is not free to be evil. That would be nonsense. Further, his freedom in determining creation, and in particular, his choice to create other moral agents with the freedom of choice, means that he has voluntarily limited his own freedom in relation to these other moral beings. Thus, from the time of creation God has limited his freedom in part so as not to override the free will of his creatures.

Omnipotence. The final relative attribute that seems closely associated with God's work in creation is that of his omnipotence. He is the one who has all power and is able to do that which he pleases. This is particularly related to his self-sufficiency. His omnipotence is clearly demonstrated in his power to create the universe (Gen 1—2). "To whom then will you compare me, that I should be like him? says the Holy One. Lift up your eyes on high and see: who created these? He who brings out their host by number, calling them all by name; by the greatness of his might, and because he is strong in power not one is missing" (Is 40:25-26; cf. 44:6).

In addition, his omnipotence is closely related to his role as sovereign Ruler of the universe and also as powerful Redeemer.[76] But it is in his role as Creator that Jeremiah identifies him: "It is he who made the earth by his power" (Jer 10:12). At the end of Scripture God is described in the revelation to John as the "Almighty" (Rev 1:8), so the praise to God includes the declaration, "Holy, holy, holy, is the Lord God Almighty, who was and is and is to come!" and this omnipotence is emphasized again when they sing to him, "Worthy art thou, our Lord and God, to receive glory and honor and power, for thou didst create all things, and by thy will they existed and were created" (Rev 4:8, 11). Thus, the one who is described in the beginning of Scripture as the one powerful enough to create the whole universe, is praised at the end of Scripture as the one worthy of glory and honor and power because he did create and bring all things into existence.

God as Physician/Healer

Within the concept of God's role as the Creator, with a focus on giving life, there

---

[76] See also relationship of "omnipotence" to these roles in chapters 4 and 9.

are several subcategories that describe God when he does Creator-like things, but in a different language figure. We have already looked at three of these: God as Cultivator, God as Builder and God as Potter. However, the most significant of these is God's role as Physician or Healer. Whereas the focus of God's work as Creator is the giving of life, the *focus* of God's role as Physician is the *restoration of life* or health. The *language* of this *figure* relates to the *medical field* and has to do with matters of sickness and health.[77] It is a figure of speech designed to show that the one who has the capacity to give life also has the capacity to restore life and health in his creatures.[78]

The first and perhaps the only direct reference to God as Healer, comes in Exodus 15 where the Lord declares to Israel that he "will put none of the diseases upon you which I put upon the Egyptians; for I am the LORD, your healer" (Ex 15:26).[79] The context of this reference has to do with praise to God for his deliverance during the Exodus and is commonly known as the Song of Moses. It is also the chapter with the first reference to the holiness of God, where the people are taught to sing, "Who is like thee, O LORD, among the gods? Who is like thee, majestic in holiness?" (15:11). The holy one, whom Israel is beginning to learn to know during the time of their first wandering in the desert, is also the one who describes himself as able to heal them.[80] When Israel is later called by David to bless God's holy name because of all his benefits, one of those benefits listed is that he "heals all your diseases" (Ps 103:3). Also Isaiah speaks of the "high and lofty One who inhabits eternity, whose name is Holy," who gives the breath of life. The Holy One becomes angry because Israel "went on backsliding in the way of his own heart." God promises, "I have seen his ways, but I will heal him" (Is 57:15, 17-18; cf. Jer 51:5-9).

Father. With the exception of Exodus 15:26, God himself is not called either Physician or Healer in Scripture. Nevertheless, he does act like a physician in terms of his healing work among people. There are a number of general references to healing by God such as his statement to Israel, "I kill and I make alive; I wound and I heal" (Deut 32:39).[81] There are also significant examples of

---

[77] *TWOT*, p. 857.

[78] On biblical healing, see *TWB*, pp. 103-4; *ISBE*, 2:640-47.

[79] The word רָפָא is not in a substantive but in a verbal form here.

[80] Cf. Deut 7:6, 15, where God looks for a holy people (because he is holy, Lev 11:44-45) and promises to take away their sickness.

[81] That Jer 8:22 refers to God is problematic.

God's work in physical healing of his people, like the healing of Abimelech in answer to Abraham's prayer (Gen 20:17), or the healing of Miriam of her leprosy in response to Moses' plea for her (Num 12:13). There is a healing of God's people from the effects of the fiery serpents in the wandering in the wilderness (Num 21:4-9) and the healing of Hezekiah in response to his own prayer (2 Kings 20:5; Is 38:1-8).[82]

God's spiritual healing is not quite as obvious in the Old Testament, although it certainly may be included in the general references to healing by God. Nevertheless, it is clear that "he heals the brokenhearted, and binds up their wounds" (Ps 147:3).[83] In certain of the Old Testament predictions of the coming of the Messiah, spiritual healing is certainly connected to dealing with sin in the life of the individual. "He was wounded for our transgressions, he was bruised for our iniquities; upon him was the chastisement that made us whole, and with his stripes we are healed" (Is 53:5). Malachi at the end of the Old Testament, looking forward to the new messianic age, can declare God's word, "For you who fear my name the sun of righteousness shall rise, with healing in its wings" (Mal 4:2).

Son. When the Messiah comes in the person of Jesus, he does the things a physician or healer would do, but most of the references to Jesus as physician are indirect. One comes in Jesus' first sermon at Nazareth when he said to them, "Doubtless you will quote to me this proverb, 'Physician, heal yourself'" (Lk 4:23). Jesus' other indirect reference to himself as a physician comes at the dinner given for him by Matthew for his tax collector friends. When the Pharisees object to Jesus' disciples, he responds, "Those who are well have no need of a physician, but those who are sick" (Mt 9:12).

Although Jesus is not often called a physician or healer, there are many references to his general healing ministry. Thus Matthew, at the beginning of Jesus' ministry, summarizes his activity when he describes Jesus going about all Galilee "teaching in their synagogues and preaching the gospel of the kingdom and healing every disease and every infirmity among the people" (Mt 4:23). [84] Mark, in his introductory description of Jesus' early ministry, describes how the

---

[82]See also 2 Chron 7:14; 2 Kings 2:21, 22; Ps 107:20; Is 30:26; Jer 30:17; 50:8-9; Ezek 47:8-9, 11; Hos 6:1; 11:3; Mal 4:2.

[83]See also Ex 15:26; Is 19:22; 1 Sam 6:3.

[84]See also Mt 8:16; 9:35; 12:15; 14:14; 15:30-31; 19:2; 21:14.

whole city gathered together at the door of the house of Simon and Andrew, and Jesus "healed many who were sick with various diseases, and cast out many demons" (Mk 1:34; cf. 3:10; 6:5). Further, Luke records that after the first leper was cleansed, the report spread about regarding him was so significant that "great multitudes gathered to hear and to be healed of their infirmities" (Lk 5:15; also 4:40; 5:17, 6:7, 17-19; 9:6, 11).

In addition to the general references to healing there are many specific passages that deal with Jesus' physical healing during his ministry. Thus, Jesus heals a man with a shriveled hand (Lk 6:6-11); he heals a centurion's servant (7:1-10); he heals the woman with the issue of blood (8:43-48); he heals the woman who had been sick for eighteen years (13:11-17); he heals a man of dropsy (14:1-6); he heals the ten lepers (17:11-19); he heals the blind men at Jericho (18:35-43); and he heals the right ear of the servant of the High Priest (22:51).[85]

Often mentioned in connection with physical healing, but clearly as a distinct, specific category, is demonic healing. Examples include Luke's references to a certain women who had been healed of evil spirits and infirmities (8:2, 3). A man called Legion is healed of many demons (8:26-33), and an unclean spirit is cast out of a boy (9:37-43).

Healing metaphor in the atonement. Spiritual healing has its basis in the death of the Messiah and therefore becomes one additional element in the atonement. This is seen in the great Messianic passage in Isaiah 53:5: "He was wounded for our transgressions, he was bruised for our iniquities; upon him was the chastisement that made us whole, and with his stripes we are healed." Peter echoes this passage when he writes about Jesus, who "bore our sins in his body on the tree, that we might die to sin and live to righteousness. By his wounds you have been healed" (1 Pet 2:24). This means that the healing metaphor related to Jesus' role as Physician is connected in Scripture with his death. While this has not become a full-blown theory of the atonement, it certainly is one additional element that is necessary for a full picture of the atonement. One pictorial way in which the death of Christ is seen is his being wounded in our place so that we might receive healing. As with many of the other elements of the atonement, it involves a dimension of substitution. He clearly is wounded and bruised in our place so that we might not have to suffer—so that out of his woundedness we

---

[85]Other references to physical healing: Mt 9:1-8; 12:9-15; 15:29-31; Jn 4:47; 5:3, 7, 8, 14-17; 9:1-34.

might be healed of sin, described as our own spiritual bruises and wounds.

Examples of spiritual healing would include that of the paralytic who was first forgiven of his sins and then healed of his physical sickness as a demonstration of God's power to heal the heart (Mk 2:1-12). Isaiah 6:10 talks about people who do not understand or perceive because their ears are heavy and their eyes shut and therefore they cannot understand with their heart and turn to be healed. This passage is quoted several times in the New Testament (Mt 13:14-15; Jn 12:40, Acts 28:27). The context of each of these passages makes clear that the reference is to a kind of spiritual healing that God desires to bring to the lives of individuals.

Sin: Spiritual sickness. Almost all the references in both the Old Testament and New Testament to sickness refer to physical sickness. There are a few references to emotional or heart-sickness.[86] There are, however, a few exceptions that speak of sickness in spiritual categories. The most well known and often quoted is that of Isaiah when he gives God's evaluation of the spiritual state of Israel. "The whole head is sick, and the whole heart faint. From the sole of the foot even to the head, there is no soundness in it, but bruises and sores and bleeding wounds; they are not pressed out, or bound up, or softened with oil" (Is 1:5-6). This would seem to be a clear reference to the sinful state of man as a result of original sin. Ezekiel has a more general reference to sin in the figurative sense of the word when he challenges the leadership of Israel: "The weak you have not strengthened, the sick you have not healed, the crippled you have not bound up" (Ezek 34:4). There may be a reference to the healing of infirmities when the psalmist proclaims "the LORD sustains him on his sickbed; in his illness thou healest all his infirmities" (Ps 41:3). But he may also include deliberate acts of sin, for the psalmist continues, "O LORD, be gracious to me; heal me, for I have sinned against thee!" (Ps 41:4). And a New Testament exception seems to refer to both spiritual and physical sickness in the story of a paralytic being forgiven and healed by Jesus (Mt 9:3-12; cf. Mk 2:17; Lk 5:31-32).

The same is true with regard to references to wounds. Almost all of them are physical wounds, although there are some Old Testament exceptions. God observes of Jerusalem that "violence and destruction are heard within her; sickness and wounds are ever before me" (Jer 6:7). In describing Israel's spiritual

---

[86]Prov 13:12; Song 2:5; 5:8.

state the Lord exclaims, "Your hurt is incurable, and your wound is grievous. There is none to uphold your cause, no medicine for your wound, no healing for you" (Jer 30:12-13; also 30:15-17; Is 1:6; 53:5; Mic 1:9). Nevertheless, the Lord can be gracious and is the one who "heals the brokenhearted, and binds up their wounds" (Ps 147:3).

Salvation: Spiritual healing. The Old Testament references to spiritual healing have to do principally with recovery from backsliding. Thus the Lord can exhort Israel, "Return, O faithless sons, and I will heal your faithlessness" (Jer 3:22). But the people need to cry out to God, "Heal me, O LORD, and I shall be healed; save me, and I shall be saved" (17:14). Hezekiah prayed for the Lord to pardon the people of Israel who set their hearts to seek the Lord, and the Lord heard Hezekiah and healed the people (2 Chron 30:18-20).[87] That seems to be the import as well of two New Testament references to spiritual healing. Hebrews exhorts Christians to "make straight paths for your feet, so that what is lame may not be put out of joint but rather be healed" (Heb 12:13). James, when he calls for the elders to anoint a believer and pray for his physical recovery, implies the importance of confessing one's sins for purposes of spiritual healing as well. "Therefore confess your sins to one another, and pray for one another, that you may be healed" (Jas 5:16).

Salvation as spiritual healing is not described in a straightforward manner. The closest reference is to the healing of the paralytic whose sins are also forgiven (Mk 2:12; Mt 9:2-8; Lk 5:17-26). But even here the word *healing* is not used of the forgiveness of sins, but only of the physical miracle. Spiritual healing seems to be implied in the three New Testament quotations from Isaiah 6:10 (Mt 13:14-15; Jn 12:40; Acts 28:27). The passage states that if people had ears to hear and eyes to see and turned with their hearts, God would heal them. Its original context may have reference to a return to a proper spiritual state from backsliding, and it may carry some of those overtones in the New Testament.

Yet it needs to be recognized that the whole picture of spiritual healing in Scripture is not very extensive. It is closely related to the implied restoration of the moral image of God in people. Nevertheless, of the many healings done by the Father and the Son, the vast majority refer to physical and demonic healing, and very few have reference to spiritual healing. Thus, I have chosen to describe

---

[87]See also Is 6:10; 57:15; Hos 7:1; 144.

this figure as a subcategory of a major role (i.e., God as Creator) that may be understood as an object lesson of God's re-creation of his image in the spiritual experience of his creatures.

Conclusion

An examination of the biblical materials indicates that there is a wealth of data describing God as Creator of the universe. The language category of creation is a helpful tool throughout Scripture that describes not only the Father, Son and Holy Spirit, but also creation, people, sin, salvation, growth, the church, full sanctification and glorification. It is also the category under which a significant number of the attributes of God are best understood. Because it is the first picture of God we encounter in Scripture, it is appropriate that we treat the role of God as transcendent Creator first in our discussion. It lays a foundation for understanding many of the other roles.

It is also clear that this role is closely tied to the holiness of God. The concept of holiness as separation is particularly apropos for understanding a God who is separate from and therefore transcends the universe that he made. Not only is holiness as separation important for understanding this role, but we have also seen how it permeates the other categories described in creation language (e.g., salvation as the re-creating of the moral [holiness] image of God in people). It is clear that the holiness of God is intimately intertwined with his role as Creator.

It seemed appropriate to discuss God's role as Physician or Healer as a subrole under creation language. The physician is one who heals and therefore sustains life that is made by the Creator. We have seen while this category does not have extensive biblical development, it is closely related to the role of God as Creator.

Both the role of God as Creator and the subrole of Physician should be helpful to us in understanding who God is and how we relate to him. Since the other roles presuppose this one, we must be sure we understand how God works in this way and how he desires for us to relate to him. It is particularly important in the age in which we live that often encourages people to find God within creation or within themselves. This role is a healthy reminder that God is not to be confused either with our own inner consciousness or with the created order. He made both, but he is separate and distinct from both. Once we understand this, we can certainly relate to him more adequately.

Four

Holy God as Sovereign King

The Unity Factor

Holiness as separation. The concept of holiness is clearly linked with separation and separateness. In the previous chapter we saw the concept of holiness as separation in relation to God's role as a separate or transcendent Creator. The focus was on the one who gave life to the universe and to people, but who himself was separate and distinct from his creation. Closely intertwined with this picture of God as the Creator is his government of the universe. The Creator not only makes a world, but he rules over it. Not surprisingly, therefore, many of the passages that relate holiness to separation appear to be connected, not with God's role as transcendent Creator, but with his role as sovereign King over the universe.

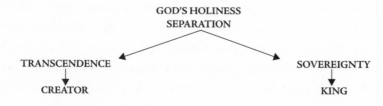

Figure 4.1. Holiness related to separation

Holy God as sovereign. The first reference to the holiness of God in Scripture is set in the context of his majestic rule. "Who is like thee, O LORD, among the gods? Who is like thee, majestic in holiness?" (Ex 15:11). In this song of Moses, by which the children of Israel praised God for his deliverance from Pharaoh, they exclaim, "In the greatness of thy majesty thou overthrowest thy adversaries," and

"The LORD will reign for ever and ever" (15:7, 18). So the initial presentation of the holiness of God is set in the context of his rule over his people as opposed to the rule of Pharaoh and the Egyptians. John gives us a similar view at the close of Scripture as he pictures God seated on his throne where the living creatures around him cry day and night saying, "Holy, holy, holy, is the Lord God Almighty" (Rev 4:8).[1] He is the holy King from the beginning of the establishment of Israel, and he is the same holy King at the end of time.

The Role of God as Sovereign King

The *language figure* for this role relates to *royalty.* It is the language of kingship derived from the royal court and was readily borrowed from the cultural milieu of the Middle East.[2] It describes God as the sovereign King over the universe in general and over people in particular as his subjects.

The *focus* of this language figure is on *authority.* It is the *king (melek)* who is one who exercises authority over those under his dominion. The basic question is, who is in charge? God wants the last word, just like a ruling king, making this language relate to both the majesty of a king and his ruling power.[3]

The Father

King over Israel. This language category begins to develop with the establishment of the people of God in the book of Exodus. A central question is whether the Egyptians will rule over Israel or whether God will rule over them. God delivers his people so that they might be a people of his own possession and therefore live under his direction. So it is not surprising to see Israel beginning to praise his majestic power in their song of deliverance from Egypt (Ex 15). Nor is it surprising when God offers them a covenant at Mount Sinai that he should tell Israel that he is looking for a "kingdom of priests" (19:6).[4] The whole concept of cove-

[1]Cf. the repeated references to God's throne for emphasis on his kingship (Rev 4:2-6, 9); see also Rev. 6:10 for the description of God as "Sovereign Lord, holy and true."

[2]See Martin Buber, *Kingship of God* (New York: Harper & Row, 1967), pp. 85-93; Henri Frankfort, *Kingship and the Gods* (Chicago: University of Chicago Press, 1948); Ivan Engnell, *Studies in Divine Kingship* (Oxford: Basil Blackwell, 1967).

[3]For God as מֶלֶךְ, see *TWOT*, 1:507-10 and *TDNT*, 1:565-71. For God as βασιλεύς see *BTLNT*, pp. 131-37; *TDNT*, 1:576-93; *NIDNTT*, 2:372-90.

[4]Cf. Buber, "The unconditioned claim of the divine Kingship is recognized at the point when the people proclaim JHWH Himself as King, Him alone and directly (Ex 15:18) and JHWH Himself enters upon the kingly reign (Ex 19:6)" (*Kingship of God*, p. 119).

nant is based on the ancient Near Eastern pattern of suzerainty treaties by which an overlord enters into an agreement with a vassal and his people. The overlord assumed certain responsibilities, while the vassal submitted to his direction and rule.[5] God makes it quite clear at Mount Sinai that he is the one who is to rule over Israel. Thus, for some centuries they do not have their own monarch, because they are living under a theocracy with God as King.[6] When Israel finally does become a monarchy, it is out of a wrong motivation to be like other nations. Thus, the Lord instructs Samuel to give them a king, because, he says, "they have rejected me from being king over them" (1 Sam 8:7).[7]

Israel a constitutional monarchy. Even when God does allow Israel to have a king, it is clearly a different sort of kingship from that of surrounding nations. Other kings could operate within their own sphere of rule as absolute sovereigns. They might be subject to some emperor or another king over them, but that was simply because someone had greater power. Within their own context, however, they did not know the bounds of any law except that of their own making. This is the reason for Jezebel's foreign attitude toward her husband Ahab, the King of Israel. When Ahab desires Naboth's vineyard, Jezebel does not understand why he does not take it. The fact that the king is under a higher law than himself is foreign to her understanding. She has no hesitancy in arranging the death of Naboth in order to get his field for her husband (1 Kings 21).

But in Israel the king is not an absolute sovereign. God is still the ultimate King, and he alone has complete sovereignty over the affairs of people.[8] Rather, Israel has something like a constitutional monarchy. Their king is limited by the character of God as revealed in his law. There are thus carefully delineated limits to the authority of the king in Israel.[9] So when Saul is crowned as the first king of Israel, "Samuel told the people the rights and duties of the kingship; and he

---

[5]See George E. Mendenhall, *Law and Covenant in Israel and the Ancient Near East* (Pittsburgh: The Biblical Collo-quium, 1995), pp. 24-50.

[6]See Buber, *Kingship of God*, pp. 136-62.

[7]Kingship was apparently in God's plan for Israel, however, because of its significant relationship to the coming Messiah. The reluctance of God to give Israel a king in 1 Samuel must be understood in the light of their unworthy motive, i.e., to be like other nations (1 Sam 8:5) rather than be under God's direct rule.

[8]See John Eaton, *Kingship and the Psalms* (Naperville, Ill.: A. R. Allenson, 1975), p. 135.

[9]See Edmond Jacob, *Theology of the Old Testament,* trans. Arthur W. Heathcote and P. J. Allcock (New York: Harper & Row, 1958), p. 237; Louis Berkhof, *Systematic Theology* (Edinburgh: Banner of Truth, 1958), p. 407. It is clear that God is understood as King before the establishment of the monarchy. Cf. Buber, *Kingship of God*, pp. 93, 99-107.

wrote them in a book and laid it up before the LORD" (1 Sam 10:25). Samuel makes it quite clear to both king and the people, "If both you and the king who reigns over you will follow the LORD your God, it will be well; but if you will not hearken to the voice of the LORD, but rebel against the commandment of the LORD, then the hand of the LORD will be against you and your king" (12:14-15). When Saul disobeys the clear commandments of God, he is rejected from his role as king (13:13-14).

A graphic illustration of the practical limits of a constitutional monarchy is the story of David's sin with Bathsheba (2 Sam 11—12). Elsewhere in the ancient Near Eastern world a king could have almost any woman in his realm. But in Israel there is a wrongness about this action because the king, as well as the people, lived under God's moral law, a higher authority than the king's own person. Thus, Nathan can appear before the king and accuse him of sin. A prophet in any other land would have forfeited his life for such boldness, but in Israel both the prophet and the king recognize that there is a higher law. David as well as everyone else is subject to its authority, and Nathan, aware that David is committed to living under a higher authority than himself, is able to make his rebuke in relative safety (12:1-15).

Purpose of kingship. The purpose of kingship in Israel was not just to rule over the land. Rather, it had a theological design, i.e., to point people to God, who was the real King. Although God granted Israel a monarchy, he still expected to be the ultimate Ruler of his people. From God's perspective a king in Israel is the representative of the King of the universe, not his replacement.[10]

Symbolic of the king as the representative of God is the declaration of the psalmist that pictures the king as God's son.[11] This obviously carries Messianic connotations, and in due course the Messianic hope becomes patterned after the ideal kingship of David. The picture is one of a son ruling under or with his father, but not over him or without his superior authority.[12]

The kings of Israel and Judah regularly abused their privilege. Consider King Uzziah. Early in his reign he sought after God and received God's blessing on his

---

[10]For the king as God's servant see Ps 78:70-72; 132:10; 89:3, 20; 35:27; 116:16; 143:12; 69:17.

[11]Ps 2:7; 22:9-10ff.; 89:27; 110; Also 2 Sam. 7:14. cf. Eaton, *Kingship of God*, pp. 146-150.

[12]Although the king in Israel is spoken of metaphorically as God's son, the king is never understood to be divine as he was in other nations. Yehezkel Kaufmann, *The Religion of Israel* (Chicago: University of Chicago Press, 1960), p. 266; Jacob, *Theology of the Old Testament*, 238.

rule. But in his latter years he grew proud and tried to usurp the prerogatives of the priests by offering incense in the temple. The judgment of God comes on him, making him a leper, as a reminder to him and to Israel that even the king is not a final authority among God's people (2 Chron 26).

Nevertheless, because of Uzziah's long reign and success in directing the nation, it is likely that many forgot who was the real king in Judah. Perhaps this is the import of the picture in Isaiah 6 that takes place the year King Uzziah dies. As he comes into the temple the prophet declares, "I saw the Lord sitting upon a throne high and lifted up; and his train filled the temple" (Is 6:1). Isaiah's vision comes to him as a sharp reminder of who is the real king of the people, and he exclaims, "My eyes have seen the King, the Lord of Hosts!" (6:5). The experience is a significant declaration that while earthly kings come and go, not so with God. He is the permanent King over his people and the universe!

Character of king: Holy. Isaiah's vision also gives us the key to understanding how Israel viewed the character of their heavenly King. Around his throne stand the seraphim who call to one another saying, "Holy, holy, holy is the LORD of Hosts; the whole earth is full of his glory" (6:3). The repeated reference to his holiness is for emphasis, and the clear implication is that when one, like the prophet, sees God as King and sees him as he really is, the overwhelming impact of his presence is tied to his holiness. God's role as King relates to what he does in ruling over Israel and the universe, but his holiness relates to what he is. The King's character and being are holy.[13]

In the light of this experience, it is no wonder that the prophet develops his own characteristic name for the God of Israel when he designates him as the Holy One of Israel (1:4).[14] The prophet has recognized that the essence of God's nature is his holiness, and this holy one does not change, as is clear from the almost identical vision in Revelation 4. There the living creatures around the throne cry day and night, "Holy, holy, holy, is the Lord God Almighty, who was and is and is to come!" (Rev 4:8).[15]

Numerous other biblical passages relate God's holiness to his kingship. Psalm 99 speaks about the reign of the Lord who sits enthroned on the cherubim. What

---

[13]John N. Oswalt, *The Book of Isaiah Chapters 1-39* (Grand Rapids, Mich.: Eerdmans, 1986), 1:180-82.

[14]Other references in Isaiah to the Holy One: Is 5:19, 24; 10:17, 20; 12:6; 17:7; 29:19, 23; 30:11-12, 15; 31:1; 37:23; 40:25; 41:14-16; 45:11; 47:4; 48:17; 49:7; 54:5; 55:5; 60:9, 14.

[15]Cf. another vision of God on his throne with an accent on his appearance as brilliance (Ezek 1:26-28).

is this "mighty king" like? The psalmist repeatedly declares, "Holy is he!" So Israel is to praise God's great and terrible name, extol his presence and worship at his holy mountain, "For the LORD our God is holy!" (Ps 99:1, 3, 5, 9).[16] Kingship and holiness are early tied together in biblical revelation as God capsules his purposes for Israel at Mount Sinai when he tells them he is looking for a kingdom of priests and a holy nation (Ex 19:6). Clearly he is looking for a kingdom over whom he will rule, and he is looking for a holy people to reflect his own holiness (Lev 11:44-45). Thus, the prophet can declare on behalf of God, "I am the LORD, your Holy One, the Creator of Israel, your King" (Is 43:15).[17]

Lord. Closely bound up with God's role as sovereign King is the terminology which describes him as Lord or Master. God's title in this category is *adon* (אָדוֹן) or *adonai* (אֲדֹנָי), which means "Lord" or "Master," and is frequently equated with God's kingship.[18] So Isaiah can claim, "I saw the Lord sitting upon a throne, high and lifted up" (Is 6:1), and the psalmist can cry, "O LORD, our Lord, how majestic is thy name in all the earth!" (Ps 8:1, 9). Furthermore, it is the Lord who rules over the universe. "The LORD reigns; let the earth rejoice; let the many coastlands be glad! . . . The mountains melt like wax before the LORD, before the Lord of all the earth" (Ps 97:1, 5).[19] The connection is made complete when Isaiah connects the Holy One with the Lord (Is 10:16-17). One of the final ties in Scripture between God's kingship and his role as Lord comes in the vision of the elders falling down and worshiping before the throne of God and crying out, "The Lord our God the Almighty reigns" (Rev 19:4-6).[20]

In the New Testament two words designate God's role as Lord. The first and most common is *kurios* (κυριός) and is a frequent designation of God the Father (e.g., Mt 5:33; Mk 5:19; Lk 1:6).[21] The second word is *despotes* (δεσπότης) which is a word that designates absolute ownership and uncontrolled power.

---

[16]The Psalms give ample praise to God as King: Ps 5:2; 10:16; 24:2, 7-8; 44:3-4; 68:24, 34-35; 95:3, 5-6; 96:7, 10; 97:1-2; 98:5-6; 149:2.

[17]On God's holiness with his kingship: Zech 14:9, 16-20; Ps 47; 48:1-2; 93; 102:12-19; 103:1, 19-22; 145:1, 10-13, 21.

[18]For אֲדֹנָי, as title for God: *TDOT*, 1:59-72; *TWOT*, 1:12-13; *NIDNTT*, 2:510-13.

[19]For the enthronement motif for understanding Israel's history see Sigmond Mowinckel, *The Psalms in Israel's Worship* (Oxford: Blackwell, 1962); and Mowinckel, *He That Cometh* (New York: Abingdon, 1954); also Jacob, *Theology of the Old Testament*, pp. 234-235, and Keith R. Crum, *The Royal Psalms* (Richmond, Va.: John Knox Press, 1962).

[20]For God as Lord see Emil Brunner, *Christian Doctrine of God* (London: Lutterworth, 1949), pp. 137-50; and CD 3/3, pp. 154-288.

[21]*TDNT*, 3:1039-95.

It is the word from which the English "despot" is derived. John connects this title with both God's sovereign kingship and his holiness: "O Sovereign Lord, holy and true" (Rev 6:10).[22]

Lord of hosts/God of the armies. Another closely related designation for God in the Old Testament is the title "Lord of hosts" or "God of the armies." It is connected both with the holiness of God and his kingship. Thus, Isaiah in describing his vision of the one whom he has seen as holy, exclaims, "My eyes have seen the King, the LORD of hosts!" (Is 6:5). Further, he can speak about "the LORD, the King of Israel and his Redeemer, the LORD of hosts" (Is 44:6). Malachi reports the Lord's declaration, "I am a great King, says the LORD of hosts, and my name is feared among the nations" (Mal 1:14).[23] The language of this title is from the military, a picture of a general leading an army. In the ancient world the king often led his military forces into battle, so the overlap between the two figures of speech was readily understood.

In Hebrew, *tsaba* (צָבָא), which we are translating "hosts," means "armies." It can refer to a human army (Judg 4:2), the heavenly hosts of celestial beings (1 Kings 22:19) or the celestial bodies, such as the sun and the moon (Gen 2:1; Deut 4:19).[24] When God rules over these heavenly bodies, they are referred to as the hosts of heaven, and it corresponds primarily to his governing of the creative order he has made. When it refers to the inhabitants of heaven, on the other hand, it speaks of angelic hosts over which God gives direction.

Frequently the term *hosts* is used to describe the armies of Israel, and this use relates God to his people as Warrior King or Commander of his military forces. Thus God acknowledges the Israelites, when he brings his people out of Egypt, as his hosts (Ex 6:26; 7:4; 12:17, 51). Likewise, the tribes of Israel are sometimes numbered as armies or companies of God (Num 1:3; 2; 33:1). David refers to Goliath as the one who would "defy the armies of the living God" (1 Sam 17:26, 36). David recognizes that it is God who wins battles and therefore is able to confront Goliath with the cry, "I come to you in the name of the LORD of hosts, the God of the armies of Israel, whom you have defied" (1 Sam 17:45). Since

---

[22]It is also used in Lk 2:29 and Acts 4:24 (and possibly 2 Tim 2:21) of God. It is used twice of Jesus in 2 Pet 2:1 and Jude 4. See Richard C. Trench, *Synonyms of the New Testament* (Grand Rapids, Mich.: Eerdmans, 1966), pp. 96-98.

[23]For other references connecting the Lord with the Lord of hosts see Is 1:24; 3:1; 10:16, 33; 19:4.

[24] *TWOT*, 2:750-51; *TDNT*, 2:705-7.

Yahweh is viewed ultimately as the head of all armies, unless he chooses to go to war with Israel's army, the battle will not be successful (Ps 49:9; Prov 21:31).

Without directly using the title "Commander" the Lord is often pictured as the one who is the leader of the army of his people. "I am the LORD, your Holy One, the Creator of Israel, your King. . . . who brings forth chariot and horse, army and warrior"(Is 43:15, 17). Just before Israel crosses the Jordan to begin its conquest for the land of Canaan, God sends his own commander to lead the army of Israel (Josh 6:13-15). John describes Jesus as a warrior King who leads the armies of heaven on a white horse to smite his enemies (Rev 19:11-14).

God as warrior king. Frequently in Scripture God is described as one who fights on behalf of his people. "Who is the King of glory? The LORD, strong and mighty, the LORD, mighty in battle!" (Ps 24:8). The prophets picture him as the one who "will go forth and fight against those nations as when he fights on a day of battle" (Zech 14:3). The priests proclaim that the "LORD your God is he that goes with you, to fight for you against your enemies, to give you the victory" in order to encourage the people of Israel and guard their hearts so they would not become faint or fearful during battle (Deut 20:3-4). The Lord demonstrated his power by fighting for his people against the armies of Pharaoh who desired to re-enslave them. By delivering them at the Red Sea the Lord proved that he is the one who fights for them (Ex 14:14, 25) and as a result the Israelites describe the Lord as "a man of war" (15:3). Elsewhere, the Lord is depicted as the one who comes down to fight for his people (Ps 35:1; Is 31:4). Clearly God uses the metaphor of the warrior king to help clarify that he is on the side of his people, he is one who has power, and he is coming to their aid like one who would fight on their behalf against enemies of any sort. The multiple references to God leading the armies of Israel and the close identification of Israel with the church of God in the Old Testament provides the foundation for Christian churches to sometimes identify themselves as the army of God (Ex 12:41).

The Son

Messiah. The references to Jesus as King begin with certain Old Testament prophecies that predict the coming of the Messiah or the Anointed One.[25] Thus,

---

[25]For background on the Messiah in Judaism and early Christianity see N. T. Wright, *Jesus and the Victory of God* (Minneapolis: Fortress, 1992), pp. 477-539; and N. T. Wright, *The Challenge of Jesus* (Downers Grove, Ill.: InterVarsity Press, 1999), pp. 78-95.

Zechariah cries, "Rejoice greatly, O daughter of Zion! Shout aloud, O daughter of Jerusalem! Lo, your king comes to you ... and he shall command peace to the nations; his dominion shall be from sea to sea, and from the River to the ends of the earth" (Zech 9:9, 10; Mt 21:1-11). Isaiah in his great Messianic prophecy declares, "Of the increase of his government and of peace there will be no end, upon the throne of David, and over his kingdom, to establish it, and to uphold it with justice and with righteousness from this time forth and for evermore. The zeal of the Lord of hosts will do this" (Is 9:7; Mt 4:12-17).[26]

Christ. In the New Testament the word Messiah from the Hebrew is translated into Greek as "Christ," meaning the Anointed One, and therefore, carrying kingly connotations.[27] Thus, the very name of Christ used throughout the New Testament is a constant reminder of his kingly role on the earth. Matthew, writing to the Jews, is particularly at pains to point out that the Jesus whom he is going to describe in his Gospel is the Christ or Messiah for whom the Hebrews have been waiting (Mt 1:1, 6, 16-18; 2:2-4 etc.). Thus, one of the early introductions to Jesus comes in the form of a question of the magi seeking him when they ask, "Where is he who has been born king of the Jews?" (2:2). The answer was given from Micah 5:2, "But you, O Bethlehem Ephrathah, who are little to be among the clans of Judah, from you shall come forth for me one who is to be ruler in Israel." Jesus is clearly understood as the fulfillment of this prophecy of a ruler who will govern God's people.

King. Luke also opens his Gospel with the declaration of the angel to Mary that the one to be born to her will be the Son of the Most High, and "The Lord God will give to him the throne of his father David, and he will reign over the house of Jacob for ever; and of his kingdom there will be no end" (Lk 1:32-33). The angel also makes clear the connection between this kingly one and his holiness when he says to Mary, "The child to be born will be called holy" (1:35). John opens his Gospel with a declaration of Jesus' kingship when Nathaniel exclaims, "Rabbi, you are the

---

[26]On Jesus as Messiah see Emil Brunner, *The Christian Doctrine of Creation and Redemption* (London: Lutterworth, 1952), pp. 334-38; Hans Conzelmann, *Outline of the Theology of the New Testament* (London: SCM Press, 1969), pp. 72-75, 129-30; W. G. Kummel, *Theology of the New Testament According to Its Major Witnesses: Jesus-Paul-John* (Nashville: Abingdon, 1973), pp. 66-72, 107-8; Oscar Cullmann, *The Christology of the New Testament* (London: SCM Press, 1963), pp. 111-36; John Bright, *The Kingdom of God* (Nashville: Abingdon, 1953), pp. 187-214.

[27]See *BTLNT,* pp. 580-81; *NIDNTT,* 2:334-43; Wolfhart Pannenburg, *Jesus, God and Man,* trans. Lewis L. Wilkins and Duane A. Priebe (Philadelphia: Westminster Press, 1968), p. 215.

Son of God! You are the King of Israel!" (Jn 1:49).[28]

Not only is Jesus introduced at the beginning of the Gospels as one who comes as a king, but the close of his ministry is punctuated by the story of his triumphal entry into Jerusalem. He comes with all the kingly regalia in fulfillment of the Messianic prophecy (Zech 9:9-10). Most significant is the cry of the multitude, "Blessed is the King who comes in the name of the Lord!" (Lk 19:38; Mt 21:5, 9; Mk 11:10; Jn 12:13). The end of this week in Jesus' life closes with a different focus on his kingship. He is challenged with the question, "Are you the King of the Jews?" (Mt 27:11). He is mocked by the soldiers who kneel before him crying, "Hail, King of the Jews!" (27:29), and they place the charge over his head on the cross which reads, "This is Jesus the King of the Jews" (27:37). The chief priests and leaders of Israel mocked him further, saying, "He saved others; he cannot save himself. He is the King of Israel; let him come down now from the cross, and we will believe in him" (27:42).

This kingship Jesus does not deny, but rather affirms. When Pilate asks him whether he is the King of the Jews, Jesus replies, "My kingship is not of this world; if my kingship were of this world, my servants would fight, that I might not be handed over to the Jews; but my kingship is not from the world." When Pilate persists, "So you are a king?" Jesus answers, "You say that I am a king. For this I was born, and for this I have come into the world" (Jn 18:33-37; cf. 18:39; 19:14-15, 19, 21).

The New Testament also pictures Jesus in his ascension as being exalted to the right hand of God and being given there a kingly position of rule in the universe (Acts 2:33-35). It is this one who will be the final conqueror of the forces of evil that is described as the "Lord of lords and King of kings" (Rev 17:14; 19:16), and he is also the one who will return to rule and judge the earth (Mt 25:31).[29]

Prince. One variation of Jesus' kingly role is that he is sometimes referred to as a Prince.[30] In the Old Testament the Messiah is known as the "Prince of Peace"

---

[28]For a fresh approach to Jesus and the kingdom see Wright, *Jesus and the Victory of God*, pp. 198-474; cf. also *TDNT*, 1:577-90.

[29]For discussion of the kingly office of Jesus see John Calvin, *Institutes*, trans. John Allen (Philadelphia: Westminster Press, 1936), 1:542-48; Charles Hodge, *Systematic Theology* (London: James Clarke, 1960), 2:596-609; William Burt Pope, *A Compendium of Christian Theology* (London: Wesleyan-Methodist Book Room, 1880), 2:249-53; Berkhof, *Systematic Theology*, pp. 406-11; Pannenburg, *Jesus, God and Man*, pp. 217-19; Brunner, *Creation*, pp. 298-305.

[30]"Prince," ἀρχηγός is also translated "author" in some places; Heb 2:10; 12:2. *TDNT*, 1:487-88.

(Is 9:6), and the "Prince of princes" (Dan 8:25), while in the New Testament he is called the Prince (Author) of life (Acts 3:15) whom God exalted "to his right hand as Leader and Savior" (5:31 NIV).[31]

Lord. One of the most frequent titles for Jesus in the New Testament is that of *kurios* or "Lord," which certainly carries kingly or ruling connotations.[32] As we have seen the title is also used of God the Father, but its most common designation in the New Testament is in its reference to Christ.[33] So Thomas exclaims on seeing the risen Christ, "My Lord and my God" (Jn 20:28). The New Testament writers make frequent use of Psalm 110:1 in a description of the Father speaking to the Son: "The LORD says to my lord: 'Sit at my right hand, till I make your enemies your footstool'" (Mt 22:44; Mk 12:36; Lk 20:41-43; Acts 2:34-35; Heb 1:13). Further, Paul declares that "no one can say 'Jesus is Lord' by the Holy Spirit" (1 Cor 12:3), and at the close of the New Testament Jesus' Lordship is connected with his kingly role through the titles he is given as "King of kings and Lord of Lords" (Rev 19:16; 17:14).

Head. One variation of God's role as sovereign ruler of the universe and of his people is the picture of Christ as the head of the church.[34] Just as the focus of God as King is on his authority, the focus of Christ as the head of the church is also on his authority and leadership. The language figure that is used is that of the human physique, so that Christ serves as the head of the body. The analogy relates the way the head rules over the body, as well as the way the body functions with its several parts coordinated into one whole.[35]

Paul makes the connection between Christ's kingly role and that as the head of the church when he talks about what God did when he raised Christ from the dead and "made him sit at his right hand in the heavenly places, far above all rule and authority and power and dominion." Then when God had put all things under Christ's feet, he "made him the head over all things for the church, which

---

[31]See Rev. 1:5 where Jesus is described as *archōn* (ἄρχων), ruler or prince.

[32]See *NIDNTT*, 2:510-20; *TDNT*, 3:1039-95; *EDT*, pp. 647-48.

[33]For discussion of the lordship of Christ see Brunner, *Christian Doctrine of Creation and Redemption*, pp. 338-40; Cullmann, *Christology of the New Testament*, pp. 195-237; Pannenburg, *Jesus, God and Man*, pp. 365-78; Conzelmann, *Outline of the Theology of the New Testament*, pp. 82-84; Kummel, *Theology of the New Testament*, 157-60.

[34]On καφαλή as "head" see Berkhof, *Systematic Theology*, pp. 406-7; Pope, *Compendium of Christian Theology*, vol. 2, p. 253; Emil Brunner, *The Mediator* (London: Lutterworth, 1934), pp. 587-88.

[35]See *TDNT*, 3:673-82; *NIDNTT*, 2:156-63; *CD* 3/2, pp. 309-16; *CD* 3/4, pp. 168-76; *EDT*, pp. 496-97.

is his body" (Eph 1:20-23). He who sits in the royal position of authority is also he who is head of the church.

Paul is the biblical writer most responsible for describing Christ as the head of the church. In encouraging the Ephesians to speak the truth in love, he relates this to growing up "in every way into him who is the head, into Christ" (Eph 4:15). In his discussion of family relationships, he makes clear that "the husband is the head of the wife as Christ is the head of the church, his body" (5:23). This one who is the head of the church is also head of all rule and authority in the universe (Col 2:9-10; cf. 1:18; 1 Cor 11:3). Several of the New Testament writers quote Psalm 118:22 to describe Jesus as the head of the corner (Mt 21:42; Mk 12:10; Lk 20:17; Acts 4:11; 1 Pet 2:7). The reference to the head of the corner seems to be more of the building figure of speech than one that relates to the physical body, and yet the same word is used for both.

The Holy Spirit

Executive of Godhead. Most of the data regarding the Holy Spirit in the role of King or Ruler is indirect. For example, Israel rebelled against God's rule in their lives and "grieved his holy Spirit" (Is 63:10). It is the Spirit of God on Moses that is also transferred to the seventy elders in order to assist Moses in governing the people (Num 11:17, 25), and it is the same Spirit that comes on Othniel and gives him the power to judge Israel (Judg 3:10). In like manner it is the Spirit of God that comes first on Saul (1 Sam.10:6, 10) and then David (16:13) that gives them the anointing to rule as kings over Israel. In the New Testament it is Jesus who declares, "If it is by the Spirit of God that I cast out demons, then the kingdom of God has come upon you" (Mt 12:28).

Jesus is also the One who is directed by the Spirit of God (Lk 4:1, 14), and who declares, "The Spirit of the Lord is upon me, because he has anointed me to preach good news" (4:18). In Acts the Holy Spirit clearly has a directing role in the affairs of the church. When the disciples asked about the restoration of God's kingly rule to Israel, Jesus responds with a promise of the Holy Spirit (Acts 1:6, 8), and it is the church's declaration that God as "Sovereign Lord" is the One who spoke by the Holy Spirit (4:24-25).

It is in harmony with a king's directing role that the Spirit of God leads Philip to join the chariot of the Ethiopian eunuch (Acts 8:29), and it is the Spirit that leads Peter to go with emissaries of Cornelius to preach for the first time to the

Gentiles (10:19; 11:12). Further, it is the Holy Spirit that speaks to the pastoral team at Antioch and directs them to set aside Barnabas and Saul for the first missionary journey (13:2, 4). It is the Holy Spirit that forbids Paul and his team from speaking in the region of Phrygia and Galatia, and also keeps them from going into Bithynia (16:6-7). Toward the end of his third missionary journey Paul goes to Jerusalem "bound in the Spirit," even when it is the Spirit that reveals to him that in every city imprisonment and afflictions await him (20:22, 23). It is this kind of data that has led to a description of the Holy Spirit as the executive of the Godhead, i.e., the immediate ruling presence of God in the world. It is this directing power of the Spirit that stands behind Paul's references to the importance of being "led by the Spirit" (Gal 5:18; Rom 8:14) as well as the necessity to "walk by the Spirit" (Gal 5:16, 25; Rom 8:4).

The trinitarian nature of God's kingly rule is implied in John's opening greetings to the churches in Asia. "Grace to you and peace from him [God] who is and who was and who is to come, and from the seven spirits [Holy Spirit] who are before his throne, and from Jesus Christ the faithful witness, the first-born of the dead, and the ruler of kings on earth. To him . . . be glory and dominion for ever and ever" (Rev 1:4-6). It is clear that the Father, Son and Holy Spirit are introduced in their role as the royal rulers of the world.[36]

Man and Woman

Relationship to king: A subject, a servant. A person's relationship to God as a sovereign King is to be one of a subject living under the authority of the Sovereign. A slight variation of this is the figure of a servant or a slave who is living in submission to properly constituted authority. God wants to rule over the lives of people, and he expects them as his servants to be submissive to his will as a servant would be to his Lord (Jas 4:7; Eph 6:5-9).

Model servant: Jesus. The model for this relationship comes in the person of Jesus. In his divinity Jesus gives us the model of the kingly rule of God in the lives of individuals. He is Lord and Master as well as Prince and Ruler. In this role he is a reflection of God as sovereign King. But in his humanity Jesus models for us

---

[36]For the trinitarian nature of the kingdom see Jürgen Moltmann, *The Trinity and the Kingdom*, trans. Margaret Kohl (New York: Harper & Row, 1981), pp. 202-12.

the role of a subject or servant.[37] As the Son of man he demonstrates for his
followers what it means to be a servant of the King and to live in submission to
God's authority over his life. He makes clear to his disciples that "the Son of man
also came not to be served but to serve" (Mk 10:45). Paul puts it graphically
when he states that Jesus did not count equality with God something to be
grasped, "but emptied himself, taking the form of a servant, being born in the
likeness of men" (Phil 2:6-7), and as a servant under God's authority "he
humbled himself and became obedient unto death" (2:8). Jesus' own example
becomes, then, the pattern for the leaders in the early church who describe
themselves as servants of God or Jesus Christ.[38]

The picture of Jesus in a servant role in the New Testament comes as the
fulfillment of Old Testament prophecy regarding the Messiah as a suffering
servant. The servant songs of Isaiah are a mixture of references to Israel as the
servant of God and a coming Messianic servant who will fulfill the role that Israel
has not played (Is 42:1-4; 49:1-6; 50:4-9; 52:13—53:12).[39] The New Testament
writers also understand many of these passages to find their completion in the
person of Jesus (Mt 8:17 [Is 53:4]; Mt 12:18-21 [Is 42:1-4]; Lk 22:37 [Is 53:12];
Jn 12:38 [Is 53:1]). The book of Acts also picks up on this theme and clearly
identifies Jesus as the servant of God (Acts 3:13, 26; 4:27-30).[40]

Teaching on kingdom. Jesus is not only demonstrating the role of a servant, but
he is proclaiming the kingly rule of God in his teaching on the kingdom of God.
The kingdom of God, and its synonymous phrase "kingdom of heaven," are at
the very heart of Jesus' teaching in the New Testament.[41] Its focus is not
primarily to a geographical location or to political rule, but has to do with the
kingship of God. The Greek word *basileia* might better be translated "kingship"
or "reign" of God as sovereign King.[42] Jesus comes to proclaim God's desire to

---

[37]Donald Guthrie, *New Testament Theology* (Downers Grove, Ill.: InterVarsity Press, 1981), pp. 258-68.

[38]Paul (Rom 1:1; Gal 1:10; Phil 1:1; Tit 1:1); James (Jas 1:1); Peter (2 Pet 1:1); Jude (Jude 1); also Epaphras
(Col 4:12).

[39]On the role of Isaiah 40—55 for understanding Jesus as servant see Wright, *Jesus and the Victory of God*, pp.
588-91; John Oswalt, *The Book of Isaiah Chapters 40-66* (Grand Rapids, Mich.: Eerdmans, 1989), pp. 285-300.

[40]For further discussion of Jesus as the suffering servant see Cullmann, *Christology of the New Testament*, pp. 51-
82.

[41]See Brunner, *Mediator*, pp. 420-23; C. H. Dodd, *The Parables of the Kingdom* (London: Collins, 1963), pp. 29-
61; Bright, *Kingdom of God*, pp. 187-214; *EDT*, pp. 607ff.; Conzelmann, *Outline of the Theology of New Testament*,
pp. 106-15; Kummel, *Theology of the New Testament*, pp. 33-38.

[42]See *TDNT*, 1:564-93; *BAGD*, p. 134; *NIDNTT*, 2:372-90.

reign over the hearts and lives of people. This is the thrust of his opening proclamation at the beginning of his ministry, "The time is fulfilled, and the kingdom of God is at hand; repent, and believe in the gospel" (Mk 1:15; Mt 4:17). Jesus continues to make this central to his proclamation as he goes about "teaching in their synagogues and preaching the gospel of the kingdom" (Mt 4:23; 9:25). Much of Jesus' early teaching to his disciples centers on the kingdom (Mt 5:3, 10, 19, 20; 7:21), as he instructs them concerning the nature of the kingdom, commands them to pray for it (6:10), and exhorts them to seek it before all things (6:33).[43] This emphasis on God's kingship continues throughout Jesus' ministry right up to the time of his ascension (Acts 1:3, 6-8).

The focus of Jesus' teaching calls attention to God's desire to be King over people's lives.[44] The picture of God as King and believers as his subjects is graphically illustrated in the series of parables that appropriately follow the story of Jesus' triumphal entry into Jerusalem where the people are crying, "Behold, your king is coming to you" (Mt 21:5). The section includes the parables of the householder who let out his vineyard to tenants (21:33-43), that of the king who gave a marriage feast for his son (22:1-14), that of the faithful and wise servant whom his master set over his household (24:45-51), and that of the master who entrusted certain talents to his servants while on a journey (25:14-30). The group of parables is concluded with the picture of the Son of man serving as King on his glorious throne at the final judgment (25:31-46).[45]

Master—servant: Jesus—the Twelve. An additional pattern for the master-to-servant relationship is given between Jesus and his disciples. As Jesus gives instructions to the Twelve on their first mission assignment, he tells them that "a disciple is not above his teacher, nor a servant above his master; it is enough for the disciple to be like his teacher, and the servant like his master" (Mt 10:24-25; Jn 13:16; 15:20).[46] At the end of his time with them Jesus reminds his disciples, "If any one serves me, he must follow me; and where I am, there shall my servant be also" (Jn 12:26). Although as disciples the Twelve are learners,

---

[43]See Wright, *Challenge of Jesus*, pp. 34-53.

[44]For discussion of the present and future dimension of the kingdom see George Eldon Ladd, *The Gospel of the Kingdom* (Grand Rapids, Mich.: Eerdmans, 1959), pp. 24-51. For its value for theology see G. E. Ladd, *Jesus and the Kingdom* (New York: Harper & Row, 1964), pp. 327-35.

[45]For other references to servants of God see Mt 20:10ff.; Lk 2:29; 17:7; Acts 2:18; 4:29; Rom 6:18, 22; Rev 1:1; 2:20; 7:3; 10:7; 11:18; 19:2, 5; 22:3, 6.

[46]Cf. Col. 3:23; 4:1.

they are also under Jesus' authority and expected to be servants as well.

Sin

While God's desire as King is to rule over a submissive people, in actual practice they often do not submit. So the doctrine of sin in this category is described as an unwillingness to submit or in terms of rebellion. Isaiah captures God's perspective on sin when he records in his theme verses how God exclaims, "Sons have I reared and brought up, but they have rebelled against me. . . . Ah, sinful nation, a people laden with iniquity, offspring of evildoers, sons who deal corruptly! They have forsaken the LORD, they have despised the Holy One of Israel, they are utterly estranged" (Is 1:2, 4). God offers to deal with their sin, but even in the midst of his invitation he is aware that they may "refuse and rebel" against him continually (1:20).[47]

Act of sin: Rebellion. Under the rubric of rebellion, sin may be described both as an action and as a state. As an action it appears as a deliberate act of rebellion or in terms of a specific instance of the rejection of God's authority. So when the people of Israel are first being directed by God in the conquest of Canaan and they draw back at the report of the ten spies, they are warned by Caleb, "Do not rebel against the LORD" (Num 14:9; Deut 1:26, 43; 9:23). Samuel describes this rebellion when the people of Israel asked for a king to be over them. "If you will not hearken to the voice of the LORD, but rebel against the commandment of the LORD, then the hand of the LORD will be against you and your king (1 Sam 12:15).[48]

State of sin: Rebelliousness. When Saul rejects God's authority, Samuel tells him that he has been rejected from being king because he has "rejected the word of the LORD," and that in God's eyes "rebellion is as the sin of divination, and stubbornness is as iniquity and idolatry" (1 Sam 15:23). That which is characteristic of the king also becomes characteristic of the people, and throughout Israel's history their sins are regularly described in terms of rebellion against God's authority.[49]

Sin as rebellion is not only descriptive of deliberate acts of sin against the

---

[47]On מָרַד as rebellion (*mered*) see *TWOT,* 1:524-25; Brunner, *Christian Doctrine of Creation and Redemption,* pp. 90-2, 124-28.

[48]On rebelling against the commandment of the Lord see Deut 1:26, 43; 9:23; Ps 107:11.

[49]See 2 Chron 13:6; Ps. 5:10; Ezek 20:8; 13:21; Dan 9:9; Hos 13:16.

authority of a sovereign King, but it also describes a state of sin in terms of rebelliousness. The focus here is on a will that has a bent toward rebellion. This rebelliousness of heart stands behind the acts of rebellion, but is distinguished from it in that it relates primarily to a state of sinfulness. This rebelliousness describes Israel's sin with the golden calf (Deut 9:12-16), and it was this consistent stubbornness of heart that causes Moses to evaluate them after forty years, "You have been rebellious against the LORD from the day that I knew you" (9:24). The psalmist, in reviewing Israel's unfaithfulness to God, describes them as "a stubborn and rebellious generation, a generation whose heart was not steadfast, whose spirit was not faithful to God" (Ps 78:8, 17, 40, 56; 66:7; Deut 10:16). Further, the prophets are faithful to call attention to this rebellious nature. Jeremiah accuses, "This people has a stubborn and rebellious heart; they have turned aside and gone away. They do not say in their hearts, 'Let us fear the LORD our God'" (Jer 5:23, 24). Although Israel is described as "rebellious children" (Is 30:1, 9), Isaiah delivers God's invitation to them. "I spread out my hands all the day to a rebellious people, who walk in a way that is not good, following their own devices" (65:2). Ezekiel is warned that he is being sent to a "nation of rebels" who are "impudent and stubborn," and he is told that they will refuse to hear God's message "for they are a rebellious house" (Ezek 2:3-7). It is probably significant that it is Ezekiel, the prophet of the exile, who has the most to say about Israel's rebellious heart (3:9, 26; 12:2-3, 9; 17:12; 24:3; 44:6).

Stiff-necked. Sometimes Israel's state of rebellion is described in terms of its being stiff-necked.[50] Moses at the end of his life describes Israel by saying, "I know how rebellious and stubborn you are" (Deut 31:27). Being stiff-necked or stubborn was a sign of an unwillingness to submit to authority in the ancient world. It first appears as a description of Israel in their sin with the golden calf at Mount Sinai. The Lord said to Moses, "I have seen this people, and behold, it is a stiff-necked people" (Ex 32:9).[51] It is this posture of resistance to the authority of God that stands behind Stephen's charge to the Sanhedrin. "You stiff-necked people, uncircumcised in heart and ears, you always resist the Holy Spirit" (Acts 7:51).[52]

---

[50]For further discussion of קָשֶׁה see *TWOT*, 2:818; for κληροτράχηλος see *TDNT*, 5:1029.

[51]See also Ex 33:3, 5; 34:9; Deut 9:6, 33; 10:16; 2 Chron 30:8; Jer 17:23.

[52]For further discussion of σκληροκαρδία, "hardness of heart," see *TDNT*, 3:613-14.

Salvation

Pardon. Coming into a right relationship with God who is a holy King is described in more than one way. In the Old Testament, God, in his kingly office, provides a pardon for his subjects who have been rebellious against him. While Moses can acknowledge that Israel is a "stiff-necked people," at the same time he entreats the Lord to "pardon our iniquity and our sin" (Ex 34:9). Moses asks for God's pardon at Mount Sinai, but he has to repeat his request during the rebellion of Israel at the report of the ten spies when the people refuse to go into the land of Canaan. "Pardon the iniquity of this people, I pray thee, according to the greatness of thy steadfast love, and according as thou hast forgiven this people, from Egypt even until now" (Num 14:19). Isaiah, speaking for the Holy One of Israel, invites the wicked to forsake his way. "Let him return to the LORD, that he may have mercy on him, and to our God, for he will abundantly pardon" (Is 55:7). To the Israelite, who says in his heart, "I shall be safe, though I walk in the stubbornness of my heart," the word is quite clear: "The LORD would not pardon him" (Deut 29:19-20).

Hezekiah, in his attempt to bring about spiritual reform in Israel, exhorts the people, "Do not now be stiff-necked as your fathers were, but yield yourselves to the LORD." It is for these people he prays that "the good LORD pardon every one who sets his heart to seek God" (2 Chron 30:8, 18-19). Further, the prophet declares, "Who is a God like thee, pardoning iniquity and passing over transgression?" (Mic 7:18).[53]

Although pardon represents coming into a right relationship with the sovereign who grants amnesty to his subjects, it is more often used to restore a subject to a right relationship with his king. This means that the concept of pardon is more often used in terms of a recovery from backsliding than it is used in terms of an initial entrance into a relationship with the king. It may be significant that the references to pardon are all found in the Old Testament.

Entering the kingdom. In the New Testament the initial coming under the rule of God as holy King is described in terms of entering the kingdom of God. So Jesus opens his public ministry with the proclamation that "the kingdom of heaven is at hand" and travels all over Galilee "preaching" the gospel of the

---

[53]For other references to pardon see 2 Kings 5:18; 24:4; Job 7:21; Ps 25:11; Is 40:2; Jer 5:1, 7; 50:20.

kingdom" (Mt 4:17, 23). A call to respond to Jesus is depicted as coming under the kingly rule of God.

Conditions: Repentance and faith. The conditions for entering the kingdom he spells out when he declares, "The time is fulfilled, and the kingdom of God is at hand; repent, and believe in the gospel" (Mk 1:15; Mt 4:17). Repentance of sins and faith in the gospel (as it is bound up with the person of Jesus) are the two essential ingredients for entrance into the kingdom of God. Jesus makes it plain that some will not enter the kingdom of heaven. He tells his disciples that unless their righteousness exceeds that of the scribes and Pharisees, "You will never enter the kingdom of heaven" (Mt 5:20). Nor, he says, will everyone who says to him "Lord, Lord" enter the kingdom of heaven, "but he who does the will of my Father who is in heaven" (7:21).

While repentance and faith may lead to the righteousness necessary to enter the kingdom of heaven, apparently an ongoing obedience to the will of God is necessary for continuing in the kingdom in this world and for a final entrance into the kingdom of the future. Jesus' statements reflect the fact that his use of the kingdom of God has a dual reference to time. It has a present reference regarding coming under the rule of God in this life, but it also has a future reference to living in God's kingdom in eternity. One begins to live under God's rule in this world, but this rule continues past death and into eternity.

It is the childlike quality of trust that Jesus refers to when he says to his disciples, "Unless you turn and become like children, you will never enter the kingdom of heaven" (Mt 18:3; cf. 19:14). It is because the wealthy man tends to trust in his riches rather than in God that makes it so difficult "for a rich man to enter the kingdom of heaven" (19:23-24). The same is true of the chief priests and the elders of the people who do not believe the message of God through John the Baptist. Thus Jesus says, "The tax collectors and the harlots go into the kingdom of God before you," and the reason is because they repented and believed (21:31-32).

Role of Spirit. The spiritual nature of entering into the kingdom of God is emphasized by the role of the Spirit in bringing people into the kingdom. Jesus said to Nicodemus, "Truly, truly, I say to you, unless one is born anew, he cannot see the kingdom of God," and he is more explicit that "unless one is born of water and the Spirit, he cannot enter the kingdom of God." The reason, says Jesus, is because "that which is born of the flesh is flesh, and that which is born of the Spirit is spirit" (Jn 3:3, 5-6). Apparently, it is the Spirit of God working in the heart of the believer through the process of repentance and faith that brings him in under the kingly rule of God.[54]

Kingdom of God verses kingdom of darkness. The kingdom of God is contrasted with the kingdom of darkness when Paul declares that God "has delivered us from the dominion of darkness and transferred us to the kingdom of his beloved Son, in whom we have redemption, the forgiveness of sins" (Col 1:13-14). From his perspective everyone is in one kingdom or another, either Satan's kingdom of darkness or God's kingdom of his Son. There is no neutral ground.

Satisfaction theory of the atonement. The basis for pardon and entering the kingdom of God is in the work of satisfying the honor and upholding the righteousness of the King. This is why the sovereign majesty of God and his divine honor are the special focus of attention in Anselm's satisfaction theory of atonement. In the 1090s the archbishop of Canterbury wrote his famous book *Cur Deus Homo* (*Why God Became Man*) in which he argued that sin was the dishonoring of the majesty of God. God must uphold his justice and the law (note the overlap with the role of God as righteous Judge), but the focus seemed to be on the necessity of restoring his lost honor. As a Sovereign he simply cannot forgive an offense; there must be appropriate satisfaction offered. As a Ruler it would not be proper for God to permit this kind of irregularity in his kingdom. While it is man who owes the satisfaction, only God is able to pay it. Therefore, Anselm concluded that only one who was both God and man could provide the necessary satisfaction. Jesus, as the God-man, could do this. As the perfect man, Christ did not deserve to die for his own sins, and therefore his death earns him merit which can then serve as a suitable satisfaction for human sins.

Christ's death then serves to pay the debt owed to God (this is why the theory sometimes called the commercial theory). Anselm saw paying the debt in terms of making reparations to God, so that satisfaction of God's justice meant Christ paying exactly the penalty for all sin. The death of Christ becomes equivalent all the demands of righteous justice against all those for whom Christ died. But by paying this debt, Christ honors God in his majesty.[55]

---

[54]For further discussion see Berkhof, *Systematic Theology*, pp. 407-8.

[55]Anselm, *Cur Deus Homo* (Albany, N. Y.: Magi, 1969); Donald M. Baillie, *God Was in Christ* (London: Faber & Faber, 1960), pp. 157-71; Thomas Oden, *The Word of Life* (San Francisco: Harper & Row, 1989), pp. 409-10; *EDT,* 101-2; *NDT,* 26-28.

It is clear that the satisfaction theory as described by Anselm relates both to God's role as sovereign King and righteous Judge. We will see in the chapter on God as righteous Judge how this theory was used by the Reformers to formulate their Penal Substitution theory. In that theory the focus is on the satisfaction of the penalty due to sin, with an emphasis on God's work as Judge. Here the emphasis is on atoning for God's honor as the sovereign Ruler of the universe. The multiple roles of God help us see why there is an element of truth in both of these understandings of the atonement.

Governmental theory of atonement. A second view of the atonement related to God as King is the governmental theory, and it emerges from one of the functions of God's role as Sovereign, viz., in the upholding of the moral order of the universe. Because God has established the moral order by giving the law, then the use of rewards and punishments helps establish questions of right and wrong in a moral universe. When a King establishes moral law, then penalty must follow to uphold both the righteousness and the goodness of his government.

This understanding of God's role begins as early as Genesis 2:17, when he warns that if "you eat of it [the tree of the knowledge of good and evil] you shall die." The prophets continually reiterate the same principle. "The soul that sins shall die" (Ezek 18:4, 20). Paul echoes the same sentiment. "For the wages of sin is death" (Rom 6:23), and "Cursed be every one who does not abide by all things written in the book of the law" (Gal 3:10). This giving of the law involves a strong overlap with the role of God as the righteous Judge. The Judge also helps establish law and thus exhibits the righteousness of God. So the governmental theory of the atonement begins by taking very seriously the question of the moral law and the righteousness of God as sovereign King. God cannot as sovereign King overlook disobedience to his law or fail to punish sin and still maintain a moral universe.

Paul describes God's work in the atonement of Christ in this way: "This was to show God's righteousness, because in his divine forbearance he had passed over former sins; it was to prove at the present time that he himself is righteous" (Rom 3:25-26). The point is that ultimately God's righteous character and his righteous government of the universe must be vindicated. Even if he waits for a period of time to punish sin, ultimately it must be punished if he is to maintain moral order in the universe. Christ's death is that which pays the penalty in our place, and thus God can be shown to be righteous and just.

Hugo Grotius (1583-1645) has been one of the primary promoters of this theory in which the preservation and example of divine order is of primary importance. With Christ's death on the cross, it would not be necessary for justly deserved punishment to be distributed to individuals. By Christ's death God is morally able to fulfill the principle "those who sin must die" and not undermine the moral order of the universe. In this theory God is seen as the Ruler (Rector) of the moral order, and for that reason it is sometimes called the rectoral theory.[56]

Assurance: God's seal. Assurance of salvation in the royal category is described by the king's placing his seal on those under his rule.[57] Thus, Paul declares that God "has put his seal upon us and given us his Spirit in our hearts as a guarantee" (2 Cor 1:22). He further elaborates: "In him you also, who have heard the word of truth, the gospel of your salvation, and have believed in him, were sealed with the promised Holy Spirit, which is the guarantee of our inheritance until we acquire possession of it" (Eph 1:13-14; cf. 4:30; 2 Cor 5:5; Rom 4:11).[58] In essence Paul is saying that God has given to us his seal or pledge regarding our future salvation and that this pledge comes by the witness of his Spirit in our hearts. So by the agency of the Holy Spirit people are given an internal conviction of their salvation and this subjective experience is like the seal or stamp of the Spirit. As the king's seal was evidence of his approval of any document in the ancient world, so God's seal as King comes as a guarantee of the salvation he has given.

Growth in Christian Experience

Implications of kingly rule. Coming into the kingdom of God and having God's royal seal of assurance on one's life is only the beginning of the process of living in a right relationship to a holy King. Growth in one's relationship to God is described in terms of the increasing implications of God's kingly rule over one's life. For those who enter the kingdom and begin to follow Jesus, he very quickly begins to explain to them its nature. In his first major teaching, references to the

---

[56]Hugo Grotius, *On the Truth of the Christian Religion*, 6 vols. trans. Simon Patrick (London: Rich Royston, 1680); *A Defense of the Catholic Faith Concerning the Satisfaction of Christ Against Faustus Socinus* (London: Draper, 1889); Pope, *Compendium of Christian Theology*, 2:279-81; John Miley, *Systematic Theology* (New York: Methodist Book Concern, 1894), 2:155-94; Oden, *Word of Life*, pp. 377, 407-8.

[57]For σφραψίς, "seal," see *NIDNTT*, 3:497-501; *TDNT*, 7:939-53; *ZPEB*, 5:319-24.

[58] For the seal as a sign of the king's possession or ownership see Esther 8:8.

kingdom of heaven bracket Jesus' statements about the beatitudes (Mt 5:3, 10). In particular, it is those who are "poor in spirit" and those who are "persecuted for righteousness' sake" who have the kingdom of heaven. It may well be that all the other beatitudes are also bound up with living under the kingly rule of God.

Obedience. On the same occasion Jesus begins to show how crucial obedience is to living under God's authority. Explaining to his disciples that he had not come to abolish the law and the prophets, he declares, "Whoever then relaxes one of the least of these commandments and teaches men so, shall be called least in the kingdom of heaven; but he who does them and teaches them shall be called great in the kingdom of heaven" (Mt 5:19). While obedience to God is also closely bound up with the category of God as the righteous Lawmaker/Judge, it is certainly a part of the kingly rule of God. God spells this out at Mount Sinai when, in order to be "a kingdom of priests" to God, they have to be willing to "obey [his] voice and keep [his] covenant" (Ex 19:5-6). It is also clear that obedience is a conditional element for entering the future kingdom of heaven. "Not every one who says to me, 'Lord, Lord,' shall enter the kingdom of heaven, but he who does the will of my Father who is in heaven" (Mt 7:21).

Growing rule. The growing implications of God's kingly rule get graphic expression in several parables. The focus of the parable of the soils has to do with those who hear "the word of the kingdom" and respond to it. While three classes of soil do not bear fruit, among the good soil some yield thirtyfold, some sixtyfold and others one hundredfold. Since the point of the parable has to do with receptivity to the word, apparently some are more receptive to the word of the ruling King than others and are accordingly more fruitful (Mt 13:18-23; Mk 4:13-20; Lk 8:4-15). The metaphor of growth in relation to the kingdom is also described in the parable of the mustard seed which grows from the smallest of the seeds to the greatest of shrubs and is parabolic of the growing implications of God's rule in the life of the believer (Mt 13:31-32; Mk 4:30-32; Lk 13:18-19). A third parable is the one in which the kingdom of heaven is described as leaven hidden in the three measures of meal until all was leavened. Again the implications are the increasing influence of the kingship of God over the lives of individuals (Mt 13:33; Lk 13:20).[59] A further illustration is the growing grain that is first scattered on the ground, then the seed sprouts and grows, "first the

---

[59]See also the parable of the wheat and tares Mt 13:24-30, 36-43.

blade, then the ear, then the full grain in the ear" (Mk 4:26-29).

The apparent purpose of the growth figures of speech in relation to God as King is that he desires greater and greater control over our lives. The longer one lives as a believer and the more one understands of the King's commands, the more he is expected to obey. So as a believer grows in grace, there is an increasing awareness of God's authority in every area of his life. It is this growing implication of the rule of God over the lives of believers that is usually described as progressive sanctification. Jesus said, "He who is greatest in the kingdom of heaven" is the one who "humbles himself like [a] child." Apparently, God's kingly rule should lead to an increasing sense of dependence and trust, and a decreasing self-sufficiency and arrogance. He who is most trusting in God and least confident in himself (i.e., least self-centered) is greatest in the kingdom (Mt 18:1-4).

Other implications of God's rule are variously described. For example, a servant having been forgiven by the King must learn to have mercy on those who are in his debt (18:23-35). Also the rewards of living under God's kingly rule do not depend just on service or effort, but on the gracious gift of the King (20:1-16; 22:1-14). Further, those living in the kingdom need to be prepared for the coming of the King at any time and be ready to render an account of their stewardship (25:1-30, 31-46). Finally, there is the growing awareness that as King, God desires to be more important in the life of the believer than houses, possessions or family. Yet, Jesus says that there is a specific reward for those who are paying the price to live under the kingship of God. "Truly, I say to you, there is no man who has left house or wife or brothers or parents or children, for the sake of the kingdom of God, who will not receive manifold more in this time, and in the age to come eternal life" (Lk 18:29-30).

Losing the kingdom. Paul makes it quite clear that those living in the kingdom of God cannot continue in sin. "Be sure of this, that no immoral or impure man, or one who is covetous (that is an idolater), has any inheritance in the kingdom of Christ and of God" (Eph 5:5; cf. 1 Cor 6:9-10). This is a strong statement by which Paul clearly means that a believer cannot continue the habitual practice of sinning. Those who have been delivered from the kingdom of darkness and transferred to the kingdom of God's Son may on occasion fall into sin, but they cannot continuously live in sinful disobedience in a regular pattern as they did before entering into the kingdom.

He also states that living under God's rule and being worthy of the kingdom of God will involve suffering (2 Thess 1:5). Finally, those who are living under the present rule of God must be "zealous to confirm your call and election" so that they will not fall from grace and will be able to enter "into the eternal kingdom of our Lord and Savior Jesus Christ" (2 Pet 1:10-11). Apparently, it is possible to fall from grace and withdraw from God's kingly control in this world and lose the eternal kingdom in the future.

The Church

As a King, God rules over his people and provides sovereign direction to those who constitute his church. There are four major ways in which his sovereignty over the church is described, three of which are illustrated in the establishment of the Old Testament church at Mount Sinai. God's offer of a covenant relationship with Israel is like a king offering a treaty to a people and binding himself to them for the future. He says to Israel, "You shall be my own possession among all peoples; for all the earth is mine, and you shall be to me a kingdom of priests and a holy nation" (Ex 19:5-6) In this context we see the people who have just begun to follow after God described as "the people of God" and as a "kingdom" or "nation." It is in this context that Moses assembles the people for God to meet them in a dramatic way. From this event, then, the church of God may be described as (1) the people of God, (2) the assembled congregation of God and (3) the kingdom/nation of God. The fourth category, the church as citizens under God's rule, will be described last.

People of God. The first category, the people of God, raises the question of ownership or sovereignty. Israel in the Old Testament and Christians in the New Testament belong to God as citizens of a nation or subjects of a king. Peter puts it succinctly: "But you are a chosen race, a royal priesthood, a holy nation, God's own people" (1 Pet 2:9). The Lord repeatedly states throughout Scripture, "I will be the God of all the families of Israel, and they shall be my people" (Jer 31:1; Ezek 37:27; 2 Cor 6:16). This focus on sovereign ownership is also revealed in the references to the people of God as the church of God (Acts 20:28; 1 Cor 1:2), and sometimes the church of Christ (Rom 16:16).

Assembly. The people of God are also frequently described in Scripture as the assembly of God's people. The word church in Scripture normally refers to "assembly." In the Old Testament the Hebrew word *qahal* (קָהָל) means "assembly," "company" or "congregation." It may be any sort of designated assembly for civil affairs (1 Kings 2:3; Prov 5:14; 26:26) or war (Num 22:4; Judg 22), so it frequently is connected with the sort of rule a king or leader would have over a group of people. It normally refers to the assembly for religious purposes. So the assembly at Mount Sinai to receive the law was described "as the day of assembly" (Deut 9:10; 10:4; 18:16). The references to *qahal* seem to designate particularly the gathering of the totality of the people of God.[60]

The *qahal* may also indicate the congregation as an organized body. At times it refers to the assembly of Israel (Deut 31:30), the assembly of Yahweh (Num 16:3), the assembly of the congregation of Israel (Ex 12:6) and the assembly of the people of God (Judg 20:2). Similar to the New Testament pattern is the reference to the congregation of the Lord or the assembly of Yahweh (Num 16:3; 20:4; Deut 23:2-4; 1 Chron 28:8; Mic 2:5). This probably is the closest Old Testament equivalent to the church of the Lord. In the Septuagint the phrase *ekklēsia kuriou*, "assembly of the Lord," is used in these instances which closely parallels the term *ekklēsia*, or the "called out ones," which is the normal designation of the church in the New Testament. The word in general may be used of any kind of assembly of citizens (Acts 19:32, 41), but the general use of the public assembly of citizens is carried over to the assembly of God's people who have been called out to follow after him as his church.

The birthday of the New Testament church comes on the day of Pentecost, when the Holy Spirit comes to take full sovereign control over the lives of the assembled disciples (Acts 2). From this point the Lord added to the church daily those who are being saved (2:47).

Kingdom/nation. Sometimes the people who make up the church are identified as a kingdom under God's rule or as a nation of God (Ex 19:6; 1 Pet 2:9). Some care needs to be taken about a complete identification of the church of God and the kingdom of God. The kingdom of God certainly includes all of those who make up his church, so that the invisible church of all believers is the heart of God's kingdom in this world and the basis of his eternal kingdom as well. But the kingdom of God sometimes is bigger than the church and carries an implication of God's rule politically, socially and culturally in the world over entities in addition to the church. So there is not a perfect correlation between the kingdom

---

[60] For קָהָל see *TWOT,* 2:790.

of God and the church of God, although the phrase "kingdom of God" is certainly a part of the language that relates to God's church in this world.

In the Old Testament since the church of God was more coextensive with the nation of Israel, the reference to kingdom and church overlap more easily. In the New Testament the kingdom of God is not limited to one political or geographical entity but includes God's reign over people in every tribe and nation. So the focus is clearly on God's reign, his *basileia* (βασιλεία).

God's kingdom is where God rules. God certainly rules over his people, and they in turn become an instrument of spreading his rule to others. So while the kingdom cannot be seen as synonymous with the church, the church is certainly at the heart of the kingdom. In the Old Testament the reign of God was seen clearly by the faithful people of Israel. Under the New Covenant the reign of God is expressed by the faithful people of the church. It is this group that is responsible for extending the kingdom of God on the earth.

Citizens. The fourth way in which those living under the kingship of God are sometimes described is in terms of citizens who live in a state under God's rule. Paul writes to the Gentiles about the time when they were "separated from Christ, alienated from the commonwealth of Israel, and strangers to the covenants of promise, having no hope and without God in the world." But now in Christ, he continues, "you are no longer strangers and sojourners, but you are fellow citizens with the saints and members of the household of God" (Eph 2:12, 19).[61] It is as a group of citizens that believers form the church of God.

Full Sanctification

Total submission. The concept of entire sanctification is dealt with in this metaphor in terms of a total submission to the authority of God as King in every area of life. It deals principally with the surrender of self-will to the total will of God. This involves a definite act of consecration or yielding to God and his full sovereignty over the individual. The standard for this kind of full consecration is set by Joshua in his farewell address to Israel, when he exhorts them to observe the commandments of God, to love the Lord and cleave to him, and also, "to serve him with all your heart and with all your soul" (Josh 22:5). This total surrender to God's service is echoed in David's closing instructions to Solomon: "Know the

---

[61]Paul refers to a heavenly commonwealth, Phil 3:20.

God of your father, and serve him with a whole [perfect] heart and with a willing mind" (1 Chron 28:9).

God is looking for servants who will live under this full sovereignty and therefore be entirely dedicated to do his will. It is the picture of the King who has absolute control over the will and therefore the life of his servant. This seems to be where Isaiah comes in his experience with God in the temple. After catching the vision of the holiness of God who is "the King, the Lord of hosts," he allows God to do a work of purging and cleansing in his life. The evidence of his submission to God's deeper work in his heart is manifested in his willingness to serve when God raises the question, "Whom shall I send, and who will go for us?" Isaiah responds, "Here am I! Send me." There is apparently a surrender of self-will to the full will of the holy King, so that God may send Isaiah to preach to a people who will not respond to his preaching (Is 6:8-10). Yet, in spite of this knowledge, Isaiah faithfully fulfills his task in obedience to the will of his sovereign Lord. It is to this place that sanctifying grace brings the individual.[62]

Lordship of Christ. In the New Testament the total sovereignty of God may also be described in terms of the Lordship of Christ. For example, in a series of stories and parables in Matthew 21—22 the whole question of Jesus' full lordship over people is discussed. The section opens with the triumphal entry of Jesus into Jerusalem and the shouts of the people, "Behold, your king is coming to you" (Mt 21:5). In this context the authority of Jesus is challenged by the chief priests and elders (21:23-27), and in response Jesus tells three parables. The first has to do with the two sons debating whether or not to do the will of their father, that is, whether they were going to live under his authority. The second is the parable of the wicked tenants who rejected the authority of the owner of the vineyard instead of submitting to his direction over their work. Jesus concludes the story with the remark, "The kingdom of God will be taken away from you and given to a nation producing the fruits of it" (21:33-43). The third parable is that of the king who prepared a marriage feast for his son, only to have his authority insulted and rejected by those who refused his invitation (22:1-14).

After these parables the issue of the authority of God versus the authority of the emperor is raised by the Pharisees, who ask Jesus about paying taxes to Caesar (Mt 22:15-22). Next the Sadducees raise the question about the

---

[62]See Oswalt, *Isaiah 1-39*, pp. 185-86.

resurrection, and Jesus turns the question into an issue of the authority of the Scriptures (Mt 22:23-33). Jesus is then asked a question about submission to the commandment of the law and what is the greatest commandment, and he responds, "You shall love the Lord your God with all your heart, and with all your soul, and with all your mind." Further, he says, you are to "love your neighbor as yourself." On these commandments, says Jesus, "depend all the law and the prophets" (22:34-40).

The whole section dealing with the authority of Jesus and the Father closes with Jesus' question to the Pharisees about whose Son is the Christ. When they respond, "David's," He challenges them, "How is it then that David . . . calls him Lord, saying 'The Lord said to my Lord, sit at my right hand, till I put thy enemies under thy feet'? If David thus calls him Lord, how is he his son?" (Mt 22:43-45). Jesus is apparently identifying himself as a greater king than David and expecting a corresponding recognition of a more complete lordship over individuals.

Entire consecration. If from God's perspective the fullness of sanctification involves his total sovereignty or lordship over people, from a human perspective it involves a total submission of one's will, and therefore one's life, to God's control. Jesus begins to spell out this entire consecration of the will for his disciples early in their association. When he first begins to teach them how to pray and recognize the holiness of their Father's name, he instructs them to pray, "Thy kingdom come, thy will be done, on earth as it is in heaven" (Mt 6:10). His instructions are that they are to learn to pray for God's full kingship in their lives so that God's total will can be done on earth in their lives as perfectly as it is done in heaven.

In the same discourse Jesus challenges his disciples not to be caught between the service of two masters. For that will lead to hate for the one and love for the other (6:24). Therefore, his disciples are not to be concerned with money or even the necessities of life that money could buy, but rather they are exhorted to "seek first his kingdom and his righteousness" and all other things will be provided by God (6:33). It is the seeking of God's total kingship and the righteousness of his character that runs parallel to the submission of one's will in the prayer, "Thy kingdom come, thy will be done, on earth as it is in heaven." While Jesus' disciples do not start out with this full submission of their wills to God's kingly control, it is the standard that Jesus sets for them when they first begin to follow him. It's only at Pentecost that we find the disciples coming to this yielding of their wills to God's total rule in their lives.

Full yielding. Paul pictures this total submission of the life to God in his letter to the Romans. After describing their justification by faith (Rom 3:21-5:11) and then the problem of their sinful nature (5:12-21), he talks about the death to their "old self," a death which was implicit in the death and resurrection of Christ that they first began to experience in their conversion. But then he makes quite clear by his exhortations that this sinfulness is still a problem in the life of the believers (6:1-11). Therefore, he exhorts them not to yield their members to sin as instruments of wickedness, but he says, "yield yourselves to God as men who have been brought from death to life, and your members to God as instruments of righteousness." This is because people are slaves of the one whom they obey, and he exhorts them to become the full slaves of God. "For just as you once yielded your members to impurity and to greater and greater iniquity, so now yield your members to righteousness for sanctification" (6:13, 16, 19). The result is that "now that you have been set free from sin and have become slaves of God, the return you get is sanctification and its end, eternal life" (6:22).

Paul repeats the same exhortation at the beginning of his final section in Romans that deals with living by faith in a totally surrendered life. "I appeal to you therefore, brethren, by the mercies of God, to present your bodies as a living sacrifice, holy and acceptable to God, which is your spiritual worship" (Rom 12:1). The word *parastēsai* (παραστήσαι), that is used for presenting or yielding of their bodies (i.e., their lives) in both Romans 6 and 12 is an aorist imperative, implying a definite act of surrender of the will to God. The totality of yielding the life is reflected in the phrase "a living sacrifice." It is expressive of something that is totally given to God. It is this definite point of yielding one's life in this way that is the experience of full sanctification.

Model: Jesus. The model for this entire submission of the will and the life to God's sovereign control comes in the person of Jesus. Repeatedly in his ministry Jesus declared, "I can do nothing on my own authority," because, he said, "I seek not my own will but the will of him who sent me" (Jn 5:30). "For I have come down from heaven, not to do my own will, but the will of him who sent me" (6:38). Thus, Jesus did not even teach on his own authority. "I do nothing on my own authority but speak thus as the Father taught me" (8:28). At the end of his ministry he repeats, "I have not spoken on my own authority; the Father who sent me has himself given me commandment what to say and what to speak" (Jn 12:49; cf. 7:16-18; 14:10, 24, 31).

Not only did Jesus exemplify the full submission of his life to God's will during his lifetime, but also in his death. Thus, in the garden he prays, "Let this cup pass from me; nevertheless, not as I will, but as thou wilt" (Mt 26:39, 42). While he makes his request known to the Father, he is fully submissive to God's will, even in relationship to the cross. This is why Paul describes him as one who "emptied himself, taking the form of a servant, being born in the likeness of men. And being found in human form, he humbled himself and became obedient unto death, even death on a cross" (Phil 2:7- 8). Jesus empties himself and assumes the form of a servant so that he might become a model of obedience unto his Father, and serving as an example for people he becomes fully obedient even to death on a cross. It is this kind of total submission and willingness to obey even to death that becomes the pattern for all Jesus' disciples. It is this kind of surrender of the will that leads to God's full sanctifying grace and power.

Further Growth

Paul's call for a total presentation of one's life as a living sacrifice in Romans 12:1 is followed by three chapters of teaching that relate to the implications of a life totally yielded to God's sovereign rule. It begins with Paul's statement in 12:2, "Do not be conformed to this world but be transformed by the renewal of your mind, that you may prove what is the will of God, what is good and acceptable and perfect." After one has totally presented his life in entire consecration, there are still some things to be learned about not being conformed to the world. There is some further transformation that comes with the renewal of the mind. This renewal of patterns of thinking makes it possible to know the full will of God. The verb for "transformed" that Paul uses is a present imperative of the word *metamorphoomai* (μεταμορφοῦσθε), from which we get "metamorphosis." Paul is saying there should be a continual or habitual transformation of the mind growing out of a total consecration as a living sacrifice to God.

This is followed by some examples of how this transformed thinking impacts a life fully submitted to God. This includes a discussion of basic spiritual gifts (Rom 12:3-8), growth in personal relationships (12:9-21), relating to the authority of the state (13:1-7), and self-denial as walking in love (14:1—15:6). Paul indirectly alludes to himself as an example of one who is working out the implications of being a living sacrifice (15:14-32). The key to this lifestyle comes with his discussion of the royal law of love. "Love is the fulfilling of the law" (13:8-14).

Glorification

Eternal kingdom of heaven. At the close of Jesus' ministry he discusses the future dimension of the kingdom of heaven that is related to his second coming. In the parable of the ten virgins Jesus links the coming kingdom to himself as the bridegroom and exhorts his disciples to watch and be ready for this event (Mt 25:1-13). In the same discourse he describes the occasion, "When the Son of man comes in his glory, and all the angels with him, then he will sit on his glorious throne." Then Jesus "the King will say to those at his right hand, 'Come, O blessed of my Father, inherit the kingdom prepared for you from the foundation of the world.'" The King will judge people on the basis of how well they have met the basic needs of those around them. The righteous will have met those needs and thus inherit the future kingdom, which Jesus says leads to eternal life. The unrighteous are those who will not have met the physical needs of those around them, and the King sends them away to eternal punishment (25:31-46; cf. 26:29).

Paul also connects the kingdom of God with Jesus' second coming, when he writes to the Thessalonians that they are being made worthy of the kingship of God through their suffering. When Jesus comes as a King from heaven, he will bring justice on those who are afflicting the believers by meting out eternal punishment (2 Thess 1:5-10).

Finally, John, in his description of heaven, places the picture of God on his throne at the very center of everything that is happening. It is as the kingly ruler of the universe that he is recognized as the Holy One who judges as well as rules the earth (Rev 4). Both the Father and the Son sit on the throne to rule as King for all eternity.

Attributes of God

Most of the attributes of God related to his kingly role are included under the category of "relative attributes." These refer to the qualities of God arising out of the relationship that exists between the Creator and the created, and which of necessity require the creature for their manifestation. These relative attributes include God's omnipotence, omnipresence, omniscience and wisdom. As a group of attributes they are particularly related to God's providential direction of the universe and especially the affairs of people. Because they are closely associated with questions having to do with God's providence, they fall under the role of God as the sovereign King who rules over his creation. God's omnipotence, omnipresence and omniscience are also related to his transcendence.

Omnipotence. God's omnipotence speaks of him as all-powerful, and so early in Scripture he appears as *El Shaddai,* God Almighty (Gen 17:1; Ex 6:3). At the close of Scripture this attribute is closely intertwined with God's kingship as well as his holiness, for it is the One who is sitting on the throne of whom the creatures cry day and night "Holy, holy, holy, is the Lord God Almighty, who was and is and is to come!" (Rev 4:8). The omnipotence of God means that he is able to do all that he pleases to do in harmony with his nature and will. It is the relative attribute that is closely associated with the absolute attribute of his self-sufficiency. It is also tied to his infinity, i.e., his being without bound or limits in terms of power.

If God is going to effectively rule over the creation, he needs power to accomplish his own purposes. We have already seen how his omnipotence is related to his role as Creator, and it naturally follows that he who has power to create, has the power to govern, i.e., coordinate circumstances and people for the accomplishment of his purposes. According to the formula of the prophets, "Nothing is too hard for thee" (Jer 32:17). The psalmist agrees: "He does whatever he pleases" (Ps 115:3). Jesus reinforces this concept with his statement that certain things with human beings are impossible, "but with God all things are possible" (Mt 19:26). This is because "whatever the Lord pleases he does, in heaven and on earth" (Ps 135:6).[63]

Omnipresence. The omnipresence of God has to do with his immensity in relationship to the universe. Because God is a spiritual being and not limited by space and time, he may be everywhere present at the same time.[64] This attribute begins to connect his transcendence with his immanence. The supranatural God who rules

---

[63]On the omnipotence of God see Pope, *Compendium of Christian Theology,* 1:311-13; Miley, *Systematic Theology,* 1:211-13; Hodge, *Systematic Theology,* 1:406-11; Berkhof, *Systematic Theology,* pp. 79-80; Brunner, *Christian Doctrine of God,* pp. 248-55; CD 2/1, pp. 522-607; EDT, pp. 457-58; Carl F. H. Henry, *God, Revelation and Authority* (Waco, Tex.: Word, 1983), 5:307-30.

[64]On the omnipresence of God see Pope, *Compendium of Christian Theology,* 1:314-15; Miley, *Systematic Theology,* 1:217-20; Berkhof, *Systematic Theology,* pp. 60-61; Brunner, *Christian Doctrine of God,* pp. 256-61; CD 2/1, pp. 461-90.

over the universe is not contained in his creation, but he must nevertheless be present in it for its providential government. So the psalmist can exclaim, "Whither shall I go from thy Spirit? Or whither shall I flee from thy presence? If I ascend to heaven, thou art there! If I make my bed in Sheol, thou art there! If I take the wings of the morning and dwell in the uttermost parts of the sea, even there thy hand shall lead me, and thy right hand shall hold me" (Ps 139:7-10). Obviously, he feels there is an intimate connection between his omnipresence and his power, and they are both bound up with his role as the sovereign King of the universe.[65]

Omniscience. Closely associated with the omnipresence of God is the omniscience of God. This has to do with God's perfect knowledge of himself and all things.[66] "His understanding is beyond measure" (Ps 147:5). This attribute describes God's infinite mind in terms of the intuitive, simultaneous and perfect knowledge of all that can ever be the object of knowledge. It relates both to the eternal cognizance of the actual and to the possible and the contingent.[67] "The Lord ... has made these things known from of old" (Acts 15:18). The divine omniscience relates to knowledge of the past, the present and the future. God's omniscience, like his omnipotence and omnipresence, is essential to his ability to govern the universe. In terms of his providence, God must direct and order the circumstances of the creation to accomplish his purposes. Knowledge of all things is necessary for the accomplishment of this objective. While his omniscience may be related to other roles as well, it is particularly important in terms of God's work as King.[68]

Wisdom. The application of God's omniscience in all his relations is described in terms of his wisdom. God's wisdom coordinates the implications of his knowledge with his infinite skills for the accomplishment of his ends by the most appropriate means.[69] "O the depth of the riches and wisdom and knowledge of God! How unsearchable are his judgments and how inscrutable his ways!" (Rom 11:33). Like the other three relative attributes, God's wisdom is closely bound up with his sovereign direction of the universe.[70] The questions of providence have to do with God's use of

---

[65]For additional references to his omnipresence see Job 28:24; Ps 33:13-14; Is 57:15; 66:1.

[66]For additional references to his omniscience see 1 Chron 28:9; Ps 139:2-6; Is 42:9; Ezek. 11:5.

[67]For further discussion of the omniscience of God see Pope, *A Compendium of Christian Theology,* 1:315-19; Miley, *Systematic Theology,* 1:180-92; Berkhof, *Systematic Theology,* pp. 66-68; Brunner, *Christian Doctrine of God,* pp. 256-65; *EDT,* p. 454; Henry, *God, Revelation and Authority,* 5:268-85.

[68]For the relation between omniscience and kingly role see Ps 33:13-15; Is 41:21-23, 26-27.

[69]On his wisdom see Job 36:5; Prov 8; Jer 51:1; Dan. 2:20; 1 Cor 1:24, 30; Eph 3:10.

[70]For the relation between wisdom and kingship or government of universe see 1 Tim 1:17.

knowledge in terms of ends and means. God needs wisdom to know how to apply knowledge and power to accomplish his purposes in the universe. "With God are wisdom and might; he has counsel and understanding" (Job 12:13).[71]

Conclusion

The role of God as sovereign King is fairly extensive in Scripture. It begins with the establishment of the people of God at Mount Sinai (though some functions of the kingly role appear earlier), and it continues until the pictures of God's final reign in Revelation. Its extensiveness accounts in part for the overruling influence this role plays in some theological traditions, where God as King is dominant over all of theology or certain key ingredients, such as the doctrine of the church. This role is *historically* significant because it accents God's purposes for his people throughout history. He rules over the affairs of nations and cultures, ultimately to accomplish his ends both for individuals and for his people. It is also *personally* significant. Within God's overall historical purposes he directs the lives of individuals. God's rule over individuals throughout history highlights the basic principles of God's rule over persons in *every* generation. Finally, it is *theologically* significant in its focus on God's providential work to accomplish his will in the lives of his people and his church. The accent at each of these levels is on God's authority and providential direction of those who belong to him.

The subrole of God as Lord of hosts or warrior king is a reminder that serving the God of Scripture is much like being in a battle. This is true at the corporate level—the church of God desires to be heard in the world, to win people to God and to influence culture—as well as at an individual level with spiritual battles in the life of faith. Theologically this subrole reminds us that God ultimately will be the victor of these battles. God's ultimate future victory gives hope to the people of God that at all levels he will accomplish his overriding purposes.

So both the role of God as King and the subrole of God as Lord of hosts provide people with a basis for confidence: God is in charge of the present and ultimately of the future. He can therefore be trusted, even in the midst of the difficulties and battles of our present experience.

---

[71]On the wisdom of God see Pope, *Compendium of Christian Theology*, 1:319-21; Miley, *Systematic Theology*, 1:193; Berkhof, *Systematic Theology*, pp. 68, 69; Brunner, *Christian Doctrine of God*, pp.282-85; CD 2/1, pp. 422-39; Walther Eichrodt, *Theology of the Old Testament*, trans. J. A. Baker (London: SCM Press, 1967), 2:80-92; Guthrie, *New Testament Theology*, pp. 94-9; C. Hodge, *Systematic Theology*, 1:401-2.

Five

Holy God as Personal Revealer

The Unity Factor

The element that relates God as Personal Revealer to his other roles is holiness. The concept of holiness as brilliance is the dimension of holiness most closely associated with God's work as Revealer, and it is to this meaning of holiness that we now turn our attention. After exploring holiness as brilliance, we will then look at the multifaceted role of God as Personal Revealer.

Holiness as brilliance. In our earlier discussion of the Hebrew word *qodesh*, we have seen that its root meaning has been a matter of extended debate among scholars. While a large number feel that it comes from the root which means "to divide" or "to separate," there are also a number of authors who believe it comes from the Babylonian *quddushi*, meaning "bright" or "clear." Accordingly, this second group tends to understand the root meaning of holiness in terms of brilliance. It must be remembered, however, that etymological meanings must be treated with some care. Of greater significance is the use of words in their immediate context, and since holiness is certainly used in the Scripture in some contexts as brilliance, then in terms of usage this meaning must be given significant consideration.

When we examine the passages that relate holiness and brilliance in their relationship to God, we find, as in the case with holiness as separation, that there appear to be two categories. Oftentimes holiness as brilliance is related to the immanence of God and so is closely bound up with his role as Personal Revealer. But at other times holiness as brilliance is associated with purity and grace, and

in those cases it seems to be related to God's role as a Priest. Both categories can
be pictured as in figure 5.1.

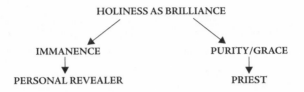

Figure 5.1. Holiness as brilliance

We will save the discussion of holiness as brilliance in terms of purity and
grace for the following chapter when we will discuss God's role as a Priest. In this
chapter we will focus our attention on God as immanent Personal Revealer.[1]

The Role of God as Personal Revealer

In one sense God's role as Personal Revealer relates to all of the roles of God. God
reveals himself in a personal, metaphorical way in each major role. There are minor
roles in which God reveals himself using animal metaphors (Lion of tribe of Judah)
or physical metaphors (rock), but all the primary metaphors are from "personal"
categories. Yet there are many occasions when God is not using one of the other
seven roles as the means of his self-revelation, but he is still revealing himself person to person. At times one person of the Godhead reveals himself not as King,
Judge, Father, etc., but as one person to another. While that fact leaves the role of
Personal Revealer the most amorphous and the most difficult to categorize of the
eight we are discussing, it is important to recognize this role's existence and identify this key role by which God is revealing himself in this personal way.[2] In some
ways this role may be considered the most extensive in Scripture.

It is in his personal role that God becomes known to people. He is not just a

---

[1] On the relationship between holiness and immanence see Emil Brunner, *The Christian Doctrine of God* (London: Lutterworth, 1949), pp. 163, 165; Gustave Friedrich Oehler, *Theology of the Old Testament*, ed. George E. Day (Grand Rapids, Mich.: Zondervan, 1883), p. 107; Snaith, *Distinctive Ideas of the Old Testament*, pp. 83ff. On the immanence of God see Carl F. H. Henry, *God, Revelation and Authority* (Waco, Tex.: Word, 1983), 6:35-51; Joshua Abelson, *The Immanence of God in Rabbinic Literature* (London: Macmillan, 1912), pp. 77-149.

[2] The specificity of the personal subroles—God as Teacher, Prophet and Friend, discussed below—provides more concreteness to this role.

transcendent Creator who sovereignly rules over his subjects. In this personal role he becomes immanent and draws near to his people. There is always a biblical balance between God's transcendence and his immanence. This role helps emphasize the place of his immanence, just as the roles of Creator and King focused on his transcendence. One value of the whole discussion of these several roles is that it helps keep the balance between transcendence and immanence. Too much focus on transcendence makes God very distant and too much immanence leads to monism and pantheistic thinking.[3]

Within God's role as immanent Personal Revealer, the concept of holiness as brilliance is expressed in two subcategories, both of which help us understand the person-to-person nature of this role and give it more concreteness. The first has to do with God's immanent appearing within the created order that he has made. Here the focus is on God's personal presence in this world. Three symbols represent the holy presence of God in this category.

Glory of God. The first of these is God's glory. As Emil Brunner puts it, the "holy name and the glory of God are inseparable."[4] When Isaiah describes the threefold vision of God's holiness, he reports, "The whole earth is full of his glory" (Is 6:3). The glory of God as an expression of his holy presence is also described in terms of the glory that fills the tabernacle and especially the holy of holies at Mt. Sinai (Ex 40:34-35). The picture is repeated when the glory of God fills the temple in Jerusalem (1 Kings 8:11; 2 Chron 5:14; 7:1-2), and so it is not surprising that Ezekiel in his vision of the return of God's presence to his temple describes it in terms of God filling the temple with his glory (Ezek 43:2, 4-5; 44:4).

The glory of God symbolizes the holy presence of God in the visions of God in Isaiah 6 and Ezekiel 1, and also represents the departure of the presence of God from the temple in Ezekiel 10-11. The same glory is identified with the presence of Jesus on the Mount of Transfiguration (Lk 9:32), and finally, the holy city of Jerusalem that comes down from heaven is identified as having the glory of God in it (Rev 21:11, 23).[5] Edmond Jacob is right when he describes

---

[3]For discussion on how these two concepts have influenced contemporary theology see Stanley Grenz and Roger Olson, *20th-Century Theology* (Downers Grove, Ill.: InterVarsity Press, 1992).

[4]Brunner, *Christian Doctrine of God*, p. 161.

[5]For other references to the glory of God see "Glory of the Lord" (YHWH): Ex 16:7-10; 24:16-17; 33:18-23; Lev 9:6, 23; Num 14:10, 22; 16:19, 42; 20:6; Deut 5:24; Josh 7:19; 1 Chron 16:23-25; 2 Chron 5:14; 7:1-3; Ps 104:31; 138:5; Is 35:2; 40:5; 58:8; 60:1-2; Ezek 3:12, 23; 10:4, 18; 11:23; 43:4-5; 44:4; Hab 2:14; Lk 2:9; 2 Cor 3:18; 8:19; 2 Thess 2:14. "Glory of God": Ps 19:1; 29:3; Prov 25:2; Ezek 8:4; 9:3; 10:19; 11:22; 43:2-3;

God's glory as the visible extension of the holiness of God. The glory of God, he says, is "uncovered holiness."[6]

Glory symbolized by cloud. If the glory of God is often used synonymously with the holiness of God's presence, it is also oftentimes symbolized by a cloud or by fire. It is a cloud, representing the glory of God, that fills the holy of holies at the location of the tabernacle and the temple (Ex 40:34-35; 1 Kings 8:10; 2 Chron 5:13-14). It is a cloud that symbolizes God's holy presence on Mt. Sinai (Ex 19:9, 16; 24:15), and Ezekiel has his vision of God's presence related to a cloud (Ezek 1:4; 10:3-4). Jesus and the disciples are surrounded by a cloud of God's presence on the Mount of Transfiguration (Mt 17:5; Lk 9:34). When Jesus ascends into heaven, it is a cloud that receives him out of their sight (Acts 1:9), and they are informed that when he returns it will be on the clouds (Rev 1:7; Acts 1:9-11).[7]

Glory symbolized by fire. Fire is also used as a symbol of the glory of God and of God's holy presence. It is from the burning bush that God speaks to Moses and informs him that he is on holy ground, i.e., he is in the presence of a holy God (Ex 3:5). God comes to reveal himself to a holy people on Mt Sinai in terms of fire and lightning (19:16, 18; 24:15, 17). Whereas God leads the children of Israel in the wilderness in the day by a pillar of cloud, in the night it is by a pillar of fire (13:21-22; 40:36-38), and when the glory of the Lord fills the temple, fire representing God's holy presence comes down and consumes the offering and the sacrifices (2 Chron 7:1). In the great story of the contest between Elijah and the prophets of Baal, it is the God of Israel who answers by fire, and not Baal, the storm god of the Canaanites (1 Kings 18). The coals of fire from the altar and the smoke representing his presence

---

Jn 11:4, 40; 12:43; Acts 7:55; Rom 1:23; 3:23; 5:2; 6:4; 15:7; 1 Cor 10:31; 11:7; 2 Cor 1:20; 4:6; 4:15; Phil 1:11; 2:11; Rev 15:8; 21:11; 21:23.

[6]Edmond Jacob, *Theology of the Old Testament*, trans. Arthur W. Heathcote and P. J. Allcock (New York: Harper & Row, 1958), pp. 79-80. For further discussion of glory as an expression of holiness see *NSRE*, 5:317; Theodorus Vriezen, *An Outline of Old Testament Theology*, trans. S. Neuijen (Bristol: John Wright, 1911), p. 150; Thomas K. Cheyne, *The Origin of the Psalter* (New York: Thomas Whittaker, 1891), p. 331; Donald Guthrie, *New Testament Theology* (Downers Grove, Ill.: InterVarsity Press, 1981), pp. 90-94; Knight, *Christian Theology of the Old Testament*, pp. 94-100; I. Efros, "Holiness and Glory in the Bible," *Jewish Quarterly Review* 41 (April 1951): 365; A. M. Ramsey, *The Glory of God in the Transfiguration of Christ* (New York: Longmans, Green, 1949), p. 22.

[7]For other references to a cloud as a symbol of the holy presence/glory of God see Ex 14:19-20; 16:10; 24:15-16, 18; 33:9-11; Lev 16:2; Num 9:15-16, 17-23; 10:11-12, 33-34; 11:25; 12:5, 9-10; 14:13-14; 16:42; Deut 1:32-33; 4:11; 5:22; 31:15; 2 Chron 5:13-14; Neh 9:12, 19; Ps 78:14; 97:1-2; 99:7; 105:39; Is 4:5; Ezek 1:4; 10:3-4; 30:3; Joel 2:1-2; Nahum 1:3; Zeph 1:14-15; Mt 17:5; 24:30; 26:64; Mk 9:7; 13:26; 14:62; Lk 9:34-35; 21:27; 1 Cor 10:1-2; 1 Thess 4:17; Rev 1:7; 14:14-16.

appear in the visions of Isaiah (Is 6:4) and Ezekiel (1:4, 13-14, 27). Fire certainly symbolizes the coming of the full presence of God on the disciples on the day of Pentecost (Acts 2:3), and in one of the final pictures of God in Scripture there are the seven torches of fire, representing the Spirit of God before the throne of God (Rev 4:5).[8]

Both the cloud and fire then represent the holiness and the glory of God.[9] The cloud may be symbolic of the mystery of God's holiness and suggests that while God is making his presence known and revealing his will, he is not known exhaustively. True knowledge of him or his presence does not require exhaustive knowledge. Fire, on the other hand, is an apt symbol for the holy presence of God in that it represents either a purifying force or a force for judgment. God's holy presence can either bring destruction, that is, judgment, or it can cleanse and refine.

Personal presence. The coming of God to reveal himself to his people was certainly not the norm in the ancient Near Eastern world. In that era people sought after gods, but there is little about any god seeking after them. The biblical view is unique in this sense, that God desires to come and know people and to be known by them.

While the symbols of his glory (a cloud and fire) may represent his coming, the chief purpose of his appearing is for God to know and be known by his people. The language category therefore that dominates this emphasis is that of personal relationships. The focus is on God's faithfulness in personal relationships. The subrole that most succinctly captures a concrete picture of God personally making himself known is that of God as Friend. We will return to his faithfulness and his friendship later. The combination of language, focus and subrole looks like figure 5.2.

---

[8]For other references to fire as a symbol of the holy presence/glory of God see Gen 15:17; Ex 3:2-6; 13:21-22; 14:24; 40:38; Lev 9:22-24; 10:1-3; Num 3:4; 9:15-16; 11:1-3; 14:14; 16:35; 21:28; 26:10; Deut 1:33; 4:11-12, 15, 24, 33-36; 5:4-5, 22-26; 9:3, 10, 15; 10:4; 32:22; 33:2; 2 Sam 22:9, 13; 1 Kings 18:24-25, 28; 2 Kings 1:10-14; 1 Chron 21:26; 2 Chron 7:1-3; Neh 9:12, 19; Ps 18:8, 12-13; 50:3; 78:14, 60-63; 97:1-4; 105:39; 106:16-18; Is 4:5; 9:18-19; 10:16-17; 29:6; 66:15-16; Lam 4:11; Ezek 1:4, 13; 3:2-4; Lk 12:49; Acts 7:30; Heb 12:29; Rev 1:14; 2:18; 19:12; 20:9.

[9]On the glory of God see *TWOT*, 1:426-28; *TDNT*, 2:233-53; *EDT*, pp. 443-44; *IDB*, 2:410ff.; *NIDNTT*, 2:44ff.; Alan Richardson, *An Introduction to the Theology of the New Testament* (London: SCM Press, 1958), pp. 64-67; H. L. Brockington, "The Presence of God, A Study of the Use of the Term 'Glory of Yahweh,'" *ExpT* 57 (1945): 21-25; G. B. Berry, "The Glory of God and the Temple," *JBL* 56 (1937): 115-17; *ZPEB*, 2:730-35; John Calvin, *Institutes of Christian the Religion*, 1:90-92; 2:68-70, 273; Brunner, *Christian Doctrine of God*, pp. 285-87; Bernard Ramm, *Them He Glorified* (Grand Rapids, Mich.: Eerdmans, 1963), pp.10ff.; Walther Eichrodt, *Theology of the Old Testament*, trans. J. A. Baker (London: SCM Press, 1967), 2:29-35; *HDB*, 2:183; *CD* 2/1, pp. 640-77.

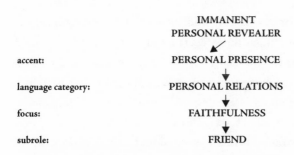

Figure 5.2. The personal presence of God as Personal Revealer

Immanent Personal Revealer: Communicator of Truth

Even though God's personal presence is one major part of his role as Revealer, it is not the whole of it. The symbols of his presence involve some revelation, but the chief purpose of his presence is to make himself known in terms of verbal communication. This is the key ingredient in person-to-person relationships.

The second subcategory, then, within God's role as immanent Personal Revealer is that which has its *focus on truth*. Here external or visible symbols are not what get attention but rather the spoken word. The *language figure* most specifically related to this category is that of *interpersonal communication*. God comes in personal presence in order to establish and maintain personal relationships. But personal relationships involve significant understanding based on verbal communication, so that the chief means of God's revealing himself in this category is his spoken word. While the symbols of God's presence may be understood in various ways, truth revealed in words is much more exact. No one will pretend that linguistic communication is perfect, but it is certainly the most precise form of communication available.

People are capable of this verbal communication because they are made in the image of God, including the capacity to reason and speak. A person's language skills reflect his capacity to exercise reason, logic and memory, and they are one of the unique factors in his makeup that make it possible to communicate with God. Since human beings are the only creatures in the universe who are made in the image of God, they are therefore the only ones who are capable of verbally communicating with their Creator.[10] It is not an accident that Adam's first

---

[10]See Carl Henry, *God, Revelation and Authority*, 2:124-42; Francis Schaeffer, *Genesis in Space and Time* (Downers Grove, Ill.: InterVarsity Press, 1972), pp. 46-48.

human experience is to hear God speak to him (Gen 1:28), while at the end of Scripture people are warned about the importance of keeping the words of the revelation that God has given (Rev 22:7, 18). When people hear and respond positively to God's revelation, there comes blessing (1:1-3), but when there is "a want of knowledge" because they "have despised the word of the Holy One of Israel," then comes the judgment of God (Is 5:13, 24).[11]

The purpose of God's verbal revelation is twofold. It has to do with the revelation of truth, and particularly the truth about God, about people and about the relationship between the two. However, God is not just concerned about the revelation of knowledge; rather, he is concerned that knowledge lead to personal relationships and that truth be applied to life. He desires re-establishment of personal fellowship with people, and therefore, the design of truth is to lead to the redemption of people, continued fellowship with God and the living out of the implications of God's truth in everyday life. Both the beginning of this relationship between God and people, and continued fellowship between them, demands a significant level of verbal communication.[12] So in this subcategory God most often is seen when he is speaking to individuals person to person. Sometimes his speaking is couched in the role of a Prophet (Jer 2:1-4) but more often in that of a Teacher (Ps 32:8). The roles of both Teacher and Prophet are primarily related to the verbal communication of God's message, so it is not surprising that God at times is seen in these roles. We have already mentioned that God is seen as one

[11]See John Frame, "Scripture Speaks for Itself," in *God's Inerrant Word*, ed. J. W. Montgomery (Minneapolis: Bethany Fellowship, 1973), pp. 178-92; Leon Morris, *I Believe in Revelation* (Grand Rapids, Mich.: Eerdmans, 1976), pp. 109-26; Francis Schaeffer, *He Is There and He Is Not Silent* (Wheaton, Ill.: Tyndale House, 1972), pp. 37-88; J. I. Packer, *"Fundamentalism" and the Word of God* (Grand Rapids, Mich.: Eerdmans, 1970), p. 75-114; Carl Henry, *God, Revelation and Authority*, 2:151-66.

[12]On verbal revelation see John J. Davis, *Foundations of Evangelical Theology* (Grand Rapids, Mich.: Baker, 1984), pp. 75-116; Clark Pinnock, *Biblical Revelation* (Chicago: Moody Press, 1971), pp. 19-52; B. B. Warfield, *The Inspiration and Authority of the Bible* (London: Marshall Morgan & Scott, 1959), pp. 71-102; CD 1/1, pp. 98-140, 223-54; Emil Brunner, *Revelation and Reason*, trans. Olive Wyon (London: SCM Press, 1942); Emil Brunner, *The Christian Doctrine of Revelation and Reason* (London: SCM Press, 1946); *Truth as Encounter* (Philadelphia: Westminster Press, 1964); James Barr, *The Semantics of Biblical Language* (London: Oxford University Press, 1961); G. C. Berkouwer, *General Revelation* (Grand Rapids, Mich.: Eerdmans, 1955); P. Helm, "Revealed Propositions and Timeless Truths," *RelS* 8 (1972): 127-36; C. F. H. Henry, ed., *Revelation in the Bible* (Grand Rapids, Mich.: Baker, 1958); H. D. McDonald, *Ideas of Revelation: An Historical Study A.D. 1700-1960* (Grand Rapids, Mich.: Baker, 1979); H. D. McDonald, *Theories of Revelation: An Historical Study 1700-1960* (Grand Rapids, Mich.: Baker, 1979); E. L. Mascall, *Words and Images* (New York: Longmans, Green, 1957); Bernard Ramm, *Special Revelation and the Word of God* (Grand Rapids, Mich.: Eerdmans, 1961); Edward J. Young, *Thy Word Is Truth* (London: Banner of Truth, 1963).

who speaks in other roles as well. We see speaking as a significant part of his activity, particularly in the roles of King, Judge and Father.

The Dual Role

Our survey indicates that God makes himself known as the immanent Personal Revealer in two complementary ways. The first has to do with the living, personal presence of God among his people. In this area the language category is about personal relationships. The focus of God's coming is bound up with his faithfulness to people, and the subrole that most effectively captures the essence of God's coming together in close personal relationship with people is the picture of God as Friend.

As the immanent Personal Revealer, God not only comes to make his living presence known to individuals, but when he comes, he speaks. So the word of God becomes a central focus with regard to his personal relations. Here the language category is that of interpersonal communication, as people relate to people. The focus is on truth about God and the truth of what he has to say. The subroles that most succinctly capture God's personal revelation in this category are those of Teacher and Prophet.

The Bible is very careful not to separate the person of God from the truth of God. It knows nothing of a separation of knowledge from personal being. There is no abstract body of truth by itself, nor is there any personal relating to God apart from spoken communication. These two are always held together in the persons of the triune Godhead who speaks to us.

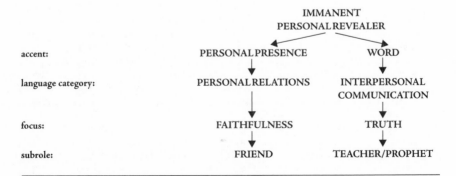

Figure 5.3. God's personal presence and word as Personal Revealer

The Father

Old Testament. In the Old Testament God's personal presence has already been discussed in terms of the revelation of his glory in the symbols of a cloud and fire. But God also makes himself known by means of theophanies, that is, visible appearances of God (e.g., Gen 12:7ff.).[13] Further, God reveals himself through the use of visions (e.g., 15:1),[14] in which a recipient who is awake is transported beyond his material environment; and dreams (e.g., 28:12), which involve one who receives God's revelation when he is asleep and therefore more passive.[15]

God also reveals himself by certain acts that indicate his presence among his people. Thus the Exodus, the wilderness wandering, the conquest, the exile, and the return to Jerusalem are all among the events in which God manifests his presence in the midst of his people. He promises them, "I will make my abode among you" (Lev 26:11) and that I "will be your God, and you shall be my people" (26:12)[16] But his actions are almost always accompanied by some verbal explanation of what he has done. Thus, in Genesis 2 he plants a garden for Adam, and then he gives him a commandment with regard to its proper use (Gen 2:15-17). God delivers his people from Egypt (Ex 12) and then he explains his actions, purpose and demands for Israel (19—20).

New Testament. In the New Testament God's audible revelation is very specific in his witness to Jesus. It happens three times. The first of these occasions comes at the baptism of Jesus when he says, "This is my beloved Son, with whom I am well pleased" (Mt 3:17; cf. Mk 1:11; Lk 3:22). This inaugurates the beginning of Jesus' public ministry. The second comes after the confession of Peter at Caesarea Philippi and in confirmation of his testimony that Jesus is "the

---

[13]For other references to theophanies see Gen 15:17; 18; 28:12-17; 32:22-32; Ex 3:2-6; 19:16-25; 20:18; 23:20-23; 24:9-11; 32:34; 33:12-23; 34:5-9; Josh 5:13-15; Judg. 6:11-24; 13:6-23. See also Eichrodt, *Theology of the Old Testament,* 2:20-29; Vriezen, *Outline of Old Testament Theology,* pp. 246-49; ZPEB, 4:719-21; EDT, p. 1087.

[14]References to visions: Gen 15:1-5; 46:1-4; Num 24:1-24; 1 Sam 3:10-15; 1Chron 17:3-15; Ezek 1:1-28; 8:3; 40:2; Dan 8:1-27; 9:20-27; 10:1-21; 11:1-12; 12:13; Acts 9:10-19; 10:1-8, 9-23; 16:9-10; 18:9-11. Others: Gen 15:12-21; Is 6:1; Dan 7:11-14; Amos 7:1-9:15. See also Vriezen, *Outline of Old Testament Theology,* pp. 244-46.

[15]For other references to dreams see Gen 20:3-7; 28:10-17; 31:10-16, 24; 37:5-11; 41:1-32; 42:9; Judg 7:13-18; 1 Kings 3:5-15; Dan 2:1-49; 4:4-33; 7:1-28; Mt 1:20-21; 2:12, 13-15, 19-23; 27:19. See also TDNT, 5:220-238; NIDNTT, 1:511-12; Leo Oppenheim, *The Interpretation of Dreams in the Ancient Near East* (Philadelphia: American Philosophical Society, 1956); EBT, 1:214-16; ZPEB, 2:162-64.

[16]For discussion of God's acts in history see George E. Wright, *God Who Acts* (London: SCM Press, 1964), pp. 70, 80-86, 107-11; George Ernest Wright, *Old Testament Against Its Environment* (London: SCM Press, 1950); Henry, *God, Revelation and Authority.* 1:247-80.

Christ, the Son of the living God." On this occasion God speaks from heaven saying, "This is my beloved Son, with whom I am well pleased; listen to him" (Mt 17:5; cf. Mk 9:7; Lk 9:35). The last occasion occurs at the very close of Jesus' ministry when he is facing the cross and declares that he has come to the world for this purpose. At his request, "Father, glorify thy name," God answers from heaven, "I have glorified it, and I will glorify it again" (Jn 12:28). Thus, at three very crucial times in the life of Jesus the Father verbally witnesses to his relationship to Jesus. At these strategic points in the life of Jesus, the Father has made clear his relationship to his Son.

Prophetic role. Within God's speaking role, there are three ways in which God as Revealer is known. These are the subroles or minor roles that particularly pertain to God's personal communication with people. One of these roles is that of the Prophet. God the Father is not called a prophet, but he speaks very frequently in Scripture, especially in the Old Testament, through the prophets. The prophet in fact becomes like the mouthpiece of God (Is 1:2ff; Jer 1:4; Ezek 1:3). As Hebrews 1:1 puts it, "In many and various ways God spoke of old to our fathers by the prophets." The identification of God with the prophets is so close that when the prophet of God speaks, it often becomes identical with what God says. Yet, because God himself is not called a prophet, the role identification is still indirect. With the coming of Jesus the prophetic dimension of God's speaking role becomes much clearer.[17]

Teacher. A second, and more extensive, subrole of God as Personal Revealer is the picture of God as Teacher. The clear identification begins with God's call on Moses to lead the children of Israel out of Egypt when he instructs him, "Now therefore go, and I will be with your mouth and teach you what you shall speak" (Ex 4:12). With the giving of the law at Mount Sinai God's role as Teacher is seen when he describes the content of the Torah as his instruction to his people (e.g., 24:12). The psalmist understands well this role when he cries out, "Make me to know thy ways, O LORD; teach me thy paths. Lead me in thy truth, and teach me." He could make such a request because of his conviction that the Lord, "instructs sinners in the way" and "teaches the humble his way" (Ps 25:4-5, 8, 9). God's role as a teacher is intimately bound up with his omniscience and wisdom as well as his ability to instruct. This is

---

[17]For references to God in a prophetic role see Ex 4:21-23; 7:14-18; Judg 6:7-10; Num 14:26-30.

what causes Job to exclaim, "Who is a teacher like him?" (Job 36:22).[18]

God's instruction is never purely academic; its purpose is to show people how to live. This is why he says, "I will instruct you and teach you the way you should go" (Ps 32:8). Teaching provides truth which is the basis of right living and right relationships.

Friend. The third subrole of God as immanent Personal Revealer is the picture of God as a Friend. The concept of friendship is a natural extension of person-to-person communication in an atmosphere of fellowship. A proper respect for God is the basis of friendship, and out of that friendship God reveals things to his people. "The friendship of the LORD is for those who fear him, and he makes known to them his covenant" (Ps 25:14). It is interesting that this reference to "the friendship of the LORD" comes in Psalm 25, which is the Psalm that is most explicit about God's role as Teacher (25:4, 5, 8, 9, 12). Obviously the communication of truth and the developing of close personal relationships are very intimate components both in revelation from God and in relating to him.

The most explicit reference to the friendship of God with an individual is in his relationship to Abraham. Jehoshaphat in his prayer to the Lord mentions "Abraham thy friend" (2 Chron 20:7). God himself speaks of "Abraham, my friend" (Is 41:8).[19] The New Testament indicates that the basis of this friendship is Abraham's belief in God. "'Abraham believed God, and it was reckoned to him as righteousness'; and he was called the friend of God" (Jas 2:23). Apparently, trust in God leads to Abraham's righteousness, which is the basis for the continuing intimacy with God so that he might be described as the "friend of God."[20] The whole concept of friendship with God implies the kind of intimacy that comes out of a developing close personal relationship between an individual and God as the immanent Personal Revealer.

---

[18]For God in a teacher's role see Ex 4:12-15; 24:12; 2 Sam. 22:35; Job 6:24; 36:22; Ps 18:34; 25:4-12; 27:11; 32:8; 86:11; 90:12; 94:10, 12; 119:12, 26, 33, 64, 66, 68, 108, 124, 135; 143:10; 144:1; Is 1:10; 2:3; 28:9, 26; 48:17; 54:13; Mic. 4:2; Jn 6:45; 1 Thess 4:9. See also *NIDNTT,* 3:778; *ZPEB,* 5:608-11.

[19]The normal word for "friend" in the Old Testament, *rea,* רֵעַ, is not used of God. The word used is the word *ahab,* אָהַב, which is the basic word for love. The *qal* participle is sometimes translated "friend."

[20]God may be referred to as a friend in the parable in Lk 11:5-8, where a man comes to his friend at midnight to say, "Friend, lend me three loaves."

The Son

Personal presence. In the New Testament Jesus is described as the One who is the personal presence of God in the world. Matthew quotes Isaiah, "His name shall be called Emmanuel (which means, God with us)" (Mt 1:23).[21] The whole meaning of the incarnation is that God has taken on human flesh and come into our midst, so that he who has seen Jesus has seen God (Jn 14:9).[22] Peter captures the essence of the fact that the two are one when he addresses Jesus by the characteristic title for God from Isaiah as "the Holy One of God" (6:69). Paul describes the essence of God's revelation through his Son when he tells how in Jesus "all the fulness of God was pleased to dwell" (Col 1:19). Finally, the writer of Hebrews makes clear that Jesus "reflects the glory of God" (Heb 1:3). God has made himself fully known in his Son.[23]

Word of God. Jesus comes not only as the personal presence of God in the midst of his people, but also as God's verbal communication to his people. Thus, Jesus is described as the "Word of God" (Jn 1:1-5, 11-14, 18).[24] The title reflects the fact that God is speaking to people through his Son by means of both teaching and the events of his life. So God's communication comes jointly through the message as well as the life of Jesus. Truth is conveyed in both his word and flesh. The incredible implication is that the person of Jesus demonstrates that for God truth always has a personal character to it.

Prophet. The personal presence of God is connected with his verbal communication in all of the three subroles in which Jesus appears as immanent Personal Revealer. The first is the prophetic role. Moses was the first to describe the coming Messiah as a prophet like unto himself, and since the New Testament

[21]See William DeBurgh, *The Messianic Prophecies of Isaiah* (Dublin: Hodges, Smith, 1863), pp. 41-78; E. Braeling, "The Emmanuel Prophecy," *JBL* 1 (1931): 277-97; ZPEB, vol. 3, pp. 259-61.

[22]See Thomas F. Torrance, *The Trinitarian Faith* (Edinburgh: T & T Clark, 1995), pp. 146-90; Emil Brunner, *The Mediator*, trans. Olive Wyon (London: Lutterworth, 1934), pp. 285-327.

[23]See Thomas F. Torrance, *The Mediation of Christ* (Grand Rapids, Mich.: Eerdmans, 1983), pp. 11-33.

[24]On Jesus as the Word of God see R. G. Bury, *The Fourth Gospel and the Logos Doctrine* (Cambridge: W. Heffer & Sons, 1940); K. E. Lee, *The Religious Thought of St. John* (London: SPCK, 1950), pp. 74-108; E. C. Hoskyns, *The Fourth Gospel* (London: Faber & Faber, 1956), pp. 154ff.; F. E. Walton, *The Development of the Logos Doctrine on Greek and Hebrew Thought* (Bristol: John Wright, 1911); Oscar Cullmann, *The Christology of the New Testament* (London: SCM Press, 1963), pp. 249-69; ISBE, 3:1911-17; Guthrie, *New Testament Theology*, pp. 331, 329; Werner Georg Kummel, *The Theology of the New Testament According to Its Major Witnesses* (Nashville: Abingdon, 1973), pp. 277-82; Hans Conzelman, *Outline of the Theology of the New Testament* (London: SCM Press, 1969), pp. 332-35; Eichrodt, *Theology of the Old Testament*, 2:69-89; Brunner, *Mediator*, pp. 201-31; CD 1/1, pp. 98-282; Wolfhart Pannenberg, *Jesus, God and Man*, trans. Lewis L. Wilkins and Duane A. Priebe (Philadelphia: Westminster Press, 1968), pp. 160-67; George Eldon Ladd, *Theology of the New Testament* (Grand Rapids, Mich.: Eerdmans, 1974), pp. 237-42.

sees Jesus as the fulfillment of this prediction, it sometimes describes him as "the prophet" (Jn 7:40; Mt 21:11).[25] Jesus alludes to this role when he says of himself, "A prophet is not without honor except in his own country" (Mt 13:57).[26]

Teacher. The second subrole of Jesus as immanent Personal Revealer is that of the Teacher. While Jesus' role as a Teacher is subsumed under his larger responsibility as Revealer, it really is a major way in which Jesus is described in the Gospels. His disciples first begin to call him *Rabbi*, meaning "teacher," as soon as they begin to relate to him (Jn 1:38).[27] As the disciples begin to follow him, sitting under the teaching ministry of Jesus is one of the major dimensions of being his disciples (Mt 5:1-2ff). The teaching of Jesus is connected with his preaching and healing, and is presented as one of the three major activities of his public ministry (4:23; 9:35).[28] It is in his role as a Teacher that Jesus accomplishes one of God's major purposes in terms of the verbal communication of God's word to people. As a Teacher he is providing through the use of human language personal communication from God.[29]

The teaching of Jesus seems to have two focal points. One is his public ministry of teaching to the multitudes and the other is the private, more concentrated teaching with the Twelve and a few other select individuals, (e.g.,

---

[25]For Jesus as a prophet see Mt 21:46; Mk 6:4, 15; Lk 4:24; 7:16; 13:33; Jn 4:19, 44; 6:14; 9:17; also N. T. Wright, *Jesus and the Victory of God* (Minneapolis: Fortress, 1992), pp. 147-97; Joachim Jeremias, *New Testament Theology: The Proclamation of Jesus* (New York: Scribners, 1971), pp. 76-84; Guthrie, *New Testament Theology*, 269-70; Cullmann, *Christology of the New Testament*, pp. 13-50; C. H. Dodd, "Jesus as Teacher and Prophet," in *Mysterium Christi*, eds. G. K. A. Bell and G. A. Deissman (London: Longmans, Green, 1930), pp. 53-66; V. F. Filson, *Jesus Christ the Risen Lord* (Nashville: Abingdon, 1941), pp. 137ff.; Kummel, *Theology of the New Testament*, pp. 65-66.

[26]For more on the prophetic office of Jesus see William Burt Pope, *A Compendium of Christian Theology* (London: Wesleyan-Methodist Book Room, 1880), 2:207-16; Charles Hodge, *Systematic Theology* (London: James Clark, 1960), 2:462-63; Louis Berkhof, *Systematic Theology* (Edinburgh: Banner of Truth, 1958), 356-60; Brunner, *Christian Doctrine of Creation and Redemption*, pp. 275-80; Pannenburg, *Jesus, God and Man*, pp. 215-70.

[27]On Jesus as Rabbi see *TDNT*, 4:961-65; Géza Vermès, *Jesus the Jew* (Philadelphia: Fortress, 1981), pp. 113-28; George F. Moore, *Judaism* (Cambridge: Harvard University Press, 1940), 3:15ff.; A. J. Feldman, *The Rabbi and his Early Ministry* (New York: Bloch, 1941); A. Finkle, *The Pharisees and the Teacher of Nazareth* (Leiden: Brill, 1964).

[28]On Jesus as Teacher see Mt 4:23; 5:2; 7:29; 13:54; 21:23; 22:16; 26:55; Mk 1:21; 2:13; 4:1-2; 6:2, 6, 34; 8:31; 9:31; 10:1; 11:17; 12:14, 35; 14:49; Lk 4:15; 5:3, 17; 6:6; 11:1; 13:10, 22; 19:47; 20:1, 21; 21:37; Jn 1:38, 49; 3:2; 6:25, 59; 7:14, 28; 8:2, 20; 18:20; 20:16; Acts 1:1.

[29]For further discussion of Jesus' role as Teacher see *NIDNTT*, vol. 3, pp. 759-81; Gunter Bornkamm, *Jesus of Nazareth* (New York: Harper, 1960); Brunner, *Mediator*, pp. 417-23; R. Montague, "The Dialectic Method of Jesus," *Bsac* 41 (1884): 549-72; G. Stevens, "The Teaching of Jesus," and "The Method of His Teaching," *BibW*, vol. 5 (1885): 106-13; Herman Horne, *Jesus, the Master Teacher* (Grand Rapids, Mich.: Kregel, 1964); Walter Squires, *The Pedagogy of Jesus in the Twilight of Today* (Philadelphia: Westminster Press, 1927); Charles McKoy, *The Art of Jesus as a Teacher* (Boston: Judson, 1930); Ray Carter, *The Eternal Teacher: a Guide to Jesus' Teaching Methods* (New York: Exposition, 1960).

Mary, Martha, and Lazarus). With Jesus we get a much more graphic picture of the teaching role of God because he functions like the rabbis of his day in a training capacity.

Friend. The third subrole of Jesus as immanent Personal Revealer is that of Friend. There is a certain general friendship Jesus has with those who are interested and respond in some way to him. Thus he may be described as "a friend of publicans and sinners" (Mt 11:19; Lk 7:34). But the normal use of the friendship category is Jesus' relation to the Twelve (Lk 12:4; Jn 15:14-15). On his final evening with his disciples Jesus makes clear the depth of the friendship they have developed over the last three years. One evidence is his willingness to die on their behalf. "Greater love has no man than this, that a man lay down his life for his friends" (Jn 15:13). The second evidence is his willingness to share with them what God has made known to him. "No longer do I call you servants, for the servant does not know what his master is doing; but I have called you friends, for all that I have heard from my Father I have made known to you" (Jn 15:15).

The basis of their friendship is the disciples' continued obedience to Jesus. "You are my friends if you do what I command you" (15:14). The ongoing obedience of the disciples to Jesus is based on an ongoing trust and confidence in him (cf. 14:1). Whereas the friendship figure is not used very extensively in the Old Testament, apparently, Jesus' relationship to his disciples is modeling under the New Covenant a kind of intimacy and closeness that is possible between very close friends who live and work together over a period of years. The figure is designed to indicate that God wants just this kind of intimate personal friendship with everyone who is a follower of Jesus.

Witness. As Personal Revealer Jesus is sometimes described as the one who is a faithful Witness unto God, i.e., who is accurately reflecting the revelation of God to the world (Rev 1:5). So Jesus can say to Nicodemus, "We speak of what we know, and bear witness to what we have seen" (Jn 3:11). Jesus makes a similar declaration before Pilot, "For this I have come into the world, to bear witness to the truth. Every one who is of the truth hears my voice" (18:37). The role of Witness also pertains to the legal category as we will discuss again under the category of the righteous Judge.[30] It is mentioned here because of its clear

---

[30]For Jesus as a witness see Jn 5:31; 8:18; 1 Tim 6:13; Rev 3:14. See also *NIDNTT,* 3:1045-47.

connection with speaking the truth. This is certainly one of Jesus' assignments in his work of making God known (Jn 1:14, 17-18).

Word became flesh. John gives graphic representation to the revealing role of Jesus when he writes, "The Word became flesh and dwelt among us, full of grace and truth; we have beheld his glory, glory as the only Son from the Father. . . . For the law was given through Moses; grace and truth came through Jesus Christ. No one has ever seen God; the only Son, who is in the bosom of the Father, he has made him known" (Jn 1:14, 17-18).[31] He makes it clear that Jesus is the One who brings us both grace and truth. When we behold his glory, we behold that of the Father. While no one has seen God, Jesus is the one who has made him known to us. Much of the rest of John's Gospel is built around this revelation of God in Jesus Christ. Hebrews reminds us that God has spoken to our fathers in many and various ways through the prophets; "but in these last days he has spoken to us by a Son" (Heb 1:1-2). His point is that the revelation of God comes through one who is speaking to people in the person of Jesus. This was possible because, as Paul puts it, "In him the whole fulness of deity dwells bodily" (Col 2:9).

To bring the picture of Jesus as the immanent Personal Revealer full circle we must remember that the purpose of the full divinity of God being revealed in Jesus and God's word being accurately made known by Jesus has to do in large measure with God's desire to be known personally in this world. God desires personal relationships between people and himself, and Jesus comes to make this possible, both the initial establishment of the relationship and the ongoing development of it. It is Jesus' personal relationship with the disciples that symbolizes the close personal relationship that God desires with every person. The intimacy that Jesus has with the Twelve and the development of those close personal ties that involve both the heart and the mind in personal commitment is symbolic of what God desires to do with everyone who is a believer.

One of the purposes of Jesus' discipleship during his earthly ministry is to model the fact that God desires a close, intimate, personal relationship with everyone whom he has made in his own image. While in the Old Testament God has come to his people to relate to them in a personal way, in a far richer and more intimate manner than other gods in the ancient Near Eastern world, it is

---

[31]Cf. Barth's comments, CD 1/2, pp. 1-44, 132-202.

particularly in the New Testament that we see the full revelation of this person-
to-person relationship God desires as it is revealed by the incarnation of Jesus. It
is Jesus, the Word made flesh, the God-man who reveals to us the full revelation
of God's desire for fellowship, communication, interaction, love and intimacy
with other persons. The warm, personal, close relationship Jesus has with the
Twelve is a model revealed to us so that every individual might have this kind of
relationship with God.[32]

The Holy Spirit

Personal presence of God. In the Old Testament the Holy Spirit often times represents the personal presence of God in the lives of individuals.[33] Joseph is described
as one "in whom is the Spirit of God" (Gen 41:38). The first man in Scripture who
is described as being "filled" with the Spirit of God is the artisan Bezalel (Ex 31:3;
35:31), while Joshua is also described as one "in whom is the spirit" (Num 27:18;
Deut 34:9). During the period of the Judges the Spirit of God is especially at work
in providing the presence of God to empower certain leaders to give ruling direction to Israel. The Spirit comes on Caleb's younger brother Othniel, and he judges
Israel (Judg 3:10). The Spirit of the Lord takes possession of Gideon, and he leads
the children of Israel in the defeat of the Midianites (6:34ff.). In like manner the
Spirit comes on Jephthah, giving him power to lead Israel to a defeat of the Ammonites (11:29-33), and at different times he comes on Samson, giving him unusual
prowess against a lion and the Philistines (14:6, 19; 15:14).

With the inauguration of the monarchy, the Spirit of God comes on kings.
The Spirit comes on Saul shortly after his anointing to the kingship (1 Sam
10:6, 10), but the Spirit also departs from Saul after his disobedience to God
(16:14). The Spirit comes mightily on David at his ascension as king over
Israel (16:13), and after his sin with Bathsheba he prays for God not to take his
Holy Spirit from him (Ps 51:11). In a similar vein Israel looks forward to the
Spirit serving as the presence of God with the Messiah, so that Isaiah can
declare "the Spirit of the LORD shall rest upon him" (Is 11:2). Speaking of the
servant Messiah, God declares, "Behold my servant, whom I uphold, my

---

[32] Torrance, *Trinitarian Faith*, pp. 52-65; Walter Kasper, *The God of Jesus Christ*, trans. Matthew J. O'Connell
(New York: Crossroad, 1999), pp. 184-89.
[33] See Vriezen, *Outline of Old Testament Theology*, pp. 249-51; Eichrodt, *Theology of the Old Testament*, 2:46-58;
ZPEB, 3:184.

chosen, in whom my soul delights; I have put my Spirit upon him, he will bring forth justice to the nations" (42:1). In addition there is the great Messianic passage that Jesus quotes concerning himself, "The Spirit of the Lord GOD is upon me, because the LORD has anointed me" (Is 61:1; Lk 4:18).

The presence of the Spirit is made known not only to leaders, judges and kings but also to prophets. The Spirit of God often comes on a prophet for the dual purpose of making the presence of God felt and revealing a word from God (e.g., 2 Chron 15:1; 20:14; 24:20). Ezekiel speaks of the Spirit of God entering into him (Ezek 2:2; 3:24), and it is the Spirit that lifts him up and transports him to places where he may see further visions from God (3:12, 14; 11:1, 5, 24). In God's promises of the New Covenant, one of the things he says he will do to vindicate his holiness in the lives of his people is to put his Spirit within them (36:27; 37:14; 39:29). In the same vein he promises through Joel "that I will pour out my Spirit on all flesh" (Joel 2:28-29). Apparently, the availability of the full presence of God through his Holy Spirit is to be one of the privileges for those under the New Covenant.

Revelation of God's word. The Spirit of God represents not only the personal presence of God in the Old Testament but is also intimately bound up with God's revelation to his people. When the Spirit of God comes, the most frequent result is proclamation of the word of God.[34] It begins as early as the wilderness experience when God puts some of the Spirit from Moses on the seventy elders, and they begin to prophesy (Num 11:25ff.). When the Spirit comes on Balaam, he begins to give his oracles regarding Israel (24:2-3). The Spirit of the Lord comes on Saul for the purpose of ruling Israel, and at the same time he begins to prophesy (1 Sam 6:10; 11:6; 19:23). The Spirit comes on Azariah and sends him out to meet Asa and deliver to him a word from God (2 Chron 15:1-2) and then later on Jahaziel, giving him the power to speak the word of God in the assembly (20:14-15). When the Spirit of God takes possession of Zechariah, the prophet speaks to the children of Israel saying, "Thus says God" (2 Chron 24:20).

Some of the prophets connect the filling of God's Spirit with the power to declare his word to God's people. Thus Micah declares, "But as for me, I am

---

[34]On the function of the Spirit in revelation see Thomas F. Torrance, *The Trinitarian Faith* (Edinburgh: T & T Clark, 1995), pp. 193, 247-51; and Torrance, *Christian Doctrine of God*, pp. 59-70.

filled with power, with the Spirit of the LORD, and with justice and might, to declare to Jacob his transgression and to Israel his sin" (Mic 3:8). In spite of this anointing many do not respond to God's message. Zechariah explains, "They made their hearts like adamant lest they should hear the law and the words which the LORD of hosts had sent by his Spirit through the former prophets" (Zech 7:12).

The coming of the revealing Spirit of God in the Old Testament seems particularly related to two functions. One is the leading of the people of God and is related to those who will have governing responsibilities (e.g., Joseph, the seventy elders, Joshua, Othniel, Gideon, Jephthah, Samson, Saul, David, the Messiah). Here there is a close tie to the kingly/ruling role. The other function is the proclamation of the word of God. This would seem particularly true with prophets who are the means of speaking God's message to God's people (e.g., Saul, Micaiah, Azariah, Jahaziel, Zechariah, Ezekiel, Micah).[35] This is more intimately bound up with the role of God as Personal Revealer.

Indwelling of Spirit. The event that sets the stage for all understanding of the indwelling of the Spirit in the New Testament comes at the baptism of Jesus. In this significant trinitarian passage the Father audibly identifies Jesus as his Son, and the Spirit of God descends on Jesus like a dove (Mt 3:16-17; Mk 1:10-11). Jesus is modeling for future disciples that God's plan is that no one enter into ministry without the full control of God over the individual through his Spirit. Luke clarifies the implication of this baptism when immediately after this event he accents Jesus' life as "full of the Holy Spirit" and being "led by the Spirit" (Lk 4:1). Luke also illustrates that this was a part of God's original plan under the New Covenant when he has Jesus apply directly to himself the messianic passage from Isaiah about the Spirit's coming: "The Spirit of the Lord is upon me, because he has anointed me to . . ." (Lk 4:17-19; Is 61:1-2).

In the life of Jesus, the Spirit's two major functions in the Old Testament come together. When the Spirit comes on Jesus, it is a part of the identification of the personal presence of God in his life for leading the people of God (like the Spirit coming on leaders in the Old Testament), but it is also symbolic of God's coming to speak to his people and thus is related to the prophetic role Jesus will play throughout his ministry. Not surprisingly then, when Jesus gets ready to

---

[35]On the Spirit and Scripture see Thomas Oden, *Life in the Spirit* (San Francisco: Harper & Row, 1992), pp. 67-75.

send his disciples out to replicate his own ministry, he takes his last evening with them to prepare them for his departure and the role of the Spirit for their lives in ministry. They will no longer have his physical presence with them, but he promises that they will have the indwelling presence of the Holy Spirit. The world, said Jesus, cannot receive the presence of the Spirit because it does not know him. But "you know him, for he dwells with you, and will be in you" (Jn 14:17). Jesus' first two references to the coming of the Holy Spirit bracket his statements to the disciples that he will not leave them desolate but will come to them. He promises them that those who are walking in obedience as evidence of their love for him will know his presence through the Holy Spirit. Jesus himself will manifest himself to the disciples through the Spirit, and both Jesus and the Father will make their home in the disciples. The clear implication is that this is to be done through the full indwelling power of the Holy Spirit in their lives. After the departure of Jesus, the personal dwelling of God with individuals is represented by the presence of the Holy Spirit in the lives of believers.[36]

Spirit of truth. Intimately bound up with God's personal presence in the lives of believers is God's ongoing revelation of himself through the Holy Spirit. This revelation of God's truth is emphasized by the description of the Holy Spirit as the "Spirit of truth" (Jn 14:17; 15:26; 16:13; 1 Cor 2:13; Lk 12:12). This One who is the bearer of God's truth will serve in a *teaching role* according to Jesus. "The Holy Spirit, whom the Father will send in my name, he will teach you all things, and bring to your remembrance all that I have said to you" (Jn 14:26). His role as teacher is to direct them into all truth as the Spirit speaks for the whole Trinity. "When the Spirit of truth comes, he will guide you into all the truth; for he will not speak on his own authority, but whatever he hears he will speak, and he will declare to you the things that are to come" (16:13).[37] This conviction is certainly behind the New Testament understanding of the Holy Spirit as the One through whom God has spoken in the Old Testament. Even before Pentecost Peter can declare to the others, "Brethren, the scripture had to be fulfilled, which the Holy Spirit spoke beforehand by the mouth of David" (Acts 1:16; also 4:25; Heb 3:7; 10:15). Yet, the Holy Spirit's speaking is not just limited to the Old

---

[36]See Brunner, *Christian Doctrine of God*, p. 215.

[37]On the Holy Spirit in revelation see CD 1/1, pp. 203-17, 515-22; Hodge, *Systematic Theology*, 1:531-2; Warfield, *Inspiration and Authority*, pp. 71-102, 131-66; Guthrie, *New Testament Theology*, p. 23; Pinnock, *Biblical Revelation*, p. 57.

Testament. In the New Testament the Holy Spirit speaks and gives God's revelation as well (Acts 13:2; 15:28; 20:23; 21:11). Further, the Holy Spirit speaks through Jesus (1:2) and those who have been filled with his presence (2:4; 4:8, 31; 6:3, 10; 7:55-56; 10:44-45; 11:23-24; 13:9; 19:6).

Witness. The work of the Holy Spirit speaking through believers is also closely tied to a description of his role as a witness to the truth. Jesus prepares his disciples for this when he first describes this "Spirit of truth" as one who "will bear witness to me" (Jn 15:26). But this is immediately followed by his statement, "You also are witnesses, because you have been with me from the beginning" (15:27). Accordingly, in his last promise to them he tells them they "shall receive power when the Holy Spirit has come upon you" and that "you shall be my witnesses" (Acts 1:8). Thus, the Holy Spirit is a witness to God's truth, and through his fullness the disciples of Jesus also become witnesses to God's truth. So Peter can declare to the Sanhedrin, "We are witnesses to these things, and so is the Holy Spirit whom God has given to those who obey him" (Acts 5:32).[38] One of the very specific things to which the Holy Spirit bears witness is that we have become children of God (Rom 8:16; 1 Jn 3:24; 4:13; 5:7-12).

Man and Woman

Desired relationship: Fellowship. Genesis 1 makes clear that men and women are made in the image of God (Gen 1:26-27). This image includes the capacity to think and speak like God. It is this ability within them that makes it possible for God to address them by verbal communication in a way he does not address any other part of the created order. People were made for interpersonal communication, both with God and with each other. Further, the picture of God's relationship with them in Genesis 1-2 makes it clear that man and woman were made for an intimate relationship with God. While God's relationship to Adam and Eve is anthropomorphically described, they are clearly designed for intimate fellowship with the personal presence of this God (Gen 2; 3:8). God is looking for fellowship with these whom he has made in his social image. The fellowship within the triune God is the basis for fellowship between God and people as well as the fellowship persons have with each other.

Appropriate response. In general two kinds of response are proper to a God

---

[38]For the close relationship between the witness of the Spirit and the testimony of God see 1 Jn 5:7-12.

who is revealing his personal presence to people. The first is a receptivity to the word of God that is revealed. It is the kind of receptivity that leads to obedience to the truth of God (Jn 1:14-18). The second is a receptivity to the truth that leads to a personal relationship with God. God made individuals for a right relationship to himself, and so the proper response for which he is looking is that personal knowledge of and relationship with him. This is why Jesus can say, "This is eternal life, that they know thee, the only true God" (17:3). Some receptivity to God's word is essential before one can respond in a personal relationship with him. But once that personal relationship is established, this should produce a greater receptivity to the word of God throughout one's life. Finally, increasing receptivity to the word of God leads to even deeper personal relationships with him, so that the two kinds of expected personal response to God as the Personal Revealer are designed to strengthen and reinforce one another.

These two responses parallel two of the key subroles under God as Personal Revealer. This God in his role as Teacher expects people to respond to him as students or learners. This is the kind of receptivity to understanding the Word of God that then should lead to obedience. But it is in his role as Friend that God desires a relationship with individuals, and it is a receptivity to the Word that cultivates this personal friendship with God that is the second crucial response. Jesus, who is both Teacher and Friend to disciples, is the key model of the way God works. The disciples in their responses to him become the illustration for the future believer's response as they listen to his words so they might walk in obedience and develop a closer personal relationship with him.[39]

Sin

Alienation. With the entering of sin into the world in Genesis 3, there is a break in the personal relationship between God and people.[40] While it does not render all interpersonal communication void, it does break the relationship between God and individuals, and consequently the personal communication between them. This involves an alienation and hostility that leaves people without regular verbal communication with their Creator. The symbol of this separation and bro-

---

[39]See Allan Coppedge, *The Biblical Principles of Discipleship* (Grand Rapids, Mich.: Zondervan, 1989).
[40]For sin as separation from God see Pope, *Compendium of Christian Theology,* 2:29-32.

ken relationship is the expulsion of Adam and Eve from the garden, i.e., from the immediate presence of God in their lives (Gen 3:23-24). Sin not only causes a break in relationship with God, it produces estrangement between a man and his wife (3:12).

Sin as alienation and as a broken relationship with God is graphically described in Ezekiel 10—11, where there is a symbolic withdrawing of the presence of God from his temple and from Jerusalem. The prophet gives a very vivid picture of the departure of the glory (i.e., presence) of God from the midst of his people because of their habitual and repeated sin. This kind of sin is described as that which makes us enemies of God (Rom 5:10), for it is built on the mind of the flesh that is "hostile to God" (8:7). Paul reminds the Ephesians that for a time they were "separated from Christ, alienated from the commonwealth of Israel, and strangers to the covenants of promise, having no hope and without God in the world" (Eph 2:12), and the Colossians he describes as those who "once were estranged and hostile in mind, doing evil deeds" (Col 1:21).[41]

It is obvious that intimacy with sin and the world are mutually exclusive to an intimate relationship with God. James pointedly states, "Do you not know that friendship with the world is enmity with God? Therefore, whoever wishes to be a friend of the world makes himself an enemy of God" (Jas 4:4). Sin in this figure of speech is obviously more closely related to the state of sinfulness (i.e., separation) than to an act of sin, although an act of sin might be understood in terms of deliberately breaking the relationship by refusing to hear a personal word from God. Alienation then gives a picture of sin as separating friends and destroying personal relationships. It is a key category for understanding sin.

Salvation

Reconciliation. An experience of saving grace in this category is described as the establishment of or the restoration of personal relationships with God. These new relationships are described in terms of all three members of the Trinity. With God the Father the separation and broken relationships are described in terms of reconciliation. So Paul writes, "For if while . . . we were reconciled to

---

[41]For *sin* as "to alienate" (ἀλλοτρίοω) see *NIDNTT,* 1:684-85; Guthrie, *New Testament Theology,* pp. 193-94.

God by the death of his Son, much more, now that we are reconciled, shall we be saved by his life" (Rom 5:10-11). This new relationship is possible because "God was in Christ reconciling the world to himself" (2 Cor 5:18-20). By means of this reconciliation the hostility between man and God is brought to an end (Eph 2:16). The figure of reconciliation of course is used with regard to restoring a broken relationship between friends.[42]

Reconciliation as atonement. Reconciliation needs to be understood not only as the experience of salvation where one responds to God and is reconciled to him (2 Cor 5:20) but also as a part of the atoning work of Christ. From God's perspective the broken relationship between people and himself is effectively changed at the cross, so that sin no longer remains an obstacle to the divine-human relationship. The initiative is all on God's side. "While we were enemies we were reconciled to God by the death of his Son" (Rom 5:10). People are not being reconciled to God by their own initiative but by God's initiative. It is his work on the cross to which they are being called to respond. People are invited to an experience of reconciliation after God has made reconciliation possible through the atonement (2 Cor 5:18-21).[43]

The atonement as reconciliation then is both a means and an end. Atonement is the means initiated by God to deal with the sin that breaks relationships. But reconciliation is also God's desired end where there is a rejoining of people to himself in mutual commitment to one another. This reconciliation is the new relationship in which people stand with God (the end) because of what Christ has done (the means). Those who have been separated from him are now reconciled to him (Col 1:21-22). In other words

---

[42]For further discussion of initial salvation as reconciliation see *TDNT*, 1:251-59; 3:300-323; Donald M. Baillie, *God Was in Christ* (London: Faber & Faber, 1960); CD 4/1, pp. 79-154; Rudolf Bultmann, *Theology of the New Testament* (New York: Charles Scribner's Sons, n.d.), 1:285ff., 292-305; Cullmann, *Christology of the New Testament;* James Denney, *The Death of Christ* (London: Tyndale Press, 1961); *The Christian Doctrine of Reconciliation* (New York: George H. Doran, 1918); Peter Taylor Forsyth, *Cruciality of the Cross* (London: Hodder & Stoughton, 1909); David Hill, *Greek Words and Hebrew Meaning* (New York: Scribner, 1975), pp. 23-48; *EBT*, 2:730-38.

[43]Denney, *Death of Christ*, pp. 85-86; G. W. H. Lampe, *Reconciliation in Christ* (London: Longmans, Green, 1956); Leon Morris, *The Apostolic Preaching of the Cross* (London: Tyndale Press, 1965); Gerhard von Rad, *Old Testament Theology*, trans. D. M. G. Stalker (New York: Harper & Row, 1962), vols. 1-2; A. B. Ritschl, *A Critical History of the Christian Doctrine of Justification and Reconciliation* (New York: Charles Scribner's, 1900); *The Christian Doctrine of Justification in New Testament Teaching* (New York: Charles Scribner's Sons, 1900); *HDB*, 4:204-7; *ZPEB*, 5:144-45; Kummel, *Theology of the New Testament*, pp. 203-5; John Miley, *Systematic Theology* (New York: Methodist Book Concern, 1894), 2:81-83; Pope, *Compendium of Christian Theology*, pp. 282-87; *NIDNTT*, 3:145-76.

God reconciles and is reconciled. Those who have responded by faith to his offer for reconciliation are those who are able to "rejoice in God through our Lord Jesus Christ, through whom we have now received reconciliation" (Rom 5:11). Those who have not so responded are invited. "We beseech you on behalf of Christ, be reconciled to God" (2 Cor 5:20).[44]

Fellowship. The new relationship that solves the problem of separation/alienation between God and persons may also be described in terms of fellowship. It is a restored relationship that makes intimate personal fellowship possible in grace. John writes that he is proclaiming what he has seen and heard "so that you may have fellowship with us; and our fellowship is with the Father and with his Son Jesus Christ" (1 Jn 1:3).[45] Paul tells us that we are called into this special relationship. "God is faithful, by whom you were called into the fellowship of his Son, Jesus Christ our Lord" (1 Cor 1:9).

Receiving Christ. The establishment of this new relationship with God the Son may be described in terms of receiving or accepting Christ. "To all who received him, who believed in his name, he gave power to become children of God" (Jn 1:12). This acceptance of Jesus is graphically described by the Lord when he said, "Behold, I stand at the door and knock; if any one hears my voice and opens the door, I will come in to him and eat with him, and he with me" (Rev 3:20). And he who receives the Son, also receives a new relationship with the Father. This is why Jesus says, "He who receives you receives me, and he who receives me receives him who sent me" (Mt 10:40). Since receiving Christ is just the beginning, Christians are exhorted to continue to live in this relationship with him. "As therefore you received Christ Jesus the Lord, so live in him, rooted and built up in him and established in the faith" (Col 2:6, 7).

Having the Holy Spirit. The new relationship with the Holy Spirit begins when one is born of the Spirit (Jn 3:5, 6, 8). This may be described in terms of "having the Holy Spirit," as when Jesus told his disciples that the world could not receive the Spirit of truth because it neither saw him nor knew him but "you know him, for he dwells with you" (14:17). Jesus is trying to make clear that every believer

---

[44]Thomas Oden, *Word of Life* (San Francisco: Harper & Row, 1989), pp. 354-55.

[45]For discussion of fellowship between God and persons see *TDNT*, 3:789-809; *NIDNTT*, 1:635ff.; *IDB*, pp. 664ff.; *EDT*, p. 414; Alfred R. George, *Communion with God in the New Testament* (London: Epworth, 1953); Vriezen, *Outline of Old Testament Theology*, p. 240.

has a relationship with the Holy Spirit, because "God has sent the Spirit of his Son into our hearts" (Gal 4:6). Thus, the Scripture is clear, "Any one who does not have the Spirit of Christ does not belong to him" (Rom 8:9). This Spirit is received in the establishment of this new relationship with God, so that Paul could write, "We have received not the spirit of the world, but the Spirit which is from God" (1 Cor 2:12). In the light of a trinitarian understanding of God this is not surprising. When you receive one member of the Trinity, you receive all three. So receiving Christ (cf. previous section) means receiving in some sense the Father and the Spirit. God is not divided.

Inhabitation. Sometimes this new relationship with the Holy Spirit is described as believers being the temple of the Holy Spirit. Just as the tabernacle and the temple in the Old Testament are the symbols of the dwelling place of the personal presence of God in Israel, believers in Christ become the temples of the Holy Spirit in the new age. "Do you not know that you are God's temple and that God's Spirit dwells in you? If any one destroys God's temple, God will destroy him. For God's temple is holy, and that temple you are" (1 Cor 3:16-17; cf. 6:19). Christians are those who are built into a holy temple "for a dwelling place of God in the Spirit" (Eph 2:22). The figure of Christians as temples of the Holy Spirit goes beyond just a relationship with God and graphically describes the presence of God indwelling his people. It may be accurately depicted as the inhabitation of God in people and is therefore one of the most intimate pictures of relationship with God in Scripture.

Growth in Christian Experience

Developing relationship based on receptivity to word. Growth after an experience of saving grace is described as continued receptivity to the word of God that leads to a more intimate relationship with him. The more one knows what God is saying, the better he knows the God who is speaking. Jesus could say to those who believe in him, "If you continue in my word, you are truly my disciples, and you will know the truth, and the truth will make you free" (Jn 8:31). The continued receptivity to the word of God is pictorially taught by Jesus in the parable of the soils. There the good soil produces three kinds of fruit: thirtyfold, sixtyfold and one hundredfold (Mk 4:1-20). Since the whole thrust of the parable relates the receptivity of the soil to the word, the productiveness of the good soil must also be understood as closely bound up with this receptivity to God's word. The implication is that those who are somewhat receptive produce thirtyfold, those who are more receptive produce sixtyfold and those who are the most receptive and open to God's word produce one hundredfold. All three kinds of good soil are receptive to some degree and are producing fruit, but obviously Jesus prefers the greatest receptivity and fruitfulness which seems to be in direct proportion to believers' openness to the word of God.

A slight variation of the same figure is given by Jesus in John 15:1-11 during his last night with the disciples when he pictures himself as the true vine and his disciples as the branches. "As the branch cannot bear fruit by itself, unless it abides in the vine, neither can you, unless you abide in me. I am the vine, you are the branches. He who abides in me, and I in him, he it is that bears much fruit, for apart from me you can do nothing" (Jn 15:4-5). But the abiding in Christ is intimately bound up with the word of Christ abiding in the disciples (15:7, 10; cf. 14:21-26; 16:12-19). Again, it seems to be receptivity and obedience to the word of Christ that make possible abiding in him and bearing fruit for him.

Growth in grace builds on continued reception of the word of truth, and this is the reason Paul is constantly praying and exhorting new believers to be open to more knowledge and understanding from God. He desires that God "may give you a spirit of wisdom and of revelation in the knowledge of him, having the eyes of your hearts enlightened" (Eph 1:17, 18). For others he prays that their love "may abound more and more, with knowledge and all discernment" (Phil 1:9), while to still another group he longs that they may be "filled with the knowledge of his will in all spiritual wisdom and understanding, to lead a life worthy of the Lord, fully pleasing to him, bearing fruit to every good work and increasing in the knowledge of God" (Col 1:9-10). For Paul increasing knowledge of God is the basis for an ever-increasing intimacy in one's relationship with him.

Model: Jesus and the Twelve. The growing personal intimacy with God is illustrated in the relationship of the Twelve with Jesus. Their relationship begins with him after some initial understanding of who he is and what he is like (Jn 1:35-51; Mk 1:16-20). But as the disciples continue to spend time with Jesus over the next three years, their relationships with him and the Father grow in closeness. This is due to two factors. One is the constant hearing of the preaching and teaching of Jesus so that they are continually exposed and are receptive to the word of God (Mt 4:23; 9:35). The other factor is the personal intimacy they develop with him through their time spent in his presence day and night. So at the end of their time together there is a closeness between Jesus and the Twelve that does not exist between Jesus and others in the same way (e.g. Jn 13:1, 23, 34-35). The pattern of Jesus' relationship with the disciples in the Gospels serves as a model for what God desires in terms of a growing personal intimacy with everyone who believes in him.

The Church

Old Testament characteristics: Truth and fellowship. The church in the Old Testament as well as in the New is characterized by two dimensions that repeatedly appear under this role. One has to do with its commitment to truth and the other to its focus on fellowship.

Both of these are dramatized at Mount Sinai when God offers Israel a covenant based on the Ten Words (Ex 20:1). Here is the emphasis on truth. He instructs Moses, "These are the words which you shall speak to the children of Israel" (19:6). Their response is, "All that the LORD has spoken we will do" (19:8). God then comes down on the mountain in a vivid demonstration of his personal presence to enter into fellowship with his people (19:9, 16-20).

Then at the ratification of this covenant, Moses again tells the people "all the words of the LORD" and writes them down (24:3-4). The words are read again to the people, and they respond for the third time, "All that the LORD has spoken we will do" (24:7). Next, the sacrificial blood is thrown on the people, sealing their commitment to truth from this time forth as a people of the word of God. Then Moses, the leaders and the elders of the people come into the presence of God where "they beheld God, and ate and drank" (24:11). Moses, representing the people, then goes into the personal presence of God on the mountain where the glory of the Lord settles on the mountain for another forty days and nights. Not only do the leaders have fellowship with God but Moses, representing all Israel, has a special entrance into the personal presence of God.

From this point on throughout the Old Testament, Israel is known as a people of the Torah. They live under the word of God and the instruction of God as he keeps revealing himself to them. But the purpose of this revelation is so that they might be in a right relationship with God and enjoy fellowship with him. Further, they are a community in relationship with God, which means they are in relationship with one another. The word of God builds up all relationships.

New Testament characteristics: Truth and fellowship. In the New Testament this same dual emphasis on truth and fellowship is highlighted right after the birthday of the church on Pentecost where the new believers "devoted themselves to the apostles' teaching and fellowship" (Acts 2:42). The commitment of the early church is to the word of God that comes through the apostles' teaching, but it is also connected to their fellowship with apostles and one another. The commitments to truth and to personal relationships are never separated. So when Paul writes to the church at Philippi, he can celebrate their fellowship in the gospel (Phil 1:5). This fellowship or *koinōnia* (κοινωνία), with one another is clearly based on their fellowship with God. John writes his own eyewitness account of the Word, "so that you may have fellowship with us; and our fellowship is with the Father and with his Son Jesus Christ" (1 Jn 1:3). The fellowship with the Father and the Son as well as the fellowship with other believers is based on the fellowship within the Trinity itself. The theological basis for the fellowship of the church is in the triune Godhead. God has fellowship and personal relationships in the Trinity, and men and women, created in the image of God, need the same with others who are in fellowship with God.

All through the New Testament it is clear that the church is bound by the Word of God and is under its instruction. "Every day in the temple and at home they did not cease teaching and preaching Jesus as the Christ" (Acts 5:42). The apostles declare that they cannot "give up preaching the word of God" for any other task. Rather, they devote themselves to prayer and "the ministry of the word" (6:2, 4). But this communication of the word to the church is not merely the transmission of knowledge from the apostles to the church. Rather, it is transmission plus application of God's word for the purpose of transformation, and it is embedded in the context of the fellowship of the body of Christ's ministry to one another (6:1-7).

The fellowship of the church is expressed concretely, for example, in terms of meeting the physical needs of members of the church from its earliest days (2:44-46). Later, Paul writes about the extended fellowship of the church in terms of relief to the saints (2 Cor. 8:4; 9:13).

The second area where an expression of *koinonia* as fellowship takes place relates to the reception of the Lord's Supper. In the same context where Paul talks about things that "were written down for our instruction" (1 Cor. 10:11), he talks about the believers' fellowship (participation/communion) in the blood and body of Christ (10:16). The reception of the Lord's supper is clearly one symbol of the fellowship they have with Christ and at the same time with one another. In this very context Paul describes the church as the body, emphasizing the communion among the believers in the church (10:17).[46]

So the church in this language category is described as a community under the word of God and committed to God's truth. At the same time it is a *communio sanctorum*, the communion of the saints. It may be valuable for the contemporary church to notice how closely wed these two things are in the Scripture lest we be tempted to be committed either to proclamation and teaching truth on the one side or to times of fellowship and developing relationships on the other. These two things must never be separated, and the model for it is in the Godhead, who himself is truth but who is characterized by fellowship within members of the Trinity.

Full Sanctification

Full presence of God. The concept of full sanctification in this category is a description of the full presence of God among his people. God, who has made himself known to his people in many ways, at times manifest himself in a fuller way. It happens at Mount Sinai and on the completion of the tabernacle (Ex 19—20; 40) and again at the dedication of the temple in Jerusalem (1 Kings 7—8; 2 Chron 5—7). It comes in the visions of Isaiah (Is 6) and Ezekiel (Ezek 1), and in the picture of God's return to his temple (Ezek 43). It is seen in the New Testament at the Mount of Transfiguration (Mt 17:1-13) and on the day of Pentecost (Acts 2). The Old Testament manifestations focus primarily on God the Father, whereas in the New Testament they focus on Jesus on the Mount of Transfiguration and on the Holy Spirit at Pentecost. In all cases where these special full manifestations of the presence of God appear, they come to those who are already believing followers of God.

Coming of Holy Spirit. The concept of full sanctification is particularly related to the coming of the Holy Spirit at Pentecost. The coming of the Holy Spirit is an answer to Jesus' prayer for the sanctification of his disciples (Jn 17:17). Further, Pentecost must be understood as the fulfillment of Jesus' teaching to his

---

[46]See John D. Zizioulas, *Being as Communion* (Crestwood, N.Y.: St. Vladimir's Seminary Press, 1997), pp. 143-69.

disciples about the coming of the Spirit in their lives. On the last night Jesus had with his disciples, we find that between Jesus' first two promises about the coming of the Spirit is a discussion of how the Father and the Son are going to manifest themselves to the disciples in the days to come (14:16-26). It is clear from the context that the disciples already have a significant relationship with the Father, the Son and the Holy Spirit. What Jesus is talking about is a fuller manifestation of the Trinity in the lives of his disciples. That manifestation comes with their sanctification in Acts 2.[47]

Full manifestation of God in Old Testament. While Pentecost represents the full manifestation of the presence of the Trinity in the lives of disciples under the New Covenant, this event cannot be properly interpreted except in the light of the other full manifestations of the presence of God in prior ages. In particular, the symbols and the language surrounding the full presence of God in the midst of his people must not be overlooked. At Mt. Sinai when God comes down to meet with his people, his immediate presence is symbolized by a cloud (Ex 19:9, 16; 24:15) and fire (19:18; cf. lightning, 19:16; 24:17; smoke, 19:18; 20:18). Certain sounds accompany the immediate presence of God such as thunder (19:16, 19; 20:18) and the trumpet (19:16, 19; 20:18). Further, God comes down to reveal himself by speaking to his people (19:19, 22; 20:1-17). After the initial offer of the covenant and the response of Israel to God's revelation of himself and his word, the glory of the Lord settles on Mt. Sinai (24:16), and the glory, symbolizing the presence of the Lord, is represented again by both the cloud and the fire (24:16-18).

When the tabernacle is constructed, God's full presence among his people is symbolized by the descent of his glory that fills the tabernacle (40:34). It is the glory of the Lord that is again symbolized by both a cloud and fire (40:35-38). The fact that the presence of the Lord symbolically dwells in the Holy of Holies of the tabernacle, is indicative of the centrality of holiness for understanding the presence of God. His presence is also bound up with the testimony of the revealed commandments of God that reside in the ark in the Holy of Holies. When you get closest to a holy God, he speaks to you. It is the Holy One that dwells in the midst of his people and speaks to them to make himself known.

A similar pattern is seen at the dedication of the temple of Solomon, where

---

[47]See Allan Coppedge and William Ury, *In His Image* (Franklin, Tenn.: Providence House, 2000), chaps. 7-9.

the presence of God comes as his glory and fills the temple (1 Kings 8:10-11; 2 Chron 5:14; 7:1-2). To these believing Israelites the glory of God is also symbolized by the cloud, which fills the house (1 Kings 8:10; 2 Chron 5:13-14), and the fire that comes down from heaven (2 Chron 5; 7:1-3). The presence of God, again, comes to dwell in the Holy of Holies, and again, the ark is also kept there as the symbol of both his immediate presence and his written revelation to his people (1 Kings 8:1, 6-10). Solomon then begins to declare to Israel a picture of God and to pray for the people (1 Kings 8:12-61; 2 Chron 6). It is interesting to observe that in the midst of this very Jewish occasion, Solomon reminds them about the universal purpose of God's coming: "that all the peoples of the earth may know that the LORD is God; there is no other" (1 Kings 8:60). The full manifestation of the presence of God is related, not only to the communication of God's word to Israel but also to the whole world. It is also on this occasion that Solomon exhorts the people, "Let your heart therefore be [perfect] to the LORD our God, walking in his statutes and keeping his commandments" (8:61). Evidently, keeping one's heart perfect before the Lord and walking in full obedience to his revealed word is bound up with the enjoyment of God's full presence in their lives.

In the visions of God's holy presence to the prophets, the brightness of his presence is manifested in his glory (Is 6:3; Ezek 1:27-28; 3:12, 23). Isaiah in particular describes his train (presence) that fills the temple (Is 6:1) and the earth as full of his glory (6:3). For both Isaiah and Ezekiel, fire is one of the symbols of the glorious presence of the Holy One (Is 6:4, 6; Ezek 1:4, 13-14, 27), and for Ezekiel the cloud is also coupled with the wind (Ezek 1:4). The wind, as a symbol of the presence of God, is related to the cloud in that both symbolize an element of mystery. But wind is also the same Hebrew word *ruach* that is translated "breath" or "spirit," and so is an accurate representation of the presence of the breath or Spirit of God. Certain sounds accompany the presence of God in both visions. Isaiah hears the voice of him who called (Is 6:4), while Ezekiel hears wings like many waters and also sounds like thunder and the tumult of a host (Ezek 1:24; 2:12). Both visions culminate in the explicit revelation of God's will for the prophet that they go forth to proclaim his word to his people (Is 6:8-13; Ezek 2:3-11).

Ezekiel 10 and 11 give a graphic and anthropomorphic picture of the departure of the full presence of God from among his people. Again his presence is symbolized by his glory (Ezek 10:4, 18-19; 11:22-23) and is represented by fire (10:2, 6-7) and the cloud (10:3-4). The Spirit of God which enters the prophet as a symbol of the full presence of God in his life for proclaiming God's message to Israel in an early vision (2:2; 3:24) also falls on the prophet as he speaks God's word of judgment against Israel (11:5-12). Ezekiel later has a vision of the return of the full presence of God to dwell in the midst of his people. His glory comes again (43:2, 4-5) and fills a new temple (43:5; 44:4). His presence is to be accompanied by the sound of many waters and in the brightness of his holy presence the earth shines (43:2). It is the Spirit of God in the prophet that lifts him up and makes it possible for him to behold the glory of the Lord entering the temple. God declares again that his purpose for dwelling in the midst of his people is that they should no more defile his holy name (43:7). It is interesting that while Ezekiel has this vision of God's glory returning to the temple, there is no record of this ever happening at the return from exile. It is possible the full return of God's presence is reserved for the coming of Jesus in the incarnation and the Holy Spirit at Pentecost.

Full manifestation of God in Jesus. In the New Testament the full coming of the personal presence of God among people is first bound up with the presence of Jesus. He is Emmanuel, "God with us" (Mt 1:23).[48] A special vision of the relationship between the Father and the Son is given to three of the disciples on the Mount of Transfiguration. It happens after their declaration of faith that Jesus is "the Christ, the Son of the living God" (Mt 16:16) and so comes as confirmation of their faith in Jesus. In this fuller revelation of the presence of God in Jesus, the disciples see his glory (Lk 9:32), and the brilliance of his presence is symbolized in that "his face shone like the sun, and his garments became white as light" (Mt 17:2). They are overshadowed by a bright cloud (17:5) from which a voice speaks, "This is my beloved Son, with whom I am well pleased; listen to him." God addresses the disciples by means of verbal communication as well as the symbols of his personal presence. Perhaps it is also reminiscent of God's manifestation at Mt. Sinai that Jesus takes them up on a high mountain for the purpose of receiving this revelation. The symbolic presence of Moses, representing the revelation of God in the law, and Elijah, representing the revelation of God through the prophets, is also a reminder of God's manifesting his presence to Moses at Mt. Sinai and to

---

[48]On Jesus as full manifestation of God see Torrance, *Christian Doctrine of God*, pp. 13-18.

Elijah on Mt. Carmel (1 Kings 18). The disciples get to share this vision with others, but they are warned not to do so until after Jesus is raised from the dead (Mt 17:9; cf. 2 Pet 1:16-18).

Full manifestation of God in the Holy Spirit. The full manifestation of the presence of God through the third person of the Trinity comes on the day of Pentecost. The full presence of God in the person of Jesus has just departed from them at the Ascension (Acts 1:9), and the disciples have been instructed to wait for the promise of the Father concerning the coming of the Holy Spirit (Is 59:21—61:3). It is significant that the Spirit comes on the day of Pentecost, the feast the Jews had come to associate with the giving of the law of God at Mt. Sinai. The festival of Pentecost represented God's full revelation of his word and his presence to his people. So when the disciples are filled with the Holy Spirit, they represent under the New Covenant what it means to experience the full manifestation of God's presence in the lives of believers. As temples of the Holy Spirit, they are filled with his presence in the same way that the tabernacle and the temple were filled with the presence of God in the previous age. While it is a cloud symbolizing the mysterious presence of God that receives Jesus into heaven (Acts 1:9), this symbol is replaced by the wind on the day of Pentecost (2:2). This wind fills all the house where they are sitting as a symbol of the Spirit of God that fills the disciples. The fire that had so frequently symbolized the presence of God is seen in the tongues of fire that are distributed and rest on the heads of each of those present. There is also the sound of the presence of God in the rush of a mighty wind filling the house, and immediately following the full manifestation of God's presence in the disciples, they begin to proclaim his word. This is symbolized by their speaking in other languages "the mighty works of God" (2:6-11). Peter, representing the whole group, stands before the multitude proclaiming the word of God in his great Pentecostal sermon (2:14-41).

Fullness of the Spirit. God has been preparing his people for understanding that the full manifestation of his presence to believers in the new age would be through the fullness of the Holy Spirit by connecting the work of the Holy Spirit in a fuller way with all the privileges promised in the New Covenant (Is 59:19-21). Through Ezekiel, God promises that he will put his Spirit within believers as a part of vindicating the holiness of his name (Ezek 36:27; 37:14), and it is his promise through Joel to pour out his Spirit on all flesh that Peter cites on the day of Pentecost as an explanation for the first coming of the Holy Spirit in this fullness (Joel 2:28-29; Acts 2:17-21).

The fullness of God's Spirit in the lives of the disciples brings them to the place, like it had Isaiah and Ezekiel, of total obedience to God's direction for their lives. His personal presence assumes control of their character and their conduct in a way not even accomplished with the physical presence of Jesus. God's full presence within them symbolizes an internal control over their total being.[49]

The full presence of God through his Holy Spirit is described earlier in the New Testament. John the Baptist is described as being "filled with the Holy Spirit" from his mother's womb (Lk 1:15). His mother Elizabeth is "filled with the Holy Spirit" before his birth (1:41), and his father Zechariah is "filled with the Holy Spirit" subsequent to John's birth (1:67). With slightly different language Simeon is described as one who is "righteous and devout" and "the Holy Spirit was upon him" (2:25). At his baptism Jesus has the Holy Spirit descend on him (3:21-22) and after this he is described as "full of the Holy Spirit" (4:1). Jesus himself describes this phenomenon in the language of Isaiah: "The Spirit of the Lord is upon me, because he has anointed me to preach good news to the poor" (Lk 4:18; Is 61:1). Jesus is not only described as full of the Holy Spirit early in the Gospel record, but he is also the one who baptizes with the Holy Spirit (Mt 3:11; Mk 1:8; Lk 3:16; Jn 1:33; Acts 1:5). Being baptized with the Holy Spirit and being filled with the Holy Spirit are used both to refer to this experience at Pentecost (Acts 1:5; 2:4).[50]

The day of Pentecost in one sense is a unique historical event just as much as Jesus' first call to his disciples. But in another sense it also becomes a pattern of

---

[49]For further discussion of the fullness of the Holy Spirit see Coppedge and Ury, In His Image, chaps. 8-9; NIDNTT, 1:735, 738-40; Charles W. Carter, The Person and Ministry of the Holy Spirit: A Wesleyan Perspective (Grand Rapids, Mich.: Zondervan, 1983), pp. 157-89; Asa Mahan, The Baptism of the Holy Ghost (New York: W. C. Palmer, 1870); Richard S. Taylor, Life in the Spirit (Kansas City, Mo.: Beacon Hill, 1966), pp. 78-90; Donald Metz, Studies in Biblical Holiness (Kansas City, Mo.: Beacon Hill, 1971), pp. 178-84; Daniel Steele, The Gospel of the Comforter (Apollo, Penn.: West, n.d.), pp. 247-50; J. A. Huffman, The Holy Spirit (Winona Lake, Ind.: Standard, 1944), pp. 217-31; Frederick D. Brunner, A Theology of the Holy Spirit (Grand Rapids, Mich.: Eerdmans, 1970), pp. 56-76, 155-218.

[50]For the debate about the baptism/fullness of the Spirit in relation to salvation or sanctification see James D. G. Dunn, Baptism of the Holy Spirit (Naperville, Ill.: A. R. Allenson, 1970); Laurence W. Wood, Pentecostal Grace (Wilmore, Ky.: Francis Asbury, 1980), pp. 19-35, 61-100, 177-239, 258-74; WTJ 14, no. 1 (1979); WTJ 14, no. 2 (1979); WTJ 15, no. 1 (1980). For those who separate the baptism of the Holy Spirit from the fullness of the Spirit see Billy Graham, The Holy Spirit (Waco, Tex.: Word, 1978), 62-73, 96-122; René Pache, The Person and Work of the Holy Spirit (Chicago: Moody Press, 1954), pp. 68-93, 114-49.

what Jesus would like to see in the lives of every individual. Just as he would like to call all persons to follow him, so he would like to have all disciples filled with the Holy Spirit. Certain Christians in the New Testament are described as full of the Holy Spirit, like Stephen (Acts 6:3, 5; 7:55) and Barnabas (11:24). The very fact that these Christians are described as having some unique things about them, including the fact that they are full of the Holy Spirit, means that not all Christians are full of the Holy Spirit. Further, there are a number of other examples in Acts of believers who are filled with the Holy Spirit. In Acts 4:31 a group of Jewish Christians are filled with the Holy Spirit when they recognize their lack of boldness in being a witness to Jesus as Peter was before the Sanhedrin. They pray for the power to speak the word with all boldness and are filled with the Holy Spirit (4:24-31). Three days after Paul's conversion on the road to Damascus, Ananias comes to pray for him that he might regain his sight and be filled with the Holy Spirit (9:17).[51]

Receiving the Holy Spirit. The fullness of God's personal presence through the Holy Spirit is sometimes described as receiving the Holy Spirit. Care must be exercised, however, not to imply that all believers have not received the Holy Spirit in an initial sense. The flexibility of language makes this terminology appear to mean in Acts the receiving of the Holy Spirit in a fuller sense than that which comes at the new birth. Thus the Samaritans, after believing the good news preached by Philip, responding to the kingdom of God and being baptized, "receive the Holy Spirit" when Peter and John come down from Jerusalem and pray for them (Acts 8:12-17). The disciples of Jesus in Ephesus have the Holy Spirit come on them when Paul lays his hands on them (19:1-6). Apparently, there is a telescoping of the works of grace in the lives of Cornelius and the god-fearing Gentiles in Acts 10. These, who already have a faith in God, respond to the preaching of Peter about Jesus, and the Holy Spirit falls on them. It is described in terms of the Holy Spirit been poured out on the Gentiles and their having "received the Holy Spirit" as the apostles have (10:44-47; 11:15-16; 15:8-9). For Cornelius and his family the recognition of Jesus as the basis of their faith in God comes simultaneously with the full manifestation of God's presence in their lives through the Holy Spirit. Whereas those two things are normally separated by time in others' experiences, they tend to merge for these believing Gentiles.

---

[51]For more on these comings of the Spirit see Coppedge and Ury, *In His Image*, chap. 11.

Fullness of God. The fullness of God's presence in the lives of believers is a part of Paul's desire for all Christians. After describing the whole concept of salvation by grace through faith in the lives of the Ephesians, he comes to pray for a deeper work of God's grace in their hearts. One part of that prayer is that they "may be filled with all the fulness of God" (Eph 3:19). This is certainly related to his subsequent exhortation to the Ephesians that they "be filled with the Spirit" (5:18). While his exhortation may be understood in terms of continuing to be filled with the Spirit, such an experience is not possible unless one has been initially filled at some point in time. This is most naturally understood in connection with Paul's earlier prayer for the fullness of God in their lives (3:19). A trinitarian understanding of how to relate to God explains the connection. To be filled with God the Father is the same as being filled with God the Holy Spirit.

Further Growth

Increasing knowledge of God and his will. Growth after full sanctification, when the full presence of God's Spirit indwells the believer, is related to God's further revelation of himself to an individual and the working out of God's revealed will in everyday life. So Paul may exhort the fully sanctified to "let the word of Christ dwell in you richly, as you teach and admonish one another in all wisdom" (Col 3:16). Even those who have experienced the fullness of God's sanctifying presence need further revelation of God through his word to their lives and additional working out of the implications of God's will in everyday living. For example, after praying for the Ephesians to be "filled with all the fulness of God" so they might enjoy the full fellowship of God's presence in their lives, Paul goes on to talk about three areas of working out the implications of that full manifestation in their fellowship with other individuals. The first has to do with fellowship within the body of Christ, i.e., the church (Eph 4:1-16), then he talks about personal ethical relationships in general (4:17—5:21), and finally, the personal relationships within the Christian household (5:22—6:9). There is obviously ample room for further growth after experiencing all the fullness of God.

Surrender of self-will and growing intimacy. While continued growth is related in part to increased understanding of the Word of God, a second factor relates to the ongoing development of one's intimate relationship with God. The coming of the fullness of God's presence in the life of the believer means God's total control of his will and therefore his life. But all person-to-person relationships must be cultivated and developed, and it is this ongoing development of a personal intimacy with God that is part of growth after sanctification. Because full sanctification involves the surrender of self-will in order to be filled with the fullness of God, it is now possible for the relationship with God to develop on an entirely different plane. Now there is a purity about the relationship that does not involve a self-centeredness on the part of the believer in the same way as previously. This means the will is wholly set to do the whole will of God and live under his complete control. The result is that the chief barrier for an even closer relationship to God, namely independent self-will, has now been removed, and so the possibility of greater and greater intimacy is opened. This developing closeness will come out of continued time in the presence of God, listening to his word and talking to him in prayer. Just as there is a depth and a closeness of human relationships that develops with much time spent together over a period of years, more and more time spent with God and living in his presence will produce an ever-increasing intimacy with him.

Glorification

Eternal fellowship. Glorification in this category is understood in terms of having an eternal relationship with God. It has to do with continuous intimate fellowship in the presence of God, like that which Jesus described to the thief on the cross when he said, "today you will be with me in Paradise" (Lk 23:43). Paul talks about those who will be alive when Christ returns as being "caught up together with them in the clouds to meet the Lord in the air; and so we shall always be with the Lord" (1 Thess 4:17). This eternal living in the immediate presence of God in eternity is symbolized in Revelation by the twenty-four elders who are seated around the throne of God and continually worshiping him (Rev 4:4, 10). Living in the fellowship of his presence begins in this world and continues throughout eternity.

Attributes of God

Truth. Two attributes are closely interwoven in the picture of God as Personal Revealer. One has to do with the revelation of God's word. This is the attribute of God's truth. It has particularly to do with veracity and relates to the fact that God's revelation of his word to his creatures is in exact conformity to his own will and nature. So the psalmist can exclaim, "Thou has redeemed me, O LORD, faithful God" (Ps 31:5), and "Thy law is true" (119:142). Jesus as the incarnate Word of God describes himself as truth (Jn 14:6), while he also declares that God's written word is truth (17:17). The rest of the New Testament echoes the sentiment that "it is impossible that God should prove false" (Heb 6:18), but "let God be true though every man be false" (Rom 3:4).[52]

Faithfulness. Closely bound up with the attribute of truth is that of faithfulness. Indeed, certain of the Hebrew words for truth may also be translated as "faithful" or "faithfulness," like *emet* (אֶמֶת) and *emuna* (אֱמוּנָה). In fact different translations of these words will sometimes use them with reference to God and other times in reference to his faithfulness (e.g., Ps 117:2). Likewise, in the New Testament *alētheia* (ἀλήθεία) is sometimes translated "truth" and at other times "faithfulness." So in both the Old Testament and the New Testament these two concepts are intimately bound together by the terms used to describe them.

God's faithfulness is particularly bound up with his own divine holy nature. By God's faithfulness the biblical writers mean consistency in God's character that is related to his immutability. His character, purposes and plans do not change. This consistency makes God a worthy object of the faith of individuals. In fact the Hebrew word *amen* is translated in the kal and niphal as "faithful," and in hiphil as the verb "believe." He who is faithful is a worthy object of the faith of his creatures. When God speaks a word, he is faithful to fulfill his promises. Even before the word faithful appears in reference to God in the Old Testament, he has demonstrated this quality of his character by his making and keeping of covenants. Beginning with Deuteronomy 7:9, which describes how a holy God is looking for a holy people, he begins explicitly to be described as "the faithful God who keeps covenant." Throughout the Old Testament he is repeatedly designated as faithful,[53] while Psalm 89 in particular relates his faithfulness to his holiness (89:2, 14-18, 24, 33-35, 49).

In the New Testament, God's faithfulness is often related to protection against temptation and evil (1 Cor 1:9; 10:13; 2 Thess 3:3). This faithfulness is

---

[52]For further discussion of truth, ἀλήθεία, as an attribute of God see *EDT*, pp. 1113-14; *NIDNTT*, 3:874-902; *TDNT*, 1:232-51; *TDOT*, 1:292-323; L. J. Kuper, "Grace and Truth: An Old Testament Description of God and Its Use in the Johannine Gospel," *Interpretation* 18 (1964): 3-19; Vriezen, *Outline of Old Testament Theology*, pp. 160-61; Miley, *Systematic Theology*, 1:210-11; Pope, *Compendium of Christian Theology*, 1:342-44; Hodge, *Systematic Theology*, 1:436-38.

[53]See Ps 40:10; 89:1, 2, 5, 8; 92:2; 100:5; 119:75, 90; 143:1; Is 49:7; Jer 42:5; Lam 3:23.

also bound up with the fellowship that Christians enjoy in the Lord, so that Paul can write, "God is faithful, by whom you were called into the fellowship of his Son, Jesus Christ our Lord" (1 Cor 1:9). Further, he is described as faithful in terms of his willingness to forgive sins (1 Jn 1:9) and to entirely sanctify (1 Thess 5:24). Jesus is also repeatedly described as faithful both to God (Heb 2:17; 3:2, 6) and to people (2 Tim 2:13; Heb 10:23). In one of the final pictures of Jesus, Revelation captures the duality of this attribute when it describes Jesus as "the Faithful and True" (Rev 19:11).[54]

So both truth as veracity and faithfulness as commitment are attributes that are intimately bound up with the holiness of God's character in terms of his role as Personal Revealer. The concept of truth is perhaps more directly related to the revelation of God's word, while that of faithfulness seems to be more closely tied with the personal presence of God in relationship with individuals. But the two are very difficult to divide.

Conclusion

The role of God as Personal Revealer appears first in the first chapter of Scripture and continues all the way to the last. Because it is behind all of the other major roles and subroles of God, it is in one sense the most extensive in the Bible. It accents the personal nature of God, who desires to communicate and relate to the persons he has created. While this role relates to those many places in Scripture where no other specific role identifies God in relation to persons, it also includes three subroles that give it more specifity: God as Prophet, God as Teacher and God as Friend.

There is historical significance in how God reveals himself personally throughout the Old Testament, in Jesus through the Gospels and through the Holy Spirit in the book of Acts. Likewise, all three persons of the triune God are seen interacting personally in the Epistles. The personal significance of God as Personal Revealer is obvious. God wants to enter into person-to-person relations with us; this role provides a theological foundation for understanding the three persons of the Trinity in interpersonal relationships.

The subroles of God as Personal Revealer further highlight this role's

---

[54]On the faithfulness of God see *EDT,* p. 402; *ISBE* (rev), 2:273-75; Bultmann, *Theology of the New Testament,* 1: 314-24; *NIDNTT,* 1:593-606; *TDNT,* 6:174-228; *ZPEB,* 2:479-91; Brunner, *Christian Doctrine of God,* pp. 271-75; *TWOT,* 1:51-52.

significance. Throughout history God has spoken to his people as both a Prophet and a Teacher. He continues to speak at the personal level as Teacher and Friend. Jesus fills both these roles uniquely as a disciple maker. Through Jesus' model God makes himself known as the God of truth and faithfulness in all personal relationships, showing us how these characteristics can be held together and, by our understanding of Jesus as being of one essence (*homoousia*) with the Father and the Spirit, representing these characteristics for the whole Trinity.

Six

Holy God
as Priest

The Unity Factor

The activities of God as Priest are connected to his various other roles by means of his holiness. Therefore, it is important that we begin by examining how God's holiness is expressed as brilliance in purity and grace. After such an examination we will be in a better position to understand how holiness as purity and grace are tied to the priestly role. Lastly, we will explore the various aspects of God's priestly role in relationship to a holy people.

Holiness as Brilliance: Purity and Grace

In the last chapter we dealt with the concept of holiness as brilliance in terms of God's immanence. We saw how this holiness as brilliance was expressed in terms of his personal presence and his personal communication. God's personal holy presence was evidenced in his glory and symbolized by cloud and by fire. His personal communication had to do particularly with his verbal communication of truth. This dual focus on God's brilliance led to a discussion of his role as Immanent Personal Revealer, i.e., the holy one who makes his personal presence known and can speak his word to his people. The focus of holiness as brilliance then was on God's presence and on God's truth, as is illustrated in figure 6.1.

HOLINESS ⟶ BRILLIANCE ⟶ IMMANENCE ⟨ PRESENCE / TRUTH ⟩ PERSONAL REVEALER

Figure 6.1. God's holiness as brilliance in his immanence

In this chapter we come to the closely associated concepts of holiness as brilliance in terms of purity and grace. While the brilliance of God's holiness is sometimes expressed in terms of both his presence and his communication of truth, at other times it is tied up with the language of purity and grace. Both purity and grace are closely woven together in the priestly role of God. Let's look at each in turn.

Purity. In our earlier discussion of the etymology of the Hebrew word *qodesh* we noted that one possible meaning might be derived from the Babylonian *quddushi* meaning "bright" or "clear." The concept of brightness or brilliance is closely associated with the symbol of fire and also easily associated with the concept of purification. Whether this is the best etymological meaning of the word or not, in Scripture the concept of God's holiness as brilliance certainly is often used in relationship to purity.[1] Not only is this true in the Old Testament with *qodesh* but in the New Testament the concepts of holiness and purity are combined in the word hagnos (αγνος).[2] Holiness and purity are so closely intertwined that Edmond Jacob can declare that purity "becomes the principle content of holiness. This is shown sometimes in the realm of morals and sometimes in that of ritual, and most often in both at once."[3] When this holiness has to do with God, it refers mainly to "separation from the impurity and the sinfulness of the creature, or, expressed positively, the clearness and purity of the divine nature."[4]

The fact that holiness as brilliance is related to the concept of God's immanence and also to the concept of purity means that there will be a number of very close ties between the discussion of holiness in this chapter and in the previous one. For example, the brilliance of God's personal presence (particularly as revealed in his glory) is often identified with purity or cleanness. And fire, which was one of the symbols of the personal presence and glory of God (as well as reflecting the focus on holiness as brilliance), is also closely tied with the concept of purification. It is fire that comes to burn away that which is impure and unclean and leaves the pure behind.

---

[1]For more on the concept of αγιος and purity see *TDNT,* 1:89; for קֶֹדשׁ see *TWOT,* 2:786-88; Norman H. Snaith, *Distinctive Ideas of the Old Testament* (New York: Schoken, 1964), pp. 24-5; *IDB,* 2:619; *HDB,* 2:397.

[2]On *hagnos* in terms of purity and holiness see *NIDNTT,* 3:100-102; *TDNT,* 1:122.

[3]Edmond Jacob, *Theology of the Old Testament,* trans. Arthur W. Heathcote and P. J. Allcock (New York: Harper & Row, 1958), p. 92; see also discussions of *katharos,* in connection with holiness and cleanness in *NIDNTT,* 3:102-8; *TDNT,* 3:413-31.

[4]Gustave Friedrich Oehler, *Theology of the Old Testament,* ed. George E. Day (Grand Rapids, Mich.: Zondervan, 1883), p. 110.

Grace. We will see that this holiness as brilliance is also expressed in terms of God's grace. There are two ways God's grace is joined with purity in changing people's lives. It is the grace of God that makes provision for sin in the atonement and so stands behind God's cleansing and purification of the individual. Grace makes purity possible. Further, it is grace that is expressed in the mercy of God and leads to the forgiveness of sins. So the holiness of God as purity leads to the expression of God's grace in terms of his transforming power to individuals. This happens subjectively in terms of cleansing that leads to a pure and holy life, and objectively in terms of mercy which leads to forgiveness, as illustrated in 6.2.

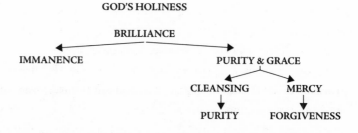

Figure 6.2. God's holiness leads to purity and grace

The Role of God as Priest

The description of God in terms of holiness as purity and grace relates to his role as Priest. The *language figure* for this *category* is derived from the sanctuary and the responsibilities of the priesthood in the tabernacle/temple. It is the language of the house of God, of sacrifice and of worship that describe the way God relates to people in terms of worship and religious ceremony.

There is a dual *focus* in this role on both *purity* and *grace*. Purity is that part of God's nature that says he is not like some things. In some ways it is the negative side of holiness, which indicates God is free from certain characteristics. In the Old Testament God identifies the holy with the pure and the clean and these reflect what has his approval. This is contrasted with the unholy, the common, the impure or the unclean. This is that which reflects ungodliness and does not have his approval. God uses the ceremonial law under the Old Covenant as an object lesson for teaching moral law. Things that were ceremonially pure, clean and holy lay the groundwork for a holy people to understand there are certain things that according to God's standard are holy, clean and pure. This means by contrast that there are other things that are common, unholy, impure and unclean in the moral realm. God's nature is the standard for that which was holy/clean/pure in moral conduct, attitudes and personal relationships. The ceremonial law that deals with issues of purity versus impurity are designed to help reinforce this crucial distinction in the minds of God's people.

The second part of the dual focus of this role is God's grace. There are three aspects of this grace. The first is that it symbolizes God's unmerited favor toward people. The second is that it refers to God's self-giving to persons. The third has to do with the resulting empowering of God so the people are able to do certain things that he asks. All three components of grace overlap and keep showing up repeatedly throughout Scripture. Regularly, we will see grace as unmerited favor, self-giving and as enabling power.

God as the gracious Priest mediates this grace in two ways. First, by making provision in the atonement for the possibility of cleansing from sin, and second, by exercising mercy and offering forgiveness to those who respond properly to him. For it is the grace of God that makes the atonement possible, and then that atonement becomes the basis for grace expressed in terms of mercy toward individuals. So God's grace provides a basis for purity on the one side and forgiveness on the other. Grace is behind the transformation of individuals in terms of the subjective purification of their lives as well as the objective change in their standing before God. Both cleansing and forgiveness are evidences of God's gracious reaching to people.[5]

The Father

Not called priest. The role of a priest is not seen equally in all three members of the Trinity. Neither the first nor the third persons of the Trinity is called a priest in Scripture, and it is really only with the second person of the Trinity that we see this role fully developed. Nevertheless, both the Father and the Holy Spirit function in the priestly role, and how they function in this capacity needs to be noted.

Mediator. A priest's basic function is that of a mediator. He is one who

---

[5]For further discussion of the grace of God in terms of both *hesed,* חֶסֶד, and *hen,* חֵן see *EDT,* pp. 479-82; *TDNT,* 10:372; *NIDNTT,* 2:115-23; *ZPEB,* 2:799-804; Guthrie, *New Testament Theology* (Downers Grove, Ill.: InterVarsity Press, 1981), pp. 105-7, 602-40.

represents God to people and people to God. In other words he stands between God and people and mediates between the two. When the mediator represents God to people, he does so principally in terms of teaching or communicating the word of God and in terms of making provision for atonement for sin so that sin might be removed as a barrier between God and people. When a mediator represents the people before God, he does it in terms of intercession or prayer for them and their needs and in seeking God's will on their behalf. But the mediator also assists people in seeking God through God's provision of the atonement. This involves the priestly role of making sacrifices, assisting people in seeking forgiveness and teaching them to worship God.

We need to understand which of these categories apply to God the Father. His teaching role in communicating his word to men has already been dealt with under the role of God as Personal Revealer. Further, the Father is not praying for people in the same way that the Son and the Spirit will be seen to do. The basic reason for this is that he is the ultimate, and there is not another god or force above or beyond him to which he needs to intercede on behalf of people. Nevertheless, God does play a mediating role in terms of making provision for the atonement and in helping people seek him based on that provision. Both of these need further exploration.

Provision of the atonement. In his mediating role as priest God basically makes the provision of atonement for sin which makes possible a new relationship between God and people. Just as a mediator would take initiative in this area from God to the people, so God takes the initiative in salvation to reach out to people. In the Old Testament it is God who initiates the establishment of covenants with Abraham (Gen 12) and with Moses and the children of Israel (Ex 3:1-10). In the New Testament it is the Father who initiates sending Jesus into the world to provide salvation for all. "But God shows his love for us in that while we were yet sinners Christ died for us" (Rom 5:8).

Not only does God take the initiative in salvation in his priestly role, but he provides the basis of salvation in the atonement. He first sets the pattern for this atonement in the Exodus, where he allows the provision of a sacrifice as a substitute for the life of the oldest son. Under the threat of death the oldest sons in Israel could be saved through the sacrifice of a lamb. The blood of the lamb put on the doorpost of the house was to be the evidence that a life had been offered for a life. Accompanying the substitute life-for-life was the covenant meal symbolizing the fellowship between God and his people (Ex 11—12). By means of the annual celebration of this Passover event God taught Israel some basic theology of the atonement. They learned the reality of the threat of spiritual death but also that God would allow a substitute death through a sacrifice. They learned that the symbol of life given up for life was the blood and that by this means God would deliver his people spiritually as well as physically from the powers of evil. The Passover meal was then eaten to symbolize God's provision of redemption, and also to indicate the fellowship available between God and people.

At Mount Sinai God provided the day of atonement (Lev 16) as a symbol of how Israel was to deal with sin. This annual reminder of sin had the high priest dress in holy garments to come into the holy place of the temple where God said he would "appear in the cloud upon the mercy seat" (16:2). There the high priest was to offer a sin offering for himself and one for the people, with the blood of the offerings symbolizing life shed on behalf of those represented. Then over the head of the scapegoat the priest was to confess the sins and iniquities of the people, and then send the goat away into the wilderness as a symbol of the forgetfulness of God's mercy. Israel's sins were to be put away from them and forgotten by God while his anger at their sin was propitiated. God said his purpose was that "this day shall atonement be made for you, to cleanse you; from all your sins you shall be clean before the LORD" (16:30).

Since God provided direction in the Old Testament as to how the atonement was to be based, it is not surprising that he also provided the atonement in the New Testament. As John put it, "God so loved the world that he gave his only Son, that whoever believes in him should not perish but have eternal life" (Jn 3:16). Paul declared that this salvation is "by his grace as a gift, through the redemption which is in Christ Jesus, whom God put forward as [a propitiation] by his blood, to be received by faith" (Rom 3:24-25).

By means of taking initiative toward people in providing the basis of salvation, God basically is mediating between himself and individuals. While God the Father is not described by the term *mediator*, he in fact does serve a priestly mediating role between individuals and himself. That is the whole purpose of his provision of the atonement as a means to bring about reconciliation and fellowship between himself and people.

Appropriation of the atonement. A priest also serves the mediating role of assisting people in taking advantage of the atonement and its provisions. Part of this role is to pronounce the forgiveness and cleansing of God on individuals when they properly come seeking God, appropriating by faith the sacrifices made on their behalf. While a priest can only pronounce God's forgiveness and cleansing to worshipers, God can actually forgive and cleanse. This is his function and where we see him filling his priestly role.

God offers forgiveness based on atonement (Lev 16:21-22); thus the psalmist can exclaim, "Blessed is he whose transgression is forgiven, whose sin is covered. Blessed is the man to whom the LORD imputes no iniquity" (Ps 32:1-2; Rom 4:7-8). Paul clearly connects the forgiveness of iniquities with the atonement of Christ's death (Rom 3:24, 26; 4:6-7). He states that in Christ "we have redemption through his blood, the forgiveness of our trespasses, according to the riches of his grace" (Eph 1:7). And the writer of Hebrews reminds the Christians that "almost everything is purified with blood, and without the shedding of blood there is no forgiveness of sins" (Heb 9:22).

In addition to God offering forgiveness, he also fulfills the priestly role of purifying and cleansing. This role is first inaugurated through the responsibility of the Hebrew priests in Leviticus, but it is clear from the rest of Scripture that it is God who does the actual purification (Is 1:18; 6:7; Ezek 36:25, 29, 31, 33; Ps 51:2, 7). While a priest may declare that a person is clean based on the individual having met certain requirements in terms of sacrifice and worship, it is God who actually makes the person pure. Ultimately, the human priest is only speaking to declare verbally what God does *in fact* in the individual.

In summary we may say that the chief way in which God the Father is understood as a priestly mediator is in terms of providing the atonement for people and pronouncing the benefits of the atonement on them in terms of forgiveness and cleansing.

The Son

High priest. While God the Father is not called a priest in Scripture, Jesus is designated under the New Covenant as our High Priest,[6] and this is where the real picture of the divine priestly role must be understood. His priestly role is described in various passages throughout the New Testament, but it is particu-

---

[6]For further discussion of Jesus as High Priest see *NIDNTT*, 3:404-2; George Eldon Ladd, *A Theology of the New Testament* (Grand Rapids, Mich.: Eerdmans, 1974), pp. 578-84; William Pope, *A Compendium of Christian Theology* (London: Wesleyan-Methodist Book Room, 1880), 2:218-21.

larly in the book of Hebrews that he is given this title (Heb 3:1; 8:1).[7] The many parallels between Hebrews and Leviticus regarding priestly responsibilities and matters dealing with the sanctuary and sacrifice make it natural for the writer to describe Jesus in this way.

Makes atonement. In his priestly role Jesus is the one who makes atonement as a basis for the forgiveness of sins and cleansing. He is described as "a merciful and faithful high priest in the service of God, to make expiation for the sins of the people" (Heb 2:17). It is this high priest who "entered once for all into the Holy Place, taking not the blood of goats and calves but his own blood, thus securing an eternal redemption" (9:12). Unlike other priests, Jesus had to offer a sacrifice only once: "He has appeared once for all at the end of the age to put away sin by the sacrifice of himself" (9:26).[8]

Sacrifice. The New Testament makes it clear that Jesus not only serves as a High Priest but he also serves as a sacrifice to be offered unto God. John the Baptist introduces him, "Behold, the Lamb of God, who takes away the sin of the world" (Jn 1:29). As the Lamb of God he becomes the substitutionary sacrifice for the lives of those who deserve to die. So Jesus "gave himself up for us, a fragrant offering and sacrifice to God" (Eph 5:2).[9] The sacrifice Jesus made was not for his own sin but the sins of others. "He did this once for all when he offered up himself" (Heb 7:27). All the sacrificial system in the Old Testament, which was designed to teach that a substitute sacrifice could be offered for life, finds its fruition in the work of Jesus in his once-and-for-all death on the cross. This sacrifice never has to be repeated. "He has appeared once for all at the end of the age to put away sin by the sacrifice of himself" (Heb 9:26, 28; see also 10:10, 12, 14).[10] Thus Jesus becomes "the last sacrifice" because he fulfills in reality what the Old Testament sacrifices only did symbolically. After the cross both the symbolic and the teaching functions of sacrifice are over. This is part of what it means for the atonement for sin to be a finished work.[11]

---

[7]Cf. Heb 10:21 where Jesus is called a "great priest."

[8]See also Heb 7:26-27; 13:12. Cf. Mt 26:28.

[9]On Jesus as the sacrificial Lamb of God see Leon Morris, *The Apostolic Preaching of the Cross* (London: Tyndale Press, 1965), pp. 129, 143.

[10]See Thomas Oden, *Word of Life* (San Francisco: Harper & Row, 1989), pp. 362-73.

[11]On the use of sacrificial language in the church subsequent to the cross see Colin Gunton, "The Sacrifice and the Sacrifices: From Metaphor to Transcendental?" in *Trinity, Incarnation and Atonement,* ed. Ronald J. Feenstra and Cornelius Plantinga Jr. (Notre Dame, Ind.: University of Notre Dame Press, 1989), pp. 210-29.

Propitiation theory of the atonement. This picture of Jesus as the High Priest making atonement and of Jesus being the sacrifice for sin is at the heart of atonement in terms of propitiation and expiation. These are terms borrowed from the temple language of worship and have to do with the whole question of sacrifice. Any view related to this understanding of the atonement involves a heavy element of substitution. Christ himself is the substitutionary or vicarious sacrifice. But the focus of the sacrifice and its purposes need a further word.

In four different places the propitiation word group *hilaskomai* (ἱλάσκομαι) appears in the New Testament, emphasizing its importance for understanding the death of Christ on the cross. Paul in his major discussion of salvation by faith talks about Jesus Christ "whom God put [forth to be a propitiation] by his blood, to be received by faith" (Rom 3:25). Hebrews describes Jesus in his role as "merciful and faithful high priest in the service of God, to make [propitiation] for the sins of the people" (Heb 2:17). And John twice speaks of this ministry of Jesus. "If any one does sin, we have an advocate with the Father, Jesus Christ the righteous; and he is [a propitiation] for our sins, and not for ours only but also for the sins of the whole world" (1 Jn 2:1-2). John particularly emphasizes that this work was done out of God's love for people. "In this is love, not that we loved God but that he loved us and sent his Son to be the [propitiation] for our sins" (1 Jn 4:10).

The focus of this propitiation is to deal with the wrath of God. The wrath of God is possibly one of the most avoided concepts in contemporary Christian thought. But it need not be so. Its avoidance perhaps comes from thinking that this response of God is unworthy of him. In reality it is the divine righteous rejection of all that is evil and wrong. It is motivated by love and a desire of God to free his people from that which would destroy them. The focus of the wrath of God is on sin, so that propitiation averts the wrath of God from the sinner by propitiating him or making him favorable toward the sinner. It is the substitute life offered for life that allows for the satisfaction of God's righteous anger against sin and allows him then to respond in a more favorable and gracious way to individuals.[12]

The complementary side of propitiation is expiation. The focus of expiation is the covering of sin so that it no longer is a barrier between God and people. Sin is the object here, and expiation involves the covering, putting away or rubbing out of

---

[12]For a very significant discussion of the key propitiation words, see Morris, *Apostolic Preaching of the Cross*, pp. 144-213.

sin so that it cannot hinder the fellowship between God and individuals. Since expiation involves less discussion of the wrath of God, it is sometimes used in place of the word propitiation to soften the impact of the propitiation concept (See RSV, NEB translations of the above texts). Scripture seems to indicate that both of these elements are involved in the sacrificial work of Christ in the atonement.[13]

Order of Melchizedek. Just as the high priest in the Old Testament did not exalt himself to that position, so Jesus also was appointed to this responsibility by God who said to him, "Thou art a priest for ever, after the order of Melchizedek" (Heb 5:6, 10; Ps 110:4; also Heb 6:20; 7:17). This appointment to the Melchizedekian priesthood is significant, because unlike other high priests, who were prevented from continuing in their office because of death, Jesus continues forever, and is therefore able to save those who come to God through him (Heb 7:23-25). The effectiveness of his priesthood is also related to his character. This high priest is "holy, blameless, unstained, separated from sinners, exalted above the heavens. He has no need, like those high priests, to offer sacrifices daily, first for his own sins and then for those of the people; he did this once for all when he offered up himself" (7:26-27). He who is holy and therefore sinless does not need a sacrifice for himself but is able to give himself as a perfect sacrifice for others.[14]

Purifier. The Scripture also speaks of a purifying role that any priest plays in relationship to individuals. In one of the Old Testament references to the coming of the Messiah, he is described as "like a refiner's fire and like fullers' soap; he will sit as a refiner and purifier of silver, and he will purify the sons of Levi and refine them like gold and silver" (Mal 3:3). Hebrews declares that if the blood of goats and bulls sanctifies for the purification of the flesh, "how much more shall the blood of Christ, who through the eternal Spirit offered himself without blemish to God, purify your conscience from dead works to serve the living God" (Heb 9:14). This purification or cleansing is also based on the atonement because "under the law

---

[13]For an excellent discussion of the relationship of propitiation to expiation and the relationship of both to the wrath of God see J. I. Packer, *Knowing God* (Downers Grove, Ill.: InterVarsity Press, 1973), pp. 161-72; Oden, *Word of Life*, pp. 392-93.

[14]For further discussion of the priestly office of Jesus see *EDT*, pp. 875-76; *ISBE*, 1:654-55; Oscar Cullmann, *The Christology of the New Testament* (London: SCM Press, 1963), pp. 83-107; Emil Brunner, *The Christian Doctrine of Creation and Redemption* (London: Lutterworth, 1952), pp. 281-97; Charles Hodge, *Systematic Theology* (London: James Clark, 1960), pp. 464-79; Louis Berkhof, *Systematic Theology* (Edinburgh: Banner of Truth, 1958), pp. 361-66; Pope, *Compendium of Old Testament Theology*, 2:216-49; Wolfhart Pannenberg, *Jesus, God and Man*, trans. Lewis L. Wilkins and Duane A. Priebe (Philadelphia: Westminster Press, 1968), p. 219; John Calvin, *Institutes of the Christian Religion*, trans. John Allen (Philadelphia: Westminster Press, 1936), 1:548-50.

almost everything is purified with blood" (9:22).

Mediator. It is the role of Jesus as High Priest in making atonement for the sins of the world that makes him a mediator. As Paul puts it, "there is one God, and there is one mediator between God and men, the man Christ Jesus, who gave himself as a ransom for all" (1 Tim 2:5-6). Hebrews closely relates Christ's mediatorial work with the giving of the New Covenant. "Christ has obtained a ministry which is as much more excellent than the old as the covenant he mediates is better" (Heb 8:6), and "therefore he is the mediator of a new covenant" (9:15).[15]

God-man. Jesus is uniquely suited to be mediator between God and humans because he is the unique God-man. The combination of divinity and humanity in the person of Jesus allows him to serve in this role. This is why he is the mediator *par excellence*, in an even fuller way than either the Father or the Holy Spirit. Neither the first nor the third members of the Trinity are divine and human in the same way that Jesus is, and therefore cannot play the same mediating role in the perfect way that he does. One dimension of this mediating role is that in his divinity he is the one who forgives and cleanses, but in his humanity he is the one who calls individuals to an experience of forgiveness and cleansing. Because of the uniqueness of his person, he is the only one able to do this work in this way.[16]

Intercessor. As High Priest Jesus not only mediates between God and individuals in terms of establishing a relationship between them, that is, making reconciliation, but he also continues to serve as the means of maintaining this relationship. Thus he helps us "hold fast our confession." He is able to do this because as our High Priest he is able to sympathize with our weaknesses having "been tempted as we are, yet without sinning" (Heb 4:14-15; also 2:17-18). Part of this ongoing mediatorial role for Jesus is in terms of his intercession for believers. "Consequently he is able for all time to save those who draw near to God through him, since he always lives to make intercession for them" (7:25). A graphic picture of Jesus in this role comes in his high priestly prayer in John 17, where Jesus prays not only for his disciples (Jn 17:9-19) but also for others who were

---

[15]See also Heb 12:24. On Jesus as Mediator see *EDT*, pp. 701-2; *ZPEB*, 4:150-58; Jacob, *Theology of the Old Testament*, p. 249; Theodorus Vriesen, *An Outline of Old Testament Theology*, trans. S. Neuijen (Bristol: John Wright, 1911), p. 265; Alan Richardson, *An Introduction to the Theology of the New Testament* (London: SCM Press, 1958), pp. 229, 232; Emil Brunner, *The Mediator*, trans. Olive Wyon (London: Lutterworth, 1934), pp. 490-514; Hodge, *Systematic Theology*, 2:455; Calvin, *Institutes* I:506-17; CD 4, pp. 122-28.

[16]On the hypostatic union see Oden, *Word of Life*, pp. 164-94; Thomas F. Torrance, *Mediation of Christ* (Grand Rapids, Mich.: Eerdmans, 1984), pp. 57-82; Brunner, *Mediator*, pp. 490-514.

to believe in him (17:20-21). After his death, resurrection and ascension Jesus continues to pray for believers. It is "Christ Jesus, who died, yes, who was raised from the dead, who is at the right hand of God, who indeed intercedes for us" (Rom 8:34).[17]

In summary, we may say that Jesus is able to uniquely fulfill the role of a mediating priest because of his unique person. As the God-man he is able to represent God to people and people to God as no one else has ever been able to do. In representing God to people he does so in his role as Teacher and more particularly for our purposes in this chapter as the Priest who makes atonement for his people. Further, he is the one who is the sacrifice by which atonement is made. But he also uniquely represents individuals to God in calling men and women to follow him and come into a personal relationship with God based on forgiveness and cleansing. He not only calls people to this experience but has the prerogative of pronouncing them forgiven and clean as no one else is able to do. Once they respond to God in forgiveness and with a clean heart, he continues his mediatorial ministry for them in prayer.

The Holy Spirit

Mediator. The Holy Spirit, like the Father, is not referred to directly as a priest in Scripture. He does however serve in some of the priestly functions. For example, the Spirit has a mediating function with Christ in the atonement. Paul can write that through Christ "we both have access in one Spirit to the Father" (Eph 2:18). The Spirit helps apply the work of the atonement to individual lives and thus assists Jesus in mediating between people and God.

Intercessor. Closely related is the role of the priest in terms of intercession. We need the Spirit's priestly ministry in our prayer lives "for we do not know how to pray as we ought, but the Spirit himself intercedes for us with sighs too deep for words." The Spirit is an excellent mediator in this function because he knows both the hearts of individuals as well as the mind of God, and therefore "intercedes for the saints according to the will of God" (Rom 8:26-27).

Purifier. The priestly ministry of the Spirit is related to initial cleansing in the passage where Paul writes, "You were washed, you were sanctified, you were

---

[17]For further discussion of Jesus as Intercessor see Hodge, *Systematic Theology*, 2:592-94; Berkhof, *Systematic Theology,* pp. 400-405; Pannenberg, *Jesus, God and Man*, pp. 219, 221.

justified in the name of the Lord Jesus Christ and in the Spirit of our God" (1 Cor 6:11). It is also related to a deeper cleansing of the heart in sanctifying grace. Thus David couples his cry for the creation of a clean heart with his plea that the Holy Spirit of God not be taken from him. "Create in me a clean heart, O God, and put a new and right spirit within me. Cast me not away from thy presence, and take not thy holy Spirit from me" (Ps 51:10-11). Peter, describing the work of the Holy Spirit among the Gentiles, can declare to the Jerusalem conference, "God who knows the heart bore witness to them, giving them the Holy Spirit just as he did to us; and he made no distinction between us and them, but cleansed their hearts by faith" (Acts 15:8-9).

Temple of the Holy Spirit. The final place where the Holy Spirit is closely bound up with the role of the priest is in connection with the use of the language of the sanctuary in describing Christians as the temple of the Holy Spirit. References to the tabernacle or temple are certainly related to his work as a Priest. So Paul challenges the Corinthians, "Do you not know that you are God's temple and that God's Spirit dwells in you? If any one destroys God's temple, God will destroy him. For God's temple is holy, and that temple you are" (1 Cor 3:16-17; also 6:19). Like the priest representing the presence of God in his temple, the Holy Spirit represents the presence of God in the lives of individuals. Further, the Holy Spirit continues to indwell the temple of the believer's life and stands for the ongoing ministry of the presence of God to him.

Man and Woman

Worshipers of God. In the language of the sanctuary, men and women are seen as worshipers of God. This is part of who they are. People were created to worship the God who made them. Individuals have a built-in need to praise God, to pray to God and to rejoice in God. Because persons are social beings, made for relationships with other people, they need to worship God in community. So the sanctuary is designed for the worshiping community to seek God and to praise him.

Conditional element: Holiness as purity. But there is a conditional factor related to worshiping God, and that is reflecting his holy nature. It is in the middle of a discussion with Israel about how they are to worship him that God makes it clear that they are to be holy for he is holy. "For I am the LORD your God; consecrate yourselves therefore, and be holy, for I am holy" (Lev 11:44-45). So a holy God desires worshipers of himself to be holy as well.

A holy God, who is pure from all unholiness and uncleanness, desires a relationship with worshiping people that requires them to be pure. It is within the same context that God charges his people to distinguish between the holy and the common that he makes them differentiate between the clean and the unclean (Lev 10:10). Therefore, the psalmist can question, "Who shall stand in his holy place?", i.e., in his holy presence. And the answer is, "He who has clean hands and a pure heart" (Ps 24:3-4).

This pattern of purity continues in the New Testament when Jesus gives his description of the character he wants to see in his disciples in his statement, "Blessed are the pure in heart" (Mt 5:8). It is clear that it will be the pure in heart who will see God, and this seems to be synonymous with the holiness that Hebrews describes as necessary to see him (Heb 12:14). So because God is holy and pure and he made people to be like himself, he desires for them to be holy and pure as well. It will be those whose hearts are pure from sin, i.e., unholiness, that will be ready to see God and enjoy his presence eternally. As J. C. Moyer puts it, "The laws of cleanness were indirect aids to remind the ancient Israelite of the purity and holiness of his God."[18] Ritual purity was intertwined with moral purity to effect God's holy purposes in the lives of his people.

Sin

Impurity. While a holy God who is pure desires a holy people who are pure, people are actually found to be in a different state. In reality men and women are impure and unclean, i.e., unholy or unlike the character of a holy God. Sin therefore in this category is sometimes described as an offense against a pure God which needs his forgiveness.[19] Leviticus goes to great length to describe how a priest shall make atonement for these sins against God's purity as a basis for forgiveness (Lev 4:26, 31, 35; 5:10, 13, 16, 18; 6:7).[20] Atonement must be made for sin against a pure God and only on the basis of such an atonement is God able to grant forgiveness. Yet the means must not be confused with the ends. "It was not the ritual purification from the officiating priest which ultimately mattered, but the forgiveness from God which rendered men clean

---

[18] *EDT,* p. 253.

[19] *EDT,* p. 421; John Miley, *Systematic Theology* (New York: Methodist Book Concern, 1894), 2:310-11.

[20] On atonement and forgiveness see Walther Eichrodt, *Theology of the Old Testament,* trans. J. A. Baker (London: SCM Press, 1967), 2:443-64, 465-85.

before him."[21] There is an impurity related to transgressions and sins that requires atonement to cleanse and hallow it (Lev 16:16-19).

Uncleanness. Sin is also described in terms of uncleanness that needs cleansing. So Leviticus states that the purpose of the day of the atonement was "to cleanse you; from all your sins you shall be clean before the LORD" (Lev 16:30). The psalmist says "Wash me thoroughly from my iniquity, and cleanse me from my sin!" (Ps 51:2, 6-7, 10). Jesus uses this same category when he describes the source of defilement as the heart (Mk 7:18-23).[22]

Sin described as being an offense against a pure God that requires forgiveness refers more to the objective description of sin in terms of the individual's relationship with God. There is a ritual uncleanness that relates to acts of sin. This kind of sin relates more to specific acts against God. However, when sin is described as uncleanness and needing cleansing, it has to do more with the subjective nature of sin within the individual. Sin, thus described, relates both to the uncleanness of guilt that results from individual transgressions and to the deeper state of uncleanness that is a part of one's fallen sinful nature. The deeper biblical description of uncleanness in terms of sin normally relates to the sin principle imbedded within the heart. It refers more to a state of sin rather than to individual transgressions.

Salvation

Initial cleansing. Saving grace is described in the priestly category as an experience of initial cleansing of the individual from guilt, condemnation and punishment. God says of his people, "I will cleanse them from all the guilt of their sin . . . and rebellion against me" (Jer 33:8). To restore them to this right relationship God commands them, "Wash yourselves; make yourselves clean; remove the evil of your doings from before my eyes" (Is 1:16). And if they will do this, he promises, "Though your sins are like scarlet, they shall be as white as snow; though they are red like crimson, they shall become like wool" (Is 1:18). Isaiah declares God's people will then be called holy, "when the Lord shall have washed away the filth of the daughters of Zion and cleansed the bloodstains of Jerusalem from its midst by a spirit of judgment and by a spirit of burning" (4:3-4). Many of the

---

[21] *TWOT,* 1:344.
[22] For more on ἀκάθαρτος, "uncleanness," and ἀκαθαρσία, "impurity," see *TDNT,* 3:427-29; *BDT,* pp. 21.

Old Testament references to this initial cleansing relate to a recovery of Israel from a condition of backsliding. Thus God can say to Ezekiel, "I will save them from all the backslidings in which they have sinned, and will cleanse them; and they shall be my people, and I will be their God" (Ezek 37:23).

In the New Testament Hebrews talks about how through the blood of Christ it is possible to "purify your conscience from dead works to serve the living God" (Heb 9:14), and Peter declares that the Christians have purified their souls by their "obedience to the truth" (1 Pet 1:22). When God gives Peter a vision of the Gentiles coming to Christ, he reminds him, "What God has cleansed, you must not call common" (Acts 10:15, 11:9). Paul connects a first cleansing with an initial sanctification and justification when he writes, "And such were some of you. But you were washed, you were sanctified, you were justified in the name of the Lord Jesus Christ and in the Spirit of our God" (1 Cor 6:11). Paul also describes the cleansing power of regeneration when he reminds Titus that God "saved us, not because of deeds done by us in righteousness, but in virtue of his own mercy, by the washing of regeneration and renewal in the Holy Spirit" (Tit 3:5).[23]

This initial cleansing at conversion deals not so much with the deeper depravity of our sinful nature but of our acquired depravity due to our own sinful actions. This subjective cleansing is closely aligned with the work of God in regenerating our natures. In a sense it is the negative side of regeneration that removes from of our lives guilt, defilement and condemnation. As Richard Taylor puts it, "There is a feeling of cleanness and of newness in the assurance of forgiveness. Pollution in the sense of defilement, guilt and condemnation is gone."[24] While cleansing is the more negative side of saving grace, the positive side is subsumed under the categories of the renewal of the moral image of God within us, the regenerating of our nature and the experience of being born again to new life. All of this happens concomitantly in the experience of saving grace, but within the priestly category of the sanctuary, it is the cleansing of our acquired depravity that receives the focus.

Forgiveness. Cleansing is often closely related to forgiveness in the language of the sanctuary (Jer 33:8; 1 Jn 1:9). The language of forgiveness is not in any way exclusively related to the vocabulary of the sanctuary. It also relates to the family

---

[23]For further discussion of salvation as an initial cleansing from guilt and defilement see Pope, *Compendium of Christian Theology*, 3:29-31; *BDT*, pp. 121-23; Miley, *Systematic Theology*, 2:356-62.

[24]*BDT*, p. 122.

terminology of the household. However, it is important to notice that there is a very close relationship between cleansing and forgiveness. Forgiveness is part of the blessing of a right relationship with God, as the psalmist declares, "Blessed is he whose transgression is forgiven, whose sin is covered" (Ps 32:1; Rom 4:7-8). This forgiveness is part of God's promise of blessings under the New Covenant (Jer 31:34). When John the Baptist begins to preach repentance for the forgiveness of sins, he is preparing the way in the hearts of many for the coming of the Messiah as the fulfillment of the New Covenant (Mk 1:4).

From Jesus' perspective the wholeness of forgiveness is even more crucial than physical healing (Mt 9:2; Mk 2:5; Lk 5:20). It is not surprising then that after the ascension of Jesus he instructs his disciples that part of their responsibility is "that repentance and forgiveness of sins should be preached in his name to all nations, beginning from Jerusalem" (Lk 24:47). This is the message not only of the apostles but also of the early church, as seen in the ministry of Barnabas and Paul on their missionary journeys (e.g., Acts 13:38). Paul declares that in his Damascus Road experience he was called by God to the Gentiles "that they may receive forgiveness of sins" (Acts 26:18). This forgiveness he believes is a product of the grace of God through the death of Christ. "In him we have redemption through his blood, the forgiveness of our trespasses, according to the riches of his grace" (Eph 1:7; see 4:32; Col 1:14; 2:13; 3:13).

1. *Conditions: Repentance and Faith.* One of the conditions for receiving the forgiveness of God is repentance (Lk 3:3; 24:47; Mk 1:4; Acts 2:38). Repentance involves an acknowledgement of sin, a confession of sin and a turning away from that sin. It is the confession of sin about which John writes when he says, "If we confess our sins, he is faithful and just, and will forgive our sins" (1 Jn 1:9). The second condition for receiving the forgiveness of God is an act of faith. This is the proximal condition for receiving God's forgiveness. This means that when a person exercises faith in God to forgive him for Christ's sake, that is the point at which he receives forgiveness. While repentance may be a secondary or remote condition for forgiveness, faith is the immediate condition. The connection between faith and God's forgiveness is illustrated in the story of Jesus forgiving the sins of the sinful woman, when he says to her, "Your faith has saved you; go in peace" (Lk 7:48-50; cf. Mk 2:5).

2. Symbol: Baptism. The symbol for this initial cleansing and forgiveness is water. Thus John the Baptist, who is preaching a repentance for the forgiveness of sins, declares, "I baptize you with water for repentance" (Mt 3:11). The apostles proclaim in the days of the early church, "Repent, and be baptized every one of you in the name of Jesus Christ for the forgiveness of your sins" (Acts 2:38), and Ananias can say to Paul after his Damascus Road experience, "Rise and be baptized, and wash away your sins, calling on his name" (22:16).[25] As water cleanses away physical uncleanness (as in the washing of hands), so it becomes an apt symbol for removal of spiritual uncleanness in baptism.

Growth in Grace

Maintaining purity. The new relationship to God that results from a cleansing of guilt and a receiving of forgiveness must be maintained. Part of growth has to do with maintaining this purity or cleanliness that is established in salvation. The continuousness of this cleansing is founded on an ongoing need for the atonement (Lev. 16:30). Accordingly, the psalmist can pray, "Clear thou me from hidden faults. Keep back thy servant also from presumptuous sins; let them not have dominion over me! Then I shall be blameless, and innocent of great transgression" (Ps 19:12-13). This continued purity is based on a commitment to live under the authority of the word of God (19:7-13). To the question "How can a young man keep his way pure?" the response is, "By guarding it according to thy word" (119:9). Growth after conversion is dependent not only on a continued appropriation of the atonement but on the cleansing power of the word. The Scripture seems to be the agent by which one maintains purity.

This same standard of ongoing purity is clearly set before believers as well in the New Testament. Thus Paul warns Timothy to keep himself pure (1 Tim 5:22) but also challenges him to set the believers an example in purity (4:12), while John states that "everyone who thus hopes in him purifies himself as he is pure" (1 Jn 3:3).[26] God expects his people to sustain the purity that comes out of a relationship with himself.

Ongoing forgiveness. Growth after conversion is further characterized in terms

---

[25]For water in baptism as a symbol of initial cleansing see *EDT*, p. 112-4.
[26]For more on gradual purification see Pope, *Compendium of Christian Theology*, 3:36-38.

of a continuous forgiveness of sins. After the establishment of the covenant on Mount Sinai (Ex 19—24), Israel falls into sin (32—34). More grace is needed which leads to Moses' intercession for their forgiveness (32:32). This need is also reflected at the dedication of the temple when God promises, "If my people who are called by my name humble themselves, and pray and seek my face, and turn from their wicked ways, then I will hear from heaven, and will forgive their sin and heal their land" (2 Chron 7:14). Some take God seriously and pray for his forgiveness (Ps 25:18).

In like manner when Jesus teaches his disciples to pray, "Forgive us our debts, as we have forgiven our debtors," he is recognizing the ongoing need for believers to forgive and receive forgiveness (Mt 6:12; Lk 11:4). When Simon the Magician longs for the power to give the Holy Spirit to others after his own conversion, he is exhorted by Peter, "Repent therefore of this wickedness of yours, and pray to the Lord that, if possible, the intent of your heart may be forgiven you" (Acts 8:22). This continuous forgiveness is described by James in a situation where one needs to pray for healing. If sins have been committed, they need to be confessed, and they will be forgiven (Jas 5:15-16).

John makes it clear that it is the death of Jesus that continues to provide propitiation for a believer when he does commit an act of sin. "I am writing this to you so that you may not sin; but if any one does sin, we have an advocate with the Father, Jesus Christ the righteous; and he is the [propitiation] for our sins, and not for ours only but also for the sins of the whole world" (1 Jn 2:1-2). The biblical writers were realists. They knew that even after an experience of saving grace people could again fall into sin, become partially unclean, and need forgiveness and further cleansing. They believed God has made provision for this ongoing cleansing and forgiveness in the atonement, and thus they exhort believers who have committed sins to seek further forgiveness and cleanness of heart.

The Church

In the language of the sanctuary the church is described in three ways. First, the body of believers may be described as a priesthood of God. Second, collectively as well as individually, believers may be called the temple of God. Third, those who come before God in the sanctuary are coming as a worshiping community.

Kingdom of priests. The concept of the church as priesthood finds its roots in

God's call to his people at Mount Sinai to be a kingdom of priests (Ex 19:6). This vision continues throughout the Old Covenant as God's desire for his people to "be called the priests of the LORD" (Is 61:6). Jesus designates believers under the New Covenant to serve in the same capacity when he makes us "a kingdom, priests to his God and Father" (Rev 1:6).

The purpose of this priestly role is to serve as a mediator between God and others. As priests, the Israelites are to spend time in the presence of God, receiving the word of God and proclaiming the word of God to other nations. The task does not change under the New Covenant, but Christians are selected as "a chosen race, a royal priesthood, a holy nation, God's own people, that you may declare the wonderful deeds of him who called you out of darkness into his marvelous light" (1 Pet 2:9). So part of the priestly task is spending time with God and then communicating God's message to the world.

The other part of the mediator role is to assist people in responding to God. This means helping them come into the presence of God through the sacrificial system in the Old Testament and through the atonement of Christ in the New Testament. It is extended as the church under the New Covenant assists people in bringing spiritual sacrifices unto God. "Like living stones be yourselves built into a spiritual house, to be a holy priesthood, to offer spiritual sacrifices acceptable to God through Jesus Christ" (1 Pet 2:5). In helping people to respond to God, the priestly role relates to sacrifice, worship (including prayer and praise) and bringing one's life before God as a spiritual sacrifice to him. Thus the church's priestly role involves mediating God's word to people and assisting people in proper response to God.

The close relationship between God's kingdom and the priestly role of his people continues to be emphasized throughout Scripture (Rev 5:10). God is looking for a kingdom of priests because he is concerned about all the kingdoms and nations of the world. He first chooses Israel as his priestly vehicle for reaching the world. While much of the Old Testament focuses on the role of priests within Israel, Israel as a church is called to be a priesthood of God to touch the whole world for him. The same is true under the New Covenant. The believing church is to constitute a priesthood to touch everyone in the world with the gospel of Jesus Christ.

Priesthood of all believers. This concept of the church as the priesthood of God is the basis of the Reformation doctrine of the priesthood of all believers. Every individual Christian has direct access to God without the intervention of any priest, but every believer also bears the responsibility to be in ministry to other people. Every Christian is to be a mediator between God and others, as a priest had been previously. The implication is that every believer in God has a responsibility to be in ministry to other people and a mandate to be involved in both communication of God's word to others and assisting others to responding to God.

Temple of God. The second way the language of the sanctuary is related to the church is in the description of the believers as the temple of God. Paul challenges the Corinthians, "What agreement has the temple of God with idols? For we are the temple of the living God" (2 Cor 6:16). While some of the references in the New Testament to God's temple refer to the indwelling presence of the Holy Spirit in individuals, there are some places this may refer to both individuals and the collective group of believers that make up the church (1 Cor 3:16-17). Thus Paul writes about the new believers "built upon the foundation of the apostles and prophets, Jesus Christ himself being the cornerstone, in whom the whole structure is joined together and grows into a holy temple in the Lord; in whom you also are built into it for a dwelling place of God in the Spirit" (Eph 2:20-21).

The theological significance of the church as the temple of God is that God's personal presence dwells in the community of his people. If the tabernacle/ temple under the Old Covenant represented God's personal presence among his people, in the New Testament it is the people of God who represent the presence of God wherever they are. To understand the church as the temple of God is to understand the people of God indwelt by the presence of God.

Worshiping community. The third description of the church is as a worshiping community. While there is some indication of individual worship in Scripture (Gen 24:26ff.; Ex 33:9-38), the normal pattern is to worship with other believers as a community. The Old Testament pattern is symbolized in the call to "worship the LORD in the beauty of holiness"(Ps 29:2 KJV); the New Testament exhortation becomes "Let us offer to God acceptable worship, with reverence and awe"(Heb 12:28).

This repeated commandment to worship the Lord comes because people are made to be a worshipers of God, and to effectively do so as social beings they need to worship in community. So the church as a worshiping community meets needs both for the individual and for the collective body of believers.

Jesus made it clear that God was seeking those "true worshipers [who] will worship the Father in spirit and truth"(Jn 4:23, 24). This call to worship him in spirit and truth reflects the two major parts of worship. Worshiping in truth relates to God showing himself to people. This is especially true in the revelation of his word, and it is the preaching and teaching of his word that constitutes a major part of biblical worship in both the Old and New Testaments. Since this dimension of God's character has been dealt with more fully under his role as Personal Revealer, it only needs to be noted here that this is an essential ingredient for public worship. It is the reason why the Reformers made the proclamation of the word of God central to the whole of public worship.

But Jesus was not only interested in people worshiping him in truth but also in spirit. This refers to the second part of worship, which is people's response to God in their own inner spirit. People cannot just worship with external forms but must do so within their hearts. This response to God in both the Old Testament and New Testament seems to include elements of prayer or communication with God, and praise or thanksgiving to God.

The sacrificial system as a major part of worship under the Old Covenant is described fully in the book of Leviticus. The whole sacrificial system was elaborately designed to show people how to come into the presence of God and that God meant for sin to be dealt with as a basis of proper worship of him. So the sacrifice of animals was a regular part of Old Testament worship. In the New Testament this sacrificial system is brought to fulfillment in the perfect sacrifice of Christ on the cross (1 Pet 1:18-19; Heb 9:26). While the sacrificial offering of the Lord himself cannot be repeated, the remembrance of the event in the Lord's Supper is a regular part of Christian worship (1 Cor 11:17-34).

Because the death of Christ has provided grace that makes forgiveness and the community's access to God possible, worshipers are then able to pray and respond to God (1 Cor 14:14-16) and praise God by singing psalms, hymns and spiritual songs (Eph 5:19; Col 3:16). Prayer and praise of course have been characteristic of the church under the Old Covenant as well. The Psalms particularly illustrate the call to continuous praise of God. The New Testament picks up on this call for praise, exhorting us to "continually offer up a sacrifice of praise to God, that is, the fruit of lips that acknowledge his name"(Heb 13:15).

Scripture shows Christians worshiping in homes (Acts 2:46; 5:42; 12:12), in public halls (19:9), in synagogues (13:14-15; 14:1; 17:1-2) and in the temple

(2:46; 3:1—4:2). Whatever the location, the focus of the worshiping community is listening to God and responding to him.

Full Sanctification

Cleansing from all sin. The atonement is clearly the basis for all sanctification. "Jesus also suffered outside the gate in order to sanctify the people through his own blood" (Heb 13:12; see 9:13-14; 10:10, 14). Full sanctification is described in this priestly category as a cleansing or a purification of the sinful nature. Since this purification from all sin is rooted in the atonement, the stated principle is: "The blood of Jesus his Son cleanses us from all sin" (1 Jn 1:7).

One of the early pictures of full sanctification in terms of cleansing of sinfulness comes in Psalm 51. Here David has a dual plea in relationship to his sin. He prays that God will be merciful and blot out his transgressions (v. 1-3). He asks God to hide his face from his sins and to blot out his iniquities (v. 9). In these verses he is talking about his individual acts of transgression. But he is also praying for a deeper work of God that has to do with his sinful nature. So he asks God to deal with his iniquity and with his sin (in the singular, v. 2). This deeper sinfulness he understands as a part of his own sinful nature inherited from his parents. "Behold, I was brought forth in iniquity, and in sin did my mother conceive me" (v. 5). It is of this deeper sinful nature that he prays, "Wash me thoroughly from my iniquity, and cleanse me from my sin!" (v. 2). He realizes God wants to see truth in the innermost part of his being, and he prays, "Purge me with hyssop, and I shall be clean; wash me, and I shall be whiter than snow" (v. 7). So he is asking for a deep cleansing or purification from this sinful nature, and at the same time expressing his longing for a full cleanness of heart. "Create in me a clean heart, O God, and put a new and right spirit within me" (v. 10). It is clear that David not only wants forgiveness for his individual transgressions, but he also wants God to do a more complete work of grace in his heart that is described in terms of cleansing and purification from that sinful nature.

A similar picture is found in the vision of Isaiah. Having seen the holiness of God, the prophet's reaction is an awareness of his own sinfulness. He cries out, "Woe is me! For I am lost; for I am a man of unclean lips, and I dwell in the midst of a people of unclean lips" (Is 6:5). The reference to the uncleanness of the lips is certainly an indication of the uncleanness of his heart. He is not referring so much to individual sins as to his own sinfulness in the light of the holy nature of

God. Purification comes when one of the seraphim brings a burning coal from the altar and touches his mouth, symbolic of a purging of his life. "Behold, this has touched your lips; your guilt is taken away, and your sin forgiven" (Is 6:6-7). This symbolic purification of Isaiah is not primarily related to the forgiveness of specific acts of sin but rather to the deeper work required to cleanse the iniquity of sinfulness and to purge his sinful nature. That sinful nature is closely bound up with his self-centeredness, which in the light of the subsequent conversation appears to have been transformed. When God asks who will go, Isaiah responds, "Here am I! Send me." (6:8). What has been radically altered by the cleansing has been his self-centered orientation. His pride and self-will have been purged, and he is now willing to do the whole will of God.[27]

Fire as one of the symbols of the holy presence of God is used as a symbol of cleansing in Isaiah's vision. It is not surprising that that same symbol should be used as representative of the cleansing of the apostles on the day of Pentecost (Acts 2:3). Peter describes the significance of this symbol by likening the event to the giving of the Holy Spirit to another group. "God who knows the heart bore witness to them, giving them the Holy Spirit just as he did to us; and he made no distinction between us and them, but cleansed their hearts by faith" (15:8-9).

John talks about the privilege of being cleansed from all sin. "If we walk in the light, as he is in the light, we have fellowship with one another, and the blood of Jesus his Son cleanses us from all sin" (1 Jn 1:7). For God not only desires to forgive us our sins but also to "cleanse us from all unrighteousness" (1:9). In the light of this privilege Paul exhorts the Corinthians, "Let us cleanse ourselves from every defilement of body and spirit, [perfecting] holiness . . . in the fear of God" (2 Cor 7:1). His use of the aorist imperative in this exhortation strongly suggests that he meant for this to be a definite experience that could be completed in this life. In a like manner he prays for the Christians at Thessalonica that God "may establish your hearts unblamable in holiness" (1 Thess 3:13). This was part of God's will for them regarding their sanctification, "for God has not called us for uncleanness, but in holiness" (4:3, 7). It is for a sanctification that keeps believers from uncleanness and establishes hearts unblamable in holiness that Paul prays at the end of his

---

[27]John N. Oswalt, *The Book of Isaiah Chapters 1-39* (Grand Rapids, Mich.: Eerdmans, 1986), 1:182-84.

letter, "May the God of peace himself sanctify you wholly" (5:23).[28]

This full cleansing is one of the elements promised in the prophetic description of the new covenant. In his desire to validate his holiness in his people God promises, "I will sprinkle clean water upon you, and you shall be clean from all your uncleanness, and from all your idols will I cleanse you" (Ezek 36:25; also 36:29, 33). Paul says this is possible because "Christ loved the church and gave himself up for her, that he might sanctify her, having cleansed her by the washing of water with the word, that he might present the church to himself in splendor, without spot or wrinkle or any such thing, that she might be holy and without blemish" (Eph 5:25-27). So the grace of God comes through Jesus Christ "to redeem us from all iniquity and to purify for himself a people of his own" (Tit 2:11-14).

While an initial cleansing begins to fulfill the promise of what would happen under the New Covenant, it clearly does not do all that was promised. This accounts for the exhortations in the New Testament to believers to go on to a deeper experience of cleansing in their lives (2 Cor 7:1; 1 Jn 1:7).

Baptism of the Holy Spirit. In the previous chapter we discussed the work of God making his full presence known in the lives of disciples at Pentecost. In that discussion it was noted that the fullness of the Holy Spirit is used synonymously with the phrase "the baptism of the Holy Spirit" (Acts 1:5; 2:4). Because the whole concept of baptism is particularly related to the priestly language of the sanctuary, a further word needs to be added about the use of this phrase in reference to full sanctification.

Jesus makes a clear distinction between baptism with water and being baptized with the Holy Spirit (Acts 1:5). The first relates to the experience of God's saving grace, but the second is clearly connected with the work of the Spirit on the day of Pentecost in full sanctification. The first use of *baptism* in relation to salvation implies a washing away of the guilt of sin. The second use of *baptism* in connection with the Holy Spirit suggests a deeper cleansing of the sinful nature. The need for this cleansing in the Twelve even after three years of

---

[28]For more on entire sanctification as purification from the sin nature see *BDT,* p. 121; Pope, *Compendium of Christian Theology,* 3:34-35, 45-50; Miley, *Systematic Theology,* 2:356-58; Wilber Dayton, *A Contemporary Wesleyan Theology,* ed. Charles W. Carter (Grand Rapids, Mich.: Francis Asbury Press, 1985) 1:529-30; W. T. Purkiser, *Conflicting Concepts of Holiness* (Kansas City, Mo.: Beacon Hill, 1972), pp. 15-21; Mildred Wynkoop, *A Theology of Love* (Kansas City, Mo.: Beacon Hill, 1972), pp. 249-67; H. Orton Wiley, *Christian Theology* (Kansas City, Mo.: Beacon Hill, 1941), 2:487-91.

discipleship is graphically illustrated in their self-centeredness on their last evening with Jesus in the upper room. Their failure to wash his and one another's feet clearly comes out of a self-protective unwillingness to take the role of a servant (Jn 13). It is the self-centeredness of the sinful nature that is being cleansed by a baptism with the Holy Spirit. This cleansing work deals with the self-centered focus of a sinful nature, so that one is then available for the fullness of the presence and the will of God. This means there is a complementariness between the phrases "baptism with the Holy Spirit" and "being filled with the Holy Spirit." The first deals with the problem of the self-centered nature. It cleanses away the self-centered focus so that one is then in a position to being filled with the full presence and will of God.[29]

Living sacrifice. While cleansing and purification are the chief ways that entire sanctification is described under the categories of the sanctuary, Paul also describes it in terms of a living sacrifice. He exhorts the church at Rome "by the mercies of God" to present their bodies "as a living sacrifice, holy and acceptable to God" (Rom 12:1). The sacrifice is something entirely given over to God, and this is reinforced by Paul's use again of the aorist imperative in calling them to "present" themselves. Further, the sacrifice is to be holy and acceptable to God, implying that which is like his own nature and pleasing to him. While sacrifices under the Old Covenant were normally killed and consumed, Paul is using the analogy to describe a living individual who is wholly sacrificed to God, so that his life is lived out as something totally given to God.[30] A living sacrifice is another way of speaking about absolute consecration to God.

Circumcision of heart. Still another figure of speech in the priestly category that is used to describe full sanctification is the concept of the circumcision of the heart. The rite of circumcision throughout the Old Testament is linked with that of cleansing. The circumcision of the flesh under the Old Covenant is paralleled by the New Testament concept of being cleansed from original sin "by putting off the body of flesh in the circumcision of Christ" (Col 2:11). Therefore, circumcision is the physical language used to describe the process of purification

---

[29]For more on the baptism of the Spirit in relation to Pentecost and full sanctification see Allan Coppedge and William Ury, *In His Image* (Franklin, Tenn.: Providence House, 2000), chap. 9.

[30]See also Donald Metz, *Studies in Biblical Holiness* (Kansas City, Mo.: Beacon Hill, 1971), pp. 123-24, 143; H. Orton Wiley, *Hebrews* (Kansas City, Mo.: Beacon Hill, 1959), 2:445-46; Daniel Steele, *Milestone Papers* (Minneapolis: Bethany Fellowship, 1966), p. 69; Adam Clark, *Commentary on the Bible*, (London: William Tegg, 1949), 4:136.

and cleansing of the inner nature of the heart. As Oehler describes this, "It binds him through obedience to God, whose covenant sign he bears on his body, and to a blameless walk before him. Thus it is the symbol of the renewal and purification of heart." Thus, circumcision was a "symbol of the purification and sanctification of the whole life" because it symbolized living in the presence of God. This meant that cutting away the flesh in circumcision was a symbol of removing the "inborn guilt and impurity of human nature." To live in a covenant with a holy God "presupposed that the natural life" which is "tainted by impurity" is removed. Because God is holy, he desires his people to be holy, and it was circumcision that typified this holiness.[31]

This connection between the circumcision of the heart and full sanctification was made by Wesley in one of his early sermons. "I preached a sermon on circumcision of the heart, which contains all that I now teach concerning salvation from all sin, and loving God with an undivided heart."[32] Wesley defined this experience of being circumcised of heart as "that habitual disposition of the soul which, in the sacred writing, is termed holiness; and which directly implies, the being cleansed from sin, 'from all filthiness both of flesh and spirit'; and, by consequence, the being endued with those virtues which were also in Christ Jesus; the being so 'renewed in the spirit of our mind,' as to be 'perfect as our Father in heaven is perfect.'" Laurence Wood agrees that the biblical concept of circumcision of the heart is identical to that of full sanctification. "This bodily purification by which the inherited 'unclean' flesh is excised thus became the symbol of the spiritual circumcision by which the impurity of sin is cleansed."[33]

Theological implications. The theological implications of the cleansing language in Scripture has to do with the purification of our sinful nature. Since our sinful nature focuses on self-will, the purification of our sinfulness has to do with a cleansing from self-centeredness. It is a cleansing from an independent self-orientation that has the ego as the center of the decision-making process. What is cleansed is not the ability to exercise the will, but it is the independence of the will from God's will that is removed. It is a cleansing from self-will so that the individual no longer is choosing his own will in any given situation but is choosing God's will

---

[31]Oehler, *Theology of the Old Testament*, pp. 193-94.

[32]John Wesley, *Wesley's Standard Sermons*, ed. Edward H. Sugden (London: Epworth, 1921), 1:265, 267-68.

[33]Laurence W. Wood, *Pentecostal Grace* (Wilmore, Ky.: Francis Asbury, 1980), pp. 38-39; for a thorough discussion see pp. 137-75.

in all circumstances. The choice to do this in the experience of full sanctification produces a reorientation of the life, from a self- orientation to a God-orientation. Now not self-will but God's will is the determining factor in any decision.

The difficulty for some with this language arises from the fact we are using a metaphor from the physical world to describe a spiritual phenomenon. In the physical world when something is cleansed or purified, it stays that way unless it is polluted again from the outside. But in the spiritual realm there can be a cleansing of self-will that does not imply an absolutely permanent, irreversible state. The capacity to exercise the will is not destroyed in this experience, and thus one may willfully choose again to begin to make a single decision or multiple decisions based on one's own self-interest rather than on God's will. In other words it is possible to draw back from a totally pure heart seeking only God's will to a state of seeking one's own will either in part or in whole. So while the figure of speech is a useful one, the analogy of cleansing must not be pressed too far or the theology that the figure was intended to convey will be distorted. One is never so permanently cleansed that he cannot reassert his will and choose to be self-centered again at some future time. Yet it is possible to be cleansed and to maintain a cleansing that is pure from self-centeredness and continues to seek God's will in every choice in the life of the individual.

Further Growth in Grace

Growth after an experience of full sanctification may be described by a continual living in a state of cleanness or purity of heart. Job, in making his defense of a blameless heart, declares, "My doctrine is pure, and I am clean in God's eyes" (Job 11:4). He elaborates, "I am clean, without transgression; I am pure, and there is no iniquity in me" (Job 33:9). It is those living in this state of purity about which the psalmist speaks when he declares, "Truly God is good to the upright, to those who are pure in heart" (Ps 73:1; see 73:13). This is surely the same state that Jesus describes when he said, "Blessed are the pure in heart, for they shall see God" (Mt 5:8).

The focus in this area is maintaining a state of purity of life. As with growth after conversion it will involve a continued dependence on the atonement and the agency of the Word of God as the means for continuing in this state of purity. Whereas the focus after salvation is maintaining purity in terms of individual acts of sin and resultant guilt, the focus here is maintaining the cleansing from the self-will of the sin nature. It involves guarding one's life from the reassertion of that self-will and independence of God at any point.[34]

Glorification

The language of the sanctuary describes glorification in three ways. The first way is in reference to the heavenly temple of God. The second refers to God's people as priests, and finally, the activity of eternal worship by God's people is mentioned.

The temple of God. The first description of glorification appears in the midst of one of the pictures of heavenly worship. God's temple is described as being opened and the ark of his covenant seen. This probably represents the continuing centrality of the word of God in terms of relating to God and worshiping God (Rev 11:19). The servants of the Lord have come out of the great tribulation to "serve him day and night within his temple," a representation of eternally dwelling in his presence (7:14-15).

Priests to God. In the heavenly vision that Jesus gives to John, his people are described as "a kingdom, priests to his God" (Rev 1:6). While this echo of Exodus 19:6 that refers to a kingdom of priests may describe the ministry of God's people on the earth, it also seems to imply some priestly role with him in heaven. In the midst of another occasion of heavenly worship, God's people as the priests are described as those who will reign with him on the earth. "God has made them a kingdom and priests to our God, and they shall reign on earth" (Rev 5:10). This may also be a reference to God's people who continue to serve in the role of priests to him and will reign with him during the millennium. Those who share in the first resurrection are described as those over whom "the second death has no power, they shall be priests of God and of Christ, and they shall reign with him a thousand years" (20:6). So some priestly ministry is maintained by the people who belong to God even in heaven.

Eternal worship. Although references are made to both the temple and a priestly ministry, the chief way in which glorification is described is in terms of heavenly worship. Worship apparently is characteristic of heaven according to the book of Revelation (5:14; 7:11-12; 11:16-18; 15:4; 22:3). This worship is led

---

[34]As to the question of whether the biblical concept of cleansing implies that sin is to be understood as something physical to be extracted from a person see Wood's excellent discussion in *Pentecostal Grace*, pp. 161-68.

by the twenty-four elders, who probably represent the leaders of the twelve tribes of Israel and the twelve apostles, that is, the leaders of the Old Testament church and the New Testament church (4:10; 5:8, 14; 7:11; 11:16; 19:4). The elders are joined in worship by heavenly creatures and angels, who also believe God is worthy to be praised (4:8, 9; 5:11). Their worship involves singing before God.

> Worthy art thou, our Lord and God, to receive glory and honor and power,
> For hou didst create all things, and by thy will they existed and were created. (Rev 4:11)

Singing involves some new songs (5:9-10), as well as the song of Moses and the song of the Lamb (15:3-4). The singing is also described as praise unto God: "Praise our God, all his servants, you who fear him, small and great" (19:5). In addition to praise the prayers of the saints are mentioned as that which comes up before God. This may be the prayers of believers on earth, but nonetheless it is the congregation in heaven that apparently joins in with this prayer or communication with God (5:8).

Finally, we not only find examples of eternal worship in the presence of God, but twice there are explicit exhortations to "worship God" (22:9; 19:6). The implication of this focus on heavenly worship is that people are created to worship God. They have been exhorted and taught how to do so on the earth as a part of being the people of God, but this need does not stop when one is translated into the immediate presence of God in heaven. Part of their createdness incorporates a need to worship and praise God, and they are not functioning as they were made unless they are worshiping him, both on the earth and in heaven.

Grace : undeserved favor of God

Attributes of God

Grace. We have seen that one of the attributes of God closely bound up with his role as the holy Priest is that of his grace. In the Old Testament the word for grace, *hen* (חֵן), is understood in terms of the undeserved favor of God. It is a word closely tied to God's love and mercy, as well as his kindness toward people. "If I have found [grace] in thy sight, show me now thy ways that I may know thee and find [grace] in thy sight" (Ex 33:13). Grace and mercy are very closely intertwined in the biblical picture. God declares, "I will be gracious to whom I will be gracious, and will show mercy on whom I will show mercy" (33:19). This grace/mercy is the part of the character of God that leads to forgiveness. "The LORD, a God merciful and gracious, slow to anger, and abounding in steadfast love and faithfulness, keeping steadfast love for thousands, forgiving iniquity and transgression and sin" (34:6-7).[35]

One classic expression of God's grace toward Israel is his deliverance of them from the bondage and threat of extinction in Egypt. They did not deserve his favor, but he graciously set them free. In the light of many contemporary understandings of the relationships between law and grace, it is important to note that this particular event, as evidence of God's grace, comes before the giving of the law at Mount Sinai. In God's pattern, grace always precedes law. When grace has already worked in the lives of individuals, God then gives law as a means of indicating how people may continue to live in a right relationship with a gracious God. But the relationship is begun because of God's initiative in gracious favor.[36]

In the New Testament grace is intimately bound up with what God has done for people through the life, death and resurrection of Jesus Christ. "The Word became flesh and dwelt among us, full of grace and truth" (Jn 1:14, 17). From Christ's fullness we all "received, grace upon grace" (1:16). Here grace, χάρις, is an expression of God's love, mercy, and kindness toward all, without the least thought of merit on the part of individuals.[37] Grace is God's free and unmerited way of dealing with sinful people. The whole concept of salvation is based on this

[35]For more on *hen* (חֵן) and the Hebrew word group related to *hanan* (חָנַן), see *TWOT*, 1:302-4; *TDNT*, 10:376-81; *THAT*, 1:587-96; W. L. Reed, "Some Implications of Hen for Old Testament Religion," *JBL* 73 (1954): pp. 36-41; E. E. Flack, "The Concept of Grace in Biblical Thought." In *Biblical Studies in Memory of H. C. Allemen.* Ed. Jacob Martin Myers (Locust Valley, N. Y.: J. J. Augustine, 1960), pp. 137-54; T. F. Torrance, "The Doctrine of Grace in the Old Testament," *SJT* 1 (1948): 55-65.

[36]The other Hebrew word that contains an element related to grace is *hesed* (חֶסֶד). It is normally translated in the English by words like "loving-kindness" and "steadfast love." It includes elements of love, mercy and grace, and is often used as an expression of God's gracious favor to people. We will explore this more thoroughly in the context of holiness as love, but it should be noted that it is clearly related to the work of God's grace. On *hesed* see *TWOT*, 1:305-7; *TDNT*, 1:696-701; *THAT*, 1:599-622; W. Lofthouse, "Hen and Hesed in the Old Testament," *ZAW* 51 (1933): 29-35; Nelson Glueck, *Hesed in the Bible* (Cincinnati, Ohio: Hebrew Union College Press, 1967); Katherine D. Sakenfeld, *The Meaning of Hesed in the Hebrew Bible: A New Inquiry* (Missoula, Mont.: Scholars Press, 1978); Glen Yarborough, "The Significance of Hesed in the Old Testament," Ph.D. diss., The Southern Baptist Theological Seminary, 1959.

[37]For more on *charis,* χάρις, see *TDNT*, 9:372-402; *NIDNTT*, 2:115-23; Rudolf Bultmann, *Theology of the New Testament* (New York: Charles Scribner's, 1955), vol. 1; D. Doughty, "The Priority of Charis," *NTS* (1972-1973):163-80; James Moffatt, *Grace in the New Testament*; *EBT*, 1:337-44; C. Ryder Smith, *The Bible Doctrine of Grace and Related Doctrines* (London: Epworth, 1956); N. P. Williams, *The Grace of God* (London: Longmans, Green, 1930).

grace in Christ. "By whom also we have access by faith into this grace wherein we stand" (Rom 5:2 KJV).[38] So Paul can write, "They are justified by his grace as a gift, through the redemption which is in Christ Jesus" (3:24).[39] And to the Ephesians he declares, "For by grace you have been saved through faith; and this is not your own doing, it is the gift of God—not because of works, lest any man should boast" (Eph 2:8-9). Indeed the grace of God is not only the basis of all of salvation but it is the attribute of God's nature that stands behind every gift and blessing given to people.

Purity. The second key attribute closely bound up with God's role as Priest is his purity. We have already discussed the connection between the holiness of God and purity. What needs to be emphasized is that the purity of God describes his freedom from sin. When a creature is being impure or unholy, it has to do with its deviation from the standard of God's holy and pure character. This means that purity is frequently related to cleanness by the standard that God sets before his people. As early as Mount Sinai, God identifies his own holiness with that which is clean and pure, and he contrasts it with the unholy, the unclean, and the impure. Since the unclean or unholy is also the impure, it is the opposite of God and his holiness, who is sometimes described as pure. It can be said of God, "With the blameless man thou dost show thyself blameless; with the pure thou dost show thyself pure" (2 Sam 22:26-27; Ps 18:25-26). John, who tells us that "when he appears we shall be like him," reminds us that "he is pure" (1 Jn 3:2-3). Purity and cleanness must be understood as synonymous with the holiness of God's character while the common, the unclean and the impure must be understood as that which is contrary to his nature.[40]

In addition to the connection between purity and cleanness, purity is also by implication the complement of righteousness. If righteousness is the standard of doing that which is right, purity is a characteristic of not doing wrong. To be pure from sin is to be kept from sin, so that purity is the obverse of righteousness. Purity is the negative statement that God is free from sin, while righteousness is the positive statement of his nature that sets the standard for right living.

---

[38]See also 2 Tim 2:1; 1 Pet 5:12; 2 Pet 3:18.

[39]See also Rom 4:16; 5:15.

[40]For other references to holiness as purity see Is 6:3-7, Ezek 36:23-25, 29, 31, 33; 37:23; Acts 15:8-9; 2 Cor 7:1; 1 Thess 4:7-8; Heb 9:13-14.

Conclusion

In the Old Testament God takes the initiative to provide a way for otherwise impure people to relate to him: a sacrificial system. He makes atonement possible and invites people to deal with sin and thus live in right relation to him. But the role of Priest is emphasized more highly with the coming of the person of Jesus. He is explicitly called our High Priest—the one who can bring God to us and us to God.

Historically, Jesus comes in parallel to the high priests of the Old Testament, who by making atonement open the way for people to draw near to God and for God to draw near to people. On a personal level, through the atonement Jesus provides grace so that people can be brought into a relationship with God. Theologically, Jesus as Priest serves as a mediator between God and people while also becoming the sacrifice by which mediation is possible. So at the center of this role the sacrificial mediation of a vicarious atonement makes grace available to men and women so that purity may become a reality in their lives.

SEVEN

HOLY GOD
AS RIGHTEOUS JUDGE

The Unity Factor

One central component of the concept of moral holiness is the idea of the righteousness of God. His righteousness is that part of his holiness that has to do with what is moral or right. God does not choose a standard for morality or a law to regulate righteousness which is above or beyond himself, but rather within the very nature and being of God there is a standard of right. It is his holiness as righteousness that determines all that is right, and it is rooted in his own nature, his own essence.[1]

Holiness as Righteousness

This holiness as righteousness is most clearly seen when God in his holy nature relates to his own creation. As A. H. Leitch puts it, "God is, in his essence, by his very nature, holiness itself; and righteousness is the mode or way by which his essence is expressed toward his created world or toward anything apart from himself."[2] Emil Brunner agrees, "Righteousness, therefore, is simply the holiness of God, as it is expressed and confronted with the created world. The nature of God which is Holy, manifests itself over against his creature as the divine quality of righteousness."[3] God, who is holy, is in himself the standard of all holiness, and when this is expressed toward people, one key element is in terms of his righteousness.[4]

---

[1]TWOT, 5:754.
[2]ZPBD, 5:105.
[3]Emil Brunner, *The Christian Doctrine of God* (London: Lutterworth, 1949), p. 278.
[4]On holiness as righteousness see *ISBE(rev)*, 2: 726; *HDB*, 2:397-98; Gustave Friedrich Oehler, *Theology of the Old Testament*, ed. George E. Day (Grand Rapids, Mich.: Zondervan, 1883), pp. 112-13; Theodorus Vriezen, *An Outline of Old Testament Theology*, trans. S. Neuijen (Bristol: John Wright, 1911), pp. 159-62; Edmond Jacob, *Theology of the Old Testament*, trans. Arthur W. Heathcote and P. J. Allcock (New York: Harper & Row, 1958), p. 96.

[handwritten margin note: Gods of Holiness ↗ Manifestations of]

• *Righteousness as expression of God's character.* The concept of holiness as righteousness (*tsedeq*) is manifested in two different ways in Scripture. The first of these relates to the righteousness of God's holy character wherein righteousness is one of the major expressions of God's moral holiness.[5] Thus, Isaiah writes, "The LORD of hosts is exalted in justice, and the Holy God shows himself holy in righteousness" (Is 5:16). Likewise, when the psalmist exalts the Holy One of Israel he declares, "Righteousness and justice are the foundation of thy throne," so that God's people are those "who exult in thy name all the day, and extol thy righteousness" (Ps 89:14-18). The Holy One is righteous in himself.[6]

• *Righteousness as standard for people.* The second manifestation of God's holiness as righteousness comes in the standard of righteousness that he gives to people. Since righteousness is an expression of God's holy character, it becomes the standard by which God expects everyone to live if they are to be a holy people, i.e., a people reflecting his own character. Thus, the righteous law of God becomes a written description of the holy character of God, to which people must conform their lives if they are to be called by his holy name. Accordingly, the Lord can instruct Israel, "You shall remember and do all my commandments, and be holy to your God" (Num 15:40). God's people cannot be holy without conformity, i.e., obedience, to the law of God. "The LORD will establish you as a people holy to himself . . . if you keep the commandments of the LORD" (Deut 28:9). From the beginning God declares that this conformity to his standard is to be both external and internal if his people are to be holy. "This day the LORD your God commands you to do these statutes and ordinances; you shall therefore be careful to do them with all your heart and with all your soul," so that "you shall be a people holy to the LORD your God" (26:16, 19).

This standard of righteousness as an expression of God's holy character is the basis of both the Old and the New Covenants. It is in the establishment of the Old Covenant at Mount Sinai that God first tells Israel that he is looking for a

---

[5]On the basic words for righteousness, צֶדֶק, see *TWOT*, 2:752-55; Snaith, *Distinctive Ideas of the Old Testament*, pp. 72-73; R. B. Girdlestone, *Synonyms of the Old Testament* (Grand Rapids, Mich.: Eerdmans, 1897), p. 101; *TWB*, 202-4; *ZPEB*, 5:104-18; Walther Eichrodt, *Theology of the Old Testament*, trans. J. A. Baker (London: SCM Press, 1961), 1:240. For δικαιοσύνη, "righteousness," see *TDNT*, 2:198; *NIDNTT*, 3:352-77; *BTLNT*, pp. 190-93.

[6]On the righteousness of God see Snaith, *Distinctive Ideas of the Old Testament*, pp. 51-78; Eichrodt, *Theology of the Old Testament*, 1:239-49; Brunner, *Christian Doctrine of God*, pp. 275-81; CD 2/1, pp. 375-406; Donald Guthrie, *New Testament Theology* (Downers Grove, Ill.: InterVarsity Press, 1981), pp. 99-104; Hans Conzelmann, *Outline of the Theology of the New Testament* (London: SCM Press, 1969), pp. 214-20; Werner Georg Kummel, *The Theology of the New Testament According to Its Major Witnesses* (Nashville: Abingdon, 1973), pp. 196-98.

holy people (Ex 19:6). When Israel responds positively to God's invitation to this covenant relationship, he then makes more explicit the implications of being a people of his "own possession." He does this by giving them the Ten Commandments (Ex 20) as an expression of what a holy people will be like. All this is based on the assumption that he is looking for a people like himself (Lev 11:44, 45). This standard is reiterated at the end of Moses' life before the children of Israel enter into the land of Canaan (Deut 5:1-21). It is obedience to God's holy law that brings blessing and continuation of spiritual life in one's relationship to God. "You shall walk in all the way which the LORD your God has commanded you, that you may live, and that it may go well with you" (5:33). "The LORD commanded us to do all these statutes, to fear the LORD our God, for our good always, that he might preserve us alive, as at this day. And it will be righteousness for us, if we are careful to do all this commandment before the LORD our God" (6:24-25).

The place of obedience. Some care must be exercised, however, in understanding the above statements about obedience producing life. A superficial reading of these texts led some throughout the history of Israel to conclude that obedience alone to the law is what produced spiritual life and blessing from God. What they sometimes failed to recall was that God was looking for *an obedience that arose out of faith in him* as a response to his gracious acts of redemption. The law was not given to Israel to earn their salvation, it was given to them so that they might learn how to live in a right relationship with a holy God. The grace of God in redeeming his people, both physically and spiritually, had already been demonstrated in the exodus. It received further confirmation during God's gracious provision for his people during the three months in which they traveled from Egypt to Mount Sinai (Ex 13-18). Israel had responded to God's gracious acts with at least some measure of faith, and God had proven himself to be the kind of God who was trustworthy. Therefore, it is on the basis of God's demonstrated grace and power that he invites them in Exodus 19 into a deeper covenant relationship with him. But it is a relationship that already had its beginning based on God's grace and Israel's faith in him.

The law was given against this background. The biblical pattern is always that *grace comes before law*. Grace redeems and provides for those who respond to God in faith, and then law is given so that one might continue to live in a right relationship with a holy God. J. A. Motyer aptly describes how the redeemed people of God were brought to the place where the law was given when he writes, "Grace precedes law; the law of God is not a system of merit whereby the unsaved seek to earn divine favor but a pattern of life given by the Redeemer to the redeemed so that they might know how to live for his good pleasure. Such is the biblical understanding of the place and function of law."[7]

The obedience to his law that God expects is the result of a continuation of faith. God is looking for a people who not only trust him for redemption but continue to trust his judgment about the ordering of their character as it is expressed in their behavior, attitudes and personal relationships. Those who walk in obedience out of a trusting heart are those who will find that the commandment continues to give life and allows God to produce multiple blessings in the lives of his people (Deut 6:24-25).

Many throughout the history of Israel (as well as in the history of the Christian church) have tended to reverse God's order. Some would like to put law before grace, so that men and women might try to earn God's favor by their obedience. Consequently, they tend to put obedience before or in place of faith, again reversing God's pattern. The result of this nonbiblical order has always been some form of works righteousness. Instead of producing a holy people, it tends to lead to legalism and self-justification.

Righteousness under the New Covenant. In the New Testament Jesus makes it very clear that God's standard of righteousness is also part of the basis of the New Covenant. Very soon after his call to repentance and belief (Mt 4:17; Mk 1:15), Jesus begins to gather around him his disciples as the new Israel of God (Mt 4:18-22; Mk 1:16-20). At the very outset of his time with these disciples he takes them up on the mountain where he gives them the content of the New Covenant (Mt 5—7). In Matthew's mind this is obviously a deliberate parallel to Moses going up on the mountain to receive from God his law as the content of the Old Covenant (Ex 19; 24). Jesus declares to his disciples that they have got to have in their lives a quality of righteousness that is different from that of the Pharisees. "For I tell you, unless your righteousness exceeds that of the scribes and Pharisees, you will never enter the kingdom of heaven" (Mt 5:20). Jesus then begins to give them some particular examples of the standard of righteousness that he expects of his disciples. He uses several representative commandments,

---

[7]*EDT,* p. 624. See also *ZPEB,* 5:109; *TDNT,* 2:200-201.

some from the Ten Commandments and some from other parts of the moral law. When he finishes, there is no doubt that there is a standard of righteous living that is to be characteristic of those who are his followers.[8]

There have been many from the New Testament time onward who have tended to categorize the Old Testament as law and the New Testament as grace, and since they saw themselves living under grace, they felt they could dispense with God's law. Jesus clearly rules out this option for his disciples when he declares to them, "Think not that I have come to abolish the law and the prophets; I have come not to abolish them but to fulfil them. For truly, I say to you, till heaven and earth pass away, not an iota, not a dot, will pass from the law until all is accomplished" (Mt 5:17-18). He then proceeds to give them the representative examples of the moral law under which his disciples must continue to live. He can do this to those who have already responded to him in faith, so that their obedience to the law serves as a continued expression of their trust in the Father and the Son. The clear implication is that the faith of the disciples as they first start to follow Jesus is in response to the grace of God that is beginning to work in their lives. So again, the pattern is that grace precedes the giving of law, and faith precedes a response of obedience.

So a holy God is one who is righteous within himself and who expresses that righteousness in a standard of law. W. H. Diehl summarizes the connections nicely in his discussion of righteousness as an attribute of God's nature which is the eternally perfect standard of what is right. "It is closely related to God's holiness (or moral perfection), on the one hand, and to God's moral law or will as an expression of his holiness, on the other hand."[9]

The Role of God as Righteous Judge

In the biblical world the figure of a judge is not limited to the concept of judicial responsibilities as it is in the modern world, but it is also bound up with responsibilities for making law and ruling people. In many instances a judge embodies the three major responsibilities of government in one person, viz.,

---

[8]For more on standards of righteousness see *TDNT*, 2:198-200; Girdlestone, *Synonyms of the Old Testament*, pp. 166-69; Snaith, *Distinctive Ideas of the Old Testament*, pp. 76-77; Eichrodt, *Theology of the Old Testament*, 2:316-49.
[9]*EDT*, p. 953.

the executive, the legislative and the judicial.[10]

When God is described as a Judge in Scripture there is a correspondence with all three of these functions. We have already dealt with God's ruling function in the discussion of God as sovereign King, an area closely related to his executive responsibilities as Judge. In the discussion of God's role as Judge it should be remembered that there is a good deal of overlap within the biblical materials between God's role as King and his role as Judge. This is due to the fact that in the ancient world judges also carried governing responsibilities and likewise kings had responsibility toward law and some judicial decisions. So sometimes God as Judge acts like a judge-executive who takes on ruling responsibilities.

The connection between God's righteousness and the concept of God as Judge, however, focuses more on the other two major responsibilities of a judge as lawmaker and judicator. As lawmaker God's law is based on his own holy character. Therefore, the righteousness of the law is an expression of the nature of God's holiness. As Pope expresses it, God's law is "perfect as an expression of the divine holiness; perfect therefore as the standard of right."[11] This is why Paul can say, "The law is holy, and the commandment is holy and just and good" (Rom 7:12). As a result God sets a standard of holiness expressed as righteousness for people based on his own being. This is part of his legislative responsibility for making laws for his people. As kings occasionally also make laws, this function is sometimes entwined with God's role as King of his people.

God, however, is not limited to simply making laws but has the authority to actually judge whether or not people keep his law. This judicial or forensic responsibility places him in the role of the righteous Judge and is the more extensive responsibility. God is the one who judges people with regard to their obedience in conforming their lives to the nature of God as expressed in his moral law. Therefore the predominant *language figure* for this role is that of the courtroom. Relationships are described in legal terms as they would be in a court of law.

The *focus* of this role is on the *law*. Because the whole concept of the law is very significant to the life of God's people, especially in the Old Testament, it is important to see how the vocabulary relates to each of these distinct judicial

---

[10]On the biblical judge see *shaphat* (שָׁפַט) *TWOT*, 2:947-49; *TDNT*, 3:923-25; *ZPEB*, 3:739, 758-60. For *din* (דִּין), see *TWOT*, 1:188.

[11]Pope, *Compendium of Christian Theology*, 1:336. See also *TDNT*, 2:205.

responsibilities. At times God's law is expressed as a "testimony" (Ps 119:2) when the Lord has testified concerning himself and what he requires. At other times it is referred to in terms of "teaching" (119:1). This teaching or "torah" is also closely related to God's role as Revealer and his responsibility as a teacher of his people. The teachings may then become a "word" (119:28) by which one is to live. Testimonies, teachings and words all relate to God's role as lawmaker.

But other language relates more to God's judicial function as the righteous Judge. Certain laws may be described as "statutes" (Ps 119:5), "judgments" (119:7), "precepts" (119:4) and "commandments" (119:10). So the concept of law serves as a basis of the "way" of God as well as the standard by which individuals are judged by him.[12]

The connection between God as the righteous Judge and the role of the law is found in the concept of judgment (*mishephat, krinō*). God is the righteous Judge who judges equitably, i.e., justice is applied with fairness across the board. The God who pronounces judgment is also the one who will give to individuals what they justly deserve, i.e., either punishment or reward. Thus the whole concept of the judgment of God in this world and the world to come is closely bound up with this figure of speech.[13]

The Father

Both the Old Testament and the New Testament testify to the dual role of the Father as both lawgiver and Judge. So Isaiah can write, "For the LORD is our judge, the LORD is our ruler" (Is 33:22). James gives us the identical picture when he says, "There is one lawgiver and judge" (Jas 4:12).

Old Testament. God's role as lawmaker begins in the garden of Eden when he gives Adam and Eve specific direction about the tree from which they could not eat (Gen 2:16-17). From this point on God regularly speaks, giving people commandments by which to live. Its more structured and legislative character

---

[12]On law for God's people see *TDNT,* 2:174; *EDT,* pp. 623-25; Paul Heinisch, *Theology of the Old Testament,* trans. William G. Heidt (St. Paul: North Central Press, 1955), pp. 14-17; Eichrodt, *Theology of the Old Testament,* 1:74-97; Emil Brunner, *The Christian Doctrine of Creation and Redemption* (London: Lutterworth, 1952), pp. 214-30; Conzelmann, *Outline of the Theology of New Testament,* pp. 220-28.

[13]On judgments, מִשְׁפָּט, see *TDNT,* 3:923-33; Girdlestone, *Synonms of the Old Testament,* pp. 101-2; Snaith, *Distinctive Ideas of the Old Testament,* pp. 74-5. For κρίνω, see *TDNT,* 3:921-54; *NIDNTT,* 2:361-71. See also *EDT,* pp. 590-91; Leon Morris, *The Biblical Doctrine of Judgment* (Grand Rapids, Mich.: Eerdmans 1960; *ISBE(rev),* 2:1161-62; Guthrie, *New Testament Theology,* pp. 848-74.

appears particularly at Mount Sinai with the giving of the law as a part of the Old Covenant (Ex 19—Lev 27), but it also continues as God speaks through the Prophets and Writings of the Old Testament.

The Lord who made men and women in his image in Genesis begins to give them an image of his character in written form through the law beginning in the book of Exodus. Therefore, we are given a dual reflection of the divine image within persons and within the written law of God. J. A. Motyer writes,

> Man is the living personal image of God; the law is the written, perceptual image of God. The intention of Leviticus 19 is declared at the outset: "You shall be holy, for I the Lord your God am holy" (v. 2). The Lord longs for his people to live in his image, and to that end he has given them his law. When man in the image of God and law in the image of God come together in the holy obedient life, then man is indeed "being himself." His nature is the image of God, and the law is given both to activate and to direct that nature into a totally human life; any other life is sub-human. Old Testament law, has, to a far greater extent, the function of liberating man to live according to his true nature.[14]

The Father's role as Judge of those who are to respond to his commandments begins in Genesis 3. It continues throughout the Scripture each time God has to decide whether or not an individual has been obedient to his law. The first explicit connection between God's judgeship and his righteousness is found when Abraham intercedes on behalf of Sodom and requests that God spare the city if a certain number of righteous persons are found within it. Abraham's argument rests on the connection between judgeship and righteousness. "Shall not the Judge of all the earth do right?" (Gen 18:25). Abraham is confident that God who acts as the Judge of all human conduct is also righteous in his own judgments and will do the right thing, particularly with regard to those who are righteous within the city of Sodom.

In the same way, the psalmist makes explicit what is clear throughout all of Scripture that "God is a righteous judge" (Ps 7:11), for "He judges the world with righteousness, he judges the peoples with equity" (9:8). "The heavens declare his righteousness, for God himself is judge" (50:6). God is the one who "comes to judge the earth. He will judge the world with righteousness, and the peoples with

---

[14]EDT, p. 624. For further discussion of God as lawmaker, see *TWOT*, 2:948; *TDNT*, 3:925; *ZPEB*, 3:896; *ISBE(rev)*, 3:92; Pope, *Compendium of Christian Theology*, 1:336-37.

his truth" (96:13). He is able to judge in that manner because "righteous art thou, O LORD, and right are thy judgments. Thou hast appointed thy testimonies in righteousness" (119:137-138). Further, the great judgment announced by Israel's prophets is based on the same conviction that God is the "LORD of hosts, who judgest righteously, who tries the heart and the mind" (Jer 11:20).[15]

New Testament. The New Testament also presents a strong picture of the judgment of God (e.g., Rom 2:2-3). It is God who "judges the secrets of men" as well as "the world" (Rom 2:16; 3:6; also 1 Cor 5:13). Christians are not exempt from the judgment of God, because Scripture says "the Lord will judge his people" (Heb 10:30). However, this is the one to whom Jesus could trust himself because he "judges justly" (1 Pet 2:23). Finally, in the book of Revelation, in the end time, God is the one who will judge the whole earth (Rev 18:8; 19:2, 20:12-13; also Heb 10:30).

The connection between holiness as righteousness and the character of God in his role as Judge comes with the equal (and right) ruling of reward and punishment. This distributive justice of God is remunerative on the one hand, as it provides rewards for those who have been obedient, and punitive on the other, as it provides punishment for those who have transgressed the law of God. This administration of righteousness as a Judge is what is best termed the justice of God. His justice is the application of righteousness in the affairs of people.[16] It must be remembered that as the just Judge, God is administrating righteousness but that this standard of righteousness is not a law above or separate from himself. Rather, he is applying a standard of righteousness that is a reflection of his own character and being. So the judicial function of God as Judge can never be completely separated from his legislative role as the one who makes law or from his basic being, that is, the *justitia interna*, or essential righteousness of the God of holiness. Because of who he is, he lays down a law for the good of all and judges whether or not people are in accord with that law.[17]

---

[15]For other references to God as Judge, see 1 Sam 2:10; Ps 50:4; 67:4; 94:1-2 .

[16]The justice of God is intimately tied up with the righteousness of God; indeed some of the basic biblical words may be translated either "righteousness" or "justice." Yet, strictly speaking, justice may be understood as the more immediate application of righteousness in the affairs of men and women. See *TWOT*, 2:948; *NIDNTT*, 2:363; Heinisch, *Theology of the Old Testament*, pp. 85-91; John Miley, *Systematic Theology* (New York: Methodist Book Concern, 1892), 1:201-4.

[17]Pope, *Compendium of Christian Theology*, 1:335-39. On the role of God as Judge, see *TWOT*, 2:947; *TWB*, p. 118; *EDT*, p. 952; *EDT*, 595; *ZPEB*, 3:758-59; Jacob, *Theology of the Old Testament*, pp. 96-98; Guthrie, *New Testament Theology*, pp. 87-88; Kummel, *Theology of New Testament*, pp. 39-40; Calvin, *Institutes*, 1:822-31; Charles Hodge, *Systematic Theology* (London: James Clark, 1960), 1:416-7; *CD* 2/1, p. 381.

The Son

The holiness and righteousness of Jesus are tightly knit together as is revealed in the title given to Jesus in the preaching of the early church as "the Holy and Righteous One" (Acts 3:14). When this is joined with John's description of him as "Jesus Christ the righteous" (1 Jn 2:1), it is obvious that the New Testament writers understood Jesus to have the same character as the Father in his righteousness. By revealing moral holiness and clarifying for men and women God's standards of right and wrong, Jesus is certainly modeling the holy character of God in terms of righteousness.[18]

Judge. Under the category of this legal terminology Jesus plays several roles. In his divinity, the first is his role as Judge. In one of his strongest claims to equality with God, Jesus declares that the Father has given him two prerogatives of deity, viz., to give life and to exercise judgment. "The Father judges no one, but has given all judgment to the Son, that all may honor the Son, even as they honor the Father." For God "has given him authority to execute judgment, because he is the Son of man" (Jn 5:22-23, 27). It is this authority from the Father that serves as a basis for Jesus' role as Judge. "As I hear, I judge; and my judgment is just, because I seek not my own will but the will of him who sent me" (5:30).

The statements of Jesus should not have been unexpected in the light of Jeremiah's prophecy regarding the coming Messiah. "In those days and at that time I will cause a righteous Branch to spring forth for David; and he shall execute justice and righteousness in the land. . . . And this is the name by which it will be called: 'The LORD is our righteousness'" (Jer 33:15-16). Isaiah also describes the Messiah as one who "shall not judge by what his eyes see, or decide by what his ears hear; but with righteousness he shall judge the poor, and decide with equity for the meek of the earth" (Is 11:3-5). Accordingly, Peter declares to the Gentiles that the apostles were commanded to "testify that he is the one ordained by God to be judge of the living and the dead" (Acts 10:42).

Jesus' role as judge does not terminate at his ascension. He is the one who will judge the earth at the close of the age. So Paul warns, "We must all appear before the judgment seat of Christ" (2 Cor 5:10). He alerts us of "Christ Jesus who is to judge the living and the dead by his appearing and his kingdom." Just as God the Father judges in righteousness, so Revelation depicts Christ as being "Faithful

---

[18]On the righteousness of Christ, see *NIDNTT,* 3:362.

and True, and in righteousness he judges" (Rev. 19:11).[19] Since judgment relates to reward as well as to punishment, Paul can in confidence write regarding his own status, "There is laid up for me the crown of righteousness, which the Lord, the righteous judge, will award to me on that Day, and not only to me but also to all who have loved his appearing" (2 Tim 4:8).

Advocate. While the major accent of the legal language pictures Jesus as a Judge, there is a minor role where he is described as an Advocate. This comes in the description of Jesus as the "paraclete." The word is best translated as "advocate" or "counselor" rather than in some of the older translations, "comforter." It is really legal terminology that places Jesus in the position of defender. As Paraclete or Counselor, Jesus is the one called alongside to plead our case, so that "if any one does sin, we have an advocate with the Father, Jesus Christ the righteous" (1 Jn 2:1). He is able to plead our case as the Son of man, because he is the only one who has been fully obedient to all the law and the will of God.[20]

Witness. There is a third role within the legal category in which Jesus is described as a witness. As a witness Jesus gives testimony to the character and work of God and to himself. Jesus sees his own witness to himself as that which is joined with his Father's so that the dual witness required in the Old Testament to confirm a matter may be fulfilled. "In your law it is written that the testimony of two men is true; I bear witness to myself, and the Father who sent me bears witness to me" (Jn 8:17-18; cf. 5:31-37). The concept of giving testimony is also closely bound up with Jesus' role as Revealer. He gives witness to God and testifies to people regarding God's character and word, and as such he is the One who reveals and makes known God's will and nature to men and women.[21] But the role of the witness is also a part of legal terminology and a part of the normal procedure within any courtroom. It is in this capacity that Jesus is able to testify for the truth. He is a witness to God regarding human activity and a witness to people of the way God is working.

The Holy Spirit

The relationship between righteousness and the Holy Spirit is found within the

---

[19]For further discussion of Jesus as Judge, see *TDNT*, 3:937, 943; *ZPEB*, 3:759.
[20]For Jesus as advocate, see *BDT*, p. 30; *TDNT*, 5:800-814; *ZPEB*, 1:66; *ISBE(rev)*, 1:60.
[21]Cf. chapter five on Jesus as Personal Revealer.

promise of the giving of the Spirit in the New Covenant. When "the Spirit is poured upon us from on high, . . . then justice will dwell in the wilderness, and righteousness abide in the fruitful field. And the effect of righteousness will be peace, and the result of righteousness, quietness and trust for ever" (Is 32:15-17). The promise of the coming of the Spirit is coupled with the expectation that righteousness of conduct will pervade the relationships between people. The Holy Spirit then becomes the agent which practically works out righteousness in human relationships.[22]

Judge. In the Old Testament the Holy Spirit is not directly called a judge, but the functions of this role may be properly inferred when the Spirit of God comes on some to give them the power to exercise judgment, especially in terms of punishment on God's enemies (Judg 14:19; 15:14).[23] Further, it is the Spirit of the Lord that shall rest on the Messiah, empowering him to judge with righteousness and equity (Is 11:2-5). It is this servant Messiah of whom God declares, "I have put my Spirit upon him, he will bring forth justice to the nations" (Is 42:1; see 42:3-4; Mic 3:8). There is clearly a close connection between the Spirit and the Messiah in exercising judgment.

Paraclete. In the New Testament when Jesus is preparing his disciples for his departure, he describes the coming Holy Spirit as the Paraclete. "I will pray the Father, and he will give you another Counselor [Paraclete], to be with you, . . . even the Spirit of truth" (Jn 14:16-17, 26). When this Counselor/Advocate arrives, he will "convince the world of sin and of righteousness and of judgment" (16:8). So the role of the Holy Spirit to the nonbelievers is to convict them of their transgressions, making them conscious that they are not living according to God's standard of righteousness and that they will come under the judgment of God if they do not change. But for those who are believers in Jesus, the Paraclete becomes a counselor alongside them to plead their cases before the Father and minister to them according to God's standard of truth.[24]

The Scripture refers to both Jesus and the Spirit as "paraclete." While the same is not true of God the Father, he is described as *paraklēseous*, (παρακλήσεους). This may be translated as "the God of all encouragement."

---

[22]On the Holy Spirit and righteousness, see *TWOT*, 2:753; *NIDNTT*, 3:362.

[23]Is 40:7 may refer to the Spirit of the Lord who brings judgment on Israel.

[24]On Spirit as advocate, see *BDT*, p. 30; *ISBE(rev)*, 3:659ff.; *TDNT* 5, p. 300; Kummel, *Theology of the New Testament*, pp. 314-17.

The verbal form of this is also used extensively of God by Paul in 2 Corinthians 1:3-7. Many translations deal with this as God's comforting role. It might be better translated as "encouragement," which would be closer to the role of a counselor or advocate in legal categories. However, the context here is the role of God the Father who is doing the encouragement, and there is nothing to suggest any legal overtones. This may be one of the occasions where some words bleed from one language category to another, and in this case it would be a conjoining of both legal and family language as a description of God the Father.

Witness. The Holy Spirit, who is described as a Counselor/Advocate by Jesus, is also referred to in legal language as a witness. "When the Counselor comes, whom I shall send to you from the Father, even the Spirit of truth, who proceeds from the Father, he will bear witness to me" (Jn 15:26). In a similar vein John declares that "the Spirit is the witness, because the Spirit is the truth" (1 Jn 5:7). So the Holy Spirit serves in the New Testament as a legal Advocate to stand alongside the believer and plead his case before God but also as a witness to Jesus and to the truth of God.

The Holy Spirit also bears witness to believers with respect to giving them assurance regarding their own salvation. Thus Paul writes, "It is the Spirit himself bearing witness with our spirit that we are children of God" (Rom 8:16). The Spirit witnesses God's truth to the heart, and in particular witnesses to the truth of saving grace in the heart of the children of God. It is part of the internal testimony of the Spirit that brings a deep conviction that an individual has come to an experience of God's saving grace. This assurance is often described in terms of "the witness of the Spirit."[25]

Man and Woman

Old Testament. There is no question that from the beginning of God's establishment of a relationship with the people of Israel that he is looking for righteous people. This means those who will be obedient to his law. He desires an obedience based on faith and an obedience that leads to the conformity of life to his own holy character. "Therefore, if you will obey my voice and keep my covenant, you shall be my own possession among all peoples" (Ex 19:5). Israel does not

---

[25]On the witness of the Spirit, see Wesley, *Standard Sermons*, 1:199-236; 2:341-59; Pope, *Compendium of Christian Theology*, 3:115-22; Miley, *Systematic Theology*, 2:342-47.

always obey, and on one occasion their disobedience leads to their wandering in the wilderness for forty years (Num 13—14). When they finally are ready to enter God's promised land, God repeatedly reminds them of his call to obedience and the consequences of disobedience.

> And now, O Israel, give heed to the statutes and the ordinances which I teach you, and do them; that you may live, and go in and take possession of the land which the LORD, the God of your fathers, gives you. You shall not add to the word which I command you, nor take from it; that you may keep the commandments of the LORD your God which I command you. (Deut 4:1-2)

Part of God's purpose has to do with the missionary responsibility of Israel to other peoples. He desires for other nations to say of Israel, "What great nation is there, that has statutes and ordinances so righteous as all this law?" (Deut 4:8). However, God also desires that his people walk in obedience so that they might then be recipients of his multiple blessings. "You shall walk in all the way which the LORD your God has commanded you, that you may live, and that it may go well with you, and that you may live long in the land which you shall possess" (Deut 5:33).[26]

New Testament. Jesus expresses the same desire for obedience for those living under the New Covenant. One of his earliest commandments to his disciples, "Follow me," requires a decision on their part as to whether or not to obey. For those who begin to follow him in obedience, he quickly begins to show how they are to continue to live in obedience to the law of God (Mt 4:19; 5:17-19). They are to be obedient not only to the Old Testament as the written word of God but also to the words of Jesus. Thus, he closes his earliest teaching to his disciples with the parable about the wise and the foolish man. It was the wise man who heard the words of Jesus and did them, whereas the foolish man heard the words but did not do them (Mt 7:24-27). Jesus drives the significance of this point home with the statement, "Not every one who says to me, 'Lord, Lord,' shall enter the kingdom of heaven, but he who does the will of my Father who is in heaven" (Mt 7:21).

Peter learned this lesson well and so he can write to the Christians that if they are to be holy in their conduct as God is holy, they cannot be conformed to the

---

[26]See Deut 6:1, 3, 17, 24-25; *TWOT,* 1:752-54; *BDT,* pp. 69-70; *TDNT,* 1:216; *EDT,* p. 624.

passions of their former ignorance as unbelievers, but they must be "as obedient children" (1 Pet 1:14-16). In the New Testament, as in the Old Testament, obedience is understood to be based on one's faith. It is not a substitute for trust but rather the logical expression of faith exercised in God (1:7-9).[27]

While the concept of obedience is particularly apropos to the legal category in which an individual must relate to God as the Righteous Judge, this is not the only category to which obedience applies. It is certainly implied in the relationship between an individual and God as King. A citizen must be subject to the laws of his sovereign and in that sense be obedient. In the parallel figure between master and slave the concept of obedience is even more pronounced. Further, it appears in the relationship between a shepherd and his sheep. The sheep must follow the shepherd in obedience to his voice commands. Lastly, and perhaps most importantly, obedience relates to the family category. Children are clearly to live in obedience to their parents, and believers must walk in obedience to their heavenly Father. So the idea of obedience is widespread across several of the roles that relate God to individuals and must be understood in terms of its relevance for each one. Within legal language obedience has as its primary focus conformity to God's law as an expression of holy character.

Sin

State of sin: Lawlessness. While it is clear from Scripture that God desires a relationship of obedience to his law and, therefore, conformity to his nature, in actual practice what we find is people walking in disobedience to the law of God. In consequence, one of the definitions of sin in this category is lawlessness. "Everyone who commits sin is guilty of lawlessness; sin is lawlessness" (1 Jn 3:4). Thus, those who sin may be described as the ones who "do not obey the truth, but obey wickedness" (Rom 2:8). Lawlessness refers here to a state of the heart that is rejecting the law, that is, the will of God. It is a spirit of rejection of the law of God that leads to external acts of disobedience, but in itself lawlessness constitutes a basic reaction against God and any authority conveyed through his law.

This spirit of lawlessness may be expressed by either those who have the written law or those who do not. God declares that all will be "judged by the law"

---

[27]For discussion of obedience, see *EDT*, pp. 784-85; *ZPEB*, 4:482-84.

for breaking the law. This applies to the Jews and those who have had the written law of God but also to the Gentiles who have some of that law written on their conscience (Rom 2:12-24).[28] The judgment of God clearly will come on different groups of people depending on their obedience to their understanding of the will of God. Judgment will be most severe on those who have had the written law and therefore more light, but it will also apply to those who have had the light of conscience and nature, depending on their response to God through those.[29]

Act of sin: Transgression. A variation of the description of sin as lawlessness is the concept of sin as transgression of the law of God (Rom 4:15). Paul mentions Eve as the first transgressor, implying that she clearly knew the law of God and yet disobeyed (1 Tim 2:14). James explains sin as a transgression of the law when he warns, "If you show partiality, you commit sin, and are convicted by the law as transgressors" (Jas 2:9, 11).[30] Similarly, the writer of Hebrews declares "every transgression or disobedience received a just retribution" (Heb 2:2). Indeed, it was because of "the transgressions under the first covenant" that Christ came as a mediator of a New Covenant to redeem humankind (9:15).

Unrighteousness. There are several results that follow from breaking the righteous law. One is that a person is not in conformity to the righteousness of God's holy nature, and therefore, is described as not being righteous. "None is righteous, no, not one" (Rom 3:10). The sin of disobedience and transgression does not produce righteousness, because it is the opposite of righteousness. This is the obvious conclusion of the fact that sin is the opposite of the law of God, that is, of that which reflects the righteousness of his holy character.[31]

Guilt. In addition to the lack of righteousness, the breaking of the law produces guilt. "For whoever keeps the whole law but fails in one point has become guilty of all of it" (Jas 2:10). Guilt, of course, has to do with being held accountable to the standard of God's law (Rom 3:19).[32] When one breaks the

[handwritten marginal note: Breaking Law Produces]

---

[28]For sin as lawlessness, see also Rom 2:25 and 1 Tim 1:9.

[29]For further discussion of sin as lawlessness, see *TDNT*, 2:191; Hodge, *Systematic Theology*, 2:180-91.

[30]Louis Berkhof, *Systematic Theology* (Edingburgh: Banner of Truth, 1958), p. 231. For sin as transgression/ rebellion, see *TWOT*, 2:741-42, 863-64.

[31]On unrighteousness, see the words related to *adikos* (ἄδικος), *BTLNT*, pp. 200-202; *TDNT*, 1:149-63.

[32]On the words and concept of guilt, see *NIDNTT*, 2:18-38, 142; *TDOT*, 1:429-37; *TDNT*, 1: 279-80; *BDT*, p. 244; *EDT*, pp. 489-90; *ZPEB*, 2:852-53; *ISBE(rev)*, 2:580-81; Leon Morris, "'Asham," *EvQ* 30, no. 4 (1958): 196-210; Eichrodt, *Theology of the Old Testament*, 2:413-22; Kummel, *Theology of the New Testament*, pp. 181-4.

law one becomes guilty of transgression. The guilt has an objective component in terms of one's standing before God as the Righteous Judge and his law. But it also has the subjective components that are usually identified with guilt feelings and shame that grow out of an awareness that one has done wrong. The objective side of guilt can only be dealt with by punishment for sin, and that is why the biblical picture of Christ's substitutionary atonement is so significant. It is Christ himself who has born our guilt and paid the penalty for it by his own death on the cross (3:24-25). The subjective side of guilt is God's gift to individuals to make them conscious of the fact they have disobeyed his law and that they are under the threat of punishment until they receive forgiveness for their sin.

Punishment. A third result of disobedience to the law of God is that of punishment. It comes in the form of the judgment of God on unrighteousness or sin. Paul in his discussion of God's righteous judgment declares, "All who have sinned without the law will also perish without the law, and all who have sinned under the law will be judged by the law" (Rom 2:12). He declares that in the light of the justice of God the condemnation of the sinner is just (3:5-8). When he says that "the law brings wrath" (4:15), he means that those who know God's decrees as recorded in his law but do not do them "deserve to die" (1:32). Punishment then is the just reward of God for those who have transgressed his law. Because he is righteous and has made a universe to conform to his nature, all unrighteousness must be punished.[33]

Jesus makes clear that it is not just external disobedience that brings the judgment of God but also internal disobedience. "You have heard that it was said to the men of old, 'You shall not kill; and whoever kills shall be liable to judgment.' But I say to you that every one who is angry with his brother shall be liable to judgment" (Mt 5:21-22). Jesus is concerned with both outward and inward righteousness and therefore both outward and inward obedience. God, who knows the heart, will judge men and women according to their internal obedience to his righteous standard as well as their external conformity to his law.[34]

---

[33]On the concept of punishment, see *TDNT*, 1:181; 3:814; Girdlestone, *Synonyms of the Old Testament*, pp. 254-55; *NIDNTT*, 3:98; *ZPEB*, 5:954-57; Eichrodt, *Theology of the Old Testament*, 2:423-33; Roland de Vaux, *Ancient Israel* (New York: McGraw-Hill, 1961), 1:143-63; CD 2/1, pp. 390-93.

[34]For eternal punishment/judgment, see Mt 25:46; Jn 16:8, 11; Heb 6:2, 9:27; 10:26-31.

Salvation

Penal theory of the atonement. Under this role with its focus on righteousness, the atonement of Christ can be viewed as both active and passive obedience to the righteous standard that God has set forth. Obedience is the expected response to God's righteous standard. Christ's active obedience was his conforming of his life to the law of God throughout his lifetime. This active obedience in a sense counteracts that of Adam's disobedience. "For as by one man's disobedience many were made sinners, so by one man's obedience many will be made righteous" (Rom 5:19). By this active obedience Jesus fulfilled all the law of God and thus atoned for our failure to fulfill it. So from God's perspective believers are viewed as recipients of Christ's active righteousness (Gal 4:4-5; Rom 5:8; 8:3; 10:4; Phil 3:9; Mt 5:17). This means the righteousness demanded by the law and rendered by Christ might become ours by faith. Accordingly, "Christ is the end of the law so that there may be righteousness for everyone who believes" (Rom 10:4 NRSV). By his active obedience Christ in our place fulfills the law and satisfies the just demand of God for righteousness.

The complementary side of Jesus' active obedience is his passive obedience in his death on the cross when he took on himself the full punishment of the sins and guilt of everyone. His passive obedience means a willingness to suffer and die and to render full satisfaction for the punishment that sin rightly deserves according to the law. "Christ redeemed us from the curse of the law, having become a curse for us" (Gal 3:13).

This view of the atonement (i.e., the death of Christ to satisfy the righteousness of God) begins with the premise that God takes sin very seriously. "The wages of sin is death" (Rom 6:23). Someone has to die so that righteousness and justice may be fulfilled. This view focuses on Christ's death to pay that penalty in place of sinners. "For our sake he made him to be sin who knew no sin, so that in him we might become the righteousness of God" (2 Cor 5:21). Since it is clear that Christ died for us and in our stead, the exchange metaphor accents the fact that the atonement involves an element of substitution (Mt 20:28; 2 Cor 5:21; Gal 2:20; 1 Pet 3:18; 1 Cor 11:23-24). Paul especially emphasizes this. "God demonstrates his own love for us in this: while we were still sinners, Christ died for us" (Rom 5:8 NIV). It is this focus on Christ dying for another that has led to this emphasis of the atonement sometimes being described as the substitutionary theory of the atonement. In reality substitution is also involved in a number of the other theories of the atonement, but it takes a very central role in this one.

Because the emphasis in this language figure is on Christ's dying to take the penalty we deserve for sin, it is frequently referred to as the penal substitution theory. It involves not only the substitute for the penalty but a satisfaction of the justice of God. It is therefore very closely allied to Anselm's satisfaction theory discussed earlier in chapter four. The slight difference in focus was that Anselm's emphasis was a satisfaction of God's honor as majestic King, whereas in this role the focus is on the satisfying of divine justice with God in his role of righteous Judge. The two emphases obviously contain significant overlap.

The Reformers borrowed much of Anselm's language, but their focus on legal categories from Scripture had them put the emphasis on the penal substitution element in the atonement. Many Protestants following their lead tend to identify this as *the* orthodox view of the atonement. While it is right at the center of any such view of the atonement, an evangelical or orthodox view must be described broadly enough to include elements of the satisfaction theory, propitiation theory and ransom theory.[35] We are distinguishing these various theories to show the relationship of different biblical data to the different roles of God, but in reality there certainly is an overlap of these elements in several different ways.[36]

Justification. An understanding of God's saving grace in the legal category centers in the concept of justification. It is first introduced by Jesus when he talks about the parable of the Pharisee and the publican. It was the publican who cried out, "God, be merciful to me a sinner!" Jesus said that the result of this recognition of sin, confession of sin, and implicit cry of faith was that "this man went down to his house justified" (Lk 18:9-14). Paul picks up on this legal language used by Jesus and elaborates at length on the concept of justification by faith (Rom 3:21—5:11). Although the Old Testament bears witness to the righteousness of God, Paul says God's way is to manifest this righteousness in those who have faith in Jesus Christ. Since all have sinned and fallen short of the glory of God, i.e., the righteousness of God's holy character, there is no way they may justify themselves or make themselves righteous. But God by his grace has justified

[35]Wayne Grudem, *Systematic Theology* (Grand Rapids, Mich.: Zondervan, 1994), pp. 577-81.

[36]Emil Brunner, *The Mediator,* trans. Olive Wyon (London: Lutterworth, 1934), pp. 455-74; Thomas Oden, *The Word of Life* (San Francisco: Harper & Row, 1989), pp. 358, 362, 376, 382.

sinners as a gift based on the atonement. It is the death of Jesus as the propitiation for sin that demonstrates God's righteousness. Because of God's divine forbearance, for a time he passes over sins, but his righteousness ultimately demands that there be judgment on sin. With that judgment placed on Jesus at the cross, God has proved himself to be righteous and has made it possible for him to justify those who have faith in Jesus (Rom 3:21-26).

Paul is at pains to show that this righteousness comes not by obedience to the law of God but rather springs from faith (Rom 3:26, 28, 30). Since God's original plan had always been that faith should precede obedience, Paul clarifies the relationship between obedience to the law and faith by saying, "Do we then overthrow the law by this faith? By no means! On the contrary, we uphold the law" (3:31).

By faith. To make clear his case that justification or the making of people righteous has always been based on faith and not just on obedience to the law of God, Paul cites the case of Abraham. He is one who "believed God, and it was reckoned to him as righteousness." He then points out that this declaration of his righteousness came before Abraham's obedience to the law of circumcision. So he concludes, "The promise to Abraham and his descendants, that they should inherit the world, did not come through the law but through the righteousness of faith." It is faith as a human response to God that makes it possible for God's saving grace to make righteousness manifest in people. "That is why it depends on faith, in order that the promise may rest on grace" (Rom 4:3, 9-13, 16). Paul concludes that just as Abraham's faith was reckoned to him as righteousness, so "it will be reckoned to us who believe in him that raised from the dead Jesus our Lord, who was put to death for our trespasses and raised for our justification" (4:22-25; see 5:1, 9, 16; 8:30).

Paul reiterates his classic argument on justification again in his letter to the Galatians. He says that we are those "who know that a man is not justified by works of the law but through faith in Jesus Christ, even we have believed in Christ Jesus, in order to be justified by faith in Christ, and not by works of the law, because by works of the law shall no one be justified" (Gal 2:16). Paul again uses Abraham as the example of one who believed God, and it was reckoned to him for righteousness (3:6-9). "Now it is evident that no man is justified before God by the law; for he who through faith is righteous shall live" (3:11).[37] It is God the

---

[37]See also 1 Cor 6:11; Tit 3:7. On justification, see *TDNT*, 2:202-10, 214-19; *NIDNTT*, 3:362-65; *TWB*, pp. 118-19; *BDT*, pp. 296-98; *EDT*, pp. 593-97.

righteous Judge who justifies people before the law, and it is their faith, enabled by prevenient grace, that is the instrumental cause that makes that justification possible.[38]

Imputed and imparted righteousness. Because justification is a legal pronouncement by God the righteous Judge there is some question as to the extent of the effect of this experience on the life of a new believer. Justification certainly gives a person a new legal standing before God as one who is free from guilt and punishment. It also gives him a new relationship with God as one who is not any longer a transgressor of the law but one who is righteous. This new standing with God is a genuine change, but it is a change of relationship. The question is, does the concept of justification also include actually making the individual righteous while at the same time declaring him to be righteous? In other words, is righteousness imparted subjectively as well as imputed declaratively? Is a person actually made righteous or just pronounced righteous? Many insist that the legal categories allow only for an imputed or declared righteousness. They see justification as a purely judicial or forensic function of God the righteous Judge, and therefore the only possibility is an imputed righteousness.[39]

The actual impartation of a holy and righteous nature in the individual at conversion seems to be more closely related to the work of God in regeneration, the new birth and sanctification. Within those categories the actual subjective change of a new believer's nature falls most naturally then under discussions of God as the Creator who regenerates and the Father who begets children. But at the same time there seems to be some overlap of roles with the picture of God as the righteous Judge who justifies. Certainly both must be included in any holistic understanding of salvation by faith. But it seems that the way Paul uses the language in Romans and Galatians to describe the concept of justification implies more than just a change of standing or relationship with God. He suggests that God was actually making Abraham righteous and therefore actually makes new believers righteous, i.e., imparts righteousness as holiness.

---

[38]On justification and faith, see *TDNT*, 2:206-7; Calvin, *Institutes*, 1:792-821; 2:11-18; Guthrie, *New Testament Theology*, pp. 501-7; George Eldon Ladd, *A Theology of the New Testament* (Grand Rapids, Mich.: Eerdmans, 1974), pp. 437-50; Kummel, *Theology of the New Testament*, pp. 198-202; Hodge, *Systematic Theology*, 1:423ff.; Miley, *Systematic Theology*, 2:309-13.

[39]See *TDNT*, 2:215-16; Leon Morris, *The Apostolic Preaching of the Cross* (London: Tyndale Press, 1965), pp. 249ff.; Ladd, *Theology of the New Testament*, 443-47.

This perspective is reinforced in Paul's writing to the Corinthians about being in Christ as a "new creation." He then spells out the meaning of this new creation in terms of reconciliation and not counting their trespasses against them. So a renewed relationship with God is a part of this along with the forgiveness of their trespasses. But he closes the argument with a description of God's making them righteous. "For our sake he made him to be sin who knew no sin, so that in him we might become the righteousness of God" (2 Cor 5:17-21). While some want to make being "in him" only an imputed righteousness, the same statement is used earlier about being "in Christ" as God's instrument of making "a new creation" (5:17). The implication is that God is making something new from the inside out and this includes the actual righteousness of God's holy character that is administered by being subjectively appropriated by a believer in the experience of reconciliation and forgiveness.

From a strictly forensic or judicial understanding of the role of Judge, it would be difficult to say that God as the righteous Judge actually makes individuals righteous. Nevertheless, Paul seems to imply just that, and this is probably due to his holistic understanding of God. He is not only an impartial, just Judge, he is also one who is concerned with making people new in themselves as well as changing their relationship to him. Thus when Paul talks about a person's faith being reckoned to him as righteousness, he is talking about more than just imputed righteousness but actual imparted righteousness as well.[40]

Growth in Christian Experience

Faith leads to obedience. Jesus declares to his followers that those who respond by faith in him must continue to give evidence of that faith by their obedience to God's word. "Jesus then said to the Jews who had believed in him, 'If you continue in my word, you are truly my disciples'" (Jn 8:31). While a person begins to trust in Christ in a moment of time, the evidence of continued trust is expressed in terms of obedience. So Jesus reiterates to his disciples when he is ready to leave them that if they are to continue the intimate relationship that they have, involving trust and love, they must continue to obey. "If you love

---

[40]On imputed versus imparted righteousness see Pope, *Compendium of Christian Theology*, 1:335-36; 2:404-6, 409-11; *BDT*, 296-98; *TDNT*, 2:204-5; *NIDNTT*, 3:271; *BDT*, pp. 276-77; Vincent Taylor, *Forgiveness and Reconciliation* (London: Macmillan, 1948), p. 57; Wesley, *Standard Sermons*, 2:420-41.

me, you will keep my commandments" (Jn 14:15).[41]

This pattern is consistent with Paul's statement of the gospel in the theme of the book of Romans, when he declares that the gospel is the power for salvation to everyone who has faith (Rom 1:16). That seems to have specific reference to the initial act of faith in Christ. But it is followed by his statement, "For in it the righteousness of God is revealed through faith for faith; as it is written 'He who through faith is righteous shall live' " (1:17). His second statement focuses on the manifestation of God's righteousness in the life of the individual as he continues in faith. The righteousness of God is both imputed and imparted as one begins to believe, but there is an implication of ongoing trust in Christ by the statement "the righteous shall live by faith." This is consistent with the whole book of Romans that begins with the discussion of how one comes to justification by faith (3:21—5:11) but also includes a discussion of the implications of living a life of faith (12—15).

Faith and law. In Galatians Paul addresses the question of justification by faith versus justification by works of the law. He reiterates that we are "to be justified by faith in Christ, and not by works of the law" (Gal 2:16). Paul certainly means that no one can be justified by keeping either the moral or the ceremonial law. "If a law had been given which could make alive, then righteousness would indeed be by the law" (3:21). He makes the case so strongly in his letter that a superficial reading of Galatians has left some with the impression that there is no place for the law or obedience to the law of God for those who have been justified by faith. An understanding of the context in which he is writing makes that interpretation problematic.

The problem the Galatians were facing related to a group of Judaizers who were insisting that the Gentile Christians not only believe in Christ by faith but also keep the ceremonial law of the Jews. The question of the Gentile Christians keeping the moral law of God was not really an issue, as is clear from the fact that all the problem areas that Paul addresses in his letter to the Galatians have to do with ceremonial law. The kind of ceremonial regulations the Judaizers wanted to impose upon the Gentile Christians included dietary regulations (2:12), the keeping of certain Jewish festival occasions (4:10), and circumcision (5:2-12). It is the freedom from obedience to the ceremonial law that Paul declares Christ

---

[41]See also Jn 14:21, 23-24; 15:10.

has given to those who believe in him (5:1). In no way does he mean to imply that freedom from the ceremonial law also provides a license to disobey the moral law of God. Indeed, nothing in the letter leaves one with the impression that anybody involved, whether Peter, Paul, the Judaizers or the Galatians, had any question about their responsibility to walk in obedience to the moral law of God.

Law and love. Paul does in fact caution the Galatians that their freedom from ceremonial law should not lead them to consider "freedom as an opportunity for the flesh" (Gal 5:13). He exhorts them rather that through love they be servants of one another. He substantiates this exhortation with the statement, "For the whole law is fulfilled in one word, 'You shall love your neighbor as yourself'" (Gal 5:14). Paul clearly means that the expressions of their love ought to be in harmony with and expressed through the whole of the moral law, not as a substitute for it. He is encouraging the Galatians to love their neighbor as a means of expressing their obedience to the moral law of God. This is paralleled by John in his statement, "By this we know that we love the children of God, when we love God and obey his commandments" (1 Jn 5:2).

Law and walking by Spirit. Paul continues in his discussion of how one fulfills the law of God by describing obedience in terms of walking by the Spirit (Gal 5:16). He says, "If we live by the Spirit, let us also walk by the Spirit" (5:25). If one comes to life by the Spirit, then one needs to walk in obedience to the moral law of God through the power of the Spirit. Thus, when Paul says, "If you are led by the Spirit you are not under the law," He certainly cannot mean that you are not under the moral law of God but rather that you are not under the ceremonial law of God. In the very next verse he describes the works of the flesh that are clear violations of the moral law of God, and he closes his list with the warning "that those who do such things shall not inherit the kingdom of God" (5:18-21). The implication is plain that any who are involved in immorality, impurity, licentiousness, idolatry, sorcery, enmity, strife, jealousy, anger, selfishness, dissension, party spirit, envy, drunkenness, carousing and the like will not inherit the kingdom of God, are not walking by the Spirit, are not loving their neighbors as themselves and are not fulfilling the whole moral law of God. But those who are trying through Christ's love to be servants to one another, to fulfill the whole moral law of God, to love their neighbors as themselves and to walk by the Spirit of God will reap the fruit of the Spirit (5:22-23) and the ability to "bear one another's burdens, and so fulfill the law of Christ" (6:2; also Col 2:16; 2 Cor 10:5).

Faith and works. The picture of justification by faith and its relationship to obedience after conversion is further clarified by James. He also speaks of fulfilling the royal law of Scripture, "You shall love your neighbor as yourself" (Jas 2:8). However, the chief focus of James's discussion about fulfilling the law has to do not with the ceremonial law but with the moral law. For example, he discusses the questions of adultery and murder as representative examples of the moral law (2:11). So when he begins to talk about the question of works in relationship to faith, it is clearly a question of works in terms of obedience to the moral law. If one is not meeting his responsibility according to the moral law to meet the physical needs of his neighbor, then he is not walking according to love and his declaration of faith is dead (2:14-17). Real faith, declares James, manifests itself in expression of obedience to God that is seen in our works. "Show me your faith apart from your works, and I by my works will show you my faith" (2:18).

James, like Paul, uses Abraham as his example in his discussion of justification. He declares that Abraham's faith was manifested in his works when he was willing to obey the word of God and offer his son Isaac on the altar. "You see that faith was active along with his works, and faith was completed by works." According to James, this is the proper understanding of the expression, "Abraham believed God, and it was reckoned to him as righteousness" (2:21-23). When James says, "You see that a man is justified by works and not by faith alone," he clearly means that the works in terms of obedience to the moral law of God are the evidence that a person has believed and continues to walk by faith. "For as the body apart from the spirit is dead, so faith apart from works is dead" (2:24, 26).[42]

Walking in obedience. John also describes a walk of obedience as evidence that one is continuing to live by faith in a right relationship with the Lord. In the context of his discussion of Christians having an advocate with the Father, namely Jesus Christ the righteous, he declares that "by this we may be sure that we know him, if we keep his commandments. He who says, 'I know him,' but disobeys his commandments is a liar, and the truth is not in him" (1 Jn 2:1-4). From John's perspective one cannot walk in disobedience to the clear

---

[42]For further discussion of the relationship of righteousness to faith and works in both Paul and James, see *TDNT,* 2:200-210; *NIDNTT,* 3:369-70.

commandment of the Lord and claim to actually know him, i.e., be in a right relationship of faith with him. For John one of the tests of our assurance that we abide in Christ is that we are walking in obedience. "By this we may be sure that we are in him: he who says he abides in him ought to walk in the same way in which he walked" (2:5-6). Thus, abiding in Christ is contingent on our obedience. "All who keep his commandments abide in him, and he in them" (1 Jn. 3:24; cf. Jn. 7:10; 15:4-5). Further, answers to prayer are also dependent on continued obedience. "We receive from him whatever we ask, because we keep his commandments and do what pleases him" (1 Jn 3:22). This is not difficult for John, because from his perspective God's "commandments are not burdensome" (5:3).

Peter echoes the same concern that those who would be holy as God is holy express it in their conduct by obedience. "As obedient children, do not be conformed to the passions of your former ignorance, but as he who has called you is holy, be holy yourselves in all your conduct." This obedience is expected in the light of God, "who judges each one impartially according to his deeds," and therefore Christians should "conduct yourselves with fear throughout the time of your exile" (1 Pet 1:14-17). In the light of the rest of Peter's letter it is clear that obedience as an expression of God's holiness will be manifest in circumstances that involve submission to proper authorities and a willingness to suffer for one's faith.[43]

Obedience out of faith. So within the legal category spiritual growth after conversion is described principally in terms of obedience as evidence that one is living by faith. The evidence that one is truly continuing to trust in God is the willingness to abide by his decisions and therefore live in obedience to his law. Learning what the commandments are and how to walk in obedience to them is part of the growth process. Very few new believers come into the experience of justification by faith aware of the full implications of what it means to walk in obedience to God. Discovering what God's commandments are and learning to apply his word to their lives in a trust which leads to obedience is a crucial dimension in one's experience of Christian growth. A believer is justified by God's grace and through the believer's faith he is able by the grace of God to live according to God's law in order to continue in fellowship with God and have his

---

[43]See Pope, *Compendium of Christian Theology*, 2:415-18.

life more perfectly conformed to God's character. This is how the law of God assumes its proper place in his life as he learns the implications of living by faith.

The Church

Since the church is a people under the authority of God, whatever God says to them becomes the standard for obedience. Therefore, they are always known as a people of the Word. Under the Old Covenant this is especially illustrated in the fact that Israel is a people committed to the Torah. The Torah includes both instruction and commandments. The instruction is more closely tied to the role of God as Personal Revealer and is seen particularly in the teaching office of God and those in spiritual leadership. The commandments and ordinances that also come under the Torah are more directly related to the role of God as the righteous Judge who gives statutes spelling out what righteous conduct entails. The use of the English word *law* emphasizes the latter of these two, but both are important to a proper understanding of the Torah or the Word of God. Since we have already dealt with the role of God as Personal Revealer of Torah as instruction in a previous chapter, our focus here is on the people living under the word of God as law.

Old Testament. The establishment of the church as a people under the word of God comes clearly at Mount Sinai. At the ratification of the covenant in Exodus 24 "all the words of the LORD and all the ordinances" are told to the people and they respond with a commitment to obey. Then "Moses wrote all the words of the LORD," and "he took the book of the covenant, and read it in the hearing of the people" (Ex 24:3-4, 7). From this point in the life of God's people, they are known as a people under the law or Torah, that is, under the authority of God through his written word.

A reiteration of the importance of God's people understanding themselves as a people of the law appears in Deuteronomy. "Moses summoned all Israel and said to them, 'Hear O Israel, the statutes and the ordinances which I speak in your hearing this day, and you shall learn them and be careful to do them'" (Deut 5:1). One of the key themes of the entire book is the crucial importance of walking in obedience to all the commandments of God (4:40, 44-45; 5:31-32; 6:1-3, 17-18, 20-25; 7:11-12; 8:1, 6, 11; 11:1, 8, 13, 22, 26-28; 28:1-2, 9; 30:16; 31:9). At the end of his life, as he is beginning to transfer leadership responsibility to Joshua, Moses again writes the law of the Lord as it has been given to him up to that point and presents it to the priests and elders of the nation (31:9, 12-13). Moses then commands the Levites to guard the law in the Ark of the Covenant that it may be a witness against them (31:24, 26). They are commanded to regularly read the law before all Israel so that it will continue to be familiar to them as the standard by which they live (31:11).

The importance of the word of God for the whole church of God is seen in the responsibility of the king in Israel to have his own copy of the law, to read it and to walk in obedience to it (Deut 17:18-20). When this is coupled with Samuel writing down the rights and duties of the kingship at the establishment of the monarchy, it is indisputable that Israel understood herself as the people of God under the Word of God. Everyone understood this meant all of the Israelites, including the king (1 Sam 10:25). This is the basis for establishing a constitutional monarchy: the king rules but under a higher authority, that is, God speaking through his word.

While at times Israel did not give the attention to the law of God as they should, God repeatedly calls their attention to it as a priority. During certain times of revival there is a special reemphasis on the book of the law (2 Kings 22:8-14). During the exile when the temple and the sacrificial system are destroyed, there is a fresh emphasis on the word of God as the basis for the identity of the people of Israel. The development of the synagogue during the exilic and intertestamental periods focused primarily on the reading and exposition of the word.

At their return from the exile both Ezra and Nehemiah lead the people in the fresh covenant commitment to obey the Lord as he has spoken in his law. It is particularly the reading and expounding of the law of God so that people can understand what God is saying that forms the basis of their identity (Ezra 7:6, 10; Neh 8:1-13). Because the church and the nation are so closely woven together under the Old Covenant, the word of the Lord that comes as law for the nation comes also as his law for the church.

New Testament. Under the New Covenant we have already noted that Jesus expects his disciples to live under the authority of the written word of God.

> Think not that I have come to abolish the law and the prophets; I have come not to abolish them but to fulfil them. For truly, I say to you, till heaven and earth pass away, not an iota, not a dot, will pass from the law until all is accomplished. Whoever then relaxes one of the least of these commandments and teaches men so,

shall be called least in the kingdom of heaven; but he who does them and teaches them shall be called great in the kingdom of heaven. (Mt 5:17-19)

Alongside the Old Testament Jesus very quickly begins to place his own words as the standard of authority for the church. "Every one then who hears these words of mine and does them will be like a wise man." (7:24, 28). At the end of this time with them he sends forth the Twelve as the nucleus of the church to make disciples of all nations, and one part of their responsibility is teaching others "to observe all that I have commanded you" (28:20).

Followers of Jesus in the New Testament did a better job of understanding the dual nature of the word of God than Israel did under the Old Covenant. There is a heavy focus on the word in the New Testament as teaching or instruction. It is very much like the Torah of the Old Covenant that was to instruct the people of Israel. But the word of God in the New Testament does carry clear specific commandments, and these also get attention, in a proper balance with the word of God as teaching (e.g., 5:21-48). As we discussed earlier, it is particularly the moral law of God that is not questioned in the New Testament. The only issue about law that appears negatively in the early church is the references to the ceremonial law or keeping the law as a means of justification. The law in terms of moral obedience is not questioned. The people of God continue to be under the authority of God at every stage of their development.

Full Sanctification

Holy living. Full sanctification in the legal language of Scripture is described primarily in terms of a state of holy, righteous living. The focus is not so much on a momentary experience in the life of a Christian that makes possible this level of righteous living as it is on the fact that such a state exists and that it is the privilege of Christians by the grace and power of God to live in it. This state of righteous living is based on a standard of righteousness given by God as an expression of his holy character. Therefore, all that has been said in terms of a standard that God sets for a holy people is related to this experience. "So the law is holy, and the commandment is holy and [righteous] and good" (Rom 7:12). The reason this is so is because it is based on the character of a holy God. In revealing this righteous character as an expression of his own holiness, God has set a standard by which he desires for his people to live, and consistent conformity to this standard, or full obedience to the commandments it contains, constitutes living in an experience of holiness of heart and life. That is the essence of what the New Testament means by full sanctification.

When God called Israel to "obey his voice" so they might be his own possession among all peoples, he gave them the moral law as the standard of righteous living. What he desired from Israel was a total commitment to be fully obedient, and the Scripture records that "all the people answered together and said, 'All that the LORD has spoken we will do' " (Ex 19:8; 24:7).

After an initial commitment to the covenant, God then begins to give his people the Ten Words, or Ten Commandments. The first of these sets the tone for the other nine: "You shall have no other gods before me" (Ex 20:3). This is the umbrella commandment that serves as a great declaration of monotheism. god is telling his people that he is the only God and that they are not to have any other god before or besides him. This is a particularly remarkable statement in a polytheistic world where people looked to multiple gods to meet multiple needs. Yahweh is now saying that in fact there are not any other gods and therefore people are not to look elsewhere for their needs to be met but to look to him to meet every need in their lives. So obedience to this commandment in the fullest sense of the word is that which makes full reflection of the righteous and holy character of God possible. For if he is the only God in one's life, then he becomes the controlling, directing force in their lives. This is what God desires from his people in every generation.

While it was God's obvious desire that his people walk in full obedience to his standard of righteousness and it was Israel's intention to do so when they first established the covenant at Mount Sinai, it quickly becomes clear that they did not fully walk according to this standard (Ex 32—34). Throughout the history of Israel it is evident that many times both the nation as a whole and individuals are walking in obedience to God's commandments, but numerous other times they do not. The fact that they often do obey makes it very difficult to say there was not grace or power available for them to be obedient. Certainly some individuals seem to walk before God blameless in the light of his law (e.g., Job, Daniel). Yet, there does seem to be a lack of power available to fully obey on a consistent long-term basis for a large number of people.

Law written on the heart. It is in this light that we must understand the promises of the New Covenant. Israel's repeated failure to walk in full obedience to the law of God was certainly permitted in part to make God's people in all ages aware of a need for a fuller grace and power. This seems to be what is promised in the predictions of a New Covenant. At the heart of this covenant God declares, "I will put my law within them, and I will write it upon their hearts" (Jer 31:33). In the New Testament age God provides a grace that will allow for an internalization of his law and therefore of his righteous character in a way that was not actualized for many under the Old Covenant. God does not say he will do away with his moral law but rather that he will inscribe it on their hearts. Apparently, he is describing an imparted righteousness that will make it possible for the individual to walk in full obedience to God's moral law and, therefore, be fully conformed to his holy character. According to the writer of Hebrews the privilege of living in this state of spiritual experience is possible under the New Covenant (Heb 8:10).

The Spirit and full obedience. The Old Testament hints that having this law within the heart is also related to a new availability of the Spirit of God under the New Covenant. "This is my covenant with them, says the LORD: my spirit which is upon you, and my words which I have put in your mouth, shall not depart out of your mouth" (Is 59:21). Ezekiel predicts this experience will come when under the New Covenant God takes out a stony heart, gives a heart of flesh and puts his Spirit within them "that they may walk in my statutes and keep my ordinances and obey them" (Ezek 11:19-20). When God desires to vindicate his holiness in the lives of believers, he promises that "I will put my spirit within you, and cause you to walk in my statutes and be careful to observe my ordinances" (36:27). So it seems as though the Old Testament writers expect a fuller standard of obedience to be possible under the New Covenant and tend to relate it to the new availability and fullness of the Spirit of God in that age.

This full standard of godly living is set before the disciples of Jesus very soon after they begin to follow after him in repentance and faith. In the Sermon on the Mount Jesus makes clear the kind of standards of righteous conduct that he wants to see in his followers (Mt 5—7). But it is just as evident that the disciples are not able to live up to this high standard according to the description that we have of them in the Gospels, even though they are living in the immediate presence of Jesus. But full conformity to that standard of godliness does appear to be evident in their character after Pentecost. The obvious conclusion is that it is the fullness of God's Spirit, like the prophets predicted, that is what gives power and grace for full obedience to the full will of God.

This seems to be what Paul is describing in his call for those who have been justified not to obey their passions any longer but rather: to yield their members and themselves to God as instruments of righteousness. This is possible because they are now living under a grace that has the power to enable them to fully obey. Thus, he exhorts them to be obedient slaves of God and to yield a kind of full obedience that leads to righteousness (Rom 6:12-16). The return that you get he says is sanctification. Before completing his letter he sets before the Romans the standard of godly living if one is walking in full obedience based on full faith in a righteous God (12—15).

Paul does the same thing for the Ephesians after his prayer that they may be filled with all the fullness of God. When he lays before them the challenge to "lead a life worthy of the calling to which you have been called" (Eph 4:1), he then gives them a standard for righteous living in the church (4:1-16), in personal ethical conduct (4:17-5:21) and in the Christian household (5:22—6:9). All of this is bound up with understanding and obeying the full will of the Lord and also continuing to "be filled with the Spirit" (5:17-18).[44]

Holiness as godliness. Sometimes, Paul describes this standard of holiness in terms of godliness (1 Tim 4:7; 6:3, 6, 11). Peter also equates holiness and godliness (2 Pet 3:11) and states that God has made available a power to live according to this standard of holiness. "His divine power has granted to us all things that pertain to life and godliness" (1:3; cf. 1:4, 6-7). It may well be this is the full standard of complete obedience that Peter is describing when he calls on Christians "as obedient children" not to be conformed to the passions of their former ignorance but to be holy—as God is holy—in *all* their conduct (1 Pet 1:14-15). From the perspective of the New Testament writers, complete obedience leading to total conformity of conduct to God's standard of holiness is possible, even if they do not always describe how one comes into this state of holy living. Clearly it is not automatic for all believers, or they would not have to exhort the Christians regarding their privileges of living a holy life. Just as clearly they view it as a realistic possibility that is available under the New Covenant.

Blamelessness. A final concept under the legal category that relates to full

---

[44]For further discussion of full sanctification as full obedience, see *BDT*, p. 370.

sanctification is blamelessness. To be free from blame means to be innocent or guiltless and so carries forensic connotations.[45] Under the Old Covenant God set a standard for his people and wanted them to be free and clear of any guilt and therefore blameless with regard to the law. Under the New Covenant the focus is also on the state of blamelessness.

Paul speaks of this in his prayer for the Thessalonians. He first connects blamelessness with holiness of heart when he asks that God "may establish your hearts unblamable in holiness" (1 Thess 3:13). Then he includes it in his prayer for their full sanctification. "May the God of peace himself sanctify you wholly; and may your spirit and soul and body be kept sound and blameless at the coming of our Lord Jesus Christ" (5:23).

This standard of godliness is earlier realized in Elizabeth and Zechariah (Lk 1:6) and is the same character which Paul desires the Philippians to possess when he wishes, "that you may be blameless and innocent, children of God without blemish in the midst of a crooked and perverse generation" (Phil 2:15). Paul declares this as part of God's purposes for his people before creation, "that we should be holy and blameless before him" (Eph 1:4), and it is to make this possible that Christ died for his people, "that he might present the church to himself in splendor, without spot or wrinkle or any such thing, that she might be holy and without blemish" (Eph 5:27; cf. Col 1:22; Jude 24).

It is the same standard of blamelessness that Paul indicates is a key mark of leadership in the church. Both bishops and deacons are to be blameless before the Lord in character (1 Tim 3:2, 10; 5:7; Tit 1:6-7). This clearly implies a freedom from condemnation in relationship to the righteous standard of God and his law. If one is free from any guilt or condemnation, this is the full state of God's sanctifying work that he desires for his people.[46]

A realizable experience. The standard for those living in an experience of full sanctification is pervasive throughout the New Testament. While it is certainly not the standard in which all believers begin to live immediately following their experience of saving grace, it is a standard that Jesus and the apostles set before believers, and it is one that God certainly expects of those who are committed to him. The most dangerous attitude toward this standard

---

[45] On *ni* (נִי) as "blameless," "innocent," "guiltless," see *TWOT*, 2:597-98.
[46] On *amemptos* (ἄμεμπτος) and *amōmos* (ἄμωμος) as "blameless," see *TDNT*, 4:572-73; 830-31.

of righteous living is to make it an unreachable ideal. While it is not an automatic possession for believers, neither is it a distant goal for them either. Jesus sets this standard before his own disciples, and after the infilling of the Holy Spirit, this is the level of Christian experience in which they do live. Not only that, but it is the level that they set before the early church. While some do not live up to this standard, others do. From the New Testament perspective, it is clearly possible to get into this state of sanctifying grace and live there on a consistent basis. It is this picture that needs to be the standard for all Christians of every age.

Further Growth

Based on understanding. The concept of growing after one gets into an experience of full obedience to God's standard of holy living is related more to knowledge and understanding than to questions of willful choices of right and wrong. Having already chosen to fully obey, one needs only to understand more perfectly God's will through his law in order to conform one's life to his holy character. "His divine power has granted to us all things that pertain to life and godliness, *through the knowledge* of him who called us to his own glory and excellence. . . . For this very reason make every effort to supplement your faith with virtue, and virtue *with knowledge.* . . . For if these things are yours and abound, they keep you from being ineffective or unfruitful in *the knowledge* of our Lord Jesus Christ" (2 Pet 1:3, 5-8; italics added). This divine power for godliness begins with a faith that leads to virtue and righteous living. That needs to be further supplemented with more knowledge that should lead to greater self-control. Then knowledge and self-control should be coupled with steadfastness or perseverance as one moves toward godliness, brotherly affection and love.

Likewise, in the midst of two of Paul's major discussions of the standard of righteous living, he talks about the importance of continued growth and understanding of the will of God. In Romans 12—15 Paul opens by exhorting the saints not to be conformed to this world, "but be transformed by *the renewal of your mind,* that you may prove what is the will of God, what is good and acceptable and perfect" (Rom 12:2; italics added). He wants those who have wholly presented themselves to God to continue to be transformed in their minds and therefore in their understanding. Then, starting with instruction about spiritual gifts, he begins to explain more fully what some of that advanced knowledge will mean for the believer living at this state of spiritual experience (Rom 12:3-8).

Similarly, in setting the standard for the Ephesians (Eph 4—6), Paul is concerned that the believers "no longer be children, tossed to and fro and carried about with every wind of doctrine," and so they need to hear the truth in love (4:14-15). He further exhorts them to "be renewed in the spirit of your minds" as a part of putting off their old nature and putting on the new nature "created after the likeness of God in true righteousness and holiness" (4:22-24). Continued renewal of the mind and therefore understanding of God's will and character ought to lead to a greater conformity to the image of the holy God who expresses himself in righteousness.

Glorification

Holy before God. One of the New Testament's chief concerns about the return of the Lord is that believers may be found to be holy and, therefore, fit for living eternally in his presence. Paul wants to see their hearts established unblamable in holiness at the coming of our Lord Jesus Christ (1 Thess 3:13). When he begins to describe this holiness, it is clear that it has to do with full conformity to the moral law and particularly the standard of righteousness in terms of sexual purity (4:1-8). Paul desires not only that the Thessalonians be sanctified wholly but that their total spirits, souls and bodies "be kept . . . blameless at the coming of our Lord Jesus Christ" (5:23). He prays for this so that men and women will be ready to stand before the righteous judgment of God in the last day (2 Thess 1:5-12). In a similar view, John closes his Revelation with the reminder that at the final day the evildoer and the filthy will continue in their state, while the righteous and the holy will continue in theirs (Rev 22:11). So the biblical picture is that God is crucially concerned that individuals reflect his holy character by the righteousness of their lives. This of course is part of God's preparation for people to live eternally in his holy presence.

Final judgment. Another major focus on the legal category regarding glorification is the final judgment of God. While the Old Testament looks forward to the Day of the Lord when God will finally judge the earth, the New Testament elaborates on this picture by including both the Father and the Son in the judgment of all.[47] Since we have already discussed some of the role of the Father

---

[47]See *TDNT*, 3:936; *ISBE(rev)*, 2:1162-63; Donald Bloesch, *Essentials of Evangelical Theology*, (San Francisco: Harper & Row, 1978) 2:211-34; J. P. Martin, *The Last Judgment* (Grand Rapids, Mich.: Eerdmans, 1963); Berkhof, *Systematic Theology*, pp. 728-34.

and the Son in this process earlier, we will not elaborate their roles here. It suffices to say that Scripture is very clear that there will be a future final judgment with the Father and the Son serving as righteous Judges of humanity to reward some and punish others.[48]

Attributes of God

Righteousness. Our study makes it obvious that the chief attribute of God related to the legal description of God as the Lawmaker and Judge is his righteousness. Righteousness is the manifestation of his holy character (Is 5:16), and it becomes the standard for the character he desires to see in people. Therefore righteousness is ultimately bound up with the giving of the law as an expression of what God is like on the one hand, and what his people are to be like on the other.

The justice of God is the administration of God's law in accordance with his holy character. Justice becomes the reaction of God toward people in the light of their response to his righteousness. Justice rewards conformity to God's standard of righteousness and punishes disobedience to that standard. The judgments of God in his justice are always based on the righteousness of his own nature. "The judgments of the LORD are true and righteous altogether" (Ps 19:9 KJV). Because justice is the administration of the standard of God's righteousness, justice and righteousness are often closely woven together in Scripture (89:14).[49]

Conclusion

The role of God as Righteous Judge appears explicitly at Mount Sinai and continues through Scripture to the book of Revelation. This role connects the functions of God as lawmaker, enforcer and arbiter under one title. The legal focus is modified, however, by the concept of law as Torah. Torah is instruction that may include law; its scope is bigger than mere legal language.

Historically, God has graciously given his law/word to redeemed people to show them how to live in accord with his character. Personally, therefore, each member of the people of God has explicit direction about attitudes, conduct and relationships that reflect the righteous character of a holy God. Theologically,

---

[48]Pope, *Compendium of Christian Theology,* 1:339-42; 3:412-23; Miley, *Systematic Theology,* 2:454-61; A. A. Hoekema, *The Bible and the Future* (Grand Rapids, Mich.: Eerdmans, 1979); *EDT,* 620-21.

[49]On the justice of God, see Carl F. H. Henry, *God, Revelation and Authority* (Waco, Tex.: Word, 1983), 6:402-17.

the role of God as Righteous Judge reminds us that God is righteous, and right relations are crucial to all interpersonal relationships. Righteousness is not imposed from above, creating something abnormal; rather it is offered by grace as that which enables us to function as persons rightly related to other persons. It further serves to reassure us that we live in a moral universe where there are some clear distinctions between right and wrong. What is right is ultimately rewarded; what is wrong is correctly punished.

EIGHT

HOLY GOD
AS LOVING FATHER

The Unity Factor

Since the picture of God as loving Father is tied to his other roles by means of his holiness, we will first see how love and fatherhood are connected to holiness. Then we shall be in a position to examine the language of God's role as Father.

Holiness as Love

The concept of the love of God is one of the dominant themes in the Bible. While it receives significant attention in the Old Testament, it is in the New Testament that its full importance is revealed. Some feel that the concept of holiness is the dominant characteristic of God in the Old Testament, whereas love becomes the dominant attribute in the New. Thus Emil Brunner writes, "As in the Old Testament everything turns on the holiness of God, so in the New everything turns on the love of God." But he rightly points out that the New Testament concern is "with the love of the *holy* God."[1]

The relationship between God's holiness and his love will properly be understood only when the New Testament is properly related to the Old Testament. This is part of the interpretive task of theology to relate the two testaments of biblical truth. If we follow Jesus and the New Testament writers as our pattern, we will understand the Old Covenant to be preparatory for the new. The Old Testament picture of God is laying the groundwork for further revelation in the New. There is preparation and elaboration, promise and fulfillment, but not opposition or contradiction. The picture of God in the Old

---

[1] Emil Brunner, *Christian Doctrine of God* (London: Lutterworth, 1949), p. 183, emphasis added.

Covenant is expanded in the New but in harmony with what has already been revealed. Jesus' further revelation of the Father is built solidly on the Old Testament understanding of the nature and character of God. He is speaking to Hebrews who know God as the Holy One of Israel.[2]

The implication of this proper relating of the Old Testament to the New is that the picture of God's love in the New Testament must be understood as being built on the picture of God's holiness in the Old Testament. The statement "God is love" presupposes God's declaration, "I am holy." The New Testament writers do not have to elaborate the picture of the holiness of God again because this is a "given" in their understanding of what he is like. They build on this accepted premise by showing more fully what that holy character is, namely, that it is holy love. So Brunner is right, "The holiness which the Bible teaches is the holiness of the God who is love, therefore the truth of the holiness of God is completed in the knowledge of his love. This indissoluble connection between holiness and love is the characteristic and decisive element in the Christian idea of God."[3]

While some would argue that holiness and love are correlative, love is better understood as an expression of God's holy nature. This is suggested by the emphasis on the character of God in progressive revelation. The concept of the love of God is not absent in the early part of Scripture, but the primary picture of God from Mount Sinai on is built on his holiness. Some of the Old Testament writers such as Isaiah clearly show a picture of God's love as an expression of his holiness. As Eichrodt puts it, "Hence for him love is a part of the perfection of Yahweh's nature and a basic element in holiness."[4] It is in the New Testament that the full expression of God's love is manifested through the person of God's Son. With the coming of the Son the family categories that describe God and our relationship to him come to the fore, and it is possible to arrive at a much more complete understanding of the love of God and its implications. But this knowledge of God's love will be fundamentally unsound if it is not pictured against the backdrop of God's holy character as revealed under the Old

---

[2]For connecting the Old Testament with the New Testament and both with systematic theology see Francis Watson, *Text and Truth* (Grand Rapids, Mich.: Eerdmans, 1997); Christopher Seitz, *Word Without End* (Grand Rapids, Mich.: Eerdmans, 1998); Joel Green and Max Turner, *Between Two Horizons* (Grand Rapids, Mich.: Eerdmans, 2000).

[3]Brunner in *Christian Doctrine of God* correctly writes, "Thus the holiness of God is the basis of the self-communication which is fulfilled in love" (p. 164).

[4]Walther Eichrodt, *Theology of the Old Testament*, trans. J. A. Baker (London: SCM Press, 1961), 1:281.

Covenant. As we explore the following biblical materials it will be clear that God's love comes as a natural expression of his moral holiness. As Skevington Wood describes it, "The supreme manifestation of holiness is in love."[5]

Love from a holy Father. The picture of God as a loving Father is one of the most pervasive figures of speech used in the Scripture. The reference to God as Father is so strongly emphasized by Jesus that it has become in effect the normative title for God and it may be the most widely used figure of speech among Christians. If we begin looking in Scripture for the kind of things a loving Father does for his children, then the first pictures of God in this category would come with the opening chapters of Genesis, which depict God caring for Adam and Eve, providing for their protection and meeting their needs for love and fellowship. God continues to do fatherlike things for others throughout the early chapters of the Bible. The specific words or language that describe the role of a loving Father, however, do not come until somewhat later in Scripture. One of the first references to God's role as Father is the indirect reference to Israel as his "first-born son" in Exodus 4:22-23. It occurs during the same event in which God speaks to Moses through the burning bush and makes him aware that he is on holy ground because he is in the presence of a holy God. It is a holy God who begins to identify Israel as his first-born son and thus begins to address his people in family categories.

Holiness and love: Hesed. God's love is related to his holiness in the first passage that speaks about the holiness of God. "Who is like thee, O LORD, among the gods? Who is like thee, majestic in holiness? . . . Thou hast led in thy steadfast love the people whom thou hast redeemed, thou hast guided them by thy strength to thy holy abode" (Ex 15:11, 13). In the midst of Israel's experience of deliverance from Egypt, God is identified as "majestic in holiness," and at the same time described as the one who leads his people in "steadfast love." The word translated "steadfast love" in the RSV is the Hebrew word *hesed* (חֶסֶד), and is one of the two major Hebrew words that describe the love of God. It is a covenant word whose meaning is one of the richest in Scripture. It refers to not only his love but also his grace, mercy, faithfulness and goodness, and therefore has various translations such as steadfast love, faithful love, loving kindness,

Hesed

---

[5]ZPEB, 3:183. On love as an expression of holiness see *NSRE*, 5:318; *IDB*, 2:622; Dale Moody, *The Word of Truth* (Grand Rapids, Mich.: Eerdmans, 1981), p. 104; *TDNT*, 1:93; *TWOT*, 2:788.

mercy and so forth. Thus, it is a word that does not exclusively relate to love but has love at its center, and therefore, it is one of the terms that appropriately describes a loving Father.[6]

After God calls Israel to be a holy people (Ex 19:6) and begins to spell out for them what that holiness will mean in their lives (20:1-17), he talks about manifesting his steadfast love to thousands of those who are responding properly to this standard of holiness (Ex 20:6; Deut 5:10). The psalmist views this relationship from a human perspective when he exclaims, "Yea, our heart is glad in him, because we trust in his holy name. Let thy steadfast love, O LORD, be upon us, even as we hope in thee" (Ps 33:21-22). It is from the holy name or nature of God that the writer expects to see an expression of God's steadfast love. Isaiah describes the same phenomenon from God's viewpoint when "the Holy One of Israel" declares, "My steadfast love shall not depart from you, and my covenant of peace shall not be removed, says the LORD, who has compassion on you" (Is 54:5, 10; also 54:7-8). Further, some the Psalms give an expression of the particulars of God's "holy name," of which his steadfast love is one prominent manifestation (e.g., Ps 103:1, 4, 17; 145:8, 21). Other passages that closely bind together holiness and steadfast love include 1 Chronicles 16:33, 35; Psalm 33:21-22; 89:14-18, 33-35; and Isaiah 63:7-11.[7]

The steadfast love of God as an expression of his fatherhood is seen in texts like God's promise to David. "I will be his father, and he shall be my son. . . . I will not take my steadfast love from him" (2 Sam 7:14-15). In the passage in Isaiah that has two of the three references to the Holy Spirit of God in the Old Testament, there is repeated reference to the steadfast love of the Lord toward his "sons" (Is 63:7-8, 10). "For thou art our Father, though Abraham does not know us and Israel does not acknowledge us; thou, O LORD, art our Father" (63:16). Jeremiah, who looks forward to the New Covenant, quotes God describing himself as a Father and saying, "I am a Father to Israel, and Ephraim is my first born." It is this God who declares, "I have loved you with an everlasting love" (Jer 31:9, 3).[8]

The concept of the *hesed* of the Lord, which focuses on his steadfast love but

---

[6]On the concept of *hesed* see Norman H. Snaith, *Distinctive Ideas of the Old Testament* (New York: Schoken, 1964), pp. 94-130; *EDT*, pp. 661-62; Nelson Glueck, *Hesed in the Bible* (Cincinnati: Hebrew Union College Press, 1967); Katherine D. Sakenfeld, *Meaning of Hesed in the Hebrew Bible* (Missoula, Mont.: Scholars Press, 1978); *TWOT*, 1:305-7; *TDNT*, 1:696-701.

[7]For more on God's holiness and steadfast love see Neh 13:22; Ps 5:7; 106:45-47, 138:2; cf. Ps 115:1; Jer 2:2-3.

[8]For the relation between God's steadfast love and his role as Husband see Is 54:5-10 and Hos 2:19.

also includes elements of grace, mercy and faithfulness, is best understood as a major expression of the holiness of God. This seems to be true from the passages that describe a holy God expressing his steadfast love and also from those where the fatherhood of God is expressed by his steadfast love. In both it is the picture of a holy God relating in covenant love to his people.

Holiness and love: Aheb. The second Hebrew word that describes the love of God is the more common word for love, *aheb* (אָהֵב). This word is not used to describe God's love until the book of Deuteronomy when God has Moses look back over the history of Israel from Mount Sinai up to the end of their wilderness wandering. This book comes not only as a second account of Israel's history but also as a reflective and interpretive evaluation of the way in which God has worked and the implications of this for Israel in the future. It is at this point that *aheb* is first used to describe God's love for Israel (Deut 4:37). Here God tells Israel that they "are a people holy to the LORD your God" and "a people for his own possession" (7:6). Immediately, we are reminded of God's declaration to Israel at Mount Sinai regarding the reason that he wants a holy people. Because God is holy, he desires a holy people (Lev 11:44-45). Then God begins to explain his motivation for choosing Israel as his own people.

> It was not because you were more in number than any other people that the LORD set his love upon you and chose you, for you were the fewest of all peoples; but it is because the LORD loves you, and is keeping the oath which he swore to your fathers, that the LORD has brought you out with a mighty hand, and redeemed you. (Deut 7:7-8)

It is evident from this passage that God's love is a clear expression of his holy character as he seeks a holy people. Therefore, love becomes a manifestation of God's holiness, particularly at the point of the election of Israel. This passage not only relates holiness and love but also parallels God's love (*aheb*) and God's steadfast love (*hesed*). For those who respond properly to God, "the LORD your God will keep with you the covenant and the steadfast love (*hesed*) which he swore to your fathers to keep; he will love you (*aheb*), bless you, and multiply you" (Deut 7:12-13; also 7:9).

When Moses speaks about this One who must be revered as holy, he declares, "He loved his people" (Deut 32:51—33:3). Isaiah quotes the Holy One of Israel who promises to redeem his people, "because you are precious in my eyes, and honored, and I love you, I give men in return for you, peoples in exchange for your life" (Is 43:4). In like manner when God describes himself to Hosea as "God, and not man, the Holy One in your midst," he does so in the context of his love for Israel. "When Israel was a child, I loved him, and out of Egypt I called my son" (Hos 11:9).[9] Other passages also indicate that love was the key motivation for a holy God electing his people (Is 43:4; 63:9; Jer 31:3; Mal 1:2).[10] At the same time Deuteronomy makes clear that the Lord sets his love not only on Israel and their descendants, but also on the sojourner, that is, the non-Israelite (Deut 10:15, 18). This picture of his concern for both Israel and the world stands behind the central New Testament declaration of God's love as the basis of redemption for all in Christ. "For God so loved the world that he gave his only Son, that whoever believes in him should not perish, but have eternal life" (Jn 3:16).

Holiness and love: Agapē. The third biblical word that describes the love of God is the Greek term *agapē* (αγάπη). *Agapē* is a unique word adopted by the New Testament writers to express that unconditional self-giving love of God. It is distinct from *eros* which relates more to a romantic and physical love which must possess its object. It differs further from *phileō,* which better describes friendship, companionship and family love. *Agapē* is a supranatural love that has the special good and concern of the love object as its focus. It has an unconditionalness and an other-centeredness about it that is distinct from the other words used for love in Greek. It is particularly used in the New Testament to describe the love of God the Father, Son and Holy Spirit and the kind of love God implants in the hearts of those who become his spiritual children.[11]

The picture of *agapē* as an expression of God's holy character is seen most clearly in John 17. Here Jesus addresses God as "holy Father." The intimacy of

---

[9] For other Old Testament references to God's love see Deut 23:5; 2 Sam 12:24; 1 Kings 10:9; 2 Chron 2:11, 9:8; Ps 47:4; 146:8; Prov 3:12, 12:9; Is 43:4; 48:14; 63:9; Jer 31:3; Hos 3:1; 11:4; 14:4; Zeph 3:17; Mal 1:2; .

[10] On love (*aheb*) see Snaith, *Distinctive Ideas of the Old Testament*, pp. 131-42; *TWOT,* 1:14-15; *TDNT,* 1:21-25; *TDNT,* 9:124-27, 154-59; *TDOT,* 1:99-117; Dennis McCarthy, "Notes on the Love of God in Deuteronomy and the Father-Son Relationship between Yahweh and Israel," *CBQ* 27 (April 1965): 144-47; J. W. McKay, "Man's Love for God in Deuteronomy and the Father/Teacher-Son/Pupil Relationship," *VT* 22 (October 1972): 426-35.

[11] On agape see *TDNT,* 1:21-55; *NIDNTT,* 2:542-47; Walter Harrelson, "The Idea of Agape in the New Testament," *JR* 31 (1951): 169-82; Leon Morris, *The Testaments of Love* (Grand Rapids, Mich.: Eerdmans, 1981); Anders Nygren, *Agape and Eros,* trans. Philip S. Watson (Philadelphia: Westminster Press, 1953); Gene Outka, *Agape: An Ethical Analysis* (New Haven, Conn.: Yale University Press, 1972); Ceslas Spicq, *Agape in the New Testament,* 3 vols. (St. Louis: B. Herder, 1963-1966); B. B. Warfield, "The Terminology of Love in the New Testament," *PTR* 16 (1918): 1-45.

the love relationship between the Father and the Son is seen when Jesus talks about how the Father has loved him (Jn 17:23-24, 26). This love relationship between the Father and the Son must be understood in reference to Jesus' request of the Father to keep his disciples "in thy name" (17:11). The name of God refers to his nature, which is described in the same verse as holy. Within this holy nature the chief relationship between the first and second members of the Trinity is their love for one another. So through his prayer Jesus reveals that the heart of the holy nature of God is his love for the Son and his love for those who are becoming his disciples (17:22, 26).

All three of the major biblical words for the love of God are seen most clearly in the context of his holy character. The relationship between holiness and love in the character of God is best understood if holiness is viewed as the essence of his being and love as one of the major expressions of that essence in relationship to other persons, whether that be within the Trinity or without it.[12]

God's holiness and fatherhood. Another expression of the concept of God's love as a manifestation of his holiness comes in the biblical connection between God's holiness and his fatherhood. For example, Deuteronomy not only gives us an understanding of the love of God as an expression of his holy character seeking a holy people, but it is also the first place that connects explicitly God's holiness with his role as Father. "You are the sons of the LORD your God. . . . For you are a people holy to the LORD your God, and the LORD has chosen you to be a people for his own possession" (Deut 14:1-2). A holy Father is clearly seeking holy sons. Similarly, the Holy One of Israel says of David, "He shall cry to me, 'Thou art my Father, my God, and the Rock of my salvation.' And I will make him the firstborn, the highest of the kings of the earth." God further attests to these words with an oath. "Once for all I have sworn by my holiness" (Ps 89:26-27, 35). And David, while exhorting himself to bless God's holy name, describes God as "a father" who "pities his children" (103:1, 13), a "Father of the fatherless and protector of widows" (68:5).

---

[12]On the biblical concepts of love see *EDT*, pp. 656-69; *NIDNTT*, 2:538-51; *CD* 1/2, pp. 371-401; *CD* 4/2, pp. 727-840; C. S. Lewis, *The Four Loves* (New York: Harcourt, Brace, 1960); William Burt Pope, *A Compendium of Christian Theology* (London: Wesleyan-Methodist Book Room, 1880), 1:344-46; D. D. Williams, *The Spirit and Forms of Love* (New York: Harper and Row, 1968); Snaith, *Distinctive Ideas of the Old Testaments*; Martin C. D'Arcy, *The Mind and Heart of Love, Lion and the Unicorn: A Study of Eros and Agape* (New York: Meridian, 1956); Günther Bornkamm, *Jesus of Nazareth* (New York: Harper, 1960), pp. 109-17; Rudolf Bultmann, *Theology of the New Testament* (New York: Charles Scribner's Sons, 1951-1955); W. Lillie, "The Christian Conception of Love," *SJT* 7 (1959): 226-42.

Jesus at the beginning and again at the end of his ministry closely ties God's fatherhood to the holiness of his character. When he first begins to teach his disciples, he exhorts them to pray, "Our Father who art in heaven, hallowed be thy name" (Mt 6:9). "Hallowed" is an old English word for holy and so the passage may be translated "sanctified be thy name" (or nature). Jesus is clearly instructing his disciples that God is their Father while reminding them that the basic nature of their Father is holy. Jesus himself prays, "Holy Father" in his high priestly prayer at the end of his time with his disciples (Jn 17:11). During this prayer Jesus talks about the love of God being an expression of his holiness. It is to the holy Father that he prays that the world may know that God "hast loved them even as thou hast loved me." Further, it is to the holy name of the Father that he refers in his last petition: "I made known to them thy name, and I will make it known, that the love with which thou hast loved me may be in them" (17:23, 26). Finally, Peter, citing the Old Testament, states clearly that God is like a holy Father looking for holy children.

> As obedient children, do not be conformed to the passions of your former igno-
> rance, but as he who called you is holy, be holy yourselves in all your conduct; since
> it is written, "You shall be holy, for I am holy." And if you invoke as Father him
> who judges each one impartially according to his deeds, conduct yourselves with
> fear throughout the time of your exile. (1 Pet 1:14-17)

As the New Testament begins to amplify the picture of God as a Father it is evident that this is understood to be in close relationship to his basic holy nature. The one who is to be invoked as the Father is the same as the one who declares that he is holy, so that when the love of God is expressed as a direct manifestation of the fatherhood of God, it also comes as a major dimension of the Father's holy character.

The Role of God as Loving Father

Jesus' prayer to his Father in John 17 gives us the key to this particular role. When he addresses God as "Holy Father," he capsules for his disciples this unique understanding of God (Jn 17:11). It focuses on *his* relationship to God as Father, but also reminds his disciples that they are to look to God as *their* Father.

In the use of the fatherhood figure of speech God draws from the everyday experience of almost every individual. Everyone is born into some kind of family, and those very few who do not have a father of their own grow up in a world where they do know something of fathers and families. Thus, the language figure that characterizes this role is that of the family and the home. It was chosen deliberately by God because this structure of human existence is so pervasive for all humankind. While there may be many distorted views of family, home and fatherhood, these categories are at least basic to almost all human experience. They need to be sharpened and corrected in the light of biblical revelation, but they provide a beginning point for almost everyone to understand some things about God.

The family and the home, as God would have us understand them, has its focus on love and centers around an atmosphere of acceptance and close relationships. It is based on the assumption that God is looking for an intimate fellowship with people that is best described in terms of love.

The Father

Old Testament. The earliest references to God as a Father are indirect, and they speak of him as one who has children. Thus, God instructs Moses, "You shall say to Pharaoh, 'Thus says the LORD, Israel is my first-born son, and I say to you, "Let my son go that he may serve me"; if you refuse to let him go, behold, I will slay your first-born son'" (Ex 4:22-23). God is also likened unto a father who corrects his son. "As a man disciplines his son, the LORD your God disciplines you" (Deut 8:5). The people who are "holy to the LORD your God" are in the same paragraph described as "the sons of the LORD your God" (14:2, 1). Elsewhere in the Old Testament the people of God are described as sons or children. Isaiah quotes the Lord as saying, "Sons have I reared and brought up, but they have rebelled against me. . . . They have forsaken the LORD, they have despised the Holy One of Israel, they are utterly estranged" (Is 1:2, 4).

The first explicit reference to God as Father comes in the Song of Moses. Moses sets out to "proclaim the name of the LORD," and the Lord reminds him at the close that his name is holy (Deut 32:3, 51). Moses declares this God to be "a God of faithfulness and without iniquity, just and right is he. They have dealt corruptly with him, they are no longer his children." To these foolish and senseless people he asks, "Is he not your father who created you, who made you and established you?" (32:4-6). He reminds Israel that they are the heritage of the Lord (32:8-9), and he rebukes them that they have forgotten "the God who gave you birth." "His sons and daughters" provoke the Lord to hide his face from them "for they are a perverse generation, children in whom there is no faithfulness" (32:18-20).

This picture of a holy Father is expressed again by the psalmist. "Father of the fatherless and protector of widows is God in his holy habitation" (Ps 68:5). Again, the Holy One of Israel says of David, "He shall cry to me, 'Thou art my Father, my God, and the Rock of my salvation.' And I will make him the first-born, the highest of the kings of the earth" (89:26-27). While blessing God's holy name, David exclaims, "As a father pities his children, so the LORD pities those who fear him" (103:1, 13).

The prophets also speak of God as a loving Father. Isaiah recounts God's love to sons who deal falsely with him. In the same passage that describes God as having a *Holy* Spirit, Isaiah records the cry of God's people. "For thou art our Father, though Abraham does not know us and Israel does not acknowledge us; thou, O LORD, art our Father" (Is 63:7-11, 16). Isaiah also likens God's role as Father to that of the potter. "Yet, O LORD, thou art our father; we are the clay, and thou art our potter; we are all the work of thy hand" (64:8). Jeremiah describes God's evaluation of Judah: "I thought how I would set you among my sons, and give you a pleasant land, a heritage most beauteous of all nations. And I thought you would call me, My Father, and would not turn from following me. . . . Return, O faithless sons, I will heal your faithlessness" (Jer 3:19, 22). But while Israel has been faithless in responding properly to God as a Father, God continues to fulfill this role in the restoration of his people. "With weeping they shall come, and with consolations I will lead them back, I will make them walk by brooks of water, in a straight path in which they shall not stumble; for I am a father to Israel, and Ephraim is my first-born" (31:9, 20, 23). This family figure of speech is not only picked up by the prophets but also in the wisdom literature. In Proverbs we read, "For the LORD reproves him whom he loves, as a father the son in whom he delights" (Prov 3:12).

Our survey of the figure of God as Father in the Old Testament indicates a number of direct references to God as Father. Many of these refer to his role as the Father of Israel (Deut 32:6, 18; Jer 3:14, 19; 31:9; Is 63:16; 64:8; Mal 1:6; 2:10; 1 Chron 29:10). But it is also evident that God may be understood as the Father of certain individuals within the nation of Israel (Ps 68:5; 89:26-27; 103:13; 2

Sam 7:14). In particular, the king is sometimes explicitly referred to as God's son, representing the nation as a whole, but so are other individuals within the nation who must directly relate to God (2 Sam 7:14; Ps 89:26-27).

The indirect references to God as Father come as allusions in reference to his sons or children. Israel is his "firstborn son" (Ex 4:22; Jer 31:9). Clearly Israel as a people and as individuals within the nation are sometimes understood as having a family relationship with God.[13]

Both the direct and indirect references to God as Father in the Old Testament are tied to God's covenant relationship with Israel. He is the Father of those whom he has elected to be his own, and nowhere does the Old Testament speaks of a universal fatherhood of God. At first glance, Malachi 2:10 seems to imply such a universal fatherhood. "Have we not all one father? Has not one God created us?" But the context of Malachi's prophecy is clearly "the oracle of the word of the LORD to Israel by Malachi" (Mal 1:1). He is talking to the people who are in a covenant relationship with God, and the God who has elected them is referred to both as Father and Creator. When he says "One God created us," he is clearly referring to the nation of Israel.[14] So he is not referring to God as the Father of all creation but to him as the Father of those who enter into a special covenant relationship with himself.

Cremer feels that the use of Father as a distinctively New Testament designation of God can only be understood as the proper equivalent of the Old Testament designation Yahweh. Yahweh is the special personal name by which God makes himself known to his people under the Old Covenant, and Cremer feels it is the closest parallel to the intimacy invited by the use of the concept of Father in the New Testament.[15]

In the light of the pervasive use of the figure of God as Father in the New Testament, the question naturally arises as to why it does not receive more attention in the Old Testament. There are two major reasons for this. One of

---

[13]See George A. F. Knight, *A Christian Theology of the Old Testament* (Richmond, Va.: John Knox Press, 1959), pp. 169-74.

[14]*TWOT*, 1:5-6. On the possible universal fatherhood of God see Robert S. Candlish, *Discourses Bearing Upon the Sonship and Brotherhood of Believers* (Edinburgh: Adam & Charles Black, 1872), pp. 14-19; Charles H. H. Wright, *The Fatherhood of God: and Its Relationship to the Person and Work of Christ and the Operations of the Holy Spirit* (Edinburgh: T & T Clark, 1967), pp. 1-29, 62-79; W. B. Selbie, *The Fatherhood of God* (New York: Charles Scribner's Sons, 1936), pp. 44-62.

[15]H. Cremer, *The Biblical-Theological Lexicon of New Testament Greek* (Edinburgh: T & T Clark, 1895), p. 173.

these will be discussed in the following section about the role of God as Father in the New Testament. The other has to do with the unique picture of God which Israel is called on to establish in the ancient Near Eastern world.

Israel is called on to make the case that Yahweh, the God of Israel, is the supranatural creator of the entire universe. He is not a natural god, as are the other gods of the ancient world, and thus he is not a part of the universe of space and time. In other words he is not a natural force within the universe itself but stands outside it as the transcendent Creator of everything. To the ancient world a god that is a father is most naturally associated with the natural gods which beget by means of natural processes. Human beings are begotten as a part of emanations from gods. But in Israel no part of the natural world is an emanation from God in a physical or biological sense. The universe and people are created separate and distinct from God so that there is a clear discontinuity between Yahweh and the natural world. It may well be that the use of the figure of God as Father could have blurred this distinction in the minds of some, and this accounts in part for its limited use in the Old Testament, especially in Genesis.[16] The Old Testament clearly indicates that God is not to be understood as Father in any biological sense but in a soteriological sense, that is, by election and salvation.[17] This clearly involves a moral identification of children with God as Father, but does not involve a physical or natural generation as would be the case in many places in the ancient Near Eastern world.[18]

Husband. The alternative family model that continues to focus on love, acceptance and intimate fellowship is the picture of God as a loving Husband and his people as a wife. It is graphically portrayed in the picture of the prophet Hosea's relationship to his wife Gomer. Their marriage became a living parable of God's relationship to Israel. Gomer's adultery after her marriage to Hosea is a picture of Israel's spiritual idolatry in following after other gods. Judgment is promised to Israel like the judgment that comes on Gomer, but at the same time restoration is also promised. As Hosea in his covenant love is willing to take Gomer back as his wife and make her a part of his family again, so the Lord says Israel again will call him "my husband." God then promises Israel another covenant when "I will

---

[16]*TDNT,* 5:967; see also pp. 945-1014.

[17]*NIDNTT,* 1:617-18.

[18]Knight, *Christian Theology of the Old Testament,* p. 172. For further discussion of the role of God as Father in the Old Testament see *TDOT,* 1:1-18, 52-8; George F. Moore, *Judaism* (Cambridge: Harvard University Press, 1940), 2:201-11.

betroth you to me for ever; I will betroth you to me in righteousness and in justice, in steadfast love, and in mercy. I will betroth you to me in faithfulness; and you shall know the LORD" (Hos 2:16, 18-20). Although the new relationship between prophet and wife and between God and his people is one of covenant accepting love, it is also built on a combination of righteousness, justice, steadfast love, mercy and faithfulness. It will require some proper response from God's people for the enjoyment of a newly accepted relationship between them.[19]

The role of God as a husband is also connected with the holiness of his character by Isaiah.

> For your Maker is your husband, the LORD of hosts is his name; and the Holy One of Israel is your Redeemer, the God of the whole earth he is called. For the LORD has called you like a wife forsaken and grieved in spirit, like a wife of youth when she is cast off, says your God. For a brief moment I forsook you, but with great compassion I will gather you. In overflowing wrath for a moment I hid my face from you, but with everlasting love I will have compassion on you, says the LORD, your Redeemer. (Is 54:5-8)

Jeremiah picks up the same theme in his discussion of God as a Father who is calling for the return of his faithless sons. He then shifts to the husband and wife metaphor: "Surely, as a faithless wife leaves her husband, so have you been faithless to me, O house of Israel, says the LORD" (Jer 3:20). He uses this figure a second time, again in the same chapter as a reference to God as Father (31:9).

Like Hosea, Jeremiah describes the New Covenant that God is going to make with the house of Israel and Judah, and in the process describes the Old Covenant "which they broke, though I was their husband, says the LORD" (Jer 31:32). The same theme is graphically portrayed in Ezekiel 16 in the story of God and his saving the foundling child, who grew up to be a beautiful woman and who then is married to God as a wife. As in the case with Hosea and Gomer, God's people turned to harlotry, leading God to exclaim, "Adulterous wife, who receives strangers instead of her husband!" (Ezek 16:32). This is followed by a picture of the coming judgment on the spiritual unfaithfulness of Judah along with the promise of restoration and a New Covenant (16:1-63).[20]

---

[19]Gerhard von Rad, *Old Testament Theology*, trans. D. M. G. Stalker (New York: Harper & Row, 1962), 2:138-42.

[20]On the picture of Israel as the bride of God see Knight, *Christian Theology of the Old Testament*, pp. 177-84, 323-24.

The alternative role of God as a Husband continues the same family focus with an emphasis on love, acceptance and close intimate relationships. Yet, it shifts the analogy from parent and child to that of a husband and wife, and thus adds a slightly different dimension to the picture of intimacy that God desires with his people. Of all human relationships, that between a husband and wife is surely the most intimate, and it is this kind of close relationship God seeks with his people.[21]

New Testament. While there are far more references to God as Father in the Old Testament than many people acknowledge, there is certainly a much fuller picture of God as Father in the New Testament. This should not be unexpected in the light of the fact that Jesus comes in the New Testament as God's Son, and with the coming of a Son, it is possible to get a much fuller understanding of the Father's role. While some understanding has been possible up to this time, a much more significant perspective is given in the light of the incarnation of the Son of God.

This relationship between Jesus and God is first described in the New Testament in terms of a fulfillment of that which was spoken by the prophet, "Out of Egypt have I called my son" (Mt 2:15). In Jesus' earliest major teaching of his own disciples in the New Testament, he begins to refer to God as Father (Mt 5:16, 48; 6:4, 6, 9, 18, 32; 7:11, 21). The strong emphasis on God as the Father of the disciples of Jesus continues throughout Matthew's Gospel. At the end of his time with his disciples (as recorded in Matthew) he sends them forth to make more disciples, "baptizing them in the name of the Father and of the Son and of the Holy Spirit" (Mt 28:19).

In the Synoptics Matthew clearly has the larger number of references to God as Father. Matthew records 43 references to God as Father, whereas Mark has only 5 and Luke 14. John, on the other hand, has the greatest number of references with 115. The references are pervasive enough throughout the Gospels to make it clear that Jesus' use of "Father" is widespread and dominant. It is also evident that the references to God as Father have to do with God's role in relation to the disciples of Jesus and not to the people in general. There has been some debate over the question of a universal fatherhood of God, as opposed to his being the Father of only

---

[21]For further discussion of God as Husband see *NIDNTT,* 2:540-42.

believers in Jesus, because of places like the Sermon on the Mount where a larger group of people seem to be listening to the teachings of Jesus. But the Sermon on the Mount is clearly addressed first of all to the disciples, and this seems to be the dominant focus of Jesus' use of the references to God as Father.[22]

John's pattern is similar in that in his preface he begins to talk about the relationship of Jesus to God in terms of Father and Son. "The Word became flesh and dwelt among us, full of grace and truth; we have beheld his glory, glory as of the only Son from the Father" (Jn 1:14). From John's perspective it is clear that it is the Son who is giving us an image of the Father and reflecting his likeness to the world. "No one has ever seen God; the only Son, who is in the bosom of the Father, he has made him known" (1:18). On Jesus' last night with his disciples, John records that he speaks of God more than fifty times as his Father. He emphasizes again the oneness between himself and the Father and the fact that he has been the One revealing the full character of the Father. "He who has seen me has seen the Father" (14:6-11). Because of the pervasive use of this title for God by Jesus, it becomes then the normative title for God among Christians throughout the rest of the New Testament. Every New Testament Epistle but three open with a reference to God as Father, and two of those three have a reference to the Father in the first paragraphs of the book. Only 3 John does not refer to God in this way. The New Testament writers did not miss the lesson that the normative role by which God is to be understood is that he is a loving Father.

This brings us to the second major way in which the Father-Son figure is used in the New Testament. If the first relates Jesus to God the Father, the second relates his disciples to God as a Father. Jesus makes this clear as he begins to instruct his disciples when they first begin to follow him. He begins by referring to their spiritual Father with repeated reference to God as "Father, who is in heaven" or "heavenly Father" (Mt 5:16, 45, 48; 6:1, 9, 14, 26, 32; 7:11, 21). At the same time he makes it clear through the use of the phrase "your Father" that his disciples are to understand God in terms of his being their Father (Jn 5:16, 44, 6:32).[23] Further, when he begins to teach them to

---

[22]*NIDNTT,* 1:618-21; Joachim Jeremias, *New Testament Theology,* trans. John Bowden (New York: Scribner, 1971), p. 180.

[23]For a different evaluation see Jeremias, *New Testament Theology,* pp. 179-80.

relate to God in prayer, his first instructions are that they are to refer to him as "Our Father" (Mt 6:9).[24] The same focus on God as the Father of disciples as well as the Father of Jesus is seen again at the end of the Gospel record when Jesus instructs Mary to "go to my brethren and say to them, I am ascending to my Father and your Father, to my God and your God" (Jn 20:17).

While the father-son figure applies to both Jesus' relationship to God as well as his disciples', there is clearly a distinct theological difference between these two. Jesus' relationship to the Father has to do with his being and nature. We will explore this further in the next section on the relationship of the Son to the Father in the context of the Trinity. God is the Father of Jesus in a metaphysical sense that is tied with the essence of both. But when the analogy is used to describe the relationship of God to disciples of Jesus, it has to do with the spiritual relationship, not an ontological relationship. God as Father of believers in Jesus is the source of their life and the one who provides a family context for the development of that spiritual life, especially in terms of righteousness and love. He disciplines them according to his righteous standards. But he also loves them and that is the context of his training (Heb 12:5-6).[25]

God as Abba Father. The unparalleled element of intimacy in the references to God as Father is nowhere seen more clearly than in Jesus' use of the word "Abba" (Mk 14:36). This was the Aramaic form of address used by children in the most familiar way to refer to God as "dear Father" or "Daddy." It is clear that this is a unique form used by Jesus which finds no other parallel in the Old Testament or in Judaism as an address to God. The Abba form conveys a sense of intimacy, familiarity and close fellowship that brings an entirely new dimension into the relationship with God. It begins to be used by Jesus but is picked up by the early church (Rom 8:25; Gal 4:16).[26] With this form Jeremias declares, "We are confronted with something new and unheard of which breaks the limits of

---

[24]On the fatherhood of God in the Lord's Prayer see Ernest Lohmeyer, *"Our Father:" An Introduction to the Lord's Prayer*, trans. John Browden (New York: Harper and Row, 1965), pp. 32-62; Bultmann, *Theology of the New Testament*, 1:23ff.

[25]See Donald Guthrie, *New Testament Theology* (Downers Grove, Ill.: InterVarsity Press, 1981), p. 83. On the fatherhood of God see pp. 80-84. On the New Testament picture of God as Father see *BTLNT*, pp. 469-73; *TDNT*, 5:945-1014; Werner Georg Kummel, *Theology of the New Testament According to Its Major Witnesses* (Nashville: Abingdon, 1973), p. 75; T. W. Manson, *The Teaching of Jesus: Studies of its Form and Content* (Cambridge: Cambridge University Press, 1963), pp. 89-115; A. T. Robertson, *The Teaching of Jesus Concerning God the Father* (New York: American Tract Society, 1904).

[26]Guthrie, *Theology of the New Testament*, p. 84.

Judaism."[27] It certainly is used by Jesus and the early Christians as an indicator of the more intimate fellowship that is possible now between every believer and the God who reveals himself as a loving Father.

Centrality of Father role. The uniqueness of the role of God as Father in the New Testament has made it possible for some to consider it a "central principle of Christianity."[28] It certainly has become the dominant figure to describe God in his relationship both to Jesus and to the followers of Jesus. The New Testament clearly does not ignore other roles such as God as Creator, King and Judge, but the new dimension of the Fatherhood of God radically alters the character of the other roles. When there is a synthesis between God as Father and God as Judge or between God as Father and God as King, there is no lessening of respect or submission to his authority or commitment to his righteous standards, but the entire relationship is covered by an intimacy of fellowship and a blanket of love. The whole atmosphere of the total relationship between people and God has been changed.[29] This new dimension preserves obedience, submission and respect, but also adds affection, fellowship, acceptance and affirmation. With this fuller revelation by Jesus of God the relation of everyone to God is forever on an entirely different footing.[30]

The Son

Son of God. Jesus' role as the Son of God emphasizes the family relationship within the Trinity and the spiritual family relationship God desires to have with those who are his people. It gets emphasized early in Jesus' life at his baptism where a voice from heaven speaks saying, "This is my beloved Son, with whom I am well-pleased" (Mt 3:17). The same attestation of the Father to the Son comes after Peter's confession at Caesarea Philippi. Peter, speaking for the rest of the disciples, is able to declare, "You are the Christ, the Son of the living God" (16:16). This is followed by the experience of the three disciples with Jesus on the Mount of Trans-

---

[27]Joachim Jeremias, *The Central Message of the New Testament* (London: SCM Press, 1965), p. 30. See also pp. 9-30 and Jeremias, *New Testament Theology*, pp. 36-37, 61-68. For further discussion of the use of Abba see *TDNT,* 1:5-6, 5:984-85; *NIDNTT,* vol. 1, pp. 614-15.

[28]See A. M. Fairbairn, *Christ in Modern Theology* (London: Hodder & Stoughton, 1893), p. 452.

[29]On the relationship of the role of God as Father to his other roles see *TDNT,* 5:984-85, 995-96, 1010-11; Jeremias, *New Testament Theology,* p. 179.

[30]On the role of God as Father see *EDT,* p. 408; John Wesley, *Explanatory Notes on the New Testament* (London: Epworth, 1966), p. 374 (Jn 17:1); CD 1/1, pp. 448-56; Pannenberg, *Jesus, God and Man,* pp. 229-332; R. W. Candlish, *The Fatherhood of God* (Edinburgh: Adam Charles Black, 1979); R. A. Webb, *The Reformed Doctrine of Adoption* (Grand Rapids, Mich.: Eerdmans, 1947), pp. 19-20, 168-69; Wright, *Fatherhood of God,* pp. 45-61.

figuration when they receive from God a confirmation of their testimony of faith. A bright cloud overshadows them and the Father speaks, saying, "This is my beloved Son, with whom I am well-pleased; listen to him" (17:5). The same confirmation is received a final time at the close of Jesus' ministry when he cries out, "Father, glorify thy name," and a voice from heaven replies, "I have glorified it, and I will glorify it again" (Jn 12:28). These three supranatural experiences which come at crucial times in the gospel story reinforce for us the intimate relationship between Jesus as a Son and God as a Father.

Jesus' own recognition of his unique sonship is described in various passages throughout the Gospels. When Jesus was a boy, we see evidence that he recognized something of this unique relationship through his response to his parents questioning of his whereabouts. "Did you not know that I must be in my Father's house?" (Lk 2:49). There are also a number of references in both the synoptics and John where Jesus refers to God as "my Father" (Mt 7:21; 10:32-33; 20:23; Jn 5:17; 6:40; 8:54; 10:18; 15:15). When the High Priest questions Jesus, "Are you the Christ, the Son of the Blessed?" Jesus responds simply, "I am" (Mk 14:61-62). But perhaps his most direct statement regarding his sonship is found in John 10:36, when he says, "I am the Son of God."

The relationship of Jesus to God as Son to Father carries a much deeper significance than the other figures of speech used to describe God in relationship to the world. This figure is used to describe the essence of the Trinity and so affects not only our understanding of the essence of the personhood of God but is determinative for our Christology as well. The uniqueness of the relationship between the Father and the Son and its implications as understood by the church has been succinctly captured by Robert Candlish:

> It is essential to the very being of the Supreme that he should be a Father, and that of him there should be a Son. From all eternity, accordingly—in the terms of the Creed of the Council of Nicea,—the Son is of the Father; "begotten of the Father before all worlds; God of God, Light of Light, Very God of Very God." He is "the everlasting Son of the Father," "begotten not made." The relation therefore of paternity or fatherhood in God precedes creation, as well as redemption; and is indeed from everlasting. From the very necessity of his nature;—not by any voluntary act in time, but by the eternal mode of his subsistence, the Highest is everlastingly a Father; and has in his bosom, of his own substance and as his fellow, a Son whom he loves, and with whom in the community of the Holy Spirit, he is one. This is what is implied in the

doctrine of the eternal and necessary existence of the Son, as distinct from the Father in respect to personality, though one with him in nature and substance, in attributes, works, and ways. It is what is brought out in the descriptions which Scripture gives of the Son's fellowship with the Father from everlasting.[31]

Within the Godhead, the Father and the Son must be understood to be in eternal relationship with each other.

The application of human language to describe the supranatural always has some limits. The limit of the Father-Son analogy to describe the first and second persons of the Trinity comes with a description of Jesus as the "only begotten son." In the natural world fathers beget sons and everyone understands that there was a time when sons did not exist. The early church understood that this is not what is being implied with this analogy when Jesus is described in this way. While the Arian Christians wanted to make Jesus a created being, Athanasian Christology properly prevailed within the church to establish the fact that Jesus is an uncreated being and in that sense unlike the natural relationship between a father and son.[32] The church did not discard the analogy, however, but described it in terms of Jesus' eternal Sonship.[33] Some of the debate over this question and some of the issues involved might have been dealt with more easily with a more realistic recognition of the fact that while this category may most aptly describe the essence of the Godhead, it still uses human language to describe divinity. As such it has limitations and is an analogy that cannot be pressed to the extreme in every detail.[34]

---

[31]Candlish, *Discourses Bearing Upon the Sonship and Brotherhood of Believers*, pp. 6-7. For more on the Nicean explication of the relation of Fatherhood and Sonship see Thomas F. Torrance, *Trinitarian Faith* (Edinburgh: T & T Clark, 1995), pp. 47-65, 110-45.

[32]See Athanasius, *On the Incarnation* (Crestwood, N.Y.: St. Vladimir's Seminary Press, 1944), pp. 31-48; Walter Kasper, *God of Jesus Christ*, trans. Matthew J. O'Connell (New York: Crossroad, 1999), pp. 173-97; Thomas F. Torrance, *Christian Doctrine of God* (Edinburgh: T & T Clark, 1995), pp. 13-72.

[33]On the Sonship of Jesus see Emil Brunner, *The Christian Doctrine of Creation and Redemption* (London: Lutterworth, 1952), pp. 340-56; CD 1/1, pp. 474-512; Webb, *Reformed Doctrine of Adoption*, 28ff.; Hill, *Three-Personed God*, pp. 6-16.

[34]See Wright, *Fatherhood of God*, pp. 98-122; CD 2/1-2; J. N. D. Kelley, *Early Christian Doctrines* (London: Adam & Charles Black, 1965); R. Grant, *The Early Christian Doctrine of God* (Charlottesville: University of Virginia Press, 1966); Jürgen Moltmann, *Trinity and the Kingdom*, trans. Margaret Kohl (New York: Harper & Row, 1981); Brunner, *Christian Doctrine of God*, pp. 204-40; Pannenberg, *Jesus, God and Man*, pp. 158-60, 179-83; William Rausch, *The Trinitarian Controversy* (Philadelphia: Fortress, 1980); EDT, pp. 462-64; Olin Curtis, *The Christian Faith* (Grand Rapids, Mich.: Kregel, 1971), pp. 504-10; Jarislov Pelikan, *The Emergence of the Catholic Tradition (100-600)* (Chicago: University of Chicago Press, 1971); George L. Prestige, *Fathers and Heretics: Six Studies in Dogmatic Faith* (New York: Macmillan, 1940); *God in Patristic Thought* (London: SPCK, 1952); A. Rawlinson, ed., *Essays on the Trinity and the Incarnation* (London: Longmans, Green, 1928); Arthur W. Wainwright, *The Trinity in the New Testament* (London, SPCK, 1962).

A contemporary example of this same phenomenon is the attempt to sometimes describe the Holy Spirit as feminine or as the mother figure within the Trinity.[35]

Not only do the Father and Jesus witness to this divine Sonship, but others bear the same testimony from the very earliest days of Jesus' ministry. John the Baptist claims that he has seen "the Son of God" (Jn 1:34), and Nathaniel on his first encounter with Jesus is able to exclaim with at least some initial understanding, "Rabbi, you are the Son of God!" (1:49). John's entire Gospel is written to include signs that lead people to believe "that Jesus is the Christ, the Son of God," so that they might have life in his name (20:30-31). The Jews of Jesus' day recognized that his claim for God to be his Father meant that in a unique kind of way he was making himself equal with God, and it became the occasion for several lively debates (e.g., 5:17-27; 8:18-19, 27-59; 10:29-38). This title was also picked up by the early church and became a keynote of their proclamation of Jesus (e.g., Acts 9:20; 13:33). For example, Paul opens his letter to the Romans with a description of Jesus as God's Son "who was descended from David according to the flesh and designated Son of God in power according to the Spirit of holiness by his resurrection from the dead" (Rom 1:3-4; cf. 5:10; 8:29). Much of the theology of the epistles is both informed with the concept of Jesus as the divine Son of God and presupposes it as the basis for its explication of salvation.[36]

Son of man. The family figure of speech includes references to Jesus, not only as the Son of God, but also the Son of man. The first of these titles focuses on his divinity, whereas the second centers on his humanity. It is this dual relationship

---

[35]On contemporary feminist theology's attempt to jettison of the Father-Son language to describe the first two persons of the Godhead see Donald Bloesch, *The Battle for the Trinity: The Debate over Inclusive God-Language* (Ann Arbor, Mich.: Vine, 1985); G. F. Gilder, *Sexual Suicide* (New York: Quadrangle, 1973); Vernard Eller, *The Language of Cannan and the Grammar of Feminism* (Grand Rapids, Mich.: Eerdmans, 1982); W. A. V. Hooft, *The Fatherhood of God in an Age of Emancipation* (Philadelphia: Westminster Press, 1982); Sallie McFague, *Metaphorical Theology* (Philadelphia: Fortress, 1982); Rosemary Ruether, *Sexism and God-Talk* (Boston: Beacon, 1983); Virginia Mollenkott, *The Divine Feminine* (New York: Crossroad, 1983).

[36]For further discussion in Christology on Jesus as the Son of God see *TDNT,* 5:99-101, 8:334-97; Vincent Taylor, *The Names of Jesus* (New York: St. Martin's, 1962); pp. 53ff.; Guthrie, *New Testament Theology,* pp. 301-20; Cullmann, *Christology of the New Testament,* pp. 270-305; Stauffer, *Theology of the New Testament;* R. H. Fuller, *The Foundations of New Testament Christology* (London: Lutterworth, 1965); R. N. Longenecker, *The Christology of Early Jewish Christianity* (Grand Rapids, Mich.: Baker, 1981); Bultmann, *Theology of the New Testament,* vol. 1; I. H. Marshall, "The Divine Sonship of Jesus," *Interp.* 21 (1967): 87-103; Ferdinand Hahn, *The Titles of Jesus in Christology: Their History in Early Christianity* (London: Lutterworth, 1969); Alan Richardson, *An Introduction to the Theology of the New Testament* (London: SCM Press, 1958), pp. 147-53; Webb, *Reformed Doctrine of Adoption,* pp. 93-110.

due to the incarnation that describes the unique character of Jesus as the God-man. This Christological title (Son of man) occurs 69 times in the synoptic Gospels and 13 times in John. It is used almost exclusively by Jesus to refer to himself. The Son of man sayings are sometimes employed by Jesus as a substitute for the pronoun "I," when he makes unusual claims for his own authority to do things on the earth. For example, Jesus claims authority for the Son of man to forgive sins on the earth (Mk 2:10) and to have authority over the Sabbath (2:28).[37]

A second group of the Son of man sayings refer to Jesus' prophecies of his upcoming suffering. They start to appear immediately after Peter's confession at Caesarea Philippi when Jesus begins to describe to his disciples his inevitable suffering and death on the cross (Mk 8:31; Lk 9:22).[38] The final category to which these sayings refer is his future glorification. Jesus speaks of the Son of man "when he comes in the glory of his Father with the holy angels" (Mk 8:38; Mt 16:27; Lk 9:26).[39]

While the title Son of man is one of Jesus' favorite means of referring to himself, it is displaced by others in the early church. It appears only a few times in the rest of the New Testament. It is used once on Stephen's lips, "Behold, I see the heavens opened, and the Son of man standing at the right hand of God" (Acts 7:56). Hebrews, as a citation from Psalm 8:4-6, clearly applies it to Jesus (Heb 2:6-8). Twice in the book of Revelation the person of Christ is referred as one "like a son of man" (Rev 1:13; 14:14). The fact that this title is rarely used by the early church indicates that it had a particularly unique use on the lips of Jesus in reference to himself and his identification with humankind, but after his ascension its use was no longer as necessary for the early church. Nevertheless, it clearly reflects the use of family language to describe the humanity of Jesus and is very significant in understanding the

---

[37]For other references to the Son of man in this category see Mk 2:28 (Mt 12:8, Lk 6:5); Mt 11:19 (Lk 7:34); Mt 8:20 (Lk 9:58); Mt 12:32 (Lk 12:10); Mt 5:11; 13:37; 16:13; Mk 8:27; Lk 6:2; 19:10; 22:48. See also Guthrie, *New Testament Theology*, pp. 275-78.

[38]For further references to the Son of man in relationship to his sufferings see Mk 9:9 (Mt 17:9); Mk 9:12 (Mt 17:12); Mk 9:31 (Mt 17:22-23; Lk 9:44); Mk 10:33 (Mt 20:18; Lk 18:31); Mk 10:45 (Mt 20:28); Mk 14:21 (Mt 26:24; Lk 22:22); Mk 14:41 (Mt 26:45); Mt 12:40 (Lk 11:30).

[39]For further references to the Son of man with reference to his future glorification see Mk 8:38 (Mt 16:27; Lk 9:26); Mk 13:26 (Mt 24:30; Lk 21:27); Mk 14:62 (Mt 26:64; Lk 22:69); Mt 24:27 (Lk 17:24); Mt 24:37-39 (Lk 17:26-27); Mt 24:44 (Lk 12:40); Mt 10:23; 13:41; 16:28; 19:28; 24:30; 25:31; Lk 12:8; 17:22, 29-30; 18:8; 21:36. On three categories of the "Son of man" sayings see *EDT*, 1034-36.

God-man and his work of redemption.[40]

Brother. The Son of man references to Jesus in the Gospels are a part of Jesus' self-identification with all humanity, so that as people become children of God, they might be not only heirs of God but also "fellow heirs with Christ" (Rom 8:16-17). The focus on family relationships is still maintained when Jesus is described as an elder brother. Paul talks about God's desire for his children to be "conformed to the image of his Son, in order that he might be the first-born among many brethren" (8:29). Becoming a child of God makes one like his divine Son. While the uniqueness of Jesus' divine sonship is preserved, the same family analogy is used to include others who come into a new relationship with God. It is by this second use of the word son or children that Jesus may be described as an elder brother within the family of God.[41] One basis for this use of family terminology is found in Jesus' resurrection appearances when he said to the women, "Go and tell my brethren" (Mt 28:10; Jn 20:17).

Bridegroom/Husband. Within the family figure of speech another role for Jesus is a description of him as a Bridegroom or Husband. It first occurs when the disciples of John ask Jesus why his disciples do not fast. To this question Jesus replies, "Can the wedding guests mourn as long as the bridegroom is with them?" (Mt 9:15; Mk 2:19; Lk 5:34). Jesus is clearly, if indirectly, referring to himself as the Bridegroom who is with his disciples for only a short period of time. John also identifies Jesus with this description when he himself disclaims that he is the Christ. "He who has the bride is the bridegroom; the friend of the bridegroom, who stands and hears him, rejoices greatly at the bridegroom's voice" (Jn 3:29). Paul picks up this metaphor when he writes; "For I betrothed you to Christ to

---

[40]On the Son of man see *TDNT*, 8:402; Knight, *Christian Theology of the Old Testament*, pp. 174-77; I. Howard Marshall, "The Synoptic Son of Man Sayings in Recent Discussions," NTS 22 (1966): 327-51; R. Marlow, "The Son of Man in Recent Journal Literature," CBQ 28 (1966): 20-39; A. J. B. Higgins, *Jesus and the Son of man* (Philadelphia: Fortress, 1964); Manson, *The Teaching of Jesus*, 211-34; Richardson, *Theology of the New Testament*, pp. 128-46; Ethelbert Stauffer, *New Testament Theology* (London: SCM Press, 1955), pp. 108-11; Morris, *The Lord from Heaven*; Barnabas Lindars, "The Son of Man in Johannine Christology," in *Christ and Spirit in the New Testament*, ed. Barnabas Lindars and Stephen S. Smalley (Cambridge: Cambridge University Press, 1973), pp. 43-60; Jeremias, *New Testament Theology*, pp. 257-66; F. J. Moloney, *The Johannine Son of Man* (Rome: LAS, 1976); C. H. Dodd, *The Interpretation of the Fourth Gospel* (Cambridge: Cambridge University Press, 1965); Leon Morris, *The Gospel According to John* (Grand Rapids, Mich.: Eerdmans, 1971); Oscar Cullmann, *The Christology of the New Testament* (London: SCM Press, 1963), pp. 137-92; Howard, *Christianity According to St. John*, 110ff.; C. K. Barrett, *The Gospel According to St. John* (London: SPCK, 1965).

[41]On Jesus as Brother see Candlish, *Discourses*, pp. 21-4; *TDNT*, 1:145; *EDT*, p. 217. Hebrews also pictures Jesus calling his followers brethren and places an Old Testament quotation (Ps 22:22) in the mouth of Jesus, "I will proclaim thy name to my brethren" (Heb 2:11-12, 17).

present you as a pure bride to her one husband" (2 Cor 11:2), and he hints at Jesus' role as a bridegroom to the church in his description of how husbands are to love their wives (Eph 5:25-28).[42] When the book of Revelation describes Jesus as the Bridegroom, it refers to the church as his bride and the marriage of the lamb as the union that will lead to an eternal fellowship (Rev 18:7, 9). The holy city, that is, the New Jerusalem, is also described as being "prepared as a bride adorned for her husband." In this context it is the holy city, representing the people of God, that is described as "the bride, the wife of the Lamb" (21:2, 9).[43]

When the relationship of Jesus to the church is described in terms of a bridegroom to a bride, special emphasis is placed on the relationship of love, intimacy and coming together for a permanent union. Marriage reflects the closest of all human relationships, and when the relationship of husband and wife is described with bridal language, it places a key accent on the freshness of their love and on their coming together to be joined in a permanent commitment.

The Holy Spirit

Old Testament. In Isaiah 30, which speaks three times of God as the Holy One of Israel, there is a reference to God speaking to "rebellious children" who carry out plans and make leagues but not by God's Spirit. Here we have an indirect reference to the Spirit of God in relation to God's role as Father (Is 30:1, 9).

Agent of the conception of Jesus. In the New Testament the Holy Spirit is uniquely related to the family figure of speech by his relationship to the person of Jesus. In the incarnation it is Jesus who is conceived in Mary "of the Holy Spirit" (Mt 1:18, 20; Lk 1:35). The Holy Spirit is obviously very significantly involved in the conception of Jesus as the agent of his birth. At the baptism of Jesus it is the Spirit of God that descends on him like a dove, while the voice of the Father speaks, "This is my beloved Son" (Mt 3:16-17). Paul understands this unique relationship between the second and third persons of the Trinity when he declares that Jesus was "designated Son of God in power according to the Spirit of holiness" (Rom 1:4). The same picture is seen when Paul talks about people who believe in Jesus and have become sons of God. These are those for

---

[42]For other references in the parables to the Bridegroom/bride analogy with reference to Jesus and the church see Mt 22:1-14; 25:6; Lk 12:35-40.

[43]On Christ as Bridegroom of the church see Richardson, *Theology of the New Testament*, pp. 256-58; Claud Chavasse, *The Bride of Christ* (London: Religious Book Club, 1940).

whom "God has sent the Spirit of his Son into our hearts, crying, 'Abba! Father!'" (Gal 4:6). So within the family category the Spirit of God is very closely bound up to Jesus' role as the Son of God.[44]

Agent of new birth. The Holy Spirit's relationship to people is primarily through his role as the agent of the new birth. In responding to Nicodemus's question about being born again, Jesus says, "Unless one is born of water and the Spirit, he cannot enter the kingdom of God. That which is born of the flesh is flesh, and that which is born of the Spirit is spirit" (Jn 3:5-6). The Spirit *(pneuma)* is like the wind. It contains a mysterious element that is not controlled by people, but it does accomplish its work. Thus, says Jesus, "is everyone who is born of the Spirit" (3:8).[45]

The context of John 3 makes it clear that being born of the Spirit is related to believing in Jesus Christ and receiving eternal life (3:15-16). If it is the Spirit that makes possible being born into the family of God, then the Spirit is certainly operative in the exercising of faith that leads to this life (cf. Jn 3:34-35). The Spirit is not only responsible for bringing the non-Christian to a conviction of sin, righteousness and judgment (Jn 16:7-11), but he is also responsible for giving the individual power to believe on Christ and, thus, be born of the Spirit and enter the kingdom of God to possess eternal life. This is why Paul can refer to "the Spirit of life" which is in Christ Jesus (Rom 8:2). So as believers "we serve not under the old written code but in the new life of the Spirit" (7:6). This is also related to the love of God that is put into our lives through the agency of the Holy Spirit in the experience of conversion. Paul writes of those who have come to saving grace: "God's love has been poured into our hearts through the Holy Spirit which has been given to us" (5:5).

Guarantor of inheritance. The Holy Spirit also appears in the family figure of speech as the guarantee of our inheritance. "In him you also, who have heard the word of truth, the gospel of your salvation, and have believed in him, were sealed with the promised Holy Spirit, which is the guarantee of our inheritance until we acquire possession of it, to the praise of his glory" (Eph 1:13-14). Again, God

---

[44]On the relationship of the Spirit to the Sonship of Jesus see Guthrie, *Theology of the New Testament,* p. 318; James D. G. Dunn, "Jesus as Flesh and Spirit: An Exposition of Romans 1, 3, and 4," *JTS* 24 (1973): 40-68; J. I. Packer, *Knowing God* (Downers Grove, Ill.: InterVarsity Press, 1973), pp. 198-200.
[45]On the Holy Spirit as the agent of the new birth see *NIDNTT,* 1:179; Guthrie, *Theology of the New Testament,* p. 527.

is described as the One who has "put his seal upon us and given us his Spirit in our hearts as a guarantee" (2 Cor 1:22). With salvation understood as culminating in a final inheritance in heaven, the Holy Spirit is an inward witness to the hearts of God's children that God is going to fulfill his promises to them and take them to his eternal home.

The Spirit and the family. The relationship between the Spirit and the Father becomes more explicit when Jesus talks about "the Spirit of your Father" to his disciples (Mt 10:20). Paul says that only those who "are led by the Spirit" are the sons of God (Rom 8:14). One begins to be led by the Spirit when he comes to receive "the spirit of sonship." It is this Spirit that leads us to cry, "Abba! Father!" The reason for this is that "it is the Spirit himself bearing witness with our spirit that we are children of God, and if children, then heirs, heirs of God and fellow heirs with Christ" (8:15-16). So the Spirit himself is the Spirit of sonship that makes it possible to call unto God as Father, and at the same time it is the Spirit that bears witness to the hearts of believers that they are children of God and, therefore, have assurance of their relationship and their heritage in the family of God.[46] The Spirit's involvement in the family atmosphere is also described when Paul talks about the love of the Spirit (Rom 15:30) and "the fellowship of the Holy Spirit" (2 Cor 13:14).

In summary, it may be said that the Spirit is the one who leads a person through a conviction of sin, of righteousness and of judgment, and brings him to the place where he may be born into the family of God. At this point the love of God as a Father is poured out into the hearts of the believers through the Holy Spirit, and the Spirit makes it possible for the individual to cry, "Abba! Father!" The Spirit then leads those who are the children of God, bearing witness to their hearts and giving assurance of their relationship to God, while serving as the guarantor of their inheritance in an atmosphere of love and fellowship. Finally, Jesus sets the gift of the Holy Spirit clearly in a family context when he says to his disciples, "If you then, who are evil, know how to give good gifts to your children, how much more will the heavenly Father give the Holy Spirit to those who ask him!" (Lk 11:13).

---

[46]On the Spirit bearing witness that we are children of God see John Wesley, "Marks of the New Birth," in *Wesley's Standard Sermons*, ed. Edward H. Sugden (London: Epworth, 1921), 1:289-91.

Man and Woman

Desired relationship with Father. It is certainly God's desire that those who are his people be related to him as children are related to a father, and so the family figure of speech describes the people of God in this way (e.g., Ex 4:22-23; Jn 1:12; 1 Jn 3:1).[47] Because all believers are children of God, their relationship to one another is described in terms of brothers and sisters in Christ (e.g., Acts 1:16; Rom 12:1; 16:1, 14-15, 17).[48] Sometimes other members of the family of God are referred to as kinsmen (e.g., Rom 16:7, 11, 21). The focus on the family figure of speech means that the language in this category is borrowed from the home. The purpose of the analogy is to emphasize an atmosphere of love and acceptance.

The Father relates to his children in two major areas. One is in terms of his authority as the one who sets a righteous standard for the family, provides instruction and enforces discipline. But judges and kings may also do those things. The new dimension that is provided with the family analogy is the atmosphere in which this authority is exercised. It is the atmosphere of a home which focuses on loving relationships and intimate fellowship. God desires that we relate to him in an intimate way in love and in the joy of fellowship with him. Further, he desires that we relate to other members of his spiritual family in the same way. John captures it well when he writes, "These things write we unto you that you may have fellowship with us and truly our fellowship is with the Father and with his Son Jesus Christ" (1 Jn 1:3-4 author's translation).[49]

Family relationships. The family analogy is extended so that Christians are to relate to other Christians like they are members of their own family. The purpose again is to focus on an atmosphere of loving acceptance and fellowship for those who together call themselves children of God. Thus Paul addresses Timothy as his "true child in the faith" (1 Tim 1:2; also 2 Tim 1:2; Tit 1:4) and exhorts him to treat the elders in the church "as you would a father." Then he elaborates the relationship with other members of the family of God: "Treat younger men like brothers, older women like mothers, younger women like sisters" (1 Tim 5:1-2).

The family figure of speech means that sometimes the concept of salvation is described as an inheritance from God the Father (e.g., Deut 4:20; Is 19:25). Paul

---

[47]For an excellent discussion on "being a child" see Jeremias, *New Testament Theology*, pp. 188-203.

[48]On the term *brother* to designate fellow believers in Christ see *BDT*, p. 83; *EDT*, p. 217.

[49]For further discussion of the concept of fellowship within the family see Candlish, *Discourses*, pp. 24-27.

talks about "the riches of his glorious inheritance in the saints," (Eph 1:18), and Peter speaks of being born anew "to an inheritance which is imperishable, undefiled, and unfading, kept in heaven for you, who by God's power are guarded through faith for a salvation ready to be revealed in the last time" (1 Pet 1:3-5).[50]

Sin

While the doctrine of man and woman describes the desired relationship with God the Father, the doctrine of sin expresses the actual relationship.

State of sin: Absence of life. The principle of sin is described in this category in terms of the absence of the life that comes from a father. The absence of life and family relationships from a holy God is described as a state without life, i.e., death. Often the word death itself is not used but is implied in statements that have to do with the giving of life in a family context (Jn 3:15-16). At other times it is quite clear that when one comes into life he is moving out from under the wrath of God or out of spiritual death. "He who believes in the Son has eternal life; he who does not obey the Son shall not see life, but the wrath of God rests upon him" (Jn 3:36). Jesus clarifies this shift when he said, "He who hears my word and believes him who sent me, has eternal life; he does not come into judgment, but has passed from death to life" (5:24). The reason for this is that the Father has given the Son the power to give "life to whom he will" (5:21).

Paul describes the principle of sin and its concomitant of death in his comparison and contrast of Adam with Christ. "Therefore as sin came into the world through one man and death through sin, and so death spread to all men because all men sinned." He tells how death reigned and that many had died through one man's trespass, meaning that many had experienced spiritual death because of inherited sin. He discusses how one man's trespass led to the condemnation for all and how one man's disobedience ended up making many sinners. But he closes with the reminder that "as sin reigned in death, grace also might reign through righteousness to eternal life through Jesus Christ our Lord" (Rom 5:12-21). This seems to be the same sin principle that Paul is discussing in Romans 7 when he talks about "the body of death" (7:24).[51]

---

[50]See also Acts 20:32 and Col. 3:24. On salvation as inheritance see *TDNT,* 3:758ff.; *TDNT,* 4:294ff.; *NIDNTT,* 2:295-304; *EDT,* p. 561; James D. Hester, *St. Paul's Concept of Inheritance* (London: Oliver & Boyd, 1968); Richardson, *Theology of the New Testament,* pp. 266-67; Rad, *Old Testament Theology,* 1:296-305; *ZPEB,* 3:277ff.; *IDB,* 2:701ff.

Paul describes sin as a state of death using family language in his discussion with the Ephesians. He reminds them there was a time

> when you were dead through the trespasses and sins in which you once walked, following the course of this world, following the prince of the power of the air, the spirit that is now at work in the sons of disobedience. Among these we all once lived in the passions of our flesh, following the desires of body and mind, and so we were by nature children of wrath, like the rest of mankind. (Eph 2:1-3)

It is interesting to observe in this context Paul's reference to nonbelievers as a part of the family of the devil. He describes them as "sons of disobedience" or those who were "by nature children of wrath" (Eph 2:2-3). This is the same position that John takes when he contrasts the children of God with the children of the devil (1 Jn 3:10). This may be an echo of Jesus' description of the devil as a father. When certain Jews claim to have God as their Father, Jesus responds, "You are of your father the devil, and your will is to do your father's desires. . . . When he lies, he speaks according to his own nature, for he is a liar and a father of lies" (Jn 8:41, 44).[52] Apparently, the early church is following Jesus' categorization and places everyone either in the family of the devil or the family of God.

Self-love. While self-giving love is the desired standard within the family, the perversion of this has love turned back on itself. Self-love means a self-centered focus—another significant way of understanding our sinful nature. Accordingly, Paul warns Timothy that in the last days there will be some who "will be lovers of self" (2 Tim 3:2-5). This description of self-love, *philautos* (φίλαυτος) comes at the head of a list of characteristics of people who Paul says hold "the form of religion but deny the power of it." Some parts of Paul's additional description give a definiteness to what is meant by "lovers of self." These are people who are also described as "lovers of money," suggesting a focus on financial resources that provide power for people to accomplish their own will. They are also described as "proud, arrogant," which reinforces the focus on self-centeredness and the need to have one's own way. Finally, they are described as "lovers of pleasure

---

[51]On sin as death see *EDT*, pp. 299-300; Pope, *Compendium of Christian Theology*, 2:37-41; H. Orton Wiley, *Christian Theology* (Kansas City, Mo: Beacon Hill, 1941), 2:91-95. See also *NIDNTT*, 1:435-41; Robert Martin-Achard, *From Death to Life* (Edinburgh: Oliver & Boyd, 1960); O. Kaiser and E. Lohse, *Death and Life* (Nashville; Abingdon, 1981).

[52]For further discussion see Webb, *The Reformed Doctrine of Adoption*, pp. 79-92.

rather than lovers of God" (3:4). Because they are focused on themselves, they are
not focused on God. This means they are interested in their own concerns, i.e.,
pleasure, rather than the things of God.

All of this self-centered love is exactly the opposite of the design of the family,
which was put together so that people might enjoy the experience of self-giving
to those persons with whom they are closest. So the alternative to loving people
as God loves them, that is, unconditionally, is a sinfulness that now has their love
turned back on themselves and focused on individual power and pleasure. While
this term, "lovers of self," is only used once in the New Testament, as a
theological concept it is an apt description of multiple other situations in which
people are first concerned about themselves rather than others, even others in
the family of God (e.g., 2 Tim 4:10; 1 Tim 6:10; cf. Gal 5:13-21; Rom 1:29-31).

Act of sin: Deliberate disobedience. Whereas in the legal category disobedience was
primarily to the law of God, in the family category an act of sin is described as a
deliberate disobedience to the person and will of God as Father. The difference
becomes evident in that a judge looks at an individual to see whether or not they
have obeyed the letter of the law, but a father looks at the intent of the heart and
is concerned with the motivation of his child. With a legal definition of an act of
sin, any act of disobedience to a law of God, willful or otherwise, constitutes sin.
But with a family or ethical definition of sin, it is only a voluntary transgression of
the known will of the Father that describes an act of sin.[53] We see this kind of
definition alluded to in Jesus' discussion with the Pharisees about his coming into
the world for judgment. "Some of the Pharisees near him heard this, and they said
to him, 'Are we also blind?' Jesus said to them, 'If you were blind, you would have
no guilt; but now that you say, "We see," your guilt remains'" (Jn 9:40-41). Jesus
is saying that guilt is incurred only when there is a willful knowledge of
disobedience. Again Jesus speaks of those who will persecute his disciples because
they did not know his Father. "If I had not come and spoken to them, they would
not have sin; but now they have no excuse for their sin" (15:22). He clearly
indicates that sin is related to one's understanding of right and wrong.

Paul also addresses this question when he states, "Where there is no law there

---

[53]See John Wesley, *Works*, 12:394; *A Plain Account of Christian Perfection* (London: Epworth, 1952), p. 45. On the
difference between the legal and ethical definition of an act of sin see Merne A. Harris and Richard S. Taylor,
"The Dual Nature of Sin," in *The Word and the Doctrine*, ed. Kenneth Geiger (Kansas City, Mo.: Beacon Hill,
1965), pp. 91-101.

is no transgression" (Rom 4:15). He does not mean that sin is relative or subjectively dependent on one's understanding or that people do not do wrong in an absolute sense, but rather that disobedience is not considered transgression where there is no knowledge of wrong. "Sin indeed was in the world before the law was given, but sin is not counted where there is no law" (5:13).

This ethical or family definition of an act of sin fits the picture of a loving Father who is not primarily concerned with external obedience from his children, but who wants to know the intent of their hearts. The real judgment of God as a Father depends on his discernment of the internal motivation and not the external performance only.[54]

Salvation

New birth. The family figure of speech describes salvation in terms of the new birth. This experience of being born again is described in a conversation with Nicodemus when Jesus explains to him, "Unless one is born anew, he cannot see the kingdom of God" (Jn 3:3). Nicodemus is confused about the spiritualization of this birth language, and so asks, "How can a man be born when he is old?" Jesus then indicates that one has to be born physically as well as spiritually. "I say to you, unless one is born of water and the Spirit, he cannot enter the kingdom of God" (3:4-5). He explains that everything properly belongs to its own order, and thus, "that which is born of the flesh is flesh, and that which is born of the Spirit is spirit" (3:6). Jesus notes that Nicodemus should not marvel at his explanation of a new birth, as there is an element of mysteriousness about the powerful experience of being born of the Spirit into the family of God just as there is in natural birth. "The wind blows where it wills, and you hear the sound of it, but you do not know whence it comes or whither it goes; so it is with every one who is born of the Spirit" (3:8).

In the immediate context Jesus explains that being born of the Spirit also means having eternal life, and that one can only have this life, and consequently only be born again, when one believes in Jesus as the Son of God. " 'Whoever believes in him may have eternal life.' For God so loved the world that he gave his only Son, that whoever believes in him should not perish but have eternal life" (3:15-16).

---

[54]For further discussion on the family definition of an act of sin see Donald Metz, *Studies in Biblical Holiness* (Kansas City, Mo.: Beacon Hill, 1971), pp. 76-83; Charles Carter, *Contemporary Wesleyan Theology* (Grand Rapids, Mich.: Zondervan, 1983), 1:270-72.

John elsewhere speaks about two of the results of being born of God. The first is the family experience of being able to love other members of the family. "Beloved, let us love one another; for love is of God, and he who loves is born of God" (1 Jn 4:7). Further, those who are born of God can also victoriously overcome the world through their faith in God the Father. "For whatever is born of God overcomes the world; and this is the victory that overcomes the world, our faith" (5:4).

While the predominant focus on the new birth comes in the writings of John, Peter also uses this metaphor. "By his great mercy we have been born anew to a living hope through the resurrection of Jesus Christ from the dead, and to an inheritance which is imperishable, undefiled, and unfading, kept in heaven for you" (1 Pet 1:3-4). Coming into the family of God makes it possible for one to look forward to a future spiritual inheritance from God the Father. Further, Peter makes it clear that the experience of the new birth comes through the Word of God. "You have been born anew, not of perishable seed but of imperishable, through the living and abiding word of God" (1:23).[55]

Becoming children of God. Sometimes the experience of the new birth is described as becoming children of God. "To all who received him, who believed in his name, he gave power to become children of God; who were born, not of blood nor of the will of the flesh nor of the will of man, but of God" (Jn 1:12-13). John declares that becoming children of God is contingent on "believing in his name," and he echoes the same principle elsewhere. "Everyone who believes that Jesus is the Christ is a child of God" (1 Jn 5:1). Paul agrees that we are all sons of God through faith (Gal 3:26), but he also indicates the added dimension of grace as the other side of the divine process (Tit 3:7).[56]

---

[55]On the new birth see Wesley, "Marks of the New Birth," *Standard Sermons*, 1:280-97; "The Great Privilege of Those Who Are Born of God," *Standard Sermons*, vol 1:298-312; "The New Birth," *Standard Sermons*, 2:226-43; Webb, *Reformed Doctrine of Adoption*, 181-85; Wright, *Fatherhood of God*, pp. 171-77; Peter Toon, *Born Again* (Grand Rapids, Mich.: Baker, 1987), pp. 24-36, 37-46; Moody, *Word of Truth*, pp. 319-22; Donald Bloesch, *Essentials of Evangelical Theology* (San Francisco: Harper & Row, 1982), 2:6-11; William Cannon, *The Theology of John Wesley* (Nashville: Abingdon, 1946), pp. 122-25, 130-34; Harald Lindstrom, *Wesley and Sanctification*, pp. 83-86, 98-100; Pope, *Compendium of Christian Theology*, 3:7; TWB, p. 31; E. G. Selwyn, *The First Epistle of Peter* (London: Macmillan, 1946), p. 122; Richardson, *Theology of the New Testament*, pp. 34-36; R. A. Harrisville, *The Concept of Newness in the New Testament* (Minneapolis: Augsburg, 1960); Guthrie, *New Testament Theology*, pp. 585-87; Timothy Smith, *Whitefield and Wesley on the New Birth* (Grand Rapids, Mich.: Zondervan, 1986); H. A. Slaatte, *Fire in the Brand* (New York: Exposition, 1963), pp. 137-40; James M. Boice, *Awakening to God* (Downers Grove, Ill.: InterVarsity Press, 1979), pp. 51-59.

[56]On the sons/children of God see Packer, *Knowing God*, pp. 181-208; Richardson, *Theology of the New Testament*, p. 36; NIDNTT, 1:289-90; TDNT, 4:912-23; TDNT 5:636-54; TDNT, 8:334-400; Webb, *Reformed Doctrine of Adoption*, pp. 28-40, 167-77.

Theological implications. The experience of the new birth provides both a new objective and a new subjective dimension to salvation. When one is born into a family, there is a new relationship created between father and son. Thus, when anyone is born into the family of God, there is a new relationship established between himself and God. But the new birth also implies a new subjective beginning for the individual. Just as new life begins at birth, so a new spiritual life and nature begin in the new birth. God's grace is so radically transforming that it is described in terms of beginning life all over again. One now (at least initially) becomes like God in the same sense a son is like a father, and that is why this experience may be described in terms of initial sanctification: beginning to be made holy as God is holy. The subjective dimension of the new birth in terms of inward transformation means it is very close to the biblical description of the same experience in terms of regeneration. The picture of God as the Creator who regenerates or gives life has already been discussed in chapter three. The phraseology of the new birth refers to this same internal change of nature within the individual but is related primarily to the work of God as Father. Because both regeneration and the new birth are so closely tied with the subjective transformation of the individual, they are often discussed together as complementary ways of explaining the same phenomena.

Adoption. An alternative means of describing what it is like to come into the family of God is Paul's description of salvation as adoption. The adoption language is a mixture of the family figure of speech with legal categories, but the principal focus is in terms of relating to God as Father. He declares that by the Spirit of God we did not receive a new spirit of slavery that leads to fear, but we received the spirit of adoption or sonship. This comes when we cry unto God, "Abba! Father!" It is at this point that the Spirit of God bears witness with our spirits "that we are children of God, and if children, then heirs, heirs of God and fellow heirs with Christ" (Rom 8:14-17). This adoption as sons means we not only have the privilege of crying, "Abba! Father!" but also "through God you are no longer a slave but a son, and if a son then an heir" (Gal 4:5-7). In a similar vein Paul describes the experience of salvation through grace and faith to the Ephesians and likens it to becoming a member of God's household. "So then you are no longer strangers and sojourners, but you are fellow citizens with the saints and members of the household of God" (Eph 2:19).[57]

Eternal life. The experience of the new birth that results in being a part of the family of God is closely related in Scripture to the description of salvation as being given life or eternal life. New birth means new life and therefore the passages that deal with life in the spiritual sense are closely bound up with being born again. We have already seen how life is associated with God's role as Creator in that God both creates physical life and regenerates individuals so that they may have spiritual life. But the concept of life is not exclusive to God's role as Creator. Since it is God as Father who begets life, there is a clear overlap of the roles of Creator and Father in describing the concept of life.

Sometimes it is not possible to determine whether a passage deals with life in reference to God's role as Creator or his role as Father (e.g., Col 2:13). But there are some passages that can clearly be understood in terms of the family figure of speech. When Jesus discusses the new birth with Nicodemus, it is placed within the context of life being dependent on one's belief in the Son (Jn 3:1-8, 15, 16, 36).[58] Similarly, when Jesus declares that it "is the will of my Father, that everyone who sees the Son and believes in him should have eternal life," the concept of life is embedded in the language of family (6:40).[59] John writes in his first letter that "God gave us eternal life, and this life is in his Son" (1 Jn 5:11-13). This description of eternal life is given in the verses that follow John's declaration that "everyone who believes that Jesus is the Christ is a child of God" and that whoever "is born of God overcomes the world" (5:1-4).

Moral influence theory of the atonement. Many in the history of the Christian church have understood the centrality of the love of God behind all provision of

---

[57]On the concept of adoption see Wesley, *Standard Sermons*, 1:178-98; Packer, *Knowing God*, pp. 186-208; Webb, *Reformed Doctrine of Adoption*, pp. 17-27, 169-70, 173-75; Candlish, *Fatherhood of God*, pp. 54-65; *EDT*, p. 13; Richardson, *Theology of the New Testament*, p. 264; Cannon, *Theology of John Wesley*, pp. 120-21; Pope, *Compendium of Christian Theology*, 3:13-16; Richard Watson, *Theological Institutes* (London: John Mason, 1832), 2:478-80; T. M. Ralston, *Elements of Divinity* (Nashville: Southern Methodist Press, 1976), pp. 435-37; H. C. Thiessen, *Introductory Lectures on Systematic Theology* (Grand Rapids, Mich.: Eerdmans, 1949), pp. 373-74; *TDNT*, 8:397-99; J. I. Cook, "The Concept of Adoption in the Theology of Paul." In *Saved by Hope*, ed. J. I. Cook (Grand Rapids, Mich.: Eerdmans, 1978); W. H. Rosell, "New Testament Adoption: Graeco-Roman or Semitic?" *JBL* 71 (1952): 233-34; D. J. Theron, "'Adoption' in the Pauline Corpus," *EQ* 28 (January-March 1956): 6-14.

[58]On the concept of eternal life see Toon, *Born Again*, p. 31; David Hill, *Greek Words and Hebrew Meanings* (New York: Scribner, 1975), p. 192ff.; Guthrie, *New Testmament Theology*, p. 643; *EDT*, 368-69; *ISBE*, 3:1888-90; Lewis S. Chafer, *Systematic Theology*, ed. John F. Walvoord (Wheaton, Ill.: Victor, 1988), 4:24-28, 389, 400-401; 7:142, 227.

[59]See also Jn 5:20-21, 24, 26; 6:62-69; 11:25-27; 14:6; 20:31; Eph 5:1-5. Note the category that describes life in legal language as aquittal from the condemnation of death: Rom 5:17-18, 21; 7:6.

salvation in the atonement. Throughout the history of the church the death of Christ has been seen as a demonstration of the love of God desiring to seek a positive response from individuals. Thus Paul writes, "For Christ's love compels us, because we are convinced that one died for all, and therefore all died. And he died for all, that those who live should no longer live for themselves but for him who died for them and was raised again" (2 Cor 5:14-15 NIV). Christ's love then is demonstrated on the cross in order to motivate people to respond to God in love and to walk in love in their behavior toward others. So Christ's death in one sense is designed to exercise a moral influence on believers. "Be imitators of God, therefore, as dearly loved children and live a life of love, just as Christ loved us and gave himself up for us as a fragrant offering and sacrifice to God" (Eph 5:1-2 NIV). The cross reveals the love of God for lost humanity and makes a challenging appeal for a loving response including repentance for sin.[60]

While there clearly is a scriptural basis for seeing all of Jesus' life and death as an example, several Christian traditions have used this as an occasion for overemphasizing the subjective response to Christ's work on the cross. They hold that the purpose of Christ's death is to provide an example of divine love that will then elicit love from people and so draw humanity toward the Father. Christ's death on the cross is viewed as an example of a martyrdom that ought to serve as an incentive for moral responsibility.

Usually this moral influence theory concerning the atonement is connected to Peter Abelard (1079-1142), who taught that the exemplary effect of Christ's death was designed to move sinners to repentance, faith and love for God. The fact that people can respond to God's love implies that they have the power to love God and therefore no longer have to live in selfishness and sin.

More radical still are the theories of Faustus Socinus, the father of universalism (1539-1604), who sees Christ as a teacher and prophet instructing students and setting an example of godly living. The death of Jesus is viewed as an act of moral heroism that should serve as an example for others in patience, and which ought to produce repentance and faith as a

---

[60]Ignatius, "Ephesians 1," in *Ante-Nicene Fathers* (New York: Charles Scribner's Sons, 1925), 1:49. These dimensions of moral influence theory (sometimes called example theory) of the atonement are found throughout classical Christianity. Augustine, *Trinity*, trans. Stephen McKenna (Washington, D.C.: Catholic University of America Press, 1963), 1:6-13; Thomas à Kempis, *Imitation of Christ* (London: Collin, n.d.); Isaac Watts, "When I Survey the Wondrous Cross."

response. In the same tradition is Frederick Schleiermacher, the father of modern liberal theology (1768-1834), who believes Christ's life is an identification with the suffering of sin, both in life and in death. As people respond in faith to Jesus, they are drawn into Christ's God consciousness, sharing a sense of sonship and being freed from any sense of God's anger or wrath. The key to Schleiermacher's view of the atonement is Christ's sympathy for sinners that becomes an example to draw people into vital fellowship with the Father.

All of these responses have too strong an emphasis on the subjective side of what happened at the cross and not enough emphasis on the objective work of Christ in changing the divine-human relationship. Thomas Oden very helpfully points out that this perspective was condemned by the Council of Sens (A.D. 1141) when Abelard was charged with giving too much attention to the subjective appropriation of Christ's death to the neglect of the objective transformation that occurs in relationship between God and humans.[61] The underlying problem is a failure to see a holistic picture of God from his multiple roles, and consequently there is neglect of much biblical data on themes in the atonement from the roles that accent the objective work of Christ on the cross (e.g., Priest, Judge and Redeemer). A fuller, more complete picture of God protects from this kind of imbalance, while not denying the insights from the role of God as loving Father.

Assurance of salvation. The role of God as a loving Father theologically explains the reason God is concerned about giving assurance of salvation to those who believe in him. Some of the roles by which God identifies himself, if seen in isolation, could imply that God is rather distant from those who relate to him. Kings or judges may not particularly care how people feel about their relationship to them. It is different with the role of Father. A father not only loves but desires to be loved. He desires for his children to understand his personal commitment to them as well as his affection for them, in order to provide a basic security for them as they grow in maturity. One of the most anxiety-producing situations in anyone's life is a lack of assurance about relationships. It is just this assurance that God wants to give to his children. An

---

[61]Thomas Oden, *The Word of Life* (San Francisco: Harper & Row, 1989), pp. 404-5. On moral influence theories see Wiley, *Christian Theology*, 2:237-41, 259-69.

assurance based on a right relationship to him is what makes it possible for God to give them the security they need for spiritual growth. A father desires for his children to know exactly where they stand with him. It would be a cruel (and unbiblical) picture of a father who wanted to keep his children in the dark as to whether or not they were in a relationship of acceptance, love and commitment with him.

Witness of the Spirit. The biblical picture is that God as Father desires for his children to know their standing with him, and no question is more central to any individual than the matter of his or her salvation. This is why Paul is so strong about the Spirit bearing witness with our spirits that we are the children of God. He declares, "You did not receive the spirit of slavery to fall back into fear, but you have received the spirit of sonship." Thus, because the Spirit has brought this spirit of sonship or adoption, it is possible for us to cry "Abba! Father!" and to know that we are God's children. "And if children, then heirs, heirs of God and fellow heirs with Christ" (Rom 8:15-17). When the Spirit comes into the heart of a believer, it is possible to know that he is a child of God. This is what Paul means when he writes to the Galatians, "Because you are sons, God has sent the Spirit of his Son into our hearts, crying, 'Abba! Father!' " (Gal 4:6).

John relates this internal testimony to God's Spirit who gives assurance to the believer in the matter of receiving eternal life. "The Spirit is the witness. . . . This is the testimony, that God gave us eternal life, and this life is in his son. He who has the Son has life; he who has not the Son of God has not life" (1 Jn 5:7, 11-12). It is also John who gives us the strongest picture of God as a Father and this is why he is so convinced that God wants to give assurance of salvation to his children. Indeed, this is one of the chief reasons for writing his first letter. "I write this to you who believe in the name of the Son of God, that you may know that you have eternal life" (1 Jn 5:13). It is this knowledge of eternal life that constitutes the heart of the assurance the Father desires to give to every member of his spiritual family. It is in this knowing that one is free to develop a love relationship with God and grow up spiritually in the context of acceptance and affirmation.

Growth in Christian Experience

Growth as maturity. The language of the home is very apt to describe Christian experience, because it not only speaks of being born into the family of God but also of growing up in the family. A father not only begets children, he raises them to maturity. God is not only concerned that we be born again but that we grow up in spiritual maturity to the place we are able to reproduce ourselves spiritually in the lives of other people. Thus, John can talk about levels of spiritual experience in terms of some being little children, some young men, and some fathers in the faith (1 Jn 2:12-14). Paul also speaks of that spiritual growth which should lead us to the point when "we may no longer be children, tossed to and fro and carried about with every wind of doctrine," but rather reach "mature manhood" and experience "the measure of the stature of the fullness of Christ." According to him, this occurs when we "grow up in every way into him" (Eph 4:13-15). This growth he relates to being properly joined to other members of the family in order to learn how to speak the truth in love, to understand true doctrine, and to be equipped by spiritual leadership for the work of ministry (4:11-16).

In the same vein Peter declares that after we have been born anew by the word of God, we are to grow up in Christ, longing for the spiritual milk of the word. "Like newborn babes, long for the pure spiritual milk, that by it you may grow up to salvation" (1 Pet 1:23—2:2). Likewise Hebrews describes the need for not just living on milk but for moving on to solid food that results in greater spiritual growth. "You need milk, not solid food; for every one who lives on milk is unskilled in the word of righteousness, for he is a child. But solid food is for the mature, for those who have their faculties trained by practice to distinguish good from evil" (Heb 5:12-14).[62]

Family atmosphere for growth. The proper biblical context for a father to raise his children is in an atmosphere of discipline and love. This is parallel to the moral holiness that expresses God's holy nature in terms of righteousness and love. One of the earliest references to God as Father in Scripture comes in the context of a holy God seeking a holy people when he describes his holiness to them in terms of love and a standard of righteousness (Deut 7:6-11). He is the holy One who loves his people and gives to them a standard of righteousness (i.e., his commandments). Within this context we read: "Know then in your heart that, as a man disciplines his son, the LORD your God disciplines you" (8:5). The chief purpose of the discipline of God is that they might obey his

---

[62]On spiritual growth after birth see Moody, *Word of Truth*, pp. 319-22; *NIDNTT*, 2:128-30.

commandments (8:3, 6). A father sets a standard for his son, and then he disciplines and corrects him to see that he conforms to it. Yet, it is clearly discipline within the context of love. This context provides some of the clearest expressions of the love of God for his people (7:7-8), and it also provides a picture of God dealing with people like a father deals with his son, that is, in love. (8:5). The expression of God's holy character in love and righteousness, then, provides the basis of the context for a father to raise his children in discipline and love, so that the children, like the father, may be holy.

Proverbs captures this dual emphasis within the family context in succinct form. "My son, do not despise the LORD's discipline or be weary of his reproof, for the LORD reproves him whom he loves, as a father the son in whom he delights" (Prov 3:11-12). This is the passage quoted by the writer of Hebrews when he encourages the Christians to see God's discipline/chastening as evidence that they are legitimate children of a heavenly Father.

> It is for discipline that you have to endure. God is treating you as sons; for what son is there whom his father does not discipline? If you are left without discipline, in which all have participated, then you are illegitimate children and not sons. Besides this, we have had earthly fathers to discipline us and we respected them. Shall we not much more be subject to the Father of spirits and live? (Heb 12:7-9)

Hebrews speaks equally about love as the motivation behind God's correction as well as the context in which it is exercised. "For the Lord disciplines him whom he loves, and chastises every son whom he receives" (Heb 12:6). The writer further emphasizes that this discipline in love is for the purpose of developing holiness of character. For God "disciplines us for our good, that we may share his holiness. For the moment all discipline seems painful rather than pleasant; later it yields the peaceful fruit of righteousness to those who have been trained by it" (12:10-11).

In describing the training of children in a context of discipline and love, Hebrews uses the words *paideuō* and *paideia* (παιδεύω and παιδεία). They are the words specifically used for the training of children, and therefore, they connote learning, instruction and teaching on the one hand, but also chastening, discipline and correction on the other. Just as a father, who sacrificially loves his wife (and by implication his family), is not to provoke his children to anger, but to "bring them up in the discipline and instruction of the Lord" (Eph 6:4), so God both loves and disciplines his spiritual children. "Those whom I love, I reprove and chasten" (Rev 3:19).[63] This context for growth in the family is diagrammed in figure 8.1.

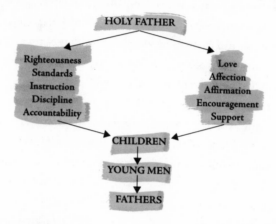

Figure 8.1. Growth of God's children

The reason this (training up of children in a context of discipline and love) is so significant is because it meets two basic human needs for structure and security. God, like a father, sets before individuals a standard for right conduct and behavior, and then he disciplines his children to help them learn to conform to it. The teaching and the discipline provide a standard by which to live, some structure for life and the security of knowing that God is true to his word and will punish disobedience. But the love of God provides the other half of the equation that meets people's need for fellowship and acceptance in relationships. A person is loved by a God who desires to have an intimate relationship with him.[64]

God also has means for accomplishing his purposes through both of these emphases. On the one hand, it is the Word of God that serves as the standard for expressing God's righteousness and the commandments by which one must live and be trained in godly character. "All scripture is inspired by God and profitable for teaching, for reproof, for correction, and for training in righteousness" (2 Tim 3:16).

---

[63]On discipline and love as meeting basic human psychological needs see M. Scott Peck, *The Road Less Traveled* (New York: Simon & Schuster, 1978).

[64]For further discussion see *TDNT*, 5:596-625; *NIDNTT*, 3:775-81; *EDT*, p. 320.

On the other hand, God's love expresses itself through his grace in the training process. Paul says it is the grace of God that is "training us to renounce irreligion and worldly passions and to live sober, upright, and godly lives in this world" (Tit 2:12). So the standards of righteousness and love which provide the context of discipline and love also are the areas in which God has provided the means of Scripture and grace to train up his spiritual children to reflect his own holy character.

Family model for discipleship. The application of this family context for spiritual growth is found in the discipleship process and modeled for us first by Jesus and the Twelve. When Jesus first begins to instruct his disciples about their understanding of God as their Father, he repeatedly emphasizes that God is their "heavenly Father." This is to distinguish God from any earthly father, but is also to explain that disciples are to understand themselves as part of a spiritual family under God's fatherly direction. Jesus limits the size of the discipleship group to twelve, in part because of its symbolic significance relative to the twelve tribes of Israel, but also because of the need for intimacy within the discipleship group that parallels the intimacy within a family. Jesus is saying by implication that just as it is in the physical family that one experiences the closest personal relationships, this should now be understood to be taking place in a deeper way with a spiritual family. There is one sense in which the spiritual family of God covers all believers in Christ, but with the designating of the Twelve into a special relationship with him, Jesus is also pointing out the crucial need for all believers to be part of a small group about the size of a large family. Twelve would be about the maximum for the make-up of such a spiritual group.

One of Jesus' key purposes for training disciples in a spiritual family context is the development of close personal relationships. This takes time and spiritual energy and can only be done with a few people. The closer their relationships are previous to their commitment to this spiritual family, the faster their intimacy will develop. This is probably the reason Jesus chose at least two sets of brothers to form the nucleus of his spiritual family (cf. Jn 1; Mt 4). Early in his life, Jesus mixes his physical and spiritual families, like the occasion he retreats to Capernaum to spend time with his mother and brothers as well as his disciples (Jn 2:12). At least part of Jesus' physical family (particularly his brothers) do not believe in him until after the resurrection and so do not come into Jesus' spiritual family until after the close of the Gospel record (cf. Jn 7:3-10). It is evident that for Jesus the spiritual family takes precedence over his own physical family. Thus when his mother and brothers come to take him home, he responds by questioning, "Who is my mother, and who are my brothers?" Then pointing to his disciples he says, "Here are my mother and my brothers! For whoever does the will of my Father in heaven is my brother, and sister, and mother" (Mt 12:46-50). This understanding of spiritual family is why at the end of his three years with the disciples Jesus can refer to them in the true spiritual sense as "my brethren" (Jn 20:17; Mt 28:10).

When Jesus begins to form his spiritual family, one of the things he does immediately for them is to set before them a context that includes a standard of righteousness (Mt 5:20-42) and a commitment of love (Mt 5:43-48). He continues throughout his three years with the disciples to elaborate for them his standard of righteousness while he disciplines and corrects them within the context of love when they are wrong. John the apostle recognizes this when he describes Jesus' last night with the disciples. "Having loved his own who were in the world, he loved them to the end" (Jn 13:1). It is within this dual context that real spiritual nurture takes place inside the discipleship group. Here is where Jesus sets before them standards, provides instruction, exercises discipline and corrects and rebukes when necessary, but at the same time he does all of these things in an atmosphere of unconditional love, acceptance, affirmation, encouragement and commitment. These ingredients form the basis for the most significant growth within a physical family, and they provide just the proper context for maturity as well within the spiritual family.

The disciples learn their lessons well, and when the first people respond in faith to Jesus after Pentecost, the disciples immediately place them in small groups (Acts 2:46) as a part of the process of building certain basic spiritual lessons into their lives. It is significant to note that the first two things they set before the three thousand new believers are the apostles' teaching (standard of righteousness) and fellowship (context of love) (2:42). It is this model that provides the paradigm for the theological understanding of the family as the context for spiritual growth that we have seen earlier reflected in John, Paul, Peter and the writer to the Hebrews. The New Testament writers make it clear that there is no real growth to spiritual maturity without the context of a spiritual family on the model of Jesus' discipleship band.[65]

---

[65]On the discipleship model as a context for spiritual growth, maturity and training for Christian service see Allan Coppedge, *The Biblical Principles of Discipleship* (Grand Rapids, Mich.: Zondervan, 1989), pp. 61-93.

The Church

Family of God. It should not be surprising that all we have discovered under the language category of the home implies that the church is to be understood as the family of God. The whole cluster of concepts of the new birth, receiving life, assurance and growing up in one's spiritual life are wrapped in family language. The whole focus of this language figure is on the church as the family of God.

Paul indicates that this is the standard understanding of the early church when he instructs Timothy about relating to the individual members of a congregation. "Do not rebuke an older man but exhort him as you would a father; treat younger men like brothers, older women like mothers, younger women like sisters, in all purity" (1 Tim 5:1-2). Members of the New Testament church are to treat one another like they are part of the same family and relate to one another as though they are mothers, fathers, brothers and sisters in the faith.

Even under the Old Covenant the church is sometimes described in family categories. The promise to the people of Israel is that they shall be "sons of the living God" (Hos 1:10). Under the New Covenant when people believe in the Lord Jesus and "become children of God" (Jn 1:12), they then are regularly described as sons and daughters in relationship with a father. "I will be a father to you, and you shall be my sons and daughters, says the Lord Almighty" (2 Cor 6:18; cf. Is 43:6).

Those who are "all sons of God, through faith" are the real offspring of Abraham and "heirs according to promise" (Gal 3:26, 29). If they are children of God, they are also heirs (Gal 1:5-7), and collectively the members of the church may be described as fellow heirs. Paul says "the Gentiles are fellow heirs, member of the same body, and partakers of the promise in Christ Jesus through the gospel" (Eph 3:6). He makes the connections, "if children, then heirs, heirs of God and fellow heirs with Christ" (Rom 8:17).

The family analogy for the church is reinforced by the frequent reference in the New Testament to Christians as brethren. Jesus says to his disciples, "you are all brethren . . . for you have one Father" (Mt 23:8-9). If God is their Father, Christ is like an elder brother, for he describes his disciples as his brethren (Mt 28:10; Jn 20:17).

The early church picks up on this family analogy by frequently describing Christians as "the brethren" (e.g., Acts 6:3; 9:20; 10:23; 11:1, 12; 15:1, 7). Christians both in the Jewish church in Jerusalem and among the newly birthed

Gentile believers are described as brethren by the apostles and elders (Acts 15:22-23). The family nature of the church becomes so pervasive that reference to the brethren becomes the major way that Christians are addressed in the New Testament (Rom 1:13). Most of the references to brethren in Acts and the epistles are generic references to both brothers and sisters in the faith, while sisters in the spiritual sense are referred to specifically in a number of occasions (Rom 16:1; 1 Cor 7:15; 9:5; 1 Tim 5:2; Jas 2:15; 2 Jn 13).

Household of God. A slight variation on the use of family terminology is to describe the church as the household of God. Peter warns that judgment begins with the household of God (1 Pet 4:17), and Paul writes instructions to Timothy about how members of the church "ought to behave in the household of God" (1 Tim 3:15). Christ is described as one who is over the house of God (Heb 3:6). Paul says that new Gentile Christians are not only fellow citizens but also "members of the household of God" (Eph 2:19). The Christians are exhorted to make these members of the church the special objects of their good deeds. "As we have opportunity, let us do good to all men, and especially to those who are of the household of faith" (Gal 6:10).

The emphasis on the church as the family of God or the household of God carries significant theological implications for the believers in the early church. Because this understanding of the church is the predominant one (especially if the numerous references to "the brethren" are given their proper weight), then this view affects the way Christians understand their relationship to one another. They do not relate to each other primarily in business, legal or royal categories but in family categories. This means every person is important, regardless of his or her ability to perform. Relationships are based on mutual commitment in a family atmosphere, and not on whether or not a person "produces" for someone else. Obviously, in a family the very young and the very old (and sometimes the sick) cannot produce at all. Yet they are all of infinite value, to be honored because of who they are. The family atmosphere means that everybody is both honored and loved because they are part of a family. Relationships are characterized by affection and mutual self-esteem. The family does not have the same temptation to "use" people as the world does, and the basic needs of individuals are met in a church that sees itself as the family of God in terms of structure and discipline on the one side and love and affirmation on the other.

Bride/Wife. The alternative biblical pattern of describing the church in the language of family is to see it as a bride or wife to God. The analogy of a bride's relationship to a bridegroom gets special emphasis in the Old Testament in the Song of Songs. In the New Testament Jesus is introduced very early as a bridegroom (Jn 3:29; Mt 9:15). Similarly Paul writes to the Corinthian church, "For I betrothed you to Christ to present you as a pure bride to her one husband" (2 Cor 11:2). The espousal of the church (the bride) to Jesus (the bridegroom) is to come to consummation in glorification with the marriage supper of the Lamb. "Let us rejoice and exult and give him the glory, for the marriage of the Lamb has come, and his Bride has made herself ready" (Rev 19:7; cf. 19:9; 21:9).

The focus of the bride and bridegroom analogy is on the developing love relationship between a man and a woman. It is the growing closeness that comes before marriage and is one symbol of the growing intimacy that God desires with people who make up his church. This then comes to greater fruition with another alternative way of describing the family, viz., in terms of a relationship between a husband and wife.

The husband and wife figure of speech also has a significant Old Testament background. It is often related to the unfaithfulness of a wife who belongs to her husband (Hos 1—3). While the church is seen as an unfaithful wife, God is seen as one who continually reaches out to her and desires to draw her back into a right relationship with himself (Ezek 16, 23). The church may look at times like a wife who is forsaken because of her sin, but God declares that this is only in appearance and for a brief period of time. "With great compassion I will gather you. . . . With everlasting love I will have compassion on you" (Is 54:5-8).

It is clearly God's love, in a covenant family relationship, that does not let his people go. It is the same unconditional covenant love that Paul describes in his discussion of a family comparison of Christ's relationship to the church. Husbands are exhorted to love their wives "as Christ loved the church and gave himself up for her." The purpose is that "he might present the church to himself in splendor, without spot or wrinkle or any such thing, that she might be holy and without blemish." So husbands are to love and cherish their wives "as Christ does the church" (Eph 5:25-29).

The focus in the husband and wife relationship has to do with the closest possible human ties that are available, and Christ desires this with individual members of the church and with the church as a whole. The emphasis is on intimacy, closeness, love, sacrificial giving, and a bonded permanent commitment. If this is true of natural families, God desires the same kind of relationship with his church.

Full Sanctification

Perfect love. The concept of full sanctification is described in the family category by the state of the heart. It has to do with total or perfect love, like that of a child who loves his father with all his heart. It is this perfect love that describes the state in which one lives when he has had an experience of full sanctification. This means that many times it is the state of this experience that is described and not the experience of moving into such a state. So in this figure of speech full sanctification may often be described as a level of Christian experience where Christians ought to live and for which provision is made by grace.

Jesus sets this state of perfect love before his disciples very early in his relationship to them (Mt 5:43-48). His challenge to them is not only to love their neighbor (which is obvious and already previously commanded) but to "love your enemies" as well. He is concerned that his disciples learn to love those who do not love them back and then in this sense "be perfect, as your heavenly Father is perfect" (Mt 5:44, 48). With the setting of this standard before his own spiritual family (i.e., the disciples) Jesus indicates that the biblical data related to full sanctification in the family role relates both to the concept of perfectness as well as to the concept of love.

Perfectness in the Old Testament. In the Old Testament the concept of perfectness is related chiefly to two Hebrew words *shalem* (שָׁלֵם) and *tamim* (תָּמִים). *Shalem* comes from the same Hebrew root as the word *shalom*, meaning peace, wholeness or completeness. It is rendered in some English translations as "perfect" in certain contexts, like that of Deuteronomy 25:15, where it describes a perfect and just weight. Perfect in this context means that it weighs exactly what it is supposed to weigh. There is no specification regarding a weight in terms of its color, shape or appearance; but with regard to its weight, it is to be exactly what it is supposed to be. The implications are that something may not be perfect in an absolute sense, but it may be perfect in a more limited sense with regard to its principle purpose and intent. When the word is used with regard to the heart, it means a complete heart or a heart that loves as fully as it is possible to love. Clearly, it refers to the perfectness of love for which the heart is intended. In several places a perfect heart is related to full obedience to God or, conversely, a failure to fully obey God's commandments leads to an imperfect heart before God (1 Kings 8:54-61; 11:1-13; 1 Chron 28:1-10). A perfect heart is also related to a perfect desire or will to do something (1 Chron 12:38; 29:9), and sometimes it is related to a perfect trust or complete faith in God (2 Chron 16:9; 19:9).[66]

The word *tamim* is also used to describe perfectness in the Old Testament. It is particularly used in Leviticus as a description of perfect animals. A perfect animal does not have a spot or blemish, and it may be described as blameless. In an absolute sense, of course, no animal will be perfect, but in the limited sense one that is free from defect or blemish may be described as a perfect animal. This again implies that the word is not used in Scripture in an absolute way, but that there is a relative perfection that indicates both animals and people may be perfect in the sense of being complete, whole or being what they were created to be.

In this sense several people are described as perfect in the Scripture. Noah is described as "a just man and perfect in his generations" (Gen 6:9 KJV). This clearly relates to righteousness and obedience (7:1-5) and is also closely bound up with a complete desire to please God and a total trust in God. Abraham is commanded to walk before God and be "perfect" (17:1). Again, this includes obedience to God and a total trust in God with regard to his method of fulfilling his covenant promises to Abraham. In Deuteronomy 18:9-14 the command to be perfect or blameless is connected with ethical behavior, and Job is repeatedly described as "[perfect] and upright, one who feared God and turned away from evil" (Job 1:1, 8; 2:3). His perfectness is certainly related to righteousness of character, total trust in God and a willingness to separate himself from the world of evil.[67]

The Old Testament picture of perfectness, then, relates to the heart and describes one who is walking in full obedience to God's commandments and who has a righteousness of character like God's character. It involves a will or desire to wholly please God and serve him, as well as a total trust or confidence in God to accomplish his purposes in one's life. It is related not primarily to outward performance but to the motivation of the heart.

---

[66]On *shalem* as perfectness see John Oswalt, *A Call to Be Holy: A Biblical Perspective* (Nappance, Ind.: Evangel, 1999), pp. 52-63; *TWOT,* 2:930-31; *TDNT,* 2:402-6; George A. Turner, *The Vision Which Transforms* (Kansas City, Mo.: Beacon Hill, 1964); pp. 44-45.

[67]On תָּמִים as perfect see *TWOT,* 2:973-74; Turner, *Vision Which Transforms,* pp. 42-44; A. Deissley, "Perfection," *Sacramentum Verbi* 2 (1970), pp. 653-58; *THAT,* 2:1045-50. On the total Old Testament picture of perfection see Turner, *Vision Which Transforms,* pp. 41-51.

Perfectness in the New Testament. In the New Testament the concept of perfectness centers around the word *telios* (τέλειος). The basic word has to do with design, completeness, wholeness and purpose. Often it means "mature," especially when contrasted with *nepios* (νήπιος), meaning "children, childlike." In some places its meaning is certainly mature or grown-up in a moral sense (1 Cor 14:20; Eph 4:13-14), while in other places the concept of maturity, which implies continual growth, does not seem to do justice to this usage.[68]

It may be significant that five times in the Septuagint *telios* is used to translate *shalem* (שָׁלֵם), where it refers to a perfect heart (1 Kings 8:61; 11:4; 15:3, 14; 1 Chron 29:9). This shade of meaning coupled with the Old Testament background forms the standard for perfectness that Jesus sets before his disciples in the Sermon on the Mount. When Jesus exhorts his disciples, "You, therefore, must be perfect, as your heavenly Father is perfect" (Matt 5:48), the concept of perfectness (*telios*) must be understood in the light of its Old Testament counterparts. Perfectness relates to righteousness, to the will and desire of the heart and to faith in God.

But Jesus also accents another dimension in the immediate context of his command. It is the addition of a more complete understanding of love in relation to perfectness. While this may have been implied in the description of people in the Old Testament who had a perfect heart, it becomes more evident in Jesus' statement, "But I say to you, Love your enemies and pray for those who persecute you" (Mt 5:44). This love is to be that which makes his disciples reflect the love of their heavenly Father, "so that you may be sons of your Father who is in heaven" (Mt 5:45). The evidence of God's love is that he keeps loving people and doing good things for them whether they respond appropriately to him or not (5:45-47). It is in this sense that Jesus desires for his disciples to be perfect, i.e., that they should love perfectly or unconditionally, not only those who will love them back, like their neighbors, but those who are their enemies and who will hate them. This is an unconditional love that does not depend on the response of the recipients in order to continue to be expressed. This is the sense in which Jesus desires for his disciples to have a heart of perfect love, and it is the way in which they may be perfect like their heavenly Father. Jesus is not talking

---

[68]On *telios* in the New Testament see Turner, *Vision Which Transforms*, pp. 132-34; *BTL*, pp. 541-45; *TDNT*, 8: 49-87.

about an absolute perfection where people are like God in terms of capacities, knowledge, ability and so on, but according to Jesus it is possible to love like God loves.[69]

Loving God with all the heart. It is this kind of love for God and for people that Jesus describes in the "Great Commandment." "You shall love the Lord your God with all your heart, and with all your soul, and with all your mind. This is the great and first commandment. And a second is like it, you shall love your neighbor as yourself" (Mt 22:37-39; Deut 6:5; Lev 19:18). Jesus desires a complete devotion from the heart toward God and also an unconditional, self-giving love toward others. This is the standard for the hearts of those who know and experience full sanctification.[70]

While Jesus sets the standard before his disciples during his days with them on earth, it is not until his ascension and the coming of the Holy Spirit at Pentecost that we see the evidence of this kind of heart in the lives of his disciples. In preparation for this Jesus meets his disciples in the upper room and gives them a new commandment that they are to love one another as he has loved them (Jn 13:34-35). This is the self-giving, unconditional love that Jesus has demonstrated for them on this very occasion by his washing of the feet of all the disciples, including those of Judas (13:1ff.). The same evening Peter tries to express his less-than-perfect love for Jesus by declaring his willingness to lay down his life for his Master, but Jesus knows that his love is not complete enough to motivate him fully to do this yet and so predicts his denial (13:36-38). Thus, when Jesus comes to pray for his Father to sanctify his disciples, one of the results of this sanctification should be the perfect love that God has for the Son. "I have made known to them thy name, and I will make it known, that the love with which thou hast loved me may be in them, and I in them" (17:17, 26).[71]

This same motivation of the heart is reflected in the epistles. After calling for a total surrender of one's life as a living sacrifice to God (Rom 12:1), Paul sets this standard for Christians as they learn to live by total faith (13:8-10). For him all the commandments are summed up in the sentence, "You shall love your

---

[69]On references of *telios* that carry the sense of completeness as perfectness and usually connected with love see Jn 17:23; 1 Jn 2:5; 4:12, 17-18. See also Mt 19:21.

[70]On what biblical perfection does and does not mean see Wesley, "Christian Perfection," in *Wesley's Standard Sermons*, 2:47-77. See also "On Perfection," and "On Patience," in *Works*, 7.

[71]On Jesus' preparation for this kind of love see Allan Coppedge and William Ury, *In His Image* (Franklin, Tenn.: Providence House, 2000), chaps. 7-8.

neighbor as yourself." The reason for this is that "love does no wrong to a neighbor; therefore love is the fulfilling of the law" (13:9-10). This is the same standard he sets before the Corinthians when he warns them about seeking spiritual gifts instead of a heart that reflects the character of God. "Love is patient and kind; love is not jealous or boastful; it is not arrogant or rude. Love does not insist on its own way; it is not irritable or resentful; it does not rejoice at wrong, but rejoices in the right" (1 Cor 13:4-6). The heart of this kind of love, reflecting the love of God, is that it "does not insist on its own way." It is not self-centered love, but it is God-centered love expressed unconditionally toward both God and others. The carnal Corinthians are not living at this standard of Christian experience, but Paul reminds them that this is God's desire for them.[72]

Appropriation. In addition to the description of this state of love in which Christians should be living, there are also certain prayers and exhortations to move into this level of Christian experience. One of these comes in Paul's letter to the Ephesians after his discussion of the whole question of salvation by grace through faith (Eph 2). In his prayer to the Father for these believers, Paul prays that they "might be strengthened with might through his Spirit in the inner man" (3:16), that Christ might continue to dwell in their hearts through faith and that they might be filled with all the fullness of God. In the midst of this prayer, he asks that they might know a fuller dimension of the love of Christ than they have ever known before. It is clear that he is praying for Christians and that this level of Christian love is not that of beginning to love, but a level that would be consistent with the "fullness of God" and his Spirit in their lives. He prays that "you, being rooted and grounded in love, may have power to comprehend with all the saints what is the breadth and length and height and depth, and to know the love of Christ which surpasses knowledge" (3:17-19). It is to those who know this experience that he continues to exhort, "be filled with the Spirit" (5:18); in their family contexts the husbands are to love their wives "as Christ loved the

---

[72]On perfect love or Christian perfection see Lindstrom, *Wesley and Sanctification*, pp. 126-60; Ralston, *Elements of Divinity*, pp. 457-72; Turner, *Vision Which Transforms*, pp. 129-59; Metz, *Studies in Biblical Holiness*, pp. 221-28; Leo G. Cox, *John Wesley's Concept of Perfection* (Kansas City, Mo.: Beacon Hill, 1964); Mildred Bangs Wynkoop, *A Theology of Love* (Kansas City, Mo.: Beacon Hill, 1972), pp. 268-301; W. T. Purkiser, *Sanctification and its Synonyms* (Kansas City, Mo.: Beacon Hill, 1961), pp. 63-74; Bloesch, *Essentials of Evangelical Theology*, 2:47-53; François Fénelon, *Christian Perfection* (New York: Harper & Brothers, 1947); Samuel Chadwick, *The Call to Christian Perfection* (Kansas City, Mo: Beacon Hill, 1943); Andrew Murray, *Be Perfect* (Minneapolis: Bethany Fellowship, 1965); Asa Mahan, *Christian Perfection* (Salem, Ohio: Schmul, 1975); Newton F. Flew, *The Concept of Perfection* (London: Oxford University Press, 1934).

church and gave himself up for her, that he might sanctify her" (5:25-26). The kind of sacrificial love expected of husbands is identical to that of Jesus who loved enough to give of himself completely. This is the kind of love for which Paul is praying in Ephesians 3:17-18. It is the same kind of love in which he wants to see the Ephesians continuing to live when he exhorts them "walk in love, as Christ loved us and gave himself up for us, a fragrant offering and sacrifice to God" (5:2). He emphasizes that they are to love in this way as children of God (5:1).

Paul prays that the Philippians might experience this deeper love as well as its concomitants of purity and righteousness, and that all three of these parts of moral holiness be to the glory of God. "And it is my prayer that your love may abound more and more, with knowledge and all discernment, so that you may approve what is excellent, and may be pure and blameless for the day of Christ, filled with the fruits of righteousness which come through Jesus Christ, to the glory and praise of God" (Phil 1:9-11).

It is this standard of godliness or holiness that God intends for the believer when he first reconciles him to Christ. So Paul can write to the Colossians that they are the ones "he has now reconciled in his body of flesh by his death, in order to present you holy and blameless and irreproachable before him" (Col 1:22). Though the Colossians have begun to be made holy, Paul continues to work to produce the kind of full holiness he believes God desires to see in their lives. He sees his task as "warning every man and teaching every man in all wisdom, that we may present every man mature in Christ" (1:28). It is to these Christians that he gives explicit exhortation to "put to death therefore what is earthly in you" (3:5), and he spells out what the evil conduct is that represents the earthly. The aorist imperative used here indicates a definiteness regarding the putting of something to death. This is followed by mention of the new nature that has been "put on" (3:9-10), along with the exhortation to keep on being renewed (present tense) in knowledge after the image of the Creator (3:10). A progressive renewal of the image is obviously indicated. This is followed by another definite aorist imperative about certain things that Christians ought to "put on" (3:12-13), and this list is summarized with the exhortation to "put on love, which is the bond of perfectness" (3:14 KJV). There is a definiteness about the quality of love that is possibly acquired at a point in time.

Finally, Paul prays for the Thessalonian Christians that the Lord would make them "increase and abound in love to one another and to all men, as we do to you, so that he may establish your hearts unblamable in holiness before our God and Father" (1 Thess 3:12-13). For him, being established unblamable in holiness is intimately bound up with the increase in abounding love toward others. This is related to his closing prayer that sums up his requests from 3:11—5:22 when he prays, "May the God of peace himself sanctify you wholly [entirely]; and may your spirit and soul and body be kept sound and blameless at the coming of our Lord Jesus Christ" (5:23). The definiteness of this prayer, along with the others mentioned, continues to confirm the conviction that it is possible by a definite act of commitment to move into this level of Christian experience known as entire or full sanctification that provides a heart abounding in love that is like the unconditional, self-giving love of God the Father and God the Son.[73]

Further Growth

Family context for perfect heart. The concept of perfectness in the life of a Christian is only possible in the context of the family analogy. In the context of the other roles of God, perfection is not be possible, because placing the concept of perfectness within most of the other language categories makes it sound as though the Bible is speaking about an absolute perfection. This is particularly true if we speak in legal categories where God looks on people as a Judge or in the royal categories where he views them as the sovereign King. Those within the Christian tradition who think primarily in these categories cannot but view all perfection as an absolute perfection or perfectionism.[74]

Within the family category, however, the whole concept of perfectness takes on an entirely different cast. While no perfection is possible before a judge or a king, it is possible for a father who judges his children, not so much on their outward performance, but with regard to the inward intent of the heart. A father is concerned primarily about two things. He wants to know the deliberate intention of his children, i.e., are they trying to obey, and is there a will or desire with the intent to please? The second (an alternative means of asking the same question) is whether the child is motivated by a heart of love, even if his outward actions are not perfect in performance. So first a father asks about whether or

---

[73]On commands and exhortations related to this Christian experience, see Wesley, *Plain Account,* pp. 36-38.

[74]E.g., B. B. Warfield, *Perfectionism* (Philadelphia: Presbyterian & Reformed, 1958).

not a child's will wholly desires to please and be in submission to his father's will, and second, he asks whether or not the motivation is out of a heart of love. In terms of having a will wholly desirous to obey God and to please him and to have a heart that loves him completely, it is possible to speak of a Christian being perfect in a limited sense.[75]

Relative perfectness allows for growth. Because this perfection in the family category is not of an absolute nature, it allows for continuous growth. Growth in perfectness has to do particularly with the areas of righteous conduct and loving other people. More maturity after an experience of Christian perfection or full sanctification is possible as one grows in his understanding of the perfect will of God and makes application of this understanding in his own life. Additional growth has to do with understanding the full implications of loving as God loves and applying this in all areas of life. Maturity is always related to increased knowledge and understanding, and this is true for those who have had an experience of Christian perfection as well. As they continue in the family context of discipleship, their knowledge of God's will and the implications of his love will continue to increase, and their ability to apply this understanding in their own lives is further developed, particularly with the assistance of a small group of the body of Christ that serves as their spiritual family. Ongoing nurture continues to be a significant need in the lives of those who have come to an experience of having a heart wholly desirous to please God and by grace have been enabled to love like God loves.

Glorification

Final inheritance. Glorification is described in the family category as a final inheritance reserved for the children of God. Thus, Peter writes about having been "born anew to a living hope through the resurrection of Jesus Christ from the dead, and to an inheritance which is imperishable, undefiled, and unfading, kept in heaven for you" (1 Pet 1:3-4). Obviously, Peter means that those who have been born again can look forward to a future inheritance in heaven that comes to them as one of the rights of being a member of the family of God. The same thought is reiterated when Paul speaks about working heartily "as serving the Lord and not men, knowing that from the Lord you will receive the inheritance

---

[75]On the meaning of Christian perfection see Metz, *Studies in Biblical Holiness*, pp. 21-43.

as your reward" (Col 3:23-24). It is the Spirit of God who witnesses to this future inheritance. Those who have believed in Christ "were sealed with the promised Holy Spirit, which is the guarantee of our inheritance until we acquire possession of it" (Eph 1:13-14). So while salvation as an inheritance within the family of God in one sense is a present possession, in another sense its full implications will not be realized until glorification."[76]

Final adoption. In addition to final inheritance the concept of glorification may be described in family categories as a future adoption. Thus Paul, speaking about looking forward to being glorified with Christ, also speaks of the glorious liberty of the children of God who groan inwardly as they "wait for adoption as sons" (Rom 8:17, 21, 23). This final adoption will also mean the redemption of our bodies as a part of the transformation of all creation. This future adoption must be understood in the light of believers having "received the spirit of sonship" and having learned to cry, "Abba! Father!" (8:15-17).[77] The combination of inheritance and adoption is found in God's description of the new heavens and the new earth. For anyone who responds to "the fountain of the water of life" God promises, "he who conquers shall have this heritage, and I will be his God and he shall be my son" (Rev 21:6-7).

Marriage of the Lamb. The family language (particularly the husband and wife relationship) is used to describe God's ultimate blessing for those who were gathered together with him in a new heaven for all eternity. This is called the marriage supper of the Lamb, where the church of Christ as his bride is forever joined to the Lord. "Let us rejoice and exult and give him the glory, for the marriage of the Lamb has come, and his Bride has made herself ready." For those who are privileged to be a part of this great event he writes, "Blessed are those who are invited to the marriage supper of the Lamb" (Rev 19:7, 9). This is the group who will be referred to as "brethren" (19:10).

In the midst of the same eschatological picture of the future heaven and earth, the bride of Christ is identified with the "holy" city, that is, the New Jerusalem. "I saw the holy city, New Jerusalem, coming down out of heaven from God, prepared as a bride adorned for her husband" (21:2). Again, the angel says to John, "Come, I will show you the Bride, the wife of the Lamb" (21:9). Finally, at

---

[76]Cf. also Rom 8:17; 1 Cor 15:15. On eschatological inheritance see Richardson, *Theology of the New Testament,* p. 267; *NIDNTT,* 2:300; Selwyn, *First Epistle of Peter.*

[77]On glorification as a future adoption see *EDT,* p. 13; J. I. Packer, *Knowing God,* pp. 196-98.

the very end of the visions in Revelation, it is the Spirit and the bride who say to Jesus, "Come" (22:17).[78]

Eternal life. A final way that glorification is described in the family category relates to certain passages that deal with eternal life. Eternal life often refers to life that begins in the present and continues for eternity. While it does not have only a future orientation, it does have a future dimension, and in glorification one will continue to enjoy life in God as a part of the family of God. Jesus refers to this life with an eternal dimension in John 3. In the context of describing the significance of being born of the Spirit into the family of God, he declares, "Whoever believes in him may have eternal life" (Jn 3:15). This is also the context for the great statement of God's love in sending Jesus into the world. "For God so loved the world that he gave his only Son, that whoever believes in him should not perish but have eternal life" (3:16). It is clear from the way life is contrasted to perishing that both have a future dimension to them. John intends for us to understand that the spiritual life that comes to those who are born again will last, not only throughout this life, but also for eternity.

Because the concept of life is not only related to the role of God as Father but also to the role of God as Creator, this is one of the concepts that provides an overlap between these two figures of speech. Sometimes a passage that refers to eternal life indicates whether it should be understood in terms of God's role as Father (as is often the case in the Johannine writings) or his role as Creator. But sometimes life is referred to without specifically indicating one or the other of these roles and so serves as a reminder of the frequent overlap of language with regard to these metaphors.[79]

Attributes of God

Love. In our survey of God as Father and the use of the family analogy to describe his relationship to persons, it is evident that the dominant attribute related to his fatherhood is that of love. We have seen that by the use of the Old Testament words for love, *ḥesed* (steadfast love) and *'aheb* (love), as well as God's

---

[78]The marriage supper of the Lamb may be prefigured in certain of Jesus' parables. See Mt 22:1-14; Lk 14:15-24; cf. Mt 25:1-13.

[79]For further references to eternal life see Mt 19:16, 29; 25:46; Mk 10:17, 30; Lk 10:25; 18:18, 30; Jn 3:36, 4:14, 36; 5:24; 6:27, 40, 47, 54, 68; 10:28; 12:25, 50; 17:2-3; Acts 13:36, 48; Rom 2:7; 5:21; 6:22-23; Gal 6:8; 1 Tim 1:16; 6:12, 19; Tit 1:2; 3:7; 1 Jn 1:2; 2:25; 3:15; 5:11, 13, 20; Jude 21.

loving action (especially toward Israel), he has made his loving character known to people from the earliest times. With the coming of Jesus as his Son and the much fuller family picture available, the focus on his love has been clarified more and more in New Testament revelation. This focus on God's love has also become sharper with the use of the concept of agape as a supranatural love of God for men and women. In Scripture the complete picture is of a God with a covenant-electing love that longs to choose every individual for a personal relationship with himself. This means he loves the whole world and in this sense his love is unconditional. He keeps on loving all, even those who do not love him back.

Yet there is a conditional enjoyment of his love, for only those who have responded to him in faith and obedience are drawn into a right relationship with him as a Father. It is only within the spiritual family of God that one has the opportunity to enjoy most the fruits of his love. There are certain blessings that come from the love of God even outside his covenant family (Mt 5:43-48), but the full extent of his love is only experienced by those who have trust in him and are beginning to develop a love relationship with him.

It is this supranatural love that God desires to impart into all his children, so that they might reflect his image and character to the world. It is the grace of God that is the vehicle for implanting his love in the hearts of his children. This supranatural love is not natural to mankind, but it is available by the renewing of their natures through transforming grace. When this happens, beginning with an experience of the new birth, people can begin the process of loving as God loves. The maturity of this love grows throughout their lives and arrives at a greater point of purity when they choose to love God with all their hearts and are empowered to love others from a pure heart and with a total will.

The love of God as Father is frequently associated with his righteousness. This is to prevent God's love from becoming pure sentimentalism or indulgence. It is a love that has moral character to it and is tied with righteous conduct and behavior. There is a very significant balance in God's character between righteousness and love, and he desires individuals to respond to him in both areas, in terms of obedience to his righteousness and love to his love. But he also expects his children to reflect his holy character to other people by being like him in terms of righteous conduct and love. The holding together of these two elements of God's moral holiness is one of the chief functions of the image of God as Father.[80]

Conclusion

The historical emphasis of the role of God as Father begins with his relation to Israel and to key individuals (e.g., the king) within the nation. The role comes to fruition in the New Testament with the arrival of Jesus the Son, and it then becomes the dominant role of God for the Christian church. The personal emphasis comes from Jesus as he teaches his followers to relate to God as Father as he does. Such an invitation accents the availability of intimacy with God that is not as clearly represented in the other roles by which God has made himself known.

Theologically, Jesus the Son takes the church straight to the doctrine of the Trinity, helping us to understand what God was like before creation. A focus on the ontological Trinity (what God is in his own inner being) helps us to see the essence of God as relational, as illustrated between Father and Son. This interaction sets the pattern for those made in the image of a triune God to be joined together with other persons in intimate relationships. Thus the role of God as Father sets the parameters for understanding every other doctrine of Christian thought.[81]

---

[80]On love as an attribute of God see Snaith, *Distinctive Ideas of the Old Testament*, pp. 131-32; Pope, *Compendium of Christian Theology*, 1:344-46; Brunner, *Christian Doctrine of God*, pp. 183-99; A. B. Davidson, *The Theology of the Old Testament* (Edinburgh: T & T Clark, 1904), pp. 170-74; J. Barton Payne, *Theology of the Older Testament* (Grand Rapids, Mich.: Zondervan, 1962), pp. 161-65; Paul Heinisch, *Theology of the Old Testament*, trans. William G. Heidt (St. Paul: North Central Press, 1955), pp. 92-101; Guthrie, *Theology of the New Testament*, pp. 104-5; *EDT*, pp. 656-59; A. W. Argyle, *God in the New Testament* (Philadelphia: Lippincott, 1965); Spicq, *Agape in the New Testament*; James Moffat, *Love in the New Testament* (London: Hodder & Stoughton, 1929); Moody, *The Word of Truth* pp. 104-15.

[81]On the impact of God as Father on Christian theology, see Thomas Smail, *The Forgotten Father* (London: Hodder & Stoughton, 1980).

NINE

HOLY GOD
AS POWERFUL REDEEMER

The Unity Factor

The role of Redeemer requires a God who has enough power to set people free. Power is related to some other roles (e.g., Creator and King), but it is essential for this one. Therefore, our first inquiry will be into the source of this power, viz., the holiness of God. An understanding of holiness as power will then prepare us for seeing clearly the work of a holy God as powerful Redeemer.

Holiness as Power

Old Testament. The earliest pictures of a holy God reveal that the concept of his holiness contains an element of power. The very first reference to his holiness in the Song of Moses is a celebration of God's deliverance of Israel from the army of Pharaoh. They praise the one who is "majestic in holiness," who is the strength of his people and whose right hand is "glorious in power." The whole thrust of the song rests on a celebration of the power of the Holy One to deliver his people from the Egyptians (Ex 15:1-18).

At Mount Sinai when God first calls Israel to be a holy nation, he descends on the mountain to give them the covenant. This picture of God coming to his people is laden with overtones of power, symbolized by the thunder, the lightning, the loud trumpet blasts, the fire and the quaking mountain. An awesome sense of the presence of a powerful one in their midst is apparent, and they tremble with fear in response (Ex 19:16-19). During their wilderness wandering they often had to be reminded of the power of the Holy One who led them. "They tested him again and again, and provoked the Holy One of Israel. They did not keep in mind his power, or the day when he redeemed them from the foe" (Ps 78:41-42). Consistently Israel is reminded throughout their history that "Holy is he!" whom they are to praise as their mighty King (99:3-5, 9; also 71:16-23; 145:1, 21).

The prophets provide the same picture of a holy God who reveals himself in power. Isaiah's vision, in which "the foundations of the thresholds shook at the voice of him who call" (Is 6:3-4), depicts the power of the One who is holy. It is this "Holy One" who not only creates men and women but delivers them "by the greatness of his might, and because he is strong in power" (40:26). Ezekiel reminds God's people that they profaned God's holy name by giving the impression to other nations that their holy God was not powerful enough to protect his people in their land. The other nations interpreted Israel's captivity as a reflection of God's lack of power to protect his people, whereas in reality it was a result of God's holy judgment on them (Ezek 36:20). The prophet predicts a time when God will vindicate his holiness before the nations when he demonstrates his power to redeem them from all the countries and bring them again into their own land (36:23-24). As Ringgren observes, "The holiness of God is his greatness and power and his capability of protecting and saving his people."[1]

Skinner feels the connection between God's holiness and power is particularly prominent in the book of Ezekiel. There, he says, "the divine holiness appears to denote no other attribute than that of majesty, exhibited in the exercise of irresistible power. When he is said to 'sanctify himself' (i.e., show himself to be holy), or to 'sanctify his name,' which is profaned, the meaning always is that by display of might he produces the recognition of his true majesty."[2]

New Testament. One of the earliest connections between the holiness of God and his power in the New Testament is seen in the announcement of the birth of Jesus. The angel declares to Mary, "The Holy Spirit will come upon you, and the power of the Most High will overshadow you; therefore the child to be born will be called holy, the Son of God" (Lk 1:35). In anticipation of Jesus' birth and in response to what God has done, Mary sings God's praise. "For he who is mighty

---

[1]Helmer Ringgren, *The Prophetical Conception of Holiness* (Uppsala: A. B. Lundequistska Bokhandeln, 1948), p. 28.

[2]HDB, 2:397.

has done great things for me, and holy is his name" (1:49). During Jesus' ministry with his disciples, when he prays "Hallowed be thy name," he reminds them of the holiness of God's nature, and juxtaposes God's holiness with the petition for God to exercise his power to deliver them from evil (Mt 6:9, 13 mg.). After Jesus is resurrected and ascends to heaven, Paul also shows the relationship between Jesus' holiness and power by describing him as the one who was "designated Son of God in power according to the Spirit of holiness" (Rom 1:4). One of the final connections made between God's holiness and power is depicted in John's vision of God's holiness when the four living creatures sing, "Holy, holy, holy, is the Lord God Almighty" (Rev 4:8). The connection between holiness and power runs straight through the biblical materials.

Original Ideas of Holiness

The element of power related to the biblical picture of holiness is singled out for special treatment by Rudolf Otto in his book *The Idea of the Holy*. Otto attempts to connect the concept of holiness in Israel with holiness in other religions in the ancient world. By definition he wants to reduce the concept of the holy to that which *does not* include either a cognitive or a moral element. The holy, then, becomes what he calls "the numinous," something that can only be experienced by feeling but not rationally apprehended. The strong emotions that one has in the presence of this "numinous" he describes as the *mysterium tremendum*. This expression is intended to convey the element of mystery with regard to God and the whole concept of holiness. In his analysis of the content of the *tremendum* Otto includes elements of awfulness, overpoweringness and energy or urgency. All three of these aspects of the *tremendum* are closely wrapped up with the dimension of holiness as power.

However, this presentation of the Holy One as a force without rational or moral dimensions is very problematic. Otto has been helpful in pointing out that when one is in the presence of a holy God, he experiences dimensions of awfulness, overpoweringness and energy. Otto leaves the impression that "the holy" constitutes raw power which neither makes itself known nor is rationally understandable and which may or may not have or demand moral character.[3] As

---

[3]Rudolf Otto, *The Idea of the Holy* (London: Oxford University Press, 1928), pp. 12-24. On Otto and his work see *EDT*, pp. 809-10.

Emil Brunner points out, "In the biblical revelation, however, we are concerned not with 'the holy' (as an abstract conception), but with the Holy One (as personal)."[4] The God who makes himself known, even in the earliest strands of biblical data, is not one who is merely tremendous energy. He is a personal God who comes down to enter into personal relationships with men and women and to create a people of his own possession. A personal revelation of himself by a holy God must therefore color every understanding of the concept of power in relationship to his holy nature.

While Otto's concept of the holy as simply overpoweringness must be seriously modified, the element of power as part of holiness remains very significant. Thus Skinner notes, "Of all the uses of the word this is the most widely prevalent and in nearly every part of the literature we find expressions where holiness conveys no other thought than the might and majesty of the God of Israel."[5] The connection is so strong that Skevington Wood can describe holiness as "a synonym for power."[6] This power God uses to control the forces of the universe, not as a tyrannical overlord for his own selfish ends, but to convey life and blessing. Thus Edmund Jacob concludes, "The essential aspect of holiness is that of power, but of power in the service of a God who uses all things to make his kingdom triumph." This holiness of God is expressed "in the power which communicates itself in order to bestow life."[7] It is this power of a holy God to give life and blessing that brings us to a discussion of the Holy One as powerful Redeemer.

Holiness as power for other roles. The concept of holiness as power is related to several different roles of God. In one sense it might be related to every role, if understood in terms of God having power to carry out the functions of that particular role. However, the biblical materials seem to more closely bind it with certain roles than with others. As Creator, God clearly has the power to plan and create the universe according to his own purposes (Is 40:25-26). We have already seen how power is intimately bound up with his responsibilities for ruling the universe, and so it is often connected with his role as King (Is 6:3-5; Ex. 15:11; Ps 99:3-4; Rev 4:9). Further, it is sometimes closely related to the exercise of

---

[4] Emil Brunner, *The Christian Doctrine of God* (London: Lutterworth, 1949), p. 157.
[5] *HDB,* 2:397.
[6] *ZPEB,* 3:175, 181. See also Gerhard von Rad, *Old Testament Theology,* trans. D. M. G. Stalker (New York: Harper & Row, 1962), 1:205.
[7] Edmond Jacob, *Theology of the Old Testament,* trans. Arthur W. Heathcote and P. J. Allcock (New York: Harper & Row, 1958), p. 87.

righteousness and therefore is closely tied with God's role as the righteous Judge (Ps 71:16, 18, 19, 22, 24; Ex 19:1—20:26). Likewise, as both Father and Shepherd, God has certain power to care for, provide for and protect those who are his responsibility.

The Role of God as Redeemer

Yet the chief role of holiness as power seems to be bound up with God's responsibility as Redeemer of his people. The psalmist states that God's people, in relating to the "Holy One of Israel," did not always "keep in mind his power, or the day when he redeemed them from the foe" (Ps 78:41-42). God comes as Deliverer of his people in his powerful, holy character, which explains why the *language figure* most often used to describe this is that of *slavery* and *freedom*. People are understood to be in bondage and slavery (whether physical or spiritual), and God has the power to set them free.

The *focus*, therefore, of this particular role has to do with *freedom*, and the metaphor used is that of manumission. Freedom includes four elements. The first is the state of bondage from which one needs to be set free. The second is the actual event of deliverance that accomplishes the redemption. The third is the state of freedom resulting from being set free. The last is the free choice to serve another after one's deliverance. This last dimension accents the fact that freedom and service are inseparably connected, so that it is impossible to speak of one without the other.

The real issue at stake is the matter of ownership. The theological use of the redemption metaphor in Scripture was readily understood because of the institution of slavery throughout the ancient world. This is true of the ancient Near East during the Old Testament times as well as during the Greek and Roman empires which set the stage for the New Testament era. The idea of slaves who were owned but who could be set free was a very graphic one that spoke readily to those who lived in the biblical world.[8] Yet all slaves were not

---

[8]On the institution of slavery see *NBD*, 1195-98; Isaac Mendelsohn, *Slavery in the Ancient Near East* (New York: Oxford University Press, 1949); Roland de Vaux, *Ancient Israel* (New York: McGraw-Hill, 1961); William W. Buckland, *The Roman Law of Slavery* (London: Cambridge University Press, 1908); R. H. Barrow, *Slavery in the Roman Empire* (New York: Barnes & Noble, 1968); William L. Westermann, *The Slave Systems of Greek and Roman Antiquity* (Philadelphia: American Philosophical Society, 1955); Thomas Wiedemann, *Greek and Roman Slavery* (Baltimore: John Hopkins University Press, 1981); Joachim Jeremias, *Jerusalem in the Time of Jesus* (Philadelphia: Fortress, 1975), pp. 312-16.

freed when purchased. Some were bought by another owner and so served a new master. This second use of this figure appears in the transfer of ownership of an individual to God. As the new Master, God now expects the person to serve him. So there are mixed implications under this metaphor. A person in bondage to evil can be set free, but this freedom is not seen in absolute terms but rather as a freedom to serve God.

The concepts of Savior, being saved and salvation are often closely intertwined with the metaphor of redemption. They are not as definite with regard to the focus of the redemption metaphor, which specifically relates to "buying something at a price." Yet the vocabulary related to salvation often overlaps with that of redemption, ransom and deliverance. We will include some discussion of these terms under this category, while at the same time recognizing that the cluster of terms related to "salvation" is much more general in nature.

The redemption metaphor has received increased attention in recent years due to its use by the movement known as liberation theology. The key biblical data that serves as a basis of this movement is an understanding of the centrality of the exodus event as the principal biblical paradigm of salvation as liberation. This movement is committed to the political and material nature of biblical liberation, both in the Old and New Testaments, and they attribute any "spiritualizing" of liberation language to Hellenistic philosophy and its impact on the early centuries of the Christian church.

One of the key problems of liberation theologians is their selective use of Scripture. They focus on this metaphor and use it as a description of salvation that happens to fit their revolutionary ideology. Unfortunately, they leave virtually untouched most of the other major roles in Scripture as a means of describing a holistic picture of God, persons and salvation. Even in their understanding of the exodus event they have ignored the spiritual side of redemption, where God is clearly setting Israel free to be his people and to follow him, so that both the Hebrews and the Egyptians might know that he is God. While much of liberation language in the Old Testament does refer to the physical or material nature of deliverance, rescue and salvation, as we will see in our study, it sometimes implies spiritualized meanings even under the Old Covenant. But in the New Testament the language is predominantly used in a figurative sense to describe the spiritual dimensions of God's saving grace.

The failure of liberation theologians to take seriously other figures of speech to describe God, persons and salvation, and their almost exclusive focus on the physical side of the redemption language in Scripture, seriously limits their ability to speak biblically to these major areas of theology. This approach starts with their understanding of Scripture as basically a human book rather than God's revelation to humanity and with their interpretive principles that begin primarily with social analysis rather than theological or philosophical principles. Their selective use of Scripture and the roles of God is grounded on their a priori ideological principles.[9] Those who take a stronger view of the reliability of Scripture as God's revelation will come at basic theological questions from a much more holistically biblical view.[10]

The Father

Old Testament. One of the earliest names by which God makes himself known in the Old Testament is *El Shaddai,* the Almighty One (Ex 6:2-6).[11] God continues to carry this designation at the very end of Scripture where the creatures cry, "Holy, holy, holy, is the Lord God Almighty" (Rev 4:8). It is this powerful One who comes to Moses and the children of Israel to set them free from bondage and slavery in Egypt. In celebration of God's power to deliver, Moses praises him who is "majestic in holiness" on behalf of the people whom he has "redeemed" (Ex 15:11, 13). Later praises recorded by the psalmist echo the same theme. "Yet thou art holy, enthroned in the praises of Israel. In thee our fathers trusted; they

---

[9]For a discussion of the liberationists' view of Scripture and hermeneutical principles for Scripture's interpretation see R. C. Hundley, *Radical Liberation Theology* (Wilmore, Ky.: Bristol, 1987), pp. 23-34; "A Study of the Hermeneutical Theories and Methods of Selected Latin American Theologians" (master's thesis, Cambridge University, 1982).

[10]For further discussion of liberation theology see C. Emilio A. Nuñez, *Liberation Theology* (Chicago: Moody Press, 1985); Andrew Kirk, *Liberation Theology: An Evangelical View from the Third World* (Atlanta: John Knox Press, 1979); Samuel Escobar, *La Fe Evangelica y Los Teologios de la Liberacion* (El Paso, Tex.: Casa Bautista, 1987); Rosino Gibellini, ed., *Frontiers of Theology in Latin America* (Maryknoll, N.Y.: Orbis, 1979); Gustavo Gutiérrez, *Theology of Liberation: History, Politics, and Salvation* (Maryknoll, N.Y.: Orbis, 1973); José Miguel Bonino, *Doing Theology in a Revolutionary Situation* (Philadelphia: Fortress, 1975); *Christians and Marxists* (Grand Rapids, Mich.: Eerdmans, 1976); Hugo Assmann, *Theology for a Nomad Church* (Maryknoll, N.Y.: Orbis, 1975); Stephen Phillips, "The Use of Scripture in Liberation Theology" (Ph. D. Diss., The Southern Baptist Theological Seminary, 1978); José S. Croatto, *Exodus: A Hermeneutic of Freedom* (Maryknoll, N.Y.: Orbis, 1981).

[11]For additional references to El Shaddai see Gen 17:1; 28:3; 35:11; 43:14; 48:3; 49:25; Ezek 10:5. On this name for God see *TDOT*, vol. 1, pp. 255-57; W. F. Albright, "The Names Shaddai and Abram," *JBL* 54 (1935): 175-92; Lloyd Bailey, "Israelite El Sadday and Amorite Bel Sade," *JBL* 87 (1987): 434-38; G. H. May, "El Shaddai," *JBL* 60 (1941): 114-45; Robert D. Wilson, "The Names of God in the Old Testament," *PTR* 18 (1920): 460-92.

trusted, and thou didst deliver them. To thee they cried and were saved" (Ps 22:3-5). Elsewhere the Israelites were exhorted to "bless his holy name . . . who redeems your life from the Pit" (Ps 103:1, 4). This connection between God's holiness and his role as Redeemer is summarized by Isaiah. "I will help you, says the LORD; your Redeemer is the Holy One of Israel" (Is 41:14).[12]

The connection, then, between God's role as Redeemer and his holiness is clear.[13] Two of the major ways in which God functions as Redeemer are related to the deliverance from Egypt and from the Babylonian captivity. So the redeeming God presents himself in the introduction to the Ten Commandments, "I am the LORD your God, who brought you out of the land of Egypt, out of the house of bondage" (Ex 20:2). When Jeremiah looks forward to the time God will deliver his people from those who have held them as captives, he reminds Israel that "their Redeemer is strong" (Jer 50:34).

While these two major events of exodus and return from exile relate God's redemption to Israel as a nation, it should also be remembered that God continues to relate to individuals within the nation as well. National redemption provides a covering for an understanding of personal redemption. The fact that individuals as well as the nation are clearly personally related to God is illustrated in the fact that the Ten Commandments, which are introduced with a reference to Israel being delivered from the house of bondage, are addressed to individuals. At other times God is referred to as personal Redeemer, as in the case of Job, when he declares, "I know that my Redeemer lives" (Job 19:25; see Prov 23:10-11). H. Wheeler Robinson summarizes the meaning of redemption in the Old Testament: "The Old Testament idea of redemption, then, lays emphasis on the divine initiative, comprehends within itself the deliverance from material as well as from spiritual perils and constraints, and deals primarily with Israel as a people, though growingly concerned with the relation of the individual to God, within that social solidarity."[14]

The holiness of God is not only connected to his role as Redeemer, but also to his title of Savior. "For I am the LORD your God, the Holy One of Israel, your Savior" (Is 43:3, 11-13). Not only is God the Savior, he is the only Savior. "You know no God but me, and besides me there is no savior" (Hos 13:4; cf. Lk 1:68-

---

[12]On the connection of Redeemer with the Holy One see Is 43:14; 47:4; 48:17; 49:7; 54:5.

[13]See Theodorus C. Vriezen, *An Outline of Old Testament Theology*, trans. S. Neuijen (Bristol: John Wright, 1911), pp. 270-71.

[14]H. Wheeler Robinson, *Redemption and Revelation in the Actuality of History* (London: Nisbet, 1942), p. 227.

69). There were times in Israel's history when "they forgot God, their Savior" (Ps 106:21), as they did in the desert, and yet he continued to desire to redeem them.

New Testament. The New Testament picks up this theme that pictures God as Savior and reiterates that "holy is his name" (Lk 1:47, 49). Paul makes it clear that it is "God our Savior, who desires all men to be saved and to come to the knowledge of the truth" (1 Tim 2:3-4). There is also a strong emphasis on the availability of God's saving work for everyone. "We have our hope set on the living God, who is the Savior of all men, especially of those who believe" (4:10).[15]

The Son

Savior. Not only is God the Father referred to as Savior, but so is Jesus. We are prepared for this in the Gospel record by the connection of both Father and Son to this title in the Lukan birth narrative. Mary magnifies the Lord by exclaiming, "My spirit rejoices in God my Savior." Then the angels announce Jesus' birth to the shepherds saying, "To you is born this day in the city of David a Savior, who is Christ the Lord" (Lk 1:47; 2:11). During Jesus' ministry, the Samaritans recognize him as "the Savior of the world" (Jn 4:42), and in proclaiming the death, resurrection and exaltation of Jesus the early church describes him as "leader and Savior" who makes possible repentance and forgiveness of sins (Acts 5:30-31; 13:23).

In like manner, Paul gives both Father and Son this title in his opening greeting to Titus where he talks about being entrusted with the gospel "by command of God our Savior" and then he sends greetings of grace and peace from "God the Father and Christ Jesus our Savior" (Tit 1:3-4). The Son is again connected with the Father where the title is used for both in Paul's description of salvation based on God's mercy and the Holy Spirit given through Jesus. "When the goodness and loving kindness of God our Savior appeared, he saved us, . . . by the washing of regeneration and renewal in the Holy Spirit, which he poured out upon us richly through Jesus Christ our Savior" (Tit 3:4-6). Peter

---

[15]For God as Savior see Deut 13:14; 1 Sam 10:19; Ps 24:5; 27:1; 35:3; 62:2, 6; 65:5; 79:9; Is 12:2; 17:10; 43:3, 11; 45:15, 21; 60:16; 62:11; 63:8; Jer 14:8; Mic 7:7; Hab 3:18; 1 Tim 1:1; Tit 2:10; 3:4; Jude 25. See also F. F. Bruce, "Our God and Savior: A Recurring Biblical Pattern," in *The Savior God*, ed. Samuel G. F. Brandon (New York: Barnes & Noble, 1963), pp. 54-65; Guthrie, *Theology of the New Testament*, p. 88; Oscar Cullmann, *The Christology of the New Testament* (London: SCM Press, 1963), p. 239.

also closely connects the titles of Savior and Lord and their relationship to Jesus. "So there will be richly provided for you an entrance into the eternal kingdom of our Lord and Savior Jesus Christ" (2 Pet 1:11; also 1:1-2; 2:20; 3:2). Finally, John makes it clear that it is the Father who "has sent his Son as the Savior of the world" (1 Jn 4:14).[16]

Jesus. In the angel's announcement of the Lord's birth he reveals that Jesus was to fulfill a saving role by giving him the name "Jesus," which is derived from the Hebrew יֵשׁוּעַ meaning "God saves" (Mt 1:21). That means everywhere in the New Testament where the name "Jesus" is used, there are the obvious implications of his name being intimately bound up with his saving and redeeming mission in the world. Because the Eastern world places so much importance on the meaning of a name of person, it becomes that much more significant in terms of Jesus' work in the world.[17]

Redeemer. Jesus' redeeming role in the New Testament is usually expressed in terms of the vocabulary of Savior rather than of Redeemer. Although the title Redeemer is not given to Jesus, he clearly is the subject of the verb "to redeem, ransom" in several places (e.g., Tit 2:13-14). So the theological use of the title "Redeemer" for Jesus has a very solid biblical base.[18] Coupled with his role as Redeemer is the picture of Jesus as the power of God in the world to deliver from the forces of evil, sickness and sin (Lk 4:18; Is 61:1). So Paul is able to write that it was Jesus "who gave himself for our sins to deliver us from the present evil age" (Gal 1:4), and from Paul's own experience he cries out, "Who will deliver me from this body of death? Thanks be to God through Jesus Christ our Lord!" (Rom 7:24-25). Further, Paul says it is "Jesus who delivers us from the wrath to come" (1 Thess 1:10), which makes it clear that Jesus not only delivers us in this world but also from the threat of future punishment.[19]

The Holy Spirit

Old Testament: Spirit of power. The Holy Spirit in this language category may be referred to as the Spirit of power. In the Old Testament when the Spirit of God

---

[16]For Jesus as Savior see Phil 3:20; 2 Tim 1:10; Tit 2:13; see *NIDNTT*, 3:219-21; Cullmann, *Christology of the New Testament*, pp. 238-45; Taylor, *Names of Jesus*, p. 109; *EDT*, p. 975.

[17]On the name Jesus see *TDNT*, 3:284-93; *TWB*, p. 116.

[18] See Alan Richardson, *An Introduction to the Theology of the New Testament* (London: SCM Press, 1958), p. 219.

[19] On Jesus as the Power of God see Werner Georg Kummel, *Theology of the New Testament According to Its Major Witnesses* (Nashville: Abingdon, 1973), pp. 121-23; Richardson, *Theology of the New Testament*, pp. 62-64.

comes on people, he sometimes provides power for them to bring about a physical deliverance of the people of Israel from the bondage of some neighboring people. Thus, the Spirit of the Lord "took possession of Gideon," and he raised up a people to throw off the yoke of the Midianites and the Amalekites (Judg 6:33-34). In like manner when "the Spirit of the LORD came upon Jephthah," he raised up the people of God and was given power for the defeat of the Ammonites (11:29). For similar purposes "the spirit of God came mightily upon Saul" empowering him for a defeat of the Ammonites (1 Sam 11:6-11), for which Saul rightly gave the credit to God. "For today the LORD has wrought deliverance in Israel" (11:13). This is consistent with the Lord's reminder to his people that it is not through their own ability that he works, but rather through the power of his own Spirit. "Not by might, nor by power, but by my Spirit, says the LORD of hosts" (Zech 4:6).[20]

New Testament: Spirit of power. In the New Testament the Holy Spirit, along with the Father, is intimately involved in making the incarnation possible. Thus, the angel declares to Mary, "The Holy Spirit will come upon you, and the power of the Most High will overshadow you; therefore, the child to be born will be called holy, the Son of God" (Lk 1:35). The connection between the Holy Spirit and power is reinforced by Jesus in his last words to his disciples. "You shall receive power when the Holy Spirit has come upon you" (Acts 1:8). When the Holy Spirit does descend on the disciples, it is with symbols of power (wind, fire, languages). Later as the early church looked back at Jesus, they were convinced that God annointed him with the Holy Spirit and power (10:38). So Paul declares that Jesus was "designated Son of God in power according to the Spirit of holiness by his resurrection from the dead" (Rom 1:4).

This power of the Spirit brings various blessings to the lives of believers. For example, Paul connects it with hope. "May the God of hope fill you with all joy and peace in believing, so that by the power of the Holy Spirit you may abound in hope" (Rom 15:13). In accordance with Jesus' promise of power from the Holy Spirit (Acts 1:8), the early church experienced a special anointing from the Spirit for witnessing and proclamation. Thus when Paul writes to the Corinthians, he says, "My speech and my message were not in plausible words of wisdom, but in demonstration of the Spirit and power, that your faith might not

---

[20] For the Spirit as the agent of salvation history see Walther Eichrodt, *Theology of the Old Testament*, trans. J. A. Baker (London: SCM Press, 1967), 2:50-57.

rest in the wisdom of men but in the power of God" (1 Cor 2:4-5). Likewise, he reminds the Thessalonians that his gospel came to them "not only in word, but also in power and in the Holy Spirit and with full conviction" (1 Thess 1:5). This is not altogether unlike the Old Testament prophet who could declare, "I am filled with power, with the Spirit of the LORD, and with justice and with might, to declare to Jacob his transgression and to Israel his sin" (Mic 3:8).

This power from the Spirit of God, however, not only relates to proclamation but also to freedom from sin and to an internal transformation of a person's character to that like the Holy Spirit's. "Now the Lord is the Spirit, and where the Spirit of the Lord is, there is freedom. And we all, with unveiled face, beholding the glory of the Lord, are being changed into his likeness from one degree of glory to another; for this comes from the Lord who is the Spirit" (2 Cor 3:17-18). Clearly the Spirit of God is setting men and women free to be transformed into the likeness of the Lord Jesus so they might reflect the glory of his holy character.

This very closely parallels the Old Testament prophecy of how the Messiah would set people free. The New Testament writers saw the fulfillment of this prophecy when "Jesus returned in the power of the Spirit into Galilee" (Lk 4:14). Jesus interprets this event to those of his hometown when he declares, "The Spirit of the Lord GOD is upon me, because the LORD has anointed me to bring good tidings to the afflicted; he has sent me to bind up the brokenhearted, to proclaim liberty to the captives, and the opening of the prison to those who are bound" (Is 61:1; Lk 4:18-19). Jesus is clearly using the redemption metaphor and transferring it from the physical realm of freedom to the spiritual deliverance of individuals. The freedom that he brings is through the agency of the power of the Holy Spirit. Skevington Wood notes how the Spirit works in transforming power in the redemption process. "It is the Spirit who makes possible such conformity to the Master's image." He aptly summarizes the role of the Spirit in this phenomenon. "The close association of the Spirit with power would seem to suggest that in him this power is brought directly down to earth and made available for the purposes of godly living."[21]

Man and Woman

Freedom from sin. The heart of this relationship is God's desire for people to be

---

[21]ZPEB, 3:181.

free from the bondage and slavery of sin and to be active as his servants. It is a two-sided relationship. One has to do with the freedom and deliverance from sin. But because there is no such thing as absolute freedom, God desires people to be bond slaves to himself. So the second side of this figure has to do with being slaves to God.

Jesus describes sin and salvation in the categories of bondage and freedom. In a discussion with the Jews, Jesus said that the truth would make them free, to which they responded that they had never been in bondage to anyone. Jesus answers them by saying, "I say to you, every one who commits sin is a slave to sin. The slave does not continue in the house for ever; the son continues for ever. So if the Son makes you free, you will be free indeed" (Jn 8:34-36).

Paul elaborates on this figure of bondage when he says that "our old self was crucified with him so that the sinful body might be destroyed, and we might no longer be enslaved to sin. For he who has died is freed from sin" (Rom 6:6-7). But he also clarifies the fact that there is no absolute freedom, and that we will be slaves of someone.

> Do you not know that if you yield yourselves to any one as obedient slaves, you are slaves of the one whom you obey, either of sin, which leads to death, or of obedience, which leads to righteousness? But thanks be to God, that you who were once slaves of sin have become obedient from the heart to the standard of teaching to which you were committed, and, having been set free from sin, have become slaves of righteousness. (Rom 6:16-18)

Clearly he intends the phrase "slaves of righteousness" to be the equivalent of "slaves of God." He also clarifies the consequences of each kind of slavery. "When you were slaves of sin, you were free in regard to righteousness. . . . The end of those things is death. But now that you have been set free from sin and have become slaves of God, the return you get is sanctification and its end, eternal life" (Rom 6:20-22). Further, one can be free in Christ even though he may continue a slave in his earthly life. "For he who was called in the Lord as a slave is a freedman of the Lord. Likewise he who was free when called is a slave of Christ" (1 Cor 7:22).[22]

While God desires for all to be free from sin and slaves to Christ, this

---

[22]For Christians as slaves of God in Christ see *TDNT,* 2:273-77.

nevertheless involves a choice on the part of the individual. A person may not in effect serve both sin and God. Jesus made this clear from the beginning to his own disciples when he said, "No one can serve two masters; for either he will hate the one and love the other, or he will be devoted to the one and despise the other" (Mt 6:24).

Servants of God. While the focus of this figure of speech is on redemption from the bondage of sin, there is also a secondary focus on serving God. Here there is a strong overlap between God's role as the sovereign King, who desires subjects or servants to serve him, and God's role as Redeemer, who redeems people from sin so that they may be his slaves. In the figure of speech related directly to slavery, the relationship between individuals and God is even more strongly stated than it would be in the figure of servants under the direction of the King. According to the slavery metaphor God owns a person, who is therefore ultimately under his total control. This figure of speech is reinforced by the fairly widespread references throughout the Scripture regarding the importance of serving God (e.g., Acts 20:19; Rom 12:11; Col 3:23, 24; 1 Thess 1:9).

Sin   → aka enslavement

Bondage. While it is God's desire for people to be free from sin, in reality sin is a very powerful influence on the nonbeliever. Sin as a principle is described in terms of enslavement or bondage. So when the Jews declare to Jesus that they are "descendants of Abraham and have never been in bondage to anyone," Jesus responds, "Everyone who commits sin is a slave to sin" (Jn 8:33-34). This is the same spiritual bondage that Paul describes in Romans 6 when he declares that slavery to sin leads to death (Rom 6:6, 16, 20-22). With reference to this spiritual state he says, "When you did not know God, you were in bondage to beings that by nature are no gods" (Gal 4:8). Peter also warns about those who promise "freedom, but they themselves are slaves of corruption," and he insightfully notes that "whatever overcomes a man, to that he is enslaved" (2 Pet 2:19).[23]

Paul elaborates on this bondage metaphor when he speaks about being a captive to the law of sin (Rom 7:23). While the figure of speech used in this instance is more related to imprisonment in war than to the bondage of slavery,

---

[23]On sin as slavery see Leon Morris, *The Apostolic Preaching of the Cross* (London: Tyndale Press, 1965), p. 61; *NIDNTT,* 3:592-98.

it is a part of a larger subjection motif from which one needs to be delivered.[24]

Surrender to slavery. Sin as an act in this category would be described as the yielding to temptation or to the power of evil that enslaves. So Paul warns the Galatians about this surrender to sin, "For freedom Christ has set us free; stand fast, therefore, and do not submit again to a yoke of slavery" (Gal 5:1). He also alerts them that sin can re-enslave them. "For you were called to freedom, brethren; only do not use your freedom as an opportunity for the flesh." And "if a man is overtaken in any trespass, you who are spiritual should restore him in a spirit of gentleness. Look to yourself, lest you too be tempted" (Gal 5:13; 6:1). Paul also reminds the Corinthians to be careful about even good things, that they not be recaptured by them to sin. "'All things are lawful for me,' but not all things are helpful. 'All things are lawful for me,' but I will not be enslaved by anything" (1 Cor 6:12; 10:23). On the other hand, if one is careful, God has the power to deliver from temptation. "Therefore let any one who thinks that he stands take heed lest he fall. No temptation has overtaken you that is not common to man. God is faithful, and he will not let you be tempted beyond your strength, but with the temptation will also provide the way of escape, that you may be able to endure it" (10:12-13).

Salvation

Redemption. God's saving grace in this category is described in terms of redemption. The focus of the language is more on what Christ has done by his death on the cross than on the application of that in the life of the individual, although both are subsumed under the language of redemption. This means the language centers most heavily on Christ's work in the atonement. In the narrative that introduces the life of Jesus, the Lord God of Israel is praised because "he has visited and redeemed his people" (Lk 1:68). During Jesus' lifetime people came to hope that "he was the one to redeem Israel" (24:21).

This redemption is based on Christ's death on the cross which leads to the availability of God's grace which is able to justify all who receive it through faith. "They are justified by his grace as a gift, through the redemption which is in Christ Jesus, whom God put forward as [a propitiation] by his blood, to be

---

[24]For further reading on being a captive, *aichmalotos* (αἰχμάλωτος), see *NIDNTT*, 3:590-91; *TDNT*, 1: 195-97.

received by faith" (Rom 3:24-25). Paul declares that Jesus was "born under the law, to redeem those who were under the law." Christ redeemed us "from the curse of the law, having become a curse for us" (Gal 4:4-5; 3:13). Accordingly, it is the grace of God that makes possible our redemption through the death of Christ. "In him we have redemption through his blood, the forgiveness of our trespasses, according to the riches of his grace" (Eph 1:7). Likewise, Hebrews describes Jesus as he who "entered once for all into the Holy Place, taking not the blood of goats and calves but his own blood, thus securing an eternal redemption" (Heb 9:12). The focus of the metaphor is that redemption sets free from the slavery and bondage of sin at the point where people believe in him for this deliverance.[25]

Ransom. The biblical words in both the Old and the New Testament connected with redemption include significant components related to the idea of ransom and deliverance. In the Old Testament, for example, one of the words used is that of *gaal* (גָּאַל), meaning "redemption, ransom." It particularly carries the concept of the kinsman redeemer, where the nearest of kin is responsible for redeeming or buying back either a member of his family or something that once belonged to him. This figure illuminates the person of Jesus as a kinsman or spiritual family member who is responsible for redeeming others.[26] Hebrew also uses the word *pada* (פָּדָה), to describe ransom, rescue or deliverance. Its predominant meaning has to do with the general sense of redeeming people or things but is also used in a spiritual sense of redemption from sin (Ps 130:7-8).[27] The third Hebrew word most closely associated with this language is *kopher* (כֹּפֶר), which refers to ransom price that was paid to redeem a slave and set him free.[28] Sometimes the word *nasal* (נָצַל), is also used in terms of to deliver, rescue or save.[29]

---

[25]Origen, *In Matthaum on Matthew 20:18*. In *Ante-Nicene Fathers*, vol. 9, ed. Allan Menzies (Peabody, Mass.: Hendrickson, 1994); and Origen, *Contra Celsum*, ed. Henry Chadwick (Cambridge: Cambridge University Press, 1953) pp. 7, 17.

[26]For further discussion of *gaal* see *TWOT*, 1:144-45; *TDOT*, 2:350-55; R. A. Johnson, "The Primary Meaning of the Root G'l," *VTSup* 1:67-77; de Vaux, *Ancient Israel*, pp. 11-12, 21-23; Morris, *Apostolic Preaching of the Cross*, pp. 19-22; Jacob, *Theology of the Old Testament*, p. 292; Robinson, *Redemption and Revelation*, pp. 223-25.

[27]For a discussion on *pada*, see *TWOT*, 2:716-17; Morris, *Apostolic Preaching of the Cross*, pp. 22-24; *TDOT*, 4:329-35; David Hill, *Greek Words and Hebrew Meanings* (New York: Scribner, 1975); Jacob, *Theology of the Old Testament*, pp. 292-93; Robinson, *Redemption and Revelation*, pp. 221-23.

[28]On *kopher*, see Morris, *Apostolic Preaching of the Cross*, pp. 24-27; *TWOT*, 1:453; Jacob, *Theology of the Old Testament*, pp. 293-94.

[29]For further discussion of *nasal*, see *TWOT*, 2:594; *TDOT*, 6:99-102; *THAT*, 2:96-98.

In the New Testament the word group centered around *lutron* (λύτρον) is the basic language category. It means "loosing" but almost always for a price paid for the liberation of those in bondage.[30] Of that word group particularly *apolutrōsis* (ἀπολύτρωσις), meaning "releasing for a ransom," is particularly significant.[31]

Ransom theory of atonement. Leon Morris has convincingly shown that the whole concept of redemption involves paying a price for the release of a captive. This is why the concept of ransom is so closely bound up with the concept of redemption.[32] There has been considerable debate over the use of the metaphor, with many wanting the focus to be on the concept of deliverance and minimizing the concept of a ransom paid to effect that deliverance. The theological problem for many seems to be with the question, To whom was the ransom paid? Some in the early church, like Origen, suggested that a ransom was paid to the devil.[33] Subsequently, beginning with Anselm, many have been at pains to point out that there does not seem to be any biblical warrant for this conclusion and so the focus of the redemption metaphor should be on deliverance rather than the paying of a price.

The basic problem probably relates to pressing a metaphor as one form of analogy further than it was intended to be used. The focus of the biblical materials seems to be that God redeemed humankind by paying the price through Christ's death on the cross. "The wages of sin is death" (Rom 6:23). But within that metaphor a price or ransom has to be paid. Since the question of to whom a price was paid is never mentioned in Scripture, that may indicate the writers did not press the metaphor any further than the paying of a price to effect deliverance. Certainly there is no indication of paying a price to the devil.[34]

Because of the wide use of the ransom theory in the early centuries of the

---

[30]For further discussion of *lutron* see *BTLNT*, pp. 408-10; Morris, *Apostolic Preaching of the Cross*, pp. 11-53; *TDNT*, 4:329-35, 340-56; B. B. Warfield, "The New Testament Terminology of 'Redemption,'" *PTR* 15 (1917): 207ff.; G. A. Deissmann, *Light from the Ancient Near East* (New York: Harper & Bros, 1927); Richardson, *Theology of the New Testament*, p. 218; Robinson, *Redemption and Revelation*, pp. 228-30.

[31]For *apolutrosis* see *BTLNT*, p. 410.

[32] Morris, *Apostolic Preaching of the Cross*, pp. 11-64; *NBD*, p. 1078-79.

[33]For discussion of to whom the price was paid see Thomas Oden, *Word of Life* (San Francisco: Harper & Row, 1989), pp. 396-402.

[34]On the concept of redemption see *EDT*, pp. 918-19; *NIDNTT*, 3:177-205; *TDNT*, 4:228ff.; Robinson, *Redemption and Revelation*, pp. 219-44; Vriesen, *Outline of Old Testament Theology*, pp. 272-73; Guthrie, *New Testament Theology*, pp. 476-81; Ethelbert Stauffer, *New Testament Theology* (London: SCM Press, 1955), pp. 146-47; George Eldon Ladd, *A Theology of the New Testament* (Grand Rapids, Mich.: Eerdmans, 1974), pp. 433-34; Ludwig Hugo Koehler, *Old Testament Theology* (Philadelphia: Westminster Press, 1957), pp. 227-35.

church, it is sometimes referred to as the classical theory. Care should be taken, however, not to infer this to be the only aspect of the atonement discussed during this Patristic period. A fresh emphasis on this view in modern theology has come from Bishop Gustaf Aulen's book *Christus Victor*.[35]

The picture of the redeemer buying a slave's freedom with a ransom is certainly a crucial part of the biblical materials related to the cross. When Jesus discusses the role of a servant amongst his disciples, he remarks that "the Son of man also came not to be served but to serve, and to give his life as a ransom for many" (Mk 10:45; Mt 20:28). Paul picks up the same figure of speech when he declares that "there is one mediator between God and men, the man Christ Jesus, who gave himself as a ransom for all" (1 Tim 2:5-6). Clearly, Christ's death was to make redemption available to all by ransoming them from the bondage of sin.[36]

Paul extends the metaphor when he describes those who have been ransomed as those who were "bought with a price" and as a result their bodies are not their own. They are to glorify God in the body (1 Cor 6:19-20). He further warns that since they were "bought with a price," they should not "become slaves of men," but rather "a slave of Christ" (7:22-23).[37]

Being set free. The concept of being bought with a price is also closely related to the concept of being set free. This is bound up with a New Testament word *elutheria* (ελευθερία), dealing with liberty and freedom. The experience of saving grace is described in terms of being set free from sin, guilt and the law. This freedom is also related to liberation from spiritual powers.[38] Thus Jesus declared, "If the Son makes you free, you will be free indeed" (Jn 8:36). He not only desires to set people free, but he longs for them to continue in that freedom

---

[35]Gustaf Aulén, *Christus Victor* (London: SPCK, 1965).

[36]For "ransom" see *TDNT,* 4:340-56; Morris, *Apostolic Preaching of the Cross,* pp. 29-38; *TWOT,* 2:453; D. Hill, *Greek Words and Hebrew Meanings; TWB,* pp. 185-87; Vincent Taylor, *Jesus and His Sacrifice* (London: Macmillan, 1937); Guthrie, *New Testament Theology,* pp. 440-41, 476-80; Joachim Jeremias, *New Testament Theology* trans. John Bowden (New York: Scribner, 1971), pp. 292-94; Cullmann, *Christology of the New Testament,* pp. 65ff.; William Manson, *Jesus the Messiah* (Philadelphia: Westminster Press, 1946), pp. 182-85; Wolfhart Pannenburg, *Jesus, God and Man,* trans. Lewis L. Wilkens and Duane A Priebe (Philadelphia: Westminster Press, 1968), pp. 275-77; Robinson, *Redemption and Revelation,* pp. 235-37.

[37]For *agorazō* (ἀγοράζω), "buy," "purchase," see *TDNT,* 1:124-28; Morris, *Apostolic Preaching of the Cross,* pp. 53-55. See also I. Howard Marshall, "Development of the Concept of Redemption in the New Testament," in *Reconciliation and Hope,* ed. Robert J. Banks (Grand Rapids, Mich.: Eerdmans, 1974), p. 157ff.; Robinson, *Redemption and Revelation,* pp. 230-31.

[38]For *eleutheria* (ελευθερία), see *NBD,* pp. 732-34; *EDT,* pp. 638-39; *TDNT,* 2:487-502; Kummel, *Theology of New Testament,* pp. 186-93; Moody, *Word of Truth,* pp. 332-37.

from sin. "For freedom Christ has set us free; stand fast therefore, and do not submit again to a yoke of slavery" (Gal 5:1).

Deliverance. Another dimension of saving grace in relation to redemption is the whole matter of deliverance. Paul says that the Thessalonians were described by other Christians as those who "turned to God from idols, to serve a living and true God," and that these were now waiting for "Jesus who delivers us from the wrath to come" (1 Thess 1:9-10). This deliverance was clearly from the powers of evil and also a deliverance to God's rule in their lives. "He has delivered us from the dominion of darkness and transferred us to the kingdom of his beloved Son, in whom we have redemption, the forgiveness of sins" (Col 1:13-14).[39]

This deliverance was possible because Jesus assumed human nature, and by his death on the cross made deliverance possible to those who were enslaved. "Since therefore the children share in flesh and blood, he himself likewise partook of the same nature, that through death he might destroy him who has the power of death, that is, the devil, and deliver all those who through fear of death were subject to lifelong bondage" (Heb 2:14-15; also Lk 1:74).

Underlying the whole concept of being redeemed from sin is the idea of power made available for salvation (Rom 1:16). While on earth Jesus demonstrated his own power and authority to forgive sins by the exercise of his power in healing men and women (e.g., Mk 2:5-12). Furthermore, John introduces Jesus with the statement that "to all who received him, who believed in his name, he gave power to become children of God" (Jn 1:12). The picture we get is that Jesus, as one who is more powerful than the devil and the forces of evil, is able to effect redemption out of that strength (Mk 3:27).

Salvation from sin. Closely tied to the redemption metaphor is the description of conversion as being saved from sin. This is first attested in the New Testament by the announcement that the Son of God will be called "Jesus, for he will save his people from their sins" (Mt 1:21). So it is not surprising when Paul announces the basic theme of the gospel that he declares, "It is the power of God for salvation to every one who has faith" (Rom 1:16).

It is Christ's death on the cross that makes possible God's power to save his

---

[39]On deliverance see *NIDNTT*, 3:200-205; *TWB*, pp. 62-63; Kummel, *Theology of the New Testament*, pp. 185-86.

people. "For the word of the cross is folly to those who are perishing, but to us who are being saved it is the power of God" (1 Cor 1:18; 2:1-5; Phil 3:10). Further, God reveals in the New Testament, like he did in the Old Testament, that this salvation is available to anyone who desires it. "And it shall be that whoever calls on the name of the Lord shall be saved" (Acts 2:21; Joel 2:32; Rom 1:16). This is because it is from "God our Savior, who desires all men to be saved" (1 Tim 2:3-4).

It was for this very purpose of saving men and women that Jesus came into the world to die on the cross. "The saying is sure and worthy of all acceptance, that Christ Jesus came into the world to save sinners" (1 Tim 1:15; Mt 18:11mg.). The basis of Christ's coming as well as our salvation is the grace of God. Peter declares to the Jerusalem conference, "We believe that we shall be saved through the grace of the Lord Jesus" (Acts 15:11), and Paul makes it clear to the Ephesians that "by grace you have been saved through faith; and this is not your own doing, it is the gift of God—not because of works, lest any man should boast" (Eph 2:8-9). He emphasizes that this salvation by grace is not because of any good works they have done, but rather it is because of God "who saved us and called us with a holy calling, not in virtue of our works but in virtue of his own purpose and the grace which he gave us in Christ Jesus ages ago, and now has manifested through the appearing of our Savior Christ Jesus" (2 Tim 1:9-10). He reiterates the same theme again to Titus. "When the goodness and loving kindness of God our Savior appeared, he saved us, not because of deeds done by us in righteousness, but in virtue of his own mercy, by the washing of regeneration and renewal in the Holy Spirit, which he poured out upon us richly through Jesus Christ our Savior" (Tit 3:4-6). Thus, salvation is available to whoever desires it on the basis of God's grace and human faith in Christ, and when men and women exercise that faith, the power of God is released to bring about salvation from sin.

The whole picture of salvation and being saved from sin is much broader than the more narrow metaphor of redemption but the overlap between the two is very strong. Redemption is far more particular than the words relating to salvation, but it is at the point of an experience of initial salvation that an individual being saved by grace is often spoken of as being redeemed. Indeed, the theological language that we use to describe salvation in the manumission category takes language more heavily focused on the atonement and applies it to the individual. So we speak of being redeemed, saved, delivered from sin, set free from sin and guilt to express that people have come to an experience of saving grace and that the redemption effected on the cross has been applied to their lives.

Growth in Christian Experience

Service in love. People's continued response to God as powerful Redeemer is related to service for God in holiness. When God redeems one from the slavery of sin and evil, the resultant relationship is described in two ways. The first is that the redeemed individual is now the slave of God (Rom 6:16, 18, 22). Paul talks about those who "have been set free from sin and have become slaves of God" (6:22). As the slave of God, one needs to grow in the likeness of the character of the Master. So Luke says God's purpose in redeeming his people was "to grant us that we, being delivered from the hand of our enemies, might serve him without fear, in holiness and righteousness before him all the days of our life" (Lk 1:68, 74-75). This holiness of character is to be expressed in terms of service to others in love. "For you were called to freedom, brethren; only do not use your freedom as an opportunity for the flesh, but through love be servants of one another. For the whole law is fulfilled in one word, 'You shall love your neighbor as yourself'" (Gal 5:13-14).

Slavery to sonship. The second way a redeemed individual is described in Scripture is in terms of sonship to God. Here the manumission metaphor is mixed with the family one, and God redeems persons from the slavery of sin in order to make them free as his children. Thus Paul writes to the Galatians about a time when "we were slaves to the elemental spirits of the universe." But he announces that God sent forth his Son "to redeem those who were under the law, so that we might receive adoption as sons." The result of this action is that "through God you are no longer a slave but a son, and if a son then an heir" (Gal 4:3-7). Here the contrast is between a slave who has no rights or privileges and a son who is the heir to all the inheritance of his father. By adding the family category of adoption, the concept of growth in grace immediately shifts to family categories in terms of one's growing up in the family until he becomes of age and is able to receive his inheritance with all its rights and privileges.

Resisting reenslavement. In addition to serving God in holiness of character, a believer in Christ must continually resist re-enslavement by the forces of evil. He must, therefore, stand fast and "not submit again to a yoke of slavery" (Gal 5:1). This is possible because God has the power to keep him from being enslaved again by anything, even by those things that may be lawful (1 Cor 6:12, 14). God's purpose in redeeming his people is to free them from the curse of the law and from the bondage of slavery. Thus part of growth in grace is learning about the experience of freedom in Christ and its proper use. "For freedom Christ has set us free" (Gal 5:1). But a newly liberated slave in a spiritual sense must learn how to use that freedom. "For you were called to freedom, brethren; only do not use your freedom as an opportunity for the flesh, but through love be servants of one another" (5:13). Those free from sin must now learn how to serve God and others. While in one sense Christians are now free from the law of sin and death, they are now under the law of Christ (1 Cor 9:21; Gal 6:2; Jas 1:25; 2:12) which is sometimes described as the law of love (Gal 5:13).[40]

Power for Christian life. Coupled with the power for resisting re-enslavement is the power available for Christian living. Paul refers to this as the "immeasurable greatness of his power in us who believe, according to the working of his great might" (Eph 1:19). This power is available to give strength to believers that they might continue to endure in Christ. "May you be strengthened with all power, according to his glorious might, for all endurance and patience with joy" (Col 1:11). This power is also connected with God's grace and is fully manifested when the individual realizes his own inadequacies and weaknesses. Paul describes the Lord's word to him: "My grace is sufficient for you, for my power is made perfect in weakness" (2 Cor 12:9). Peter also talks about a power that makes possible the actualization of God's holy character in the life of the individual. "His divine power has granted to us all things that pertain to life and godliness," for the purpose of becoming "partakers of the divine nature" (2 Pet 1:3-4). Nevertheless, God's power must be matched by our faith if we are to continue to persevere and obtain that final salvation God has available for us. Thus, when Peter speaks of this final inheritance, he describes it as "kept in heaven for you, who by God's power are guarded through faith for a salvation ready to be revealed in the last time" (1 Pet 1:4-5).

---

[40]See *NBD*, pp. 733-34; William Burt Pope, *A Compendium of Christian Theology* (London: Wesleyan-Methodist Book Room, 1880), 3:171-85.

In speaking to the Christian household Paul addresses both physical and spiritual slaves, and while mixing his figures, indicates that all Christians are to be serving God in obedience to his will and doing it from the heart as a gift of service.

> Slaves, be obedient to those who are your earthly masters, with fear and trembling, in singleness of heart, as to Christ; not in the way of eye-service, as men-pleasers, but as servants of Christ, doing the will of God from the heart, rendering service with a good will as to the Lord and not to men, knowing that whatever good anyone does, he will receive the same again from the Lord, whether he is a slave or free (Eph 6:5-8).

In the midst of the discussion as to what it means to be "servants of Christ," He exhorts them to "be strong in the Lord and in the strength of his might," and then one is able to fight in spiritual warfare by putting on the whole armor of God as a servant of God fighting in God's strength (Eph 6:10-20).

The Church

The body of believers may be described as the community of the redeemed. Collectively they are a band of individuals who have each been set free from the bondage and slavery of sin. Their common redemption has given them a mutual bond with each other.

Ongoing deliverance. While Christians are a community of those who have been redeemed, they are also a community experiencing further deliverance as a part of God's ongoing work in their lives. Thus in the church at Samaria, Simon the Magician needs to be delivered from "the bond of iniquity" (Acts 8:23). The forces of evil physically capture members of the early church at various times (Acts 4, 5) and so physical deliverance is needed. Peter is the classic example. When taken into custody by Herod, the community of the redeemed pray earnestly for him and this seems to be the secret of his being set free (Acts 12). But physical deliverance is not the only ongoing kind of redemption necessary. The Christians at Ephesus come to a place where they realize they must quit practicing magic arts, and in order to be free from its influence on their new-found Christian experience, they publicly burn their books and artifacts as a testimony to their freedom in the Lord (19:18-19).

Serving God. Because members of the church have been delivered from the forces of evil, they are now free to choose to serve God. Peter states it well: "live as free men . . . live as servants of God" (1 Pet 2:16). So the body of Christ is exhorted to "serve the Lord"(Rom 12:11; Col 3:23). Sometimes believers are characterized as servants of the Lord (2 Tim 2:24) and sometimes as slaves of Christ (Eph. 6:6-7). Apparently, the church is not free to serve God until they have been delivered in the experience of redeeming grace.

Serving others. Not only is the community of the redeemed now available to serve God, but they are called to serve each other. The language used to describe this service is that normally of the work done by a slave/servant and many times in menial, manual tasks. They are to be in a community serving each other. This is their proper collective use of freedom in Christ. Paul exhorts them, "For you were called to freedom, brethren . . . but through love be servants of one another" (Gal 6:13). This is a service of love that is not rendered by compulsion, as some service is, but chosen out of a willing heart (Heb 6:10).

This service to other members of the body of Christ takes several forms. One is the meeting of basic physical needs, like when the members sell their possessions and distribute to those who have need (Acts 2:44-45; 4:32, 34, 37). Their regular acts of service toward others are well exemplified by Tabitha (Acts 9:36-43). The specific needs of the disadvantaged within the community receive special attention, like the care for widows within the church (Acts 6:1-6; 1 Tim 5:3-16). Further, the meeting of needs extends far beyond the local congregation. The classic example is when the spreading church senses its responsibility to send relief to the congregation in Jerusalem (Acts 11:27-30; Rom 15:31).

Gifts of service. The church's service to its own members is closely tied to the work of the Spirit in providing spiritual gifts for different members of the congregation. While all members are to serve one another through such things as contributing to the needs of the saints and practicing hospitality (Rom 12:13), some have a special gift for service (12:7). Peter implies that among the spiritual gifts given to the body of Christ, some of them are related to speaking gifts, while others are tied particularly to service. "Whoever speaks, as one who utters oracles of God; whoever renders service, as one who renders it by the strength which God supplies" (1 Pet 4:11). This probably covers the gift of service that Paul mentions in Romans as well as the gifts of mercy (Rom 12:7-8) and helps (1 Cor 12:28). While the church has to guard against some people feeling they are not responsible for serving others if their gifts are not closely related to the service gifts, nevertheless the fact that some members have a clear giftedness in these area indicates that this is a major part of the church's ministry to other members of the body as well as to those outside the community of faith.

Model servants. Scripture not only exhorts the church to be involved in service to God and to others, it provides some very clear examples of those with both a servant heart and servant activity. Jesus is the key example of a servant heart. The washing of the disciples' feet (Jn 13) is one of the things he both modeled and exhorted his followers to do after he left them. Paul declares that as a part of his ministry of coming into the world Jesus "emptied himself, taking the form of a servant, being born in the likeness of men" so that he might make possible the redemption of the world (Phil 2:7). Since Paul is calling the church at Philippi to follow the example of Jesus in having "this mind among yourselves" (which has to do with humility and self-giving, 2:5), he also provides them with some additional examples that they knew. Timothy is described as one who "has served with me in the gospel" (2:22), and Epaphroditus, who had been their messenger and minister to Paul's need, is described as one who had been willing to lay down his life "to complete your service to me" (2:25, 30).

Elsewhere others are lifted up as models with servant hearts who have ministered to Paul and others (Tychicus, Col 4:7; Onesiphorus, 2 Tim 1:16-17). These models clearly have major leadership positions in the church but are nevertheless seen as slaves of God (Paul, Rom 1:1; Phil 1:1; James, Jas 1:1; Peter, 2 Pet 1:1; Jude, Jude 1). Like slaves to their master, these leaders' usefulness comes out of total submissiveness to God's full will for their lives. God apparently is looking for a church of people with this kind of servant heart, and he begins with leadership.

Masters and slaves in the church. The question of the wrongness of slavery is not addressed head on in the New Testament. Paul certainly implies to Philemon that his desire is for him to set his slave Onesimus free. But the whole theological use of the figure of speech of people being set free from the bondage and slavery of sin is part of the understanding that grew in the church that God wanted people to be set free physically as well as spiritually. However, the church lived in an era where slavery was an everyday fact of life, and to deal with this the New Testament addresses both slaves and masters who have become believers and are now a part of the church of Christ.

Slaves are to continue in their state in obedience to their earthly masters, remembering that they are really serving Christ and not just human beings. They are to see themselves as "servants of Christ, doing the will of God from the heart, rendering service with a good will as to the Lord and not to men, knowing that whatever good any one does, he will receive the same again from the Lord, whether he is a slave or free" (Eph 6:6-8; Col 3:22-24). Even those who had believing masters are never to be disrespectful just because they are joined in the family of God, but rather they are to serve them even more heartily since now it is believers who would benefit from their service (1 Tim 6:1-2; Tit 2:9-10; 1 Pet 2:18).

Masters are also addressed. They are particularly exhorted to "treat your slaves justly and fairly" and the reason is because masters have their own Master in heaven (Col 4:1; Eph 6:9), and this Master shows no partiality. The implications for those who own slaves is that they in fact are to see themselves as slaves of God as their Master and to treat those under their responsibility with the same justice and love they expect from God.

So the church sees itself as people who have been freed from spiritual slavery but who now are collectively serving as slaves of God. This means they understand themselves as owned by God and under his absolute authority just like a slave is to his master. So obedience to God is a major issue for the church, and a willingness to serve God and express this in deeds toward God and other people is a part of its character (Tit 3:3-8).

Full Sanctification

Full redemption. The state of complete sanctification may be described as a full redemption from all sinfulness. This concept in Scripture of a total deliverance from sinfulness is anticipated by the promise of the psalmist in his praise to the Lord for his "plenteous redemption" when he hopes that "he will redeem Israel from all his iniquities" (Ps 130:7-8).[41] Paul seems to believe the fulfillment of this promise is found in the "Savior Jesus Christ, who gave himself for us to redeem us from all iniquity and to purify for himself a people of his own" (Tit 2:13-14). According to the pattern Paul gives, "the grace of God has appeared for the salvation of all men," and those who are saved are to be trained "to renounce irreligion

---

[41]See John Wesley, *A Plain Account of Christian Perfection* (London: Epworth, 1952), pp. 35, 41.

and worldly passions, and to live sober, upright, and godly lives in this world."
Furthermore, they are to await for the second coming of Jesus, but it is in this
context that he mentions the power of Jesus "to redeem us from all iniquity"
(2:11-14). This full destruction of the power of Satan and evil in lives parallels
John's understanding of the deepest purpose of Jesus' coming. "The reason the
Son of God appeared was to destroy the works of the devil" (1 Jn 3:8). So full
sanctification has to do with a full deliverance from the power of sin.

Total yielding. It is this fuller deliverance from sin that Paul discusses in
Romans 6. He completes his discourse on justification by grace through faith in
Romans 5:1-11, and he then talks about the sinfulness inherited from Adam in
5:12-21. This is followed by a discussion of how identification with Christ and
his death ought to be the means by which grace might abound to free us from the
slavery of sinfulness (Rom 6:1-11). Yet, while it is theoretically true that at the
cross all sin was dealt with fully, in practice one must do something deliberate to
"consider yourselves dead to sin and alive to God in Christ Jesus" (6:11). It is in
this context that Paul calls for a definite yielding/presenting of one's members
and one's self to God in entire consecration (6:13, 19). It is this total yielding of
oneself as obedient slaves that describes this experience of sanctification. While
in one sense they have "been set free from sin" and "have become slaves of
righteousness," there is another dimension to which Paul exhorts them when he
calls for them to "now yield your members to righteousness for sanctification"
(6:16-19). But when people have been fully "set free from sin" and become in a
total sense "slaves of God," then the return is "sanctification, and its end, eternal
life" (6:22).[42]

After calling for a full yielding and surrendering of oneself as a slave to God in
sanctification (Rom 6), Paul turns to the problem that Christians find as justified
believers (Rom 7). It is as though he now discusses in more detail sin's effect on
the believer after being justified by faith. The Christian begins to see the law in
its full implications as "holy and just and good" (7:12). Yet at one time in this
state Paul describes himself as "carnal, sold under sin." In this state he did not
have the power to do what he knew was right to do, but ended up doing that
which he knew to be wrong. This he attributes to the sinful principle dwelling
within him. So while he delights in the law of God in his innermost self, at the

---

[42]See William Greathouse, *Romans* (Kansas City, Mo.: Beacon Hill, 1975), pp. 107-12.

same time he sees in his members a sinfulness at war with what he knows to be right. The result is that it makes him a "captive to the law of sin," and therefore he cries out, "Who will deliver me from this body of death?" At the end of chapter seven Paul gives praise and acknowledges that Christ has the power to deliver him from this sinful principle. He further clarifies this power at the beginning of chapter eight. "For the law of the Spirit of life in Christ Jesus has set me free from the law of sin and death" (7:13—8:2). It is this freedom from the law of sin and the body of death that describes the experience to which Paul has exhorted the Christians in chapter six, and this is also related to the Spirit-filled life that he describes in chapter eight. This is that victory that sets one fully free from the power of sinfulness and empowers one to live under the full control of the Holy Spirit.[43]

Power of the Spirit. This experience also seems to be described in terms of a Christian being strengthened with power by the fullness of God's Holy Spirit. Jesus exhorts his disciples at the close of his time with them not to leave Jerusalem, because, he says, "I send the promise of my Father upon you; but stay in the city, until you are clothed with power from on high" (Lk 24:49). He repeats the same exhortation in his final appearance with them and relates it to receiving power when the Holy Spirit has come on them (Acts 1:4, 8). An illustration of this power of God on a person who is full of the Spirit comes in the life of the early church in the person of Stephen. Repeatedly he is described as "full of the Spirit" (6:3, 5, 10; 7:55), while also depicted as one who is "full of grace and power" (6:8).

This also seems to be part of the focus of Paul's petition for the sanctification of the Ephesian Christians when he prays that they might know the fullness of the love of Christ in their lives and that they may be filled with all the fullness of God. He begins this prayer with the request that God may grant them "to be strengthened with might through his Spirit in the inner man" (Eph 3:16-19). He further indicates that he is convinced God has the ability to answer his prayer: "Now to him who by the power at work within us is able to do far more abundantly than all that we ask or think" (3:20). So the Spirit of power serves as the agent of this experience of God's fuller power in sanctification.

---

[43]See A. Skevington Wood, *Paul's Pentecost* (Exeter, U.K.: Paternoster, 1963), pp. 21-24.

Further Growth

Victory over temptation. The full redemption that God makes available in sanctifying grace seems to release a power in the lives of Christians in two particular areas. The first has to do with resisting temptation and, therefore, living victoriously in the face of the powers of evil. The second has to do with a power in witness and proclamation of the gospel. Both are illustrated in Luke 4 in the life of Jesus. The chapter begins describing Jesus as "full of the Holy Spirit," and led by the Spirit of God into the wilderness to be tempted by the devil (Lk 4:1-2). He returns victoriously "in the power of the Spirit" after this encounter with Satan (4:14). In this same "power of the Spirit" he begins to teach in their synagogues, and the opportunity to teach in his home synagogue of Nazareth is given as an illustration of his wider ministry (4:16-30). It is on this occasion that he reads from Isaiah concerning himself. "The Spirit of the Lord is upon me, because he has anointed me to preach good news to the poor" (4:18). Clearly, the fullness of God's Spirit on Jesus is intimately bound up with an anointing that makes it possible for him both to resist temptation and to proclaim the gospel of God. While those in Nazareth did not respond positively to one of their own, the same teaching in Capernaum met with astonishment that one could teach with such authority (4:31-32). It was in this synagogue that the unclean spirit identified Jesus as "the Holy One of God" (4:34).

The pattern of Jesus is illustrative of the availability of God's grace through the fullness of the Spirit in order to live victoriously over all temptation. The reason this is possible is that in an experience of full sanctification there is a total surrender of the will to God as its Master. There is a freedom from sinfulness, i.e., having to have one's own way, and, therefore, a freedom from self-centeredness, which is that to which temptation normally appeals. When one is totally committed to doing all the will of God as a slave of God, a temptation to please oneself is much easier to resist.

Power for proclamation. The second part of the effect of power available to those who have experienced full redemption has to do with a total willingness to proclaim God's message to all the world. When a disciple is aware he is not his own master but is fully subservient to God, there is a fuller willingness to be obedient in proclaiming the gospel, even if the response to that proclamation should be negative. One of the greatest hindrances to the communication of the gospel is the concern of the proclaimer for what other people will think. When there is a surrender of this self-centeredness expressed in self-protection, it makes it easier for the Spirit to lead in terms of making such a person an effective tool for witness. Jesus tells his disciples that power will be available when the Holy Spirit comes on them (Lk 24:48-49; Acts 1:8), and when the Holy Spirit does come on those who had been cowering behind closed doors for fear of the Jews, they boldly stand forth proclaiming Jesus Christ (Acts 2:14-38). This applies to not only the disciples and those in the upper room but also others who later come into an experience of the fullness of God's Holy Spirit (e.g., 4:31).

Glorification

Final redemption. In this language category the concept of glorification is described as final redemption. There is an initial redemption that comes with saving grace, but there is also a final redemption that comes with glorification. Jesus describes his own second advent to his disciples. "Now when these things begin to take place, look up and raise your heads, because your redemption is drawing near" (Lk 21:28). Paul likens this to the "glorious liberty of the children of God" that will come with the final redemption of our bodies as well as our souls. At that time creation itself will be set free from its bondage to decay and obtain the glorious liberty of the children of God. "We know that the whole creation has been groaning in travail together until now; and not only the creation, but we ourselves, who have the first fruits of the Spirit, groan inwardly as we wait for adoption as sons, the redemption of our bodies. For in this hope we were saved" (Rom 8:21-24). Accordingly, he exhorts Christians not to "grieve the Holy Spirit of God, in whom you were sealed for the day of redemption" (Eph 4:30). Thus, Christians are to wait for Christ our Savior who has the power even to transform our bodies into his likeness. "Our commonwealth is in heaven, and from it we await a Savior, the Lord Jesus Christ, who will change our lowly body to be like his glorious body, by the power which enables him even to subject all things to himself" (Phil 3:20-21).[44]

Attributes of God

Omnipotence. The attribute of God most closely bound up with his role as

---

[44]For further discussion on final redemption see Morris, *Apostolic Preaching of the Cross*, pp. 47-48; Richardson, *Theology of the New Testament*, pp. 219-20; Charles Hodge, *Systematic Theology* (London: James Clark, 1960), 2:520.

Redeemer is that of his omnipotence. He is a God of all power, but it is power related to his holy being. So there is a sense in which it is a qualified power in many respects.

The concept of God's power or omnipotence is, as previously noted, closely related to several other roles. In his role as Creator, God has all power and in this sense omnipotence may be understood as *potestas absoluta*. By his "absolute power" and the choice of his absolute will God has ordered the creation and all of its parts. God has had the power to create the universe exactly as he wanted. But in relation to the other roles, the omnipotence of God does not need to be understood in terms of *potestas absoluta* but rather as a more relative power that may be described as the *potestas ordinata*. This "ordained power" of God has been limited by himself. He has chosen to plan and accomplish his purposes under certain self-imposed limits. So as King or Ruler of the universe, for example, he governs according to the laws he has made as Creator. Here his power to accomplish his purposes in the physical universe and his power to accomplish his purposes in general among mankind are conditioned by his wisdom. He has the power of course to interrupt the laws of nature that he has created and this accounts for the intervention in the universe we call miracles. But normally he limits himself to working through the laws of nature that he has created. Further, he accomplishes his purposes among people in the light of the freedom he has given to them. He had the power to create persons with a certain freedom of will, and his governing of their affairs must now be conditioned by the exercise of that freedom. Again, it is the wisdom of God that makes it possible for him to accomplish his ultimate purposes throughout history in spite of the freedom of individuals.

God's omnipotence in relation to his role as Judge and Father mean that his power is conditioned by his moral attributes of righteousness and love respectively. He has the power to judge and the power to lead in his spiritual family, but he exercises these in accordance with his holiness revealed as both righteousness and love.

Finally, his omnipotence is particularly related to his role as the Redeemer from the power of sin and evil.[45] Here God demonstrates that his power is

---

[45]On the omnipotence of God see Brunner, *Christian Doctrine of God*, pp. 248-55; Pope, *Compendium of Christian Theology*, 1:311-13; *EDT*, pp. 457-58; A. W. Tozer, *Knowledge of the Holy* (New York: Harper & Row, 1961), pp. 71-74; John Miley, *Systematic Theology* (New York: Methodist Book Concern, 1892), 1:211-13.

greater than that of the forces of evil, but again the exercise of this power is conditioned by the freedom he has given to people. They must choose to allow grace to continue to work in their lives and bring them to a place of redemption. God does not use his absolute power to force redemption, but he, by giving persons through grace the freedom of choice, has limited his own power with regard to their salvation. Many people find it difficult to reconcile God's absolute power as Creator and their own experience of him as Redeemer. God does not use his omnipotence as a means of arbitrarily forcing people to be redeemed, whether they will to or not. A proper understanding of how God has limited his own power in relation to individuals with regard to several of the roles should be helpful in understanding the way in which an omnipotent God is related to the salvation of men and women.[46]

Conclusion

The role of God as powerful Redeemer sets in the forefront of discussion both the power of God and the salvation of men and women. Historically, redemption is both effected and illustrated in the exodus and the return from exile. These events prepare a way for understanding the significant spiritual redemption to come through Christ's redeeming work on the cross. At a personal level this role highlights the freedom from sin and the privilege of serving God that is made available to everyone. Personal salvation is a part of God's larger redemptive purposes. Theologically, this role accents God's power over sin and evil, as well as his ability to bring about the salvation of men and women. God as Redeemer frees people to be all that he intended them to be.

---

[46]For further discussion of the relationship of the roles of God to his omnipotence and its impact on the concept of salvation see Allan Coppedge, *John Wesley in Theological Debate* (Wilmore, Ky.: Wesley Heritage, 1987), pp. 126-29, 132, 143.

TEN

HOLY GOD
AS GOOD SHEPHERD

The Unity Factor

The picture of God as Shepherd demands a God who cares. Being a Shepherd is about caring. Since the motivation for God's care is his goodness, our first task will be to look at this attribute. This will mean showing the relationship of goodness to God's holiness and thus how it is tied to his other attributes and roles. Then we will be able to adequately focus on his role as the Good Shepherd.

Holiness as Manifested in Goodness

The concept of a holy God as Good Shepherd is derived from a proper understanding of several pieces of interlocking biblical data. It involves (1) the connection between holiness and goodness, (2) the goodness of God, (3) the character of the shepherd described as good, and (4) a holy God's activity as a good shepherd.

Holiness and goodness. The connection between goodness and holiness begins with the synonymous use of these terms to describe God's temple. "We shall be satisfied with the goodness of thy house, thy holy temple!" (Ps 65:4). Then in describing the benefits of God's "holy name," one of the things the psalmist lists is that which is "good." For it is the one who is holy "who satisfies you with good as long as you live" (103:1, 5). Furthermore, in calling all flesh to bless God's holy name forever, he declares that the people will "pour forth the fame of thy abundant goodness" (145:21, 7). Clearly, goodness is an expression of God's holy name, that is, his nature.

There is also a connection between the goodness of God and the giving of his Holy Spirit. When Isaiah tells of "the great goodness to the house of Israel" by God who brought Israel through the Red Sea as "his flock," He describes God as the one who "put in the midst of them his holy Spirit" (Is 63:7-14). In the New Testament Luke compares the giving of good gifts by an earthly father to his children with the gift of the Holy Spirit from a heavenly Father to his children. "If you then, who are evil, know how to give good gifts to your children, how much more will your heavenly Father give the Holy Spirit to those who ask him!" (Lk 11:13).[1] The writer of Hebrews also identifies goodness with holiness when he declares that God "disciplines us for our good, that we may share his holiness" (Heb 12:10).

Goodness of God. The goodness of God has its roots in the description of God's work at creation. Repeatedly after each aspect of the creation, God declares it to be good, i.e., in accord with his purpose and plan. Since his purpose and plan is based on his own nature, the goodness of these things relates to that which is in accord with God's being. This is particularly apropos to man and woman created in God's own image (Gen 1:4, 10, 12, 18, 21, 31). The goodness of God is further expressed in his provision of the garden of Eden for Adam and Eve. God made it "pleasant to the sight and good for food," indicating the abundant provision and care God provides for his people. His goodness is related to making things beautiful, and to providing for basic needs like food, security, stability and companionship (2:9, 18).

The first direct reference to the goodness of God comes in connection with the revelation of God's glory and God's name, both of which are intimately bound up with the holiness of his character. Thus, when Moses asks for God to show him his glory, he responds, "I will make all my goodness pass before you, and proclaim before you my name" (Ex 33:18-19). The psalmist makes the same connection between God's goodness and his name or holy nature. "Praise the LORD, for the LORD is good; sing to his name, for he is gracious!" (Ps 135:3). It is possible for God's name, that is, his holy nature, to be consistently identified with goodness because, as W. B. Pope explains, holiness "is the standard of goodness." Thus it is the holy nature of God "that declares what is morally good." "The reason why good is good" is because a holy God is the eternal standard and foundation of all goodness.[2] This is why Jesus declares "No one is good but God

---

[1] Cf. Mt 7:11, which refers to the Father who gives "good things to those who ask him."

alone" (Mk 10:18; Lk 18:19; Mt 19:17). God does not choose good based on some standard higher than himself, but rather what he wills is good because goodness is an expression of his holy being. G. R. Lewis puts it well when he says:

> The good, the just, the pure, the holy is holy, not by reason of an arbitrary act of the divine will, nor of a principle independent of God, but because it is an outflow of his nature. God always wills in accord with his nature consistently. He wills the good because he is good. And because God is holy, he consistently hates sin and is repulsed by all evil.[3]

Donald Guthrie rightly warns us about defining what is good apart from the character of God. Jesus' statement that "only one is good, God," "makes clear that the character of God is such that it is itself the standard that should determine all human notions of goodness. And that goodness flows from the holy essence of God's being."[4]

Shepherd is good. The character of God in his role as Shepherd seems to be best characterized by the adjective "good." The twenty-third Psalm, which gives one of the clearest pictures of the Lord as Shepherd, closes with the statement "Surely goodness and mercy shall follow me all the days of my life" (Ps 23:6). In John 10 Jesus describes himself as the Good Shepherd who lays down his life for his sheep (Jn 10:11, 14).[5] It is clear that there is a basic goodness that is identified with the character of divinity. God is good.

Holy God's activity as good shepherd. This relationship serves to show how a holy God's activity as a good shepherd is one basis for understanding the relationship between holiness and goodness. The first reference to the holiness of God (Ex 15:11) is set in the midst of a section demonstrating God's activity in relationship to his people (Ex 13-18) and this activity includes direction, protection, provision and other shepherd-like activity. In the passage describing the journey of Israel from Egypt to Mount Sinai, there is no direct reference to God as Shepherd, but the Hebrews look back on this experience as a description of God's Shepherd role in their experience. "Oh God, when thou didst go forth

[2]William Burt Pope, *A Compendium of Christian Theology* (London: Wesleyan-Methodist Book Room, 1880), 1:333.

[3]*EDT*, p. 456.

[4]Donald Guthrie, *New Testament Theology* (Downers Grove, Ill.: InterVarsity Press, 1981), p. 108. See also *NBD*, p. 482.

[5]See also Ps 68:10; Jer 31:10-14; Zech 9:16-17.

before thy people, when thou didst march through the wilderness . . . thy flock found a dwelling in it; in thy goodness, O God, thou didst provide for the needy" (Ps 68:7, 10). Not only does he make provision for them as a Shepherd, he leads them "like a flock" (77:20). It is the "Holy One of Israel" who "led forth his people like sheep, and guided them in the wilderness like a flock. He led them in safety, so that they were not afraid; but the sea overwhelmed their enemies. And he brought them to his holy land" (78:41, 52-54). So it is that first occasion when God is called holy (Ex 15) that Israel looks back on as a time when God manifested himself in shepherd-like activity.

Furthermore, when God promises to Israel a New Covenant through which he will vindicate his holiness and his holy name in them, part of how he intends to demonstrate his holiness relates to the work of a shepherd. He will gather them from all the countries and bring them into their own land (Ezek 36:22-24), and he promises "to increase their men like a flock." The end result will be a repopulation of the land so that "the waste cities will be filled with flocks of men" and by this means they will know that he is the Lord and that he is holy (Ezek 36:37-38). Thus a part of the manifestation of his holy name and the vindication of his holy character comes when God exercises certain shepherd-like functions. Clearly, the connection between God's activity as a Good Shepherd and his holy character is a key expression of the connection between God's holiness and his goodness.

In summary, we may say that the evidence indicates that the concept of goodness is one direct manifestation of God's holiness. The biblical material sometimes demonstrates a direct connection between the two. At other times part of our theological task is to understand the indirect, but no less significant connections between holiness and the goodness of God's character, the character of goodness that relates to God's role as Shepherd and the holy God's activity as the Good Shepherd. Certainly the best understanding of the way these materials fit together is to see the goodness of God as an important expression of his holiness. There is no question then that Guthrie is right when he says that goodness "is closely linked with the moral holiness of God."[6]

---

[6]Guthrie, *New Testament Theology*, p. 108. On goodness as the moral element in the holy, see Emil Brunner, *Christian Doctrine of God* (London: Lutterworth, 1949), pp. 166-67. See also Ludwig Hugo Koehler, *Old Testament Theology* (Philadelphia: Westminster Press, 1957), p. 53.

The Role of God as Good Shepherd

The *language figure* that describes this role is drawn from the nomadic picture of a *shepherd* in relationship to his sheep. It is a pastoral role in which shepherds watch over their sheep, so the comparison pictures are vivid and clear about how God exercises these functions toward his people.

It is obvious that the *focus* of a shepherd's work is on *care*. With the people as God's sheep, the picture explicates the activity of God as a Shepherd. In this role God makes provision for his people by feeding them, he gives guidance and leads them in his pathways, he provides protection from outside forces that would destroy them, and he is involved in healing and restoring those who may be wounded under his care. On occasion it involves the responsibility of searching, seeking and gathering together those that may have wandered astray (e.g., Ps 23; Ezek 34:11-16; Zech 11:16).[7]

The Father

Old Testament. In the Old Testament God is referred to as a Shepherd on several occasions. The most famous of these comes in the psalmist's declaration, "The LORD is my Shepherd" (Ps 23:1). In other Scripture, when people call on God for help, they appeal to him as a Shepherd. "Give ear, O Shepherd of Israel, thou who leadest Joseph like a flock!" (80:1). Likewise the prophets claim that "he will feed his flock like a shepherd, he will gather the lambs in his arms, he will carry them in his bosom, and gently lead those that are with young" (Is 40:11). Not only does he provide, but he gathers his sheep. "He who scattered Israel will gather him, and will keep him as a shepherd keeps his flock" (Jer 31:10). Looking forward to the New Covenant, God declares himself to be like a Shepherd seeking his people.

> Behold, I, I myself will search for my sheep, and will seek them out. As a shepherd seeks out his flock when some of his sheep have been scattered abroad, so will I seek out my sheep; and I will rescue them from all places where they have been scattered on a day of clouds and thick darkness. And I will bring them out from the peoples, and gather them from the countries, and will bring them into their

---

[7]For further discussion of the shepherd metaphor, see *TDNT,* 4:485-502; *TWOT,* 2:852-53; *NIDNTT,* 3:564-69; *NBD,* p. 1174-76; J. G. S. S. Thompson, "The Shepherd/Ruler Concept in the Old Testament and its Application in the New Testament," *SJT* 8 (December 1955): 406-18; Edmond Jacob, *Theology of the Old Testament,* trans. Arthur W. Heathcote and P. J. Allcock (New York: Harper & Row, 1958), p. 203.

own land; and I will feed them on the mountains of Israel.... I myself will be the shepherd of my sheep, and I will make them lie down, says the Lord GOD. I will seek the lost, and I will bring back the strayed, and I will bind up the crippled, and I will strengthen the weak, and the fat and the strong I will watch over; I will feed them in justice. (Ezek 34:11-13, 15-16)

The earliest direct reference in Scripture to God as a Shepherd comes in the blessing of Jacob to his sons, where God Almighty is referred to as "the mighty one of Jacob" and in a parenthesis there is added by way of additional explanation, "the name of the Shepherd, the Rock of Israel" (Gen 49:24-25).[8] It may well be that Jacob recognized God's role as Shepherd in terms of his leading his family to Egypt and his acts of provision and protection for them during the years of famine.[9]

While some passages in Scripture refer directly to God as Shepherd, others are more indirect, referring to the people of God as sheep.[10] At the end of Moses' life he prays for God to provide another leader for Israel so "that the congregation of the LORD may not be as sheep which have no shepherd" (Num 27:17). The psalmist exclaims, "Thou has made us like sheep for slaughter, and has scattered us among the nations.... Nay, for thy sake we are slain all the day long, and accounted as sheep for the slaughter" (Ps 44:11, 22). Through Jeremiah God speaks some strong words to the leaders of Israel who have not served well as shepherds to the spiritual flock of the people of God.

"Woe to the shepherds who destroy and scatter the sheep of my pasture," says the LORD. Therefore thus says the LORD, the God of Israel, concerning the shepherds who care for my people: "You have scattered my flock, and have driven them away, and you have not attended to them. Behold, I will attend to you for your evil doings," says the LORD. "Then I will gather the remnant of my flock out of all the

---

[8]For other references to God as Shepherd see Ps 28:9; 68:8ff.; 74:1; 77:20; 78:52; 79:13; 95:7; 100:3; 121:4; 130:1; Is 49:9; Jer 23:3; 50:19; Mic 4:6; 7:14.

[9]For further discussion of God as Shepherd see NBD, p. 1176; TDNT, 6:487-88, 491-92; Alan Richardson, An Introduction to the Theology of the New Testament (London: SCM Press, 1958), p. 292; NIDNTT, 3:565; F. F. Bruce, "The Shepherd King," in This Is That: The New Testament Development of Some Old Testament Themes (Exeter, U.K.: Paternoster, 1968), pp. 100-114; Rudolf Bultmann, The Gospel of John, ed. G. R. Beasley-Murray (Oxford: Basil Blackwell, 1971), pp. 358-91.

[10]For further discussion of the people of God as sheep see TDNT, 6:499-502; NBD, p. 1174; Ethelbert Stauffer, New Testament Theology (London: SCM Press, 1955), p. 154; NIDNTT, 3:565-67; 2:413; C. H. Dodd, Interpretation of the Fourth Gospel (Cambridge University Press, 1964), pp. 358-59; Alfred Plummer, The Gospel According to St. John (Cambridge: Cambridge University Press, 1902), pp. 216-17, 220; R. V. G. Tasker, The Gospel According to St. John (London: Tyndale Press, 1964), pp. 129-30.

countries where I have driven them, and I will bring them back to their fold, and they shall be fruitful and multiply." (Jer 23:1-3)[11]

New Testament. In the New Testament Jesus shares many of the same concerns for people as Moses. He has compassion on the crowds "because they were harassed and helpless, like sheep without a shepherd" (Mt 9:36; Mk 6:34). Jesus refers to believers as a "little flock" (Lk 12:32), and the disciples are sent out in ministry "as sheep in the midst of wolves" (Mt 10:16). Further, his spiritual leaders are challenged to feed his sheep (Jn 21:16, 17; Acts 20:28-29; 1 Pet 5:2-3).[12] So it is evident that in both the Old Testament and New Testament the people of God are sometimes referred to as the sheep or flock of God.

The Son

Shepherd. In certain Old Testament predictions of the coming Messiah, Jesus is described as a Shepherd. When God describes his concern over the shepherds of Israel not caring for the flock, he promises to "set up over them one shepherd, my servant David, and he shall feed them: he shall feed them and be their shepherd. And I, the LORD, will be their God, and my servant David shall be prince among them" (Ezek 34:23-24). Because God uses David, who was both a shepherd and a king, as a pattern for the coming Messiah, he is able to declare, "My servant David shall be king over them; and they shall all have one shepherd. They shall follow my ordinances and be careful to observe my statutes" (37:24). Micah also uses this dual role when he addresses Bethlehem of Judah. "From you shall come forth for me one who is to be ruler in Israel," and it is this one that "shall stand and feed his flock in the strength of the LORD, in the majesty of the name of the LORD his God" (Mic 5:2, 4). The New Testament writers understand Zechariah's prophecy, "Strike the Shepherd, that the sheep may be scattered" (Zech 13:7), as a reference to the death of Jesus (Mt 26:31; Mk 14:27).[13]

In the New Testament Jesus' discourse about himself as the Good Shepherd in John 10 is clearly the most extensive development of this analogy. He

---

[11]For other Old Testament references to the people of God as sheep/flock see 1 Kings 22:17; 2 Chron 18:16; Ps 74:1; 77:20; 78:52; 79:13; 80:1; 95:7; 100:3; 107:41; Jer 50:6, 17; Ezek 34:2, 3, 6, 8, 10-12, 15, 17, 19, 20, 22, 31; 36:37-38; Zech 9:16; 10:2; 11:4, 7, 11, 17; 13:7.

[12]For other New Testament references to the people of God as sheep/flock see Mt 9:36; 10:6, 16; 15:24; 25:32; 26:31; Mk 14:27; Lk 12:32; Jn 10:1, 6; 11:52; Heb 13:20; 1 Pet 2:25.

[13]For further discussion of the Old Testament picture of the Messiah as Shepherd see *TDNT,* 6:48; Richardson, *Theology of the New Testament,* p. 292; *NIDNTT,* 3:566-67.

describes himself as the Shepherd of the sheep, who calls his own sheep by name and leads them out. He goes before them and the sheep follow him and know his voice (Jn 10:2-6). He continues to describe himself as the Good Shepherd who lays down his life for the sheep (10:11-18). He further clarifies that not all are his sheep but only those who continue to hear his voice and to follow him. To these he gives eternal life and protects them from all outside threats to their spiritual lives (10:26-29).[14]

Other New Testament writers capture this vivid metaphor. Hebrews refers to Jesus as the "great shepherd" (Heb 13:20), while Peter calls him "the chief Shepherd" (1 Pet 5:4). In addition, Peter, perhaps in remembrance of his own denial of Jesus, talks to those who "were straying like sheep, but have now returned to the Shepherd and Guardian of your souls" (1 Pet 2:25). Finally, Matthew's account of the great judgment where Jesus will have all the nations gathered before him quotes Jesus saying that "he will separate them one from another as a shepherd separates the sheep from the goats" (Mt 25:32).[15]

Lamb. In the pastoral figure of speech, Jesus is not only described as a Shepherd but sometimes as a Lamb. It is found with the description of his suffering in Isaiah 53 as a result of the sins of the believers who have like sheep "gone astray." Because of our sins, the Messiah is pictured as one who comes as a substitute Lamb, the one on whom all our iniquities are laid. "He was oppressed, and he was afflicted, yet he opened not his mouth; like a lamb that is led to the slaughter, and like a sheep that before its shearers is dumb, so he opened not his mouth" (Is 53:6-7). It is this passage that Philip uses to explain to the Ethiopian eunuch the gospel of Jesus (Acts 8:32-35). This Old Testament figure is certainly in the mind of John the Baptist when he identifies Jesus as "the Lamb of God, who takes away the sin of the world!" (Jn 1:29, 36).

Peter declares that it was with the precious blood of Christ, like from that "of a lamb without or blemish or spot," that Christians are ransomed from the evil

---

[14]Lesslie Newbigin, *The Light Has Come: An Exposition of the Fourth Gospel* (Grand Rapids, Mich.: Eerdmans, 1982), pp. 125-30.

[15]For further reading on Jesus as Shepherd see Joachim Jeremias, *New Testament Theology*, trans. John Bowden (New York: Scribner, 1971), pp. 297-98; *TDNT*, 6:292, 297; *NBD*, p. 1176; Richardson, *Theology of the New Testament*, p. 293; *NIDNTT*, 3:567; B. F. Westcott, *The Epistles of St. John* (Cambridge, London: Macmillan, 1892), pp. 154-55; Plummer, *Gospel According to St. John*, pp. 215-16; J. A. Bernard, *St. John* (New York: Charles Scribner's Sons, 1929), 2:356-66; Tasker, *St. John*, 2:128-31; Merrill C. Tenney, *John, the Gospel of Belief* (Grand Rapids, Mich.: Eerdmans, 1948), pp. 163-65; C. K. Barrett, *The Gospel According to St. John* (London: SPCK, 1965), pp. 304-5, 310-12; Leon Morris, *The Gospel According to John* (Grand Rapids, Mich.: Eerdmans, 1971).

ways of sin inherited from their fathers (1 Pet 1:18-19). The book of Revelation also pictures Jesus as "the Lamb who was slain" but who now lives forever (Rev 5:6-13).[16] In an interesting mixture of roles the Lamb becomes the Shepherd of those who have washed their robes in his blood. "For the Lamb in the midst of the throne will be their Shepherd, and he will guide them to springs of living water" (Rev 7:14-17).

The picture of Jesus as a lamb is related not only to the Shepherd figure of speech but also to his priestly role. In the temple metaphor Jesus is both the Priest and the sacrificial Lamb, just as in the pastoral figure of speech he is both Shepherd and Lamb. In both cases there is a unique blend in the person of Jesus of both God and man that makes him uniquely qualified to fit two figures within the same role. In the pastoral metaphor Jesus' divinity is probably more predominant in the role he plays as Shepherd, whereas as the perfect man his humanity is more dominant in his role as the Lamb. The two cannot be absolutely divided between his divinity and his humanity, but the emphasis does seem to fall in this way within this metaphor.[17]

Holy Spirit

The Holy Spirit is identified as good in the prayer of David, "Let thy good spirit lead me on a level path!" (Ps 143:10). This good Spirit of God is not normally described with the title of Shepherd, but as in the case with other roles, the Holy Spirit does certain activities that fit the pattern of this metaphor. So in the pastoral role the Holy Spirit performs shepherd-like functions. Thus, when Moses prays for a shepherd to lead the congregation of Israel, God brings forth Joshua as "a man in whom is the Spirit" to lead his people (Num 27:16-18). Nehemiah describes the Holy Spirit as God's "good Spirit" who instructs them in the way to go but also provides manna and water for his people (Neh 9:20).

In the Old Testament the passage that contains two of the three references where the adjective *holy* is connected with the Spirit of God relates to the context of God delivering his people from the Red Sea and leading them in the

---

[16]See also Rev 6:1, 16; 7:9, 10, 14, 17; 8:1; 12:11; 13:8; 14:4; 15:3; 19:9; 21:9.

[17]For further discussion of Jesus as a Lamb see *TDNT*, 1:338-41; *NBD*, p. 706; *EDT*, pp. 618-19; Morris, *Apostolic Preaching of the Cross*, pp. 129-43; *BDT*, pp. 306-7; Geerhardus Vos, *Biblical Theology* (Grand Rapids, Mich.: Eerdmans, 1948), pp. 48-51; Guthrie, *New Testament Theology*, pp. 450-52; Richardson, *Theology of the New Testament*, pp. 225-29; *NIDNTT*, 2:411-12; Dodd, *Interpretation of the Fourth Gospel*, pp. 230-38.

wilderness. Speaking of Israel as "his flock," Isaiah asks, "Where is he who put in the midst of them his holy Spirit?" It is this one "who divided the waters before them to make for himself an everlasting name." He concludes, "Like cattle that go down into the valley, the Spirit of the LORD gave them rest. So thou didst lead thy people, to make for thyself a glorious name" (Is 63:10-14). It is clear that the prophet is convinced it is the Holy Spirit who has led Israel as the flock of God by dividing the Red Sea before them and leading them through the desert to a place of rest.

The leading/guiding function of the Shepherd also appears in the work of the Spirit of God in the New Testament. Simeon is led by the Spirit to come into the temple during the occasion of the dedication of Jesus (Lk 2:27). At the beginning of Jesus' ministry he is "led up by the Spirit into the wilderness to be tempted" (Mt 4:1; Mk 1:12), and at the close of his ministry, Jesus tells the disciples that the Holy Spirit "will guide you into all the truth" (Jn 16:13). In the book of Acts there are numerous examples of the Spirit's leading function (e.g., Acts 10:19; 11:12; 13:2, 4; 16:6-7; 19:21). This leading activity is also related to a protecting/guarding responsibility, as seen when Paul cautions the spiritual shepherds at Ephesus, "Take heed . . . to all the flock, in which the Holy Spirit has made you guardians" (Acts 20:28).[18] So the Holy Spirit is not only good, but he shepherds the flock of God, particularly by leading and providing for their needs.

Man and Woman

Desired relationship with shepherd: Following. The relationship between the Shepherd and the sheep is that the Shepherd leads and the sheep follow. So God's desired relationship to people in this role is that they follow in obedience to his leading for their lives. Following in obedience strongly overlaps several other roles where obedience to God is expected (e.g., God as King, Judge, Father). But in this picture it is obedience expressed in following the Shepherd that is emphasized. So when Jesus describes "the Shepherd of the sheep," he says that "the sheep hear his voice, and he calls his own sheep by name and leads them out. When he has brought out all his own, he goes before them, and the sheep follow him, for they know his voice. A stranger they will not follow, but they will flee from

[18]On the Holy Spirit's leading role see René Pache, *Person and Work of the Holy Spirit* (Chicago: Moody Press, 1954), pp. 157-62.

him, for they do not know the voice of strangers" (Jn 10:2-5). The following of
God by his sheep is intimately bound up with a personal knowledge of him and
is particularly related to his voice. The sheep are accustomed to his presence and
vocal commands, and on this basis they follow their Shepherd and will not follow a stranger.

But not only do the sheep know the Shepherd's voice, the Shepherd knows
the sheep. Jesus says, "My sheep hear my voice, and I know them, and they
follow me; and I give them eternal life, and they shall never perish, and no one
shall snatch them out of my hand" (Jn 10:27-28). The verbs used here are in the
present tense, indicating that the sheep continually hear his voice and continue
to follow. Those that continue hearing and following in obedience are those who
receive eternal life and have the protection of the Shepherd from any who might
try to "snatch them out" of his hand.

Purpose: The sheep's good. The following of God as Shepherd in obedience is for
people's good. Thus, at the close of Israel's experience of following God in the
wilderness, Moses reminded Israel "to keep the commandments and the statutes
of the LORD, which I command you this day for your good" (Deut 10:13; cf. 6:24;
Ps 34:10). The Good Shepherd desires good things for those who follow in
obedience after him. The good things a shepherd provides include provision of
their physical needs (like grass and water), security (protection from external
threats), and care (like the binding up of wounds). These good things are
possible only when the Shepherd is able to lead the sheep to places where all
these things may be provided. In like manner, God is only able to provide,
protect and care for the basic needs of his people when they are willing to follow
his leading to places where he can provide for each of these.

Sin

Act of sin: Straying. While following the Shepherd is the desired relationship,
sheep do not always do this, and this leads us to a discussion of sin under the
pastoral role. An act of sin is described in this category as going astray or straying. The picture is that of a sheep wandering away from the rest of the flock and
the watchful eye of the Shepherd. The focus is not so much on whether or not
the straying of the sheep is deliberate but on the resultant fact that the sheep
becomes lost. When one is lost, he is separated both from the Shepherd and
from companion sheep. Isaiah pictures this: "All we like sheep have gone astray"

(Is 53:6; cf. Ezek 34:12, 16; Jer 23:1-2; 50:6). Jesus, in the parable of the lost sheep, gives us the same picture when he describes the one sheep out of the hundred that has gone astray (Mt 18:12; 24:4, 5, 11, 24; Mk 13:5, 6; Lk 21:8). This analogy is later used by Peter who speaks of some who "were straying like sheep" (1 Pet 2:25) and others who "forsaking the right way they have gone astray" (2 Pet 2:15).[19]

State of sin: Lost. In addition to the picture of sin as going astray, this category also describes sin as getting lost or being in a state of lostness. Here there is some overlap between sin as a definite act (getting lost), and sin as a principle or a state (lostness). Jeremiah describes this experience: "My people have been lost sheep; their shepherds have led them astray," (Jer 50:6). This figure is defined as meaning, "they have sinned against the LORD" (50:7).[20] When Jesus first sends his disciples out on a training mission, he does not allow them to go to the Gentiles or to the Samaritans but tells them to "go rather to the lost sheep of the house of Israel" (Mt 10:6; 15:24; 18:11-12). Probably the most well known use of the figure of lostness comes in Luke 15 when Jesus describes the lost sheep, the lost coin and the lost sons. Even though one might have a hundred sheep, says Jesus, who, "if he has lost one of them, does not leave the ninety-nine in the wilderness, and go after the one which is lost" (Lk 15:4). In like manner the prodigal son, who went into a far country, is also described as one who was lost when he was away from his home (15:24, 32). This powerful story is obviously a case of mixing metaphors, as the story of the prodigal son is told in both family and pastoral categories.[21]

Sin in the pastoral category then implies going astray, getting lost, or being in a state of lostness. The implications of being lost are theologically significant. It means that the individual like a sheep is separated from the Shepherd and therefore is separated from his leading, provision, care and protection. Without the care and protection of the Shepherd, the sheep is clearly in danger, and if it continues to be lost, it is open to the threat of death. So the language of lostness is a very apt description of the impact of sin on the individual's life.

[19]For further discussion of *planaō* (πλανάω), "going astray," see *TDNT*, 6:228-53.
[20]See also Ezek 34:6. Cf. Jer 50:17 where they are described as "hunted sheep."
[21]On sin as being lost see *BDT*, pp. 322-23; Werner Georg Kummel, *Theology of the New Testament* (Nashville: Abingdon, 1973), pp. 288-91; Alfred Plummer, *A Critical Exegetical Commentary on the Gospel According to St. Luke* (Edinburgh: T & T Clark, 1922), pp. 368-72, 376-7; *TDNT*, 1:394-96.

Salvation

Being found. If sin is described in the pastoral category in terms of going astray and being lost, then salvation is described as being found or rescued by the Shepherd. If one is lost in the wilderness, Jesus assures us that the Shepherd will leave the rest of the sheep and "go after the one which is lost, until he finds it." Upon finding the lost one he calls together his neighbors to rejoice, "for I have found my sheep which was lost" (Lk 15:4-6). Jesus indicates that to be found is like the sinner "who repents" of his sins (15:7), and it is Jesus himself who is the one who "came to save the lost" (Mt 18:11 mg.). When Zacchaeus repents and turns toward God as an example of one who has been lost, Jesus declares, "Today salvation has come to this house." Then he describes his shepherd role in redemption when he says, "the Son of man came to seek and to save the lost" (Lk 19:9-10).[22]

Following the Lord. The pastoral role also describes salvation in terms of following the Lord. Elijah challenges Israel on this issue on Mount Carmel. "How long will you go limping with two different opinions? If the LORD is God, follow him; but if Baal, then follow him" (1 Kings 18:21). Along with the call to follow after the Lord, Elijah also provides us with a model of a disciple following his teacher. When Elisha begins to follow him, Elijah is then able to train him for ministry (19:19-21). Indeed this pattern serves as a background for understanding how disciples start to follow Jesus, beginning with John the Baptist's disciples who are pointed toward Jesus by John. On being told that he is "the Lamb of God . . . they followed Jesus" (Jn 1:36-37). Jesus at the beginning of his ministry commands those who would be his disciples to "follow me" (Jn 1:43; Mt 4:19; Mk 1:17), at which point they "left everything and followed him" (Lk 5:11; Mk 1:20; Mt 4:22). The command to follow is also given to others who would be his disciples, including such figures as the reluctant follower (Mt 8:21-22), Matthew, the tax collector (Mt 9:9; Mk 2:14; Lk 5:27-28), and the rich young ruler (Mt 19:21; Mk 10:21; Lk 18:22). Unfortunately, not all respond to his challenge.

There are several references to following Jesus that go beyond an initial decision and have to do with a continued following and obedience that represent growth in grace, a total following that involves entire sanctification, and a full following in total obedience that represents growth after sanctification. But the

---

[22]For further discussion see Norvel Geldenhuys, *Luke* (London: Marshall, Morgan & Scott, 1950), pp. 401-3, 405-13.

above references seem to refer primarily to the beginning of certain relationships to Jesus and, therefore, relate in particular to the concept of initial salvation. These situations represent circumstances in which people actually begin to follow Jesus or circumstances where Jesus commands them to begin to follow him in this way.[23]

Example theory of the atonement. Some passages of Scripture have an emphasis on the work of Jesus on the cross as an example for people to follow. This, to some degree, relates the example theory of the atonement to following after God as the good Shepherd. So Peter writes, "For to this you have been called, because Christ also suffered for you, leaving you an example, that you should follow in his steps" (1 Pet 2:21). In the same paragraph Peter indicates how people like sheep need to respond to Jesus as the Shepherd. "For you were straying like sheep, but have now returned to the Shepherd and Guardian of your souls" (2:25). Between these two verses Peter also connects relating to Jesus in this way with his death on the cross. "He himself bore our sins in his body on the tree, that we might die to sin and live to righteousness" (2:24).

While there is an emphasis here on following the example of Jesus who suffered and gave his life for others, this subjective responsibility on the part of those responding to Jesus is matched with the more objective statement about Christ bearing our sins in his body. The objective dimension of the change in our relationship to God is stressed in the middle of challenge for people to follow after Jesus as our example. The holding together of both the objective and subjective dimensions of this phase of the atonement is one of the crucial differences between the biblical perspective and the example theory of Faustus Socinus and others.[24]

Initial rest. The concept of saving grace in the pastoral category may also be described in terms of an initial rest in one's relationship to the Lord. Rest for the animals is one of the things that a Shepherd provides. In like manner Jesus invites people to himself in order that he might give them rest. "Come to me, all

---

[23]For further discussion of *akoloutheō* (ἀκολουθέω), "I follow" Christ, see *BTLNT,* pp. 79-82; *TDNT,* 1:210-16; Vincent Taylor, *The Gospel According to St. Mark* (London: Macmillan, 1952), pp. 169-381; Earnest Best, *Following Jesus: Discipleship in the Gospel of Mark* (Sheffield: University of Sheffield Press, 1981), pp. 31-39; *NIDNTT,* 1:480-83.

[24]See earlier discussion of the role of example in the moral influence theory in chap. 8. Often example theories of the atonement are seen as variations of the moral influence theory. H. Orton Wiley, *Christian Theology* (Kansas City, Mo.: Beacon Hill, 1941), 2:259-66. See also Louis Berkhof, *Systematic Theology* (Edinburgh: Banner of Truth, 1958), pp. 387-88.

who labor and are heavy laden, and I will give you rest. Take my yoke upon you, and learn from me; for I am gentle and lowly in heart, and you will find rest for your souls. For my yoke is easy, and my burden is light" (Mt 11:28-30).[25]

Growth in Christian Experience

Following. The whole concept of living in an experience of grace is described as a continual following of the Lord in obedience. God calls people to begin following him, but he also expects them to continue to follow him. This pattern is established early in the monarchy, when Samuel warns both people and king that it will be necessary for them to "follow the LORD your God" if it is to be well with them (1 Sam 12:14). By this he certainly means an ongoing walk in faithfulness to God's commandments. God describes David as one "who kept my commandments, and followed me with all his heart, doing only that which was right in my eyes" (1 Kings 14:8). So when David describes his own thirsting and longing for God, he declares, "My soul followeth hard after thee" (Ps 63:1, 8 KJV).

In the New Testament it is this ongoing following of Jesus that is described in John 10: "When he has brought out all his own, he goes before them, and the sheep follow him, for they know his voice" (Jn 10:4). Of particular significance is the close relationship between the Shepherd and the sheep. The sheep know the voice of the Shepherd and for this reason will follow him but not the voice of a stranger. To know the voice of the Shepherd, however, requires a period of time. The point of the analogy for disciples in particular is the necessity of developing intimacy with the One whom they are following. There is an intimacy of knowing, hearing and understanding his voice and direction for life that is available for those who are following Jesus closely.

Conditional element: Trust. Particularly significant is the use of the present tenses of the verbs that indicate a continuous or habitual action in reference to Jesus' statement, "My sheep hear my voice, and I know them, and they follow me" (Jn 10:27). Continuing to be his sheep is related to continually hearing his voice and following in obedience. For those who meet these conditions, Jesus provides the tremendous promise of security. "And I give them eternal life, and they shall never perish, and no one shall snatch them out of my hand" (10:28).

---

[25]For further discussion of initial rest see *TWB*, p. 192; B. F. Westcott, *The Epistle to the Hebrews* (New York: Macmillan, 1906), pp. 92, 94.

But the security he promises is based on continually hearing his voice, cultivating a close personal relationship with him and following him. Implied in all three of these conditional elements in John 10:27 is the underlying assumption of faith. Because they trust the shepherd, they continue to listen to his voice, cultivate their "knowing" him, and follow him. Faith which leads to obedience provides protection from any outside force that might otherwise destroy them. Westcott rightly observes:

> If any man falls at any stage in his spiritual life, it is not from want of divine grace, nor from the overwhelming power of adversaries, but from his neglect to use that which he may or may not use. We cannot be protected against ourselves in spite of ourselves. He who ceases to hear and to follow is thereby shown to be no true believer.[26]

The incident of Jesus' confrontation with the rich young ruler provides a graphic contrast between those who refuse Jesus' invitation to follow him and those who have chosen to do so. Jesus challenges the young man to sell what he has, give it away (and by so doing indicate his choice to trust in God rather than in his possessions) and follow him. The young man chooses to continue to place his faith in himself and his possessions and so refuses Jesus' invitation. At this point Jesus explains how difficult it is for wealthy people to put their trust in God and not in their possessions. Peter points out that he and the other disciples "have left everything and followed you" (Mk 10:28). By an act of trust they began to follow Jesus and left behind their businesses, professions, and possessions (Mk 1:18, 20; Lk 5:11). According to Jesus, God will reward this kind of faithful following by providing in this world houses, family and possessions as they are needed. He also promises eternal life and additional rewards in the age to come (Mk 10:29-30; Mt 19:28-29; Lk 18:28). Those who have continued to follow Jesus will certainly be rewarded for their faithfulness.

Walking in light. Jesus also makes a connection between following him and walking in the light. "I am the light of the world; he who follows me will not walk in darkness, but will have the light of life" (Jn 8:12). Because Jesus is the light of the world, those who follow him will continue to walk in this light. This has to do with all aspects of life under Jesus' direction and not just with the initial giving of light and life. In the same passage in which Peter designates Jesus as "the

---

[26]Westcott, *St. John*, p. 158.

Shepherd and Guardian of your souls," he talks about a willingness to follow Jesus even if it means suffering. "For to this you have been called, because Christ also suffered for you, leaving you an example, that you should follow in his steps" (1 Pet 2:25, 21). He knows through firsthand experience that there is a cost to continually following Jesus. There will be some emotional, psychological and possibly even physical suffering for those who are determined to continue following Jesus. Perhaps Peter remembered Jesus' promise to those who followed him that they will receive in due time honor, family, lands, "with persecutions" (Mk 10:30).

The Church

Old Testament. The people of God in Israel are sometimes described as his flock. God is praised as one who "didst lead thy people like a flock"(Ps 77:20; 78:52; 80:1). With the Shepherd/sheep analogy controlling this understanding of the church, God is described in pastoral language."He will feed his flock like a shepherd, he will gather the lambs in his arms, he will carry them in his bosom, and gently lead those that are with young" (Is 40:11).

God's own role over the church as his flock is to seek those who are lost and bring them into the flock, to rescue those who have strayed, to gather those who are scattered, to feed those who are hungry, to bind up those with wounds, and to watch over those who need protection (Ezek 34:11-16; cf. Jer 10:21; 23:2). While God intends to perform this role himself as the Shepherd (Ezek 34:11-12, 15), there is also the promise of a coming Messiah, a servant like David, who will fill the Shepherd role for God's people (Ezek 34:23). The picture is one of God meeting basic needs for his people who are called to follow him.

New Testament. Jesus picks up on this figure of speech by describing his disciples as "a little flock" (Lk 12:32). When he refers to himself as the Good Shepherd, his followers are then collectively described as his flock (Jn 10:11-17). His resurrection instructions to Peter emphasize that a leadership role carries special responsibility for feeding and tending the sheep who belonged to Jesus (21:15-17). Peter understands this function and in turn challenges other elders in spiritual leadership to "tend the flock of God that is in your charge." They are to not do this because they are forced nor out of mercenary motives but rather they are exhorted to "be examples to the flock" (1 Pet 5:2-3).

This is the same set of instructions Paul gives to the elders at Ephesus when he exhorts them, "take heed . . . to all the flock, in which the Holy Spirit has made you guardians, to feed the church of the Lord which he obtained with his own blood." If feeding is one of their major responsibilities, a second is protection of the flock from the outside forces that would devour it. Paul warns the elders, "I know that after my departure fierce wolves will come in among you, not sparing the flock"(Acts 20:28-29).

The role of spiritual leadership over the flock as shepherds has a significant Old Testament history. The shepherds of Israel are chastised by God in very strong terms for their failure to feed and care for the church as the flock of God (Jer 23:1-2; Ezek 34:1-10). So a shepherd role in both Old and New Testament becomes a very significant model for the spiritual care and nurture that leaders are to exercise over the church of God. It is this figure of speech of course that has become so descriptive of what is often known as pastoral ministry.

Full Sanctification

Total following. Full sanctification in the category of the Shepherd's role may be described as a total or full following of the Lord. It represents a total willingness to follow wherever God leads and is based on a total trust in God as the Shepherd who knows best. Two examples from Scripture of those who are described in this way are Caleb and Joshua. They both show a complete willingness to follow God's leading into the land of Canaan at their initial approach to the Promised Land. The ten other spies caution the people to withdraw and turn back from following the Lord. But God singles out Caleb because "he has a different spirit and has followed me fully" (Num 14:24; Deut 1:36; Josh 14:14). Joshua is coupled with Caleb in this matter, "for they have wholly followed the LORD" (Num 32:12). This is Joshua's own testimony some years later when he contrasts his heart with the heart of the ten spies. "Yet I wholly followed the LORD my God" (Josh 14:8).

This kind of total following of the Lord is not only based on complete trust of the Lord but leads to a willingness to lay down one's own life in obedience to the Lord's direction if this should be necessary. It is this total trust in God that leads to a total willingness to obey God at whatever price that distinguishes Joshua and Caleb from their contemporaries.

In the New Testament this kind of whole-hearted following of the Lord is seen in Jesus' challenge to the disciples after they have been following him for a period of time. It first appears in his charge to the Twelve as he sends them out in ministry. At the close of his instructions he lays before them the cost of being his disciples in the world in terms of their willingness to love him more than any member of their family or even their own lives. "He who loves father or mother more than me is not worthy of me; and he who loves son or daughter more than me is not worthy of me; and he who does not take his cross and follow me is not worthy of me. He who finds his life will lose it, and he who loses his life for my sake will find it" (Mt 10:37-39). Jesus is asking for a devotion that makes love for him more important than the most important human relationships, and even more important than keeping or protecting one's own life.

Following to death. Jesus sets a very similar challenge before the disciples after they confess him as the Messiah, the Son of the living God at Caesarea Philippi (Mt 16:13-17). Once they have made their confession of faith, Jesus describes to them for the first time in significant measure his own death on the cross. In the light of this impending threat of death and his own willingness to lay down his life for the world, Jesus exhorts his disciples, "If any man would come after me, let him deny himself and take up his cross and follow me. For whoever would save his life will lose it, and whoever loses his life for my sake will find it" (Mt 16:24-25). Now that Jesus has begun to talk about the cross in his own life, he also begins to talk about it in a significant way for the disciples. A new dimension of self-denial is now added to the picture of following him. Self-denial is not merely doing without certain things but rather a surrender of one's self-will to the total will of God so that he has full control of one's life. This will be expressed in a willingness to follow God completely in whatever he asks, which may mean taking up the cross and giving up one's life. Jesus is laying before his disciples at this point a standard that involves a deeper level of following than they have known before this. Although the disciples themselves have not yet experienced this level of total self-denial and willingness to die, Jesus is setting before them the kind of following of himself he would like to see.

This same standard is placed before the disciples again at the very end of Jesus' time with them. At this point Jesus describes his own impending death on the cross when he says to the Twelve, "Truly, truly, I say to you, unless a grain of wheat falls into the earth and dies, it remains alone; but if it dies, it bears much fruit. He who loves his life loses it, and he who hates his life in this world will keep it for eternal life" (Jn 12:24-25). Jesus is about to die and bear much fruit, and he desires to draw disciples after him who will also be willing to totally follow him in his willingness to lay down his life for God. So he concludes, "If any one serves me, he must follow me" (12:26). Jesus is clearly looking for servants who are willing to follow him totally in his willingness to lay down his life for God. Just where the disciples are in relation to this challenge is illustrated in Peter's remarks to Jesus on their last night together. When Jesus says to him, "Where I am going you cannot follow me now; but you shall follow me afterward," Peter responds, "Lord, why cannot I follow you now? I will lay down my life for you" (13:36-37). Jesus is after a complete willingness to follow him even in death, and Peter proclaims his readiness to do this. However, Jesus knows Peter's heart better than Peter does, and he knows that before the night is over Peter will deny his Lord three times. Peter is not yet ready to fully follow Jesus in laying down his life. There is still some protection of himself and a willingness to preserve his own life that prevents Peter from totally following. But Jesus is preparing Peter to understand his own need, so that in due course he might be able to fully follow as the Lord desires.

John also records the final occasion in which Jesus lays this challenge of total following before Peter and indirectly before the rest of the disciples. It is during their breakfast beside the Sea of Galilee when Jesus asks Peter three times, "Do you love me?" (21:15-17). Jesus' question indicates his desire for a kind of love for him that is greater than Peter's self-love, greater than his love for his profession and possessions. He then speaks to Peter about how his death will also glorify God and "after this he said to him, 'Follow me'" (21:19, 22). This kind of following may involve martyrdom, but it certainly involves a self-surrender of one's own will to do the whole will of God.[27]

The Gospel record certainly indicates that none of the disciples reaches the place of total following of Jesus during his earthly time with them. It is only after an experience of the infilling of the Holy Spirit on the day of Pentecost that they are empowered to follow him in this full way. But after Pentecost it becomes evident that their love for Jesus is far greater than their love for any other human relationship, possession or profession, and that they are willing to lay down their lives for him and pay whatever price is necessary to serve him. So all the

---

[27]On a total following of Jesus that involves denying one's self and living a life of self-sacrifice, see Barrett, *St. John*, p. 487; Plummer, *St. John*, p. 253; Westcott, *St. John*, pp. 181-304.

challenges Jesus puts before the disciples in terms of totally following him using
the language of a shepherd are found in the Gospels, but the application of them
in the lives of the disciples in terms of actually following him in this way
(although without the similar pastoral vocabulary to describe it) are not found
until after the day of Pentecost.

Rest of faith. Full sanctification as described in the pastoral figure is also
called a rest of faith. In the Old Testament the experience of the exodus in
Israel's life and the experience of the conquest become types of the kind of
spiritual experience God wants to see in each of his people. The exodus
becomes symbolic of the deliverance of conversion, and the conquest
represents that deeper experience of the fullness of God's blessing and is
related to full sanctification. God not only redeems his people from spiritual as
well as physical bondage, but he also gives them his best, as symbolized by the
land of Canaan.[28] Oftentimes this conquest experience is described in terms of
the rest of the Lord. Thus, the Lord promises to Moses, "My presence will go
with you, and I will give you rest" (Ex 33:14). The same promise is reiterated
to Joshua just before he leads the children of Israel into the Land of Canaan.
"The Lord your God is providing you a place to rest, and will give you this
land" (Josh 1:13, 15).[29] This is the background behind the Hebrews
description of full sanctification as the rest of faith.

The book of Hebrews indicates the New Testament church understood the
spiritual implications of "the rest" God gave Israel on entering Canaan. Hebrews
is based around two major exhortations. One has to do with holding fast one's
confidence in the Lord and maintaining the spiritual state to which one has
attained (e.g., Heb 3:6, 12-14; 4:14). The second exhortation is to press on to a
deeper experience that involves more of what God has for each believer. One of
the ways this second exhortation is described is in terms of entering into the rest
of God. The writer reminds his readers of Israel's rebellion against the Holy
Spirit in the wilderness, and then explains that because they went astray in their
hearts, God swore in his wrath, "They shall never enter my rest" (3:7-11). But

---

[28]For an excellent discussion of the Exodus/Canaan motif see Laurence W. Wood, *Pentecostal Grace* (Wilmore, Ky.: Francis Asbury, 1980), pp. 19-60.

[29]On the concept of rest see *NBD*, p. 1085; *BTLNT*, pp. 826-29; *TDNT*, 1:350-51; *TDNT*, 3:627-28; *NIDNTT*, 3:254-58; *EBT*, 2:748ff.; Gerhard von Rad, "There Remains Still a Rest for the People of God: An Investigation of a Biblical Conception," in *The Problem of the Hexateuch and Other Essays* (New York: McGraw-Hill, 1966), pp. 94-102.

rest was available to the people of God, and Hebrews uses this in spiritual categories as well as physical. "Therefore, while the promise of entering his rest remains, let us fear lest any of you be judged to have failed to reach it" (4:1). At one point the writer describes this state as a Sabbath rest. "So then, there remains a Sabbath rest for the people of God; for whoever enters God's rest also ceases from his labors as God did from his" (4:9-10).

The secret for entering into this state of rest is faith leading to obedience. Some did not enter into the physical rest of the land of Canaan because they did not believe, and disbelief led to disobedience. "For good news came to us just as to them; but the message which they heard did not benefit them, because it did not meet with faith in the hearers. For we who have believed enter that rest" (Heb 4:2-3). So Hebrews exhorts the believers, "Let us therefore strive to enter that rest, that no one fall by the same sort of disobedience" (4:11, 6). This experience certainly constitutes a deeper level of Christian experience for those who have been redeemed by grace, and it is based on a deeper trust and a fuller obedience to God.[30]

The theological implications of the concept of rest have to do with the enjoyment of the fullness of God's blessings. A sheep at rest enjoys the place to which he has been led by a shepherd, as well as the provision of his basic needs and a protection from threatening danger. Spiritually, the rest of faith means an enjoyment of the wholeness of God's blessings in terms of full sanctification. It involves a delight in God's leading, a contentment with the circumstances in which one finds oneself, an enjoyment of God's provisions in multiple areas (physical, emotional, spiritual, social) and a place of protection from the forces of evil. Spiritual rest particularly implies contentment and delight in the best that God has to offer.

It is important to notice that this deeper relationship with God is a rest of faith. It involves a deeper level of trust in the shepherd with regard to where he is leading, what he has provided and his protection from danger. Living in this state of rest involves a cessation of labor in the sense that one is not wrestling in order to achieve his own self will but is content with the will of God. He is like one who is content with where God leads and with what God provides because

---

[30]On the concept of rest of faith see Wood, *Pentecostal Grace*, pp. 47-49; Westcott, *Hebrews*, pp. 92, 94-100; Franz Delitzch, *Hebrews* (Grand Rapids, Mich.: Eerdmans, 1952); 1:186-87, 192-202; H. Orton Wiley, *Hebrews* (Kansas City, Mo.: Beacon Hill, 1959), pp. 121-40; John Owen, *An Exposition to the Epistle to the Hebrews* (Edinburgh: J. Ritchie, 1812), p. 63; see also *NIDNTT*, 11:207-57.

of his confidence that ultimately God knows best. At heart it is again a faith matter. Out of this deeper trust in God comes contentment with life and with God's provisions, and a delight in the fullness of all God gives. It is all a part of God's plan to give his people his best.

Further Growth

Ongoing following. Growth following full sanctification may be understood as a continued following in complete obedience. It is closely bound up to the growth after conversion but seems to contain a power for a fuller measure of obedience to God's leading. This ongoing total following is the import of Jesus' challenge to his disciples, "If any man would come after me, let him deny himself and take up his cross and follow me" (Mt 16:24). In this exhortation there is a definiteness about his call to his disciples to "deny" themselves as indicated by the use of the aorist imperative. But the "follow me" is in the present imperative and suggests an ongoing or continual act of following him. We have seen that the deeper following of Jesus has its roots in the surrender of one's self-will in order to totally follow the will of God. This complete following must have a beginning, but built into the concept of following is the continuous process of growing. It is this ongoing following and total obedience that provides the context for further growth after the experience of full sanctification. The same kind of continued walk in full obedience is also implied in Jesus' other commands to believing disciples to follow him (Jn 12:26; 13:36; 21:19, 22).

Glorification

Following the Lamb. Glorification in this pastoral category is also related to following Jesus, but this time it is in terms of the second coming. Revelation describes the picture of the Lamb standing on Mount Zion with 144,000 from the tribes of Israel who have his name and the name of the Father written on their foreheads. These are those "who had been redeemed from the earth," and "it is these who follow the Lamb wherever he goes" (Rev 14:1, 3-4). Here we get a picture of Jesus as the eschatological Lamb who is returning to earth and of the redeemed who are continuing to follow him.[31]

Separation of sheep from goats. Related to the second coming is the picture of

---

[31]On Jesus as the eschatological lamb see Morris, *Apostolic Preaching of the Cross*, pp. 136-39; *EDT,* pp. 618-19.

Jesus in the final judgment who will gather all the nations before him and separate them from one another "as a shepherd separates the sheep from the goats" (Mt 25:32). Jesus as the Shepherd will bring the sheep into the inheritance of his Father and into his final kingdom because of their works that were done as an expression of their faith. But the goats, whose faith did not lead to works, are excluded to eternal punishment. In the scene of this final judgment there is clearly a mixture of the pastoral categories with those of the royal court, the family and the courtroom. Nevertheless, the shepherd metaphor is one of the significant ways in which the final judgment is described.

Final rest. Related to those who are judged by their works as an expression of their faith is the description of a final rest of the redeemed from their service of God. In John's vision he hears a voice from heaven saying, "'Write this: Blessed are the dead who die in the Lord henceforth.' 'Blessed indeed', says the Spirit, 'that they may rest from their labors, for their deeds follow them!' " (Rev 14:13). For those who have followed the Lord in obedience and served him well there will come a final "rest from their labors" as a part of their eternal reward.[32]

Attributes of God

Goodness. According to Jesus the focus of all goodness is in the being of God. In the primary sense of the word, God and God only is good. Jesus' statement to the rich young ruler that "only one is good, God" makes it clear that the character of God is the only standard that should determine any human notions of goodness (Mk 10:17; Mt 19:17).[33] Jesus' statement must be understood against the frequent reference in the Old Testament to the goodness of God. So the prophets declare that "the Lord is good;" therefore, everyone needs to give thanks unto him (Jer 33:11; Nahum 1:7). The psalmist also rejoices that he shall "see the goodness of the Lord in the land of the living!" (Ps 27:13). This goodness is manifested especially in behalf of those who fear the Lord. "Oh how abundant is Thy goodness, which Thou hast laid up for those who fear Thee" (Ps 31:19). The psalmist in particular repeatedly exhorts people to praise and give thanks to God "for he is good: for his mercy endures forever" (Ps 105:1; 107:1; 118:1; 136:1).[34]

---

[32]For further discussion of the final rest see *TDNT,* 1:350.
[33]Guthrie, *New Testament Theology,* p. 108.
[34]NBD, p. 482.

The basic Old Testament word for good is *tob* (טוֹב), meaning "pleasant, joyful, agreeable," which primarily indicates that which gratifies the senses and in a secondary sense gives aesthetic or moral satisfaction.[35] The LXX and the New Testament render *tob* by the Greek word *agathos* (ἀγαθός), meaning good as a physical or moral quality and occasionally by *kalos* (καλός), which more often means good as beautiful, noble, honorable, admirable, or worthy.[36] The focus on this goodness as applied to God has to do with beneficence and generosity. It represents the disposition of God to keep on giving to others with no mercenary motive or on the basis of what the recipients deserve, but it is simply a desire to provide that which others need and that which brings them delight and happiness.[37]

In a theological sense the goodness of God is sometimes related to a cluster of his moral perfections or attributes. This use is illustrated when God promises to make all his goodness pass before Moses (Ex 33:19). When this happens the resultant proclamation is, "The LORD, the LORD, a God merciful and gracious, slow to anger, in faithfulness, keeping steadfast love for thousands, forgiving iniquity and transgression and sin" (34:6-7). All these moral qualities of God's character are revealed to Moses as closely bound up with his goodness.

Relation to other roles. The goodness of God is expressed in relationship to several of the roles of God that we have already discussed. Thus as the Creator, it is God who makes all things good, i.e., according to his nature and plan for the world (Gen 1:4, 10, 12, 18, 21, 25). His goodness is particularly revealed in making man and woman in his own image and likeness, and when he has finished, his conclusion about them as well as the rest of the creation is that "it was very good" (Gen 1:31). Persons in particular are good because they are made like the goodness of God.

In the priestly category we frequently find the goodness of God expressed in terms of mercy, forgiveness, steadfast love and graciousness. "For Thou, O LORD, are good and forgiving" (Ps 86:5; 25:6-8). "O give thanks to the LORD, for he is good; for his steadfast love endures forever!" (25:7; 100:5; 106:1; 107:1;

---

[35]On *tob* as goodness see *TDNT*, 1:13-15; *TWOT*, 1:345-46.

[36]For further discussion of *agathos* and *kalos* see *TDNT*, 1:10-18; *TDNT*, 3:536-56; *BTLNT*, pp. 3-6, 339-42; *NIDNTT*, 2:98-105; B. B. Warfield, "The New Testament Terminology of 'Redemption,'" *PTR* 22 (1914): 177-228.

[37]*NBD*, p. 481; J. I. Packer, *Knowing God* (Downers Grove, Ill.: InterVarsity Press, 1970), pp. 146-47.

118:29; 136:1). "Praise the LORD, for the LORD is good; sing to his name for he is gracious!" (135:3). In the legal category where God is pictured primarily as a Judge, we often see the good identified with the right.

In the family figure of speech it is God as a Father who continually gives a multitude of things to his children. Thus Jesus can remark, "If you then, who are evil, know how to give good gifts to your children, how much more will your Father who is in heaven give good things to those who ask him!" (Mt 7:11). But it is in the shepherd metaphor that God's goodness seems to receive a special accent. It is his goodness as benevolence and generosity that is expressed toward his people in shepherd-like activity. Thus his goodness is behind his leading and giving guidance, his protection of his people, his provision of their physical, emotional and spiritual needs, and his general care for wounds or hurts. It is out of the goodness of his being that God as a Shepherd keeps giving of himself in these ways to those who are his sheep.

Goodness, love and holiness. The goodness of God is often overlapped with his love. Some prefer to discuss this in terms of God's love being expressed in goodness toward his people. Others reverse the order and speak of God's basic goodness of character that is expressed in a love relationship with his people. Better than either of these options is the concept of holiness being the basic essential character of God that is expressed in these two ways that often overlap each other. It is God's holiness that produces love which is often expressed in goodness. But holiness also is expressed in terms of goodness, which in its application has to do with loving human relationships. It would seem that seeing both love and goodness as two closely related expressions of moral holiness provides the best understanding for the distinctness of each while both are closely related to the essential character of God.[38]

Conclusion

David, himself a shepherd, summarizes God's history of leading and caring for Israel by describing him as a Shepherd (Ps 23). The prophets pick up on this fig-

---

[38]On the goodness of God see *TDNT*, 1:15-16; *EDT*, p. 470; *NBD*, pp. 481-82; Packer, *Knowing God*, pp. 145-48; Paul Heinisch, *Theology of the Old Testament*, trans. William G. Heidt (St. Paul: North Central Press, 1955), pp. 89-90; Guthrie, *New Testament Theology*, p. 108; Charles Hodge, *Systematic Theology* (London: James Clark, 1960), 1:427-36; B. B. Warfield, *The Person and the Work of Christ*, ed. Samuel G. Cra (Philadelphia: Presbyterian & Reformed, 1950), pp. 149ff.; CD 2/2, pp. 208-32.

ure and depict Messiah as the coming Shepherd (Jer 23; Ezek 34). Jesus identifies himself with this description as he elaborates on his role as the Good Shepherd. The role of Shepherd accents God's care for each believer: giving direction, provision protection and nurture. This personal accent brings theological focus to God's holiness as goodness in its expression as care for people, either as a nation or as individuals. Likewise, God's holiness is expressed in the self-giving care exchanged among the Trinity. God as Shepherd sets the standard for the care spiritual leaders are to extend to God's people as his flock.

Eleven

The Implications
of Roles

What God Is Doing with Multiple Roles

Making himself known. There are many ways to understand the holy God who reveals himself in Scripture. In his revelation God has chosen to make himself known in a number of significant roles in order that we might understand the fullness of his being and character. God is a supranatural being and is faced with a problem of revealing his own nature to those who are part of his created order. The natural world does not have perceptive powers to comprehend the supranatural world in the abstract. Therefore, God has condescended to make himself known in categories that are familiar to us within our own world. This involves the use of comparisons or metaphors as a teaching vehicle, and it makes it possible for God to explain the unknown in terms of the familiar. God uses our world and our experience to tell us about himself.

Thus people know from their own experience something of what it is to make and create things. Most people know about kings or political rulers. Everyone understands something of personal relationships, such as what it means to be or have a friend, and all have had teachers in some area of life. The priestly function of those who are intermediaries between ourselves and others is not unfamiliar to most, and almost all understand the role of a lawmaker and a judge.

The role of a father is probably the most universal in the experience of everyone. Most know about the world of slavery and freedom and what it means to have someone set free, and the picture of the shepherd looking after his sheep is a figure easily recognized. So God has chosen from the common everyday experiences of the vast majority of people certain figures of speech by which he chooses to reveal his own person and character.

Using general and special revelation. Because these roles of God are taken from general experience, we should understand their explication in Scripture to be special revelation's complement to what God has also revealed by general revelation in the world of nature and experience. We see here a good example of the complementariness of special and general revelation. Without special revelation, the roles that we see in general experience are not fully adequate to tell us what God is like, but with special revelation, our general experience of people in these roles does contribute to our understanding of God and the way he works. This is not to say that the description of the roles of God in special revelation is the same or on an equal basis with that of God's making himself known in general revelation, but it is to say that when special revelation in Scripture illuminates general revelation in experience and creation, there is a holistic understanding of God's truth that is very significant. There is a match between the two. It parallels the dual witness required in the Old Testament to confirm a truth.

The fact that God chooses a number of major roles in order to make himself known is important. It means that while he is like all these, he is not to be perfectly identified with any single one of them. He resembles each role in certain respects, but as in the case of most analogies, they cannot be pressed absolutely. For example, God is like a shepherd in many respects, but he is unlike a shepherd in the sense that a shepherd cannot have person-to-person relationships with sheep, while God very clearly desires person-to-person relationships with those who belong to him. So while each role is valuable, each has limits, and no one of them can be made to stand alone or be pressed too far without distorting the full picture of what God is really like.

Why God Uses Multiple Roles

Necessary for knowing God. One of the reasons for God's revealing himself in multiple roles is that if we are to properly relate to him, we must have the whole picture of what he is like. Sometimes people tend to see God in only one or two of the roles and therefore relate to him only in the way that they would relate to the particular figure that God is using to describe himself. A much more holistic understanding of God's character is necessary if one is to properly relate to him as he desires. For example, some relate to God only as a righteous Judge or a sovereign King. The problem with such an approach is that it does not allow for the intimacy and affection that God desires to express toward those who belong to him. The roles of Judge and King must be balanced with the pictures of God's immanence, which we find in his roles as Father and Shepherd.

The reverse is also true. Some try to relate to God only as a loving Father and do not understand his commitment to righteousness as the Lawmaker/Judge. In this case they often try to redefine a loving Father as a permissive parent who makes few or no demands on his children. Again, a false picture of God often leads to a very faulty relationship with him. So if we are going to know him and relate properly to him, this can only be done to its fullest effectiveness when all of the major roles are taken into consideration.

Familiarity with different roles. A second reason why God uses the multiple roles to reveal himself is that certain people are more familiar with certain categories of language than they are with others. Some may be more familiar with kings than shepherds, while others may understand fathers better than a creator. But because these figures are all drawn from the everyday human experience of life, everyone knows, at least to some significant degree, something about several of these categories. By the very nature of their experience people begin to relate to God first in certain roles. They may know him initially as a Father who gives them new life, or as a Judge who declares them not guilty. However, if they are to know him properly and fully, their understanding needs to be expanded to include all of the roles. This means that the teaching ministry of the church is very significant for the education of people to make it possible for them to respond more adequately to God. Some of this teaching may be done before people come into a believing relationship with God. Certainly a great deal more needs to be done after a person establishes a right relationship with him.

Holiness: The Unifying Attribute

Our study has demonstrated that every major role of God is connected with some aspect of his holiness. The strong implication of this is that holiness is the attribute of God that unifies these multiple descriptions of God as well as his other attributes that are closely related to each role. More than any other single characteristic of God's nature, holiness provides for us the unity of God's being. His holiness is at the essence of who he is and what he is like. As such, it ties together more of God's characteristics than any other concept. No wonder he says repeatedly in Scripture, "I am holy" (Lev 11:44; 1 Pet 1:15-16).

Meaning of holiness in the roles. In reviewing the various components of holiness it is evident that this word is pregnant with meaning. In surveying its etymology and usage we have seen that it carries with it six major dimensions: separation, brilliance, righteousness, love, power and goodness. Within each of these six parts of the meaning of holiness we have endeavored to understand how each part relates to the holiness of God and to the holiness he desires in people. The concept of holiness as *separation* focuses first on God's supranatural transcendence of (separation from) the universe as the Creator of all things. Then the focus shifts to God's desire to have a people who are *separated from* the world of things that are unholy and are *separated unto* himself. This holiness as separation includes God's sovereignty and his role as King and Ruler over the universe. It also includes the consecration of people to God in order that they might be separated unto his rule.

The meaning of holiness as *brilliance* relates first to the personal presence of the holy God who makes himself known as Personal Revealer through symbols of glory, fire, and cloud, and also through personal relationships like that of Teacher, Prophet and Friend. This brilliance is a reflection of the immanence of a holy God seeking a holy people to relate to him in an intimate, personal way. Because it is tied to personal, verbal communication, it carries a focus on truth as a significant subcategory of holiness. Not only is God's brilliance expressed in his immanence, but it is also related to his grace. This grace reflects his own purity, as well as his desire to purify his people so that they may be like a holy God. His holy brilliance is revealed in his priestly role as he comes to provide forgiveness and cleansing for his people so they can be a reflection of the grace and purity of his holy character.

Further, the holiness of God is reflected in the concept of *righteousness.* A holy God is righteous, and in his role as Judge he sets a standard for righteous conduct. A people who are to be holy must conform to this standard of righteousness in their behavior and personal relationships. If they are to be holy as he is holy, they will have to be righteous as he is righteous.

The standard of God's righteousness is balanced by the concept of holiness as *love.* A holy God is not only the basis for understanding what is right, but out of him flows an unconditional commitment called love that provides an atmosphere of warmth, acceptance and affirmation for his people. While it is God as a holy Father who most perfectly reflects this love to people, he also desires for his children to reflect his holiness by returning his love completely and loving others as he loves them.

We have seen that the concept of holiness has a dimension of *power* to it. A holy God is a powerful Redeemer and Deliverer of people form the forces of evil, and for those he wants to make holy, he gives them a power to live victoriously over sin and frees them to serve him. Finally, our study has revealed that holiness as *goodness* is a reflection of the basic nature of a holy God who keeps giving both himself and multiple blessings to individuals. The full enjoyment of the goodness of God comes to those who have chosen to follow him like sheep who follow the Good Shepherd.

While holiness has these major aspects to it, holiness cannot be completely identified with any one aspect alone. It is the sum of the parts, and it is not to be perfectly identified with only one or two parts. This should come as a word of caution to those who only identify holiness as separation or as power, and rule out its other dimensions. It is quite popular in some circles to limit holiness to these categories and exclude those that relate to God's personal presence and the moral dimensions of holiness like purity, righteousness, love and goodness. The biblical picture includes all of these, and the entire biblical perspective must be given its proper weight for the development of a truly biblically based theology.

Holiness and other attributes. We have seen that God's holiness ties together these eight major roles. While there are many attributes of God, holiness seems to be the most central of all. It allows for a proper understanding of other major categories that describe God's nature, for example, his sovereignty and his fatherhood. However, none of the other dimensions of his being fully capture the whole scope of each of these roles by which God reveals himself in the same way his holiness does. Further, his holiness seems to be the connecting link between the other attributes of God's being. This is especially obvious in the relationship of holiness to the other moral attributes, viz., grace, purity, righteousness, love, goodness and truth. Yet, it also seems to be true that holiness is the connecting tie behind his absolute and relative attributes. Holiness is that essential essence of the nature of God, that when properly comprehended, makes it possible to understand all of his other attributes. Beginning with his holiness, all the other dimensions of his existence come into a sharper focus, and we understand better how they fit together. Therefore, the centrality of the concept of holiness will have to be given appropriate attention in any significant doctrine of God.

The Overlap of Roles

As we observed at the beginning, these eight roles of God are often interwoven in any single passage of Scripture. Moreover, they "bleed" into one another, i.e., there is significant overlap in many categories with characteristics that pertain to another category. For example, there is a *law-giving, directing* function that pertains to the King as well as the Judge, and sometimes to the Father. While God has a special role as *Revealer* of himself in personal conversation, he obviously is also revealing himself in all of the other seven roles. The whole question of *servanthood* pertains not only to God's role as sovereign King but also to that of the powerful Redeemer. Both a Creator and a Father have a special responsibility for *producing life*, and a Shepherd along with a Father carries certain responsibilities for *protection, provision* and *direction*.

So at many levels of theological inquiry, the roles have significant overlap with one another. This should not surprise us in the light of the fact that there is one God revealing himself behind all of these portraits. It also is an emphatic reminder that none of the roles of God can be seen in isolation from one another. No one role is fully adequate to explain God without the others. In our study we have separated them for purposes of analysis and classification. In the practice of relating to God, they overlap in multiple ways.

Is one role dominant? While no one analogy fully explains God without the others, it is possible to understand one of the roles as more dominant than the others. The criteria that one uses to select a dominant role will, of course, make a difference in the choice. If one makes the selection purely on the basis of quantity of material, then the biblical data that pictures God in person-to-person relationships, like the role of a Personal Revealer, is obviously by far the largest. While God's role as immanent Personal Revealer is very significant, it is the least definite of the eight major roles we have studied. Nevertheless, the personal nature of God is clearly foundational for understanding God and his other roles.

Alternatively, if one begins with the Old Testament and follows the biblical materials as we have them (the *order of knowing*), then it will be possible to see God's role as Creator as dominant. The Scripture opens with a picture of God's work in creation, and it closes with a picture of a new creation. Thus his role as Creator seems to bracket all of the biblical materials. But although it stands at the beginning and the end of the biblical record, it is clearly not the most dominant of God's roles in the rest of the biblical books.

Another major picture of God revealed in the early portions of Scripture is his role as King or Ruler, on the one hand, and his role as Lawmaker and Judge on the other. The overlap between these two roles is very strong, so it is not difficult to see how many have understood the dominant picture of God to be that of a sovereign King and righteous Judge. Yet, if one begins to evaluate the Scripture in its totality, it is not clear at all that these roles are the most theologically dominant. Particularly when one looks at the New Testament, and more specifically at the role that Jesus seems to understand as most significant, then the choice of a predominant role could not be God as either King or Judge.

The best possibility appears to be the picture of God as Father. The Father image dominates the New Testament materials. If the New Testament is to be understood as the fullness of God's revelation, then the significance of this role must be understood in this light. Further, the fact that Jesus relates to God most often in this role makes a strong case that it should be considered the dominant role. The choice of Father as the preeminent role may be related to the fact that by the time we come to the end of the New Testament, we have all of the roles of God in perspective. This means we are in a position to shift from the *order of knowing* (i.e., the unfolding of God's roles in progressive revelation) to an *order of being*, (i.e., what God is in himself before he has made himself known in Scripture). With the full revelation of all of the roles of God in view, two significant things are clear about God. One is that he is a personal being, and two, he is a Father within the triune Godhead. Assuming the foundational role of personhood for understanding the concept of the roles altogether, this means that it is the role of God as Father that seems to be the most dominant of his personal roles. God is a Father before he is a Creator, King, Judge or anything else.[1]

The picture of God as Father is also the only role that adequately encompasses in some measure all of the functions of the other seven roles. Thus, God as a Father gives life. It is not the absolute creation of life as with the Creator, but

---

[1] See Thomas F. Torrance, *The Christian Doctrine of God* (Edinburgh: T & T Clark, 1995), pp. 18-21, 137-41; Walter Kasper, *The God of Jesus Christ*, trans. Matthew J. O'Connell (New York: Crossroad, 1999), pp. 140-47.

as one who begets life. A Father has a ruling and directing function like a King. He communicates person-to-person with his children, and often serves as a teacher and a friend. In the priestly role it is the Father who gives forgiveness and is full of grace. Yet, at the same time he lays down standards and makes judgments as a Lawmaker and a Judge would do. A Father is concerned about freeing his children from the forces of evil, as well as showing them how to serve. Lastly, a Father carries the same responsibility as a Shepherd does in terms of direction, provision, protection and care. Yet a Father does all of these things in a context of loving acceptance and unconditional commitment. So there is a sense in which a Father does in significant measure the things God is pictured doing in all of the other seven roles. None of the other seven may be understood to provide these same functions in quite the same way. So if the choice has to be made of one role carrying prominence over the others, it will clearly have to be the role of God as loving Father.[2]

Essentialness of Roles for Christian Theology

Once it is recognized that a great deal of Christian truth is described in each role category, then it is easier to understand how the various doctrines of Christian theology are built on this multiple terminology. Every area of systematic theology ought to use the biblical language and related concepts from each of the eight major roles. With this method the roles of God serve to show the connections between Old Testament material and New Testament data, and then how both lead into Christian theology. Since the roles appear in both testaments, in relationship to all three Persons of the Trinity, and have implications for all of the doctrines of systematic theology, they become an incredibly valuable connecting link between biblical studies and the doctrines of the church. It is the contention of this book that in fact the roles of God form an ideal unifying factor for a holistic theology that is properly grounded in the biblical materials of both the Old and New Testament. This should assist us in the task of reuniting Old Testament studies, New Testament studies and systematic theology, three disciplines

---

[2]For a reaction to the use of the role of God as Father, and especially as a dominant role (model), see Sallie McFague, *Metaphorical Theology* (Philadelphia: Fortress, 1982), pp. 145-52. For a statement about why the role of God as Father is essential for Christian theology see Colin E. Gunton, "Proteus and Procrustes: A Study in the Dialectic of Language in Disagreement with Sallie McFague," in *Speaking the Christian God*, ed. Alvin F. Kimel Jr. (Grand Rapids, Mich.: Eerdmans, 1992), pp. 74-80.

that have too long been divided. To illustrate how this method would function, let us look at how the data from biblical studies forms the foundation for building a holistic doctrine in Christian theology. Because of their central significance for other parts of systematics, we will illustrate how this procedure, using the data from the roles, could be used for constructing a doctrine of the person of Christ (christology) and then we will see how it would work with the person of the Holy Spirit (pneumatology).

Person of Christ. Christology is connected with the Old Testament by the fact that all of the roles of God revealed under the Old Covenant come to even more vivid expression in the person of Christ. The roles Jesus plays under the New Covenant parallel each of those Yahweh has demonstrated about himself under the Old. By this parallel use of roles for God and for Jesus, the "identity of God" is given fresh meaning and clearer illustration in the life and work of Jesus.[3] In other words, the categories we have for understanding Jesus come from understanding the roles of God already revealed in the Old Testament.

This means there is a natural connection between Old Testament materials and New Testament materials—Jesus is described in every major way in which God has made himself known. Further, because of the unique union of the divine with the human in Jesus (the theandric union), he is able to model these roles by illustrating more clearly who God is and God's design for human beings. Accordingly, in Jesus' case, very often both his divinity and his humanity are described in reference to each role. Since he is the God-man, parts of the language emphasize his supranatural character, while other parts accent his human nature, and in some cases there is overlap between the two. Thus Jesus, in the creation metaphor, is not only the Creator of the cosmos and the reflection of the image of God, but he is also the image of the perfect man. In other roles he has a similar dual designation. He is understood as King over the universe, but he is also the Servant (subject) of God. While he reveals God in personal categories as the Word, he frequently does this as a Prophet and more often as a Teacher. But in his humanity he models friendship with God, cultivating a relationship by listening to him in prayer and being receptive to all God has to say.

In the categories of the sanctuary Jesus serves as a High Priest, while also modeling a perfect sacrifice. His work in this role is further revealed in his

---

[3]Cf. Richard Bauckham, *God Crucified* (Grand Rapids, Mich.: Eerdmans, 1998), pp. 6-13.

activity of interceding for people before the Father. As God he is a Judge in the legal language of Scripture, but he serves as an advocate and witness while also modeling perfect obedience to the law. He is the Son of God as well as the Son of man in the family figure of speech. As divine Redeemer, Jesus is the Savior of the world, but after setting people free from sin and evil, he models for them what it is to be a human servant of God (note the overlap with the role of King). Finally, in his divinity, he is the Good Shepherd, while in his humanity he shows us how to follow God. The overall picture looks like table 11.1.

Table 11.1. Christ in the Different Roles

CHRISTOLOGY

Holiness:	Separation Transcendence	Separation Sovereignty	Brilliance Immanence	Brilliance Purity/Grace	Righteousness	Love	Power	Goodness
Role:	Creator	King	Personal Revealer	Priest	Judge	Father	Redeemer	Shepherd
Christ's Divinity:	Creator, Image of God	King of kings	Word, Teacher, Prophet	High Priest, Mediator	Judge, Advocate	Son of God	Savior	Good Shepherd
Christ's Humanity:	Image of Man	Servant of God	Friend	Perfect Sacrifice, Intercessor	Obedience to law	Son of Man	Servant	Following God

Jesus must be understood in his totality in all of these ways if we are to relate properly to him and let him do for us all he desires to do. Further, there is no holistic Christology without all this data. Any attempt to build a doctrine of the person of Christ without taking into account all these roles will be inadequate and incomplete. Jesus must be known as fully as he came to make God known (Jn 1:18).

The value of using the roles of God to describe the person of Jesus is that it allows us to use all of the traditional language regarding the titles of Jesus that have been so popular in New Testament theology, but it makes it possible to go further. In particular it ties these titles with God the Father and God the Spirit, and also it connects them with the language of the various categories of Christian theology. So the roles have the advantage over titles in that they allow the language of the titles to be seen in a much broader perspective by connecting the person of Jesus with their Old Testament background, while also moving into the theological categories which are related to the language systems. All of this increases the possibility of a much more biblically grounded, holistic Christology.

Person of the Holy Spirit. A parallel case can be made for understanding the Holy Spirit. We cannot see how the Spirit fits into this approach without realizing that one of his major responsibilities is to call attention to the Father and to the Son rather than to himself (Jn 16:13-15). This has led some to observe that the images used of the Spirit are far less noticeable than those of the other two persons of the Trinity. He is sometimes called "the imageless" member, reflecting the fact that the descriptions of the Spirit are certainly less vivid than the way the roles describe both the Father and the Son.

However, an examination of the data reveals that when we focus on the *function* of the Spirit, he works in all eight roles parallel to the Father and the Son. He begins to do this in the Old Testament, where in some ways there is more material about the Spirit as the third person of the Trinity than about the second person. Known usually as the "Spirit of God," he parallels the way God works in all eight roles. This prepares us for the fuller revelation about him in the New Testament. Under the New Covenant it is the work of Jesus that illuminates and gives life to the roles of the Spirit. Just as the incarnation makes more vivid the roles of God the Father (Jn 1:18), so in a parallel way Jesus is making known the roles of the Spirit. To know the second person of the Trinity is a way into knowing the first, and by parallel, is the same way of knowing the third member. In other words, Jesus becomes our key means of highlighting the person and work of God the Father and in the same way he becomes the way in which we know God the Holy Spirit.

The function of the Holy Spirit, then, in connecting the Old and the New Testament materials looks like this. He plays a role as Creator at the opening of Scripture, then as the ruling presence of the Godhead in the lives of believers (King). He is also the Spirit of truth that makes God's revelation possible in this world (Personal Revealer). He intercedes for people (Priest), and he serves as a Counselor and Advocate on behalf of individuals before God (Judge). At the same time he is the agent of the new birth that brings one into the family of God (Father). He is the empowerer of people to serve God (Redeemer) and also the guide that gives direction to the lives of individuals (Shepherd).

A full knowledge of the Spirit's work can only be understood in the light of all these categories. There certainly cannot be a whole biblical doctrine of the Holy Spirit without including the data from each category about who he is and how he works. You cannot develop a pneumatology unless all these perspectives are considered. The totality of revelation throughout the Old and New Testaments must be incorporated in a truly Christian theology of the Spirit (see table 11.2.).

Table 11.2. The Holy Spirit in All the Roles

PNEUMATOLOGY

Holiness:	Separation Transcendence	Separation Sovereignty	Brilliance Immanence	Brilliance Purity/Grace	Righteousness	Love	Power	Goodness
Role:	Creator	King	Personal Revealer	Priest	Judge	Father	Redeemer	Shepherd
Holy Spirit:	Agent of Creation	Executive of Godhead	Spirit of Truth	Intercessor	Advocate	Agent of New Birth	Spirit of Power	Good Spirit
	Eternal Spirit		Spirit of Glory	Spirit of Grace	Counselor	Spirit of Sonship Assurance	Spirit of Freedom	
	Spirit of Life		Spirit of Wisdom	Indwelling Spirit	Witness		Spirit of Might	

The development of systematic theology includes other steps, but it must begin with the correlation of all scriptural materials if it produces biblically grounded doctrine. Once there has been a correlation of all of the data about the person of Christ or the person of the Spirit, then the next task of systematics is to find the unity and coherence of these materials, to understand how the data fit together and what is implied by the language categories and information spelled out in Scripture. It is with this approach that the early church developed the doctrine of the Trinity. It is here that the task of systematics begins to use reason, tradition and experience as tools and secondary sources for the rounding out of the total picture of Christian truth. The final step is to package the whole for presentation to the church and the world in each succeeding generation. Classic Christian theology, however, presupposes that everything begins with a full grasp of the biblical data as it relates to each doctrinal category. While there may be other biblical materials relative to each doctrine, it is the argument of this book that every doctrine must *at least* take into account all of the roles of God as a basis for fleshing out any holistic, biblically grounded Christian theology.

Use of Roles in Knowing God

Once all three persons of the Trinity have been understood within each of the eight major roles discussed, certain implications follow. One is that we have not exhausted everything that the Scripture says about God or about how we relate to him. These eight major roles plus their subroles are not the only metaphors that the Bible uses to describe God. But while there are others, these eight are certainly the major ways in which God has made himself known. Knowledge of God in these categories does not exhaust our understanding of him, but neither is it possible to know him well without some mastery of these portraits. Failure to recognize the identity of God in any one of these categories will place a limit in some significant measure on our understanding and knowledge of him.

A second implication is that knowledge about God is not the same as "knowing him." The reason God has revealed himself in multiple ways is that we might know him in an intimate way. Factual knowledge about the way he works and about his nature is foundational for this purpose, but it is not the end of the process. An understanding of what God is like is designed to lead us to a personal relationship with him. Knowledge about him is supposed to lead to knowing him. Once we know *about* him in each of the eight categories discussed, we must ask if we really *know* him in each of them. While it is possible to understand intellectually each of the metaphors that describe him, do we really relate to him in all eight ways? Theology must relate to the spiritual lives of God's people.

It may be that some deliberate attempt in several less familiar categories will be necessary if one is going to begin to *know* God in the full way that he desires. For example, if we are not used to relating to God as the sovereign Ruler of the universe, we may have to ask ourselves, "In what way do I need to submit to God's authority and direction in my life?" Alternatively, it may be that we are not used to relating to God in a person-to-person manner as one relates to close friends. It may be that some deliberate attempt needs to be made to cultivate our relationship with him in the light of this deeper understanding of what he desires in relating to us.

The key that translates information about God into knowing God is faith. When a proper knowledge about who God is in any of these roles is coupled with a choice to trust him in the ways that role implies, then we begin to know him more fully within that particular role. So understanding God to be King must be coupled with a choice to trust him and let him make the ruling decisions in our lives. An act of faith here will lead to submission to his authority and to a relationship in which he is the ruling Sovereign of the our lives in practice as well as theory. To use another example, when we come to a proper understanding of God as a Priest who desires, on the basis of his grace, to provide mercy and forgiveness, and we couple this understanding with the choice to believe that he will actually do this for us, we may then come before his presence to ask and receive his forgiveness. When we receive his mercy, we then know him in a way we have not known him before. Again, it is faith in God that transforms an understanding of God into an actual relationship with him. This same trust factor is that which changes any of the roles from being just head knowledge into practical, relational experience.

Implications of the Roles for Theology and Ministry

We have already seen how the roles of God connect Old and New Testament materials in a way that lays the foundation for biblically based Christian doctrines like Christology and Pneumatology. We now wish to show how this paradigm functions with several other doctrines of Christian theology. The fact that we are talking about the roles of God throughout Scripture is indicative of a connection between Old and New Testament materials, since in almost all cases, concepts that lead to any doctrine are illustrated from both testaments under each of the roles. The purpose here is to illustrate how a fully biblically based theology must include *at least* this data on any subject (although it may also include other material from Scripture). No doctrine can be adequately developed without taking into account the language and concepts from each of the roles. The summaries that follow form the basis for a holistic, systematic theology on each doctrinal area.

A further task will be to indicate at various points how such a holistic view of each doctrine ought to influence the practice of ministry. Our concern is how a comprehensive understanding of any biblical truth affects the way the church ministers to people. It grows out of a conviction that theology relates to practice, and that what we believe to be true affects how we do ministry to others. It is further related to the concern that theology not be divorced from the spiritual lives of people. God gave us truth so we could properly relate to him and to each other. There must be no separation between the two. On the one hand, we must not allow theology to become an academic discipline without reference to the spiritual lives of individuals in the church. On the other, we must not develop any ministry or attempt spiritual formation of people without a sound doctrinal foundation rooted in a holistic picture of God and our relationship to him. These are never separated in the New Testament church, and they must never be separated for us.

Implications for Man and Woman

For doctrine: Anthropology. There is no full-orbed understanding of the concept of men and women as they are described in Scripture without seeing how they are depicted as relating to God in each one of the major categories discussed. Persons are creatures in the created order, but they are also the only part of creation that is made in the image and likeness of God (Creator). They are able to relate to God in an interpersonal way because of their capacity to reason, imagine, think and make choices by an act of the will. People therefore need to be understood as the climax of creation. They are also servants of the God who rules (King) over the created order, having been given dominion over the earth. Further, they are not just animals, they are made for interpersonal relationships, both in this world and with God (Personal Revealer).

Part of people's desire for a personal relationship with God flows out of their built-in need for forgiveness and their need to worship God (Priest). They are made for righteous living, and therefore they need the standard of God's law to give direction to their lives (Judge). Left on their own, individuals are incomplete and lack the security of direction for life this standard provides.

People are also made for love, and so their most natural habitat is that of the family (Father). They need a few intimate, personal relationships, like that of a family, in order to be able to give and receive love. A person's need for redemption from the bondage of sin and evil is a reality we must recognize before we can properly experience a right relationship with God in any of the other categories (Redeemer). The experience of such redemption results in freedom to serve God. However, freedom from bondage to sin does not remove our dependence on God. Rather, it makes us like sheep in that we need some protection from outside forces. We need provision for basic necessities of life, as well as direction for life (Shepherd). In other words, we are dependent. Basic human needs, arising out of what God made us to be, ought to be understood in relationship to the various biblical categories that describe people in a relationship with God. An overview of these categories appears in table 11.3.

Table 11.3. Man and Woman in Relation to All the Roles

ANTHROPOLOGY

Holiness:	Separation Transcendence	Separation Sovereignty	Brilliance Immanence	Brilliance Purity/Grace	Righteousness	Love	Power	Goodness
Role:	Creator	King	Personal Revealer	Priest	Judge	Father	Redeemer	Shepherd
Man/ Woman:	Creature	Subject	Person	Worshiper	Law-abiding person	Child	Freedman	Sheep
Made:	In the image of God	For living under authority and having dominion over the earth	For interpesonal relations and understanding truth	To worship God, For purity	For righteous living	For maturity, love and family relations	For freedom and service to God	For following and depending

For ministry. A proper anthropology is valuable for ministry, particularly pastoral care, because it gives a picture of what God intends people to be. Because of the drastic impact of sin on people, we tend to see them as broken individuals and sometimes forget that sin is not originally a part of God's created order. Humanness and sinfulness are not to be viewed as identical. A biblical anthropology that tells us how God created man and woman will give us indications both of his desires for us and our needs. It also gives us some goals for ministry to individuals, so that we know what are we trying to help them to be. Some concrete suggestions will illustrate the point.

Since people are made in the moral image of God, then God clearly intends their character to reflect his holiness in terms of righteousness and love. The challenge for us is to design ministry so that people can be re-formed again in the likeness of God, reflecting his holy character in righteous conduct and loving attitudes. Again, the fact that men and women are created to be subjects under the authority of God as King certainly indicates a need for some structure and authority in their lives. Do they have proper biblical authority, or are they submitting themselves to nonbiblical authorities?

Men and women are created as persons and clearly have a need for interpersonal relationships. Is our ministry providing the context where people can be connected with others and enable them to fight off the current cultural emphasis on rugged individualism? Since people are made to be worshipers of God, we must ask if we are providing the proper opportunity for worship. Individuals are made to make choices, to walk in obedience before God and have that obedience reflected in virtuous behavior. In ministry, are we setting before them both a standard and a model of righteous living and providing the structures that will help them make these right choices?

Every individual in their experience of the new birth comes into the family of God as one of his children. Are we providing the chance for them to grow up in this spiritual family and come to a level of maturity where in turn they may reproduce themselves in the spiritual lives of others? Are we providing the close family relationships (e.g., in small groups) that will give the necessary acceptance and encouragement for people to mature in their faith? People are made to be free from the forces of evil, so that they might be able to give themselves to the service of God. Are we providing in our ministry the opportunities for people to serve him? Like sheep, men and women are not only made for following but are clearly dependent on leadership. Are we providing the kind of pastoral care necessary to feed, protect, nurture and heal those under our care?

It may be that all those involved in pastoral ministry need to go through the list of these eight categories to see whether or not in their personal ministry (or the ministry of the church at large) the basic needs of people are being met. The point of the argument here is that without a proper understanding of how God made men and women, there will not be a sound basis for evaluating those needs or making plans to meet them.

Implications for Sin

For doctrine: Hamartiology. Closely bound up with a balanced anthropology is a proper hamartiology or doctrine of sin. Sin has had its effect on the creation, but it has especially impacted people and their relationship with God. Sin has to be understood both as an *act* and as a *state of being*. It is something people *do*, but it is also something that they *are*. It relates to their attitudes and conduct, but also to their nature. Therefore, the scriptural terms to describe sin often relate to both the act and the state of sin in each language figure. Consider the various facets of the meaning of sin when applied in each of the categories already discussed.

After being created by God, Adam uses his power of the will (part of the image of a Creator God), to commit an act of sin against God and thus destroy a right relationship with him. In his Fall he lost the moral image of God and severely marred the natural image of God. He begins to worship the creation (idolatry) more than the Creator. He finds himself in a wrong relationship to God, as well as being subject to a certain subjective impact of sin on his own nature. Consequently, sin may be described as rebellion against God's sovereign authority (King) by the free exercise of one's will. When the Scriptures describe this state of rebelliousness, people are presented as being "stiff-necked." This rebellion or rejection of God results in a broken personal relationship with God (Personal Revealer) and alienation from the personal presence of as well as the enjoyment of fellowship with God. Sin is further defined as an act which "defiles" or "makes unclean," and the resultant state of sin is described as "uncleanness" or "impurity" (Priest).

Another definition of sin as one form of disobedience or transgression is "breaking the law," with the resultant state of being guilty as a lawbreaker before the bar of justice (Judge). Sin as disobedience also occurs in the context of family, but with a more personal overtones (Father). The state of sin in the family of God is loving oneself rather than others. An act of sin may also be described as "yielding to temptation from the power of evil" (Redeemer), and this action can be understood as growing out of a state of enslavement or bondage to sin. Last, sin may be described as "going astray" and "getting lost" the pastoral category, while the state of sin may be seen as a tendency toward waywardness or straying (Shepherd). Any full-orbed picture of sin, both as an act and as a state, must include the language from all these categories if a whole doctrine is to be constructed out of a full biblical base, as illustrated in table 11.4.

The language that describes people indicates the marvelousness of a human being created by God, while the description of sin provides that which can currently be observed as wrong both within persons and in their relationships. The biblical picture in all its fullness is the only adequate explanation for understanding the positive and negative things that may be said about people from the observation of experience. People are good but they are fallen, and biblical categories are crucial for explaining this reality.

Table 11.4. Sin in Relation to All the Roles

HAMARTIOLOGY

Holiness:	Separation Transcendence	Separation Sovereignty	Brilliance Immanence	Brilliance Purity/Grace	Righteousness	Love	Power	Goodness
Role:	Creator	King	Personal Revealer	Priest	Judge	Father	Redeemer	Shepherd
Man/Woman:	Creature	Subject	Person	Worshiper	Law-abiding Person	Child	Servant Freedman	Sheep
Sin, State:	Marred Image	Rebelliousness	Alienation	Uncleanness	Guilt	Self-Love	Bondage	Lostness
Sin, Act:	Idolatry	Rebellion	Rejection	Defilement	Transgression	Disobedience	Yielding	Straying

This biblical perspective provides the only satisfactory explanation that matches life as it exists. It is a realistic view of persons: neither too optimistic ("People are basically good") nor too pessimistic ("People are basically evil"). The Bible always holds two things in tension: people are good because they are made in the image of God, but they are corrupt because of the impact of sin on their lives. The roles help us see the multiple ways these two things are repeatedly described in Scripture.

For ministry. There are very significant ministry implications for under-standing both persons and sin in the multiple categories we have discussed. The ministry of the church must speak to human needs. These needs are only going to be properly understood where there is an adequate understanding of the way God made people, i.e., his original design and purposes for them *and* the way persons currently exist, that is, what their state is as a result of the impact of sin on their lives. So a full understanding of the concepts of persons and sin provides the church a perspective on God's original purposes for people and the problem in which people now live that keeps them from realizing God's best. If ministry to people's needs is going to be adequate, it must take into account God's agenda. This means we need both a full understanding of his original plan and purposes and of the human predicament that keeps people from having what God designed for them. Any other approach will take people in unrealistic directions for which they were not originally made, or it will design solutions to something other than their basic problems.

This dual understanding is valuable for all branches of ministry to human need, but it is especially valuable in certain areas. For example, counseling people must always begin with one eye on what God's purposes are for men and women and the other on the multiple effects of sin on human lives. A counselor who does not understand these two biblical foundations may very well begin dealing with people on the basis of clinical techniques, naturalistic presuppositions or some current psychological theory. Then, even though the counselor may be a committed Christian, there will be no "Christian counseling." The integration of counseling skills with Christian faith must begin with right theology. The roles of God and their eight pictures of people and sin provide just such a basis for this.

The church must keep asking how it can more effectively meet people's needs. Often this begins with "felt needs." Since people have many felt needs, it may be that some needs occur in areas where an individual understands neither the roles of God nor the way God works. Sometimes we must begin with a better understanding of God. God can more fully meet felt needs when people clearly understand who God is in his various roles and how he is able to meet their immediate felt needs. Thus in counseling individuals it will be helpful to expand their picture of what God is like in order that they might allow him to meet the needs in their lives.

Similarly, with regard to the nature of sin, there may be sin in an individual's life that he or she does not fully comprehend. Understanding the manifestations of sin and the ways sin affects life may enable people to allow God to deal with their sin more thoroughly. The solution to sin can only be applied when the problem is understood and when God is seen as having the capacity to deal with it. It is only the God who has revealed himself in multiple ways in Scripture who is big enough to meet the multiple and complex needs of the men and women whom he has created. For example, people will be willing for God (as powerful Redeemer) to set them free from addictive sin only when they understand two things: (1) the full implications of the power of sin and evil that grips their lives and (2) that God is more powerful than any force of evil. Thus a person needs to more fully understand God and sin in order to appropriate God's solution to their problems and allow him to meet their basic needs.

Implications for Salvation

For doctrine: Soteriology. The experience of God's saving grace that reestablishes a right relationship with God and internally changes the nature of individuals is often described by the word *salvation.* This experience is described in each of the biblical roles, and without using every language category we cannot fully understand what God is doing in this experience. This is where we see how a blend of Old and New Testament materials provides a dynamic base for building a doctrine of salvation.

These are the components that must fit together. An individual who is made in the image of God and has had that image marred by sin must be remade or regenerated by a life-giving God (Creator). This subjective experience is matched by a more objective one when God as Sovereign (King) pardons an individual in order that he may enter the kingdom of God. The person then has a new personal relationship with God that may be described as reconciliation or receiving Christ into his life (Personal Revealer).

Salvation also includes the experience of God's forgiveness and initial cleansing (Priest), where one is justified by faith and therefore declared to be just and right before the law of God (Judge). Again, this objective justification is matched by the subjective experience of the new birth, as one is born into the family of God and given new life with a nature resembling that of the Father. Further, people must be delivered from the power of sin, and this experience may be described as redemption or being ransomed from the forces of evil (Redeemer). This is complemented by the pastoral description of a person as being found in his state of lostness (Shepherd).

Thus the description of initial salvation comes sometimes in terms of an objective change that takes place in one's relationship with God, and sometimes in terms of the subjective change that happens internally in the nature of the individual. Both types of changes are essential for understanding all that God does in an experience of saving grace. The full picture of both the objective and subjective experiences may be seen in table 11.5.

Table 11.5. Salvation in Relation to All the Roles

SALVATION

Holiness:	Separation Transcendence	Separation Sovereignty	Brilliance Immanence	Brilliance Purity/Grace	Righteousness	Love	Power	Goodness
Role:	Creator	King	Personal Revealer	Priest	Judge	Father	Redeemer	Shepherd
Sin, Act:	Idolatry	Rebellion	Rejection	Defilement	Transgression	Disobedience	Yielding	Straying
Salvation:	Regeneration Life	Pardon Entering kingdom	Reconciliation Accepting Christ	Forgiveness Cleansing	Justification	New Birth Life	Redemption Ransom Deliverance	Being found

For ministry. The parallel pictures of sin and salvation are valuable for several areas of ministry because they provide a framework for seeing correlations between the human problem (sin) and the divine solution (salvation). These multiple categories are especially relevant in presenting the gospel to nonbelievers in a variety of situations, such as evangelistic preaching and cross-cultural missions. It means the evangelist/missionary/apologist has available at least eight ways to speak to people's felt needs and at least eight ways to offer God's provision to meet those needs in salvation. Any proclaimer of the gospel must try and discern where people are in their sense of need, so he can present saving grace in the manner that most appeals to the listener.

Another reason that God uses the multiple figures of speech to describe himself is that certain categories initially appeal to certain individuals more than others. People can identify more easily with the pictures of God in some roles than they can with others. Some people may come to saving grace because they sense a need of forgiveness and the priestly figure of God is particularly apropos to them. Others may wrestle with guilt in their lives, so God as the righteous Judge, who justifies them and removes guilt, is particularly appealing. Many have never felt it possible to have a personal relationship with God, so that the offer of receiving Christ and living with him as a Friend on a day-by-day basis is very attractive. Those struggling with sinful habits may strongly feel the need of deliverance and a freedom from the power of sin that they know has a hold on their lives, so they respond especially to the picture of God as powerful Redeemer. Others would like to have a fresh start, so the picture of God as Creator who regenerates them or gives a new life is something to which they are strongly drawn.

Certain individuals not only feel the need for a fresh beginning in life but also the need of an atmosphere of love and acceptance in their lives, so the experience of the new birth and becoming a part of the family of God is something that speaks particularly to their life situation. These are very open to the portrait of God as loving Father. Another group knows they have lost direction in their lives, so the picture of being found by God as the Good Shepherd communicates directly to their problem. Finally, those who have rebelled against God and gone their own way may be especially attracted to God as sovereign King who offers pardon and the security of a new life under his rule.

The fact, then, that different language categories speak to different people has significant implications for evangelism, missions and apologetics. Evangelism, for example, may take its starting point from any of these figures. In reality, the presentation of the gospel can be made from all these categories, so that people may respond to that which touches their felt need most immediately. In practice, people's problems are great enough that usually more than one of the categories speaks to some need in their lives. Rare will be the case when it is necessary to present the gospel from eight different directions before it finds a responsive note in the heart of the individual. But it may have to be presented several different ways before a person is ready to respond in faith. This means those doing evangelism need to be prepared for multiple presentations of the gospel in their preaching or personal conversations, and the biblical data on each of the roles gives them the tools for this task.

With slight variations the same is true for cross-cultural presentations of the gospel in missions contexts. A missionary must discern in the culture where he is working what pictures of God are likely to be most readily understood. He must see where people feel needs and so be ready to offer the gospel from the appropriate corresponding role category.

Different cultures are likely to be more responsive to some portraits of God and certain presentations of the gospel than others. Surely this is one reason why God gives us so many. The spiritually sensitive and theologically discerning missionary will seek the guidance of the Holy Spirit as to which is the best way to bring people into a relationship with Jesus Christ. This will be an easier task, however, if he already has at hand the biblical data in these eight major categories from which to present the gospel. Great frustration will result if he only shares salvation in terms that have spoken to his own culture or his personal needs, and this finds an unresponsive audience. "More of the same" will simply not do! But more of the same gospel with different portraits and different language may connect with people's hearts and bring them to salvation. Again, understanding the multiple roles will be a key to spiritual fruit in other people's lives, no matter what their cultural context.

After a person has responded to the grace of God from any one or combination of these portraits, this new believer needs to understand the broader biblical picture, so that he might see the full implications of what has happened in his life by grace. He does not need to continue to know God only as Father or Shepherd or Redeemer but in all the ways in which God desires to relate to him. Not all the figures of speech will speak to him with the same force or meet his felt needs in the same way, but all are true, and he needs to understand them all to more perfectly know the God who has redeemed him and to more fully appreciate the multiple things God has done in the experience of saving grace.

Implications for Atonement

For doctrine. In the history of the Christian church certain major theological issues were settled when key councils of the church evaluated the scriptural data and made definitive statements against incorrect views. This was particularly true of the doctrines of the Trinity and Christology. But no such consensual formulation of the doctrine of atonement has been done in the church. As we have indicated throughout this book, the variety of biblical materials related to the atoning work of Christ has led to a significant number of "theories of the atonement." None of these have carried official sanction of the total church, although some have wanted their view to be considered the orthodox view of the atonement.

In general most churches acknowledge that the atonement, especially as it focuses on the work of Christ on the cross, has been central to the whole of Christian theology but that there are multiples ways in which this event is both described and explained in Scripture.[4] Part of the value in seeing how the various pieces of biblical data relate to each of the roles of God is that it helps explain why so many different theories of the atonement have risen. Different parts of the church have focused on different portraits of God in the way he works in salvation and thus have accented certain terms that articulate that particular picture. By seeing how the data on the atonement is related to the multiple roles of God, a much more holistic understanding of this truth is possible and a much fuller doctrine of the saving work of Christ will result.

The various roles, then, provide material either for a full-blown theory of the atonement or at least for an emphasis within the atonement. So in the creation category we find the view of Christ being made the new head of the race in the Recapitulation theory. There is also a minor focus on the atonement as healing under the subrole of God as Physician. In the royal category there have been two perspectives set forth. The satisfaction theory of Anselm focuses on the satisfaction of the divine honor of God as sovereign King. At the same time the governmental theory has centered its attention on the upholding of the moral order of the universe through the punishment of sin. In the personal category the element of God's initiative in making reconciliation with humanity gets the attention. Reconciliation is not a full blown theory of the atonement but figures in several others as a major component.

In the priestly category the emphasis is on Christ's work as a vicarious sacrifice for sin. This is usually understood in terms of a propitiation theory of the atonement that deals with the wrath of God by means of sacrifice. In the legal category the satisfaction concept of atonement has gotten a slightly different focus with what some call the penal substitution theory. Here the focus is on the satisfaction of the just penalty for sin deserved by all. Christ is the substitute who pays the price by taking the punishment.

The picture of God in the family category focuses on the Father's love that stands behind the whole concept of the atonement. In addition to love as a motivating factor for God, many see the cross as eliciting a responsive love from individuals and have accordingly constructed what some call the moral influence theory of the atonement. This is closely related to the example theory, which

---

[4]For a valuable discussion on how the multiple biblical data help to provide a holistic view of the atonement see Thomas Oden, *The Word of Life* (San Francisco: Harper & Row, 1989), pp. 344-425.

also might be connected with God's role as the Good Shepherd. Certainly the example of Christ's work on the cross is something to which men and women are called to follow in their obedience to him. Finally, in the redemption category the focus is on God's work of ransoming individuals and setting them free from the power and bondage of sin. It is the picture of Christ claiming the victory over the forces and power of evil. This is referred to as the ransom theory, sometimes called the classical theory of the atonement.

Many parts of the concept of atonement include the idea of substitution. While its name is attached to some of the theories of the atonement (e.g., penal substitution), in reality the picture of Christ dying in our place is an element in many of the theories of the atonement. This is simply the heart of the gospel: God has provided salvation for us through Christ's substitutionary death on the cross. No doctrine of the atonement is satisfactory nor is any experience of salvation possible without this reality.

For ministry. The implications of the multiple explanations of the atonement for ministry are closely bound up with those implications for salvation. The several views of the death of Christ provide a variety of ways in which the gospel may be presented, either through evangelism in one's own culture or through missions in crosscultural situations. This means that there are at least eight different ways in which the provision of salvation can be described. Certain roles will speak to some and different roles to others. At least one of the roles ought to speak to every individual.

One special value of the multiple ways to describe the atonement is that it emphasizes that salvation is a work of God. It has to do with the way that God has made provision for salvation. It is a healthy corrective to the constant tendency to form a view of salvation by works or human effort. Most of the theories of the atonement make clear that salvation is something done on God's initiative, that he has provided it and that it comes as an offer to men and women. Most of these theories also remind people of the cost to God for us to experience salvation. This is not something lightly offered or to be cheaply received. The death of Jesus reemphasizes the high price God has paid to secure our redemption. The multiple explanations of this provision help accent these truths.

For people to respond to an offer of salvation, they need some explanation as to how it is possible that such a salvation is available. Some understanding in their minds is a prerequisite for a response of the heart. The focus on the cross and the provision that God has made through the atonement for salvation provides this significant conceptual ingredient. So preaching and teaching on the cross from multiple perspectives will be part of the tools necessary to help people understand the cross, so they can properly respond to it by faith. After they come to the experience of salvation, they will need to understand it more fully in terms of its wide implications for life and for an ongoing relationship with God.

Implications for Growth in Christian Experience

For doctrine: The Christian life. The Christian life begins with salvation, but it does not end here. The next step is growth in this new relationship with God, and so one needs to understand the variety of ways in which one can grow in Christian experience. This growth in grace is described in each portrait, and the full picture provides a variety of ways in which Christians live and mature after coming to a right relationship with God. Thus, after regeneration Christians should continually be conformed more fully to the moral image of God within them. In addition to this increasing likeness to the Creator, they need to learn the significance of submission to God as sovereign King in their lives and the implications of what it means to live under his authority. Growth in relationships is significant for all of life, and those who have accepted Christ into their lives need to learn how to cultivate this relationship with him as well as with the Father and the Spirit in an intimate personal way (Personal Revealer). It will be especially significant to learn from him as Teacher and to enjoy him as Friend.

Growth also includes a continual need of the atonement from the priestly category as well as an ongoing appropriation of forgiveness and cleansing. Within the same figure, believers learn to worship and to pray in order to cultivate this relationship with God. Within the legal metaphor they must not only come to be declared just and righteous before the law, but they must work the righteousness of God's law into their lives through daily obedience to his word. The new birth brings persons into the family of God, but people need to grow up in the family, moving from being a babe in Christ to a child, then to a young man or young woman, and then to a father or mother in the faith. Growth to maturity within the family is probably the most important category for understanding spiritual development.

Further, God desires to redeem people from the slavery of sin, but then he also desires to set a person at liberty to serve as a bondslave of himself (Redeemer). Finally, in the pastoral category it is the ongoing following of the Good Shepherd that is related to continual protection, provision and guidance for life. Each category adds some new dimension to what it means to grow in the Christian life and to live in a right relationship with God. God's patterns for growth parallel his purposes for men and women, as shown in table 11.6.

Table 11.6. Growth in Christian Life in Relation to All the Roles

THE CHRISTIAN LIFE

Holiness:	Separation Transcendence	Separation Sovereignty	Brilliance Immanence	Brilliance Purity/Grace	Righteousness	Love	Power	Goodness
Role:	Creator	King	Personal Revealer	Priest	Judge	Father	Redeemer	Shepherd
Man/ Woman:	Creature	Subject	Person	Worshiper	Law-abiding Person	Child	Servant Freedman	Sheep
Growth:	Growth in image	Kingly rule	Developing Relationship	Continuous Cleansing	Obeying law	Maturity	Serving God	Following

For ministry. The implications of the multiple ways in which people grow in their Christian experience is particularly important for the church and spiritual leadership in fulfilling their responsibility of making disciples. The second half of the Great Commission involves Jesus' command that disciples be formed by "teaching them to observe all that I have commanded you" (Mt 28:20). This means that training as a part of growth is essential for all those who are believers, and it is one of the reasons the church has been given gifts for spiritual leadership—that the members of the body of Christ might be raised up in spiritual maturity (Eph 4:11-16).

So leaders in the church play a certain role within each of the eight categories discussed that help people grow. Within the creation figure leaders are to be concerned about spiritual development and helping people be more conformed to the image of Christ in their lives. In the royal category leadership carries a certain governing, leading and directing function in the lives of those under their care. But this leadership is not to be exercised at a distance but in close personal relationships that particularly involve the roles of Teacher and Friend. In the priestly category those involved in giving direction to the church are responsible for the ongoing mediation between God and his people, and especially in intercession for their needs. Leaders also are to provide opportunities for significant corporate worship of God. Further, leadership must set standards of righteousness and challenge people to godly living. Without being legalistic they are to set before God's people his word as the moral law (legal category) by which they are to live if they are to reflect the righteousness of God. At the same time the church must provide a loving context of acceptance and affirmation (such as in small groups) as an expression of people's being a part of the spiritual family of God. Leaders must be working continually to help people free themselves from the impact of sin on their lives (redemption category), as well as instructing them on how to serve God more effectively. Finally, in the pastoral role, leadership must provide direction, food, and protection from the forces of evil as well as care for the hurts of their flock.

In all these categories spiritual leadership works together with God to accomplish God's purposes in the lives of individuals, meeting their needs and assisting them in their growth in relationship to God. Not every spiritual leader will be fully able to do all of these things, but this is the purpose of the variety of gifts given to the church. There should be a team of leadership that exercises all these functions within the body of Christ, so that all of the varying needs of the people of God might be met and everyone assisted in their growth toward maturity.

Implications for the Church

For doctrine: Ecclesiology. Since the church, like many other things in Scripture, is described in multiple ways, understanding how it is depicted will help us understand its nature as well as how it ought to function. The church, in fact, cannot fully function as the church is supposed to unless it is operating in all the ways that God intended. Understanding God's multiple patterns will assist the church at large, as well as local congregations, to see how they ought to be doing ministry for God. The various roles of God provide the categories for us to understand the way God wants to work in relationship to a group of people in their collective walk with him.

Accordingly, the church's self-understanding is increased when it recognizes that it is to function as the body of Christ. This creation category also allows the church to understand itself as the building of God. These pictures are complemented from the royal category that describes believers as an assembly under a King.

Sometimes there is a strong overlap between the descriptions of the church and the kingdom of God. Further, the church must understand itself as a communion of saints who are living in fellowship with each other (personal category), and this means that developing relationships with others is one of its essential tasks. Using sanctuary language the congregation of believers is described as a kingdom of priests. This focuses on the role of the priesthood of all believers and the ministry responsibility that each one carries both to the church and to the world. This is complemented when the church understands itself from the legal category as a community under the law and word of God. They must see themselves as responsible for setting a standard for righteous living and influencing the non-Christian world with this model of godly behavior.

The church also needs to understand its function as the family of God, how we relate to God as Father and to each other as brothers and sisters in the faith. The household analogy allows the church to focus on intimate relationships and the importance of growth toward maturity. But the church is also a community of the redeemed, people who have been set free from the forces of evil and are now at liberty to serve God and do his will. This means that they must also see themselves as the flock of God, following the Good Shepherd and allowing him to care for them through pastoral shepherds who feed, lead, protect and heal. No full understanding of the church is complete that does not take into account all of these descriptions. The whole schematic that describes the church looks like table 11.7.

Table 11.7. The Church in Relation to All the Roles

ECCLESIOLOGY

	Separation Transcendence	Separation Sovereignty	Brilliance Immanence	Brilliance Purity/Grace	Righteousness	Love	Power	Goodness
Holiness:								
Role:	Creator	King	Personal Revealer	Priest	Judge	Father	Redeemer	Shepherd
Church:	Body, Building	Assembly Kingdom	Communion of saints	Kingdom of priests	Community under law	Family House-hold	Community of redeemed	Flock

For ministry. The practical implications of the multiple descriptions of the church for ministry are twofold. One is that the church is not truly functioning as the church unless it is functioning in some measure in all these ways. Both the local congregation and the church at large need to see the multiple dimensions of its work and not be satisfied until it has significant ministry to people in all of these roles.

The second implication of the roles for understanding the church has to do with the unfortunate tendency of many branches of the church to view themselves primarily in only one or two categories. Some of this is a natural result of the historical development of certain denominations. We have mentioned how Lutherans, for example, have a heavy focus on the role of God as sovereign King. This is not surprising in light of the battle over sovereign authority that they fought during the Reformation period. Calvinism, following close behind as a second generation of reformers, added to this emphasis on a strong legal language and the picture of God as the righteous Judge. The Roman Catholic and the Eastern Orthodox branches of the church provide a heavy accent on the language of the sanctuary, and the use of the mass as a focus of worship dominates much of their understanding of the function of the church. Wesleyans, on the other hand, have a strong inclination for the picture of God as a loving Father and so accent family dimensions of life and ministry in the church. Charismatics have a significant emphasis on the doctrine of the Spirit and a corresponding focus on fellowship and personal relationships. They find themselves most comfortable in relating to God as Personal Revealer. Baptists have a definite accent on initial salvation, so they tend to accent the role of God as Redeemer.

This is not to say that these branches of the church do not have any other understanding of the life and function of the church for themselves. But it does indicate that some groups very definitely focus their ecclesiology on one of the roles of God as the controlling motif for their understanding of the church. While there may be both historical and theological reasons for this, it would seem that any growing maturity of a church's self-understanding should lead to some broadening of the concept of the church and therefore its functions. This is not to deny the traditions in which God has placed us, but it may be helpful to see each tradition in light of other traditions and all of them in terms of the scriptural data that variously describe the church and its ministry. Perhaps the roles of God will help us understand something of our own distinctives, while allowing for appreciation of why other denominations accent other features of the church's understanding of itself as well as its ministry. The roles may also be helpful in determining where we need to strengthen the ministry of any local congregation to provide the full range of ministries that God has designed for his church.

Implications for Full Sanctification

For doctrine. The deeper work of God's sanctifying grace in the life of the individual is referred to by many as the experience of entire or full sanctification. It has been a focus for deeper-life movements throughout the church. It involves a second definite point of commitment, an act of the will to trust God totally in an act of full consecration. This is normally as definite and as clear as the experience of initial salvation. As with our other themes of Christian theology, the roles of God give us language from the Old Testament and New Testament that is indispensable for building a doctrine of sanctification. As a practical matter, much misunderstanding and caricature of this deeper, more total commitment to God has arisen from a failure to understand the multiple ways Scripture describes the experience.

A fuller picture of the roles of God will assist us in seeing the many sides of this rich spiritual experience, while each role also increases our understanding, so that we have a more complete doctrinal formulation of this important biblical teaching. With a view then of establishing a scriptural doctrine of full sanctification, this significant truth may be seen as a full remaking of the moral image and likeness of God in people (creation category). It involves a total submission to the full will of the sovereign King in every area of life (royal category), and so may be understood as coming under the complete Lordship of Christ. It means an enjoyment of the full presence of God that is sometimes described as the fullness of God or the infilling of the Holy Spirit (personal category). This experience involves a deeper cleansing and purifying of self-will and the sinful nature (priestly category). It is this that makes possible a total, willful obedience to the known will/law of God in everyday life (legal category).

Full sanctification also means having a heart that is wholly committed to loving God, and therefore, it can be described in terms of loving God with all the heart, mind, soul and strength, or in terms of an experience of perfect love (family category). In another sense it may be seen as a full redemption from the power of a sinful nature (redemption category), which leads to a deeper state of dependence or rest in one's relationship with God (pastoral category). Because this experience of full sanctification is particularly related to God's work in dealing with our sinful nature (problem/solution), the whole range of terms for sanctification needs to be seen in parallel to the categories for sin as a state (sinfulness), as in table 11.8.

Table 11.8. Full Sanctification in Relation to All the Roles

FULL SANCTIFICATION

Holiness	Separation Transcendence	Separation Sovereignty	Brilliance Immanence	Brilliance Purity/Grace	Righteousness	Love	Power	Goodness
Role:	Creator	King	Personal Revealer	Priest	Judge	Father	Redeemer	Shepherd
State of Sin:	Marred Image	Rebelliousness	Alienation	Impurity	Lawlessness	Death	Bondage	Lostness
Sanctification:	Full remaking of image	Full submission to lordship	Fullness of God Infilling of Holy Spirit	Cleansing from sin Baptism of Holy Spirit	Full obedience Blamelessness	Perfect love Loving God with all heart Abundant life	Full redemption	Total following Rest of faith

None of these categories perfectly describes all that happens in the experience of full sanctification, and therefore all are needed to have a complete picture of what is involved. One language figure used by itself is always inadequate and such a situation leads to the raising of unnecessary questions by those who would press any one analogy too far. But when the whole picture is given of total dependence on God and of the full grace of God working in a person as an example of the full presence of God in total control of that life, then we get a perspective on how God intends for people to live.

For ministry. One of the ministry implications of seeing the multiple ways in which full sanctification is described has to do with the proclamation of this truth. Just as in the preaching of saving grace, the use of different language categories will speak to different people's felt needs. All Christians need to come to a deeper experience of God's sanctifying grace, but one approach will appeal to some in a way that other language or terminology may not. For example, in our day there is a special interest in the infilling or baptism of the Holy Spirit to describe this experience. This is certainly one legitimate way in which people can come into God's full sanctifying grace, and it is particularly attractive currently because of the desire by many to know the third person of the Trinity in a more personal way. The neglected emphasis on the Holy Spirit has created a need, so that the proclamation of full sanctification in terms of the infilling of the Holy Spirit is very appealing. However, it is important for the body of Christ to realize that when people come into an experience of the fullness of the Spirit, they need to be taught that the Scripture describes this experience in a number of other ways. Without this, there will be a limit to their growth in maturity beyond this experience because of failure to understand the full implications of all God has done for them.

While many have responded to the proclamation of the fullness of the Spirit, others will respond to this deeper work of God from other categories. Thus many are interested in learning to love God with all their hearts, so the proclamation of this experience in the family language may be particularly apropos for them. Still others respond to the challenge of the full lordship of Christ, which places them under the total kingly control of Jesus in their lives. The Christological connection makes it very appealing to them, perhaps because they do not find this category as threatening as some of the others, and so are able to respond to it accordingly. It will be important for the church to vary its proclamation to include the use of all of these categories at some point, so that many believers might be brought into this experience from a variety of directions, depending on the language that speaks to them and the needs in their own lives.

Implications for Further Growth
For doctrine. The experience of full sanctification is followed by that of further growth in grace. One of the limits of the biblical phraseology "entire sanctification" (see 1 Thess 5:23) is that some have felt it implies that one's Christian experience is "entirely" complete at this point. Nothing could be further from the biblical view, which talks about increased growth after the point of sanctifying grace. In fact, growth after sanctification is where the full implications of God's control begin to be worked out more completely in everyday living.

The description of growth after sanctification is normally very similar to the language used for growth after conversion, so this section really serves to show how progress in the Christian life is related to both. It has to do with a continuousness in one's experience in each category. This means that people must learn to live out the implications of reflecting the moral image of a holy God (Creator) in holiness of heart (love) and life (righteousness). It will be necessary to see what is implied by a total submission to God's kingly rule in everyday living. While enjoying the full presence of the Holy Spirit, one must learn the ongoing cultivation of personal relationships with all three members of the Trinity (Personal Revealer). There is certainly much more to be learned from God as Teacher, and the further development of a relationship with him is like the deepening and maturing of a rich friendship. Further, it will be necessary to learn how to walk in a way that not only enjoys a pure heart but is able to keep the heart fully clean before the Lord (Priest).

Discovering the whole will of God will be essential to working out the implications of walking in total obedience to everything God has for a person (Judge). In addition, one must learn the implications of a heart that loves like God's heart and how to apply that full love in personal relationships (Father). In like manner those who have been set free from the bondage of sin (Redeemer), must learn the implications of serving God more totally within this freedom and how not to use this freedom as an occasion for license. Finally, one must be sensitive to God's further leading as a Shepherd, so that in a total following in every area of life, one does not miss any part of God's best but is able to seek him and receive from him all that he desires to provide.

While the language of this ongoing growth after sanctification is very similar to that of growth after initial salvation, the difference is in the totality of one's commitment to God that has been experienced in full sanctification. There is a fuller commitment, involving a deeper level of both trust and consecration, that is worked out in practice in terms of a wholeheartedness in an ongoing relationship with the Lord. Whereas after conversion growth might have been hindered at times by the struggle over whether things should be done according to God's will or one's own will, after full sanctification this issue is settled, and a person has chosen in a definite way to do God's will in every situation as soon as he understands what God is saying to him. This frees the individual from a useless drain on emotional and spiritual energy, while it empowers him for doing the whole will of God and serving him with a full heart.

For ministry. Practical implications of the multiple roles for growth after sanctification have to do with the ongoing nature of Christian experience. There is never a time when people should not be growing, both in their understanding of what God is saying and in their appropriation of his truth for their personal lives, for the church and for the world. In this ongoing spiritual development the particular areas for ministry that carry special significance are preaching, teaching and discipleship. In all three of these areas the whole range of the roles is important to the one ministering in order that further truth might be communicated. Here is the place where the question must be asked, "How do we help people develop a fuller understanding of God and how do they relate to him in categories other than those with which they are most familiar or most comfortable?" It is at this point that people can be stretched in their own spiritual experience, particularly through learning the importance of applying biblical truth to their lives. Thus the communicating ministries of preaching, teaching and discipleship should bring people to an understanding of less familiar roles and help them comprehend doctrines that require using the whole picture of God's revelation.

At this level of spiritual growth people become more and more conscious of the possibilities of intimacy with God. A proper understanding of the roles of God (and some subroles) can assist them in this process of growth by identifying the roles and the degree of intimacy each depicts. There are certain ways, connected to specific roles, in which God relates to us that leave us feeling distant. On the other hand, the way in which he relates to us in some of the other roles communicates intimacy. There is in fact a definite progression in the roles which moves from a distant relationship to that of a more intimate walk with him.

The most distant of the roles is God as Creator. Because he made the universe and therefore stands outside of it, he *seems* to be more separate from us. Next on the spectrum of distance versus intimacy would be the kingly role. Although a King does relate to citizens to a greater extent than a Creator, he is still held in an awe which creates a significant psychological distance between himself and his subjects. Much like a King, a Judge also maintains a certain distance from the people he faces in a courtroom. However, judges are more common than kings and are thus placed further along the continuum of familiarity than the royal category. God as Redeemer would follow as one who liberates people, and yet expects to be served by them. The Priestly role would be next in order, particularly the picture of Jesus who stands between us and the Father as Mediator. It is a picture that places him as much on "our side" as on "God's side," and thus communicates a greater closeness to people. The Shepherd role is much closer in terms of intimacy than any of the previous roles because there is a daily responsibility to lead his sheep, provide for them, protect them and bind up their wounds. His is a "hands on" ministry that communicates his immediate presence with the sheep.

God's role as Personal Revealer is even more intimate than the Shepherd's relationship to sheep because it is a person-to-person relationship instead of a person-to-animal one. In particular God's role as Teacher brings him into a more immediate personal contact with people, and when this is coupled with his role as Friend, it creates an even more intimate relationship. However, the category which provides the atmosphere of greatest intimacy is that of family. Here, the Father's relationship to his children is one of warmth, love and closeness, while the relationship of a Husband to his wife may illustrate the closest of all human ties. One final figure may be borrowed from the language of the sanctuary to illustrate intimacy. It is the picture of God inhabiting the tabernacle/temple of his people. In this figure of "inhabitation" God actually dwells within the lives of those who belong to him. While there is no full-blown role that gives us this phenomenon, it is a variation of the temple language. The difference is that God is not acting here as a priest, but God is actually inhabiting his people.

Figure 11.1 portrays the progression of the roles of the most distant to the most intimate.

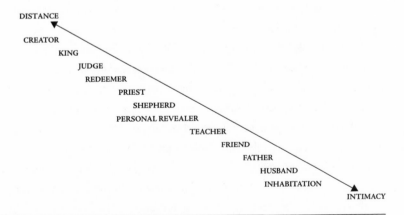

Figure 11.1. Progression of roles from distance to intimacy

It is the responsibility of those in ministry to help people grow in knowing God in all the roles. Those who want to know him with greater intimacy, but not relate to him in his more transcendent roles, need to have the balance corrected so that they relate to him in all ways. On the other hand, those who only know him in the more distant roles need to be encouraged to develop a greater intimacy with him. People need to know God in all the ways that he has revealed himself. But if they do know him in all ways, part of the resulting relationship will include an intimacy and closeness like that of a friend to friend, family member to family member or one person indwelling another.

Implications for Glorification

For doctrine: Eschatology. The concept of glorification normally uses the same language that describes our relationship to God in this world. The difference involves a projection into the future. So the language categories here are not different, but have a different time reference. We have used the term glorification to refer to the moment of the physical death of an individual, when he is immediately translated into the presence of God, and also with reference to the second coming of Christ and the events related to the glorification of people at that time.

The many ways in which glorification is described include that of giving of eternal life, which one begins to enjoy in this world but which will continue in the presence of God forever. The creation category also gives us an understanding of the final events in history as related to the creation of a new heaven and a new earth. Over this new creation the Lord will rule as King of kings and Lord of lords, and his word will be the final word in all circumstances in heaven and on earth. Individuals will enjoy an eternal fellowship with the Father, the Son and the Spirit when the glory of the Lord is fully revealed on the last day (Personal Revealer). Eternity will provide an opportunity for heavenly worship of God (Priest). It will be a time when God as the righteous Judge exercises final judgment over mankind, but it will also be an occasion for believers to continue enjoying their eternal inheritance as members of the family of God (Father). Glorification will involve the final redemption of the body and the universe from the powers of evil, as well as deliverance of people from their infirmities (Redeemer). This will be coupled in the pastoral category with a permanent rest in the presence of God and provision from him for all basic needs (Shepherd). So the concept of glorification, which is so intimately tied up with last things or the doctrine of eschatology, provides a way of describing the final eternal way in which people will continue to relate to the God who has redeemed them by his grace. The whole group of glorification terms is illustrated in table 11.9.

Table 11.9. Eschatology in Relation to All the Roles

ESCHATOLOGY

Holiness:	Separation Transcendence	Separation Sovereignty	Brilliance Immanence	Brilliance Purity/Grace	Righteousness	Love	Power	Goodness
Role:	Creator	King	Personal Revealer	Priest	Judge	Father	Redeemer	Shepherd
Glorifi- cation:	New heaven/ earth Eternal life	King of kings	Eternal fellowship	Eternal worship	Final judgment Reward/ Punishment	Final inheritance Eternal life	Final redemption	Eternal rest

For ministry. The whole question of glorification accents either our moving into the presence of God through death or the second return of Christ. In either case the focus will be on living eternally in his presence, and it will involve in some way our death to living in this world. This means that the multiple ways to describe glorification are particularly helpful to those in ministry to people or families who are facing death. The multiple roles should be a means of communicating the tremendous blessings that are available to those who belong to the Lord when they pass from this life into the next. It should be a cause for hope, thanksgiving and praise for the things that God is going to do for those who belong to him.

In ministering to individuals or families facing death there is also the opportunity to speak about the blessings God is going to provide in eternity as a means of being sure people are ready to face God at the end of their lives. So a discussion of these blessings (using the multiple roles that describe glorification) may provide an evangelistic opportunity. As people are encouraged to look forward to meeting Christ, for example, as King of Kings or as a Judge or as a Father in whose presence they will live for eternity, they may be forced to raise questions about their salvation or their assurance of salvation.

Finally, the various descriptions of glorification should be presented to believers as a reminder that we need to live in the light of eternity. Everyone needs to hear that the close of life in this world is not the end, and that there is more coming. This is particularly helpful when people have to live with suffering and injustice, some of which will not be alleviated or made right in this world. But God's good and just character will ultimately be vindicated, and we must live in the light of this eternal hope. In addition, it is important for everyone to realize that some decisions that are now being made are going to have eternal consequences. This fact should be a valuable tool in our ministry of helping people make right choices.

Implications for Attributes of God

For doctrine. Finally, with regards to the attributes of God we have seen how these are intertwined with the several portraits of God. While there is obvious overlap in many categories, certain attributes seem to be more closely associated with certain roles. The absolute attributes of his spirituality, infinity, immutability, and self-existence are intimately bound up with his role as Creator. The Creator role also is often tied with the relative attributes of freedom and omnipotence. God's role as sovereign King is connected primarily with his relative attributes, especially his omnipotence, omnipresence, omniscience, and wisdom, since all these are particularly related to his governing role over the universe. The relative attribute of his omnipotence is also closely interwoven with God's role as powerful Redeemer.

The other roles are tied to the several moral attributes of God. His role as Personal Revealer is very intimately joined with the concepts of truth, wisdom and faithfulness. God is speaking with clarity about himself and is accurately revealing himself to people. Grace, mercy and purity all seem to be heavily associated with the priestly category, in which God is ministering to people impacted by sin. Righteousness and justice are bound up with his role as Lawmaker/Judge, and love seems to be most obviously linked with his function as Father. The Shepherd category is most appropriately related to his goodness.

While there is an evident overlap between these categories, the biblical data does seem to accent these connections. Yet, all of these attributes are tied together by the holiness of God that stands behind each of these roles. All of these attributes may be rightly understood as manifestations of the holy character of God, and they need to be seen in the light of this connection. The relationship between holiness, the roles and the attributes of God looks like table 11.10.

Table 11.10. The Attributes of God in Relation to His Holiness and Roles

	ATTRIBUTES OF GOD							
HOLINESS:	SEPARATION		BRILLIANCE		RIGHTEOUS NESS	LOVE	POWER	GOODNESS
	Transcendence	Sovereignty	Immanence	Purity	Righteousness	Love	Power	Goodness
Role:	Creator	King	Personal Revealer	Priest	Judge		Father	Redeemer	Shepherd
Absolute:	Spirituality Infinity Immutability Self-Existence							
Relative:	Omnipotence Freedom	Omnipotence Omnipresence Omniscience Wisdom	Wisdom				Omnipotence	
Moral:			Truth Faithfulness	Purity Grace Mercy	Righteousness Justice	Love		Goodness

For ministry. The practical value of understanding the attributes of God in light of the roles of God comes in two ways. The first is the wealth of material available for preaching and teaching about God. This of course is true for all the other areas of Christian theology that we have covered. The whole scope of the roles and the multiple categories in Christian theology that each role describes allows those in preaching and teaching ministry an enormous amount of significant and serious biblical content to communicate to believers about who God is and how they relate to him.

The second reason the roles are important for understanding the attributes of God is that for many people the discussion of attributes seems very academic. The division into absolute, relative and moral attributes only adds to this impression for many in the church. But by connecting the attributes to the various roles of God, portraits of God are wrapped around the rational discussions of these characteristics of his being. These pictures provide an entirely different context for knowing God, and in fact they make some parts of theology more "user friendly." For example, people more easily understand omnipotence when the discussion is about God having "all power" to redeem people and set them free from the forces of evil. Alternatively, it is one thing to discuss the goodness of God in abstract philosophical categories, but when God's goodness is pictured in terms of a shepherd caring for his sheep out of a good, giving heart and providing for them by feeding, protecting, leading and binding up hurts, then the whole concept is immediately more attractive and helps people respond to a good God. In a way the roles soften the more academic discussion of the attributes of God and put them in a context that allows for an easier personal response from individuals to God.

Conclusion

The last several sections of this chapter have been focused on the implications of the roles of God both for building Christian theology and for the practice of ministry. The purpose has been to show that the synthesis of material under each of the eight roles forms the basis for a holistic Christian theology under each doctrinal category. In other words, it is essential to know what the scriptural terms are in all eight categories to have a full picture of any Christian doctrine.

At the same time, we wanted to indicate that there are practical applications for ministry with such a synthesis of truth. Theology has enormous implications for the practice of ministry. So we have tried to indicate in an initial way how these doctrinal summaries are useful for pastoral care, counseling, evangelism, missions, discipleship, deeper life ministry, preaching, teaching, etc. We have not meant to imply that the summaries under each doctrine only have practical applications in one area of ministry. Rather, we have tried to highlight one or two areas where they seemed to have a special relevance. A little creative imagination will uncover many more.

Further investigation will show that the multiple roles of God also have implications for additional areas of the study of Christian theology and in the practice of ministry. For example, some feel that one way to interpret contemporary theology is to evaluate the movements of the late nineteenth century to the end of the twentieth century in the light of a shifting focus from the transcendence of God to the immanence of God. The argument is that some theologians accent God's transcendence, while others have focused more on his immanence.[5] The history of Christian theology has always held these two truths about God in balance, and the picture of the roles of God helps with this process. It is easy to note, for example, that four of the roles (Creator, King, Judge and Redeemer) have an accent on God's transcendence, while the other four have a much stronger focus on his immanence (Personal Revealer, Priest, Shepherd and Father). The balance between transcendence and immanence is easier to maintain when a holistic picture of God is in view.

Further implications of the roles for ministry come in the shaping of a curriculum for theological seminaries or colleges. Both classical and applied disciplines will find the use of the roles helpful in both synthesizing the materials for their area of study and seeing implications of it for practical ministry. Alternatively, implications of the roles for discipleship training in a local church are very significant. Any biblical pattern for disciple making must have the disciple maker functioning in some measure in all of these roles as a part of "doing what God does" (albeit in a modified way) in order to accomplish God's purposes in the spiritual lives of men and women. These and other areas of exploration may be helpful for the church in days to come.

A final word needs to be said regarding the major purposes of this book. The first purpose was to introduce the roles of God as a means of knowing about God, about ourselves and how we relate to him. Our study has indicated that there is an enormous amount of biblical material that may be organized in this way. It has been our desire that this better intellectual conception of God, people and their relationship to each other would provide the foundation for relating to him directly. In other words, it has been our conviction that better *knowledge about* God is essential, when coupled with faith, for actually *knowing* God. If your understanding of who he is has increased throughout this book, then the next challenge is a deeper level of responsiveness to him by faith, so that he might be known more fully in personal experience.

A second purpose was to show the centrality of holiness for understanding the nature of God. Our study on the roles of God strengthens the conviction that the holiness of God is bound up both with his nature as well as with how he relates to people. He desires a holy people to reflect his character, and he is

---

[5]Stanley J. Grenz and Roger B. Olson, *20th-Century Theology* (Downers Grove, Ill.: InterVarsity Press, 1992), pp. 9-13.

looking for a way to deal with unholiness, that is, sin, and bring people to the place where they may be like a holy God. Each of the role categories discussed uses language that is descriptive not only of who he is, but of what God wants in people and the way he desires to accomplish these ends. This being true, it makes holiness a truly pervasive concept for all biblical truth. If it is true that the Bible is about God, people, the relationship between them, and people's relationship to other people and the world, then holiness must be understood to be right at the center of biblical revelation.

The final purpose of the book has been to show the connection between Old Testament materials, New Testament materials and Christian theology. The hope has been to move forward another step in reconnecting these three disciplines that have been too long divided. The roles of God seem to be an excellent way of showing how God is described in both testaments and then how each of these language categories lends itself to a study of the major themes of systematic theology. In this volume we have only been able to introduce the terms and concepts from Scripture, without having the opportunity to formulate them into whole doctrines. Nevertheless, there seems to be significant value in using a biblical method of this sort as the beginning of a correlation of materials for the work of systematic theology. It allows systematics to be grounded in biblical studies and to have as its key starting point the nature and work of the God who is making himself known. Now the next steps of systematic theology must take over to find a unity and coherence of materials revealed in Scripture and then to use other critical tools like reason, tradition and experience to work out the full implications of truth so that it might finally be packaged for ministry to the church and the world. The value of this study for systematics is that it begins the first step in the process of correlating data by giving basic terms, concepts and ideas that then must be coordinated into the whole of God's truth that will ultimately be available to influence the church and the world.

Bibliography

Abelson, Joshua. *The Immanence of God in Rabbinic Literature*. London: Macmillan, 1912.

Albright, W. F. "The Names Shaddai and Abram," *JBL* 54 (1935): 175-92.

Anselm. *Cur Deus Homo*. Translated by Joseph M. Colleran. Albany, N.Y.: Magi, 1969.

Aquinas, Thomas. *Summa Contra Gentiles*. Notre Dame, Ind.: University of Notre Dame Press, 1955-1957.

————. *Summa Theologica*. Edited by Thomas Gilby. Garden City, N.Y.: Image, 1969.

Argyle, Aubrey William. *God in the New Testament*. Philadelphia: Lippincott, 1965.

Assman, Hugo. *Theology for a Nomad Church*. Maryknoll, N.Y.: Orbis, 1975.

Athanasius. *On the Incarnation*. Crestwood, N.Y.: St. Vladimir's Seminary Press, 1944.

Augustine. *Trinity*. Translated by Stephen McKenna. Washington, D.C.: Catholic University of America Press, 1963.

Aulén, Gustaf. *Christus Victor*. London: SPCK, 1965.

————. *The Faith of the Christian Church*. Philadelphia: Muhlenberg, 1960.

Bailey, Lloyd. "Israelite El Shaddai and Amorite Bel Sade." *JBL* 87 (1987): 434-38.

Baillie, Donald M. *God Was in Christ*. London: Faber & Faber, 1960.

Barbour, Ian. *Myths, Models and Paradigms*. New York: Harper & Row, 1974.

Barr, James. *The Semantics of Biblical Language*. London: Oxford University Press, 1961.

Barrett, Charles Kingley. *The Gospel According to St. John*. London: SPCK, 1965.

Barrow, R. H. *Slavery in the Roman Empire*. New York: Barnes & Noble, 1968.

Barth, Karl. *Church Dogmatics*. Translated by G. T. Thomson and Harold Knight. Edinburgh: T & T Clark, 1963.

Bauckham, Richard. *God Crucified*. Grand Rapids, Mich.: Eerdmans, 1998.

Berkhof, Louis. *Systematic Theology*. Edinburgh: Banner of Truth, 1958.

Berkouwer, Gerrit Cornelis. *General Revelation*. Grand Rapids, Mich.: Eerdmans, 1955.

Bernard, John Henry. *St. John*. 2 vols. New York: Charles Scribner's Sons, 1929.

Berry, G. B. "The Glory of God and the Temple," *JBL* 56 (1937): 115-17.

Best, Ernest. *Following Jesus: Discipleship in the Gospel of Mark*. Sheffield, U.K.: University of Sheffield Press, 1981.

Bethune-Baker, J. F. *Introduction to the Early History of Christian Doctrine*. London: Metheun, 1942.

Bevan, Edwyn R. *Symbolism and Belief*. London: Collins, 1938.

Black, Max. *Models and Metaphors*. Ithaca, N.Y.: Cornell University Press, 1962.

Bloesch, Donald G. *The Battle for the Trinity: The Debate over Inclusive God-Language*. Ann Arbor, Mich.: Vine, 1985.

————. *Essentials of Evangelical Theology*. 2 vols. San Francisco: Harper & Row, 1978, 1982.

Boice, James Montgomery. *Awakening to God*. Downers Grove, Ill.: InterVarsity Press, 1979.

Bonino, José Miguez. *Christians and Marxists*. Grand Rapids, Mich.: Eerdmans, 1976.

————. *Doing Theology in a Revolutionary Situation*. Philadelphia: Fortress, 1975.

Bornkamm, Günther. *Jesus of Nazareth*. New York: Harper, 1960.

Braeling, E. "The Emmanuel Prophecy." *JBL* 1 (1931): 277-97.

Bright, John. *The Kingdom of God*. New York: Abingdon, 1953.

Brockington, H. L. "The Presence of God, A Study of the Use of the Term 'Glory of Yahweh.'" *Expository Times* 57 (1945): 21-25.

Brown, F., S. R. Driver and C. A. Briggs. *A Hebrew and English Lexicon of the Old Testament*. Oxford: Clarendon, 1907.

Bruce, F. F. "Our God and Savior: A Recurring Biblical Pattern." In *The Savior God*. Edited by Samuel G. F. Brandon. New York: Barnes & Noble, 1963.

Brueggemann, Walter. *Old Testament Theology*. Minneapolis: Fortress, 1992.

Brunner, Emil. *The Christian Doctrine of Creation and Redemption*. London: Lutterworth, 1952.

————. *The Christian Doctrine of God.* London: Lutterworth, 1949.

————. *Dogmatics.* 3 vols. Translated by Olive Wyon. London: Lutterworth, 1949-1952.

————. *Man in Revolt.* Translated by Olive Wyon. Philadelphia: Westminster Press, 1947.

————. *The Mediator.* Translated by Olive Wyon. London: Lutterworth, 1934.

————. *Revelation and Reason.* Translated by Olive Wyon. London: SCM Press, 1942.

————. *Truth as Encounter.* Translated by Olive Wyon. Philadelphia: Westminster Press, 1964.

Brunner, Frederic Dale. *A Theology of the Holy Spirit.* Grand Rapids, Mich.: Eerdmans, 1970.

Buber, Martin. *Kingship of God.* New York: Harper & Row, 1967.

Buckland, William Warwick. *The Roman Law of Slavery.* Cambridge University Press, 1908.

Bullinger, E. W. *Figures of Speech Used in the Bible: Explained and Illustrated.* Grand Rapids, Mich.: Baker, 1968.

Bultmann, Rudolf. *The Gospel of John.* Edited by G. R. Beasley-Murray. Oxford: Basil Blackwell, 1971.

————. *Theology of the New Testament.* 2 vols. New York: Charles Scribner's Sons, 1951-1955.

Bury, R. G. *The Fourth Gospel and the Logos Doctrine.* Cambridge: W. Heffer & Sons, 1940.

Caird, George B. *The Language and Imagery of the Bible.* Philadelphia: Westminster Press, 1980.

Cairns, David. *The Image of God in Man.* London: SCM Press, 1953.

Calvin, John. *Institutes of the Christian Religion.* 2 vols. Translated by John Allen. Philadelphia: Westminster Press, 1936.

Candlish, Robert W. *Discourses Bearing upon the Sonship and Brotherhood of Believers.* Edinburgh: Adam & Charles Black, 1872.

————. *The Fatherhood of God.* Edinburgh: Adam & Charles Black, 1879.

Cannon, William R. *The Theology of John Wesley.* Nashville: Abingdon, 1946.

Carter, Charles W. *A Contemporary Wesleyan Theology.* Grand Rapids, Mich.: Zondervan, 1983.

————. *The Person and Ministry of the Holy Spirit: A Wesleyan Perspective.* Grand

Rapids, Mich.: Baker, 1974.

Carter, Ray Cecil. *The Eternal Teacher: a Guide to Jesus' Teaching Methods*. New York: Exposition, 1960.

Chadwick, Samuel. *The Call to Christian Perfection*. Kansas City, Mo.: Beacon Hill, 1943.

Chavasse, Claud L. *The Bride of Christ*. London: Religious Book Club, 1940.

Cheyne, Thomas Kelley. *The Origin of the Psalter*. New York: Thomas Whittaker, 1891.

Childs, Brevard. *Biblical Theology of the Old and New Testaments*. Minneapolis: Fortress, 1993.

———. *Canon, Theology and Old Testament Interpretation*. Philadelphia: Fortress, 1988.

———. *Introduction to the Old Testament as Scripture*. Philadelphia: Fortress, 1979.

———. *Old Testament Theology in a Canonical Context*. Philadelphia: Fortress, 1985.

Clark, Adam. *Commentary on the Bible*. London: William Tegg, 1859.

Clayton, Philip, and Carl E. Braaten. *The Theology of Wolfhart Pannenberg*. Minneapolis: Augsburg, 1988.

Clements, Ronald E. *Old Testament Theology*. Atlanta: John Knox Press, 1978.

Conzelmann, Hans. *Outline of the Theology of the New Testament*. London: SCM Press, 1969.

Cook, James. I. "The Concept of Adoption in the Theology of Paul." In *Saved By Hope*. Edited by J. I. Cook. Grand Rapids, Mich.: Eerdmans, 1978.

Coppedge, Allan. *The Biblical Principles of Discipleship*. Grand Rapids, Mich.: Zondervan, 1989.

———. *Holy Living: Godliness in the Old Testament*. Wilmore, Ky.: Barnabas Foundation, 1999.

———. *John Wesley in Theological Debate*. Wilmore, Ky.: Wesley Heritage, 1987.

Coppedge, Allan, and William Ury. *In His Image*. Franklin, Tenn.: Providence House, 2000.

———. *A Workbook on Spiritual Gifts*. Wilmore, Ky.: Barnabas Foundation, 1999.

Cox, Leo G. "The Imperfections of the Perfect." In *Further Insights into Holiness*. Edited by Kenneth Geiger. Kansas City, Mo.: Beacon Hill, 1963.

———. *John Wesley's Concept of Perfection*. Kansas City, Mo.: Beacon Hill, 1964.

Cremer, Herman. *Biblical-Theological Lexicon of New Testament Greek*. Edinburgh: T & T Clark, 1895.

Croatto, José Severino. *Exodus: A Hermeneutics of Freedom*. Maryknoll, N.Y.: Orbis, 1981.

Crum, Keith R. *The Royal Psalms*. Richmond, Va.: John Knox Press, 1962.

Cullmann, Oscar. *The Christology of the New Testament*. London: SCM Press, 1963.

Curtis, Olin Alfred. *The Christian Faith*. Grand Rapids, Mich.: Kregel, 1971.

D'Arcy, Martin Cyril. *The Mind and Heart of Love, Lion and the Unicorn: A Study of Eros and Agape*. New York: Meridian, 1956.

Davidson, A. B. *The Theology of the Old Testament*. Edinburgh: T & T Clark, 1904.

Davis, John Jefferson. *Foundations of Evangelical Theology*. Grand Rapids, Mich.: Baker, 1984.

DeBurgh, William. *The Messianic Prophecies of Isaiah*. Dublin: Hodges, Smith, 1863.

Deissley, Alexander. "Perfection." In *Sacramentum Verbi*. 3 vols. Edited by Johannes B. Bauer. New York: Herder & Herder, 1970.

Deissmann, G. A. *Light from the Ancient Near East*. New York: Harper & Bros., 1927.

Delitzsch, Franz. *Hebrews*. Translated by Thomas L. Kingsbury. Grand Rapids, Mich.: Eerdmans, 1952.

Denney, James. *The Christian Doctrine of Reconciliation*. New York: George H. Doran, 1918.

――――. *The Death of Christ*. London: Tyndale Press, 1961.

Dodd, C. H. *The Interpretation of the Fourth Gospel*. Cambridge: Cambridge University Press, 1965.

――――. "Jesus as Teacher and Prophet." In *Mysterium Christi*. Edited by G. K. A. Bell and G. A. Deissman. London: Longmans, Green, 1930.

――――. *The Parables of the Kingdom*. London: Collins, 1963.

Dunn, James D. G. *Baptism of the Holy Spirit*. Naperville, Ill.: Alec R. Allenson, 1970.

――――. "Jesus as Flesh and Spirit: An Exposition of Romans 1, 3, and 4." *Journal of Theological Studies* 24 (1973): 40-68.

Eaton, John H. *Kingship and the Psalms*. Naperville Ill.: Alec R. Allenson, 1975.

Efros, I. "Holiness and Glory in the Bible." *Jewish Quarterly Review* 41 (April 1951): 365.

Eichrodt, Walther. *Theology of the Old Testament.* Translated by J. A. Baker. 6th ed., 2 vols. London: SCM Press, 1961, 1967.

Eller, Vernard. *The Language of Canaan and the Grammar of Feminism.* Grand Rapids, Mich.: Eerdmans, 1982.

Engnell, Ivan. *Studies in Divine Kingship.* Oxford: Basil Blackwell, 1967.

Escobar, Samuel. *La Fe Evangelica y Los Teologios de la Liberacion.* El Paso, Tex.: Casa Bautista, 1987.

Fairbairn, Andrew Martin. *Christ in Modern Theology.* London: Hodder & Stoughton, 1893.

Feensta, Ronald Jay, and Cornelius Plantinga Jr. *Trinity, Incarnation, and Atonement.* Notre Dame, Ind.: University of Notre Dame Press, 1989.

Feldman, A. J. *The Rabbi and His Early Ministry.* New York: Bloch, 1941.

Fénelon, François. *Christian Perfection.* London, New York: Harper & Brothers, 1947.

Filson, V. F. *Jesus Christ the Risen Lord.* Nashville: Abingdon, 1941.

Finkle, Asher. *The Pharisees and the Teacher of Nazareth.* Leiden: Brill, 1964.

Flack, E. E. "The Concept of Grace in Biblical Thought." In *Biblical Studies in Memory of H. C. Allemen.* Edited by Jacob Martin Myers. Locust Valley, N.Y.: J. J. Augustine, 1960.

Flew, Newton F. *The Concept of Perfection.* London: Oxford University Press, 1934.

Forsyth, Peter Taylor. *The Cruciality of the Cross.* London: Hodder & Stoughton, 1909.

————. *The Work of Christ.* Great Britain: Collins, 1965.

Frankfort, Henri. *Kingship and the Gods.* Chicago: University of Chicago Press, 1948.

Fuller, Reginald H. *The Foundations of New Testament Christology.* London: Lutterworth, 1965.

Geisler, Norman L. *Philosophy of Religion.* Grand Rapids, Mich.: Zondervan, 1974.

Geldenhuys, Norvel. *Luke.* London: Marshall, Morgan & Scott, 1950.

George, Alfred Raymond. *Communion with God in the New Testament.* London: Epworth, 1953.

Gibellini, Rosino, ed. *Frontiers of Theology in Latin America*. Maryknoll, N.Y.: Orbis, 1979.

Gilder, George F. *Sexual Suicide*. New York: Quadrangle, 1973.

Girdlestone, Robert Baker. *Synonyms of the Old Testament*. 1987. Reprint, Grand Rapids, Mich.: Eerdmans, 1948.

Glueck, Nelson. *Hesed in the Bible*. Cincinnati, Ohio: Hebrew Union College Press, 1967.

"The Gospel of Jesus Christ: An Evangelical Celebration," *Christianity Today*, June 1999, pp. 51-56.

Graham, Billy. *The Holy Spirit*. Waco, Tex.: Word, 1978.

Grant, Robert. *The Early Christian Doctrine of God*. Charlottesville: University of Virginia Press, 1966.

Greathouse, William. *Romans*. Kansas City, Mo.: Beacon Hill, 1975.

Green, Joel and Max Turner. *Between Two Horizons: Spanning New Testament Studies and Systematic Theology*. Grand Rapids, Mich.: Eerdmans, 2000.

Grenz, Stanley J., and Roger E. Olson. *20th-Century Theology*. Downers Grove, Ill.: InterVarsity Press, 1992.

Grotius, Hugo A. *Defense of the Catholic Faith Concerning the Satisfaction of Christ Against Faustus Socinus*. London: Draper, 1889.

―――. *On the Truth of the Christian Religion*. 6 vols. Translated by Simon Patrick. London: Rich Royston, 1680.

Grudem, Wayne. *Systematic Theology*. Grand Rapids, Mich.: Zondervan, 1994.

Gunton, Colin E. *The One, the Three and the Many*. Cambridge, N.Y.: Cambridge University Press, 1993.

―――. *The Promise of Trinitarian Theology*. Edinburgh: T & T Clark, 1991.

―――. "Proteus and Procrustes: A Study in the Dialectic of Language in Disagreement with Sallie McFague." In *Speaking the Christian God*. Edited by Alvin K. Kimel Jr. Grand Rapids, Mich.: Eerdmans, 1992.

―――. "The Sacrifice and the Sacrifices: From Metaphor to Transcendental?" In *Trinity, Incarnation and Atonement*. Edited by R. J. Feenstra and Cornelius Plantinga Jr. Notre Dame, Ind.: University of Notre Dame Press, 1989.

Guthrie, Donald. *New Testament Theology*. Downers Grove, Ill.: InterVarsity Press, 1981.

Gutiérrez, Gustavo. *Theology of Liberation: History, Politics, and Salvation*. Maryknoll, N.Y.: Orbis, 1973.

Hahn, Ferdinand. *The Titles of Jesus in Christology: Their History in Early Christianity.* London: Lutterworth, 1969.

Harrelson, Walter J. "The Idea of Agape in the New Testament." *Journal of Religion* 31 (1951): 169-82.

Harris, Merne A., and Richard S. Taylor. "The Dual Nature of Sin." In *The Word and the Doctrine.* Edited by Kenneth Geiger. Kansas City, Mo.: Beacon Hill, 1965.

Harrison, Everett F., ed. *Baker's Dictionary of Theology.* Grand Rapids, Mich.: Baker, 1960.

Harrisville, R. A. *The Concept of Newness in the New Testament.* Minneapolis: Augsburg, 1960.

Hart, Trevor. *Faith Thinking: The Dynamics of Christian Theology.* Downers Grove, Ill.: InterVarsity Press, 1995.

Heinisch, Paul. *Theology of the Old Testament.* Translated by William G. Heidt. St. Paul: North Central Press, 1955.

Helm, P. "Revealed Propositions and Timeless Truths." *Religious Studies* 8 (1972): 127-36.

Henry, Carl F. H. *God, Revelation and Authority.* 6 vols. Waco, Tex.: Word, 1983.

———, ed. *Revelation in the Bible.* Grand Rapids, Mich.: Baker, 1958.

Heron, Aladair I. C., ed. *The Forgotten Trinity.* London: BBC/CCBI, 1991.

Hester, James D. *St. Paul's Concept of Inheritance.* London: Oliver & Boyd, 1968.

Higgins, Angus John Brochkhurst. *Jesus and the Son of Man.* Philadelphia: Fortress, 1964.

Hill, David. *Greek Words and Hebrew Meanings.* New York: Scribner, 1975.

Hill, William J. *The Three-Personed God: the Trinity as a Mystery of Salvation.* Washington, D.C.: Catholic University of America Press, 1982.

Hodge, Charles. *Systematic Theology.* 3 vols. London: James Clarke, 1960.

Hoekema, A. A. *The Bible and the Future.* Grand Rapids, Mich.: Eerdmans, 1979.

Hooft, W. A. Visser't. *The Fatherhood of God in an Age of Emancipation.* Philadelphia: Westminster Press, 1982.

Horne, Herman Harrell. *Jesus, the Master Teacher.* Grand Rapids, Mich.: Kregel, 1964.

Hoskyns, E. C. *The Fourth Gospel.* London: Faber & Faber, 1956.

Huffman, J. A. *The Holy Spirit.* Winona Lake, Ind.: Standard, 1944.

Hughes, Philip E., *The True Image.* Grand Rapids, Mich.: Eerdmans, 1989.

Ignatius. "Ephesians 1." In *Ante-Nicene Fathers.* Edited by Alexander Roberts and James Donaldson. Peabody, Mass.: Hendrickson, 1994.

Irenaeus. "Against Heresies," In *Ante-Nicene Fathers.* Edited by Alexander Roberts and James Donaldson. Peabody, Mass.: Hendrickson, 1994.

Jacob, Edmond. *Theology of the Old Testament.* Translated by Arthur W. Heathcote and P. J. Allcock. New York: Harper & Row, 1958.

Jastrow, Marcus, ed. *A Dictionary of the Tarqumim, the Talmud Babli and Yerushalmi, and the Midrashic Literature.* 2 vols. New York: Pardes, 1950.

Jeremias, Joachim. *The Central Message of the New Testament* London: SCM Press, 1965.

———. *Jerusalem in the Time of Jesus.* Philadelphia: Fortress, 1975.

———. *New Testament Theology.* Translated by John Bowden. New York: Scribner, 1971.

Johnson, R. A. "The Primary Meaning of the Root G'l." *Supplement Vestus Testamentum* 1: 67-77.

Kaiser, O., and E. Lohse. *Death and Life.* Nashville: Abingdon, 1981.

Kaiser, Walter C., Jr. *Toward an Old Testament Theology.* Grand Rapids, Mich.: Zondervan, 1978.

Kasper, Walter. *The God of Jesus Christ.* Translated by Matthew J. O'Connell. New York: Crossroad, 1999.

Kaufmann, Yehezkel. *The Religion of Israel.* Chicago: University of Chicago Press, 1960.

Keach, Benjamin. *Preaching from the Types and Metaphors of the Bible.* Grand Rapids, Mich.: Kregel, 1972.

Kelley, John Norman Davidson. *Early Christian Doctrines.* London: Adam & Charles Black, 1965.

Kempis, Thomas à. *Imitation of Christ.* London: Collins, n.d.

Kimel, Alvin F., Jr., ed. *Speaking the Christian God.* Grand Rapids, Mich.: Eerdmans, 1992.

Kirk, J. Andrew. *Liberation Theology: An Evangelical View from the Third World.* Atlanta: John Knox Press, 1979.

Kittel, R., ed. *The New Scaff-Herzog Encyclopedia of Religious Knowledge.* 13 vols. Edited by Samuel M. Jackson. New York: Funk & Wagnalls, 1908-1914.

Knight, George A. F. *A Christian Theology of the Old Testament.* Richmond, Va.: John Knox Press, 1959.

Koehler, Ludwig Hugo. *Lexicon in Veteris Testamenti Libros.* Edited by Walter Baumgartner. Leiden: E. J. Brill, 1959.

————. *Old Testament Theology.* Philadelphia: Westminster Press, 1957.

Kummel, Werner Georg. *Theology of the New Testament According to Its Major Witnesses: Jesus-Paul-John.* Nashville: Abingdon, 1973.

Kuper, L. J. "Grace and Truth: An Old Testament Description of God and Its Use in the Johannine Gospel." *Interpretation* 18 (1964): 3-19.

Ladd, George Eldon. *The Gospel of the Kingdom.* Grand Rapids, Mich.: Eerdmans, 1959.

————. *Jesus and the Kingdom.* New York: Harper & Row, 1964.

————. *A Theology of the New Testament.* Grand Rapids, Mich.: Eerdmans, 1974.

Lakoff, George, and Mar Johnson. *Metaphors We Live By.* Chicago: University of Chicago Press, 1980.

Lampe, Geoffrey W. H. *Reconciliation in Christ.* London: Longmans, Green, 1956.

Lee, K. E. *The Religious Thought of St. John.* London: SPCK, 1950.

Lewis, C. S. "Bluspels and Flalanfferes." In *Rehabilitations and Other Essays.* New York: Oxford University Press, 1939.

————. *The Four Loves.* New York: Harcourt, Brace, 1960.

————. *Miracles: A Preliminary Study.* New York: Macmillan, 1947.

Lillie, W. "The Christian Conception of Love." *Scottish Journal of Theology* 7 (1959): 226-42.

Lindars, Barnabas. "The Son of Man in Johannine Christology." In *Christ and the Spirit in the New Testament.* Edited by Barnabas Lindars and Stephen S. Smalley. Cambridge: Cambridge University Press, 1973.

Lindstrom, Harald G. *Wesley and Sanctification.* Stockholm: Nya Bokförlags Aktiebolaget, 1946.

Lofthouse, W. "Hen and Hesed in the Old Testament." *Zeitschrift fur die Alttestamentliche Wissenschaft* 51 (1933): 29-35.

Lohmeyer, Ernest. *"Our Father": An Introduction to the Lord's Prayer.* Translated by John Bowden. New York: Harper & Row, 1965.

Longenecker, Richard N. *The Christology of Early Jewish Christianity.* Grand Rapids, Mich.: Baker, 1981.

Lyall, Francis. "Roman Law and the Writings of Paul: Adoption." *JBL* 88 (December 1969): 458-66.

MacCormac, Earl Ronald. *A Cognitive Theory of Metaphor*. Cambridge, Mass.: MIT Press, 1985.

———. *Metaphor and Myth in Science and Religion*. Durham, N.C.: Duke University Press, 1976.

Macky, Peter W. *The Centrality of Metaphors to Biblical Thought*. Lewiston, N.Y.: Edwin Mellen, 1990.

Mahan, Asa. *The Baptism of the Holy Ghost*. New York: W. C. Palmer, 1870.

———. *Christian Perfection*. 1839. Reprint, Salem, Ohio: Schmul, 1975.

Manson, Thomas Walter. *The Teaching of Jesus: Studies of Its Form and Content*. Cambridge: Cambridge University Press, 1963.

Marlow, R. "The Son of Man in Recent Journal Literature." *Catholic Biblical Quarterly* 28 (1966): 20-39.

Marshall, I. Howard. "The Development of the Concept of Redemption in the New Testament." In *Reconciliation and Hope*. Edited by Robert J. Banks. Grand Rapids, Mich.: Eerdmans, 1974.

Martens, Elmer A. *God's Design*. Grand Rapids, Mich.: Baker, 1981.

Martin, James Perry. *The Last Judgment*. Grand Rapids, Mich.: Eerdmans, 1963.

Martin-Achard, Robert. *From Death to Life*. London: Oliver & Boyd, 1960.

Mascall, Eric L. *Existence and Analogy*. Hamden, Conn.: Archon, 1967.

———. *Words and Images*. New York: Longmans, Green, 1957.

May, G. H. "El Shaddai." *JBL* 60 (1941): 114-45.

McCarthy, Dennis. "Notes on the Love of God in Deuteronomy and the Father-Son Relationship Between Yahweh and Israel." *Catholic Biblical Quarterly* 27 (April 1965): 144-47.

McDonald, H. D. *Ideas of Revelation: An Historical Study* A.D. 1700-A.D. 1860 Grand Rapids, Mich.: Baker, 1979.

———. *Theories of Revelation: An Historical Study 1860-1960*. Grand Rapids, Mich.: Baker, 1979.

McFague, Sallie. *Metaphorical Theology*. Philadelphia: Fortress, 1982.

McInerny, Ralph M. *The Logic of Analogy: An Interpretation of St. Thomas*. The Hague: Nijhoff, 1961.

McKay, J. W. "Man's Love for God in Deuteronomy and the Father/Teacher-Son/Pupil Relationship." *Vestus Testamentum* 22 (October 1972): 426-35.

McKoy, Charles. *The Art of Jesus as a Teacher*. Boston: Judson, 1930.

Mendelsohn, Isaac. *Slavery in the Ancient Near East*. New York: Oxford University

Press, 1949.

Mendenhall, George E. *Law and Covenant in Israel and the Ancient Near East*. Pittsburgh: The Biblical Colloquium, 1955.

Metz, Donald. *Studies in Biblical Holiness*. Kansas City, Mo.: Beacon Hill, 1971.

Miley, John. *Systematic Theology*. 2 vols. New York: Methodist Book Concern, 1892-1894.

Moffatt, James. *Love in the New Testament*. 2 vols. London: Hodder & Stoughton, 1929.

Mollenkott, Virginia Ramey. *The Divine Feminine*. New York: Crossroad, 1983.

Moloney, Francis J. *The Johannine Son of Man*. Rome: LAS, 1976.

Moltmann, Jürgen. *The Trinity and the Kingdom of God*. Translated by Margaret Kohl. New York: Harper & Row, 1981.

Mondin, Battista. *Principle of Analogy in Protestant and Catholic Theology*. The Hague: Martinus Nyjhoff, 1963.

Montague, R. "The Dialectic Method of Jesus." *Bibliotheca Sacra* 41 (1884): 549-72.

Moody, Dale. *The Word of Truth*. Grand Rapids, Mich.: Eerdmans, 1981.

Moore, George Foot. *Judaism*. 3 vols. Cambridge: Harvard University Press, 1940.

Morris, Leon. *The Apostolic Preaching of the Cross*. London: Tyndale Press, 1965.

———. *The Biblical Doctrine of Judgment*. Grand Rapids, Mich.: Eerdmans, 1960.

———. *The Gospel According to John*. Grand Rapids, Mich.: Eerdmans, 1971.

———. *The Testaments of Love*. Grand Rapids, Mich.: Eerdmans, 1981.

Mowinckel, Sigmund O. P. *He That Cometh*. Translated by G. W. Anderson. Oxford: Blackwell, 1959.

———. *The Psalms in Israel's Worship*. 2 vols. Translated by D. R. A. Thomas. Oxford: Basil Blackwell, 1962.

Murray, Andrew. *Be Perfect*. Minneapolis: Bethany Fellowship, 1965.

Newbigin, Lesslie. *The Light Has Come: An Exposition of the Fourth Gospel*. Grand Rapids, Mich.: Eerdmans, 1982.

Nuñez, C. Emilio Antonio. *Liberation Theology*. Chicago: Moody Press, 1985.

Nygren, Anders. *Agape and Eros*. Translated by Philip S. Watson. Philadelphia: Westminster Press, 1953.

O'Collins, Gerald, and Daniel Kendall. *The Bible for Theology: Ten Principles for the Theological Use of Scripture*. Mahwah, N.J.: Paulist, 1997.

O'Connor, Daniel. "The Human and the Divine." In *Creation: The Impact of an Idea*. Edited by Daniel O'Connor and Francis Oakley. New York: Charles Scribner's Sons, 1969.

Oden, Thomas. *Life in the Spirit*. San Francisco: Harper & Row, 1992.

————. *The Living God*. San Francisco: Harper & Row, 1987.

————. *The Transforming Power of Grace*. Nashville: Abingdon, 1993.

————. *The Word of Life*. San Francisco: Harper & Row, 1989.

Oehler, Gustave Friedrich. *Theology of the Old Testament*. Edited by George E. Day. Grand Rapids, Mich.: Zondervan, 1883.

Ollenburger, Ben, Elmer Martens, and Gehard Hasel, eds. *The Flowering of Old Testament Theology*. Winona Lake, Ind.: Eisenbrauns, 1992.

————. Origen. *Contra Celsum*. Edited by Henry Chadwick. Cambridge: Cambridge University Press, 1953.

————. *Commentary on the Gospel of Matthew*. In *Ante-Nicene Fathers*. Vol. 9. Edited by Allan Menzies. Peabody, Mass.: Hendrickson, 1994.

Orr, James. *God's Image in Man*. London: Hodder & Stoughton, 1907.

Oswalt, John N. *The Book of Isaiah Chapters 1-39*. Grand Rapids, Mich.: Eerdmans, 1986.

————. *The Book of Isaiah Chapters 40-66*. Grand Rapids, Mich.: Eerdmans, 1989.

————. *A Call to Be Holy: A Biblical Perspective*. Nappance, Ind.: Evangel, 1999.

Otto, Rudolf. *The Idea of the Holy*. London: Oxford University Press, 1928.

Outka, Gene H. *Agape: An Ethical Analysis*. New Haven, Conn.: Yale University Press, 1972.

Owen, John. *An Exposition to the Epistle to the Hebrews*. 7 vols. Edinburgh: J. Ritchie, 1812-1814.

Pache, René. *The Person and Work of the Holy Spirit*. Chicago: Moody Press, 1954.

Packer, J. I. *"Fundamentalism" and the Word of God*. Grand Rapids, Mich.: Eerdmans, 1970.

————. *Knowing God*. Downers Grove, Ill.: InterVarsity Press, 1973.

Palmer, Humphrey. *Analogy, A Study of Qualification and Argument in Theology*. London: Macmillian, 1973.

Pannenberg, Wolfhart. *Jesus, God and Man*. Translated by Lewis L. Wilkins and Duane A. Priebe. Philadelphia: Westminster Press, 1968.

————. *Systematic Theology*. Translated by Geoffrey W. Bromiley. 2 vols. Grand

Rapids, Mich.: Eerdmans, 1991.

Payne, J. Barton. *The Theology of the Older Testament.* Grand Rapids, Mich.: Zondervan, 1962.

Peck, M. Scott. *The Road Less Traveled.* New York: Simon & Schuster, 1978.

Pedersen, Johannes. *Israel: Its Life and Culture.* 4 vols. London: Oxford University Press, 1940.

Pelikan, Jaroslav. *The Emergence of the Catholic Tradition (100-600).* Chicago: University of Chicago Press, 1971.

Pfeiffer, C. F. "Figures of Speech in Human Language." *BETS* 2, no. 4 (fall 1959): 17-21.

Phillips, Stephen "The Use of Scripture in Liberation Theology." Ph.D. dissertation. The Southern Baptist Theological Seminary, 1978.

Pinnock, Clark H. *Biblical Revelation.* Chicago: Moody Press, 1971.

Plummer, Alfred. *A Critical Exegetical Commentary on the Gospel According to St. Luke.* Edinburgh: T & T Clark, 1922.

———. *The Gospel According to St. John.* Cambridge: Cambridge University Press, 1902.

Pope, William Burt. *A Compendium of Christian Theology.* 3 vols. London: Wesleyan-Methodist Book Room, 1880.

Poythress, Vern S. *Symphonic Theology.* Grand Rapids, Mich.: Zondervan, 1991.

Prestige, George Leonard. *Fathers and Heretics: Six Studies in Dogmatic Faith.* New York: Macmillan, 1940.

———. *God in Patristic Thought.* London: SPCK, 1952.

Purkiser, W. T. *Conflicting Concepts of Holiness.* Kansas City, Mo.: Beacon Hill, 1972.

———. *God, Man and Salvation.* Kansas City, Mo.: Beacon Hill, 1977.

———. *Sanctification and Its Synonyms.* Kansas City, Mo.: Beacon Hill, 1961.

Rad, Gerhard von. *Old Testament Theology.* 2 vols. Translated by D. M. G. Stalker. New York: Harper & Row, 1962.

———. "There Remains Still a Rest for the People of God: An Investigation of a Biblical Conception." In *The Problem of the Hexateuch and Other Essays.* New York: McGraw-Hill, 1966.

Ralston, Thomas N. *Elements of Divinity.* Nashville: Southern Methodist, 1976.

Ramm, Bernard. *Special Revelation and the Word of God.* Grand Rapids, Mich.: Eerdmans, 1961.

————. *Them He Glorified.* Grand Rapids, Mich.: Eerdmans, 1963.

Ramsey, A. M. *The Glory of God in the Transfiguration of Christ.* New York: Longmans, Green, 1949.

Rausch, William. *The Trinitarian Controversy.* Philadelphia: Fortress, 1980.

Rawlinson Alfred, ed. *Essays on the Trinity and the Incarnation.* New York: Longmans, Green, 1928.

Reed, W. L. "Some Implications of Hen for Old Testament Religion." *JBL* 73 (1954): 36-41.

Richards, I. A. *The Philosophy of Rhetoric.* New York: Oxford University Press, 1936.

Richardson, Alan. *An Introduction to the Theology of the New Testament.* London: SCM Press, 1958.

————, ed. *A Theological Wordbook of the Bible.* London: SCM Press, 1957.

Ricoeur, Paul. *The Rule of Metaphor.* Translated by Robert Czerny. Toronto: University of Toronto Press, 1977.

Rienecker, Fritz. *A Linguistic Key to the Greek New Testament.* Translated by Cleon Rogers Jr. Grand Rapids, Mich.: Zondervan, 1980.

Ringgren, Helmer. *The Prophetical Conception of Holiness.* Uppsala: A. B. Lundequistska Bokhandeln, 1948.

Ritschl, Albrecht B. *The Christian Doctrine of Justification in New Testament Teaching.* New York: Charles Scribner's Sons, 1900.

————. *A Critical History of the Christian Doctrine of Justification and Reconciliation.* New York: Charles Scribner's Sons, 1900.

Robinson, H. Wheeler. *Redemption and Revelation in the Actuality of History.* London: Nisbet, 1942.

Rolnick, Philip A. *Analogical Possibilities: How Words Refer to God.* Atlanta: Scholars Press, 1993.

Rosell, W. H. "New Testament Adoption: Graeco-Roman or Semitic?" *JBL* 71 (1952): 233-34.

Ruether, Rosemary Radford. *Sexism and God-Talk.* Boston: Beacon, 1983.

Sakenfeld, Katherine D. *The Meaning of Hesed in the Hebrew Bible: A New Inquiry.* Missoula, Mont.: Scholars Press, 1978.

Scalise, Charles J. *From Scripture to Theology: A Canonical Journey into Hermeneutics.* Downers Grove, Ill.: InterVarsity Press, 1996.

Schaeffer, Francis A. *He Is There and He Is Not Silent.* Wheaton, Ill.: Tyndale

House, 1972.

Schultz, Herman. *Old Testament Theology.* 2 vols. Translated by J. A. Patterson. Edinburgh: T & T Clark, 1892.

Schwöbel, Christoph. *Trinitarian Theology Today.* Edinburgh: T & T Clark, 1995.

Schwöbel, Christoph, and Colin Gunton. *Persons, Divine and Human.* Edinburgh: T & T Clark, 1991.

Seitz, Christopher. *Word Without End.* Grand Rapids, Mich.: Eerdmans, 1998.

Seitz, Christopher, and Catherine Green-McCreight, eds. *Theological Exegesis.* Grand Rapids, Mich.: Eerdmans, 1999.

Selbie, W. B. *The Fatherhood of God.* New York: Charles Scribner's Sons, 1936.

Selwyn, Edward Gordan. *The First Epistle of Peter.* London: Macmillan, 1946.

Sherry, P. "Analogy Reviewed." *Philosophy* 51 (1976): 337-45.

———. "Analogy Today." *Philosophy* 51 (1976): 431-46.

Slaatte, Howard Alexander. *Fire in the Brand.* New York: Exposition, 1963.

Smail, Thomas A. *The Forgotten Father.* London: Hodder & Stoughton, 1980.

Smith, C. Ryder. *The Bible Doctrine of Grace and Related Doctrines.* London: Epworth, 1956.

Smith, Timothy. *Whitefield and Wesley on the New Birth.* Grand Rapids, Mich.: Zondervan, 1986.

Snaith, Norman H. *The Distinctive Ideas of the Old Testament.* New York: Schocken, 1964.

Sohn, Seock-Tae. *The Divine Election of Israel.* Grand Rapids, Mich.: Eerdmans, 1991.

Soskice, Janet M. *Metaphor and Religious Language.* Oxford: Clarendon, 1985.

Spicq, Ceslas. *Agape in the New Testament.* 3 vols. St. Louis, Mo.: B. Herder, 1963-1966.

Sproul, R. C. *Holiness of God.* Wheaton, Ill.: Tyndale House, 1985.

Squires, Walter Abion. *The Pedagogy of Jesus in the Twilight of Today.* Philadelphia: Westminster Press, 1927.

Stauffer, Ethelbert. *New Testament Theology.* London: SCM Press, 1955.

Steele, Daniel. *The Gospel of the Comforter.* Apollo, Penn.: West, n.d.

———. *Milestone Papers.* Minneapolis: Bethany Fellowship, 1966.

Stevens, G. "The Teaching of Jesus: The Method of His Teaching," *Biblical World* 5 (1885): 106-13.

Swinburne, Richard. *Revelation: From Metaphor to Analogy.* Oxford: Clarendon,

1992.

Tasker, R. V. G. *The Gospel According to St. John.* London: Tyndale Press, 1964.

Taylor, Richard S. *Life in the Spirit.* Kansas City, Mo: Beacon Hill, 1966.

Taylor, Vincent. *The Gospel According to St. Mark.* London: Macmillan, 1952.

———. *Jesus and his Sacrifice.* London: Macmillan, 1937.

———. *The Names of Jesus.* New York: St. Martin's, 1962.

Tenney, Merrill C. *John: The Gospel of Belief.* Grand Rapids, Mich.: Eerdmans, 1948.

Theron, D. J. "'Adoption' in the Pauline Corpus." *Evangelical Quarterly* 28 (January-March 1956): 6-14.

Thiessen, Henry C. *Introductory Lectures on Systematic Theology.* Grand Rapids, Mich.: Eerdmans, 1949.

Thompson, J. G. S. S. "The Shepherd/Ruler Concept in the Old Testament and Its Application in the New Testament." *Scottish Journal of Theology* 8 (December 1955): 406-18.

Toon, Peter. *Born Again.* Grand Rapids, Mich.: Baker, 1987.

Torrance, Thomas F. *The Christian Doctrine of God.* Edinburgh: T & T Clark, 1995.

———. "The Doctrine of Grace in the Old Testament." *Scottish Journal of Theology* 1 (1948): 55-65.

———. *The Incarnation: Ecumenical Studies in the Nicene-Constantinopolitan Creed.* Edinburgh: Handsel, 1981.

———. *Theological Dialogue Between Orthodox and Reformed Churches.* Edinburgh: Scottish Academic Press, 1985.

———. *Theology in Reconciliation.* Grand Rapids, Mich.: Eerdmans, 1975.

———. *The Trinitarian Faith.* Edinburgh: T & T Clark, 1995.

Tozer, A. W. *The Knowledge of the Holy.* New York: Harper & Row, 1961.

Trench, Richard C. *Synonyms of the New Testament.* Grand Rapids, Mich.: Eerdmans, 1966.

Turner, George Allen. *The Vision Which Transforms.* Kansas City, Mo.: Beacon Hill, 1964.

Vaux, Roland de. *Ancient Israel.* New York: McGraw-Hill, 1961.

Vermès, Géza. *Jesus the Jew.* Philadelphia: Fortress, 1981.

Vos, Geerhardus. *Biblical Theology.* Grand Rapids, Mich.: Eerdmans, 1948.

Vriezen, Theodorus C. *An Outline of Old Testament Theology.* Translated by

S. Neuijen. Bristol: John Wright, 1911.

Wainwright, Arthur W. *The Trinity in the New Testament*. London: SPCK, 1962.

Walton, Frank Edward. *The Development of the Logos Doctrine on Greek and Hebrew Thought*. Bristol: John Wright, 1911.

Warfield, B. B. *The Inspiration and Authority of the Bible*. London: Marshall Morgan & Scott, 1959.

————. "Jesus' Alleged Confession of Sin." *Princeton Theological Review* 12 (1914): 177-228.

————. "The New Testament Terminology of 'Redemption.'" *Princeton Theological Review* 15 (1917).

————. *Perfectionism*. Philadelphia: Presbyterian & Reformed, 1958.

————. "The Terminology of Love in the New Testament." *Princeton Theological Review* 16 (1918): 1-45.

Watson, Francis. *Text and Truth*. Grand Rapids, Mich.: Eerdmans, 1997.

Watson, Richard. *Theological Institutes*. 3 vols. London: John Mason, 1829-1832.

Watts, Isaac. "When I Survey the Wondrous Cross." In *The Methodist Hymnal* (Nashville: Methodist Publishing House, 1964), p. 435.

Webb, Robert Alexander. *The Reformed Doctrine of Adoption*. Grand Rapids, Mich.: Eerdmans, 1947.

Wesley, John. *Explanatory Notes on the New Testament*. London: Epworth, 1966.

————. *A Plain Account of Christian Perfection*. London: Epworth, 1952.

————. *Wesley's Standard Sermons*. 2 vols. Edited by Edward H. Sugden. London: Epworth, 1921.

————. *Works of John Wesley*. 3rd ed., 14 vols. Edited by Thomas Jackson. London: Wesleyan-Methodist Book Room, 1831.

Westcott, B. F. *The Epistle to the Hebrews*. New York: Macmillan, 1906.

————. *The Epistles of St. John*. London: Macmillan, 1892.

Westermann, William L. *The Slave Systems of Greek and Roman Antiquity*. Philadelphia: American Philosophical Society, 1955.

White, James R. *The Forgotten Trinity*. Minneapolis: Bethany House, 1998.

Wiedemann, Thomas E. J. *Greek and Roman Slavery*. Baltimore: Johns Hopkins University Press, 1981.

Wiley, H. Orton. *Christian Theology*. 2 vols. Kansas City, Mo.: Beacon Hill, 1941.

————. *Hebrews*. Kansas City, Mo.: Beacon Hill, 1959.

Williams, D. D. *The Spirit and Forms of Love*. New York: Harper & Row, 1968.

Williams, Norman Powell. *The Grace of God*. New York: Longmans, Green, 1930.

Wilson, Robert Dick. "The Names of God in the Old Testament." *Princeton Theological Review* 18 (1920): 460-92.

Wood, Arthur Skevington. *Paul's Pentecost*. Exeter, U.K.: Paternoster, 1963.

Wood, Laurence W. *Pentecostal Grace*. Wilmore, Ky.: Francis Asbury, 1980.

Wright, Charles Henry Hamilton. *The Fatherhood of God: And Its Relationship to the Person and Work of Christ and the Operations of the Holy Spirit*. Edinburgh: T & T Clark, 1967.

Wright, George Ernest. *God Who Acts*. 2nd ed. London: SCM Press, 1964.

————. *The Old Testament Against Its Environment*. London: SCM Press, 1950.

Wright, N. T. *The Challenge of Jesus*. Downers Grove, Ill.: InterVarsity Press, 1999.

————. *Jesus and the Victory of God*. Minneapolis, Minn.: Fortress, 1992.

————. *The New Testament and the People of God*. Minneapolis: Fortress, 1992.

Wynkoop, Mildred Bangs. *A Theology of Love*. Kansas City, Mo.: Beacon Hill, 1972.

Yarborough, Glen. "The Significance of Hesed in the Old Testament." Ph.D. dissertation, The Southern Baptist Theological Seminary, 1959.

Young, Edward J. *Thy Word Is Truth*. London: Banner of Truth, 1963.

Zizioulas, John. *Being as Communion*. Crestwood, N.Y.: St. Vladimir's Seminary Press, 1997.

Subject Index by Theme